The Waite Group's
New C Primer Plus®
Second Edition

The Waite Group's
New
C
Primer
Plus

Second Edition

Mitchell Waite and Stephen Prata

SAMS
PUBLISHING

A Division of Prentice Hall Computer Publishing
11711 North College, Carmel, Indiana 46032 USA

Dedication

With love to Vicky and Bill Prata,
who, for more than fifty years,
have been showing how rewarding
marriage can be.

SP

International Standard Book Number: 0-672-30319-1

Library of Congress Catalog Card Number: 93-83470

From The Waite Group, Inc.

Editorial Director: *Scott Calamar*
Managing Editor: *John Crudo*
Technical Editors: *Bryan Costales and Harry Henderson*

From Sams Publishing

Publisher: *Richard K. Swadley*
Acquisitions Manager: *Jordan Gold*
Development Editor: *Dean Miller*
Manuscript Editors: *Diana Francoeur and Katherine Stuart Ewing*
Cover Illustrator: *Kathy Hanley*
Production Analysis: *Mary Beth Wakefield*

Production: *Christine Cook, Terri Edwards, Mitzi F. Gianakos, Howard Jones, Sean Medlock, Angela M. Pozdol, Michelle Self*

Indexer: Joelynn Gifford

96 95 94   5   4

Interpretation of the printing code: the rightmost double-digit number is the year of the book's printing; the rightmost single-digit, the number of the book's printing. For example, a printing code of 93-2 shows that the second printing of the book occurred in 1993.

Composed in AGaramond and MCPdigital by Prentice Hall Computer Publishing

Printed in the United States of America

Overview

	Preface to the Second Edition	xxi
	Preface to the First Edition	xxiii
1	Getting Ready	1
2	Introducing C	23
3	Data and C	45
4	Character Strings and Formatted Input/Output	79
5	Operators, Expressions, and Statements	119
6	C Control Statements: Looping	159
7	C Control Statements: Branching and Jumps	205
8	Character Input/Output and Redirection	249
9	Functions	277
10	Arrays and Pointers	319
11	Character Strings and String Functions	359
12	File Input/Output	403
13	Storage Classes and Program Development	433
14	Structures and Other Data Forms	469
15	Bit Fiddling	513
16	The C Preprocessor and the C Library	535
17	Advanced Data Representation	571
A	Additional Reading	641
B	C Operators	645
C	Basic Types and Storage Classes	653
D	Expressions, Statements, and Program Flow	657

E   ASCII Table   665

F   Standard I/O Functions (ANSI C)   671

G   Answers to the Review Questions   675

Index   699

Contents

1   Getting Ready   **1**

Whence C? 2
Why C? 2
   Design Features 2
   Efficiency 2
   Portability 2
   You Can Take C Home 3
   Power and Flexibility 3
   Programmer Oriented 4
   Shortcomings 4
Whither C? 4
Using C: Seven Steps 6
   Step 1: Define the Program Objectives 6
   Step 2: Design the Program 6
   Step 3: Write the Code 6
   Step 4: Compile 7
   Step 5: Run the Program 7
   Step 6: Test and Debug the Program 8
   Step 7: Maintain and Modify the Program 8
   Commentary 8
Programming Mechanics 9
   Source Code Files 10
   Object Code Files, Executable Files, and Libraries 10
   Preparing a C Program on a UNIX System 11
   Preparing a C Program on an IBM PC 13
   Integrated Development Environments (IDEs) 17
   Think C 5.0 on the Macintosh 17
   Why Compile? 18
Language Standards 18
Some Conventions 19
   Typeface 19
   Screen Output 19
   Input and Output Devices 19
Chapter Summary 20
Review Questions 20
Programming Exercise 20

2   Introducing C   23

A Simple Sample of C 24
The Explanation..24
    Pass 1: Quick Synopsis 25
    Pass 2: Details 27
The Structure of a Simple Program 33
Tips on Making Your Programs Readable 34
Taking Another Step 35
    Documentation 35
    Multiple Declarations 35
    Multiplication 36
    Printing Multiple Values 36
While We're at It...Multiple Functions 36
Debugging 38
    Syntax Errors 38
    Semantic Errors 39
    Program State 41
Keywords 41
Chapter Summary 42
Review Questions 42
Programming Exercises 43

3   Data and C   45

A Sample Program 46
    What's New in This Program? 47
Data: Variables and Constants 48
Data: Data-Type Keywords 49
    Integer Versus Floating-Point Types 50
    The Integer 50
    The Floating-Point Number 51
C Data Types 52
    The *int* Type 52
    Other Integer Types 55
    Using Characters: Type *char* 59
    Types *float* and *double* 65
    Other Types 67
    Type Sizes 71
Using Data Types 72
Arguments and Pitfalls 73
One More Example 74
    What Happens 74
    A Possible Problem 75
Chapter Summary 76
Review Questions 77
Programming Exercises 78

4   Character Strings and Formatted Input/Output   79

Introductory Program 80
Character Strings—An Introduction 81
   Type *char* Arrays and the Null Character 81
   Using Strings 82
   String Length—*strlen()* 83
Constants and the C Preprocessor 85
   Using *#define* and *#include* Together 89
   C—A Master of Disguise: Creating Aliases 89
   Manifest Constants on the Job 91
Exploring and Exploiting *printf()* and *scanf()* 91
   The *printf()* Function 92
   Using *printf()* 93
   Conversion Specification Modifiers for *printf()* 95
   The Meaning of Conversion 101
   Using *scanf()* 107
   The * Modifier with *printf()* and *scanf()* 112
Usage Tips 114
Chapter Summary 115
Review Questions 116
Programming Exercises 117

5   Operators, Expressions, and Statements   119

Introducing Loops 120
Fundamental Operators 122
   Assignment Operator: = ... 122
   Addition Operator: + ... 125
   Subtraction Operator: − 125
   Sign Operators: − and + ... 125
   Multiplication Operator: * 126
   Division Operator: / 128
   Operator Precedence 129
   Precedence and the Order of Evaluation 131
Some Additional Operators 133
   The *sizeof* Operator 133
   Modulus Operator: % 134
   Increment and Decrement Operators: ++ and −− 135
   Decrementing: −− 138
   Precedence 139
   Don't Be Too Clever 140
Expressions and Statements 141
   Expressions 141
   Statements 142
   Compound Statements (Blocks) 145

Type Conversions 147
   The Cast Operator 149
Function with Arguments 151
   K&R Function Declarations and Headings 152
An Example Program 153
Chapter Summary 155
Review Questions 156
Programming Exercises 158

6 C Control Statements: Looping   159

An Initial Example 160
   Program Comments 161
   C-Style Reading Loop 162
The *while* Statement 163
   Terminating a *while* Loop 163
   When a Loop Terminates 164
   while —An Entry-Condition Loop 165
   Syntax Points 165
Which Is Bigger: Using Relational Operators and Expressions 167
   What Is Truth? 168
   What Else Is True? 169
   Troubles with Truth 170
   Precedence of Relational Operators 172
Indefinite Loops and Counting Loops 174
The *for* Loop 175
   Using *for* for Flexibility! 177
More Assignment Operators: +=, -=, *=, /=, %= 182
The Comma Operator 183
   Zeno Meets the *for* Loop 185
An Exit-Condition Loop: *do while* 187
Which Loop? 189
Nested Loops 190
   Discussion 191
   A Nested Variation 191
Arrays 192
   Using a *for* Loop with an Array 194
A Loop Example Using a Function Return Value 195
   Program Discussion 198
   Using Functions with Return Values 198
Chapter Summary 199
Review Questions 200
Programming Exercises 202

7   C Control Statements: Branching and Jumps   205

The *if* Statement 206
    if Basics 207
Adding *else* to the *if* Statement 208
    Another Example: Introducing *getchar()* and *putchar()* 209
    Multiple Choice: *else if* 212
    Pairing *else* with *if* 215
    More Nested *ifs* 216
Let's Get Logical 221
    Precedence 223
    Order of Evaluation 223
A Word-Count Program 224
The Conditional Operator: *?:* 227
Loop Aids: *continue* and *break* 229
    The *continue* Statement 229
    The *break* Statement 231
Multiple Choice: *switch* and *break* 233
    Using the *switch* Statement 235
    Reading Only the First Character of a Line 237
    Multiple Labels 237
    switch and *if else* 239
The *goto* Statement 240
    Avoiding *goto* 240
Chapter Summary 244
Review Questions 245
Programming Exercises 247

8   Character Input/Output and Redirection   249

Single-Character I/O: *getchar()* and *putchar()* 250
Buffers 251
Terminating Keyboard Input 253
    Files, Streams, and Keyboard Input 253
    The End of File 254
Redirection and Files 257
    UNIX and DOS Redirection 257
    Comment 260
A Graphic Example 261
Creating a Friendlier User Interface...263
    Working with Buffered Input 263
    Mixing Numeric and Character Input 265
Character Sketches 269
    Analyzing the Program 271
Chapter Summary 273
Review Questions 274
Programming Exercises 275

9   Functions   **277**

Review 278
Creating and Using a Simple Function 279
Function Arguments 282
Defining a Function with an Argument: Formal Arguments 284
Prototyping a Function with Arguments 285
Calling a Function with an Argument: Actual Arguments 285
The Black Box Viewpoint 286
Returning a Value from a Function with *return* 286
Function Types 289
ANSI C Function Prototyping 290
The Problem 290
The ANSI Solution 291
No Arguments and Unspecified Arguments 293
Recursion 293
Recursion Revealed 293
Recursion Fundamentals 295
Tail Recursion 296
Recursion and Reversal 298
All C Functions Are Created Equal 299
Compiling Programs with Two or More Functions 300
UNIX 300
Microsoft C Versions 4.0–7.0 (Command-Line) 300
Microsoft C 6.0–7.0 (PWB) 300
QuickC 301
Turbo C/Borland C 301
Think C 301
Using Header Files 301
Finding Addresses: The & Operator 305
Altering Variables in the Calling Function 306
Pointers: A First Look 308
The Indirection Operator: * 309
Declaring Pointers 310
Using Pointers to Communicate Between Functions 311
Chapter Summary 316
Review Questions 317
Programming Exercises 317

10   Arrays and Pointers   **319**

Arrays 320
Initialization and Storage Classes 320
More Array Initialization 322
Assigning Array Values 325

Pointers to Arrays 326
Functions, Arrays, and Pointers 329
   Array Names as Arguments 330
   Using Pointer Arguments 331
   Comment: Pointers and Arrays 333
Pointer Operations 333
   Another Example 336
Multidimensional Arrays 337
   Initializing a Two-Dimensional Array 339
   More Dimensions 340
Pointers and Multidimensional Arrays 340
   Functions and Multidimensional Arrays 344
Planning a Program 349
   General Plan 349
   The *read_array( )* Function 350
   The *show_array( )* Function 351
   The *mean( )* Function 352
   The Result 352
Chapter Summary 354
Review Questions 355
Programming Exercises 356

11   Character Strings and String Functions   359

Defining Strings Within a Program 361
   Character String Constants 361
Character String Arrays and Initialization 362
   Array Versus Pointer 363
   Specifying Storage Explicitly 365
   Arrays of Character Strings 366
   Pointers and Strings 367
String Input 368
   Creating Space 369
   The *gets( )* Function 369
   The *scanf( )* Function 371
String Output 373
   The *puts( )* Function 373
   The *printf( )* Function 374
The Do-It-Yourself Option 375
String Functions 377
   The *strlen( )* Function 377
   The *strcat( )* Function 378
   The *strcmp( )* Function 379
   The *strcpy( )* Function 383
   The *sprintf( )* Function 386

Other String Functions 387

A String Example: Sorting Strings 388

Sorting 390

The *ctype.h* Character Functions 390

Command-Line Arguments 393

Command-Line Arguments in Integrated Environments 395

Command-Line Arguments with Think C 395

String to Number Conversions 396

Chapter Summary 397

Review Questions 398

Programming Exercises 400

12   File Input/Output   403

Communicating with Files 404

What Is a File? 404

Levels of I/O 405

Standard Files 406

Standard I/O 406

Checking for Command-Line Arguments 407

The *fopen( )* Function 408

The *getc( )* and *putc( )* Functions 409

The *fclose( )* Function 410

Standard Files 410

A Simple-Minded File-Condensing Program 410

File I/O: *fprintf( )*, *fscanf( )*, *fgets( )*, and *fputs( )* 412

The *fprintf( )* and *fscanf( )* Functions 412

The *fgets( )* and *fputs( )* Functions 414

Adventures in Random Access: *fseek( )* and *ftell( )* 416

How *fseek( )* and *ftell( )* Work 417

Binary Versus Text Mode 418

Portability 418

Using Random-Access in a Text Mode 419

Portability 421

Behind the Scenes with Standard I/O 422

Other Standard I/O Functions 422

int ungetc(int c, FILE *fp) 423

int fflush(FILE *fp) 423

int setvbuf(FILE *fp, char *buf, int mode, size_t size) 423

Binary I/O: *fread( )* and *fwrite( )* 424

size_t fwrite(void *ptr, size_t size, size_t nmemb, FILE *fp) 426

size-t fread(void *ptr, size_t size, size_t nmemb, FILE *fp) 426

int feof(FILE *fp) and *int ferror(FILE *fp)* 427

An Example 427

Chapter Summary 430
Review Questions 430
Programming Exercises 431

13 Storage Classes and Program Development   433

Storage Classes and Scope 434
   Scope, Linkage, and Storage Duration 436
   Automatic Variables 437
   External Variables 438
   Definitions and Declarations 441
   Static Variables 442
   External Static Variables 443
   Multiple Files 444
   Scope and Functions 444
   Register Variables 444
   Which Storage Class? 445
A Random Number Function 446
Roll 'Em 450
Sorting Numbers 452
   Global Decisions 453
   Reading Numeric Data 454
   The *getarray()* Function 456
   Sorting the Data 458
   Printing the Data 460
   Results 461
   Comments 462
ANSI C Type Qualifiers 462
   The *const* Type Qualifier 462
   The *volatile* Type Qualifier 463
Chapter Summary 464
Review Questions 465
Programming Exercises 466

14 Structures and Other Data Forms   469

Example Problem:
  Creating an Inventory of Books 470
Setting Up the Structure Template 471
Defining a Structure Variable 472
   Initializing a Structure 473
Gaining Access to Structure Members 474
Arrays of Structures 475
   Declaring an Array of Structures 477
   Identifying Members of an Array of Structures 477
   Program Details 479

Nested Structures 479
Pointers to Structures 481
  Declaring and Initializing a Structure Pointer 482
  Member Access by Pointer 483
Telling Functions About Structures 483
  Passing Structure Members 484
  Using the Structure Address 485
  Passing a Structure as an Argument 486
  More on the New, Improved Structure Status 487
  Structures or Pointer to Structures? 490
  Functions Using an Array of Structures 491
Saving the Structure Contents in a File 493
  Program Points 496
Structures: What Next? 497
Unions—A Quick Look 498
typedef—A Quick Look 501
Fancy Declarations 504
Functions and Pointers 505
Chapter Summary 507
Review Questions 508
Programming Exercises 510

15 Bit Fiddling   513

Binary Numbers, Bits, and Bytes 514
  Binary Integers 514
  Signed Integers 515
  Binary Floating Point 516
Other Bases 516
  Octal 516
  Hexadecimal 517
C's Bitwise Operators 518
  Bitwise Logical Operators 518
  Usage: Masks 520
  Usage: Turning Bits On 521
  Usage: Turning Bits Off 522
  Usage: Toggling Bits 522
  Usage: Checking the Value of a Bit 522
  Bitwise Shift Operators 523
  Programming Example 524
  Another Example 525
Bit Fields 527
  Bit-Field Example 528
Chapter Summary 532
Review Questions 533
Programming Exercises 534

16 The C Preprocessor and the C Library   **535**

Manifest Constants: *#define* 536
    Tokens 540
    Redefining Constants 540
Using Arguments with *#define* 541
    Including the Macro Argument in a String 543
Macro or Function? 544
File Inclusion: *#include* 545
    Header Files: An Example 546
    Uses for Header Files 547
Other Directives 548
    The *#undef* Directive 548
    Conditional Compilation 549
Enumerated Types 552
    enum Constants 553
    Default Values 553
    Assigned Values 553
    Usage 554
The C Library 555
    Gaining Access to the C Library 555
    Using the Library Descriptions 556
The Math Library 557
The General Utilities Library 559
    The *exit()* and *atexit()* Functions 560
    Memory Allocation: *malloc()* and *free()* 562
    The *calloc()* Function 565
    Storage Classes and Dynamic Memory Allocation 566
Chapter Summary 567
Review Questions 567
Programming Exercises 568

17 Advanced Data Representation   **571**

Exploring Data Representation 573
Beyond the Array to the Linked List 575
    Using a Linked List 580
    Afterthoughts 583
Abstract Data Types (ADTs) 583
    Getting Abstract 585
    Building an Interface 586
    Using the Interface 590
    Implementing the Interface 591
Getting Queued with an ADT 598
    Implementing the Interface Data Representation 599
    Testing the Queue 608

Simulating with a Queue 610
The Linked List Versus the Array 616
Binary Search Trees 620
A Binary Tree ADT 621
    The Binary Search Tree Interface 622
    The Binary Tree Implementation 624
    Trying the Tree 631
    Tree Thoughts 635
Other Directions 637
Chapter Summary 637
Review Questions 638
Programming Exercises 638

A   Additional Reading   641

C Language 641
Programming 642
Reference 643

B   C Operators   645

Arithmetic Operators 646
Relational Operators 646
    Relational Expressions 647
Assignment Operators 647
    Example 647
Logical Operators 648
    Logical Expressions 648
    Order of Evaluation for Logical Expressions 648
    Examples 648
The Conditional Operator 648
    Examples 648
Pointer-Related Operators 648
    Example 649
Sign Operators 649
Structure and Union Operators 649
    The Membership Operator 649
    Example 649
    The Indirect Membership Operator 649
    Example 650
Bitwise Operators 650
    Examples 650
Miscellaneous Operators 651
    Example 651

C   Basic Types and Storage Classes   **653**

Summary: The Basic Data Types 653

   Keywords 653

   Signed Integers 653

   Unsigned Integers 654

   Characters 654

   Floating Point 654

Summary: How to Declare a Simple Variable 654

Summary: Qualifiers 656

   Keywords 656

   General Comments 656

   Properties 656

D   Expressions, Statements, and Program Flow   **657**

Summary: Expressions and Statements 657

   Expressions 657

   Statements 658

Summary: The *while* Statement 658

   Keyword 658

   General Comments 658

   Form 658

   Examples 658

Summary: The *for* Statement 659

   Keyword 659

   General Comments 659

   Form 659

   Example 659

Summary: The *do while* Statement 659

   Keywords 659

   General Comments 659

   Form 660

   Example 660

Summary: Using *if* Statements for Making Choices 660

   Keywords 660

   General Comments 660

   Form 1 660

   Form 2 660

   Form 3 661

   Example 661

Summary: Multiple Choice with *switch* 661

   Keyword 661

   General Comments 661

   Form 661

Examples 662
Summary: Program Jumps 662
Keywords 662
General Comments 662
The *break* Command 662
The *continue* Command 663
The *goto* Command 663

E   ASCII Table   665

F   Standard I/O Functions (ANSI C)   671

G   Answers to the Review Questions   675
Chapter 1 675
Chapter 2 676
Chapter 3 677
Chapter 4 678
Chapter 5 679
Chapter 6 681
Chapter 7 683
Chapter 8 684
Chapter 9 685
Chapter 10 686
Chapter 11 687
Chapter 12 689
Chapter 13 691
Chapter 14 691
Chapter 15 693
Chapter 16 694
Chapter 17 695

Index   699

Preface to the Second Edition

The Waite Group's New C Primer Plus has, we hope, met the objectives outlined in the Preface to the first edition. We were pleased to learn that the Computer Press Association recognized *New C Primer Plus* as the best how-to book of 1990, and now we're trying to improve on that book. Here's what's new this time:

- A new chapter (Chapter 17) explores the philosophy and techniques of advanced data representations. The first sixteen chapters concentrate on presenting the C language to you, and this chapter focuses on introducing you to the science of programming.

- The book is ANSI-er than ever, with an earlier emphasis on following ANSI C precepts.

- Examples have been retested using the latest compilers from Microsoft and Borland.

- We pay greater attention to the Macintosh user by offering guidance on using Think C.

We hope you enjoy this book and that it helps you learn and take pleasure in C.

Acknowledgments for the Second Edition

The authors wish to thank John Crudo and Scott Calamar for guiding the second edition to completion and Harry Henderson for his editorial feedback.

Preface to the First Edition

C was a relatively little-known language when we wrote *C Primer Plus* in 1984. Since then, the language has boomed. Although we don't claim that our book caused the boom, it is true that the book has helped many people learn C. Now that C is getting a new standard (ANSI C), we felt it was time for a new *C Primer Plus*. So here it is, now titled *The Waite Group's New C Primer Plus*.

What's new with this edition? Here are the main changes:

- Completely revamped text to bring the book into accord with the ANSI C Standard. This standard was developed by a committee of the American National Standards Institute (ANSI) in response to a need created by C's success and its spread to a variety of computer platforms. The standard is scheduled for final adoption soon.

- Revised examples, figures, and explanations.

- New order of presentation, based on reader feedback.

- Expanded coverage of C topics, including bitwise operators, enumerated types, and the C preprocessor.

- More complete discussion of functions from the C library.

We've also retained much from the earlier editions. In particular, we've kept the philosophy that the book should be a friendly, easy-to-use, self-study guide, as is reflected in the following points:

- We don't assume that you are a professional programmer. We explain programming ideas along with the C language.

- We emphasize an interactive approach. Because you learn by doing, we often use short, easily typed examples that illustrate just one or two concepts at a time.

- We clarify ideas with figures and illustrations.

- We summarize the main C features in highlighted boxes.

- We provide review questions and programming exercises so that you can test and improve your understanding of C.

Our goal in writing this introduction to C has been to make it instructive, clear, and helpful. To gain the greatest benefit, you should take as active a role as possible. Don't just read the examples. Enter them into your system and try them. C is a very portable language, but you may find differences between how a program works on your system and how it works on ours. Experiment—change part of a program to see what the effect is. Modify a program to do something slightly different. Ignore our occasional warnings and see what happens when you do the wrong thing. Try the questions and exercises. The more you do yourself, the more you will learn and remember.

We wish you good fortune in learning C. We've tried to make this book meet your needs, and we hope it helps you reach your goals.

Acknowledgments for the First Edition

The authors wish to thank Scott Calamar of The Waite Group for guiding this book through the writing, editing, and production stages. We particularly wish to thank Bryan Costales for his useful and knowledgeable editing of the first draft.

Trademarks

All terms mentioned in this book that are known to be trademarks or service marks are listed below. In addition, terms suspected of being trademarks or service marks have been appropriately capitalized. Sams Publishing cannot attest to the accuracy of this information. Use of a term in this book should not be regarded as affecting the validity of any trademark or service mark.

Apple is a registered trademark of Apple Computer, Inc.

Borland C++ is a registered trademark of Borland International, Inc.

Cray is a registered trademark of Cray Computer, Inc.

IBM and PC are registered trademarks and PC DOS is a trademark of the International Business Machines Corporation.

Macintosh is a registered trademark of McIntosh Laboratory, Inc., licensed by Apple Computer, Inc.

Microsoft, Microsoft Word, MS-DOS, and XENIX are registered trademarks of Microsoft Corporation.

Primer Plus is a registered trademark of The Waite Group, Inc.

Think C is a registered trademark of Symantec Corporation.

Turbo C is a registered trademark of Borland International, Inc.

UNIX is a trademark of American Telephone and Telegraph Corporation.

VAX is a registered trademark and VMS is a trademark of Digital Equipment Corporation.

WordPerfect is a registered trademark of WordPerfect Corporation.

WordStar is a registered trademark of MicroPro International Corporation.

About the Authors

Mitchell Waite is president of The Waite Group, a developer of computer books. He is an experienced programmer, fluent in a variety of computer languages, including C, Pascal, BASIC, Assembly, and HyperTalk. He wrote his first computer book in 1976, and is coauthor of *C: Step-by-Step, Microsoft QuickC Programming, UNIX Primer Plus,* and many other titles.

Stephen Prata is a professor of physics and astronomy at The College of Marin in Kentfield, California, where he teaches UNIX and the C language. He received his B.S. from the California Institute of Technology and his Ph.D. from the University of California, Berkeley. His association with computers began with the computer modeling of star clusters. Dr. Prata is coauthor of *C: Step-by-Step, UNIX Primer Plus,* and author of *Microsoft QuickBasic Primer Plus, C++ Primer Plus,* and *Artificial Life Playhouse.*

Getting Ready

In this chapter you learn about C's history and features, examine the steps needed to write programs, learn a bit about compilers and linkers, and look at C standards.

Welcome to the world of C. C is a vigorous, professional programming language popular with amateur and commercial programmers alike. This chapter prepares you for learning and using this powerful and popular language, and it introduces you to the kinds of environments in which you most likely will develop your C-legs.

First, we look at C's origin and examine some of its features, both strengths and drawbacks. Then we examine some general principles for programming. Finally, we discuss how to run C programs on some common systems.

Whence C?

Dennis Ritchie of Bell Labs created C in 1972 as he and Ken Thompson worked on designing the UNIX operating system. C didn't spring full-grown from Ritchie's head, however. It came from Thompson's B language, which came from…. but that's another story. The important point is that C was created as a tool for working programmers. Thus, its chief goal is to be a *useful* language.

Most languages aim to be useful, but often they have other concerns. The main goal for Pascal, for instance, was to provide a sound basis for teaching good programming principles. BASIC, on the other hand, was developed to resemble English so that it could be learned easily by students unfamiliar with computers. These are important goals, but they are not always compatible with pragmatic, workaday usefulness. C's development as a language designed for programmers, however, has made it the modern-day language of choice.

Why C?

During the last two decades, C has become one of the most important and popular programming languages. It has grown because people try it and like it. As you learn C, you will recognize its many virtues (see Figure 1.1). Let's preview a few of them now.

Design Features

C is a modern language incorporating the control features that the theory and practice of computer science find desirable. The design of C makes it natural for users to use top-down planning, structured programming, and modular design. The result is a more reliable, understandable program.

Efficiency

C is an efficient language. Its design takes advantage of the abilities of current computers. C programs tend to be compact and to run quickly. In fact, C exhibits some of the fine control usually associated with assembly language. If you choose, you can fine-tune your programs for maximum speed or most efficient use of memory.

Portability

C is a portable language. This means that C programs written on one system can be run with little or no modification on other systems. If modifications are necessary, they can often be made just by changing a few entries in a *header* file accompanying the main program. Of course, most languages are meant to be portable, but anyone who has converted an IBM PC BASIC program to Apple BASIC (and they are close cousins) or tried to run an IBM mainframe FORTRAN program on a UNIX system will know that *porting* is troublesome at best. C is a leader in portability. C compilers are available for about 40 systems, running from 8-bit microprocessors to Cray supercomputers. Note, however, that the portions of a program written specifically to access particular hardware devices—such as a VGA monitor—or special features of an operating system—such as Windows or System 7.1—typically are not portable.

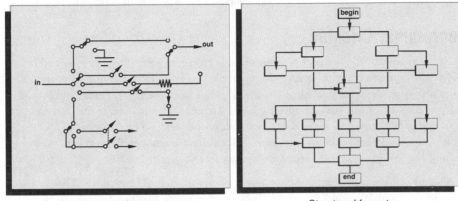

Flexible control structures   Structured format

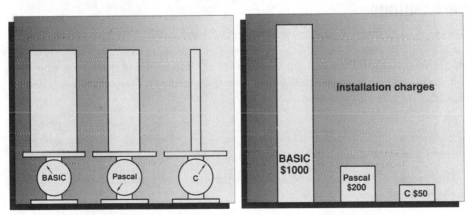

Compact code—small programs   Portable to other computers

Figure 1.1. *The virtues of C.*

You Can Take C Home

Because C is portable, you can take your UNIX C programs home to use on a personal computer. Several C compilers are available now to enable you to do that.

Power and Flexibility

C is powerful and flexible (two favorite words in computer literature). For example, most of the powerful, flexible UNIX operating system is written in C. Many compilers and interpreters for other languages—such as FORTRAN, APL, Pascal, LISP, Logo, and BASIC—have been written in C. Therefore, when you use FORTRAN on a UNIX machine, ultimately a C program has done the work of producing the final executable program. C programs have been used for solving physics and engineering problems and even for animating special effects for movies such as the *Return of the Jedi*.

Programmer Oriented

C is oriented toward the needs of programmers. It gives you access to hardware, and it enables you to manipulate individual bits in memory. It has a rich selection of operators that enable you to express yourself succinctly. C is less strict than, say, Pascal, in limiting what you can do. This is both an advantage and a danger. The advantage is that many tasks, such as converting forms of data, are much simpler in C. The danger is that C will enable you to make mistakes that are impossible in some languages. C gives you more freedom, but it also puts more responsibility on you.

Also, most C implementations have a large library of useful C functions. These functions deal with many needs commonly facing the programmer.

Shortcomings

C does have some faults. Often, as with people, faults and virtues are opposite sides of the same feature. For example, we've mentioned that C's freedom of expression also requires added responsibility. C's use of pointers, in particular, enables you to make programming errors that are very difficult to trace. As one computer preliterate once commented, the price of liberty is eternal vigilance.

C's conciseness combined with its wealth of operators make it possible to prepare code that is extremely difficult to follow. You aren't compelled to write obscure code, but the opportunity is there. After all, what other language has a yearly Obfuscated Code contest?

There are more virtues and, undoubtedly, a few more faults. Rather than delve further into the matter, let's move on to a new topic.

Whither C?

By the early 1980s, C already was a dominant language in the minicomputer world of UNIX systems. Since then, it has spread to personal computers (microcomputers) and to mainframes (the big guys). See Figure 1.2. Many software houses use C as the preferred language for producing word processing programs, spreadsheets, compilers, and other products. These companies know that C produces compact and efficient programs. More important, they know that these programs will be easy to modify and easy to adapt to new models of computers.

What's good for the companies and the C veterans is good for other users, too. More and more computer users are turning to C to secure its advantages for themselves. You don't have to be a computer professional to use C.

In the 1990s, we should point out, many software houses are turning to the C++ language for large programming projects. C++ grafts object-oriented programming tools to the C language. C++ is nearly a superset of C, meaning that any C program is, or nearly is, a valid C++ program, too. By learning C, you also learn much of C++.

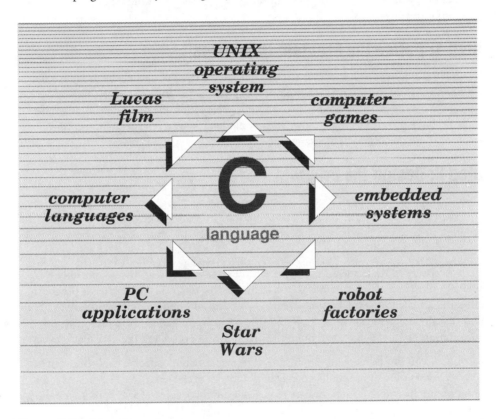

Figure 1.2. *Where C is used.*

In short, C is one of the most important programming languages and will continue to be during the next decade. It is used on mainframes, minicomputers, and personal computers. It is used by software companies, computer science students, and enthusiasts of all sorts. If you want a job writing software, one of the first questions you should be able to answer yes to is, "O say can you C."

Using C: Seven Steps

C is a *compiled language*. If you are accustomed to using a compiled language, such as Pascal or FORTRAN, you will be familiar with the basic steps in putting together a C program. If your background is in an *interpreted* language, however—such as BASIC or Logo—or if you have no background at all, you will need to learn how to compile. We'll soon guide you through that process, and you'll see that it is straightforward and sensible. First, to give you an overview of programming, we'll break down the act of writing a C program into seven steps.

Step 1: Define the Program Objectives

Naturally enough, you should start with a clear idea of what you want the program to do. Think in terms of the information your program needs, the feats of calculation and manipulation the program needs to do, and the information the program should report back to you. At this level of planning, you should be thinking in general terms, not in terms of some specific computer language.

Step 2: Design the Program

Once you have a conceptual picture of what your program ought to do, you should decide how the program will go about it. What should the user interface be like? How should the program be organized? Who will the target user be? How much time do you have to complete the program?

You also need to decide how to represent the data in the program and, possibly, in auxiliary files, and which methods to use to process the data. As you first learn programming in C, the choices will be simple, but as you deal with more complex situations, you'll find that these decisions require more thought. Choosing a good way to represent the information often can make designing the program and processing the data much easier.

Again, you should be thinking in general terms, not about specific code, but some of your decisions may be based on general characteristics of the language. For example, a C programmer has more options in data representation than, say, a BASIC programmer.

Step 3: Write the Code

Now that you have a clear design for your program, you can begin to implement it by writing the code. That is, you translate your program design into the C language. Here is where you really have to put your knowledge of C to work. You can sketch your ideas on paper, but eventually you have to get your code into the computer. The mechanics of this process depend on your programming environment. We'll present the details for some common environments soon. In general, you use a text editor to create what is called a *source code* file. This file contains the C rendition of your program design. Listing 1.1 shows an example of C source code.

Listing 1.1. An example of C source code.

```c
#include <stdio.h>
int main(void)
{
  int dogs;

  printf("How many dogs do you have?\n");
  scanf("%d", &dogs);
  printf("So you have %d dog(s)!\n", dogs);
  return 0;
}
```

As part of this step, you should document your work. The simplest way is to use C's comment facility to incorporate explanations into your source code. We'll explain more about using comments in Chapter 2, "Introducing C."

Step 4: Compile

The next step is to *compile* the source code. Again, the details depend on your programming environment, and we'll look at some common environments shortly. Here, we'll take a more conceptual view of what happens.

The compiler is a program whose job is to convert *source code* into *executable code.* Executable code is code in the native, or *machine,* language of your computer. Different computers have different machine languages, and a C compiler translates C to a particular machine language. C compilers also incorporate code from C *libraries* into the final program; the libraries contain a fund of standard routines, such as `printf()` and `scanf()`, for your use. (More accurately, a program called a *linker* brings in the library routines, but on most systems the compiler runs the linker for you.) The end result is an *executable file* containing code that the computer understands and that you can run.

The compiler also checks that your program is valid C. If the compiler finds errors, it reports them to you and doesn't produce an executable file. Understanding a particular compiler's complaints is another skill that you will pick up.

Step 5: Run the Program

Traditionally, the executable file is a runnable program. To run the program in many common environments, including UNIX and MS-DOS, just type the name of the executable file. Other environments, such as VMS on a VAX, may require a *run* command or some other mechanism. More recently, integrated environments such as Turbo C and QuickC enable you to run your executable C program from within the integrated environment by selecting names from a list or by pressing special keys.

Step 6: Test and Debug the Program

The fact that your program runs is a good sign, but it's possible that it may run incorrectly. Therefore, you should check to see that your program does what it is supposed to do. You'll find that some of your programs will have mistakes—*bugs* in computer jargon. *Debugging* is the finding and fixing of program errors. Making mistakes is a natural part of learning. It also seems inherent to programming, so when you combine learning and programming, you had best prepare yourself to be reminded often of your fallibility. As you become a more powerful and subtle programmer, your errors, too, will become more powerful and subtle.

You have many opportunities to err. You can make a basic design error. You can implement good ideas incorrectly. You can overlook unexpected input that will mess up your program. You can use C incorrectly. You can make typing errors. You can put parentheses in the wrong place and so on. You'll find your own items to add to this list.

Fortunately, the situation isn't hopeless, although there may be times when you feel it is. The compiler catches many kinds of errors, and there are things you can do to help yourself track down the ones that the compiler doesn't catch. Throughout this book we'll give you debugging advice.

Step 7: Maintain and Modify the Program

When you create a program for yourself or for someone else, that program may see extensive use. If it does, you'll probably find reasons to make changes in it. Perhaps there is a minor bug that shows up only when someone enters a name beginning with Zz, or you may think of a better way to do something in the program. You may add a clever new feature. You may adapt the program so that it runs on a different computer system. All these tasks are greatly simplified if you document the program clearly and if you follow sound design practices.

Commentary

Programming is not always as linear a process as we've just described. Sometimes you'll have to go back and forth between steps. For instance, when you are writing code, you may find that your plan was impractical, you may see a better way of doing things, or after you see how a program runs, you may feel motivated to change the design. Documenting your work will help you move back and forth between levels.

Most learners tend to neglect steps 1 and 2 (defining program objectives and designing the program) and go directly to step 3 (writing the program). The first programs you write are simple enough that you can visualize the whole process in your head. If you make a mistake, it's easy to find. As your programs grow longer and more complex, mental visualizations begin to fail, and errors get harder to find. Eventually, those who neglect the planning steps are condemned to hours of lost time, confusion, and frustration as they produce ugly, dysfunctional, and abstruse programs.

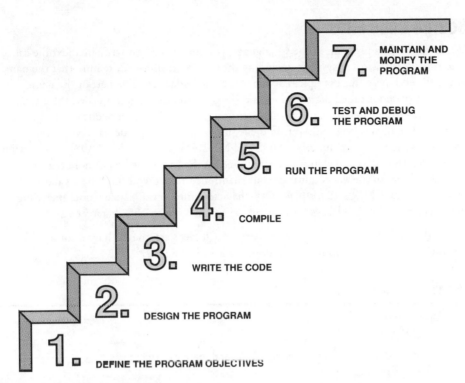

Figure 1.3. *The seven steps of programming.*

The moral here is that you should develop the habit of planning before coding. Use the ancient but honorable pen-and-pencil technology to jot down the objectives of your program and to outline the design. If you do so, you eventually will reap substantial dividends in time saved and satisfaction gained.

Programming Mechanics

The exact steps you must follow to produce a program depend on your computer environment. Currently, the most widespread environments are UNIX C on a UNIX system, Borland's Turbo C and Borland C++ on IBM PCs and clones, and Microsoft C and QuickC on IBM PCs and clones. We'll discuss all four, filling in some of the details we glossed over when summarizing the programming process.

First, however, let's look at some aspects shared by many C environments, including the four we just mentioned. You don't really need to know what follows to run a C program, but it is good background. It also may help you understand why you have to go through some particular steps to get a C program.

Source Code Files

When you write a program in the C language, you store what you write in a text file called a *source code file*. Most C systems, including the ones we mentioned, require that the name of the file end in .c: for example, wordcount.c and budget.c. The part of the name before the period is called the *basename* and the part after the period is called the *extension*. Thus budget is a basename and c is an extension. The combination budget.c is the *filename*. The name also should satisfy the requirements of the particular computer operating system. For example, PC DOS and MS-DOS (hereafter just DOS) are operating systems for IBM PCs and clones. They require that the basename be no more than 8 characters long, so the wordcount.c name mentioned earlier would not be a valid DOS filename. Some UNIX systems place a 14-character limit on the whole name, including the extension; other UNIX systems allow longer names, up to 255 characters.

So that we'll have something concrete to refer to, let's assume we have a source file called concrete.c containing the C source code of Listing 1.2.

Listing 1.2. concrete.c.

```
#include <stdio.h>
int main(void)
{
    printf("Concrete contains gravel and cement.\n");
    return 0;
}
```

Don't worry about the details of the source code file shown in Listing 1.2; you'll learn about them in Chapter 2, "Introducing C."

Object Code Files, Executable Files, and Libraries

The basic strategy in C programming is to use programs that convert your source code file to an *executable file*, which is a file containing ready-to-run machine language code. C implementations do this in two steps: compiling and linking. The *compiler* converts your source code to an intermediate code, and the *linker* combines this with other code to produce the executable file. C uses this two-part approach to facilitate the modularization of programs. You can compile individual modules separately and then combine the compiled modules later. That way, if you need to change one module, you don't have to recompile the other ones.

There are several choices for the form of the intermediate files. The most prevalent choice, and the one taken by the implementations we describe, is to convert the source code to machine language code, placing the result in an *object code file*, or *object file* for short. (We are assuming that your source code consists of a single file.) Although the object file contains machine language code, it is not ready to run. The object file contains the translation of *your* source code, but it is not yet a complete program.

The first element missing from the object code file is something called *start-up* code. This is code that acts as an interface between your program and the operating system. For example, you can run, say, an IBM AT clone under DOS or under XENIX, a UNIX variety. The hardware is the same in either case, so the same object code would work with both, but you would need different start-up code for DOS than you would for XENIX, because these systems handle programs differently from one another.

The second missing element is the code for library routines. Nearly all C programs make use of *routines* (called *functions*) that are part of the standard C library. For example, concrete.c uses the function printf(). The object code file does not contain the code for this function; it merely contains instructions saying to *use* the printf() function. The actual code is stored in another file, called a *library*. A library file contains object code for many functions.

The role of the linker is to bring together these three elements—your object code, the standard start-up code for your system, and the library code—and put them together into a single file, the executable file. For library code the linker extracts only the code needed for the functions you use from the library. See Figure 1.4.

In short, an object file and an executable file both consist of machine language instructions. The object file, however, contains the machine language translation only for the code you used, but the executable file also has machine code for the library routines you use and for the start-up code.

On some systems you must run the compile and link programs separately. On other systems the compiler starts the linker automatically, so that you have to give only the compile command.

Now let's look at some specific systems.

Preparing a C Program on a UNIX System

Because C's popularity began on UNIX systems, we will start there.

Editing on a UNIX System

Unlike BASIC, UNIX C does not have its own editor. Instead, you use one of the general-purpose UNIX editors, such as ed, ex, edit, emacs, jove or vi.

Your two main responsibilities are typing the program correctly and choosing a name for the file that will store the program. As we discussed, the name should end with .c. Note that UNIX distinguishes between upper- and lowercase. Thus, budget.c, BUDGET.c, and Budget.c are three distinct and valid names for C source files, but BUDGET.C is not a valid name because it uses an uppercase C instead of a lowercase c.

Here is an example. Using the vi editors we prepared the following program and stored it in a file called inform.c.

```
#include <stdio.h>
int main(void)
{
    printf("A .c is used to end a C program filename.\n");
    return 0;
}
```

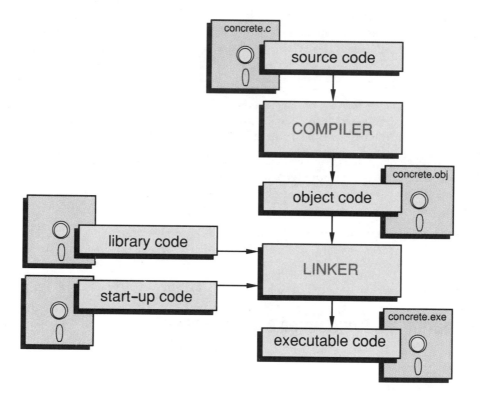

Figure 1.4. *Compiler and linker.*

The text we just typed is the *source code*, and inform.c is the *source file*. The important point here is that the source file is the beginning of a process, not the end.

Compiling on a UNIX System

Our program, although undeniably brilliant, is still gibberish to a computer. A computer doesn't understand things like #include or printf. (At this point, you probably don't either, but you will soon learn, whereas the computer won't.) As we discussed earlier, we need the help of a compiler to translate *our* code (source code) to the *computer's* code (machine code). The result of our efforts will be the executable file, which contains all the machine code that the computer needs to get the job done.

The UNIX C compiler is called cc. To compile the inform.c program, you need type only

```
cc inform.c
```

After a few seconds, the UNIX prompt will return, telling you that the deed is done. You may get warnings and error messages if you failed to write the program properly, but let's assume you did everything right. (If the compiler complains about the word void, your system has not yet updated to an ANSI C compiler. We'll talk more about standards soon. Meanwhile, just omit the word void from the example.) If you use ls to list your files, you will find that there is a new file called a.out (see Figure 1.5). This is the executable file containing the translation (or compilation) of the program. To run it, just type

```
a.out
```

and wisdom pours forth

```
A .c is used to end a C program filename.
```

If you want to keep the executable file (a.out), you should rename it. Otherwise, the file is replaced by a new a.out the next time you compile a program.

What about the object code? The cc compiler creates an object code file having the same basename as the source code but with an o extension. In our example, the object code file is called inform.o, but you won't find it, for the linker removes it once the executable program has been completed. However, if the original program used more than one source code file, the object code files would be saved. When we discuss multiple-file programs later in the text, you will see that this is a fine idea.

Preparing a C Program on an IBM PC

The first C compilers for IBM PC systems were *command-line compilers*, which means you use them by typing commands at the DOS prompt. The usual cycle was first to run an editor program to create the source code, then exit the editor, then run the compiler from the DOS command line. More recently, the trend has been toward integrated development environments (IDE), which enable you to control the editing and compiling from one integrated program. We'll take a general look at both approaches. Also, we'll assume that you are using PC DOS 3.1 or later or MS-DOS 3.1 or later.

Using Command-Line Compilers

The more recent versions of Microsoft C give you the option of using them in this command-line mode. Similarly, Turbo C and Borland C++, which feature IDEs, have command-line versions. Power C, too, is a command-line compiler.

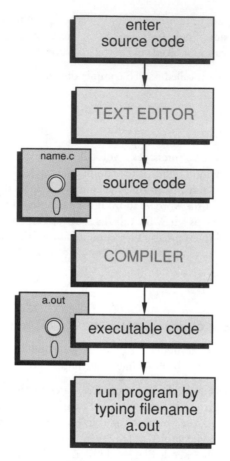

Figure 1.5. *Preparing a C program using UNIX.*

First, you need to select an editor for creating the source code. PC DOS and MS-DOS 4.0 and earlier come with a rather primitive, awkward, but adequate, editor called EDLIN. DOS 5.0 comes with a much better editor called EDIT, which works fine for editing small programs. Also, you probably have access to a word processor such as WordStar, WordPerfect, or Microsoft Word. You can use these word processors to write C programs. However, you cannot use the normal file formats that these word processors use. These files contain a lot of text formatting information in addition to the text you see when writing. This additional information will foil the compiler, so you must take care to create simple *ASCII* files, that is, files containing nothing but the text you type. If you have WordStar, for example, use the N (for nondocument) mode for program files. For WordPerfect, use the Text In/Out key to save the file as a *DOS file*. Windows versions of these programs offer text or ASCII options in the Save dialog box.

A better choice is to use an editor specifically designed for programming. Microsoft, for example, includes a programming system called Programmer's WorkBench (PWB) with its recent compiler versions. There are several commercial program editors available, including Kedit and Brief, as well as ports of the vi and emacs editors to the DOS environment. Many of these editors enable you to have several files open simultaneously, which is handy for working with large programs.

Whichever editor you use, you should, as with UNIX, use a filename ending with the c extension. Also, with DOS, the part of the name before the period is limited to 8 characters. Thus, budget.c and wordcnt.c are valid names, but countwords.c is not. DOS won't reject countwords.c; it simply trims the basename to 8 characters and saves the file as countwor.c. DOS does not distinguish between uppercase and lowercase, so both budget.c and BUDGET.C are valid names for the same file.

As an example, use the editor of your choice to create a file called inform.c having these contents:

```
#include <stdio.h>
int main(void)
{
    printf("A .c is used to end a C program filename.\n");
    return 0;
}
```

This program follows the ANSI C standard. If your compiler objects to the void, the compiler is pre-ANSI. In that case, omit the void and pay close attention to the standards discussion later.

Compiling

Once you have a source code file whose name ends in .c, you can invoke the command-line compiler. For instance, you can invoke Microsoft C compiler with this command:

```
cl inform.c
```

Turbo C uses tcc instead of cl, and Borland C++ uses bcc. Power C uses pc to create an intermediate file and pcl to create the executable file. We'll continue with the Microsoft example as a typical command-line compiler.

Like the UNIX cc compiler, the Microsoft cl compiler first produces an object code file. For DOS systems, the name of the original file is used, but with the c extension replaced by obj. Thus, for our example, the object code file would be called inform.obj. Next, the compiler requests the system linker to finish the job. On DOS systems, this is a program called link. The link program pulls in code from the C library (which comes with the compiler) and adds the start-up code to produce an executable file called inform.exe. In general, the name of the executable file is the name of the source file with the c extension replaced with exe. Unlike the UNIX compiler, cl does not erase the object file when done. Figure 1.6 shows the steps for preparing a C program using Microsoft C. Be aware that command-line compilers need to be installed properly. For example, Microsoft C requires that path be set correctly and that the environment variables INCLUDE and LIB be set properly. Usually, the installation program will modify the AUTOEXEC.BAT file so that these variables are set automatically when you start the computer.

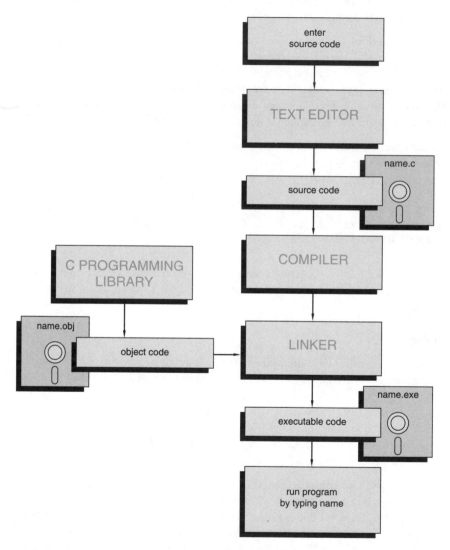

Figure 1.6. *Preparing a C program in Microsoft C.*

To run the program, type the following command at the DOS prompt:

```
inform
```

Under DOS, this is equivalent to typing `inform.exe`. The program runs, producing the following output:

```
A .c is used to end a C program filename.
```

Integrated Development Environments (IDEs)

Borland and Microsoft probably shudder at having their products lumped together, but current versions of Turbo C++, Borland C++, Microsoft C/C++, and QuickC all provide fast, integrated environments for putting together C programs. The key points are that each of these programs has a built-in editor that you can use to write a C program. Each provides menus that enable you to name and save your source code file, as well as menus that enable you to compile and run your program without leaving the IDE. Each dumps you back into the editor if the compiler finds any errors, and each identifies the offending lines and matches them to the appropriate error messages. Each enables you to create object and executable files so that you can create stand-alone programs that can be run directly from the DOS level.

These compilers follow the standard DOS naming conventions, so source code files should have a `.c` extension. Object files are given the `obj` extension, and executable files are given the `exe` extension. If you have a compiler that handles both C and C++, be sure you choose the C option. In the Borland products, just make sure the source code files have a `.c` extension. (If you use the `.cpp` extension, the compiler interprets your program as a C++ program.) With Microsoft C/C++ 7.0 and the PWB IDE, you have to use the Project menu to select a project. Select New Project from the menu, and then select Set Project Template to open a dialog box that enables you to select the language.

Think C 5.0 on the Macintosh

The usual Macintosh graphics interface requires programming that is much more sophisticated than simple PC DOS programs. However, the Think C compiler for the Macintosh enables you to emulate the simpler interface of the PC world. Here are the steps you go through. When you start Think C, you'll be prompted to open a project. Select New, and then enter a project name, for instance, NCPP. This creates a file to manage your programming project. Once that's done, go to the File menu and select New. This opens a file for you to enter your source code. Type the example and save it, using a filename ending in `.c`. Then go to the Source menu and select Add to add the source code to the project file. Next, you need to add some support libraries to the project. Select Add... from the Source menu, go to the folder called Think C 5.0 Folder, open the C Libraries, and double-click ANSI to add the standard ANSI library to your project. Then back up to the Think C 5.0 Folder, open the Mac Libraries folder, and double-click MacTraps to add it to the project. Then click Done. Macintosh code has to fit into 32 Kb segments, and the ANSI C library is so large it needs its own segment. To accomplish this, go to the project window, select ANSI, and drag it to the bottom of the list. To compile a program, go to the Project window and select Run. When you move on to the next example, just select the old example source code in the project window, select Remove from the Source menu, open a new text window, enter the new code, then add it to the project. That way you don't have to add ANSI and MacTraps for each new program.

Why Compile?

Those of you used to BASIC may wonder about going through these steps to run a program. It may seem time-consuming. It may even *be* time-consuming. Once a program is compiled, however, it will run much faster than a standard BASIC program. You trade some inconvenience in getting a program running for a swifter final product. Also, if you use an integrated package, the inconvenience is much reduced.

Language Standards

Currently, many C implementations are available. Ideally, once you write a C program, it should work the same on any implementation, providing it doesn't use machine-specific programming. For this to be true in practice, different implementations need to conform to a recognized standard.

At first, there was no official standard for C. Instead, the first edition of *The C Programming Language* by Brian Kernighan and Dennis Ritchie (1978) became the accepted standard, usually referred to as *K&R C or classic C*. In particular, the "C Reference Manual" in the book's appendix acted as the guide to C implementors. Compilers, for example, would claim to offer a full K&R implementation. However, although this appendix defined the C language, it did not define the C library. More than most languages, C depends on its library, so there is need for a library standard, too. In the absence of any official standard, the library supplied with the UNIX implementation became a de facto standard.

As C evolved and as it become more widely used on a greater variety of systems, the C community realized it needed a more comprehensive, up-to-date, and rigorous standard. To meet this need, the American National Standards Institute (ANSI) established a committee (X3J11) in 1983 to develop a new standard, which was adopted formally in 1989. This new standard (ANSI C) defines both the language and a standard C library. The International Standards Organization adopted a C standard (ISO C) in 1990. ISO C and ANSI C are essentially the same standard.

For the most part, C compiler vendors for microcomputers, such as IBM PCs and Macintoshes, took an evolutionary approach to converting to ANSI C, adding features from the early ANSI drafts as it became apparent those features would be in the final version. UNIX systems, on the other hand, stuck with K&R C until the ANSI standard became official. ANSI C, therefore, came to the UNIX world later—but fully implemented—than to the PC world. The public domain gcc UNIX C compiler, however, switched to ANSI C earlier than the standard cc UNIX C compiler, so if your UNIX system has a K&R cc compiler, check to see whether someone has installed an ANSI C gcc version.

For the most part, we will follow the ANSI C Standard. Often, ANSI C and K&R C are much the same. However, ANSI C does support some extensions and changes. We'll mention many of these where appropriate. Because you may find yourself using implementations that lack some ANSI C features, we'll point out where there are conflicts.

Some Conventions

We are almost ready to begin our study of the C language itself. Here are some of the conventions that we will use in presenting material.

Typeface

For text representing programs and computer input and output, we will use a type font that resembles what you might see on a screen or on printed output. We already have used it a few times. In case it slipped by you, the font looks like this:

```
#include <stdio.h>
int main(void)
{
    printf("Concrete contains gravel and cement.\n");
    return 0;
}
```

Screen Output

Output from the computer is printed in color. Where lines of output are interspersed with user input, only the screen output is in color. For instance, here is program output from a Chapter 14, "Structures and Other Data Forms," example:

```
Please enter the book title.
Press [enter] at the start of a line to stop.
My Life as a Budgie
Now enter the author.
Mack Zackles
```

The lines printed in color are program output, and the other lines are user input.

Input and Output Devices

There are many ways that you and a computer can communicate with each other. However, we will assume that you type in commands by using a keyboard and that you read the response on a screen.

Special Keystrokes

Usually, you send a line of instructions onward by pressing a key labeled Enter, c/r, Return, or some variation of these. We will refer to this key in the text as the Enter key.

When showing it as part of input in a program example, we use [enter]. The brackets mean that you press a single key rather than type the word enter.

We also will refer to control characters such as Control-D. This notation means to type the *D* key while you are pressing the key labeled Control (or perhaps, Ctrl).

Our System

Some aspects of C, such as the amount of space used to store a number, depend on the system. When we give examples and refer to *our system,* we speak of an IBM AT compatible running under MS-DOS 5.0 and using either a Microsoft or a Borland compiler. Most of the examples also have been tested using Think C 5.0 on a Macintosh SE/30.

We also occasionally refer to running programs on a UNIX system. The one we use is Berkeley's BSD 4.3 version of UNIX running on a VAX 11/750 computer.

Chapter Summary

C is a powerful, concise programming language. It is popular because it provides useful programming tools and good control over hardware and because C programs are easier than most to transport from one system to another.

C is a *compiled* language. C *compilers* and *linkers* are programs that convert C language source code into executable code.

Programming in C can be taxing, difficult, and frustrating, but it also can be intriguing, exciting, and satisfying. We hope that you will find it as enjoyable and fascinating as we do.

Review Questions

1. What does *portability* mean in the context of programming?

2. Explain the difference between source code file, object code file, and executable file.

3. What are the seven major steps in programming?

4. What does a compiler do?

5. What does a linker do?

Programming Exercise

We don't expect you to write C code yet, so this exercise concentrates on the earlier stages of the programming process.

1. You have just been employed by MacroMuscle, Inc. (Software for Hard Bodies). They are entering the European market and want a program that converts inches to

centimeters (1" = 2.54 cm). They want the program set up so that it prompts the user to enter an inch value. Your assignment is to define the program objectives and to design the program (steps 1 and 2 of the programming process).

Introducing C

Operator

=

Functions

```
main(), printf()
```

In this chapter you learn how to put together a simple C program, how to create integer-valued variables and assign them values, and how to display those values on-screen. Also, you find out what the newline character is, how to include comments in your programs, how to create programs containing more than one function, how to find program errors, and what keywords are.

What does a C program look like? If you skim through this book, you'll see many examples. Quite likely, you'll find that C is peculiar-looking, sprinkled with symbols like {, cp->tort, and *ptr++. As you read through this book, you will find that the appearance of these and of other characteristic C symbols grows less strange, more familiar, perhaps even welcome! In this chapter we begin by presenting a simple example program and explaining what it does. At the same time we highlight some of the basic features of C.

A Simple Sample of C

Let's take a look at a simple C program. (Figure 2.1 outlines a more extensive example.) This program, shown in Listing 2.1, serves to point out some of the basic features of programming in C. Before you read the upcoming line-by-line explanation of the program, read through Listing 2.1 to see if you can figure out for yourself what it will do.

Listing 2.1. A simple C program.

```c
#include <stdio.h>
int main(void)                  /* a simple program          */
{
    int num;                    /* define a variable called num */
    num = 1;                    /* assign a value to num      */

    printf("I am a simple ");   /* use the printf() function  */
    printf("computer.\n");
    printf("My favorite number is %d because it is first.\n",num);
    return 0;
}
```

If you think this program will print some things on your screen, you're right! Exactly what will be printed may not be apparent, so run the program and see the results. First, use your favorite editor to create a file containing the text from Listing 2.1. Give the file a name that ends in .c and that satisfies your local system's name requirements. You can use first.c, for instance. Now compile and run the program. If all went well, the output should look like this:

```
I am a simple computer.
My favorite number is 1 because it is first.
```

All in all, this result is not too surprising, but what happened to the \n's and the %d in the program? And some of the lines in the program do look strange. It's time for an explanation.

The Explanation

We'll take two passes through the program's source code. The first pass will highlight the meaning of each line, and the second will explore specific implications and details. Figure 2.1 summarizes the parts of a C program.

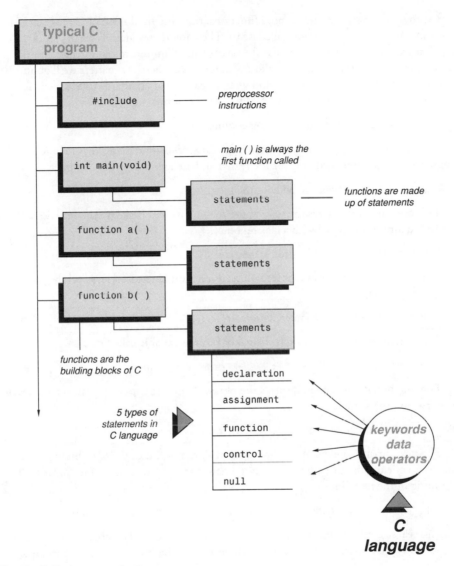

Figure 2.1. *Anatomy of a C program.*

Pass 1: Quick Synopsis

```
#include <stdio.h>      →include another file
```

This line tells the computer to include information found in the file stdio.h. The stdio.h file is a standard part of all C compiler packages.

```
int main(void)      →a function name
```

C programs consist of one or more functions, the basic modules of a C program. This program consists of one function called `main`. The parentheses identify `main()` as a function name. The `int` indicates that the `main()` function returns an integer, and the `void` indicates that `main()` doesn't take any arguments. These are matters we'll go into later. Right now, just accept the `int` and `void` as part of the standard ANSI C way for defining `main()`. (If you have a pre-ANSI C compiler, omit the void.)

```
/* a simple program */   →a comment
```

The symbols `/*` and `*/` enclose comments. *Comments* are remarks that help to clarify a program. They are intended only for the reader and are ignored by the compiler.

```
{     →beginning of the body of the function
```

This opening brace marks the start of the statements that make up the function. The function definition is ended with a closing brace, `}`.

```
int num;      →a declaration statement
```

This statement announces that we will be using a variable called `num` and that `num` will be an `int` (integer) type.

```
num = 1;   →an assignment statement
```

The statement `num = 1;` assigns the value 1 to the variable called num.

```
printf("I am a simple ");     →a print statement
```

The first `printf` statement displays the phrase `I am a simple` on your screen, leaving the cursor on the same line.

```
printf("computer.\n");   →another print statement
```

The next `printf` statement tacks on `computer` to the end of the last phrase printed. The `\n` is code telling the computer to start a new line, that is, to move the cursor to the beginning of the next line.

```
printf("My favorite number is %d because it is first.\n", num);
```

The last `printf` statement prints the value of num (which is 1) embedded in the phrase in quotes. The `%d` instructs the computer where and in what form to print the value of num.

```
return 0;     →a return statement
```

A C function can furnish, or return, a number to the agency that used it. For the present, just regard this line as part of the ANSI C requirement for a properly written `main()` function.

```
}      →the end
```

As promised, the program ends with a closing brace.

Pass 2: Details

Now take a closer look at the program.

#include Directives and Header Files

```
#include <stdio.h>
```

The effect of #include <stdio.h> is the same as if we had typed the entire contents of the stdio.h file into our file at the point where the #include line appears. *Include* files provide a convenient way to share information that is common to many programs.

The stdio.h file is supplied as part of all C compiler packages. It contains information about input and output functions, such as printf(), for the compiler to use. The name stands for *standard input/output header*. C people call a collection of information that goes at the top of a file a *header*, and C implementations typically come with several header files. One goal of ANSI C is to standardize which header files must be provided.

Some programs need to include stdio.h; some don't. The documentation for a particular C implementation should include a description of the functions in the C library. These function descriptions identify which header files are needed. For example, the description for printf() says to use stdio.h. Omitting the proper header file may not affect a particular program, but it is best not to rely on that. Each time we use library functions, we'll use the include files specified by the ANSI Standard for those functions. Because the compiler uses the information in the stdio.h to build a program, any information that the compiler does not use does not become part of the program. Therefore, including an unnecessary file does not make the final program any longer.

The #include statement is an example of a C *preprocessor directive*. In general, C compilers perform some preparatory work on source code before compiling; this is termed *preprocessing*.

Why Input and Output Are Not Built-In

Perhaps you are wondering why something as basic as input and output information isn't included automatically. One answer is that not all programs use this I/O (input/output) package, and part of the C philosophy is to avoid carrying unnecessary weight. Incidentally, the #include line is not even a C language statement! The # symbol in column 1 identifies it as a line to be handled by the C preprocessor. As you know, the preprocessor handles some tasks before the compiler takes over. We will encounter more examples of preprocessor instructions later.

The *main()* Function

```
int main(void)
```

True, `main` is a rather plain name, but it is the only choice available. A C program always begins execution with the function called `main()`. You are free to choose names for other functions you may use, but `main()` must be there to start things off. What about the parentheses? They identify `main()` as a function. You will learn more about functions soon. For now, just remember that functions are the basic modules of a C program.

The `int` is the `main()` function's return type. That means that the kind of value `main()` can return is an integer. Return where? We'll come back to this question in Chapter 6, "C Control Statements: Looping."

The parentheses following a function name generally enclose information being passed along to the function. For our simple example, nothing is being passed along, so the parentheses contain the word `void`.

Pre-ANSI C programs usually omitted the `int` and the `void`.

```
main()
```

ANSI C also accepts this form. It interprets the empty parentheses to mean that you decline to say anything about the kind of information `main()` requires. Omitting the `int` has no effect, for C (both K&R and ANSI) assumes that a function has an `int` return type unless you state otherwise, but explicitly using `int` more clearly documents what's going on.

Comments

```
/* a simple program */
```

Using comments makes it easier for someone (including yourself) to understand your program. One nice feature of C comments is that they can be placed anywhere, even on the same line as the material they explain. A longer comment can be placed on its own line or even spread over more than one line. Everything between the opening `/*` and the closing `*/` is ignored by the compiler. Here are some valid and invalid comment forms:

```
/* This is a C comment. */
/* This comment is spread over
   two lines. */
/*
  You can do this, too.
*/
/* But this is invalid
```

Braces, Bodies, and Blocks

```
{
...
}
```

Braces mark the beginning as well as the end of the body of a function. Only braces { } work for this purpose, not parentheses ( ) and not brackets [ ].

Braces also can be used to gather statements within a function into a unit or *block*. If you are familiar with Pascal, ADA, Modula-2, or Algol, you will recognize the braces as being similar to begin and end in those languages.

Declarations

```
int num;
```

The *declaration statement* is one of the most important features of C. This particular example declares two things. First, somewhere in the function, we have a *variable* called num. Second, the int proclaims num as an *integer*, that is, a number without a decimal point or fractional part. The compiler uses this information to arrange for suitable storage space in memory for the num variable. The semicolon at the end of the line identifies the line as a C *statement* or instruction. The semicolon is part of the statement, not just a separator between statements as it is in Pascal.

The word int is a C *keyword* identifying one of the basic C data types. Keywords are the words used to express a language, and you can't usurp them for other purposes. For instance, you can't use int as the name of a function or a variable.

In C *all* variables should be declared before they are used. This means that you have to provide lists of all the variables you use in a program, and that you have to show which *type* each variable is. Declaring variables is considered to be a good programming technique.

At this point, you probably have three questions. First, what are data types? Second, what choices do you have in selecting a name? Third, why do you have to declare variables at all? Let's look at some answers.

Data Types

C deals with several kinds (or types) of data: integers, characters, and *floating point*, for example. Declaring a variable to be an integer or a character type makes it possible for the computer to store, fetch, and interpret the data properly. We'll investigate the variety of available types in the next chapter.

Name Choice

We suggest that you use meaningful names for variables. The number of characters you can use will vary among implementations, but the lower limit will be at least 8 characters. The ANSI C Standard calls for up to 31 characters, except for external identifiers (see Chapter 13, "Storage Classes and Program Development"), for which only 6 characters need be recognized. Actually, you can use more than the maximum number of characters, but the compiler won't pay attention to the extra characters. Thus, on a system with an 8-character limit, shakespeare and shakespencil would be considered the same name because they have the same first 8 characters. The characters at your disposal are the lowercase letters, the uppercase letters, the digits, and the underscore _. The first character must be a letter or an underscore. Here are some examples:

Valid Names	Invalid Names
wiggles	$Z]**
cat1	1cat
Hot_Tub	Hot-Tub
_kcab	don't

C names are case sensitive, meaning an uppercase letter is considered distinct from the corresponding lowercase letter. Thus socks is different from Socks or SOCKS.

Four Good Reasons to Declare Variables

- Putting all the variables in one place makes it easier for a reader to grasp what the program is about. This is particularly true if you give your variables meaningful names (such as taxrate instead of r). If the name doesn't suffice, use the comment facility to explain what the variables represent. Documenting a program in this manner is one of the basic techniques of good programming.

- Thinking about what to put into the variable declaration section encourages you to do some planning before plunging into writing a program. What information will the program need to get started? What exactly do I want the program to produce as output? What is the best way to represent the data?

- Declaring variables helps prevent one of programming's more subtle and hard-to-find bugs, that of the misspelled variable name. For example, suppose that in some language, which lacks declarations, you made the statement

RADIUS1 = 20.4;

and that elsewhere in the program you mistyped

CIRCUM = 6.28 * RADIUSl;

You unwittingly replaced the numeral 1 with the letter l. That other language would create a new variable called RADIUSl and use whatever value it had (perhaps zero, perhaps garbage). CIRCUM would be given the wrong value, and you might have a heck of a time trying to find out why. This can't happen in C (unless you were silly enough to declare two such similar variable names) because the compiler will complain when the undeclared RADIUSl shows up.

- Your C program will not compile if you don't declare your variables. If the preceding reasons fail to move you, you should give this one serious thought.

Assignment

num = 1;

The *assignment statement* is one of the basic operations in C. This particular example means "assign the value 1 to the variable num." The earlier int num; line allotted computer space for the variable num, and the assignment line gives it its value. You can assign num a different value later on if you wish; that is why num is a variable. Note that the assignment statement assigns a value from the right side to the left side. Also, the statement is completed with a semicolon, as shown in Figure 2.2.

The *printf()* Function

```
printf("I am a simple ");
printf("computer.\n");
printf("My favorite number is %d because it is first.\n",num);
```

num = 1;

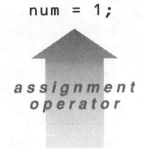

assignment operator

Figure 2.2. *The assignment statement is one of the basic C operations.*

These lines all use a standard C function called printf(). The parentheses signify that printf is a function name. The material enclosed in the parentheses is information passed from the main() function to the printf() function. For example, the first line passes the phrase I am a simple to the printf() function. Such information is called the *argument* of a function (see Figure 2.3). What does the function printf() do with this argument? It looks at whatever lies between the double quotation marks and prints that text on the screen.

printf()

argument

```
printf("That's mere contrariness!\n");
```
Figure 2.3. *The function* printf() *with an argument.*

This first print() line provides an example of how you *call* or *invoke* a function in C. You need type only the name of the function, placing the desired argument(s) within the parentheses. When the program reaches this line, control is turned over to the named function (`printf()` in this case). When the function is finished with whatever it does, control is returned to the original (the *calling*) program—`main()` in our example.

What about this next `printf()` line? It has the characters `\n` included in the quotes, and they didn't get printed! What's going on? The `\n` symbolism means to start a new line. The `\n` combination (typed as two characters) represents a single character called the *newline* character. Its meaning is "start a new line at the far left margin." In other words, printing the newline character performs the same function as pressing the Enter key of a typical keyboard. Why not just use the Enter key when typing the `print()` argument? Because that would be interpreted as an immediate command to your editor, not as an instruction to be stored in your source code. In other words, when you press the Enter key, the editor quits the current line on which you are working and starts a new one.

The newline character is an example of an *escape sequence*. An escape sequence is used to represent difficult- or impossible-to-type characters. Other examples are `\t` for tab and `\b` for backspace. In each case the escape sequence begins with the backslash character, `\`. We'll return to this subject in Chapter 3, "Data and C."

Well, that explains why our three `printf()` statements produced only two lines: the first print instruction didn't have a newline character in it, but the second and third did.

The final `printf()` line brings up another oddity: what happened to the `%d` when the line was printed? As you will recall, the output for this line was

```
My favorite number is 1 because it is first.
```

Aha! The digit `1` was substituted for the symbol group `%d` when the line was printed, and `1` was the value of the variable `num`. The `%d` is a placeholder to show where the value of `num` is to be printed. This line is similar to the BASIC statement

```
PRINT "My favorite number is "; num; " because it is first."
```

The C version does a little more than this, actually. The `%` alerts the program that a variable is to be printed at that location, and the `d` tells it to print the variable as a decimal (base 10) integer. The `printf()` function allows several choices for the format of printed variables, including hexadecimal (base 16) integers and numbers with decimal points. Indeed, the `f` in `printf()` is a reminder that this is a formatting print function.

Return Statement

```
return 0;
```

The `int` in `int main(void)` means that the `main()` function is supposed to return an integer. The ANSI C standard requires that `main()` behave that way. C functions that return values do so with a return statement, which consists of the keyword `return` followed by the returned value followed by a semicolon. If you leave out the return statement for `main()`, most compilers will chide you for the omission, but will still compile the program. At this point, you can regard the return statement in `main()` as something required for logical consistency, but it has a practical use with some operating systems, including DOS and UNIX. We'll return to that topic in Chapter 11, "Character Strings and String Functions."

The Structure of a Simple Program

Now that you've seen a specific example, you are ready for a few general rules about C programs. A *program* consists of a collection of one or more functions, one of which must be called `main()`. The description of a *function* consists of a header and a body. The *header* contains preprocessor statements, such as `#include`, and the function name. You can recognize a function name by the parentheses, which may be empty. The *body* is enclosed by braces { } and consists of a series of statements, each terminated by a semicolon (see Figure 2.4). Our example had a *declaration statement*, announcing the name and type of variable being used. Then it had an *assignment statement* giving the variable a value. Finally, there were three *print statements*, each calling the `printf()` function. The print statements are examples of *function call statements*.

In short, a simple ANSI C program should follow this format:

```
#include <stdio.h>
int main(void)
{
    statements
    return 0;
}
```

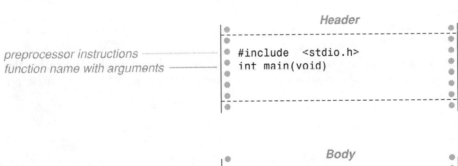

Figure 2.4. *A function has a header and a body.*

Tips on Making Your Programs Readable

Making your programs readable is good programming practice. A readable program is much easier to understand, and that makes it easier to correct or modify your program. The act of making a program readable also helps clarify your own concept of what the program does.

We've already mentioned two techniques for improving readability: choose meaningful variable names and use comments. Note that these two techniques complement each other. If you give a variable the name width, you don't need a comment saying that this variable represents a width, but a variable called video_routine_4 begs for an explanation of what video routine 4 does.

Another technique is using blank lines to separate one conceptual section of a function from another. For example, in our simple program, we had a blank line separating the declaration section from the action section. The blank line is not required by C, but it enhances readability.

A fourth technique we followed was to use one line per statement. Again, this is a readability convention, not a C requirement. C has a *free-form format*. You can place several statements on one line or spread one statement over several. The following is legitimate, but ugly, code:

```
int main(  void  ) { int four; four
=
4
;
printf(
      "%d\n",
four); return 0;}
```

The semicolons tell the compiler where one statement ends and the next begins, but the program logic is much clearer if you follow the conventions we used in our example. See Figure 2.5.

```
int main(void) /* converts 2 fathoms to feet */ ——————————— use comments

{
int feet, fathoms; ——————————————————————————— pick names
                                              ——————————— use space
fathoms=2;
feet=6*fathoms; ——————————————————————————— one statement per line
printf("There are %d feet in %d fathoms!\n", feet, fathoms);
return 0;
}
```

Figure 2.5. *Making your program readable.*

Taking Another Step

Our first example program was pretty easy, and our next example, shown in Listing 2.2, isn't much harder.

Listing 2.2. `fathm_ft.c.`

```c
/* fathm_ft.c -- converts 2 fathoms to feet */
#include <stdio.h>
int main(void)
{
    int feet, fathoms;

    fathoms = 2;
    feet = 6 * fathoms;
    printf("There are %d feet in %d fathoms!\n", feet, fathoms);
    return 0;
}
```

What's new? We provided a program description, declared multiple variables, did some multiplication, and printed the values of two variables. Let's examine these points in more detail.

Documentation

First, we began the program with a comment identifying the filename and the purpose of the program. This kind of program documentation takes but a moment to do and is helpful later on when you browse through several files or print them.

Multiple Declarations

Next, we declared two variables instead of just one in a single declaration statement. To do this, we separated the two variables (`feet>` and `fathoms`) by a comma in the declaration statement. That is,

```c
int feet, fathoms;
```

and

```c
int feet;
int fathoms;
```

are equivalent.

Multiplication

Third, we made a calculation. We harnessed the tremendous computational power of our computer system to multiply 2 by 6. In C, as in many languages, the * is the symbol for multiplication. Thus, the statement

```
feet = 6 * fathoms;
```

means "look up the value of the variable `fathoms`, multiply it by 6, and assign the result of this calculation to the variable `feet`."

Printing Multiple Values

Finally, we made fancier use of `printf()`. If you compile and run the example, the output should look like this:

```
There are 12 feet in 2 fathoms!
```

This time we made *two* substitutions. The first `%d` in the quotes was replaced by the value of the first variable (`feet`) in the list following the quoted segment, and the second `%d` was replaced by the value of the second variable (`fathoms`) in the list. Note that the list of variables to be printed comes at the tail end of the statement after the quoted part. Also note that each item is separated from the others by a comma.

This program is limited in scope, but it could form the nucleus of a program for converting fathoms to feet. All that is needed is a way to assign other values to `feet`; we will explain how to do that in later chapters.

While We're at It...Multiple Functions

So far our programs have used the standard `printf()` function. Listing 2.3 shows you how to incorporate a function of your own—besides `main()`—into a program.

Listing 2.3. `two_func.c`.

```
/* two_func.c -- a program using two functions in one file */
#include <stdio.h>
void butler(void);             /* ANSI C function prototyping */
                /* pre-ANSI C uses void butler(); instead */
int main(void)
{
   printf("I will summon the butler function.\n");
   butler();
   printf("Yes. Bring me some tea and floppy disks.\n");
}

void butler(void)             /* start of function definition */
{
   printf("You rang, sir?\n");
}
```

The output looks like this:

```
I will summon the butler function.
You rang, sir?
Yes. Bring me some tea and floppy disks.
```

The `butler()` function appears three times in this program. The first appearance is in the *prototype*, which informs the compiler about the functions to be used. The second appearance is in `main()` in the form of a function call. Finally, the program presents the *function definition*, which is the source code for the function itself. We'll look at each of these three appearances in turn.

Prototypes are an ANSI C addition, and pre-ANSI compilers may not recognize them. (We'll tell you in a moment what to do with pre-ANSI compilers.) A prototype is a form of declaration that tells the compiler that we will be using a particular function. It also specifies properties of the function. For example, the first `void` in the prototype for the `butler()` function indicates that `butler()` does not have a return value. (In general, a function can return a value to the calling function for its use, but `butler()` doesn't.) The second `void`, the one in `butler(void)` means that the `butler()` function has no arguments. Thus, when the compiler reaches the point in `main()` where `butler()` is used, it can check to see if `butler()` is used correctly. Note that `void` is used to mean empty, not invalid.

Pre-ANSI C supports a more limited form of function declaration in which you just specify the return type but omit describing the arguments.

```
void butler();
```

Most C code currently in existence uses function declarations like this instead of function prototypes. ANSI C recognizes this older form but indicates it will be phased out in time. Later chapters will return to prototyping, function declarations, and return values.

Next, we invoke `butler()` in `main()` simply by giving its name, including parentheses. When `butler()` finishes its work, the program moves to the next statement in `main()`.

Finally, the function `butler()` is defined in the same manner as `main()`, with a function header and the body enclosed in braces. The header repeats the information given in the prototype: `butler()` takes no arguments and has no return value. For pre-ANSI C, omit the second `void`.

One point to note is that it is the location of the `butler()` call in `main()`—not the location of the `butler()` definition in the file—that determines when the `butler()` function is executed. You could, for instance, put the `butler()` definition above the `main()` definition in this program, and the program would still run the same, with the `butler()` function executed between the two calls to `printf()` in `main()`. Remember, all C programs begin with `main()`, no matter where `main()` is located in the program files. However, C practice is to list `main()` first, because it normally provides the basic framework for a program.

The ANSI C Standard recommends that you provide function prototypes for all functions that you use. The standard `include` files take care of this task for the standard library functions. For example, under ANSI C, the `stdio.h` file has a function prototype for `printf()`. When we introduce defining functions with return values in Chapter 6, "C Control Statements: Looping," we'll show you how to extend prototyping to non-`void` functions.

Debugging

Now that you can write a simple C program, you are in a position to make simple errors. Listing 2.4 presents a program with some errors. See how many you can spot.

Listing 2.4. `nogood.c.`

```
/*  nogood.c -- a program with errors */
#include <stdio.h>
int main(void)
(
  int n, int n2, int n3;
    /* this program has several errors

  n = 5;
  n2 = n * n;
  n3 = n2 * n2;
  printf("n = %d, n squared = %d, n cubed = %d\n", n, n2, n3)
  return 0;
)
```

Syntax Errors

Listing 2.4 contains several *syntax* errors. You commit a syntax error when you don't follow C's rules. It's analogous to a grammatical error in English. For instance, consider the following sentence: *Bugs frustrate be can.* This sentence uses valid English words but doesn't follow the rules for word order, and it doesn't have quite the right words, anyway. C syntax errors use valid C symbols in the wrong places.

So what syntax errors did we make? First, we used parentheses instead of braces to mark the body of the function—we used a valid C symbol in the wrong place. Second, the declaration should have been this:

```
int n, n2, n3;
```

or perhaps this:

```
int n;
int n2;
int n3;
```

Next, we omitted the */ symbol pair necessary to complete a comment. Finally, we omitted the mandatory semicolon that should terminate the printf() statement.

How do you detect syntax errors? First, before compiling, you can look through the source code and see if you spot anything obvious. Second, you can examine errors found by the compiler, because part of the compiler's job is to detect syntax errors. When you compile this program, the compiler will report back any errors that it finds, identifying the nature and location of each error.

However, the compiler can get confused. A true syntax error in one location may cause the compiler to mistakenly think it has found other errors. For instance, because our example does not declare n2 and n3 correctly, the compiler may think it has found further errors whenever those variables are used. If some of the supposed errors don't make sense to you, first correct the errors before them, recompile, and see if the compiler still complains. Continue in this way until the program works.

Semantic Errors

Semantic errors are errors in meaning. For instance, consider the following sentence: *Furry inflation thinks greenly.* The syntax is fine because adjectives, nouns, verbs, and adverbs are in the right places, but the sentence doesn't mean anything. In C, you commit a semantic error when you follow the rules of C correctly but to an incorrect end. Our example has one such error.

```
n3 = n2 * n2;
```

Here, n3 is supposed to represent the cube of n, but we've set it up to be the fourth power of n.

The compiler does not detect semantic errors, for they don't violate C rules. The compiler has no way of divining your true intentions. That leaves it to you to find these kinds of errors. One way is to compare what a program does to what you expected it to do. For instance, suppose you fix the syntax errors in our example so that it now reads as shown in Listing 2.5.

Listing 2.5. stillbad.c.

```
/* stillbad.c -- a program with its syntax errors fixed */
#include <stdio.h>
int main(void)
{
  int n, n2, n3;
     /* this program has a semantic error */

  n = 5;
  n2 = n * n;
  n3 = n2 * n2;
```

continues

Listing 2.5. continued

```
printf("n = %d, n squared = %d, n cubed = %d\n", n, n2, n3);
return 0;
}
```

Its output is

```
n is 5, n squared is 25, n cubed is 625
```

If you are cube-wise, you'll see that 625 is the wrong value. The next stage is to track down how we wound up with this answer. For this example, you probably can spot the error by inspection. In general, however, you need to take a more systematic approach. One method is to pretend you are the computer and to follow the program steps one by one. Let's try that method now.

The body of our program starts by declaring three variables: n, n2, and n3. We can simulate this situation by drawing three boxes and labeling them with the variable names (see Figure 2.6). Next, the program assigns 5 to n. Simulate that by writing 5 into the n box. Next, the program multiplies n by n and assigns the result to n2, so we look in the n box, see that the value is 5, multiply 5 by 5 to get 25, and place 25 in box n2. To duplicate the next C statement (n3 = n2 * n2;), we look in n2 and find 25. We multiply 25 by 25, get 625, and place it in n3. Aha! We are squaring n2 instead of multiplying it by n.

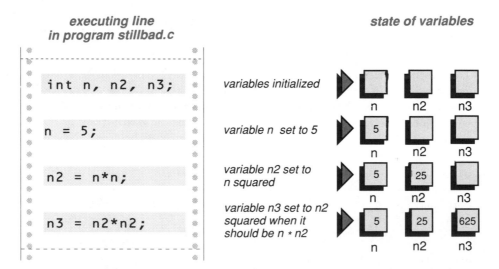

Figure 2.6. *Tracing a program.*

Well, perhaps this procedure is overkill for this example, but going through a program step-by-step in this fashion is often the best way to see what's going on.

Program State

By tracing the program step-by-step, keeping track of each variable, we monitor the *program state*. The program state is simply the set of values of all the variables at a given point in program execution. It is a snapshot of the current state of computation.

We just discussed one method of tracing the state: executing the program step-by-step yourself. In a program that makes, say, 10,000 iterations, you may not feel up to that task. Still, you can go through a few iterations to see if your program does what you intend. However, there is always the possibility that you will execute the steps as you intended them to be executed rather than as you actually wrote them, so try to be faithful to the actual code.

Another approach to locating semantic problems is to sprinkle extra `printf()` statements throughout to monitor the values of selected variables at key points in the program. Seeing how the values change can illuminate what's happening. Once you have the program working to your satisfaction, you can remove the extra statements and recompile.

A third method for examining the program states is to use a *debugger*. A debugger is a program that enables you to run another program step-by-step and to examine the value of that program's variables. Debuggers come in various levels of ease of use and sophistication. The more advanced debuggers show which line of source code is being executed. This is particularly handy for programs with alternative paths of execution, because it is easy to see which particular paths are being followed. If your compiler comes with a debugger, take time now to learn how to use it. Try it with Listing 2.4, for example.

Keywords

Keywords are the vocabulary of C. Because they are special to C, you can't use them for variable names. Many of these keywords specify various types, such as `int`. Others, such as `if`, are used to control the order in which program statements are executed. In the following list of C keywords, asterisks indicate new keywords added by the ANSI C Standard.

ANSI C Keywords

auto	double	int	static
break	else	long	struct
case	enum	register	switch
char	extern	return	typedef
*const	float	short	union
continue	for	while	unsigned
default	goto	*signed	*void
do	if	sizeof	*volatile

Chapter Summary

A C program consists of one or more C *functions*. Every C program must contain a function called `main()` because it is the function called when the program starts up. A simple function consists of a *header* followed by an opening brace, followed by the statements constituting the function *body*, followed by a terminating, or closing, brace.

Each C statement is an instruction to the computer and is marked by a terminating semicolon. A *declaration statement* creates a name for a variable and identifies the type of data to be stored in the variable. An *assignment statement* assigns a value to a variable or, more generally, to a storage area. A *function call statement* causes the named function to be executed. When the called function is done, the program returns to the next statement after the function call.

The `printf()` function can be used to print phrases and the values of variables.

The *syntax* of a language is the set of rules that governs the way in which valid statements in that language are put together. The *semantics* of a statement is its meaning. The compiler will help you detect syntax errors, but semantic errors show up in a program's behavior only after it is compiled. Detecting semantic errors may involve tracing the *program state*, that is, the values of all variables, after each program step.

Keywords are the vocabulary of the C language.

Review Questions

1. What are the basic modules of a C program called?

2. What is a syntax error? Give an example of one in English and of one in C.

3. What is a semantic error? Give an example of one in English and of one in C.

4. Ichabod Bodie Marfoote has prepared the following program and brought it to you for approval. Please help him out.

   ```
   include studio.h
   int main{void} /* this prints the number of weeks in a year /*
   (
   int s

   s : = 56;
   print(There are s weeks in a year.);
   return 0;
   ```

5. Assuming that each of the following examples is part of a complete program, what will each one print?

   ```
   a. printf("Baa Baa Black Sheep.");
      printf("Have you any wool?\n");
   ```

```
b. printf("Begone!\nO creature of lard!");
c. printf("What?\nNo/nBonzo?\n");
d. int num;

   num = 2;
   printf("%d + %d = %d", num, num, num + num);
```

6. Which of the following are C keywords? main, int, function, char, =

7. How would you print the values of words and lines in the form There were 3020 words and 350 lines.? Here, 3020 and 350 represent values for the two variables.

8. Consider the following program:

```
#include <stdio.h>
int main(void)
{
  int a, b;

    a = 5;
    b = 2;     /* line 7 */
    b = a;     /* line 8 */
    a = b;     /* line 9 */
    printf("%d %d\n", b, a);
    return 0;
}
```

What is the program state after line 5? line 6? line 7?

Programming Exercises

Reading about C isn't enough. You should try writing one or two simple programs to see if writing a program goes as smoothly as it looks in this chapter. Here are a few suggestions, but you should also try to think up some problems yourself.

1. Write a program that uses one printf() call to print your first name and last name on one line, uses a second printf() call to print your first and last name on two separate lines, and uses a pair of printf() calls to print your first and last name on one line. The output should look like this:

```
Mae West     →first print statement
Mae          →second print statement
West         →still the second print statement
Mae West     →third and fourth print statements
```

2. Write a program to print your name and address.

3. Write a program that converts your age in years to days. At this point, don't worry about fractional years and leap years.

4. Write a program that produces this output:

```
For he's a jolly good fellow!
For he's a jolly good fellow!
For he's a jolly good fellow!
Which nobody can deny!
```

Have the program use two user-defined functions in addition to main(): one that prints the *jolly good* message once, and one that prints the final line once.

5. Write a program that creates an integer variable called toes. Have the program set toes to 10. Also have the program calculate what twice toes is and what toes squared is. The program should print all three values, identifying them.

Data and C

Keywords
int, short, long, unsigned, char, float, double
Operators
sizeof
Function
scanf()

In this chapter you learn about the basic data types that C uses and about the distinctions between integer types and floating-point types. You practice writing constants and declaring variables of those types. You begin studying how to use the printf() and scanf() functions to read and write values of different types.

Programs work with data. You feed numbers, letters, and words to the computer, and you expect it to do something with the data. For example, you may want the computer to calculate an interest payment or display a sorted list of vintners. In this chapter you will do more than just read about data; you will practice manipulating data, which is much more fun.

This chapter explores the two great families of data types: integer and floating point. C offers several varieties of these types. You'll learn what the types are, how to declare them, how to use them, and when to use them. Also, you'll discover the differences between constants and variables, and as a bonus, your first interactive program will be coming up shortly.

A Sample Program

Once again we begin with a sample program. As before, you'll find some unfamiliar wrinkles that we'll soon iron out for you. The program's general intent should be clear, so try compiling and running the source code shown in Listing 3.1. To save time, you can omit typing the comments. (For reference, we've included a program name as a comment. We will continue this practice with future programs.)

Listing 3.1. goldyou.c.

```
/* goldyou.c  -- the worth of your weight in gold */
#include <stdio.h>
int main(void)
{
    float weight, value;     /* 2 floating-point variables */
    char beep;               /* a character variable       */

    beep = '\ a';
            /* assigning a special character to beep      */
    printf("Are you worth your weight in gold?\n");
    printf("Please enter your weight in pounds, ");
    printf("and we'll see.\n");
    scanf("%f", &weight);
            /* getting input from the user                */
    value = 400.0 * weight * 14.5833;
            /* assumes gold is $400 per ounce             */
            /* 14.5833 converts pounds avd. to ounces troy */
    printf("%cYour weight in gold is worth $%.2f%c.\n",
            beep,value,beep);
    printf("You are easily worth that! If gold prices drop, ");
    printf("eat more\nto maintain your value.\n");
    return 0;
}
```

When you type this program, you may wish to change the 400.0 to the current price of gold. We suggest, however, that you don't fiddle with the 14.5833, which represents the number of ounces in a pound. (That's ounces *troy*, used for precious metals, and pounds *avoirdupois*, used for people, precious and otherwise.) Note that "entering" your weight means to type your weight and then press the Enter or Return key. (Don't just type your weight and wait.) Pressing Enter informs the computer that you have finished typing your response. When we ran the program, the results looked like this:

```
Are you worth your weight in gold?
Please enter your weight in pounds, and we'll see.
175
Your weight in gold is worth $1020831.00.
You are easily worth that! If gold prices drop, eat more
to maintain your value.
```

This program also has a nonvisual aspect. You will have to run the program yourself to find out what that is, but the name of one of the variables should provide a clue.

What's New in This Program?

There are several new elements of C in this program.

- Notice that we use two new kinds of variable declarations. Previously, we used only an integer variable type (int), but now we've added a floating-point variable type (float) and a character variable type (char) so that we can handle a wider variety of data. The float type can hold numbers with decimal points, and the char type can hold characters.

- We've included some new ways of writing constants. We now have numbers with decimal points, and we have a rather peculiar-looking notation to represent the character named beep.

- To print these new kinds of variables, we use the %f and the %c codes of printf() to handle floating-point and character variables, respectively. We use the .2 modifier to the %f code to fine-tune the appearance of the output so that it displays two places to the right of the decimal.

- To provide keyboard input to the program, we use the scanf() function. The %f instructs scanf() to read a floating-point number from the keyboard, and the &weight tells scanf() to assign the input value to the variable named weight. The scanf() function uses the & notation to indicate where it can find the weight variable. We'll discuss & further in the next chapter; meanwhile, trust us that you need it here.

- Perhaps the most outstanding new feature is that this program is *interactive*. The computer asks you for information and then uses the number you type in. An interactive program is more interesting to use than the noninteractive types. More important, the interactive approach makes programs more flexible. For instance, our example program can be used for any reasonable weight, not just for 175 pounds. We don't have to rewrite the program every time we want to try it on a new person. The scanf() and printf() functions make this possible. The scanf() function reads data from the keyboard and delivers that data to the program, and printf() reads data from a program and delivers that data to your screen. Together, these two functions enable you to establish a two-way communication with your computer (see Figure 3.1), and that makes using a computer much more fun.

This chapter will explain the first two items in this list of new features: variables and constants of various data types. Chapter 4, "Character Strings and Formatted Input/Output," will cover the last three items, but we will continue to make limited use of scanf() and printf() in this chapter.

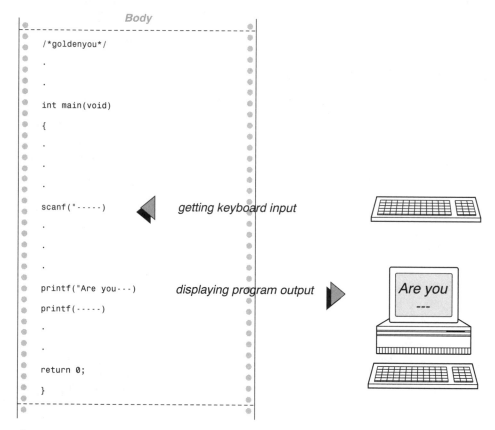

Figure 3.1. *The functions* scanf() *and* printf() *at work.*

Data: Variables and Constants

A computer, under the guidance of a program, can do many things. It can add numbers, sort names, command the obedience of a speaker or video screen, calculate cometary orbits, prepare a mailing list, dial phone numbers, draw stick figures, draw conclusions, or anything else your imagination can create. To do these tasks, the program needs to work with *data*, the numbers and characters that bear the information you use. Some data are preset before a program is used and keep their values unchanged throughout the life of the program. These are *constants*. Other data may change or be assigned values as the program runs; these are *variables*. In our sample program, weight is a variable and 14.5833 is a constant. What about the 400.0? True, the price of gold isn't a constant in real life, but our program treats it as a constant. The difference between a variable and a constant is that a variable can have its value assigned or changed while the program is running, and a constant can't.

Data: Data-Type Keywords

Beyond the distinction between variable and constant is the distinction between different *types* of data. Some data are numbers. Some are letters or, more generally, characters. The computer needs a way to identify and use these different kinds. C does this by recognizing several fundamental *data types*. If a datum is a constant, the compiler usually can tell its type just by the way it looks: 46 is an integer, and 46.100 is floating point. A variable, however, needs to have its type announced in a declaration statement. You'll learn the details of declaring variables as we move along. First, though, let's look at the fundamental types recognized by C. K&R C recognized seven keywords. ANSI C added four to the list. Two of these—void (see Chapter 2, "Introducing C") and signed—had come into general use previously. Here are the keywords:

Original K&R Keywords	Keywords from ANSI C
int	signed
long	void
short	const
unsigned	volatile
char	
float	
double	

We'll discuss the K&R keywords and the signed keyword here. The const and volatile keywords are covered in Chapter 13, "Storage Classes and Program Development."

The int keyword provides the basic class of integers used in C. The next three keywords (long, short, and unsigned) and the ANSI addition signed are used to provide variations of the basic type. Next, the char keyword designates the type used for letters of the alphabet and for other characters, such as #, $, %, and *. The char type also can be used to represent small integers. Finally, float, double, and the ANSI C combination long double are used to represent numbers with decimal points.

The types created with these keywords can be divided into two families on the basis of how they are stored in the computer. The first five keywords from the pre-ANSI C list create *integer* types, while the last two create *floating-point* types.

Bits, Bytes, and Words

The terms *bit, byte,* and *word* can be used to describe units of computer data or to describe units of computer memory. We'll concentrate on the second usage here.

The smallest unit of memory is called a *bit.* It can hold one of two values: 0 or 1. (Or we can say that the bit is set to "off" or "on.") You can't store much information in 1 bit, but a computer has a tremendous stock of them. The bit is the basic building block of computer memory.

The *byte* is the usual unit of computer memory. For nearly all machines a byte is 8 bits, and that is the standard definition. Because each bit can be either 0 or 1, there are 256 (that's 2 times itself 8 times) possible bit patterns of *0*s and *1*s that can fit in a byte. These patterns can be used, for example, to represent the integers from 0 to 255 or to represent a set of characters. Representation can be accomplished using *binary code*, which uses (conveniently enough) just *0*s and *1*s to represent numbers. (We discuss binary code in Chapter 15, "Bit Fiddling," but you can read through the introductory material of that chapter now if you like.)

A *word* is the natural unit of memory for a given computer design. For 8-bit microcomputers, such as the original Apples, a word is just 1 byte. The IBM AT and its clones are 16-bit machines. This means that they have a word size of 16 bits, which is 2 bytes. Machines like the 80386-based and 80486-based PCs and the Macintosh II have 32-bit words. More powerful computers can have 64-bit words or even larger. Our examples assume a word size of 16 bits unless noted otherwise.

Integer Versus Floating-Point Types

Integer types? Floating-point types? If you find these terms disturbingly unfamiliar, relax. We are about to give you a brief rundown of their meanings. If you are unfamiliar with *bits, bytes,* and *words,* you may wish to read the nearby box about them first. Do you *have* to learn all the details? Not really, not any more than you have to learn the principles of internal combustion engines to drive a car, not knowing a little about what goes on inside a computer or engine can occasionally help you.

For a human, the difference between integers and floating-point numbers is reflected in the way they can be written. For a computer, the difference is reflected in the way they are stored. Let's look at each of the two classes in turn.

The Integer

An *integer* is a number with no fractional part. In C, an integer never is written with a decimal point. Examples are 2, –23, and 2456. Numbers like 3.14, 0.22, and 2.000 are not integers. Integers are stored as binary numbers. The integer 7, for example, is written

111 in binary. Thus, to store this number in a byte, just set the first 5 bits to 0 and the last 3 bits to 1. See Figure 3.2.

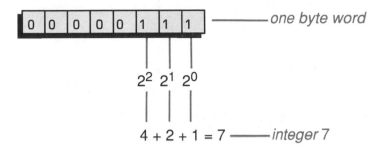

Figure 3.2. *Storing the integer 7 using a binary code.*

The Floating-Point Number

A *floating-point* number more or less corresponds to what mathematicians call a *real number*. Real numbers include the numbers between the integers. Here are some floating-point numbers: 2.75, 3.16E7, 7.00, and 2e–8. Obviously, there is more than one way to write a floating-point number. We will discuss the *E*-notation more fully later. In brief, the notation *3.16E7* means to multiply 3.16 by 10 to the 7th power; that is, by 1 followed by 7 zeros. The 7 would be termed the *exponent* of 10.

The key point here is that the scheme used to store a floating-point number is different from the one used to store an integer. Floating-point representation involves breaking up a number into a fractional part and an exponent part and storing the parts separately. Thus, the 7.00 in this list would not be stored in the same manner as the integer 7, even though both have the same value. The decimal analogy would be to write 7.0 as 0.7E1. Here, 0.7 is the fractional part, and the 1 is the exponent part. Figure 3.3 shows another example of floating-point storage. A computer, of course, would use binary numbers and powers of two instead of powers of ten for internal storage. You'll find more on this topic in Chapter 15, "Bit Fiddling." Now, let's concentrate on the practical differences, which are these:

- An integer has no fractional part; a floating-point number can have a fractional part.

- Floating-point numbers can represent a much larger range of values than integers can. See Table 3.2 near the end of this chapter.

- For some arithmetic operations, such as subtracting one large number from another, floating-point numbers are subject to greater loss of precision.

- Floating-point operations normally are slower than integer operations. However, microprocessors specifically developed to handle floating-point operations are now available, and they are quite swift.

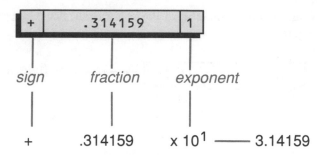

Figure 3.3. *Storing the number pi in floating-point format (decimal version).*

C Data Types

Now let's look at the specifics of the basic data types used by C. For each type, we describe how to declare a variable, how to represent a constant, and what a typical use would be. Some pre-ANSI C compilers do not support all these types, so check your manual to see which ones you have available.

The *int* Type

C offers a variety of integer types. They vary in the range of values offered and in whether negative numbers can be used. The int type is the basic choice, but should you need other choices to meet the requirements of a particular task or machine, they are available.

The int type is a *signed integer*. That means it must be an integer and it can be positive, negative, or zero. The range in possible values depends on the computer system. Typically, an int uses one machine word for storage. Thus, an IBM PC, which has a 2-byte word, uses 2 bytes (16 bits) to store an int. This allows a range in values from −32768 to +32767. Other machines may have different ranges. See Table 3.2 near the end of this chapter for examples. ANSI C specifies that the minimum range for type int should be from −32767 to +32767. Typically, systems represent signed integers by reserving 1 bit for indicating the sign.

Declaring an *int* Variable

As you saw in Chapter 2, "Introducing C," the keyword int is used to declare the basic integer variable. First comes int, then the chosen name of the variable, and then a semicolon. To declare more than one variable, you can declare each variable separately, or you can follow the int with a list of names in which each name is separated from the next by a comma. The following are valid declarations:

```
int erns;
int hogs, cows, goats;
```

We could have used a separate declaration for each variable, or we could have declared all four variables in the same statement. The effect is the same: associate names and arrange storage space for four `int`-sized variables.

These declarations create variables but don't provide values for them. How do variables get values? You've seen two ways that they can pick up values in the program. First, there is assignment

```
cows = 112;
```

Second, a variable can pick up a value from a function, from `scanf()`, for example. Now let's look at a third way.

Initializing a Variable

To *initialize* a variable means to assign it an initial, or starting, value. In C, this can be done as part of the declaration. Just follow the variable name with the assignment operator (=) and the value you want the variable to have. Here are some examples:

```
int hogs = 21;
int cows = 32, goats = 14;
int dogs, cats = 94;          /* valid, but poor, form */
```

In the last line, only `cats` is initialized. A quick reading might lead you to think that `dogs` is also initialized to `94`, so it is best to avoid putting initialized and noninitialized variables in the same declaration statement.

In short, these declarations create and label the storage for the variables and assign starting values to each. See Figure 3.4.

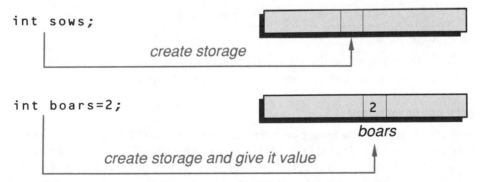

Figure 3.4. *Defining and initializing a variable.*

Type *int* Constants

The various integers (21, 32, 14, and 94) in the last example are integer constants. When you write a number without a decimal point and without an exponent, C recognizes it as an integer. Thus, 22 and −44 are integer constants, but 22.0 and 2.2E1 are not. C treats most integer constants as type `int`. Very large integers may be treated differently; see the later discussion of the `long int` type.

Printing *int* Values

You can use the `printf()` function to print `int` types. As you saw in Chapter 2, "Introducing C," the `%d` notation is used to indicate just where in a line the integer is to be printed. The `%d` is an example of a *format specifier*, for it indicates the form that `printf()` uses to display a value. Each `%d` in the format string must be matched by a corresponding `int` value in the list of items to be printed. That value can be an `int` variable, an `int` constant, or any other expression having an `int` value. Listing 3.2 presents a simple program that initializes a variable and prints the value of the variable, the value of a constant, and the value of a simple expression.

Listing 3.2. print1.c.

```
/* print1.c -- displays some properties of printf() */
#include <stdio.h>
int main(void)
{
    int ten = 10;

    printf("%d minus %d is %d\n", ten, 2, ten - 2 );
    return 0;
}
```

Compiling and running the program produces this output:

```
10 MINUS 2 IS 8
```

Thus, the first `%d` represents the `int` variable `ten`, the second `%d` represents the `int` constant 2, and the third `%d` represents the value of the `int` expression `ten - 2`.

Octal and Hexadecimal

Normally, C assumes that integer constants are decimal, or base 10, numbers. However, octal (base 8) and hexadecimal (base 16) numbers are popular with many programmers. Because 8 and 16 are powers of 2, and 10 is not, these number systems occasionally provide a more convenient way for expressing computer-related values. For example, the number 65536, which often pops up in 16-bit machines, is just 10000 in hexadecimal, but how can the computer tell whether 10000 is meant to be a decimal, hexadecimal, or octal value? In C, special prefixes indicate which number base you are using. A prefix of `0x` or `0X` (zero-exe) means that you are specifying a hexadecimal value, so 16 is written as 0x10, or 0X10, in hexadecimal. Similarly, a `0` (zero) prefix means that you are writing in octal.

For example, in C the decimal value 16 is written as 020 in octal. Chapter 15, "Bit Fiddling," discusses these alternative number bases more fully.

Be aware that this option of using different number systems is provided as a service for your convenience. It doesn't affect how the number is stored. That is, you can write 16 or 020 or 0x10, and the number will be stored exactly the same way in each case—in the binary code used internally by computers.

Printing Octal and Hexadecimal

Just as C enables you write a number in any one of three number systems, so it also enables you to print a number in any of these three systems. To print an integer in octal notation instead of decimal, use %o instead of %d. To print an integer in hexadecimal, use %x. Listing 3.3 shows a short example.

Listing 3.3. `bases.c`.

```
/* bases.c -- prints 100 in decimal, octal, and hex */
#include <stdio.h>
int main(void)
{
    int x = 100;

    printf("dec = %d; octal = %o; hex = %x\n", x, x, x);
    return 0;
}
```

Compiling and running this program produces this output:

```
dec = 100; octal = 144; hex = 64
```

We see the same value displayed in three different number systems. The `printf()` function makes the conversions. Note that the `0` and the `0x` prefixes are not displayed in the output. ANSI C provides that the specifiers %#o, %#x, and %#X generate the 0, 0x, and 0X prefixes, respectively.

Other Integer Types

When you are just learning the language, the `int` type probably will meet most of your integer needs. To be complete, however, we'll look at the other forms now. If you like, you can skim this section and jump to the discussion of the `char` type, returning here when you have a need.

C offers three *adjective keywords* to modify the basic integer type: `short`, `long`, and `unsigned`.

- The type `short int` or, more briefly, `short` may use less storage than `int`, thus saving space when only small numbers are needed. Like `int`, `short` is a signed type.

- The type `long int`, or `long`, may use more storage than `int`, thus enabling you to express larger integer values. Like `int`, `long` is a signed type.

- The type `unsigned int`, or `unsigned`, is used for variables that will have only nonnegative values. This type shifts the range of numbers that can be stored. For example, a 2-byte `unsigned int` allows a range from 0 to 65535 in value instead of from −32768 to +32767. The bit used to indicate the sign of signed numbers now becomes another binary digit, allowing the larger number.

- ANSI C and many pre-ANSI C compilers also recognize as valid types `unsigned long int`, or `unsigned long`, and `unsigned short int`, or `unsigned short`.

Declaring Other Integer Types

Other integer types are declared in the same manner as the `int` type. The following list shows several examples. Not all pre-ANSI C compilers will recognize the last two.

```
long int estine;
long johns;
short int erns;
short ribs;
unsigned int s_count;
unsigned players;
unsigned long headcount;
unsigned short yesvotes;
```

Why Three Sizes?

Why do we say that `long` and `short` types "may" use more or less storage than `int`? Because C guarantees only that `short` is no longer than `int` and that `long` is no shorter than `int`. The idea is to fit the types to the machine. On an IBM PC, for example, an `int` and a `short` are both 16 bits, and a `long` is 32 bits. On a VAX 750, however, a `short` is 16 bits, and both `int` and `long` are 32 bits. The natural word size on a VAX is 32 bits. Because this allows integers in excess of 2 billion (see Table 3.2), the implementors of C on the VAX did not see a necessity for anything larger; thus, `long` is the same as `int`. For many uses, integers of that size are not needed, so a space-saving `short` was created. The IBM PC, on the other hand, has only a 16-bit word, which means that a larger `long` was needed.

The most common practice today is to set up `long` as 32 bits, `short` as 16 bits, and `int` to either 16 bits or 32 bits, depending on the machine's natural word size. In principle, however, these three types could represent three distinct sizes.

ANSI C provides guidelines specifying the minimum allowable size for each basic data type. The minimum range for both `short` and `int` is −32767 to +32767, corresponding to a 2-byte unit, and the minimum range for `long` is −2147483647 to +2147483647, corresponding to a 4-byte unit. For unsigned short and unsigned int, the minimum range is 0 to 65535, and for unsigned long the minimum range is 0 to 4294967295.

When do you use the various int types? First, consider unsigned types. It is natural to use them for counting, because you don't need negative numbers and the unsigned types enable you to reach higher positive numbers than the signed types.

Use the long type if you need to use numbers that long can handle and that int cannot. However, on systems for which long is bigger than int, using long may slow down calculations, so don't use long if it is not essential. One further point: If you are writing code on a machine for which int and long are the same size, and if you do need 32-bit integers, you should use long instead of int so that the program will function correctly if transferred to a 16-bit machine.

Use short to save storage space or if, say, you need a 16-bit value on a system where int is 32-bit. Saving storage space usually is important only if your program uses arrays of integers that are large relative to a system's available memory.

Integer Overflow

What happens if an integer tries to get too big for its type? Let's set an integer to its largest possible value, add to it, and see what happens.

```c
/* toobig.c -- exceeds maximum int size on our system */
#include <stdio.h>
int main(void)
{
    short i = 32767;

    printf("%d %d %d\n", i, i+1, i+2);

    return 0;
}
```

Here's the result for our system:

```
32767 -]32768 -32767
```

The integer i is acting like a car's odometer. When it reaches its maximum value, it starts over at the beginning. The main difference is that an odometer begins at 0, but our short int begins at –32768. Notice that you are not informed that i has exceeded (overflowed) its maximum value. You would have to include your own programming to keep tabs on that.

The behavior described here is not mandated by the rules of C, but it is the typical implementation.

Type *long* Constants

Normally, when you use a number like 2345 in your program code, it is stored as an int type. What if you use a number like 1000000 on a system in which int will not hold such a large number? Then the compiler treats it as a long int, assuming that type is large enough. If the number is larger than the long maximum, C will treat it as unsigned long.

Sometimes you may want the compiler to store a small number as a long integer. Programming that involves explicit use of memory addresses on an IBM PC, for instance, can create such a need. Also, some standard C functions require type long values. To cause a small constant to be treated as type long, you can append an *l* (lowercase *ell*) or L as a suffix. We recommend the second form, because it looks less like the digit 1. Thus, a system with a 16-bit int and a 32-bit long treats the integer 7 as 2 bytes and the integer 7L as 4 bytes. The l and L suffixes also can be used with octal and hex integers, as in 020L and 0x10L.

Printing *long*, *short*, and *unsigned* Types

To print an unsigned int number, use the %u notation. To print a long value, use the %ld format specifier. If int and long are the same size on your system, just %d will suffice, but your program will not work properly when transferred to a system on which the two types are different. You can use the l prefix for x and o, too. Thus, you would use %lx to print a long integer in hexadecimal format and %lo to print in octal format.

ANSI C provides several additional printf() forms. First, you can use an *h* prefix for short types. Thus, %hd displays a short integer in decimal form, and %ho displays a short integer in octal form. Both the h and l prefixes can be used with *u* for unsigned types. For instance, you would use the %lu notation for printing unsigned long types. Listing 3.4 provides a sample.

Listing 3.4. print2.c.

```
/* print2.c -- more printf() properties */
#include <stdio.h>
int main(void)
{
  unsigned un = 40000;
  long ln = 2000000000;
  unsigned long uln = 2 * 2000000000; /* or 4000000000 */
  short sn = 200;

  printf("un = %u and not %d\n", un, un);
  printf("ln = %ld and not %d\n", ln, ln);
  printf("uln = %lu and not %u\n", uln, uln);
  printf("sn = %hd and, on this system, %d\n", sn, sn);
  return 0;
}
```

Here is the output:

```
un = 40000 and not -25536
ln = 2000000000 and not -27648
uln = 4000000000 and not 10240
sn = 200 and, on this system, 200
```

This example points out that using the wrong specification can produce unexpected results. It also points out that you should be wary of implementation differences. For instance, we used 2 * 2000000000 instead of 4000000000 because one of our compilers does not recognize written decimal integers beyond the long limit; in this respect, it falls short of the ANSI C Standard. (The * symbol is used in C to indicate multiplication.)

A C Oddity

You can use either the %hd or the %d specifier to print a *short* integer. That's because C automatically expands a type short value to a type int value when it's passed as an argument to a function. This may raise two questions in your mind: why does this conversion take place, and what's the use of the h modifier? The answer to the first question is that the int type is intended to be the integer size that the computer handles most efficiently. Thus, on a computer for which short and int are different sizes, it may be faster to pass the value as an int. The answer to the second question is that you can use the h modifier to show how a longer integer would look if truncated to the size of short.

Using Characters: Type *char*

The char type is used for storing characters such as letters and punctuation marks, but technically it is an integer type. Why? Because the char type actually stores integers, not characters. To handle characters, the computer uses a numerical code in which certain integers represent certain characters. The most commonly used code is the ASCII code given in Appendix E," ASCII Table." It is the code we will assume for this book. In it, for example, the integer value 65 represents an uppercase *A*. So to store the letter *A*, we actually need to store the integer 65. (Many IBM mainframes use a different code, called EBCDIC, but the principle is the same.)

The standard ASCII code runs numerically from 0 to 127. This range is small enough that 7 bits can hold it. The char type typically is defined as a 1-byte (or 8-bit) unit of memory, so it is more than large enough to encompass the standard ASCII code. Many systems, such as the IBM PC and the Apple Macintosh, offer extended ASCII codes (different for the two systems) that still stay within an 8-bit limit. More generally, C guarantees that the char type is large enough to store the basic character set for the system on which C is implemented.

Declaring Type *char* Variables

As you might expect, `char` variables are declared in the same manner as other variables. Here are some examples:

```
char response;
char itable, latan;
```

This program would create three `char` variables: `response`, `itable`, and `latan`.

Character Constants and Initialization

Suppose you want to initialize a character constant to the letter *A*. Computer languages are supposed to make things easy; we shouldn't have to memorize the ASCII code, and we don't. We can assign the character A to `grade` with the following initialization:

```
char grade = 'A';
```

A single letter contained between single quotes is a C character constant. When the compiler sees `'A'`, it converts the `'A'` to the proper code value. The single quotes are essential.

```
char broiled;          /* declare a char variable     */
broiled = 'T';         /* OK                          */
broiled = T;           /* NO! Thinks T is a variable  */
broiled = "T";         /* NO! Thinks "T" is a string  */
```

If you leave off the quotes, the compiler will think that T is the name of a variable. If you use double quotes, it will think you are using a *string*. We'll discuss strings in Chapter 4, "Character Strings and Formatted Input/Output."

Because characters really are stored as numeric values, you also can use the numerical code to assign values.

```
char grade = 65;
```

In this example, 65 is type `int`, but, because the value is smaller than the maximum `char` size, it can be assigned to `grade` without any problems. Because 65 is the ASCII code for the letter *A*, this example assigns the value A to `grade`. Note, however, that this example assumes that the system is using ASCII code. Using 'A' instead of 65 produces code that works on any system. Therefore, it's better to use character constants than numeric code values.

Nonprinting Characters

The single quote technique is fine for characters, digits, and punctuation marks, but if you look through Appendix E, "ASCII Table," you will see that some of the ASCII characters are *nonprinting*. For example, some represent actions such as backspacing or going to the next line or making the terminal bell ring (or speaker beep). How can these be represented? C offers three ways.

The first way we have already mentioned: just use the ASCII code. For example, the ASCII value for the beep character is 7, so we can do this:

```
char beep = 7;
```

The second way to represent certain awkward characters in C is to use special symbol sequences. These are called *escape sequences*. Table 3.1 shows the escape sequences and their meanings.

Table 3.1. Escape sequences.

Sequence	Meaning
\a	Alert (ANSI C)
\b	Backspace
\f	Form feed
\n	Newline
\r	Carriage return
\t	Horizontal tab
\v	Vertical tab (ANSI C)
\\	Backslash (\)
\'	Single quote (')
\"	Double quote (") (ANSI C)
\0oo	Octal value (*o* represents an octal digit)
\xhh	Hexadecimal value (*h* represents a hexadecimal digit)

Escape sequences must be enclosed in single quotes when assigned to a character variable. For example, we could make the statement

```
nerf = '\n';
```

and then print the variable nerf to advance the printer or screen one line.

Let's take a closer look at what each escape sequence does. The alert character (\a), added by ANSI C, produces an audible or visible alert. The nature of the alert depends on the hardware, with the beep being the most common. The ANSI Standard states that the alert character shall not change the *active position*. By active position, the Standard means the location on the display device (screen, teletype, printer, etc.) at which the next character would otherwise appear. In short, the active position is a generalization of the screen cursor you probably are accustomed to. Using the alert character in a program displayed on a screen should produce a beep without moving the screen cursor.

Next, the \b, \f, \n, \r, \t, and \v escape sequences are common output device control characters. They are best described in terms of how they affect the active position. A backspace (\b) moves the active position back one space on the current line. A form feed (\f) advances the active position to the start of the next page. A newline (\n) sets the active position to the beginning of the next. A carriage return (\r) moves the active position to the beginning of the current line. A horizontal tab (\t) moves the active position to the next horizontal tab stop; typically, these are found at character positions 1, 9, 17, 25, and so on. A vertical tab (\v) moves the active position to the next vertical tab position.

These escape characters do not necessarily work with all display devices. For instance, the form feed and vertical tab characters produce odd symbols on a PC screen rather than any cursor movement, but they work as described if sent to a printer instead of to the screen.

The next three escape sequences (\\, \', and \") enable you to use \, ', and " as character constants. (Because these symbols are used to define character constants as part of a printf() command, the situation could get confusing if you use them literally.) If you want to print the line

```
Gramps sez, "a \ is a backslash."
```

use

```
printf("Gramps sez, \"a \\ is a backslash.\"\n");
```

The final two forms (\0oo and \xhh) are special representations of the ASCII code. To represent a character by its octal ASCII code, precede it with a backslash (\), and enclose the whole thing in single quotes. For instance, if your compiler doesn't recognize the alert character (\a), you could use the ASCII code instead in goldyou.c (Listing 3.1).

```
beep = '\007';
```

You can omit the leading zeros, so '\07' or even '\7' will do. This notation causes numbers to be interpreted as octal even if there is no initial 0.

ANSI C and many new implementations accept a hexadecimal form for character constants. In this case, the backslash is followed by an x or X and one to three hexadecimal digits. For example, the Control-P character has an ASCII hex code of 10 (16, in decimal), so it can be expressed as '\x10' or '\X010'. Figure 3.5 shows some representative integer types.

When you use ASCII code, note the difference between numbers and number characters. For example, the character 4 is represented by ASCII code value 52. This represents the symbol 4, not the numerical value 4.

At this point you may have three questions. One, why aren't the escape sequences enclosed in single quotes in the last example (printf("Gramps sez, \"a \\ is a backslash.\"\n");)? Two, when should you use the ASCII code, and when should you use the escape sequences? Three, if you need to use numeric code, why use, say, '\032' instead of 032? Here are the answers:

1. When a character, be it an escape sequence or not, is part of a string of characters enclosed in double quotes, don't enclose it in single quotes. Notice that none of the other characters in this example (G,r,a,m,p,s, etc.) are marked off by single quotes. A string of characters enclosed in double quotes is called a *character string*. We will explore strings in Chapter 4, "Character Strings and Formatted Input/Output." Similarly, printf("Hello!\007\n"); will print Hello! and beep, but printf("Hello!7\n"); will print Hello!7. Digits not part of an escape sequence are treated as ordinary characters to be printed.

2. If you have a choice between using one of the special escape sequences, say '\f', or an equivalent ASCII code, say '\014', use the '\f'. First, the representation is more mnemonic. Second, it is more portable. If you have a system that doesn't use ASCII code, the '\f' will still work.

3. First, using '\032' instead of 032 makes it clear to someone reading the code that you intend to represent a character code. Second, an escape sequence like \032 can be embedded in part of a C string, the way \007 was in point #1.

Int Family Constants			
member	hex	octal	decimal
char	'\ x1A'	'\034'	N.A.
short	$\pm$0x23	$\pm$078	$\pm$92
unsigned short	$\pm$0x23	078	92
Long	0x23L	$\pm$078L	$\pm$92L

Figure 3.5. *Writing constants with the* int *family.*

Printing Characters

The printf() function uses %c to indicate that a character should be printed. Recall that a character is stored as a 1-byte integer value. Thus, if you print the value of a char variable with the usual %d specifier, you get an integer. The %c format specifier tells printf() to convert the integer to the corresponding character. Listing 3.5 shows a char variable both ways.

Listing 3.5. charcode.c.

```c
/* charcode.c -- displays code number for a character */
#include <stdio.h>
int main(void)
{
    char ch;

    printf("Please enter a character.\n");
    scanf("%c", &ch);    /* user inputs character */
    printf("The code for %c is %d.\n", ch, ch);
    return 0;
}
```

Here is a sample run:

```
Please enter a character.
C
The code for C is 67.
```

When you use the program, remember to press the Enter or Return key after typing the character. The scanf() function then fetches the character you typed, and the ampersand (&) causes the character to be assigned to the variable ch. The printf() function then prints the value of ch twice, first as a character (prompted by the %c code) and then as a decimal integer (prompted by the %d code). Note that the printf() specifiers determine how data is *displayed*, not how it is *stored*. See Figure 3.6.

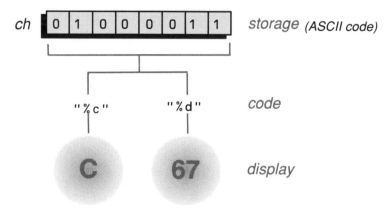

Figure 3.6. *Data display versus data storage.*

Signed or Unsigned?

Some C implementations make char a signed type. This means a char can hold values typically in the range −128 through +127. Other implementations make char an unsigned type. This provides a range of 0 through 255. Your compiler manual should tell you which type your char is.

ANSI C and many newer implementations enable you to use the keywords signed and unsigned with char. Then, regardless of what your default char is, signed char would be signed, and unsigned char would be unsigned.

Types *float* and *double*

The various integer types serve well for most software development projects. However, mathematically oriented programs often make use of *floating-point* numbers. In C, such numbers are called type float. They correspond to the real types of FORTRAN and Pascal. The floating-point approach, as we have already mentioned, enables you to represent a much greater range of numbers, including decimal fractions. Floating-point number representation is similar to *scientific notation*, a system used by scientists to express very large and very small numbers. Let's take a look.

In scientific notation, numbers are represented as decimal numbers times powers of ten. Here are some examples.

Number	Scientific Notation	Exponential Notation
1,000,000,000	$= 1.0 \times 10^9$	$- 1.0e9$
123,000	$= 1.23 \times 10^5$	$= 1.23e5$
322.56	$= 3.2256 \times 10^2$	$= 3.2256e2$
0.000056	$= 5.6 \times 10^{-5}$	$= 5.6e-5$

The first column shows the usual notation, the second column scientific notation, and the third column exponential notation, which is the way scientific notation is usually written for and by computers, with the *e* followed by the power of ten.

Often, systems use 32 bits to store a floating-point number. Eight bits are used to give the exponent its value and sign, and 24 bits are used to represent the nonexponent part. The important points are that this produces a digit precision of six or seven decimals and a range of 10^{-37} to 10^{+38}. This is handy if you like to use numbers such as the mass of the sun (2.0e30 kilograms) or the charge of a proton (1.6e–19 coulombs) or the national debt.

Figure 3.7. *Some floating-point numbers.*

C also has a `double` (for double precision) floating-point type. Although `double` is not required to be any more precise than `float` (just as `long` is not required to be bigger than `int`), it usually uses twice as many bits, typically 64. Some systems use all 32 additional bits for the nonexponent part. This increases the number of significant figures and reduces roundoff errors. Other systems use some of the bits to accommodate a larger exponent; this increases the range of numbers that can be accommodated. ANSI C requires that the `double` type can represent at least 10 significant figures.

ANSI C allows for a third floating-point type: `long double`. The intent is to provide for even more precision than `double`. However, ANSI C guarantees only that `long double` is at least as precise as `double`.

Declaring Floating-Point Variables

Floating-point variables are declared and initialized in the same manner as their integer cousins. Here are some examples:

```
float noah, jonah;
double trouble;
float planck = 6.63e-34;
long double gnp;
```

Floating-Point Constants

There are many choices open to you when you write a floating-point constant. The basic form of a floating-point constant is a signed series of digits including a decimal point, followed by an e or E, followed by a signed exponent indicating the power of 10 used. Here are two examples of valid floating-point constants:

```
-1.56E+12
2.87e-3
```

You can leave out positive signs. You can do without a decimal point (2E5) or an exponential part (19.28), but not both simultaneously. You can omit a fractional part (3.E16) or an integer part (.45E–6), but not both (that wouldn't leave much!). Here are some more valid floating-point constants:

```
3.14159
.2
4e16
.8E-5
100
```

Don't use spaces in a floating-point constant.

WRONG   1.56   E+12

By default, the compiler assumes floating-point constants are double precision. Suppose, for example, that `some` is a `float` variable, and that you have the statement

```
some = 4.0 * 2.0;
```

Then the 4.0 and 2.0 are stored as double, using (typically) 64 bits for each. The product is calculated using double precision arithmetic, and only then is the answer trimmed to regular float size. This ensures greater precision for your calculations but can slow down a program.

ANSI C enables you to override this default by using an f or F suffix to make the compiler treat a floating-point constant as type float: examples are 2.3f and 9.11E9F. An l or L suffix makes it type long double; examples are 54.3l and 4.32e4L. Note that L is less likely to be mistaken for a 1 than is l. If the floating-point number has no suffix, it is type double.

Printing Floating-Point Values

The printf() function uses the %f format specifier to print type float and double numbers using decimal notation, and it uses %e to print them in exponential notation. Listing 3.6 illustrates this.

Listing 3.6. showfpt.c.

```
/* showf_pt.c -- displays float value in two ways */
#include <stdio.h>
int main(void)
{
    float value = 32000.0;

    printf("%f can be written %e\n", value, value);
    return 0;
}
```

This is the output:

```
32000.000000 can be written 3.200000e+004
```

The preceding example illustrates the default output. The next chapter discusses how to control the appearance of this output by setting field widths and the number of places to the right of the decimal.

Those implementations that support the new ANSI C long double type use the %Lf and %Le specifiers to print that type. Note however, that both float and double use the %f or %e specifiers. That's because C automatically expands type float values to type double when they are passed as arguments to any function, including printf().

Other Types

That finishes our list of fundamental data types (see Figure 3.8). For some of you, the list must seem long. Others of you might be thinking that more types are needed. What about a Boolean type or a string type? C doesn't have them, but it still can deal quite well with logical manipulations and with strings. We will take a first look at strings in Chapter 4, "Character Strings and Formatted Input/Output."

Floating-Point Overflow and Underflow

What happens if you try to make a `float` variable exceed its limits? For example, suppose you multiply 1.0e38 by 100 (overflow) or divide 1.0e–37 by 1.0e8 (underflow)? The result depends on the system. With Microsoft C and Borland C on an IBM PC, any number that overflows will cause the program to abort and to print a `runtime error` message; any number that underflows will be replaced by 0. Early versions of Turbo C, on the other hand, aborted a program for both overflow and underflow. Other systems may not issue warnings or may offer you a choice of responses. If this matter concerns you, check the rules for your system. If you can't find the information, don't be afraid of a little trial and error.

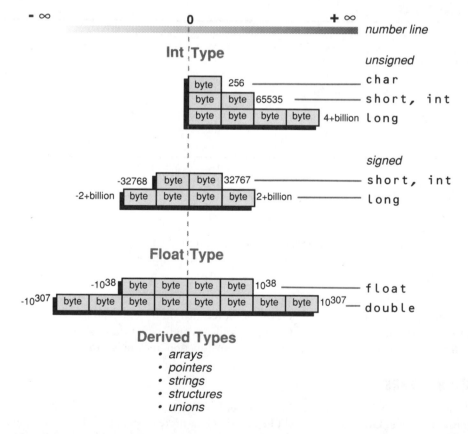

Figure 3.8. *C data types for a typical system.*

C does have other types derived from the basic types. These types include arrays, pointers, structures, and unions. Although these are subject matter for later chapters, we already have smuggled some pointers into this chapter's examples. (A *pointer* points to the location of a variable or other data object. The & prefix we used with the scanf() function creates a pointer telling scanf() where to place information.)

Floating-Point Roundoff Errors

Take a number, add 1 to it, and subtract the original number. What do you get? You get 1. A floating-point calculation, such as the following, may give another answer:

```
/* floaterr.c -- demonstrates round-off error */
#include <stdio.h>
int main(void)
{
    float a,b;

    b = 2.0e20 + 1.0;
    a = b - 2.0e20;
    printf("%f \n", a);
    return 0;
}
```

The output is

```
0.000000                    →VAX 750, UNIX
-13584010575872.000000      →Turbo C 1.5
4008175468544.000000        →Borland C 3.1, MS C 7.0
```

The reason for these odd results is that the computer doesn't keep track of enough decimal places to do the operation correctly. The number 2.0e20 is 2 followed by 20 zeros, and by adding 1, we are trying to change the 21st digit. To do this correctly, the program would need to be able to store a 21-digit number. A float number typically is just 6 or 7 digits scaled to bigger or smaller numbers with an exponent. The attempt is doomed. On the other hand, if we used, say, 2.0e4 instead of 2.0e20, we would get the correct answer because we are trying to change the 5th digit, and float numbers are precise enough for that.

Summary: The Basic Data Types

Keywords

The basic data types are set up using eight *keywords*—int, long, short, unsigned, char, float, double, and signed (ANSI C).

Signed Integers

These can have positive or negative values.

int: the basic integer type for a given system.

long or long int: can hold an integer at least as large as the largest int and possibly larger.

short or short int: the largest short integer is no larger than the largest int and may be smaller. Typically, long will be bigger than short, and int will be the same as one of the two. For example, Turbo C and Microsoft C for the PC provide 16-bit short and int and 32-bit long. It depends on the system, but ANSI C does guarantee at least 16 bits for short and int and at least 32 bits for long.

Unsigned Integers

These have zero or positive values only. This extends the range of the largest possible positive number. Use the keyword unsigned before the desired type: unsigned int, unsigned long, unsigned short. A lone unsigned is the same as unsigned int.

Characters

These are typographic symbols such as A, &, and +. Typically, only 1 byte of memory is used.

char: the keyword for this type. Some implementations use a signed char, but others use an unsigned char. ANSI C enables you to use the keywords signed and unsigned to specify which form you want.

Floating Point

These can have positive or negative values.

float: the basic floating-point type for the system.

double: a (possibly) larger unit for holding floating-point numbers. It may allow more significant figures and perhaps larger exponents than float. long double: a (possibly) even larger unit for holding floating-point numbers. It may allow more significant figures and perhaps larger exponents than double.

> **Summary: How to Declare a Simple Variable**
>
> 1. Choose the type you need.
>
> 2. Choose a name for the variable.
>
> 3. Use the following format for a declaration statement: *type-specifier variable-name;*. The *type-specifier* is formed from one or more of the type keywords; examples of declarations are `int erest;` and `unsigned short cash;`.
>
> 4. You may declare more than one variable of the same type by separating the variable names with commas, for example, `char ch, init, ans;`.
>
> 5. You can initialize a variable in a declaration statement:
>
>   `float mass = 6.0E24;`.

Type Sizes

Tables 3.2 and 3.3 show type sizes for some common C environments. What is your system like? Try running the program in Listing 3.7 to find out.

Table 3.2. Integer type sizes (bytes) for representative systems.

Type	Macintosh (Think C)	DEC VAX	IBM PC (Microsoft and Borland C)	ANSI C Minimum
char	1	1	1	1
int	2	4	2	2
short	2	2	2	2
long	4	4	4	4

Table 3.3. Floating-point facts for representative systems.

Type	Macintosh (Think C)	DEC VAX	IBM PC (Microsoft and Borland C)	ANSI C Minimum
float	6 digits −37 to 38	6 digits −8 to 38	6 digits −37 to 38	6 digits −37 to 37
double	18 digits −4931 to 4932	15 digits −38 to 38	15 digits −307 to 308	10 digits −37 to 37

continues

Table 3.3. continued

Type	Macintosh (Think C)	DEC VAX	IBM PC (Microsoft and Borland C)	ANSI C Minimum
long double	18 digits −4931 to 4932		18 digits −4931 to 4932	10 digits −37 to 37

For each type, the top row is the number of significant digits and the second row is the exponent range (base 10).

Listing 3.7. typesize.c.

```
/* typesize.c -- prints out type sizes */
#include <stdio.h>
int main(void)
{
   printf("Type int has a size of %d bytes.\n", sizeof(int));
   printf("Type char has a size of %d bytes.\n", sizeof(char));
   printf("Type long has a size of %d bytes.\n", sizeof(long));
   printf("Type double has a size of %d bytes.\n",
           sizeof(double));
   return 0;
}}
```

C has a built-in operator called sizeof that gives sizes in bytes. (Some compilers, such as Think C for the Macintosh, require %ld instead of %d for printing sizeof quantities.) Our output from this program was

```
Type int has a size of 2 bytes.
Type char has a size of 1 bytes.
Type long has a size of 4 bytes.
Type double has a size of 8 bytes.
```

This program found the size of only four types, but you can easily modify it to find the size of any other type that interests you. If you have an ANSI C compiler, you can check the limits.h and float.h header files for more detailed information on type limits.

Incidentally, notice in the last line how the printf() statement is spread over two lines. You can do this as long as the break does not occur in the quoted section or in the middle of a word.

Using Data Types

When you develop a program, note the variables you need and which type they should be. Most likely you can use int or possibly float for the numbers and char for the characters. Declare them at the beginning of the function that uses them. Choose a name for the variable that suggests its meaning. When you initialize a variable, match the constant type to the variable type.

```
int apples = 3;        /* RIGHT */
int oranges = 3.0;     /* WRONG */
```

C is more forgiving about type mismatches than, say, Pascal. C compilers allow the second initialization, but they may complain, particularly if you have activated a higher warning level. It is best not to develop sloppy habits.

Arguments and Pitfalls

The items of information passed to a function, as you may recall, are termed *arguments*. For instance, the function call printf("Hello, pal.") has one argument, "Hello, pal.". A series of characters in quotes, such as "Hello, pal.", is called a *string*. We'll discuss strings in Chapter 4, "Character Strings and Formatted Input/Output." For now the important point is that one string, even one containing several words and punctuation marks, counts as one argument.

Similarly, the function call scanf("%d", &weight) has two arguments, "%d" and &weight. C uses commas to separate arguments to a function. The printf() and scanf() functions are unusual in that they aren't limited to a particular number of arguments. For example, we've used calls to printf() with one, two, and even three arguments. For a program to work properly, it needs to know how many arguments there are. The printf() and scanf() functions use the first argument to indicate how many additional arguments are coming. The trick is that each format specification in the initial string indicates an additional argument. For instance, the statement

```
printf("%d cats ate %d cans of tuna\n", cats, cans);
```

has two format specifiers, %d and %d. This tells the program to expect two more arguments, and indeed, there are two more: cats and cans.

Your responsibility as a programmer is to make sure that the number of format specifications matches the number of additional arguments. The new ANSI C function prototyping mechanism checks to see if a function call has the correct number of arguments, but it doesn't work with printf() and scanf() because they take a variable number of arguments. What happens if you don't live up to the programmer's burden? Suppose, for example, you write a program like that of Listing 3.8.

Listing 3.8. badcount.c.

```
/* badcount.c -- incorrect argument counts */
#include <stdio.h>
int main(void)
{
```

continues

Listing 3.8. continued

```
    int f = 4;
    int g = 5;

    printf("%d\n", f, g);   /* too many arguments */
    printf("%d %d\n",f);    /* too few arguments  */
    return 0;
}}
```

None of the five compilers we tried raised any objections to this code. Nor were there any complaints when we ran the program. All four versions printed 4 for the first line. For the second line we got 4 5 (twice), 4 130, 4 936, and 4 13832. As you can see, the computer doesn't catch this kind of error during runtime, and because the program may otherwise run correctly, you may not notice the errors, either. If a program doesn't print the expected number of values or if it prints unexpected values, check to see whether you've used the correct number of `printf()` arguments.

One More Example

Let's run one more printing example, one that makes use of some of C's special escape characters. In particular, the program in Listing 3.9 shows how backspace (\b), tab (\t), and carriage return (\r) work.

Listing 3.9. escape.c.

```
/* escape.c -- uses escape characters */
#include <stdio.h>
int main(void)
{
    float salary;

    printf("Enter your desired monthly salary:");   /* 1 */
    printf(" $_____\b\b\b\b\b\b\b");               /* 2 */
    scanf("%f", &salary);
    printf("\n\t$%.2f a month is $%.2f a year.", salary,
            salary * 12.0);                          /* 3 */
    printf("\rGee!\n");                              /* 4 */
    return 0;
}
```

What Happens

Let's walk through this program step by step as it would work under an ANSI C implementation. The first `printf()` statement (the one we've numbered 1) prints the following:

```
Enter your desired monthly salary:
```

Because there is no \n at the end of the string, the cursor is left positioned after the colon.

The second `printf()` statement picks up where the first one stops, so after it is finished, the screen looks like this:

```
Enter your desired monthly salary: $_____
```

The space between the colon and the dollar sign is there because the string in the second `printf()` statement starts with a space. The effect of the seven backspace characters is to move the cursor seven positions to the left. This backs the cursor over the seven underline characters, placing the cursor directly after the dollar sign. Note that backspacing does not erase the characters that are backed over.

At this point, you type your response, say `2000.00`. Now the line looks like this:

```
Enter your desired monthly salary: $2000.00
```

The characters you type replace the underline characters, and when you press Enter (or Return) to enter your response, the cursor moves to the beginning of the next line.

The third `printf()` statement output begins with \n\t. The newline character moves the cursor to the beginning of the next line. The tab character moves the cursor to the next tab stop on that line, typically to column 9. Then the rest of the string is printed. After this statement, the screen looks like this:

```
Enter your desired monthly salary: $2000.00

        $2000.00 a month is $24000.00 a year.
```

Because the `printf()` statement doesn't use the newline character, the cursor remains just after the final period.

The fourth `printf()` statement begins with \r. This positions the cursor at the beginning of the current line. Then `Gee!` is displayed there, and the \n moves the cursor to the next line. The final appearance of the screen is this:

```
Enter your desired monthly salary: $2000.00

Gee!    $2000.00 a month is $24000.00 a year.
```

A Possible Problem

Some older C implementations do not work as we've just described. The problem lies in when `printf()` actually sends output to the screen. In general, `printf()` statements send output to an intermediate storage area called a *buffer*. Every now and then, the material in the buffer is sent to the screen. Under ANSI C, the rules for when output is sent from the buffer to the screen are clear. It is sent when the buffer gets full or when a newline character is encountered or when there is impending input. (This is called *flushing* the buffer.) For instance, the first two `printf()` statements don't fill the buffer and don't contain a newline, but they are immediately followed by a `scanf()` statement asking for input. That forces the `printf()` output to be sent to the screen.

Some older C implementations, however, do not invoke the third condition (impending input) for flushing the buffer. If you run Listing 3.9 with one of these compilers, the output of the first two `printf()` statements remains in the buffer. If you type a response anyway and then press Enter, the newline generated by the Enter key flushes the buffer. You have to type your answer before you see the question! One solution to this awkward situation is to use a newline at the end of the `printf()` statement preceding the input. That newline will flush the buffer. The code can be changed to look like this:

```
printf("Enter your desired monthly salary:\n");
scanf("%f", &salary);
```

This code works whether or not impending input flushes the buffer. However, it also puts the cursor on the next line, preventing you from entering data on the same line as the prompting string. A sample run would look like this:

```
Enter your desired monthly salary:
2000.00
```

To maintain greater portability, we'll follow this model (with the response on the line following the prompt) for the rest of this book. Another solution is to use the `fflush()` function described in Chapter 12, "File Input/Output."

Chapter Summary

C has a variety of data types. The basic types fall into two categories: *integer* types and *floating-point* types. The two distinguishing features for integer types are the amount of storage allotted to a type and whether it is signed or unsigned. The smallest integer type is `char`, which may be either signed or unsigned, depending on the implementation. ANSI C enables you to use `signed char` and `unsigned char` to explicitly specify which you want. The other integer types include `short`, `int`, and `long`. C guarantees that each of these types is at least as large as the preceding type. Each of these is a signed type, but with ANSI C you can use the `unsigned` keyword to create the corresponding unsigned types: `unsigned short`, `unsigned int`, and `unsigned long`. K&R C recognizes only `unsigned int` from this trio.

The three floating-point types are `float`, `double`, and, new with ANSI C, `long double`. Each is at least as large as the preceding type.

Integers can be expressed in decimal, octal, or hexadecimal form. A leading `0` indicates an octal number, and a leading `0x` or `0X` indicates a hexadecimal number. For example, 32, 040, and 0x20 are decimal, octal, and hexadecimal representations of the same value, respectively. An `l` or `L` suffix indicates a `long` value.

Character constants are represented by placing the character in single quotes: 'Q', '8', and '$', for example. C escape sequences, such as '\n' represent certain nonprinting characters. You can use the form '\007' to represent a character by its ASCII code.

Floating-point numbers can be written with a fixed decimal point, as in 9393.912, or in exponential notation, as in 7.38E10.

The printf() function enables you to print various types of values by using conversion specifiers, which, in their simplest form, consist of a percent sign and a letter indicating the type, as in %d or %f.

Review Questions

1. Which data type would you use for each of the following kinds of data?

   a. The population of Rio Frito.
   b. The average weight of a Rembrandt painting.
   c. The most common letter in this chapter.
   d. The number of times that the letter occurs.

2. Virgila Ann Xenopod has concocted an error-laden program. Help her find the mistakes.

```
include <stdio.h>
main
(

    float g; h;
    float tax, rate;

    g = e21;
    tax = rate*g;
)
```

3. Identify the data type (as used in declaration statements) and the print() format specifier for each of the following constants:

Constant	Type	Specifier
a. 012		
b. 2.9e05L		
c. 's'		
d. 100000		
e. '\n'		
f. 20.0f		
g. 0x44		

4. Correct this silly program. (The / in C means division.)

```
void main(int) / this program is perfect /
{
  cows, legs integer;
```

```
printf("How many cow legs did you count?\n);
scanf("%c", legs);
cows = legs / 4;
printf("That implies there are %f cows.\n", cows)
}
```

Programming Exercises

1. Find out what your system does with integer overflow, floating-point overflow, and floating-point underflow by using the experimental approach; i.e., write programs having these problems.

2. Write a program that asks you to enter an ASCII code value, such as 66, and then prints the character having that ASCII code.

3. Write a program that sounds the alert and then prints the following text:

   ```
   Startled by the sudden sound, Sally shouted, "By the Great
   Pumpkin, what was that!"
   ```

4. Write a program that reads in a floating-point number and prints it first in decimal-point notation and then in exponential notation. Have the output use the following format:

   The input is 21.290000 or 2.129000e+001.

5. There are approximately 3.156×10^7 seconds in a year. Write a program that requests your age in years and then displays the equivalent number of seconds.

6. The mass of a single molecule of water is about 3.0×10^{-23} grams. A quart of water is about 950 grams. Write a program that requests an amount of water, in quarts, and displays the number of water molecules in that amount.

Character Strings and Formatted Input/Output

Function
`strlen()`

This chapter introduces you to character strings. You see how they are created and stored and how you can use `scanf()` and `printf()` to read and display them. Also, you learn how to use the `strlen()` function to measure string lengths, and you examine the C preprocessor's `#define` directive for creating symbolic constants.

In this chapter we'll concentrate on input and output. We'll add personality to our programs by making them interactive and using character strings. We will also take a more detailed look at those two handy C input/output functions, printf() and scanf(). With these two functions, you will have the program tools you need to communicate with users and to format output to meet your needs and tastes. Finally, we'll take a quick look at an important C facility, the C preprocessor, and show you how to define and use symbolic constants.

Introductory Program

By now you probably expect a sample program at the beginning of each chapter, and we won't disappoint you. Listing 4.1 presents a program that engages in a dialogue with the user.

Listing 4.1. talkback.c.

```
/* talkback.c -- nosy, informative program */
#include <stdio.h>
#include <string.h>        /* for strlen() prototype      */
#define DENSITY 62.4        /* human density in lbs per cu ft */
int main(void)
{
  float weight, volume;
  int size, letters;
  char name[40];

  printf("Hi! What's your first name?\n");
  scanf("%s", name);
  printf("%s, what's your weight in pounds?\n", name);
  scanf("%f", &weight);
  size = sizeof name;
  letters = strlen(name);
  volume = weight / DENSITY;
  printf("Well, %s, your volume is %2.2f cubic feet.\n",
      name, volume);
  printf("Also, your first name has %d letters,\n",
      letters);
  printf("and we have %d bytes to store it in.\n", size);
  return 0;
}
```

(Recall that some compilers, such as Think C for the Macintosh, require %ld for printing sizeof quantities.) Running talkback produces results such as the following:

```
hi! what's your first name?
Angelica
Angelica, what's your weight in pounds?
102.5
```

```
Well, Angelica, your volume is 1.64 cubic feet.
Also, your first name has 8 letters,
and we have 40 bytes to store it in.
```

Here are the main new features of this program:

- We used an *array* to hold a *character string*. Here, someone's name is read into the array.

- We used the %s *conversion specification* to handle the input and output of the string. Note that name, unlike weight, does not use the & prefix when used with scanf(). (As you'll see later, both &weight and name are addresses.)

- We used the C preprocessor to define the symbolic constant DENSITY.

- We used the C function strlen() to find the length of a string.

The C approach may seem a little complex compared with the input/output of, say, BASIC. However, this complexity buys a finer control of I/O and a greater program efficiency and is surprisingly easy once you get used to it.

Let's investigate these new ideas.

Character Strings—An Introduction

A *character string* is a series of one or more characters. An example of a string is

```
"Zing went the strings of my heart!"
```

The double quotation marks are not part of the string. They inform the compiler that they enclose a string, just as single quotation marks identify a character.

Type *char* Arrays and the Null Character

C has no special variable type for strings. Instead, strings are stored in an array of char type. Characters in a string are stored in adjacent memory cells, one character per cell (see Figure 4.1).

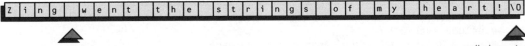

| Z | i | n | g | | w | e | n | t | | t | h | e | | s | t | r | i | n | g | s | | o | f | | m | y | | h | e | a | r | t | ! | \0 |

each cell is one byte   null character

Figure 4.1. *A string in an array.*

Note that Figure 4.1 shows the character \0 in the last array position. This is the *null character*, and C uses it to mark the end of a string. The null character is not the digit zero; it is the nonprinting character whose ASCII code value is 0. Strings in C always are stored with this terminating null character. The presence of the null character means that the array must have at least one more cell than the number of characters to be stored.

Now just what is an array? You can think of an array as several memory cells in a row. If you prefer more formal and exact language, an *array* is an ordered sequence of data elements of one type. In our example, we created an array of 40 memory cells, or elements, each of which can store one char-type value. We accomplished this with this declaration:

```
char name[40];
```

The brackets after name identify it as an array. The 40 within the brackets indicates the number of elements in the array. The char identifies the type of each element (see Figure 4.2).

Figure 4.2 *Declaring an array name of type* char

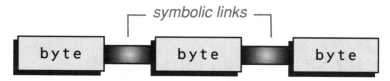

Figure 4.2. *Declaring an array name of type* char.

Using a character string is beginning to sound complicated! You have to create an array, place the characters of a string into an array one by one, and remember to add a \0 at the end. Fortunately for us, the computer can take care of most of the details itself.

Using Strings

Try the program in Listing 4.2 to see how easy it really is to use strings.

Listing 4.2. praise1.c.

```
/* praise1.c -- uses an assortment of strings */
#include <stdio.h>
#define PRAISE "My sakes, that's a grand name!"
int main(void)
{
  char name[40];

  printf("What's your name?\n");
  scanf("%s", name);
  printf("Hello, %s. %s\n", name, PRAISE);
  return 0;
}
```

The `%s` tells `printf()` to print a string. The `%s` appears twice because the program prints two strings: the one stored in the `name` array and the one represented by `PRAISE`. Running `praise1.c` should produce an output similar to this:

```
What's your name?
Porcilla Tusker
Hello, Porcilla. My sakes, that's a grand name!
```

We did not have to put the null character into the array `name` ourselves. That task was done for us by `scanf()` when it read the input. Nor did we include a null character in the *character string constant* `PRAISE`. We'll explain the `#define` statement soon; for now, simply note that the double quotation marks that enclose the text following `PRAISE` identify the text as a string. The compiler takes care of putting in the null character.

Note (and this is important) that `scanf()` just reads Porcilla Tusker's first name. After `scanf()` starts to read input, it stops reading at the first *whitespace* (blank, tab, or newline) it encounters. Thus, it stops scanning for `name` when it reaches the blank between `Porcilla` and `Tusker`. In general, `scanf()` is used with `%s` to read only a single word, not a whole phrase, as a string. C has other input-reading functions, such as `gets()`, for handling general strings. Later chapters will explore string functions more fully.

Strings Versus Characters

The string constant "x" is not the same as the character constant 'x'. One difference is that 'x' is a basic type (`char`), but "x" is a derived type, an array of `char`. A second difference is that "x" really consists of two characters, 'x' and '\0', the null character (see Figure 4.3).

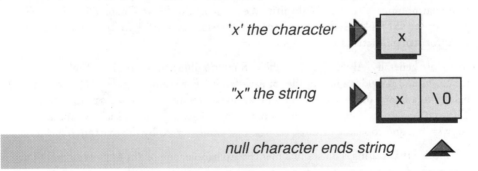

Figure 4.3. *The character 'x' and the string "x".*

String Length—*strlen()*

In the last chapter we unleashed the `sizeof` operator, which gives the size of things in bytes. The `strlen()` function gives the length of a string in characters. Because it takes 1 byte to hold 1 character, you might suppose that both would give the same result when applied to a string, but they don't. In Listing 4.3, add a few lines to our example and see why.

Listing 4.3. `praise2.c`.

```
/* praise2.c */
#include <stdio.h>
#include <string.h>        /* provides strlen() prototype */
#define PRAISE "My sakes, that's a grand name!"
int main(void)
{
  char name[40];

  printf("What's your name?\n");
  scanf("%s", name);
  printf("Hello, %s. %s\n", name, PRAISE);
  printf("Your name of %d letters occupies %d memory cells.\n",
         strlen(name), sizeof name);
  printf("The phrase of praise has %d letters ",
         strlen(PRAISE));
  printf("and occupies %d memory cells.\n", sizeof PRAISE);
  return 0;
}
```

If you are using a pre-ANSI C compiler, you may have to remove the following line:

```
#include <string.h>
```

The `string.h` file contains function prototypes for several string-related functions. Although not necessary for this particular example, this addition will make the program more harmonious with the ANSI spirit. We'll discuss this file in Chapter 12. (By the way, some pre-ANSI UNIX systems use `strings.h` instead of `string.h` to contain declarations for string functions.)

More generally, ANSI C divides the C function library into families of related functions and provides a header file for each family. For example, `printf()` and `scanf()` belong to a family of standard input and output functions and use the `stdio.h` header file. The `strlen()` function joins several other string-related functions, such as functions to copy strings and to search through strings, in a family served by the `string.h` header.

Notice that Listing 4.3 uses two methods to handle long `printf()` statements. The first method spreads one print statement over two lines. (You can break a line between arguments but not in the middle of a string, for example, not between the quotation marks.) The second method uses two `printf()` statements to print just one line. The newline character (`\n`) appears only in the second statement. Running the program could produce this interchange:

```
What's your name?
Tuffy
Hello, Tuffy. My sakes, that's a grand name!
Your name of 5 letters occupies 40 memory cells.
The phrase of praise has 30 letters and occupies 31 memory cells.
```

See what happens. The array `name` has 40 memory cells, and that is what the `sizeof` operator reports to us. Only the first 5 cells are needed to hold `Tuffy`, however, and that is what `strlen()` reports. The sixth cell in the array `name` contains the null character, and its presence tells `strlen()` when to stop counting. Figure 4.4 illustrates this concept.

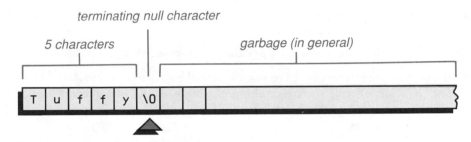

Figure 4.4. *The* `strlen()` *function knows when to stop.*

When we get to `PRAISE`, we find that `strlen()` again gives us the exact number of characters (including spaces and punctuation) in the string. The `sizeof` operator gives us a number one larger, for it also counts the invisible null character used to end the string. We didn't tell the computer how much memory to set aside to store the phrase. It had to count the number of characters between the double quotes itself.

One other point: in the preceding chapter we used `sizeof` with parentheses, and in this chapter we don't. Whether or not you use parentheses depends on whether you want the size of a type or the size of a particular quantity. Parentheses are required for types but are optional for particular quantities. That is, you would use `sizeof(char)` or `sizeof(float)`, but `sizeof name` or `sizeof 6.28`.

In the last example, our use of `strlen()` and `sizeof` was not a very important one. We merely wanted to satisfy our curiosity. Actually, however, `strlen()` and `sizeof` are important programming tools. For example, `strlen()` is useful in all sorts of character-string programs, as you'll see in Chapter 11.

Let's move on to the `#define` statement.

Constants and the C Preprocessor

Sometimes you need to use a constant in a program. For example, you could give the circumference of a circle as

```
circumference = 3.14 * diameter;
```

Here, the constant 3.14 represents the world-famous constant pi. To use a constant, just type in the actual value, as in the example. However, there are good reasons to use a *symbolic constant* instead. That is, you could use a statement like the following and have the computer substitute in the actual value later:

```
circumference = pi * diameter;
```

Why is it better to use a symbolic constant? First, a name tells you more than a number does. Compare these two statements:

```
owed = 0.015 * housevalue;
owed = taxrate * housevalue;
```

If you read through a long program, the meaning of the second version is plainer.

Second, suppose you have used a constant in several places, and it becomes necessary to change its value. After all, tax rates do change. Then you need merely alter the definition of the symbolic constant, rather than find and change every occurrence of the constant in the program.

Okay, how do you set up a symbolic constant? One way is to declare a variable and set it equal to the desired constant. You could write

```
float taxrate;
taxrate = 0.015;
```

This way is all right for a small program, but it is somewhat wasteful because the computer has to peek into the `taxrate` memory location every time `taxrate` is used. This is an example of *execution time* substitution because the substitution takes place while the program is running. Fortunately, C has a better idea.

The better idea is the C preprocessor. In Chapter 2 you saw how the preprocessor uses `#include` to include information from another file. The preprocessor also lets you define constants. Just add a line like this at the top of the file containing your program:

```
#define TAXRATE 0.015
```

When your program is compiled, the value `0.015` will be substituted everywhere you have used `TAXRATE`. This is called a *compile time* substitution. By the time you run the program, all the substitutions have already been made (see Figure 4.5). Such defined constants often are termed *manifest constants*.

Note the format. First comes `#define`. In older implementations, the # sign should be in the leftmost column; ANSI C removes this restriction. Next comes the symbolic name (`TAXRATE`) for the constant and then the value (`0.015`) for the constant.

```
#define NAME value
```

No semicolon is used, because this is a substitution mechanism, not a C statement. Why is `TAXRATE` capitalized? It is a sensible C tradition to type constants in uppercase. Then, when you encounter one in the depths of a program, you will know immediately that it is a constant, not a variable. Capitalizing constants is just another technique to make programs more readable. Your programs will still work if you don't capitalize the constants, but capitalizing them is a good habit to cultivate.

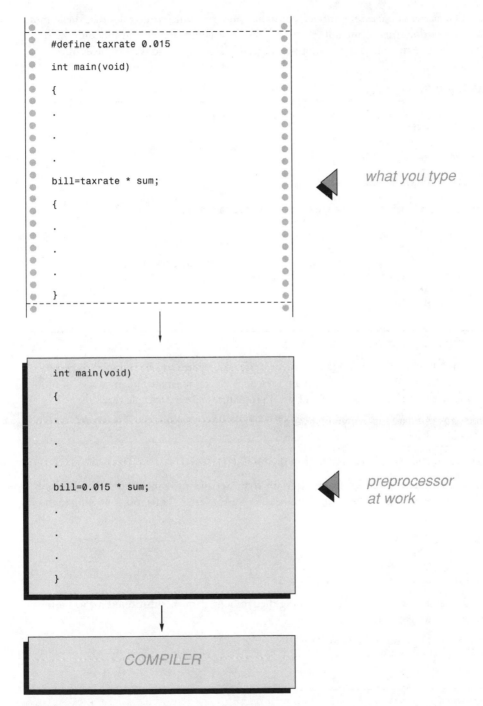

Figure 4.5. *What you type versus what is compiled.*

The names you use for symbolic constants must satisfy the same rules that the names of variables do. You can use uppercase and lowercase letters, digits, and the underscore character. The first character cannot be a digit. Listing 4.4 provides a simple example.

Listing 4.4. `pizza.c`.

```
/* pizza.c -- uses defined constants in a pizza context */
#include <stdio.h>
#define PI 3.14159
int main(void)
{
  float area, circum, radius;

  printf("What is the radius of your pizza?\n");
  scanf("%f", &radius);
  area = PI * radius * radius;
  circum = 2.0 * PI *radius;
  printf("Your basic pizza parameters are as follows:\n");
  printf("circumference = %1.2f, area = %1.2f\n", circum,
          area);
  return 0;
}
```

The `%1.2f` in the `printf()` statement causes the printout to be rounded to two decimal places. Of course, this program may not reflect your major pizza concerns, but it does fill a small niche in the world of pizza programs. Here is a sample run:

```
What is the radius of your pizza?
6.0
Your basic pizza parameters are as follows:
circumference = 37.70, area = 113.10
```

The `#define` statement can be used for character and string constants, too. Just use single quotes for the former and double quotes for the latter. Thus, the following examples are valid:

```
#define BEEP '\a'
#define TEE 'T'
#define ESC '\033'
#define OOPS "Now you have done it!"
```

Remember that everything following the symbolic name is substituted for it. Don't make this common error:

```
/* the following is wrong */
#define TOES = 20
```

If you do this, TOES is replaced by = 20, not just 20. In that case, a statement like

```
digits = fingers + TOES;
```

is converted to the following misrepresentation:

```
digits = fingers + = 20;
```

Using *#define* and *#include* Together

Here is a special treat for the lazy. Suppose you develop a whole packet of programs that use the same set of constants. You can do the following:

- Collect all your #define statements in one file; call it, say, const.h.

- At the head of each source code file of your program, insert the statement #include "const.h".

Then, when you run the program, the preprocessor will read the file const.h and use all the #define statements there for your program. Incidentally, the .h at the end of the filename is a reminder to you that the file is a *header*, i.e., full of information to be placed at the head of your program. The preprocessor itself doesn't care whether you use a .h in the name.

Note that we used "const.h", not <const.h>. The difference lies in where the compiler first looks for the include file, and it is implementation dependent. On UNIX systems, placing the filename in angle brackets causes the preprocessor to look in specific system directories for the files. Placing the filename in quotes causes the preprocessor to look in the current directory first and then in the system directories, or you can specify a full pathname, as in "/usr/tiger/myincludes/bar.h", in which case just the indicated directory (/usr/tiger/myincludes) is searched. Microsoft C and Turbo C follow similar conventions in the DOS environment. In Microsoft C you set an environmental variable called INCLUDE to the system directory that you use for the standard include files. Turbo C and Borland C use an environment menu to select the standard include directory. For both, angle brackets mean to search the standard include directory, and quotes mean to search the current directory first. Incidentally, although UNIX uses the slash (/) in pathnames, the DOS environment uses the backslash (\) for the same purpose.

C—A Master of Disguise: Creating Aliases

The capabilities of #define go beyond the symbolic representation of constants. Consider, for instance, the program in Listing 4.5.

Listing 4.5. `alias.c`.

```
/* alias.c -- users preprocessor */
#include <stdio.h>
#include "alias.h"    /* see text for more on this file */
program
  begin
    whole yours, mine then
    spitout("Give me an integer, please.\n") then
    takein("%d", &yours) then
    mine = yours times TWO then
    spitout("%d is twice your number!\n", mine) then
  end
```

Hmm, Listing 4.5 looks vaguely familiar, a little like Pascal, but it doesn't seem to be C. The secret, of course, is in the file `alias.h`. What's in it? Read on.

```
/* alias.h -- a silly abuse of preprocessing power */
#define program int main(void)
#define begin    {
#define end       return 0;}
#define then     ;
#define takein   scanf
#define spitout  printf
#define TWO       2
#define times     *
#define whole int
```

This example illustrates how the preprocessor works. Your program is searched for items defined by #define statements, and all finds are then replaced. In our example, all thens are rendered into semicolons at compilation. The resulting program is identical to what you would have received by typing in the usual C terms at the start. (By the way, this example is meant to be an entertaining illustration of how the preprocessor works; it is not intended to be a model to emulate.)

This powerful defining facility also can be used to define a *macro*, which is sort of a poor man's function. We will return to this topic in Chapter 16.

The #define feature has limitations. For example, parts of a program within double quotes are immune to substitution. The following combination wouldn't work:

```
#define MN "minimifidianism"
printf("He was a strong believer in MN.\n");
```

The printout would read simply

```
He was a strong believer in MN.
```

This is because MN is enclosed in double quotes in the printf() statement. However, the statement

```
printf("He was a strong believer in %s.\n", MN);
```

would produce

```
He was a strong believer in minimifidianism.
```

In this case, the MN was outside the double quotes, so it was replaced by its definition. (*Minimifidianism*, by the way, means having almost no belief.)

Manifest Constants on the Job

The ANSI C header files limits.h and float.h provide detailed information about the size limits of integer types and floating types respectively. Each file defines a series of manifest constants that apply to your implementation. For instance, the limits.h file contains lines similar to the following:

```
#define INT_MAX      +32767
#define INT_MIN      -32768
```

These constants represent the largest and smallest possible values for the int type. If your system used a four-byte int, the file defines minimum and maximum values for all the integer types. If you include the limits.h file, you can use code like the following:

```
printf("Maximum int value on this system = %d\n", INT_MAX);
```

If your system used a four-byte int, the limits.h file that came with that system would provide definitions for INT_MAX and INT_MIN that matched the limits of a four-byte int. More generally, limits.h and float.h that come with your system will accurately describe the type limit for your system.

Similarly, the float.h defines constants such as FLT_DIG and DBL_DIG, which represent the number of significant figures supported by the float type and the double type, DBL_MAX, which represents the maximum type double value, and FLT_MAX_10_EXP, which is the largest (base 10) exponent for a float value.

The C preprocessor is a useful, helpful tool, so take advantage of it when you can. We'll show you more applications as we move along.

Exploring and Exploiting *printf()* and *scanf()*

The functions printf() and scanf() enable you to communicate with a program. They are called *input/output* functions, or *I/O* functions for short. They are not the only I/O functions you can use with C, but they are the most versatile. Historically, these functions, like all other functions in the C library, were *not* part of the definition of C. C originally left the implementation of I/O up to the compiler writers; this made it possible to better match I/O to specific machines. In the interests of compatibility, various implementations all came with versions of scanf() and printf(). However, there were occasional discrepancies between implementations. The ANSI C Standard describes standard versions of these functions, and we'll follow that Standard. The discrepancies should disappear as the Standard is implemented.

Although printf() is an output function and scanf() is an input function, both work much the same, each using a control string and a list of arguments. We will show how these work, first with printf() and then with scanf().

The *printf()* Function

The instructions you give printf() when you ask it to print a variable depend on the variable type. For instance, we have used the %d notation when printing an integer and the %c notation when printing a character. These notations are called *conversion specifications* because they specify how the data is to be converted into displayable form. We'll list the conversion specifications that the ANSI C Standard provides for printf(), and then we'll show how to use the more common ones. Table 4.1 presents the conversion specifiers and the type of output they cause to be printed.

Table 4.1. Conversion specifiers and resulting printed output.

Conversion Specification	Output
%c	Single character
%d	Signed decimal integer
%e	Floating-point number, e-notation
%E	Floating-point number, E-notation
%f	Floating-point number, decimal notation
%g	Use %f or %e, whichever is shorter
%G	Use %f or %E, whichever is shorter
%i	Signed decimal integer
%o	Unsigned octal integer
%p	A pointer
%s	Character string
%u	Unsigned decimal integer
%x	Unsigned hexadecimal integer, using hex digits 0f

Conversion Specification	Output
%X	Unsigned hexadecimal integer, using hex digits 0F
%%	Print a percent sign

Note: The conversion specifiers in italic typeface (%E, %G, %i, %p, %X) did not appear in the first edition of Kernighan and Ritchie, and they are not yet commonly found in all implementations.

Using *printf()*

Listing 4.6 contains a program that uses some of the conversion-specification examples we will discuss.

Listing 4.6. printout.c.

```c
/* printout.c -- uses conversion specifiers */
#include <stdio.h>
#define PI 3.141593
int main(void)
{
  int number = 5;
  float ouzo = 13.5;
  int cost = 3100;

  printf("The %d women drank %f glasses of ouzo.\n", number,
         ouzo);
  printf("The value of pi is %f.\n", PI);
  printf("Farewell! thou art too dear for my possessing,\n");
  printf("%c%d\n", '$', 2 * cost);
  return 0;
}
```

The output, of course, is

```
The 5 women drank 13.500000 glasses of ouzo.
The value of pi is 3.141593.
Farewell! thou art too dear for my possessing,
$6200
```

The format for using printf() is

```
printf(Control-string, item1, item2,...);
```

Item1, item2, and so on, are the items to be printed. They can be variables or constants, or even expressions that are evaluated first before the value is printed. Control-string is a character string describing how the items are to be printed. As we mentioned in Chapter 3, the control string should contain a conversion specifier for each item to be printed. For example, consider this statement:

```
printf("The %d women drank %f glasses of ouzo.\n", number, ouzo);
```

The control-string is the phrase in double quotes. It contains two conversion specifiers corresponding to number and ouzo—the two items to be displayed. Figure 4.6 shows another example of a printf() statement.

Figure 4.6. *Arguments for* printf().

Here is another line from our example:

```
printf("The value of pi is %f.\n", PI);
```

This time, the list of items has just one member—the symbolic constant PI.

As you can see from Figure 4.7, control-string contains two distinct forms of information.

1. Characters that are actually printed.

2. Conversion specifications.

Don't forget to use one conversion specification for each item in the list following control-string. Woe unto you should you forget this basic requirement! Don't do this:

```
printf("The score was Squids %d, Slugs %d.\n", score1);
```

Here, there is no value for the second %d. The result of this faux pas will depend on your system, but at best you will get nonsense.

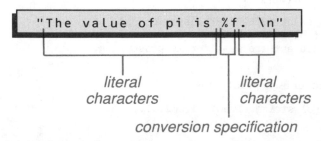

Figure 4.7. *Anatomy of a control string.*

If you want to print only a phrase, you don't need any conversion specifications. If you just want to print data, you can dispense with the running commentary. Thus, each of the following statements from Listing 4.6 is quite acceptable:

```
printf("Farewell! thou art too dear for my possessing,\n");
printf("%c%d\n", '$', 2 * cost);
```

In the second statement, note that the first item on the print list was a character constant rather than a variable and that the second item is a multiplication. This illustrates that `printf()` uses values, be they variables, constants, or expressions.

Because the `printf()` function uses the `%` symbol to identify the conversion specifications, there is a slight problem if you wish to print the `%` sign itself. If you simply use a lone `%` sign, the compiler will think you have bungled a conversion specification. The way out is simple. Just use two `%` symbols.

```
pc = 2*6;
printf("Only %d%% of Sally's gribbles were edible.\n", pc);
```

The following output would result:

```
Only 12% of Sally's gribbles were edible.
```

Conversion Specification Modifiers for *printf()*

You can modify a basic conversion specification by inserting modifiers between the `%` and the defining conversion character. Tables 4.2 and 4.3 list the characters you can place there legally. If you use more than one modifier, they should be in the same order as they appear in Table 4.2. Not all combinations are possible. The tables reflect the ANSI C Standard; your implementation may not yet support all the options shown here.

Table 4.2. `printf()` **modifiers.**

Modifier	Meaning
flag	The five flags (-, +, *space*, #, and 0) are described in Table 4.3. Zero or more flags may be present.
	Example: "%-10d"
digit(s)	The minimum field width. A wider field will be used if the printed number or string won't fit in the field.
	Example: "%4d"

continues

Table 4.2. continued

Modifier	Meaning
.digit(s)	Precision. For %e, %E, and %f conversions, the number of digits to be printed to the right of the decimal. For %g and %G conversions, the maximum number of significant digits. For %s conversions, the maximum number of characters to be printed. For integer conversions, the minimum number of digits to appear; leading zeros are used if necessary to meet this minimum. Using only . implies a following zero, so %.f is the same as %.0f. Example: "%5.2f" prints a float in a field 5 characters wide with 2 digits after the decimal point.
h	Used with an integer conversion to indicate a short int or unsigned short int value. Examples: "%hu" "%hx" "%6.4hd"
l	Used with an integer conversion to indicate a long int or unsigned long int. Examples: "%ld" "%8lu"
L	Used with a floating-point conversion to indicate a long double value. Examples: "%Lf" "%10.4Le"

Conversion of *float* Arguments

There are conversion specifiers to print floating types double and long double. However, there is no specifier for float. The reason is that, under K&R C, float values were automatically converted to type double before being used in an expression or as an argument. ANSI C, in general, does not automatically convert float to double. To protect the enormous number of existing programs that assume float arguments are converted to double, however, all float arguments to printf()—as well as to any other C function—still are automatically converted to double. Thus, under either K&R C or ANSI C, no special conversion specifier is needed for displaying type float.

Table 4.3. `printf()` **flags.**

Flag	Meaning
-	The item is left-justified; that is, it is printed beginning at the left of the field.
	Example: "%-20s"
+	Signed values are displayed with a plus sign if positive and with a minus sign if negative.
	Example: "%+6.2f"
space	Signed values are displayed with a leading space (but no sign) if positive and with a minus sign if negative. A + flag overrides a space.
	Example: "% 6.2f"
#	Use an alternative form for the conversion specification. Produces an initial 0 for the %o form and an initial 0x or 0X for the %x and %X forms. For all floating-point forms, # guarantees that a decimal-point character is printed, even if no digits follow. For %g and %G forms, it prevents trailing zeros from being removed.
	Examples: "%#o" "%#8.0f" "%+#10.3E"
0	For numeric forms, pad the field width with leading zeros instead of with spaces. This flag is ignored if a - flag is present or if, for an integer form, a precision is specified.
	Examples: "%010d" "%08.3f"

Examples

Let's put these modifiers to work. We'll begin by looking at the effect of the field width modifier on printing an integer. Consider the program in Listing 4.7.

Listing 4.7. `width.c`.

```
/* width.c -- field widths */
#include <stdio.h>
#define PAGES 336
int main(void)
{
  printf("/%d/\n", PAGES);
  printf("/%2d/\n", PAGES);
```

continues

Listing 4.7. continued

```
  printf("/%10d/\n", PAGES);
  printf("/%-10d/\n", PAGES);
  return 0;
}
```

Listing 4.7 prints the same quantity four times—but using four different conversion specifications. We used a slash (/) to show you where each field begins and ends. The output looks like this:

```
/336/
/336/
/      336/
/336      /
```

The first conversion specification is %d with no modifiers. It produces a field with the same width as the integer being printed. This is the *default* option; i.e., what's printed if you don't give further instructions. The second conversion specification is %2d. This should produce a field width of 2, but because the integer is 3 digits long, the field is expanded automatically to fit the number. The next conversion specification is %10d. This produces a field 10 spaces wide, and, indeed, there are 7 blanks and 3 digits between the /s, with the number tucked into the right end of the field. The final specification is %-10d. It also produces a field 10 spaces wide, and the - puts the number at the left end, just as advertised. Once you get used to it, this system is easy to use and gives you nice control over the appearance of your output. Try altering the value for PAGES to see how different numbers of digits are printed.

Now look at some floating-point formats. Enter, compile, and run the program in Listing 4.8.

Listing 4.8. floats.c.

```
/* floats.c -- some floating-point combinations */
#include <stdio.h>
#define RENT 1234.56
int main(void)
{
  printf("/%f/\n", RENT);
  printf("/%e/\n", RENT);
  printf("/%4.2f/\n", RENT);
  printf("/%3.1f/\n", RENT);
  printf("/%10.3f/\n", RENT);
  printf("/%10.3e/\n", RENT);
  printf("/%+4.2f/\n", RENT);
  printf("/%010.2f/\n", RENT);
  return 0;
}
```

This time we get the output

```
/1234.560000/
/1.234560e+003/
/1234.56/
/1234.6/
/   1234.560/
/1.235e+003/
/+1234.56/
/0001234.56/
```

Again, we begin with the default version, %f. In this case there are two defaults: the field width and the digits to the right of the decimal. The second default is 6 digits, and the field width is whatever it takes to hold the number.

Next is the default for %e. It prints 1 digit to the left of the decimal point and 6 places to the right. We seem to be getting a lot of digits! The cure is to specify the number of decimal places to the right of the decimal, and the next four examples in this segment do that. Notice how the fourth and the sixth examples cause the output to be rounded off.

Finally, the + flag causes the result to be printed with its algebraic sign, which is a plus sign in this case, and the 0 flag produces leading zeros to pad the result to the full field width. Note that in the specifier %010 the first 0 is a flag, and the remaining digits (10) specify the field width.

You can modify the RENT value to see how variously sized values are printed. Listing 4.9 demonstrates a few more combinations.

Listing 4.9. flags.c.

```
/* flags.c -- illustrates some formatting flags */
#include <stdio.h>
int main(void)
{
  printf("%x %X %#x\n", 31, 31, 31);
  printf("**%d**% d**% d**\n", 42, 42, -42);
  printf("**%5d**%5.3d**%05d**%05.3d**\n", 6, 6, 6, 6);
  return 0;
}
```

On a system that conforms to the ANSI C Standard, the output looks like this:

```
1f 1F 0x1f
**42** 42**-42**
**    6**  006**00006**  006**
```

First, 1f is the hex equivalent of 31. The x specifier yields a 1f, and the X specifier yields 1F. Using the # flag provides an initial 0x.

The second line illustrates how using a space in the specifier produces a leading space for positive values but not for negative values. This can produce pleasing output because positive and negative values with the same number of significant digits are printed with the same field widths.

The third line illustrates how using a precision specifier (%5.3d) with an integer form produces enough leading zeros to pad the number to the minimum value of digits. Using the 0 flag, however, pads the number with enough leading zeros to fill the whole field width. Finally, if you provide both the 0 flag and the precision specifier, the 0 flag is ignored.

Now let's examine some of the string options. Consider the example in Listing 4.10.

Listing 4.10. strings.c.

```
/* strings.c -- string formatting */
#include <stdio.h>
#define BLURB "Outstanding acting!"
int main(void)
{
    printf("/%2s/\n", BLURB);
    printf("/%22s/\n", BLURB);
    printf("/%22.5s/\n", BLURB);
    printf("/%-22.5s/\n", BLURB);
    return 0;
}
```

Here is the output:

```
/Outstanding acting!/
/   Outstanding acting!/
/                 Outst/
/Outst                 /
```

Notice how the field is expanded to contain all the specified characters. Also notice how the precision specification limits the number of characters printed. The .5 in the format specifier tells printf() to print just 5 characters. Again, the - modifier left-justifies the text.

Applying Your Knowledge

Okay, you've seen some examples. Now how would you set up a statement to print something having the following form?

The NAME family just may be $XXX.XX dollars richer!

Here, NAME and XXX.XX represent values that will be supplied by variables in the program, say, name[40] and cash.

Here is one solution:

```
printf("The %s family just may be $%.2f richer!\n",name,cash);
```

The Meaning of Conversion

Take a closer look at what a conversion specification converts. It converts a value stored in the computer in some binary format to a series of characters (a string) to be displayed. For example, the number 76 may be stored internally as binary 01001100. The %d conversion specifier converts this to the characters 7 and 6, displaying 76. The %x conversion converts the same value (01001100) to the hexadecimal representation 4c. The %c converts the same value to the character representation L.

The term *conversion* probably is somewhat misleading, because it wrongly suggests the original value is replaced with a converted value. Conversion specifications really are translation specifications; %d means translate the given value to a decimal integer text representation and print the representation.

Mismatched Conversions

Naturally, you should match the conversion specification to the type of value being printed. Often, you have choices. For instance, if you want to print a type int value, you can use %d or %x or %o. All these specifiers assume that you are printing a type int value; they merely provide different representations of the value. Similarly, you can use %f, %e, or %g to represent a type double value.

What if you mismatch the conversion specification to the type? Listing 4.11 shows some examples of mismatches within the integer family.

Listing 4.11. intconv.c.

```
/* intconv.c -- some mismatched integer conversions */
#include <stdio.h>
#define PAGES 336
#define WORDS 65616
int main(void)
{
    int num = PAGES;
    int mnum = -PAGES;

    printf("%d %u %d %u\n", num, num, mnum, mnum);
    printf("%d %c\n", num, num);
    printf("%ld %d\n", WORDS, WORDS);
    return 0;
}
```

Our system produces the following results:

```
336 336 -336 65200
336 P
65616 80
```

Looking at the first line, we see that both `%d` and `%u` produce `336` as output for the variable num; no problem there. The `%u` (unsigned) version of mnum came out as `65200`, however, not as the 336 you might have expected. This results from the way that signed integers are represented on our reference system. First, they are 2 bytes in size. Second, the system uses a method called the *two's complement* to represent signed integers. In this method, the numbers 0 to 32767 represent themselves, and the numbers 32768 to 65535 represent negative numbers, with 65535 being –1, 65534 being –2, etc. Thus, `-336` is represented by `65536 - 336`, or `65200`. Therefore, 65200 represents –336 when interpreted as a signed `int` and represents 65200 when interpreted as an unsigned `int`. Be wary! One number can be interpreted as two different values. Not all systems use this method to represent negative integers. Nonetheless, there is a moral: don't expect a `%u` conversion simply to strip the sign from a number.

The second line shows what happens if you try to convert a value greater than 255 to a character. On our system, an `int` is 2 bytes and a `char` is 1 byte. When `printf()` prints 336 using `%c`, it looks at only 1 byte out of the 2 used to hold 336. This truncation (see Figure 4.8) amounts to dividing the integer by 256 and keeping just the remainder. In this case, the remainder is 80, which is the ASCII value for the character `P`. More technically, we can say that the number is interpreted *modulo 256*, which means using the remainder when the number is divided by 256.

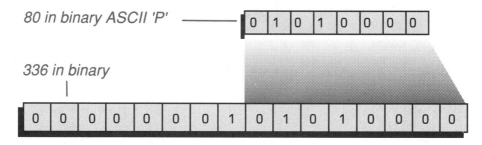

Figure 4.8. *Reading 336 as a character.*

Finally, we tried printing an integer (65616) larger than the maximum `int` (32767) allowed on our system. Again, the computer does its modulo thing. The number 65616, because of its size, is stored as a 4-byte `long` value on our system. When we print it using the `%d` specification, `printf()` uses only the last 2 bytes. This corresponds to using the remainder after dividing by 65536. In this case, the remainder is 80. A remainder between 32767 and 65536 would be printed as a negative number because of the way negative numbers are stored. Systems with different integer sizes would have the same general behavior, but with different numerical values.

When you start mixing integer and floating types, the results are more bizarre. Consider, for example, Listing 4.12.

Listing 4.12. `floatcnv.c.`

```
/* floatcnv.c -- mismatched floating-point conversions */
#include <stdio.h>
int main(void)
{
    float n1 = 3.0;
    double n2 = 3.0;
    long n3 = 2000000000;
    long n4 = 1234567890;

    printf("%.1e %.1e %.1e %.1e\n", n1, n2, n3, n4);
    printf("%ld %ld\n", n3, n4);
    printf("%ld %ld %ld %ld\n", n1, n2, n3, n4);
    return 0;
}
```

On our system, Listing 4.12 produces the following output:

```
3.0e+000 3.0e+000 3.1e+046 3.1e+046
2000000000 1234567890
0 1074266112 0 1074266112
```

The first line of output shows that using a `%e` specifier does not convert an integer to a floating-point number. Consider, for example, what happens when we try to print n3 (type `long`) using the `%e` specifier. First, the `%e` specifier causes `printf()` to expect a type `double` value, which is an 8-byte value on our system. When `printf()` looks at n3, which is a 4-byte value on our system, it also looks at the adjacent 4 bytes. Thus, it looks at an 8-byte unit in which the actual n3 is embedded. Second, it interprets the bits in this unit as a floating-point number. Some bits, for example, would be interpreted as an exponent. Thus, even if n3 had the correct number of bits, they would be interpreted differently under `%e` than under `%ld`. The net result is nonsense.

The first line also illustrates what we mentioned earlier: that `float` is converted to `double` when used as arguments to `printf()`. On our system, `float` is 4 bytes, but n1 was expanded to 8 bytes so that `printf()` would display it correctly.

The second line of output shows that `printf()` can print n3 and n4 correctly if the correct specifier is used.

The third line of output shows that even the correct specifier can produce phoney results if the `printf()` statement has mismatches elsewhere. As you might expect, trying to print a floating-point value with a %ld specifier fails, but here, trying to print a type long using %ld fails! The problem lies in how C passes information to a function. The exact details of this failure are implementation dependent, but the next box discusses a representative system.

Passing Arguments

The mechanics of argument passing depend on the implementation. This is how argument passing works on our system. The function call looks like this:

```
printf("%ld %ld %ld %ld\n", n1, n2, n3, n4);
```

This call tells the computer to hand over the values of the variables n1, n2, n3, and n4 to the computer. It does so by placing them in an area of memory called the *stack*. When the computer puts these values on the stack, it is guided by the types of the variables, not by the conversion specifiers, so for n1, it places 8 bytes on the stack (float is converted to double). Similarly, it places 8 more bytes for n2, followed by 4 bytes each for n3 and n4. Then control shifts to the printf() function. This function reads the values off the stack, but when it does so, it reads them according to the conversion specifiers. The %ld specifier indicates that printf() should read 4 bytes, so printf() reads the first 4 bytes in the stack as its first value. This is just the first half of n1, and it is interpreted as a long integer. The next %ld specifier reads 4 more bytes; this is just the second half of n1 and is interpreted as a second long integer (see Figure 4.9). Similarly, the third and fourth instances of %ld cause the first and second halves of n2 to be read and to be interpreted as two more long integers, so although we have the correct specifiers for n3 and n4, printf() is reading the wrong bytes.

The Return Value of *printf()*

As we mentioned in Chapter 2, a C function generally has a *return value*. This is a value that the function computes and returns to the calling program. For example, the C library contains a sqrt() function that takes a number as an argument and returns its square root. The return value can be assigned to a variable, can be used in a computation, can be passed as an argument—in short, it can be used like any other value. The printf() function also has a return value: under ANSI C, it returns the number of characters it printed. If there is an output error, printf() returns a negative value. (Some pre-ANSI versions of printf() have different return values.)

The return value for `printf()` is incidental to its main purpose of printing output, and it usually isn't used. One reason you might use the return value is to check for output errors. This is more commonly done when writing to a file rather than to a screen. If a full floppy disk prevented writing from taking place, you could then have the program take some appropriate action, such as beeping the terminal for 30 seconds. However you have to know about the `if` statement before doing that sort of thing. Look at a simple example, shown in Listing 4.13, that shows how you can determine the return value.

```
float n1;   /* passed as type double */
double n2;
long n3, n4;
...
printf("%1d %1d %1d %1d\n", n1, n2, n3, n4);
```

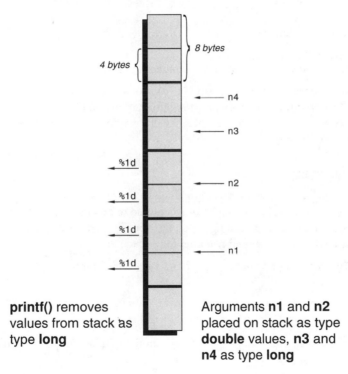

Figure 4.9. *Passing arguments.*

Listing 4.13. `prntval.c`.

```
/* prntval.c -- finding printf()'s return value */
#include <stdio.h>
int main(void)
{
  int n = 212;
  int rv;

  rv = printf("%d F is water's boiling point.\n", n);
  printf("The printf() function printed %d characters.\n",
          rv);
  return 0;
}
```

The output is as follows:

```
212 F is water's boiling point.
The printf() function printed 32 characters.
```

First, we used the form rv = printf(...); to assign the return value to rv. This statement thus performs two tasks: printing information and assigning a value to a variable. Second, note that the count includes all the printed characters, including the spaces and the unseen newline character.

Printing Long Strings

Occasionally, printf() statements are too long to put on one line. Because C ignores whitespace (spaces, tabs, newlines) except when used to separate elements, you can spread a statement over several lines, as long as you put your line breaks between elements. For instance, in Listing 4.13, we used two lines for a statement.

```
printf("The printf() function printed %d characters.\n",
        rv);
```

We broke the line between the comma element and rv. To show that the line was being continued, we indented the rv. C ignores the extra spaces.

However, you cannot break a quoted *string* in the middle. Suppose you try something like this:

```
printf("The printf() function printed %d
        characters.\n", rv);
```

C will complain that you have an illegal character in a string constant. You can use \n in a string to symbolize the newline character, but you can't have the actual newline character generated by the Enter (or Return) key in a string.

If you do have to split a string, you have three choices, as shown in Listing 4.14.

Listing 4.14. `longstrg.c`.

```
/* longstrg.c -- printing long strings */
#include <stdio.h>
int main(void)
{
    printf("Here's one way to print a ");
    printf("long string.\n");
    printf("Here's another way to print a \
long string.\n");
    printf("Here's the newest way to print a "
           "long string.\n");      /* ANSI C */
    return 0;
}
```

Here is the output:

```
Here's one way to print a long string.
Here's another way to print a long string.
Here's the newest way to print a long string.
```

Method 1 is to use more than one `printf()` statement. Because the first string printed doesn't end with a \n character, the second string continues where the first ends.

Method 2 is to terminate the end of the first line with a backslash-return combination. This causes the text on the screen to start a new line but without including a newline character in the string. The effect is to continue the string over to the next line. However, the next line has to start at the far left, as shown. If we indent that line, say, five spaces, then those five spaces become part of the string.

Method 3, new with ANSI C, is *string concatenation*. If you follow one quoted string constant with another, separated only by whitespace, C will treat the combination as a single string, so the following three forms are equivalent:

```
printf("Hello, young lovers, wherever you are.");
printf("Hello, young "    "lovers" ", wherever you are.");
printf("Hello, young lovers"
       ", wherever you are.");
```

With all these methods, you should include any required spaces in the strings: "Jim" "Smith" becomes "JimSmith", but the combination "Jim " "Smith" is "Jim Smith".

Using *scanf()*

Now let's go from output to input and examine the `scanf()` function. The C library contains several input functions, and `scanf()` is the most general of them, for it can read a variety of formats. Of course, input from the keyboard is text because the keys generate text characters: letters, digits, and punctuation. When you desire to enter, say, the integer 2002, you type the characters 2 0 0 and 2. If you want to store that as a numerical value rather than as a string, your program has to convert the string character-by-character to a numerical value, and that is what `scanf()` does! It converts string input into various forms: integers, floating-point numbers, characters, and C strings. It is the inverse of `printf()`, which converts integers, floating-point numbers, characters, and C strings to text that is to be displayed on the screen.

Like `printf()`, `scanf()` uses a control string followed by a list of arguments. The control string indicates into which formats the input is to be converted. The chief difference is in the argument list. `Printf()` uses variable names, constants, and expressions. `Scanf()` uses pointers to variables. Fortunately, you don't have to know anything about pointers to use the function. Just remember these two simple rules:

- If you use `scanf()` to read a value for one of the basic variable types we've discussed, precede the variable name with an &.

- If you use `scanf()` to read a string into a character array, don't use an &.

Listing 14.15 presents a short program illustrating these rules.

Listing 4.15. `input.c`.

```
/* input.c -- when to use & */
#include <stdio.h>
int main(void)
{
    int age;              /* variable */
    float assets;         /* variable */
    char pet[30];         /* string   */

    printf("Enter your age, assets, and favorite pet.\n");
    scanf("%d %f", &age, &assets); /* use the & here       */
    scanf("%s", pet);              /* no & for char array */
    printf("%d $%.0f %s\n", age, assets, pet);
    return 0;
}
```

Here is a sample exchange:

```
Enter your age, assets, and favorite pet.
82
8345245.19 rhino
82 $8345245 rhino
```

The `scanf()` function uses whitespace (newlines, tabs, and spaces) to decide how to divide the input into separate fields. It matches up consecutive conversion specifications to consecutive fields, skipping over the whitespace in between. Note how we spread the input over two lines. We could just as well have used one or five lines, as long as we had at least one newline, space, or tab between each entry. The only exception to this is the `%c` specification, which reads the very next character, even if that character is whitespace. We'll return to this topic in a moment.

The scanf() function uses pretty much the same set of conversion-specification characters as printf() does. Table 4.4 lists the main conversion specifiers as described in ANSI C.

Table 4.4. ANSI C conversion specifiers for scanf().

Conversion Specifier	Meaning
%c	Interpret input as a character.
%d	Interpret input as a signed decimal integer.
%e, %f, %g	Interpret input as a floating-point number.
%E, %G	Interpret input as a floating-point number.
%i	Interpret input as a signed decimal integer.
%o	Interpret input as a signed octal integer.
%p	Interpret input as a pointer (AN ADDRESS).
%s	Interpret input as a string; input begins with the first nonwhitespace character and includes everything up to the next whitespace character.
%u	Interpret input as an unsigned decimal integer.
%x, %X	Interpret input as a signed hexadecimal integer.

You also can use modifiers in the conversion specifiers shown in Table 4.4. The modifiers go between the percent sign and the conversion letter. If you use more than one in a specifier, they should appear in the same order as shown in Table 4.5.

Table 4.5. Conversion modifiers for scanf().

Modifier	Meaning
*	Suppress assignment (see text). Example: "%*d"
digit(s)	Maximum field width; input stops when the maximum field width is reached or when the first whitespace character is encountered, whichever comes first. Example: "%10s"

continues

Table 4.5. continued

Modifier	Meaning
h, l, or L	"%hd" and "%hi" indicate that the value will be stored in a short int. "%ho", "%hx", and "%hu" indicate that the value will be stored in an unsigned short int. "%ld" and "%li" indicate that the value will be stored in a long. "%lo", "%lx", and "%lu" indicate that the value will be stored in unsigned long. "%le", "%lf", and "%lg" indicate that the value will be stored in type double. Using L instead of l with e, f, and g indicates that the value will be stored in type long double. In the absence of these modifiers, d, i, o, and x indicate type int, and e, f, and g indicate type float.

As you can see, using conversion specifiers can be involved, and there are features that we have omitted. These omitted features primarily facilitate reading selected data from highly formatted sources, such as punched cards or other data records. Because we will be using scanf() primarily as a convenient means for feeding data to a program interactively, we won't discuss such unneeded features.

The *scanf()* View of Input

Look in more detail at how scanf() reads input. Suppose you use a %d specifier to read an integer. Scanf() begins reading input a character at a time. As we mentioned, it skips over whitespace characters (spaces, tabs, and newlines) until it finds a nonwhitespace character. Because it is attempting to read an integer, scanf() expects to find a digit character or, perhaps, a sign (+ or -). If it finds a digit or a sign, it saves the sign and then reads the next character. If that is a digit, it saves the digit and reads the next character. Scanf() continues reading and saving characters until it encounters a nondigit. It then concludes that it has reached the end of the integer. Scanf() places the nondigit back in the input. This means that the next time the program goes to read input, it will start at the previously rejected, nondigit character. Finally, scanf() computes the numerical value corresponding to the digits it read and places that value in the specified variable.

If you use a field width, scanf() halts at the field end or at the first whitespace, whichever comes first.

What if the first nonwhitespace character is, say, an A instead of a digit? Then scanf() stops right there and places the A (or whatever) back in the input. No value is assigned to the specified variable, and the next time the program reads input, it will start at the A again. If your program has only %d specifiers, scanf() will never get past that A. Also, if you use a scanf() statement with several specifiers, ANSI C requires the function to stop reading input at the first failure.

Reading input using the other numeric specifiers works much the same as the %d case. The main difference is that scanf() may recognize more characters as being part of the number. For instance, the %x specifier requires that scanf() recognize the hexadecimal digits *a-f* and *A-F*. Floating-point specifiers require scanf() to recognize decimal points and E-notation.

If you use a %s specifier, any character other than whitespace is acceptable, so scanf() skips whitespace to the first nonwhitespace character and then saves up nonwhitespace characters until hitting whitespace again. This means that %s results in scanf() reading a single word, that is, a string with no whitespace in it. If you use a field width, scanf() stops at the end of the field or at the first whitespace. You can't use the field width to make scanf() read more than one word for one %s specifier. A final point: when scanf() places the string in the designated array, it adds the terminating '\0' to make the array contents a C string.

If you use a %c specifier, all input characters are fair game. If the next input character is a space or a newline, then a space or a newline is assigned to the indicated variable; white-space is not skipped.

Actually, scanf() is not the most commonly used input function in C. It is featured here because of its versatility (it can read all the different data types), but C has several other input functions, such as getchar() and gets() that are better suited for specific tasks, such as reading single characters or reading strings containing spaces. We will cover some of these functions in Chapters 7, 11, and 12. In the meantime, if you need an integer or decimal fraction or a string, you can use scanf().

Regular Characters in the Format String

The scanf() function does enable you to place ordinary characters in the format string. Ordinary characters other than the space character must be matched exactly by the input string. For instance, suppose you accidentally place a comma between two specifiers.

```
scanf("%d,%d", &n, &m);
```

The scanf() function interprets this to mean that you will type a number, then type a comma, then type a second number. That is, you would have to enter two integers this way:

```
88,121
```

Because the comma comes immediately after the %d in the format string, you would have to type it immediately after the 88. However, because scanf() skips over whitespace preceding an integer, you could type a space or newline after the comma when entering the input. That is,

```
88, 121
```

and

```
88,
121
```

also would be accepted.

A space in the format string means to skip over any whitespace before the next input item. For instance, the statement

```
scanf("%d ,%d", &n, &m);
```

would accept any of the following input lines:

```
88,121
88  ,121
88 ,   121
```

Note that the concept of "any whitespace" includes the special cases of no whitespace.

Except for %c, the specifiers automatically skip over whitespace preceding an input value, so `scanf("%d%d", &n, &m)` behaves the same as `scanf("%d %d", &n, &m)`. For %c, adding a space character to the format string does make a difference. For example, if %c is preceded by a space in the format string, `scanf()` does skip to the first nonwhitespace character. That is, the command `scanf("%c", &ch)` reads the first character encountered in input, and `scanf(" %c", &ch)` reads the first nonwhitespace character encountered.

The *scanf()* Return Value

The `scanf()` function returns the number of *items* that it successfully read. If it reads no items, which will happen if you type a nonnumeric string when it expects a number, `scanf()` returns the value 0. It returns EOF when it detects the condition known as *end of file*. (EOF is a special value defined in the `stdio.h` file. Typically, a `#define` directive gives EOF the value –1.) We'll discuss end of file in Chapter 6 and make use of `scanf()`'s return value later in the book. Once you learn about `if` statements and `while` statements, you can use the `scanf()` return value detect and handle mismatched input.

The * Modifier with *printf()* and *scanf()*

Both `printf()` and `scanf()` can use the * modifier to modify the meaning of a specifier, but they do so in dissimilar fashions. First, let's see what the * modifier can do for `printf()`.

Suppose that you don't want to commit yourself to a field width in advance but that you want the program to specify it. You can do this by using * instead of a number for the field width, but you also have to use an argument to tell what the field width should be. That is, if you have the conversion specifier %*d, the argument list should include a value for * and a value for d. The technique also can be used with floating-point values to specify the precision as well as the field width. Listing 4.16 is a short example showing how this works.

Listing 4.16. `varwid.c.`

```c
/* varwid.c -- uses variable-width output field */
#include <stdio.h>
int main(void)
{
  unsigned width, precision;
  int number = 256;
  double weight = 242.5;

  printf("What field width?\n");
  scanf("%d", &width);
  printf("The number is :%*d:\n", width, number);
  printf("Now enter a width and a precision:\n");
  scanf("%d %d", &width, &precision);
  printf("Weight = %*.*f\n", width, precision, weight);
  return 0;
}
```

The variable `width` provides the `field width`, and `number` is the number to be printed. Because the `*` precedes the `d` in the specifier, `width` comes before `number` in `printf()`'s argument list. Similarly, `width` and `precision` provide the formatting information for printing `weight`. Here is a sample run:

```
What field width?
6
The number is :   256:
Now enter a width and a precision:
8 3
Weight = 242.500
```

We replied to the first question with 6, so 6 was the field width used. Similarly, our second reply produced a width of 8 with 3 digits to the right of the decimal. More generally, a program could decide on values for these variables after looking at the value of `weight`.

The `*` serves quite a different purpose for `scanf()`. When placed between the `%` and the specifier letter, it causes that function to skip over corresponding input. Listing 4.17 provides an example.

Listing 4.17. `skip2.c.`

```c
/* skip2.c -- skips over first two integers of input */
#include <stdio.h>
int main(void)
{
  int n;
```

continues

Listing 4.17. continued

```
    printf("Please enter three integers:\n");
    scanf("%*d %*d %d", &n);
    printf("The last integer was %d\n", n);
    return 0;
}
```

The `scanf()` instruction in Listing 4.17 says, "Skip two integers and copy the third into n." Here is a sample run:

```
Please enter three integers
445 345 1212
The last integer was 1212
```

This skipping facility is useful, for example, if a program needs to read a particular column of a file that has data arranged in uniform columns.

Usage Tips

Specifying fixed field widths is useful when you want to print columns of data. Because the default field width is just the width of the number, the repeated use of, say,

```
printf("%d %d %d\n", val1, val2, val3);
```

would produce ragged columns if the numbers in a column had different sizes. For example, the output could look like this:

```
12 234 1222
4 5 23
22334 2322 10001
```

(This assumes that the value of the variables has been changed between print statements.)

The output can be cleaned up by using a sufficiently large fixed field width. For example, using

```
printf("%9d %9d %9d\n", val1, val2, val3);
```

would yield

```
    12       234      1222
     4         5        23
 22334      2322     10001
```

Leaving a blank between one conversion specification and the next ensures that one number will never run into the next, even if it overflows its own field. This is so because the regular characters in the control string, including spaces, are printed.

On the other hand, if a number is to be embedded in a phrase, it often is convenient to specify a field as small or smaller than the expected number width. This makes the number fit in without unnecessary blanks. For example,

```
printf("Count Beppo ran %.2f miles in 3 hours.\n", distance);
```

might produce

```
Count Beppo ran 10.22 miles in 3 hours.
```

Changing the conversion specification to `%10.2f` would give

```
Count Beppo ran      10.22 miles in 3 hours.
```

Chapter Summary

A *string* is a series of characters treated as a unit. In C, strings are represented by a series of characters terminated by the *null character*, which is the character whose ASCII code is 0. Strings can be stored in character arrays. An *array* is a series of items, or elements, all of the same type. To declare an array called name and having 30 elements of type char, do this:

```
char name[30];
```

Be sure to allot a number of elements sufficient to hold the entire string, including the null character.

String constants are represented by enclosing the string in double quotes: "This is an example of a string."

The `strlen()` function can be used to find the length of a string (not counting the terminating null character). The `scanf()` function, when used with the `%s` specifier, can be used to read in single-word strings.

The C preprocessor searches a source code program for *preprocessor directives*, which begin with the # symbol, and acts upon them before the program is compiled. The `#include` directive causes the processor to add the contents of another file to your file at the location of the directive. The `#define` directive lets you establish *manifest constants*, that is, symbolic representations for constants.

The `printf()` and `scanf()` functions provide versatile support for input and output. Each uses a control string containing embedded *conversion specifiers*, which indicate the number and type of data items to be read or printed. Also, you can use the conversion specifiers to control the appearance of the output: field widths, decimal places, and placement within a field.

Review Questions

1. Run Listing 4.1 again, but this time give your first and last name when it asks you for your first name. What happens? Why?

2. Assuming that each of the following examples is part of a complete program, what will each one print?

    a. `printf("He sold the painting for $%2.2f.\n", 2.345e2);`
    b. `printf("%c%c%c\n", 'H', 105, '\41');`
    c. `#define Q "His Hamlet was funny without being vulgar."`

    `printf("%s\nhas %d characters.\n", Q, strlen(Q));`

    d. `printf("Is %2.2e the same as %2.2f?\n", 1201.0, 1201.0);`

3. Suppose a program starts like this:

    ```
    #define BOOK "War and Peace"
    int main(void)
    {
    float cost =12.99;
    float percent = 80.0;
    ```

    Construct a `printf()` statement that uses `BOOK` and `cost` to print the following:

    ```
    This copy of "War and Peace" sells for $12.99.
    That is 80% of list.
    ```

4. Which conversion specification would you use to print each of the following?

    a. An `unsigned long` integer in a field width of 15.
    b. A hexadecimal integer in the form 0x8a in a field width of 4.
    c. A floating-point number in the form 2.33E+02 that is left-justified in a field width of 12.
    d. A floating-point number in the form +232.346 in a field width of 10.
    e. The first 8 characters of a string in a field 8 characters wide.

5. For each of the following input lines, provide a `scanf()` statement to read it. Also declare any variables or arrays used in the statement.

    a. `101`
    b. `22.328.34E-09`
    c. `Chelsea`
    d. `catch 22`
    e. `catch 22` (but skip over `catch`)

6. Suppose that you would rather use parentheses than braces in your programs. How well would the following work?

```
#define ( {
#define ) }
```

Programming Exercises

1. Write a program that asks for your first name and then your last name, and then prints the names in the format last, first.

2. Write a program that requests your first name and does the following with it:

   a. Prints it enclosed in double quotation marks.
   b. Prints it in a field 20 characters wide, with the whole field in quotes.
   c. Prints it at the left end of a field 20 characters wide, with the whole field enclosed in quotes.
   d. Prints it in a field 3 characters wider than the name.

3. Write a program that reads in a floating-point number and prints it first in decimal-point notation and then in exponential notation. Have the output use the following formats:

   a. `The input is 21.3 or 2.1e+001.`
   b. `The input is +21.290 or 2.129E+001.`

4. Write a program that requests your height in inches and your name, and then displays the information in the following form:

   `Dabney, you are 6.208 feet tall`

   Use type `float`, and use `/` for division.

5. Write a program that requests the user's first name and then the user's last name. Have it print the entered names on one line and the number of letters in each name on the following line. Align each letter count with the end of the corresponding name, as in the following:

   ```
   Melissa Honeybee
         7        8
   ```

   Next have it print the same information, but with the counts aligned with the beginning of each name.

   ```
   Melissa Honeybee
   7       8
   ```

5

Operators, Expressions, and Statements

Keywords
    while
Operators
    = - * /
    % ++ -- (type)

This chapter introduces you to C's multitudinous operators, including those used for common arithmetic operations. You learn about operator precedence and the meanings of the terms *statement* and *expression*. Then you encounter the handy while loop. Compound statements, automatic type conversions, and type casts are next. Finally, you see how to write functions that use arguments.

Now that you've looked at ways to represent data, let's explore ways to process data. C provides a wealth of operations for that purpose. You can do arithmetic, compare values, modify variables, combine relationships logically, and more. We'll start with basic arithmetic: addition, subtraction, multiplication, and division.

Another aspect of processing data is organizing your programs so that they take the right steps in the right order. C provides several language features to help you with that task. One of these features is the loop, and in this chapter we'll take a first look at it. A loop enables you to repeat actions and makes your programs more interesting and powerful.

Introducing Loops

Listing 5.1 shows a sample program that does a little arithmetic to calculate the length in inches of a foot that wears a size 9 (men's) shoe. This first version doesn't use loops.

Listing 5.1. shoes1.c.

```
/* shoes1.c -- converts a shoe size to inches */
#include <stdio.h>
#define ADJUST 7.64
#define SCALE 0.325
int main(void)
{
  float shoe, foot;

  shoe = 9.0;
  foot = SCALE * shoe + ADJUST;
  printf("Shoe size (men's)    foot length\n");
  printf("%10.1f %15.2f inches\n", shoe, foot);
  return 0;
}
```

Here is a program with multiplication and addition. It takes your shoe size (if you wear a size 9) and tells you how long your foot is in inches. "But," you say, "I could solve this problem by hand more quickly than you could type the program." That's a good point. A one-shot program that does just one shoe size is a waste of time and effort. We could make the program more useful by writing it as an interactive program, but that still barely taps the potential of a computer.

What we need is some way to have a computer do repetitive calculations for a succession of shoe sizes. After all, that's one of the main reasons for using a computer to do arithmetic. C offers several methods to accomplish repetitive calculations, and we will outline one here. This method, called a *while loop*, will enable us to make a more interesting exploration of operators. Listing 5.2 presents our improved shoe-sizing program.

Listing 5.2. shoe2.c.

```
/* shoe2.c -- calculates foot lengths for several sizes */
#include <stdio.h>
#define ADJUST 7.64
#define SCALE 0.325
int main(void)
{
  float shoe, foot;

  printf("Shoe size (men's)    foot length\n");
  shoe = 3.0;
  while (shoe < 18.5)          /* starting the while loop */
  {                            /* start of block          */
     foot = SCALE*shoe + ADJUST;
     printf("%10.1f %15.2f inches\n", shoe, foot);
     shoe = shoe + 1.0;
  }                            /* end of block            */
  printf("If the shoe fits, wear it.\n");
  return 0;
}
```

Here is a condensed version of shoe2.c's output:

```
Shoe size (men's)    foot length
       3.0            8.61 inches
       4.0            8.94 inches
       ...             ...
      17.0           13.16 inches
      18.0           13.49 inches
If the shoe fits, wear it.
```

(Incidentally, the constants for this conversion were obtained during an incognito visit to a shoe store. The only shoe-sizer left lying around was for men's sizes. Those of you interested in women's sizes will have to make your own visit to a shoe store.)

Here is how the while loop works. When the program first reaches the while statement, it checks to see whether the condition within parentheses is true. In this case the expression is

shoe < 18.5

where the < symbol means "is less than." The variable shoe was initialized to 3.0, which certainly is less than 18.5. Thus, the condition is true and the program proceeds to the next statement, which converts the size to inches. Then it prints the results. The next statement,

```
shoe = shoe + 1.0;
```

increases shoe by 1.0, making it 4.0. At this point the program returns to the while portion to check the condition. Why at this point? Because the next line is a closing brace (}), and we have used a set of braces ({ }) to mark the extent of the while loop. The statements between the two braces are the ones that are repeated. The section of program between and including the braces is called a *block*. Now back to our program. The value 4 is less than 18.5, so the whole cycle of embraced commands (the block) following the while is repeated. (In computerese, the program is said to "loop" through these statements.) This continues until shoe reaches a value of 19.0. Now the condition

```
shoe < 18.5
```

becomes false, because 19.0 is not less than 18.5. When this happens, control passes to the first statement following the while loop. In our case, that is the final printf() statement.

You easily can modify this program to do other conversions. For example, change SCALE to 1.8 and ADJUST to 32.0, and you have a program that converts Centigrade to Fahrenheit. Change SCALE to 0.6214 and ADJUST to 0, and you convert kilometers to miles. If you make these changes, you should change the printed messages, too, to prevent confusion.

The while loop provides a convenient, flexible means of controlling a program. Now let's turn to the fundamental operators that we can use in our programs.

Fundamental Operators

C uses *operators* to represent arithmetic operations. For example, the + operator causes the two values flanking it to be added together. If the term "operator" seems odd to you, please reflect that those things had to be called something. "Operator" does seem to be a better choice than, say, "those things" or "arithmetical transactors." We'll look now at the operators used for basic arithmetic: =, +, -, *, and /. (C does not have an exponentiating operator. In a later chapter we will present a function to accomplish this task.)

Assignment Operator: =

In C, the equal sign does not mean "equals." Rather, it is a value-assigning operator. The statement

```
bmw = 2002;
```

assigns the value 2002 to the variable named bmw. That is, the item to the left of the = sign is the *name* of a variable, and the item on the right is the *value* assigned to the variable. We call the = symbol the *assignment operator*. Again, don't think of the line as saying, "bmw equals 2002." Instead, read it as "assign the value 2002 to the variable bmw." The action goes from right to left for this operator.

Perhaps this distinction between the name of a variable and the value of a variable seems like hair-splitting, but consider the following common type of computer statement:

```
i = i + 1;
```

As mathematics, this statement makes no sense. If you add 1 to a finite number, the result isn't "equal to" the number you started with, but as a computer assignment statement, it is perfectly reasonable. It means "find the value of the variable named i; to that value, add 1 and then assign this new value to the variable named i." See Figure 5.1.

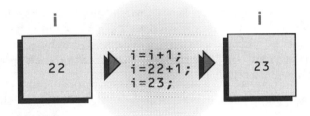

Figure 5.1. *The statement* i = i + 1;.

A statement such as

```
2002 = bmw;
```

makes no sense in C (and, indeed, is invalid) because 2002 is just a constant. You can't assign a value to a constant; it already *is* its value. When you sit down at the keyboard, therefore, remember that the item to the left of the = sign must be the name of a variable. Actually, the left side must refer to a storage location. The simplest way is to use the name of a variable, but, as you will see later, a "pointer" can be used to point to a location. More generally, ANSI C uses the term *modifiable lvalue* to label those entities to which you can assign values. "Modifiable lvalue" is not, perhaps, the most intuitive phrase you've encountered, so let's look at some definitions.

Some Terminology: Data Objects, Lvalues, Rvalues, and Operands

A *data object* is a general term for a region of data storage that can be used to hold values. The data storage used to hold a variable or an array is a data object, for instance. ANSI C uses the term *lvalue* to mean a name or expression that identifies a particular object. The name of a variable, for instance, is an lvalue, so *object* refers to the actual data storage, but *lvalue* is a label used to identify, or locate, that storage.

Not all objects can have their values changed, so ANSI C uses the term *modifiable lvalue* to identify objects whose value can be changed. Thus, the left side of an assignment operator should be a modifiable lvalue. Indeed, the *l* in *l*value comes from *left* because modifiable lvalues can be used on the left side of assignment operators.

The term *rvalue* refers to quantities that can be assigned to modifiable lvalues. For instance, consider this statement:

```
bmw = 2002;
```

Here, bmw is a modifiable lvalue, and 2002 is an rvalue. As you probably guessed, the *r* in *r*value comes from *right*. Rvalues can be constants, variables, or any other expression that yields a value.

As long as you are learning the names of things, the proper term for what we have called an "item" (as in "the item to the left of the =") is *operand*. Operands are what operators operate on. For example, you can describe eating a hamburger as applying the "eat" operator to the "hamburger" operand, or you can say that the left operand of the = operator shall be a modifiable lvalue.

The basic C assignment operator is a little flashier than most. Try the short program in Listing 5.3.

Listing 5.3. golf.c.

```
/* golf.c -- golf tournament scorecard */
#include <stdio.h>
int main(void)
{
  int jane, tarzan, cheeta;

  cheeta = tarzan = jane = 68;
  printf("                  cheeta   tarzan    jane\n");
  printf("First round score %4d %8d %8d\n",cheeta,tarzan,jane);
  return 0;
}
```

Many languages would balk at the triple assignment made in this program, but C accepts it routinely. The assignments are made right to left: first jane gets the value 68, then tarzan does, and finally cheeta does. Thus, the output is as follows:

```
                   cheeta   tarzan    jane
First round score    68       68       68
```

Addition Operator: +

The *addition operator* causes the two values on either side of it to be added together. For example, the statement

```
printf("%d", 4 + 20);
```

causes the number 24 to be printed, not the expression

```
4 + 20.
```

The values (operands) to be added can be variables as well as constants. Thus, the statement

```
income = salary + bribes;
```

will cause the computer to look up the values of the two variables on the right, add them, and assign this total to the variable income.

Subtraction Operator: –

The *subtraction operator* causes the number after the – sign to be subtracted from the number before the sign. The statement

```
takehome = 224.00 - 24.00;
```

assigns the value 200.0 to takehome.

The + and – operators are termed *binary*, or *dyadic*, operators, meaning that they require *two* operands.

Sign Operators: – and +

The minus sign also can be used to indicate or to change the algebraic sign of a value. For instance, the sequence

```
rocky = -12;
smokey = -rocky;
```

gives smokey the value 12.

When the minus sign is used in this way, it is called a *unary operator*, meaning that it takes just one operand. See Figure 5.2.

The ANSI Standard adds a unary + operator to C. It doesn't alter the value or sign of its operand; it just enables you to use statements like

```
dozen = +12;
```

without getting a compiler complaint. Formerly, this construction was not allowed.

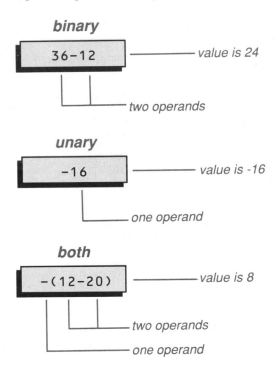

Figure 5.2. *Unary and binary operators.*

Multiplication Operator: *

Multiplication is indicated by the * symbol. The statement

```
cm = 2.54 * in;
```

multiplies the variable in by 2.54 and assigns the answer to cm.

By any chance do you want a table of squares? C doesn't have a squaring function, but, as shown in Listing 5.4, we can use multiplication to calculate squares.

Listing 5.4. `squares.c`.

```
/* squares.c -- produces a table of first 20 squares */
#include <stdio.h>
int main(void)
{
    int num = 1;

    while (num < 21)
    {
        printf("%10d %10d\n", num, num * num);
        num = num + 1;
    }
    return 0;
}
```

This program prints the first 20 integers and their squares, as you can verify for yourself. Let's look at a more interesting example.

Exponential Growth

You probably have heard the story of the powerful ruler who seeks to reward a scholar who has done him a great service. When the scholar is asked what he would like, he points to a chessboard and says, just one grain of wheat on the first square, two on the second, four on the third, eight on the next, and so on. The ruler, lacking mathematical erudition, is astounded at the modesty of this request, for he had been prepared to offer great riches. The joke, of course, is on the ruler, as the program in Listing 5.5 shows. It calculates how many grains go on each square and keeps a running total. Because you may not be up to date on wheat crops, we also compare the running total to a rough estimate of the annual wheat crop in the United States.

Listing 5.5. `wheat.c`.

```
/* wheat.c -- exponential growth */
#include <stdio.h>
#define SQUARES 64     /* squares on a checkerboard  */
#define CROP 9E14      /* US wheat crop in grains    */
int main(void)
{
    double current, total;
    int count = 1;

    printf("square   grains added   total grains   ");
    printf("fraction of \n");
    printf("                                        ");
    printf("US total\n");
```

continues

Listing 5.5. continued

```
total = current = 1.0;     /* start with one grain    */
printf("%4d %15.2e %13.2e %13.2e\n", count, current,
       total, total/CROP);
while (count < SQUARES)
{
   count = count + 1;
   current = 2.0 * current;
                       /* double grains on next square */
   total = total + current;          /* update total */
   printf("%4d %15.2e %13.2e %13.2e\n", count, current,
          total, total/CROP);
}
return 0;
}
```

The output begins innocuously enough.

square	grains added	total grains	fraction of US total
1	1.00e+00	1.00e+00	1.11e-15
2	2.00e+00	3.00e+00	3.33e-15
3	4.00e+00	7.00e+00	7.78e-15
4	8.00e+00	1.50e+01	1.67e-14
5	1.60e+01	3.10e+01	3.44e-14
6	3.20e+01	6.30e+01	7.00e-14
7	6.40e+01	1.27e+02	1.41e-13
8	1.28e+02	2.55e+02	2.83e-13
9	2.56e+02	5.11e+02	5.68e-13
10	5.12e+02	1.02e+03	1.14e-12

After ten squares, the scholar has acquired just a little over a thousand grains of wheat, but look what has happened by square 50!

```
50        5.63e+14      1.13e+15       1.25e+00
```

The haul has exceeded the total U.S. annual output! If you want to see what happens by the 64th square, you will have to run the program yourself.

This example illustrates the phenomenon of exponential growth. The world population growth and our use of energy resources have followed the same pattern.

Division Operator: /

C uses the / symbol to represent division. The value to the left of the / is divided by the value to the right. For example, the following gives four the value of 4.0:

```
four = 12.0/3.0;
```

Division works differently for integer types than it does for floating types. Floating-type division gives a floating-point answer, but integer division yields an integer answer. An integer has to be a whole number, which makes dividing 5 by 3 awkward, because the answer isn't a whole number. In C, any fraction resulting from integer division is discarded. This process is called *truncation*.

Try the program in Listing 5.6 to see how truncation works and how integer division differs from floating-point division.

Listing 5.6. `divide.c`.

```
/* divide.c -- divisions we have known */
#include <stdio.h>
int main(void)
{

    printf("integer division:  5/4   is %d \n", 5/4);
    printf("integer division:  6/3   is %d \n", 6/3);
    printf("integer division:  7/4   is %d \n", 7/4);
    printf("floating division: 7./4. is %1.2f \n", 7./4.);
    printf("mixed division:    7./4  is %1.2f \n", 7./4);
    return 0;
}
```

In Listing 5.6 we included a case of "mixed types" by having a floating-point value divided by an integer. C is a more forgiving language than some and will let you get away with this, but normally you should avoid mixing types. Now for the results.

```
integer division:  5/4   is 1
integer division:  6/3   is 2
integer division:  7/4   is 1
floating division: 7./4. is 1.75
mixed division:    7./4  is 1.75
```

Notice how integer division does not round to the nearest integer, but always truncates, that is, discards the entire fractional part. When we mixed integers with floating point, the answer came out the same as floating point. When a calculation uses both types, the integer is converted to floating point before division.

The properties of integer division turn out to be handy for some problems, and we will give an example fairly soon. First, there is another important matter: what happens when you combine more than one operation into one statement? That is our next topic.

Operator Precedence

Consider the line

```
butter = 25.0 + 60.0 * n / SCALE;
```

This statement has an addition, a multiplication, and a division. Which operation takes place first? Is 25.0 added to 60.0, the result of 85.0 then multiplied by n, and that result then divided by SCALE? Is 60.0 multiplied by n, the result added to 25.0, and that answer then divided by SCALE? Is it some other order? Let's take n to be 6.0 and SCALE to be 2.0. If you work through the statement using these values, you will find that the first approach yields a value of 255. The second approach yields 192.5. A C program must have some other order in mind, for it would give a value of 205.0 for butter.

Clearly the order of executing the various operations can make a difference, so C needs unambiguous rules for choosing what to do first. C does this by setting up an operator pecking order. Each operator is assigned a *precedence* level. As in ordinary arithmetic, multiplication and division have a higher precedence than addition and subtraction, so they are performed first. What if two operators have the same precedence? If they share an operand, they are executed according to the order in which they occur in the statement. For most operators the order is from left to right. (The = operator was an exception to this.) Therefore, in the statement

```
butter = 25.0 + 60.0 * n / SCALE;
```

the order of operations is

60.0 * n	the first * or / in the expression (assuming n is 6 so that 60.0 * n is 360.0)
360.0 / SCALE	then the second * or / in the expression and
25.0 + 180	finally (because SCALE is 2.0) the first + or - in the expression to yield 205.0

Many people like to represent the order of evaluation with a type of diagram called an *expression tree*. Figure 5.3 is an example of such a diagram. The diagram shows how the original expression is reduced by steps to a single value.

What if you want, say, an addition to take place before a division. Then you can do as we have done in this line:

```
flour = (25.0 + 60.0 * n) / SCALE;
```

Whatever is enclosed in parentheses is executed first. Within the parentheses, the usual rules hold. For this example, first the multiplication takes place and then the addition. That completes the expression in the parentheses. Now the result can be divided by SCALE.

Table 5.1 summarizes the rules for the operators we've used so far. (Appendix B, "C Operators," contains a table covering all operators.)

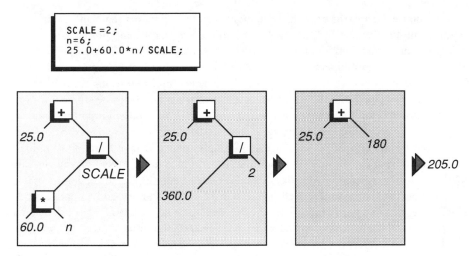

```
SCALE =2;
n=6;
25.0+60.0*n/ SCALE;
```

Figure 5.3. *Expression trees showing operators, operands, and order of evaluation.*

Table 5.1. Operators in order of decreasing precedence.

Operators	Associativity
( )	Left to right
+ - (unary)	Left to right
* /	Left to right
+ - (binary)	Left to right
=	Right to left

Notice that the two uses of the minus sign have different precedences, as do the two uses of the plus sign. The associativity column tells you how an operator associates with its operands. For example, the unary minus sign associates with the quantity to its right, and in division the left operand is divided by the right.

Precedence and the Order of Evaluation

Operator precedence provides vital rules for determining the order of evaluation in an expression, but it doesn't necessarily determine the complete order. C leaves some choices up to the implementor. Consider this statement:

```
y = 6 * 12 + 5 * 20;
```

Precedence dictates the order of evaluation when two operators share an operand. For example, the 12 is an operand for both the * and the + operators, and precedence says that multiplication comes first. Similarly, precedence says that the 5 is to be multiplied, not added. In short, the multiplications 6 * 12 and 5 * 20 take place before any addition. What precedence does not establish is which of these two multiplications occurs first. C leaves that choice to the implementor because one choice might be more efficient for one kind of hardware, but the other choice might work better on another kind of hardware. In either case, the expression reduces to 72 + 100, so the choice doesn't affect the final value for this particular example. "But," you say, "multiplication associates from left to right. Doesn't that mean the leftmost multiplication is performed first?" (Well, maybe you don't say that, but somewhere someone does.) The association rule applies for operators that share an operand. For instance, in the expression 12 / 3 * 2, the / and * operators, which have the same precedence, share the operand 3. Thus, the left-to-right rule applies in this case, and the expression reduces to 4 * 2, or 8. (Going from right to left would give 12 / 6, or 2. Here the choice does matter.) In the previous example, the two * operators did not share a common operand, so the left-to-right rule did not apply.

Trying the Rules

Let's try these rules on a more complex example—Listing 5.7.

Listing 5.7. rules.c.

```
/* rules.c -- precedence test */
#include <stdio.h>
int main(void)
{
  int top, score;
  top = score = -(2 + 5) * 6 + (4 + 3 * (2 + 3));
  printf("top = %d \n", top);
  return 0;
}}
```

What value will this program print? Figure it out; then run the program or read the following description to check your answer.

First, parentheses have the highest precedence. Whether the parentheses in -(2 + 5) * 6 or in (4 + 3 * (2 + 3)) are evaluated first depends on the implementation, as we just discussed. Either choice will lead to the same result for this example, so let's take the left one first. The high precedence of parentheses means that in the subexpression -(2 + 5) * 6, we evaluate (2 + 5) first, obtaining 7. Next, we apply the unary minus operator to 7 to obtain -7. Now, the expression is this:

```
top = score = -7 * 6 + (4 + 3 * (2 + 3))
```

The next step is to evaluate 2 + 3. The expression becomes

```
top = score = -7 * 6 + (4 + 3 * 5)
```

Next, because the * in the parentheses has priority over +, the expression becomes

```
top = score = -7 * 6 + (4 + 15)
```

and then

```
top = score = -7 * 6 + 19
```

Multiply -7 by 6 and get this expression:

```
top = score = -42 + 19
```

Then addition makes it

```
top = score = -23
```

Now score is assigned the value -23, and, finally, top gets the value -23. Remember that the = operator associates from right to left.

Some Additional Operators

C has about forty operators, but some are used much more than others. The ones we just covered are the most common, and we would like to add four more useful operators to the list.

The *sizeof* Operator

We used the sizeof operator in Chapter 3, "Data and C." To review, the sizeof operator returns the size, in bytes, of its operand. The operand can be a specific data object, such as the name of a variable, or it can be a type. If it is a type, such as float, the operand must be enclosed in parentheses. For instance, the example in Listing 5.8 shows both forms. (Think C users should replace %d with %old.)

Listing 5.8. sizeof.c.

```
/* sizeof.c -- uses sizeof operator */
#include <stdio.h>
int main(void)
{
  int n;

  printf("n has %d bytes; all ints have %d bytes.\n",
      sizeof n, sizeof (int) );
  return 0;
}
```

Modulus Operator: %

The *modulus operator* is used in integer arithmetic. It gives the *remainder* that results when the integer to its left is divided by the integer to its right. For example, 13 % 5 (read as "13 modulo 5") has the value 3, because 5 goes into 13 twice, with a remainder of 3. Don't bother trying to use this operator with floating-point numbers. It just won't work.

At first glance, this operator may strike you as an esoteric tool for mathematicians, but actually it is rather practical and helpful. One common use is to help you control the flow of a program. Suppose, for example, you are working on a bill-preparing program that is designed to add in an extra charge every third month. Just have the program evaluate the month number modulo 3 (i.e., month % 3) and check to see if the result is 0. If it is, the program adds in the extra charge. After you learn about "if statements" in Chapter 7, "C Control Statements: Branching and Jumps," you'll understand this better.

Listing 5.9 shows another use for the % operator.

Listing 5.9. min_sec.c.

```
/* min_sec.c -- converts seconds to minutes and seconds */
#include <stdio.h>
#define SEC_PER_MIN 60        /* seconds in a minute        */
int main(void)
{
    int sec, min, left;

    printf("Convert seconds to minutes and seconds!\n");
    printf("Enter the number of seconds you wish to convert.\n");
    scanf("%d", &sec);          /* number of seconds is read in */
    min = sec / SEC_PER_MIN;   /* truncated number of minutes  */
    left = sec % SEC_PER_MIN;  /* number of seconds left over  */
    printf("%d seconds is %d minutes, %d seconds.\n", sec, min,
           left);
    return 0;
}
```

Here is a sample output:

```
Convert seconds to minutes and seconds!
Enter the number of seconds you wish to convert.
234
234 seconds is 3 minutes, 54 seconds.
```

One problem with this interactive program is that it processes just one input value. Can you figure out a way to have the program prompt you repeatedly for new input values? We will return to this problem later in the "Review Questions," but if you can work out a solution first, congratulations.

Increment and Decrement Operators: ++ and --

The *increment operator* performs a simple task; it increments (increases) the value of its operand by 1. This operator comes in two varieties. The first variety has the ++ come before the affected variable; this is the *prefix* mode. The second variety has the ++ after the affected variable; this is the *postfix* mode. The two modes differ with regard to the precise time that the incrementing takes place. We'll look at the similarities first and then return to that difference. The short example in Listing 5.10 shows how the increment operators work.

Listing 5.10. add_one.c.

```c
/* add_one.c -- incrementing: prefix and postfix */
#include <stdio.h>
int main(void)
{   int ultra = 0, super = 0;

    while (super < 5)
    {
       super++;
       ++ultra;
       printf("super = %d, ultra = %d \n", super, ultra);
    }
    return 0;
}
```

Running add_one.c produces

```
super = 1, ultra = 1
super = 2, ultra = 2
super = 3, ultra = 3
super = 4, ultra = 4
super = 5, ultra = 5
```

The program counted to 5 twice and simultaneously. We confess that the same results could have been achieved by replacing the two increment statements with

```
super = super + 1;
ultra = ultra + 1;
```

These are simple enough statements. Why bother creating one, let alone two, abbreviations? One reason is that the compact form makes your programs neater and easier to follow. These operators give your programs an elegant gloss that cannot fail to please the eye. For instance, we can rewrite part of shoe2.c (Listing 5.2) this way:

```
shoe = 3.0;
while (shoe < 18.5)
{
```

```
        foot = SCALE*size + ADJUST;
        printf("%10.1f %20.2f inches\n", shoe, foot);
        ++shoe;
}
```

However, we still haven't taken full advantage of the increment operator. We can shorten the fragment this way:

```
shoe = 2.0;
while (++shoe < 18.5)
{
    foot = SCALE*shoe + ADJUST;
    printf("%10.1f %20.2f inches\n", shoe, foot);
}
```

Here we have combined the incrementing process and the `while` comparison into one expression. This type of construction is so common in C that it merits a closer look.

First, how does this construction work? Simply. The value of `shoe` is increased by 1 and then compared to `18.5`. If it is less than `18.5`, the statements between the braces are executed once. Then `shoe` is increased by 1 again, and the cycle is repeated until `shoe` gets too big. We changed the initial value of `shoe` from `3.0` to `2.0` to compensate for `shoe` being incremented before the first evaluation of `foot`. See Figure 5.4.

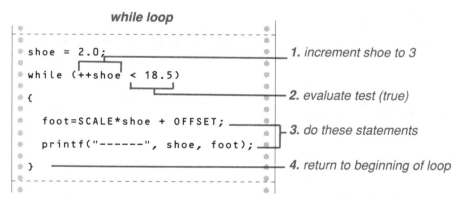

Figure 5.4. *Through the loop once.*

Second, what's so good about this approach? It is more compact. More important, it gathers in one place the two processes that control the loop. The first process is the test: do we continue or not? In this case, the test is checking to see whether the shoe size is less than 18.5. The second process changes an element of the test; in this case, the shoe size is increased.

Suppose you forgot to change the shoe size. Then `shoe` would *always* be less than 18.5, and the loop would never end. The computer would churn out line after identical line, caught in a dreaded "infinite loop." Eventually, you would lose interest in the output and have to kill the program somehow. Having the loop test and the loop change at one place instead of at separate locations helps you to remember to update the loop.

Another advantage of the increment operator is that it usually produces slightly more efficient machine language code, because it is similar to actual machine language instructions. However, as implementors produce better C compilers, this advantage may disappear. A smart compiler will recognize that x = x + 1 can be treated the same as ++x.

Finally, these operators have an additional feature that can be useful in certain delicate situations. To find out what this feature is, try running the program in Listing 5.11.

Listing 5.11. post_pre.c.

```
/* post_pre.c -- postfix vs prefix */
#include <stdio.h>
int main(void)
{
    int a = 1, b = 1;
    int aplus, plusb;

    aplus = a++;        /* postfix */
    plusb = ++b;        /* prefix  */
    printf("a    aplus   b   plusb \n");
    printf("%1d %5d %5d %5d\n", a, aplus, b, plusb);
    return 0;
}}
```

If you and your compiler do everything correctly, you should get this result:

```
a   aplus   b   plusb
2     1     2     2
```

Both a and b were increased by 1, as promised. However, aplus has the value of a *before* a changed, but plusb has the value of b *after* b changed. This is the difference between the prefix form and the postfix form. See Figure 5.5.

```
aplus = a++;  /* postfix: a is changed after its value is used */
plusb = ++b;  /* prefix: b is changed before its value is used */
```

When one of these increment operators is used by itself, as in a solitary ego++; statement, it doesn't matter which form you use. The choice does matter, however, when the operator and its operand are part of a larger expression, as in the assignment statements we just saw. In this kind of situation, you must give some thought to the result you want. For instance, recall our use of

```
while (++shoe < 18.5)
```

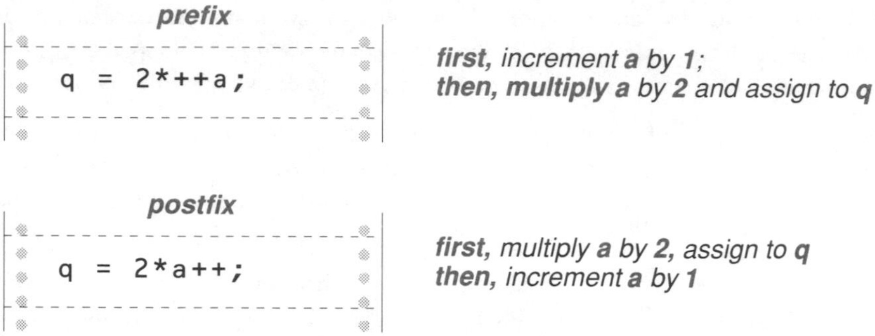

prefix

```
q = 2*++a;
```

first, increment *a* by *1;*
then, **multiply** *a* by *2* and assign to *q*

postfix

```
q = 2*a++;
```

first, multiply *a* by *2,* assign to *q*
then, increment *a* by *1*

Figure 5.5. *Prefix and postfix.*

This test condition provided a table up to size 18. If we had used shoe++ instead of ++shoe, the table would have gone to size 19, because shoe would have been increased after the comparison instead of before.

Of course, you could fall back on the less subtle form,

```
shoe = shoe + 1;
```

but then no one will believe that you are a true C programmer.

We suggest that you pay special attention to the examples of increment operators as you read through this book. Ask yourself if we could have used the prefix and the suffix forms interchangeably or if circumstances dictated a particular choice.

Decrementing: --

For each form of increment operator, there is a corresponding form of *decrement operator.* Instead of ++, use --.

```
-- count;   /* prefix form of decrement operator  */
count --;   /* postfix form of decrement operator */
```

Listing 5.12 illustrates that computers can be accomplished lyricists.

Listing 5.12. bottles.c.

```
/* bottles.c -- counting down */
#include <stdio.h>
#define MAX 100
int main(void)
{
  int count = MAX + 1;
```

```
  while (--count > 0) {
    printf("%d bottles of beer on the wall,"
           "%d bottles of beer!\n", count, count);
    printf("Take one down and pass it around,\n");
    printf("%d bottles of beer!\n\n", count - 1);
  }
  return 0;
}
```

The output starts like this:

```
100 bottles of beer on the wall, 100 bottles of beer!
Take one down and pass it around,
99 bottles of beer!
99 bottles of beer on the wall, 99 bottles of beer!
Take one down and pass it around,
98 bottles of beer!
```

It goes on a bit and ends this way:

```
1 bottles of beer on the wall, 1 bottles of beer!
Take one down and pass it around,
0 bottles of beer!
```

Apparently our accomplished lyricist has a problem with plurals, but that could be fixed by using the conditional operators of Chapter 8, "Character Input/Output and Redirection."

Incidentally, the > operator stands for "is greater than." Like < ("is less than"), it is a *relational operator*. We will take a longer look at relational operators in Chapter 6, "C Control Statements: Looping."

Precedence

The increment and decrement operators have a very high precedence of association; only parentheses are higher. Thus, x*y++ means (x)*(y++), not (x*y)++, which is fortunate, because the latter is invalid. The increment and decrement operators affect a *variable* (or, more generally, a modifiable lvalue), and the combination x*y is not itself a variable, although its parts are.

Don't confuse precedence of these two operators with the order of evaluation. Suppose you have the following:

```
y = 2;
n = 3;
nextnum = (y + n++)*6;
```

What value does nextnum get? Substituting in values yields this:

```
nextnum = (2 + 3)*6 = 5*6 = 30
```

Only after n is used is it increased to 4. Precedence tells us that the ++ is attached only to the n, not to 2 + n. It also tells us when the value of n is used for evaluating the expression, but the nature of the increment operator determines when the value of n is changed.

When n++ is part of an expression, you can think of it as meaning "use n; then increment it." On the other hand, ++n means "increment n; then use it."

Don't Be Too Clever

You can get fooled if you try to do too much at once with the increment operators. For example, you might think that you could improve on our squares.c program (Listing 5.4) to print integers and their squares by replacing the while loop with this one:

```
while (num < 21)
    {
    printf("%10d %10d\n", num, num*num++);
    }
```

This looks reasonable. We print the number num, multiply it by itself to get the square, and then increase num by 1. In fact, this program may even work on some systems, but not all. The problem is that when printf() goes to get the values for printing, it may evaluate the last argument first and increment num before getting to the other argument. Thus, instead of printing, say,

5   25

it may print

6   25

In C, the compiler can choose which arguments in a function to evaluate first. This freedom increases compiler efficiency but can cause trouble if you use an increment operator on a function argument.

Another possible source of trouble is a statement like

```
ans = num/2 + 5*(1 + num++);
```

Again, the problem is that the compiler may not do things in the same order you have in mind. You would think that it would find num/2 first and then move on, but it might do the last term first, increase num, and use the new value in num/2. There is no guarantee.

Yet another troublesome case is this:

```
n = 3;
y = n++ + n++;
```

Certainly, n winds up larger by 2 after the statement is executed, but the value for y is ambiguous. A compiler can use the old value of n twice in evaluating y and then increment n twice. This gives y the value 6, and n the value 5, or it can use the old value once, increment n once, use that value for the second n in the expression, and then increment n a second time. This gives y the value 7, and n the value 5. Either choice is allowable. More exactly, the result is undefined, which means the C standard fails to define what the result should be.

You can easily avoid these problems:

1. Don't use increment or decrement operators on a variable that is part of more than one argument of a function.

2. Don't use increment or decrement operators on a variable that appears more than once in an expression.

On the other hand, C does provide some guarantees about when incrementation takes place. We'll return to this point when we discuss sequence points.

Expressions and Statements

We have been using the terms "expression" and "statement" throughout these first few chapters, and now the time has come to study their meanings more closely. Statements form the basic program steps of C, and most statements are constructed from expressions. This suggests that we look at expressions first, and we will.

Expressions

An *expression* consists of a combination of operators and operands. (An *operand*, recall, is what an operator operates on.) The simplest expression is a lone operand, and you can build in complexity from there. Here are some expressions:

```
4
-6
4+21
a*(b + c/d)/20
q = 5*2
x = ++q % 3
q > 3
```

As you can see, the operands can be constants, variables, or combinations of the two. Some expressions are combinations of smaller expressions, called *subexpressions*. For instance, c/d is a subexpression of the fourth example.

Every Expression Has a Value

An important property of C is that every C expression has a value. To find the value, you perform the operations in the order dictated by operator precedence. The value of the first few expressions we just listed is clear, but what about the ones with = signs? Those expressions simply have the same value that the variable to the left of the = sign receives. Thus, the expression q=5*2 as a whole has the value 10. What about the expression q > 3? Such relational expressions have the value 1 if true and 0 if false. Here are some expressions and their values:

Expression	Value
-4 + 6	2
c = 3 + 8	11
5 > 3	1
6 + (c = 3 + 8)	17

The last expression looks strange! However, it is perfectly legal in C because it is the sum of two subexpressions, each of which has a value.

Statements

Statements are the primary building blocks of a program. A *program* is a series of statements with some necessary punctuation thrown in. A statement is a complete instruction to the computer. In C, statements are indicated by a semicolon at the end. Thus,

```
legs = 4
```

is just an expression (which could be part of a larger expression), but

```
legs = 4;
```

is a statement.

What makes a complete instruction? First, C considers any expression to be a statement if you append a semicolon. (These are called expression statements.) Thus, C won't object to lines such as the following:

```
8;
3 + 4;
```

However, these statements do nothing for your program and can't really be considered sensible statements. More typically, statements change values and call functions.

```
x = 25;
++x;
printf("x = %d\n", x);
```

Although a statement (or, at least, a sensible statement) is a complete instruction, not all complete instructions are statements. Consider the following statement:

```
x = 6 + (y = 5);
```

In it, the subexpression y = 5 is a complete instruction, but it is only part of the statement. Because a complete instruction is not necessarily a statement, a semicolon is needed to identify instructions that truly are statements.

So far we have encountered four kinds of statements. Listing 5.13 gives a short sample that uses all four.

Listing 5.13. addemup.c.

```c
/* addemup.c -- four kinds of statements */
#include <stdio.h>
int main(void)                 /* finds sum of first 20 integers */
{
  int count, sum;              /* declaration statement            */

  count = 0;                   /* assignment statement             */
  sum = 0;                     /* ditto                            */
  while (count++ < 20)         /* while                            */
    sum = sum + count;         /*     statement                    */
  printf("sum = %d\n", sum);   /* function statement               */
  return 0;
}
```

Let's discuss Listing 5.13. By now you must be pretty familiar with the *declaration statement*. Nonetheless, we will remind you that it establishes the names and type of variables and causes memory locations to be set aside for them.

The *assignment statement* is the workhorse of most programs; it assigns a value to a variable. It consists of a variable name followed by the assignment operator (=) followed by an expression followed by a semicolon. Note that the while statement includes an assignment statement within it.

A *function statement* causes the function to do whatever it does. In our example, the printf() function is invoked to print some results. A while statement has three distinct parts (see Figure 5.6). First is the keyword while. Then, in parentheses, is a test condition. Finally is the statement that is performed if the test is met. Only one statement is included in the loop. It can be a simple statement, as in this example, in which case no braces are needed to mark it off, or the statement can be a compound statement, like some of our earlier examples, in which case braces are required. Read about compound statements just ahead.

The while statement belongs to a class of statements sometimes called *structured statements* because they possess a structure more complex than that of a simple assignment statement. In later chapters you will encounter many other kinds of structured statements.

Side Effects and Sequence Points

Now for a little more C terminology. A *side effect* is the modification of a data object or file. For instance, the side effect of the statement

```c
states = 50;
```

is to set the states variable to 50. Side effect? This looks more like the main intent! From the standpoint of C, however, the main intent is evaluating expressions. Show C the expression 4 + 6, and C evaluates it to 10. Show it the expression states = 50, and C evaluates it to 50. Evaluating that expression has the side effect of changing the `states` variable to `50`. The increment and decrement operators, like the assignment operator, have side effects and are used primarily because of their side effects.

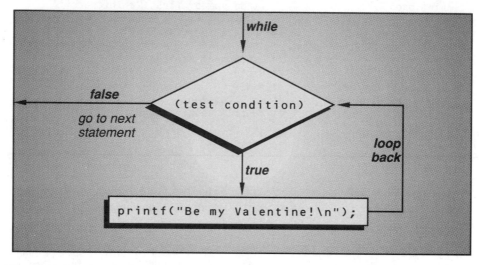

Figure 5.6. *Structure of a simple* `while` *loop.*

A *sequence point* is a point in program execution at which all side effects are evaluated before going on to the next step. In C, the semicolon in a statement marks a sequence point. That means all changes made by assignment operators, increment operators, and decrement operators in a statement must take place before a program proceeds to the next statement. Some operators that we'll discuss in later chapters have sequence points. Also, the end of any *full expression* is a sequence point.

What's a full expression? It's one that's not a subexpression of a larger expression. Examples of full expressions include the expression in a expression statement and the expression serving as a test condition for a `while` loop.

Sequence points help clarify when postfix incrementation takes place. Consider, for instance, the following code:

```
while (guests++ < 10)
    printf("%d %d\n", guests);
```

Sometimes C newcomers assume that "use the value, then increment it" means, in this context, to increment `guests` after it's used in the `printf()` statement. However, the `guests++ < 10` expression is a full expression because it is a `while` loop test condition, so the end of this expression is a sequence point. Therefore, C guarantees that the side effect (incrementing guest) takes place before the program moves on to printf(). Using the postfix form, however, guarantees that guests will be incremented after the comparison to 10 is made.

Now consider this statement:

```
y = (4 + x++) + (6 + x++);
```

The expression 4 + x++ is not a full expression, so C does not guarantee that x will be incremented immediately after the subexpression 4 + x++ is evaluated. Here the full expression is the entire assignment statement, and the semicolon marks the sequence point, so all that C guarantees is that x will have been incremented twice by the time the program moves to the following statement. C does not specify whether x is incremented after each subexpression is evaluated or only after all the expressions have been evaluated, which is why you should avoid statements of this kind.

Compound Statements (Blocks)

A *compound statement* is two or more statements grouped together by enclosing them in braces; it is also called a *block*. We used one in our shoe2.c program in order to let the while statement encompass several statements. Compare the following program fragments:

```
/* fragment 1 */
index = 0;
while (index++ < 10)
  sam = 10 * index + 2;
printf("sam = %d\n", sam);

/* fragment 2 */
index = 0;
while (index++ < 10)
{
  sam = 10 * index + 2;
  printf("sam = %d\n", sam);
}
```

In fragment 1, only the assignment statement is included in the while loop. In the absence of braces, a while statement runs from the while to the next semicolon. The printf() function will be called just once, after the loop has been completed.

In fragment 2, the braces ensure that both statements are part of the while loop, and printf() is called each time that the loop is executed. The entire compound statement is considered to be the single statement in terms of the structure of a while statement. See Figure 5.7.

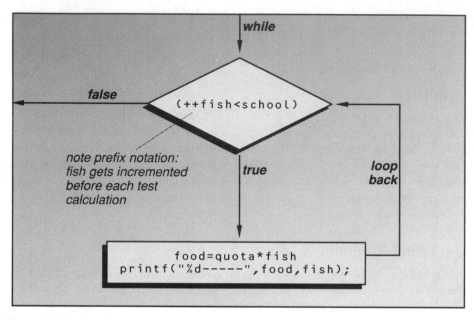

note prefix notation: fish gets incremented before each test calculation

Figure 5.7. while *loop with a compound statement.*

Style Tips

Look again at the two while fragments and notice how an indentation marks off the body of each loop. The indentation makes no difference to the compiler; it uses the braces and its knowledge of the structure of while loops to decide how to interpret our instructions. The indentation is there for us, so that we can see at a glance how the program is organized.

We have shown one popular style for positioning the braces for a block, or compound, statement. Another very common style is this:

```c
while (index++ < 10) {
  sam = 10*index + 2;
  printf("sam = %d \n", sam);
  }
```

This style highlights the attachment of the block to the while loop. The other style emphasizes that the statements form a block. Again, as far as the compiler is concerned, both forms are identical.

To sum up, use indentation as a tool to point out the structure of a program to the reader.

Summary: Expressions and Statements

Expressions

An *expression* is a combination of operators and operands. The simplest expression is just a constant or a variable with no operator, such as 22 or beebop. More complex examples are 55 + 22 and vap = 2 * (vip + (vup = 4)).

Statements

A *statement* is a command to the computer. There are simple statements and compound statements. *Simple statements* terminate in a semicolon. Examples are

Declaration statement:	`int toes;`
Assignment statement:	`toes = 12;`
Function call statement:	`printf("%d\n", toes);`
Structured statement:	`while (toes < 20) toes =`
`toes + 2;`	
NULL statement:	`; /* does nothing */`

Compound statements, or *blocks*, consist of one or more statements (which themselves can be compound) enclosed in braces. The following while statement contains an example:

```
while (years < 100)
{
    wisdom = wisdom + 1;
    printf("%d %d\n", years, wisdom);
    years = years + 1;
}
```

Type Conversions

Statements and expressions normally should use variables and constants of just one type. If, however, you mix types, C doesn't stop dead in its tracks the way, say, Pascal does. Instead, it uses a set of rules to make type conversions automatically. This can be a convenience, but it also can be a danger, especially if you are mixing types inadvertently. (The lint program, found on many UNIX systems, checks for type "clashes." Many non-UNIX C compilers report possible type problems if you select a higher error level.) It is a good idea to have at least some knowledge of the type conversion rules.

The basic rules are these:

1. When appearing in an expression, char and short, both signed and unsigned, automatically are converted to int or, if necessary, to unsigned int. (If short is the same size as int, then unsigned short is larger than int; in that case,

unsigned short is converted to unsigned int.) Under K&R C, but not under ANSI C, float automatically is converted to double. Because these are conversions to larger types, they are called *promotions.*

2. In any operation involving two types, both values are converted to the higher ranking of the two types.

3. The ranking of types, from highest to lowest, is long double, double, float, unsigned long, long, unsigned int, and int. One possible exception is when long and int are the same size, in which case unsigned int outranks long. The short and char types don't appear in this list because they would have been already promoted to int or perhaps unsigned int.

4. In an assignment statement, the final result of the calculations is converted to the type of the variable that is being assigned a value. This process can result in promotion, as described in Rule 1, or *demotion*, in which a value is converted to a lower-ranking type.

5. When passed as function arguments, char and short are converted to int, and float is converted to double. This automatic promotion can be overridden by function prototyping, as discussed in Chapter 9, "Functions."

Promotion usually is a smooth, uneventful process, but demotion can lead to real trouble. The reason is simple: the lower-ranking type may not be big enough to hold the complete number. A char variable can hold the integer 101 but not the integer 22334. When floating types are demoted to integer types, they are truncated, or rounded towards zero. That means 23.12 and 23.99 both are truncated to 23 and that -23.5 is truncated to -23. Listing 5.14 illustrates the working of these rules.

Listing 5.14. convert.c.

```
/* convert.c -- automatic type conversions */
#include <stdio.h>
int main(void)
{
    char ch;
    int i;
    float fl;

    fl = i = ch = 'A';                      /* line 8  */
    printf("ch = %c, i = %d, fl = %2.2f\n", ch, i, fl);
    ch = ch + 1;                            /* line 10 */
    i = fl + 2 * ch;                        /* line 11 */
    fl = 2.0 * ch + i;                      /* line 12 */
    printf("ch = %c, i = %d, fl = %2.2f\n", ch, i, fl);
    ch = 5212205.17;                        /* line 14 */
    printf("Now ch = %c\n", ch);
    return 0;
}
```

Running `convert.c` produces

```
ch = A, i = 65, fl = 65.00
ch = B, i = 197, fl = 329.00
Now ch = -
```

On our system, here is what happened:

Lines 8 and 9: The character 'A' is stored as a 1-byte ASCII value in `ch`. The integer variable `i` receives the integer conversion of 'A', which is `65` stored as 2 bytes. Finally, `fl` receives the floating conversion of `65`, which is `65.00`. *Lines 10 and 13*: The character variable 'A' is converted to the integer `65`, which then is added to the `1`. The resulting 2-byte integer `66` is truncated to 1 byte and stored in `ch`. When printed using the `%c` specifier, `66` is interpreted as the ASCII code for 'B'.

Lines 11 and 13: The value of `ch` is converted to a 2-byte integer (`66`) for the multiplication by `2`. The resulting integer (`132`) is converted to floating point in order to be added to `fl`. The result (`197.00`) is converted to `int` and stored in `i`. Lines *12 and 13*: The value of `ch` ('B', or `66`) is converted to floating point for multiplication by `2.0`. The value of `i` (`197`) is converted to floating point for the addition, and the result (`329.00`) is stored in `fl`. *Lines 14 and 15*: Here we try a case of demotion, setting `ch` equal to a rather large number. After truncation takes place, `ch` winds up with the ASCII code for the hyphen character.

The Cast Operator

You should usually steer clear of automatic type conversions, especially of demotions, but sometimes it is convenient to make conversions, providing you exercise care. The type conversions we've discussed so far are done automatically. However, it is possible for you to demand the precise type conversion that you want. The method for doing this is called a *cast* and consists of preceding the quantity with the name of the desired type in parentheses. The parentheses and type name together constitute a *cast operator*. The general form of a cast operator is

```
(type)
```

where the actual type desired, such as `long`, is substituted for the word *type*.

Consider these two lines, in which `mice` is an `int` variable. The second line contains two casts to type `int`.

```
mice = 1.6 + 1.7;
mice = (int) 1.6 + (int) 1.7;
```

The first example uses automatic conversion. First `1.6` and `1.7` are added to yield `3.3`. This number is then converted through truncation to the integer `3` in order to match the `int` variable. In the second example, `1.6` is converted to an integer (`1`) before addition, as is `1.7`, so that `mice` is assigned the value `1+1`, or `2`.

Normally, you shouldn't mix types; that is why some languages don't allow it, but there are occasions when it is useful. The C philosophy is to avoid putting barriers in your way and to give you the responsibility of not abusing that freedom.

Summary: Operating in C

Here are the operators we have discussed so far.

Assignment Operator

=   Assigns the value at its right to the variable at its left.

Arithmetic Operators

+   Adds the value at its right to the value at its left.

−   Subtracts the value at its right from the value at its left.

−   As a unary operator, changes the sign of the value at its right.

*   Multiplies the value at its right by the value at its left.

/   Divides the value at its left by the value at its right. Answer is truncated if both operands are integers.

%   Yields the remainder when the value at its left is divided by the value to its right (integers only).

++ Adds 1 to the value of the variable to its right (prefix mode) or to the value of the variable to its left (postfix mode).

−− Like ++, but subtracts 1.

Miscellaneous Operators

sizeof   Yields the size, in bytes, of the operand to its right. The operand can be a type-specifier in parentheses, as in `sizeof (float)`, or it can be the name of a particular variable or array, etc., as in `sizeof foo`.

(type)   As the cast operator, converts the following value to the type specified by the enclosed keyword(s). For example, `(float) 9` converts the integer `9` to the floating-point number `9.0`.

Function with Arguments

By now you're familiar with using function arguments. The next step along the road to function mastery is learning how to write your own functions that use arguments. Let's preview that skill now. (At this point you may wish to review the butler() function example near the end of Chapter 2, "Introducing C"; it shows how to write a function without an argument.) Listing 5.15 includes a pound() function that prints a specified number of pound signs (#). The example also illustrates some points about type conversion.

Listing 5.15. pound.c.

```
/* pound.c -- defines a function with an argument    */
#include <stdio.h>
void pound(int n);          /* ANSI prototype              */

int main(void)
{
  int times = 5;
  char ch = '!';            /* ASCII code is 33            */
  float f = 6.0;

  pound(times);             /* int argument                */
  pound(ch);                /* char automatically -> int   */
  pound((int) f);           /* cast forces f -> int        */
  return 0;
}

void pound(int n)           /* ANSI-style function header   */
{                           /* says takes one int argument  */
  while (n-- > 0)
      printf("#");
  printf("\n");
}
```

Running the program produces this output:

```
#####
################################
######
```

First, let's examine the function heading

```
void pound(int n)
```

If the function took no arguments, the parentheses would be empty. Because the function takes one argument, we include one variable name: n, and we indicate that this variable is type int. You can use any name consistent with C's naming rules.

Declaring an argument creates a variable called the *formal argument* or the *formal parameter*. In this case, we've created a type int variable called n. Making a function call like pound(10) acts to assign the value 10 to n. In the case of our program, the call pound(times) serves to assign the value of times (5) to n. We say that the function call passes a value, and this value is called the *actual argument* or the *actual parameter*, so the function call pound(10) passes the actual argument 10 to the function, where 10 is assigned to the formal argument.

Variable names are private to the function. This means that a name defined in one function doesn't conflict with the same name defined elsewhere. If we used times instead of n in pound(), that would create a variable distinct from the times in main(). That is, we would have two variables with the same name, but the program keeps track of which is which.

Now let's look at the function calls. The first one is pound(times), and, as we said, it causes the times value of 5 to be assigned to n. This causes the function to print five pound signs and a newline. The second call is pound(ch). Here, ch is type char. It is initialized to the ! character, which, on ASCII systems, means that ch has the numerical value 33. The automatic promotion of char to int converts this, on our system, from 33 stored in 1 byte to 33 stored in 2 bytes, so the value 33 now is in the correct form to be used as an argument to this function. The last call, pound ((int) f), uses a type cast to convert f to the proper type for this argument.

Suppose we omit the type cast. With ANSI C, the program will make the type cast automatically for us. That's because of the ANSI prototype near the top of the file

```
void pound(int n);       /* ANSI prototype                */
```

A *prototype* is a function declaration that describes a function's return value and its arguments. This prototype says two things about the pound() function:

The function has no return value

The function takes one argument, which is a type int value

Because the compiler sees this prototype before pound() is used in main(), the compiler knows what sort of argument pound() should have, and it inserts a type cast if one is needed to make the actual argument agree in type with the prototype. For instance, the call pound(3.859) will be converted to pound(3).

K&R Function Declarations and Headings

K&R C used a different syntax for function declarations and headings. The K&R function declaration specifies just the return type and is silent about arguments.

```
void pound(int n);        /* ANSI prototype                */
void pound();             /* K&R function declaration      */
```

Also, the K&R function heading looks different.

```
void pound(int n)         /* ANSI C */
{
    ...
```

```
void pound(n)              /* K&R C  */
int n;
{
   ...
```

Note that function arguments, such as n, are declared before the opening brace. Variables defined inside the function are declared after the opening brace. ANSI C recognizes both forms but may phase out the first someday. Chapter 9, "Functions," examines prototyping in more detail.

About the only reason to use the K&R forms is if your compiler doesn't support ANSI C. The ANSI C function prototype is a major improvement because it enables the compiler to check argument types. To see what prototypes do for you, consider how C behaves without them. Suppose, for example, you replace the ANSI prototype in Listing 15.15 with a K&R declaration and that you eliminate the type cast. Then, when the compiler reaches the pound() calls in main(), it knows that pound() has no return value, but it doesn't know what sort of argument pound() takes. In the absence of that knowledge, the compiler follows the usual default rules. Suppose we have this call:

```
pound(f);
```

First, the default promotion converts f to type double. On our system, this results in the function call putting an 8-byte value into the *stack*, a temporary storage area. Then the pound() function, expecting type int, reads just 2 of those bytes. The result bears little resemblance to the original value. In short, using a float or double argument when a function expects type int does not lead to an automatic type conversion; it leads to garbage. You can avoid that problem in K&R C by using an explicit type cast. With ANSI C, the problem is handled automatically.

An Example Program

Listing 5.16 is a useful program (if you're a runner or know one) that illustrates several of the ideas in this chapter. It looks long, but all the calculations are done in six lines near the end. The bulk of the program relays information between the computer and the user. We've tried using enough comments to make it nearly self-explanatory. Read through it, and when you are done, we'll clear up a few points.

Listing 5.16. running.c.

```
/* running.c -- A useful program for runners */
#include <stdio.h>
#define S_PER_M     60    /* seconds in a minute  */
#define S_PER_H   3600    /* seconds in an hour   */
#define M_PER_K 0.62137   /* miles in a kilometer */
int main(void)
{
  float distk, distm;     /* distance run in km and in miles  */
  float rate;             /* average speed in mph             */
```

continues

Listing 5.16. continued

```
int min, sec;          /* minutes and seconds of running time */
int time;              /* running time in seconds only         */
float mtime;           /* time in seconds for one mile         */
int mmin, msec;        /* minutes and seconds for one mile     */

printf("This program converts your time for a metric race\n");
printf("to a time for running a mile and to your average\n");
printf("speed in miles per hour.\n");
printf("Please enter, in kilometers, the distance run.\n");
scanf("%f", &distk);
printf("Next enter the time in minutes and seconds.\n");
printf("Begin by entering the minutes.\n");
scanf("%d", &min);
printf("Now enter the seconds.\n");
scanf("%d", &sec);
time = S_PER_M * min + sec;
                       /* converts time to pure seconds        */
distm = M_PER_K * distk;
                       /* converts kilometers to miles         */
rate = distm / time * S_PER_H;
                       /* miles per sec x sec per hour = mph   */
mtime = (float) time / distm;
                       /* time/distance = time per mile        */
mmin = (int) mtime / S_PER_M; /* find whole minutes        */
msec = (int) mtime % S_PER_M; /* find remaining seconds    */
printf("You ran %1.2f km (%1.2f miles) in %d min, %d sec.\n",
    distk, distm, min, sec);
printf("That pace corresponds to running a mile in %d min, ",
    mmin);
printf("%d sec.\nYour average speed was %1.2f mph.\n",msec,
    rate);
return 0;
}
```

Listing 5.16 utilizes the same approach that we used earlier in min_sec to convert the final time to minutes and seconds, but we also had to make type conversions. Why? Because we need integer arguments for the seconds-to-minutes part of the program, but the metric-to-mile conversion involves floating-point numbers. We have used the cast operator to make these conversions explicit.

To tell the truth, it should be possible to write the program using just automatic conversions. In fact, we did so, using mtime of type int to force the time calculation to be converted to integer form. However, that version failed to run on one of the five systems that we tried. Using type casts makes your intent clearer not only to the reader, but perhaps to the compiler as well.

Here's a sample output:

```
This program converts your time for a metric race
to a time for running a mile and to your average
speed in miles per hour.
Please enter, in kilometers, the distance run.
10.0
Next enter the time in minutes and seconds.
Begin by entering the minutes.
36
Now enter the seconds.
23
You ran 10.00 km (6.21 miles) in 36 min, 23 sec.
That pace corresponds to running a mile in 5 min, 51 sec.
Your average speed was 10.25 mph.
```

Chapter Summary

C has many operators, such as the assignment and arithmetic operators discussed in this chapter. In general, an *operator* operates on one or more operands to produce a value. Operators, such as the minus sign and sizeof, which take one operand, are termed *unary operators*. Operators requiring two operands, such as the addition and the multiplication operators, are called *binary operators*.

Expressions are combinations of operators and operands. In C, every expression has a value, including assignment expressions and comparison expressions. Rules of *operator precedence* help to determine how terms are grouped when expressions are evaluated.

Statements are complete instructions to the computer and are indicated in C by a terminating semicolon. So far we have worked with declaration statements, assignment statements, function call statements, and control statements. Statements included within a pair of braces constitute a *compound statement*, or *block*. One particular control statement is the while loop, which repeats statements as long as a test condition remains true.

In C, many *type conversions* take place automatically. The char and short types are promoted to type int whenever they appear in expressions or as function arguments. The float type is promoted to type double when used as a function argument. Under K&R C (but not ANSI C), float also is promoted to double when used in an expression. When a value of one type is assigned to a variable of a second type, the value is converted to the same type as the variable. When larger types are converted to smaller types (long to short or double to float, for example), there may be a loss of data. In cases of mixed arithmetic, smaller types are converted to larger types following the rules outlined in this chapter.

When you define a function that takes an argument, you declare a *variable*, or *formal argument*, in the function definition. Then the value passed in a function call is assigned to this variable, which can now be used in the function.

Review Questions

1. Assume all variables are of type int. Find the value of each of the following variables:

   a. x = (2 + 3) * 6;
   b. x = (12 + 6)/2*3;
   c. y = x = (2 + 3)/4;
   d. y = 3 + 2*(x = 7/2);

2. We suspect that there are some errors in the next program. Can you help us find them?

```
#include <stdio.h>
int main(void)
{
  int i = 1,
  float n;

  printf("Watch out! Here come a bunch of fractions!\n");
  while (i < 30)
    n = 1/i;
    printf(" %f", n);
  printf("That's all, folks!\n");
  return;
}
```

3. Here's a first attempt at making min_sec interactive. The program is not satisfactory; why not? How can it be improved?

```
#include <stdio.h>
#define S_TO_M 60
int main(void)
{
  int sec, min, left;

  printf("This program converts seconds to minutes and");
  printf("seconds.\n");
  printf("Just enter the number of seconds.\n");
  printf("Enter 0 to end the program.\n");
  while (sec > 0) {
    scanf("%d", &sec);
    min = sec/S_TO_M;
    left = sec % S_TO_M;
    printf("%d sec is %d min, %d sec. \n", sec, min, left);
    printf("Next input?\n");
    }
```

```
        printf("Bye!\n");
        return 0;
    }
```

4. What will this program print?

```
#include <stdio.h>
#define FORMAT "%s is a string\n"
int main(void)
{
    int num = 0;

    printf(FORMAT,FORMAT);
    printf("%d\n", ++num);
    printf("%d\n", num++);
    printf("%d\n", num--);
    printf("%d\n", num);
    return 0;
}
```

5. What will this program print?

```
#include <stdio.h>
#define TEN 10
int main(void)
{
    int n = 0;

    while (n++ < TEN)
        printf("%5d", n);
    printf("\n");
    return 0;
}
```

6. If the following fragments were part of a complete program, what would they print?

a. int x = 0;

```
    while (++x < 3)
        printf("%4d", x);
```

b. int x = 100;

```
    while (x++ < 103)
        printf("%4d\n",x);
        printf("%4d\n",x);
```

```
c. char ch = 's';

   while (ch < 'w')
      {
      printf("%c", ch);
      ch++;
      }
   printf("%c\n",ch);
```

7. Construct statements that do the following (or have the following side effects):

a. Increase the variable x by 10.

b. Increase the variable x by 1.

c. Assign twice the sum of a and b to c.

d. Assign a plus twice b to c.

Programming Exercises

1. Use a while loop to convert time in minutes to time in hours and minutes. Use a #define and a sensible method of ending the loop.

2. Write a program that asks for an integer and then prints all the integers from (and including) that value up to (and including) a value larger by 10. (That is, if the input is 5, the output runs from 5 to 15.)

3. Write a program that asks you to enter the number of days and then converts that value to weeks and days. For example, it would convert 18 days to 2 weeks, 4 days.

4. Change our program addemup.c (Listing 5.13) that found the sum of the first 20 integers. (If you prefer, you can think of addemup.c as a program that calculates how much money you get in 20 days if you receive $1 the first day, $2 the second day, $3 the third day, and so on.) Modify the program so that you can tell it interactively how far the calculation should proceed. That is, replace the 20 with a variable that is read in.

5. Now modify the program so that it computes the sum of the squares of the integers. (If you prefer, how much money you receive if you get $1 the first day, $4 the second day, $9 the third day, and so on. This looks like a much better deal!) C doesn't have a squaring function, but you can use the fact that the square of n is n * n.

6. Write a program that requests a floating-point number and prints the value of the number cubed. Use a function of your own design to cube the value and print it. The main() program should pass the entered value to this function.

C Control Statements: Looping

Keywords
    `for`
    `while`
    `do while`
Operators
    `< > >=`
    `<= != == +=`
    `*= -= /= %=`

In this chapter you learn about C's three loop structures: `while`, `for`, and `do while`. You use relational operators to construct expressions to control these loops, and you learn about several other operators, too. Arrays, which are often used with loops, are introduced. Finally, you take a first look at writing functions having return values.

Powerful, intelligent, versatile, and useful! Most of us wouldn't mind being described that way. We aren't going to tell you how to earn these accolades for yourself, but, with the help of C, your programs can earn them. The trick is controlling the *flow* of a program. According to computer science (which is the science of computers and not science by computers...yet), a good language should provide these three forms of program flow:

- Executing a sequence of statements.

- Repeating a sequence of statements until some condition is met (looping).

- Using a test to decide between alternative sequences (branching).

The first form you know well; all of the previous programs have consisted of a sequence of statements. The while loop is one example of the second form. In this chapter, you'll take a closer look at the while loop along with two other loop structures: for and do while. The final form, choosing between different possible courses of action, makes a program much more "intelligent" and increases the usefulness of a computer enormously. Sadly, you'll have to wait a chapter before being entrusted with such power. We'll begin by reviewing the while loop.

An Initial Example

You are already somewhat familiar with the while loop, but let's review it with a program (Listing 6.1) that sums integers entered from the keyboard. This example makes use of the return value of scanf() to terminate input.

Listing 6.1. summing.c.

```c
/* summing.c -- sums integers entered interactively */
#include <stdio.h>
int main(void)
{
  long num;
  long sum = 0L;        /* initialize sum to zero    */
  int status;

  printf("Please enter an integer to be summed. ");
  printf("Enter q to quit.\n");
  status = scanf("%ld", &num);
  while (status == 1)   /* == means "is equal to"    */
  {
       sum = sum + num;
       printf("Please enter next integer to be summed. ");
       printf("Enter q to quit.\n");
       status = scanf("%ld", &num);
  }
  printf("Those integers sum to %ld.\n", sum);
  return 0;
}}
```

In Listing 6.1 we use type `long` to allow for larger numbers. For consistency, we initialize `sum` to `0L` (type `long` zero) rather than to `0` (type `int` zero), even though C's automatic conversions enable us to use a plain `0`.

Here is a sample run:

```
Please enter an integer to be summed. Enter q to quit.
20
Please enter next integer to be summed. Enter q to quit.
5
Please enter next integer to be summed. Enter q to quit.
30
Please enter next integer to be summed. Enter q to quit.
q
Those integers sum to 55.
```

Program Comments

Because we are reviewing the `while` loop, let's look at it first. The test condition for this loop is the following expression:

```
status == 1
```

The `==` operator is C's *equality operator*; that is, this expression tests to see if `status` is equal to 1. Don't confuse it with `status = 1`, which *assigns* 1 to `status`. With the `status == 1` test condition, the loop will repeat as long as `status` is 1. For each cycle, the loop adds the current value of `num` to `sum`, so that `sum` maintains a running total. Once `status` gets a value other than 1, the loop terminates, and the program reports the final value of `sum`.

For the program to work properly, it should get a new value for `num` on each loop cycle, and it should reset `status` on each cycle. We accomplish this by using two distinct features of `scanf()`. First, we use `scanf()` to attempt to read a new value for `num`. Second, we use the `scanf()` return value to report on the success of that attempt. Recall (Chapter 4, "Character Strings and Formatted Input/Output") that `scanf()` returns the number of items successfully read. If `scanf()` succeeds in reading an integer, it places the integer into `num` and returns the value 1, which is assigned to `status`. (Note that the input value goes to `num`, not to `status`.) This updates both `num` and the value of `status`, and the `while` loop goes through another cycle. If you respond with nonnumeric input, such as q, `scanf()` will fail to find an integer to read, so its return value and `status` will be 0. That terminates the loop.

This dual use of `scanf()` gets around a troublesome aspect of interactive input to a loop: how do you tell the loop when to stop? Suppose, for instance, that `scanf()` did not have a return value. Then the only thing that would change on each loop is the value of `num`. We could use the value of `num` to terminate the loop, using, say, `num > 0` (num greater than 0) or `num != 0` (num not equal to 0) as a test condition, but this prevents us from entering certain values, such as –3 or 0, as input. Instead, we could add new code to the loop, such as asking "Do you wish to continue? <y/n>" at each cycle and then testing to see if the user entered a y. This is a bit clunky and slows down input. Using the return value of scanf() avoids these problems.

Now let's take a closer look at the program structure. We can summarize it thus,

```
initialize sum to 0
prompt user
read input
while the input is an integer,
     add the input to sum,
     prompt user,
     then read next input
when input is not an integer, print sum
```

This, incidentally, is an example of *pseudocode*, which is the art of expressing a program in simple English that parallels the forms of a computer language. Pseudocode is useful for working out the logic of a program. Once the logic seems right, you can translate the pseudocode to the actual programming code. The advantage of pseudocode is that it enables you to concentrate on the logic and organization of a program while sparing you from simultaneously worrying about how to express the ideas in a computer language.

Anyway, because the while loop is an entry-condition loop, the program must obtain the input and check the value of status *before* it goes to the body of the loop. That is why we have a scanf() before the while. For the loop to continue, we need a read statement inside the loop so that it can find out the status of the next input. That is why we also have a scanf() statement at the end of the while loop; it readies the loop for its next iteration.

C-Style Reading Loop

Listing 6.1 could be written in Pascal or BASIC or FORTRAN along the same design displayed in the pseudocode. C, however, offers a shortcut. The construction

```
status = scanf("%ld", &num);
while (status == 1)
{
        /* loop actions */
        status = scanf("%ld", &num);
}
can be replaced by the following:
while (scanf("%ld", &num) == 1)
{
        /* loop actions */
}
```

This form uses scanf() in two different ways simultaneously. First, the function call, if successful, places a value in num. Second, the function's return value (which is 1 or 0 and not the value of num) controls the loop. Because the loop condition is tested at each iteration, scanf() is called at each iteration, providing a new num and a new test.

Now let's take a more formal look at the while statement.

The *while* Statement

The general form of the while loop is

```
while (expression)
      statement
```

The *statement* part can be a simple statement with a terminating semicolon, or it can be a compound statement enclosed in braces.

Our examples so far have used *relational* expressions for the expression part; that is, *expression* has been a comparison of values. More generally, you can use any expression. If *expression* is true (or, more generally, nonzero), the statement is executed once, and then the expression is tested again. This cycle of test and execution is repeated until *expression* becomes false (zero). Each cycle is called an *iteration*. See Figure 6.1.

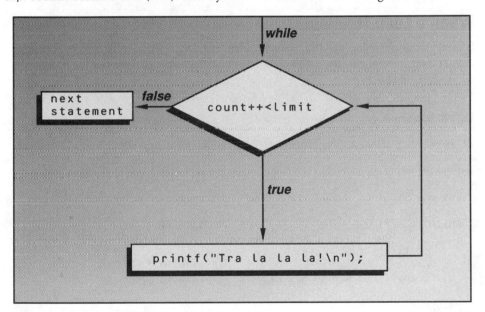

Figure 6.1. *Structure of the* while *loop.*

Terminating a *while* Loop

Here is a CRUCIAL point about while loops: when you construct a while loop, it must include something that changes the value of the test expression so that the expression eventually becomes false. Otherwise, the loop will never terminate. (Actually, you can use break and an if statement to terminate a loop, but you haven't learned about them yet.) Consider this example:

```
index = 1;
while (index < 5)
    printf("Good morning!\n");
```

The preceding fragment prints its cheerful message indefinitely. Why? Because nothing within the loop changes the value of index from its initial value of 1. Now consider this:

```
index = 1;
while (--index < 5)
    printf("Good morning!\n");
```

This last fragment isn't much better. It changes the value of index, but in the wrong direction! At least this version will terminate eventually when index drops below the most negative number that the system can handle.

When a Loop Terminates

It is important to realize that the decision to terminate the loop or to continue takes place only at the time that the test condition is evaluated. For instance, consider the program shown in Listing 6.2.

Listing 6.2. when.c.

```
/* when.c -- when a loop quits */
#include <stdio.h>
int main(void)
{
  int n = 5;

  while (n < 7)                    /* line 7  */
  {
      printf("n = %d\n", n);
      n++;                         /* line 10 */
      printf("Now n = %d\n", n);   /* line 11 */
  }
  return 0;
}}
```

Running Listing 6.2 produces the following output:

```
n = 5
Now n = 6
n = 6
Now n = 7
```

The variable n first acquires the value 7 on line 10 during the second cycle of the loop. The program doesn't quit then, however. Instead, it completes the loop (line 11) and quits the loop only when the test condition on line 7 is evaluated for the third time. (The variable n was 5 for the first test and 6 for the second test.)

while—An Entry-Condition Loop

The `while` loop is a *conditional* loop using an *entry condition*. It is called conditional because the execution of the statement portion depends on the condition described by the test expression, such as (`index < 5`). The expression is an entry condition because the condition must be met *before* the body of the loop is entered. In a situation like the following, the body of the loop is never entered because the condition is false to begin with.

```
index = 10;
while (index++ < 5)
    printf("Have a fair day or better.\n");
```

Change the first line to

```
index = 3;
```

and the loop will execute.

Syntax Points

One point to keep in mind when using `while` is that only the single statement, simple or compound, following the test condition is part of the loop. Indentation is an aid to the reader, not the computer. Listing 6.3 shows what can happen if you forget this.

Listing 6.3. while1.c.

```
/* while1.c -- watch your braces */
#include <stdio.h>
int main(void)
{
  int n = 0;

  while (n < 3)
      printf("n is %d\n", n);
      n++;
  printf("That's all this program does\n");
  return 0;
}
```

Running this program produces the following output:

```
n is 0
n is 0
n is 0
n is 0
n is 0
```

(and so on until you kill the program)

Although we indented the n++; statement, we didn't enclose it and the preceding statement within braces. Thus, only the single print statement immediately following the test condition is part of the loop. The variable n is never updated, the condition n < 3 remains eternally true, and we get a loop that goes on printing n is 0 until we kill the program. This is an example of an *infinite loop*, one that does not quit without outside intervention.

Always remember that the while statement itself, even if it uses compound statements, counts syntactically as a single statement. The statement runs from the while to the first semicolon or, in the case of using a compound statement, to the terminating brace.

Be careful where you place your semicolons. For instance, consider the program in Listing 6.4.

Listing 6.4. while2.c.

```
/* while2.c -- watch your semicolons */
#include <stdio.h>
int main(void)
{
  int n = 0;

  while (n++ < 3);                  /* line 7 */
      printf("n is %d\n", n);       /* line 8 */
  printf("That's all this program does.\n");
  return 0;
}
```

This program has the following output:

```
n is 4
That's all this program does.
```

As we said earlier, the loop ends with the first statement, simple or compound, following the test condition. Because there is a semicolon immediately after the test condition on line 7, the loop ends there, for a lone semicolon counts as a statement. The print statement on line 8 is not part of the loop, so n is incremented on each loop, but it is printed only after the loop is exited.

In this example, the test condition is followed with the *NULL statement*, one that does nothing. In C, the lone semicolon represents the NULL statement. Occasionally, programmers intentionally will use the while statement with a NULL statement, either to create a time delay or because all the work gets done in the test. For example, suppose you want to skip over input to the first character that isn't whitespace or a digit. You can use a loop like this:

```
while (scanf("%d", &num) == 1)
  ;     /* skip integer input */
```

As long as scanf() reads an integer, it returns 1, and the loop continues. Note that for clarity we put the semicolon (the NULL statement) on the line below instead of on the same line. This makes it easier to see the NULL statement when you read a program and also reminds you that the NULL statement is there deliberately. Even better, use the continue statement discussed in the next chapter.

Which Is Bigger: Using Relational Operators and Expressions

Because while loops often rely on test expressions that make comparisons, comparison expressions merit a closer look. Such expressions are termed *relational expressions*, and the operators that appear in them are called *relational operators*. We have used several already, and Table 6.1 gives a complete list of C relational operators. This table pretty much covers all the possibilities for numerical relationships. (Numbers, even complex ones, are less complex than humans.)

Table 6.1. Relational operators.

Operator	Meaning
<	Is less than
<=	Is less than or equal to
==	Is equal to
>=	Is greater than or equal to
>	Is greater than
!=	Is not equal to

The relational operators are used to form the relational expressions used in while statements and in other C statements that we'll discuss later. These statements check to see if the expression is true or false. Here are three unrelated statements containing examples of relational expressions. The meaning, we hope, is clear.

```
while (number < 6)
{
    printf("Your number is too small.\n");
    scanf("%d", &number);
}

while (ch != '$')
{
    count++;
    scanf("%c", &ch);
}
```

```
while (scanf("%f", &num) == 1)
    sum = sum + num;
```

Note in the second example that the relational expressions can be used with characters, too. The machine code (which we have been assuming is ASCII) is used for the comparison. However, you can't use the relational operators to compare strings. Chapter 11, "Characters Strings and String Functions," will show you what to use for strings.

The relational operators can be used with floating-point numbers, too. Beware though, you should limit yourself to using only < and > in floating-point comparisons. The reason is that roundoff errors can prevent two numbers from being equal even though logically they should be. For example, certainly the product of 3 and 1/3 is 1.0. If we express 1/3 as a six-place decimal fraction, the product is .999999, which is not quite equal to 1.

Each relational expression is judged to be "true" or "false" (but never "maybe"). This raises an interesting question.

What Is Truth?

We can answer this age-old question, at least as far as C is concerned. Recall that an expression in C always has a value. This is true even for relational expressions, as the example in Listing 6.5 shows. In it we print the values of two relational expressions, one true and one false.

Listing 6.5. t_and_f.c.

```
/* t_and_f.c -- true and false values in C */
#include <stdio.h>
int main(void)
{
  int true, false;

  true = (10 > 2);    /* value of a true relationship  */
  false = (10 == 2);  /* value of a false relationship */
  printf("true = %d; false = %d \n", true, false);
  return 0;
}
```

In Listing 6.5 we have assigned the values of two relational expressions to two variables. Being straightforward, we assigned true the value of a true expression, and false the value of a false expression. Running the program produces the following simple output:

```
true = 1; false = 0
```

Aha! For C, a true expression has the value 1, and a false expression has the value 0. Indeed, some C programs use the following construction for loops that are meant to run forever, because 1 always is true:

```
while (1)
{
    ...
}
```

What Else Is True?

If we can use a 1 or a 0 as a while statement test expression, can we use other numbers? If so, what happens? Let's experiment by trying the program in Listing 6.6.

Listing 6.6. truth.c.

```
/* truth.c -- what values are true? */
#include <stdio.h>
int main(void)
{
  int n = 3;

  while (n)
      printf("%d\n", n--);
  n = -3;
  while (n)
      printf("%2d\n", n++);
  return 0;
}
```

The results are

```
3
2
1
-3
-2
-1
```

The first loop executes when n is 3, 2, and 1, but terminates when n is 0. Similarly, the second loop executes when n is -3, -2, and -1, but terminates when n is 0. More generally, all nonzero values are regarded as "true," and only 0 is recognized as "false." C has a very tolerant notion of truth!

Alternatively, we can say that a while loop executes as long as its test condition evaluates to nonzero. This puts test conditions on a numeric basis instead of a true-false basis. Keep in mind that relational expressions evaluate to 1 if true and to 0 if false, so such expressions really are numeric.

Many programmers make use of this property of test conditions. For example, the phrase while (goats != 0) can be replaced by while (goats) because the expression (goats != 0) and the expression (goats) both become 0, or false, only when goats has the value 0. We think that the second form is not as clear in meaning as the first, but many C programmers prefer the second form. The popular thought has been that the second form is more efficient because it requires fewer computer processing operations when the program runs, but some compilers are clever enough to use the same efficient code for either form. The current tendency is to try for clear code and leave it to clever compilers to maximize the efficiency.

Troubles with Truth

C's tolerant notion of truth can lead to trouble. For example, let's make one subtle change in Listing 6.1, producing the program shown in Listing 6.7.

Listing 6.7. `trouble.c`.

```
/* trouble.c -- misuse of = */
#include <stdio.h>
int main(void)
{
  long num;
  long sum = 0L;
  int status;

  printf("Please enter an integer to be summed. ");
  printf("Enter q to quit.\n");
  status = scanf("%ld", &num);
  while (status = 1)
  {
      sum = sum + num;
      printf("Please enter next integer to be summed. ");
      printf("Enter q to quit.\n");
      status = scanf("%ld", &num);
  }
  printf("Those integers sum to %ld\n", sum);
  return 0;
}}
```

Running Listing 6.7 produces output like the following:

```
Please enter an integer to be summed. Enter q to quit.
20
Please enter next integer to be summed. Enter q to quit.
5
Please enter next integer to be summed. Enter q to quit.
30
Please enter next integer to be summed. Enter q to quit.
q
Please enter next integer to be summed. Enter q to quit.
Please enter next integer to be summed. Enter q to quit.
Please enter next integer to be summed. Enter q to quit.
Please enter next integer to be summed. Enter q to quit.
```

170   (and so on until you kill the program)

We made a change in the `while` test condition, replacing `status == 1` with `status = 1`. The second statement is an assignment statement, so it gives `status` the value 1. Furthermore, the value of an assignment statement is the value of the left side, so `status = 1` has the same numerical value of 1. Thus, for all practical purposes, our `while` loop is the same as using `while (1)`; that is, it is a loop that never quits. We enter q, and `status` is set to 0, but the loop test resets `status` to 1 and starts another cycle.

You may wonder why, because the program keeps looping, the user doesn't get a chance to type in any more input after entering q. When `scanf()` fails to read the specified form of input, it leaves the nonconforming input in place to be read the next time. When `scanf()` tries to read the q as an integer and fails, therefore, it leaves the q there. During the next loop cycle, `scanf()` attempts to read where it left off the last time: at the q once again. Once again `scanf()` fails to read the q as an integer, so not only does this example set up an infinite loop, it also creates a loop of infinite failure, a daunting concept. It is fortunate that computers, as yet, lack feelings. Following stupid instructions eternally is no better or worse to a computer than successfully predicting the stock market for the next ten years.

Don't use = for ==. Some computer languages (BASIC, for example) do use the same symbol for both the assignment operator and the relational equality operator, but the two operations are quite different (see Figure 6.2). The assignment operator *assigns* a value to the left-hand variable. The relational equality operator, however, checks to see if the left-hand and right-hand sides are already equal. It doesn't change the value of the left-hand variable, if one is present.

`canoes = 5`	→assigns the value 5 to canoes
`canoes == 5`	→checks to see whether canoes has the value 5

Be careful about using the correct operator. A compiler will let you use the wrong form, yielding results other than what you expect.

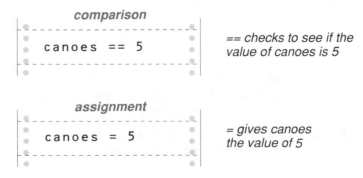

Figure 6.2. *The relational operator == and the assignment operator =.*

To sum up, the relational operators are used to form relational expressions. Relational expressions have the value 1 if true and 0 if false. Statements (such as `while` and `if`) that normally use relational expressions as tests can use any expression as a test, with nonzero values recognized as "true" and zero values as "false."

Precedence of Relational Operators

The precedence of the relational operators is less than that of the arithmetic operators, including + and -, and greater than that of assignment operators. This means, for example, that

```
x > y + 2
```

means the same as

```
x > (y + 2)
```

and that

```
x = y > 2
```

means

```
x = (y > 2)
```

That is, x is assigned 1 if y is greater than 2 and is 0 otherwise; x is not assigned the value of y.

The relational operators are themselves organized into two different priorities.

Higher-priority group: <   <=   >   =>
Lower-priority group: ==   !=

Like most other operators, the relational operators associate from left to right. Thus,

```
ex != wye == zee
```

is the same as

```
(ex != wye) == zee
```

First C checks to see if ex and wye are unequal. Then the resulting value of 1 or 0 (true or false) is compared to the value of zee. We don't anticipate using this sort of construction, but we feel that it is our duty to point out such sidelights.

Table 6.2 shows the priorities of the operators introduced so far, and Appendix B, "C Operators," has a complete precedence ranking of all operators.

Table 6.2. Operator precedence.

Operators (From High to Low Precedence)	Associativity
( )	L–R
- + ++ -- sizeof *(type)* (all unary)	R–L
* / %	L–R
+ -	L–R
< > <= >=	L–R
== !=	L–R
=	R–L

Summary: The *while* Statement

Keyword

```
while
```

General Comments

The `while` statement creates a loop that repeats until the test *expression* becomes false, or zero. The `while` statement is an *entry-condition* loop; that is, the decision to go through one more pass of the loop is made *before* the loop is traversed. Thus, it is possible that the loop is never traversed. The *statement* part of the form can be a simple statement or a compound statement.

Form

```
while (expression)
        statement
```

The *statement* portion is repeated until the *expression* becomes false or zero.

Examples

```
while (n++ < 100)
   printf(" %d %d\n",n, 2 * n + 1); /* single statement */

while (fargo < 1000)
{                                  /* compound statement */
   fargo = fargo + step;
   step = 2 * step;
}
```

> **Summary: Relational Operators and Expressions**
>
> **Relational Operators**
>
> Each relational operator compares the value at its left to the value at its right.
>
> | | |
> |-----|----------------------------|
> | < | Is less than |
> | <= | Is less than or equal to |
> | == | Is equal to |
> | >= | Is greater than or equal to |
> | > | Is greater than |
> | != | Is unequal to |
>
> **Relational Expressions**
>
> A simple relational expression consists of a relational operator with an operand on each side. If the relation is true, the relational expression has the value 1. If the relation is false, the relational expression has the value 0.
>
> **Examples**
>
> `5 > 2` is true and has the value 1.
>
> `(2 + a) == a` is false and has the value 0.

Indefinite Loops and Counting Loops

Some of our `while` loop examples have been *indefinite* loops. This means that we don't know in advance how many times the loop will be executed before the expression becomes false. For instance, when we used an interactive loop to sum integers, we didn't know beforehand how many integers would be entered. Other of our examples, however, have been *counting* loops. They execute a predetermined number of repetitions. Listing 6.8 is a short example of a `while` counting loop.

Listing 6.8. sweetie1.c.

```
/* sweetie1.c -- a counting loop */
#include <stdio.h>
#define NUMBER 22
int main(void)
{
  int count = 1;                        /* initialization */

  while (count <= NUMBER)               /* test          */
  {
```

```
        printf("Be my Valentine!\n");    /* action        */
        count++;                         /* update count   */
    }
    return 0;
}
```

Although the form used in Listing 6.8 works fine, it is not the best choice for this situation, because the actions defining the loop are not all gathered together. Let's elaborate on that point.

Three actions are involved in setting up a loop that is to be repeated a fixed number of times.

1. A counter must be initialized.

2. The counter is compared with some limiting value.

3. The counter is incremented each time the loop is traversed.

The while loop condition takes care of the comparison. The increment operator takes care of the incrementing. In Listing 6.8 the incrementing is done at the end of the loop. This choice makes it possible to omit the incrementing accidentally. Thus, it would be better to combine the test and update actions into one expression by using count++ <= NUMBER, but the initialization of the counter still is done outside the loop, making it possible to forget to initialize a counter. Experience teaches us that what *might* happen, will happen eventually, so let's look at a control statement that avoids these problems.

The *for* Loop

The for loop gathers all three actions into one place. By using a for loop, we can replace the preceding program with the one shown in Listing 6.9.

Listing 6.9. sweetie2.c.

```
/* sweetie2.c -- a counting loop using for */
#include <stdio.h>
#define NUMBER 22
int main(void)
{
    int count;

    for (count = 1; count <= NUMBER; count++)
        printf("Be my Valentine!\n");
    return 0;
}}
```

The parentheses following the keyword for contain three expressions separated by two semicolons. The first expression is the initialization. It is done just once, when the for loop first starts. The second expression is the test condition; it is evaluated before each potential execution of a loop. When the expression is false (when count is greater than NUMBER), the loop is terminated. The third expression, the change or update, is evaluated at the end of each loop. We have used it to increment the value of count, but it needn't be restricted to that use. The for statement is completed by following it with one simple or compound statement. Each of the three control expressions is a full expression, so any side effects in a control expression, such as incrementing a variable, take place before the program evaluates another expression. Figure 6.3 summarizes the structure of a for loop.

To show another example, Listing 6.10 uses the for loop in a program that prints a table of cubes.

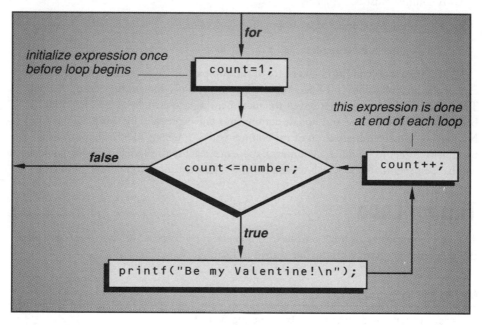

Figure 6.3. *Structure of a* for *loop.*

Listing 6.10. for_cube.c.

```
/* for_cube.c -- using a for loop to make a table of cubes */
#include <stdio.h>
int main(void)
{
  int num;
```

```
    printf("    n    n cubed\n");
    for (num = 1; num <= 6; num++)
        printf("%5d %5d\n", num, num*num*num);
    return 0;
}
```

Listing 6.10 prints the integers 1 through 6 and their cubes.

```
 n    n cubed
 1     1
 2     8
 3    27
 4    64
 5   125
 6   216
```

The first line of the for loop tells us immediately all the information about the loop parameters: the starting value of num, the final value of num, and the amount that num increases on each looping.

Using *for* for Flexibility!

Although the for loop looks similar to the FORTRAN DO loop, the Pascal FOR loop, and the BASIC FOR...NEXT loop, it is much more flexible than any of these. This flexibility stems from how the three expressions in a for specification can be used. So far we have used the first expression to initialize a counter, the second expression to express the limit for the counter, and the third expression to increase the value of the counter by 1. When used this way, the C for statement is very much like the others we have mentioned, but there are many more possibilities, and here we will show you nine variations.

1. You can use the decrement operator to count down instead of up.

```
#include <stdio.h>
int main(void)
 {
   int secs;

   for (secs = 5; secs > 0; secs--)
        printf("%d seconds!\n", secs);
   printf("We have ignition!\n");
   return 0;
}
```

Here is the output:

```
5 seconds!
4 seconds!
3 seconds!
```

```
2 seconds!
1 seconds!
We have ignition!
```

2. You can count by twos, tens, etc., if you want.

```
#include <stdio.h>
int main(void)
  {
  int n;                /* count by 13s */

  for (n = 2;  n < 60; n = n + 13)
       printf("%d \n", n);
  return 0;
}
```

This would increase n by 13 during each cycle, printing the following:

```
 2
15
28
41
54
```

3. You can count by characters instead of by numbers.

```
#include <stdio.h>
int main(void)
{
  char ch;

  for (ch = 'a'; ch <= 'z'; ch++)
       printf("The ASCII value for %c is %d.\n", ch, ch);
  return 0;
}
```

An abridged output looks like this:

```
The ASCII value for a is 97.
The ASCII value for b is 98.
...
The ASCII value for x is 120.
The ASCII value for y is 121.
The ASCII value for z is 122.
```

The program works because characters are stored as integers, so this loop really counts by integers anyway.

4. You can test some condition other than the number of iterations. In our `for_cube` program, we can replace

```
for (num = 1; num <= 6; num++)
```

with

```
for (num = 1; num*num*num <= 216; num++)
```

You would use this test condition if you were more concerned with limiting the size of the cube than with limiting the number of iterations.

5. You can let a quantity increase geometrically instead of arithmetically; that is, instead of adding a fixed amount each time, you can multiply by a fixed amount.

```c
#include <stdio.h>
int main(void)
 {
   float debt;

   for (debt = 100.0; debt < 150.0; debt = debt * 1.1)
        printf("Your debt is now $%.2f.\n", debt);
   return 0;
}
```

This program fragment multiplies `debt` by 1.1 for each cycle, increasing it by 10 percent each time. The output looks like this:

```
Your debt is now $100.00.
Your debt is now $110.00.
Your debt is now $121.00.
Your debt is now $133.10.
Your debt is now $146.41.
```

6. You can use any legal expression you want for the third expression. Whatever you put in will be updated for each iteration.

```c
#include <stdio.h>
int main(void)
 {
   int x;
   int y = 55;

   for (x = 1; y <= 75; y = (++x * 5) + 50)
        printf("%10d %10d\n", x, y);
   return 0;
}
```

This loop prints the values of x and of the algebraic expression ++x * 5 + 50. The output looks like this:

```
1        55
2        60
3        65
4        70
5        75
```

Notice that the test involved y, not x. Each of the three expressions in the for loop control can use different variables. (Note that although this example is valid, it does not show good style. The program would have been clearer if we hadn't mixed the updating process with an algebraic calculation.)

7. You can even leave one or more expressions blank (but don't omit the semicolons). Just be sure to include within the loop itself some statement that will eventually cause the loop to terminate.

```c
#include <stdio.h>
int main(void)
 {
   int ans, n;

   ans = 2;
   for (n = 3; ans <= 25; )
        ans = ans * n;
   printf("n = %d; ans = %d.\n", n, ans);
   return 0;
}
```

Here is the output:

```
n = 3; ans = 54.
```

The loop keeps the value of n at 3. The variable ans starts with the value 2, then increases to 6 and 18, and obtains a final value of 54. (The value 18 is less than 25, so the for loop goes through one more iteration, multiplying 18 by 3 to get 54.) Incidentally, an empty middle control expression is considered to be true, so the following loop goes on forever:

```c
for (; ; )
        printf("I want some action\n");
```

8. The first expression need not initialize a variable. It could, instead, be a printf() statement of some sort. Just remember that the first expression is evaluated or executed only once, before any other parts of the loop are executed.

```c
#include <stdio.h>
int main(void)
```

```
{
    int num;

      for (printf("Keep entering numbers!\n"); num != 6;  )
            scanf("%d", &num);
    printf("That's the one I want!\n");
    return 0;
}
```

This fragment prints the first message once and then keeps accepting numbers until you enter a 6:

```
Keep entering numbers!
3
5
8
6
That's the one I want!
```

9. The parameters of the loop expressions can be altered by actions within the loop. For example, suppose you have the loop set up like this:

```
for(n = 1; n < 10000; n = n + delta)
```

If after a few iterations your program decides that delta is too small or too large, an if statement (Chapter 7, "C Control Statements: Branching and Jumps") inside the loop can change the size of delta. In an interactive program, delta can be changed by the user as the loop runs.

In short, the freedom you have in selecting the expressions that control a for loop makes this loop able to do much more than just perform a fixed number of iterations. The power of the for loop is enhanced further by the operators we will discuss shortly.

Summary: The *for* Statement

Keyword

for

General Comments

The for statement uses three control expressions, separated by semicolons, to control a looping process. The *initialize* expression is executed once, before any of the loop statements are executed. Then the *test* expression is evaluated, and if it is true (or nonzero), the loop is cycled through once. Then the *update* expression is

continues

evaluated, and it is time to check the *test* expression again. The `for` statement is an *entry-condition* loop—the decision to go through one more pass of the loop is made *before* the loop is traversed. Thus, it is possible that the loop is never traversed. The `statement` part of the form can be a simple statement or a compound statement.

Form

```
for (initialize ; test ; update)
    statement
```

The loop is repeated until *test* becomes false or zero.

Example

```
for (n = 0;  n < 10 ; n++)
    printf(" %d %d\n", n, 2 * n + 1);
```

More Assignment Operators: +=, -=, *=, /=, %=

C has several assignment operators. The most basic one, of course, is =, which simply assigns the value of the expression at its right to the variable at its left. The other assignment operators update variables. Each is used with a variable name to its left and an expression to its right. The variable is assigned a new value equal to its old value adjusted by the value of the expression at the right. The exact adjustment depends on the operator, for example,

scores += 20	is the same as	scores = scores + 20
dimes -= 2	is the same as	dimes = dimes - 2
bunnies *= 2	is the same as	bunnies = bunnies * 2
time /= 2.73	is the same as	time = time / 2.73
reduce %= 3	is the same as	reduce = reduce % 3

In the preceding list, we used simple numbers on the right, but we could have used more elaborate expressions.

x *= 3 * y + 12	is the same as	x = x * (3 * y + 12)

The assignment operators we've just discussed have the same low priority that = does, i.e., less than that of + or *. This low priority is reflected in the last example, in which 12 is added to 3 * y before multiplying the result by x.

You are not required to use these forms. They are, however, more compact, and they may produce more efficient machine code than the longer form. They are particularly useful when you are trying to squeeze something complex into a `for` loop specification.

The Comma Operator

The *comma operator* extends the flexibility of the `for` loop by enabling you to include more than one initialization or update expression in a single `for` loop specification. For example, Listing 6.11 shows a program that prints first-class postage rates. (At the time of this writing, the rate is 29 cents for the first ounce and 23 cents for each additional ounce.)

Listing 6.11. `postage.c`

```
/* postage.c -- first-class postage rates */
#include <stdio.h>
#define FIRST 29
#define NEXT  23
int main(void)
{
    int ounces, cost;

    printf(" ounces  cost\n");
    for(ounces=1, cost=FIRST; ounces<= 16; ounces++,
           cost += NEXT)
       printf("%5d %7d\n", ounces, cost);
  return 0;
}}
```

The first four lines of output look like this:

```
ounces  cost
   1     25
   2     52
   3     75
```

We used the comma operator in the initialize and the update expressions. Its presence in the first expression causes `ounces` *and* `cost` to be initialized. Its second occurrence causes `ounces` to be increased by 1 and `cost` to be increased by 20 (the value of `NEXT`) for each iteration. All the calculations are done in the `for` loop specifications! See Figure 6.4.

The comma operator is not restricted to `for` loops, but that is where it is most often used. The operator has two further properties. First, it guarantees that the expressions it separates will be evaluated in a left-to-right order. (In other words, the comma is a sequence point, so all side effects to the left of the comma take place before the program moves to the right of the comma.) Thus, `ounces` is initialized before `cost`. The order is not important for this example, but it would be important if the expression for `cost` contained `ounces`. Suppose, for instance, that we had this expression:

```
ounces++, cost = ounces * FIRST
```

This would increment `ounces`, then use the new value for `ounces` in the second subexpression. The fact that the comma is a sequence point guarantees that the side effects of the left subexpression occur before the right subexpression is evaluated.

183

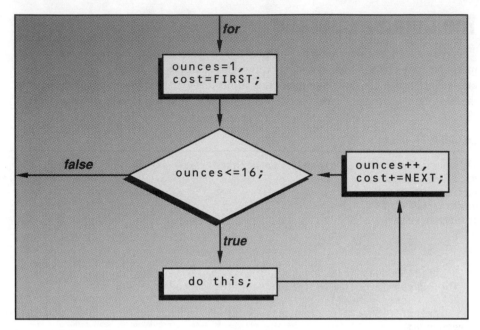

Figure 6.4. *The comma operator and the* for *loop.*

Second, the value of the whole comma expression is the value of the right-hand member. The effect of the statement

```
x = (y = 3, (z = ++y + 2) + 5);
```

is to first assign 3 to y, increment y to 4, then add 2 to 4 and assign the resulting value of 6 to z, next add 5 to z, and finally assign the resulting value of 11 to x. Why anyone would do this is beyond the scope of this book. On the other hand, suppose you get careless and use comma notation in writing a number.

```
houseprice = 249,500;
```

This is not a syntax error! Instead, C interprets the right-hand side as a comma expression, with houseprice =   249 being the left subexpression and 500 as the right subexpression. Thus, the value of the whole comma expression is the value of the right-hand expression, and this statement assigns the value 249 to the houseprice variable.

The comma also is used as a separator. Thus, the commas in

```
char ch, date;
```

and

```
printf("%d %d\n", chimps, chumps);
```

are separators, not comma operators.

Summary: Our New Operators

Assignment Operators

Each of these operators updates the variable at its left by the value at its right, using the indicated operation. We use the abbreviations *R–H* for right-hand and *L–H* for left-hand.

`+=`	Adds the R–H quantity to the L–H variable
`-=`	Subtracts the R–H quantity from the L–H variable
`*=`	Multiplies the L–H variable by the R–H quantity
`/=`	Divides the L–H variable by the R–H quantity
`%=`	Gives the remainder obtained from dividing the L–H variable by the R–H quantity

Example

`rabbits *= 1.6;`   is the same as   `rabbits = rabbits * 1.6;`

The Comma Operator

The comma operator links two expressions into one and guarantees that the leftmost expression is evaluated first. It is typically used to include more information in a `for` loop control expression. The value of the whole expression is the value of the right-hand expression.

Example

```
for (step = 2, fargo = 0; fargo < 1000; step *= 2)
        fargo += step;
```

Zeno Meets the *for* Loop

Let's see how the `for` loop and the comma operator can help solve an old paradox. The Greek philosopher Zeno once argued that an arrow will never reach its target. First, he said, the arrow covers half the distance to the target. Then it has to cover half of the remaining distance. Then it still has half of what's left to cover, ad infinitum. Because the journey has an infinite number of parts, Zeno argued, it would take the arrow an infinite amount of time to reach its journey's end. We doubt, however, that Zeno would have volunteered to be a target just on the strength of this argument.

Let's take a quantitative approach and suppose that it takes the arrow 1 second to travel the first half. Then it would take 1/2 second to travel half of what was left, 1/4 second to travel half of what was left next, etc. We can represent the total time by the following infinite series:

`1 + 1/2 + 1/4 + 1/8 + 1/16 +....`

The short program in Listing 6.12 finds the sum of the first few terms.

Listing 6.12. zeno.c.

```
/* zeno.c -- series sum */
#include <stdio.h>
#define LIMIT 15
int main(void)
{
 int count;
 float time, x;

 for (time=0, x=1, count=1; count <= LIMIT; count++, x *= 2.0)
 {
    time += 1.0/x;
    printf("time = %f when count = %d.\n", time, count);
 }
 return 0;
}}
```

The output is the sum of the first 15 terms.

```
time = 1.000000 when count = 1.
time = 1.500000 when count = 2.
time = 1.750000 when count = 3.
time = 1.875000 when count = 4.
time = 1.937500 when count = 5.
time = 1.968750 when count = 6.
time = 1.984375 when count = 7.
time = 1.992188 when count = 8.
time = 1.996094 when count = 9.
time = 1.998047 when count = 10.
time = 1.999023 when count = 11.
time = 1.999512 when count = 12.
time = 1.999756 when count = 13.
time = 1.999878 when count = 14.
time = 1.999939 when count = 15.
```

You can see that although we keep adding more terms, the total seems to level out. Indeed, mathematicians have proven that the total approaches 2.0 as the number of terms approaches infinity, just as our program suggests.

What about the program itself? It shows that you can use more than one comma operator in an expression. We initialized time, x, and count. Once we set up the conditions for the loop, the program itself is extremely brief.

An Exit-Condition Loop: *do while*

The while loop and the for loop are both entry-condition loops. The test condition is checked before each iteration of the loop, so it is possible for the statements in the loop to never execute. C also has an *exit-condition* loop in which the condition is checked after each iteration of the loop, guaranteeing that statements will be executed at least once. This variety is called a do while loop. Listing 6.13 shows an example.

Listing 6.13. dowhile.c.

```
/* dowhile.c -- exit condition loop */
#include <stdio.h>
int main(void)
{
   char ch;

   do
   {
       scanf("%c", &ch);
       printf("%c", ch);
   } while (ch != '#');
   return 0;
}
```

The program in Listing 6.13 reads input characters and reprints them until the # character shows up. How is this program different from a while loop version such as that in Listing 6.14?

The behavioral difference appears when the # character is read. The while loop prints all the characters *up to* the first # character, and the do while loop prints all the characters *up to and including* the # character. Only after it has printed the # character does the loop check to see if a # character has shown up. In a do while loop, that action comes before the test condition.

Listing 6.14. entry.c.

```
/* entry.c -- entry condition loop */
#include <stdio.h>
int main(void)
{
   char ch;

   scanf("%c", &ch);
   while (ch != '#')
```

continues

Listing 6.14. continued

```
{
     printf("%c", ch);
     scanf("%c", &ch);
}
return 0;
}
```

The general form of the do while loop is

```
do
    statement
while ( expression );
```

The statement can be simple or compound. Note that the do while loop itself counts as a statement and therefore requires a terminating semicolon. Also see Figure 6.5.

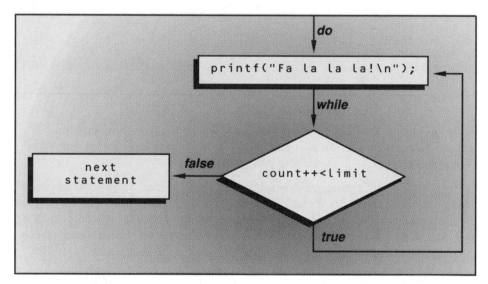

Figure 6.5. *Structure of a* do while *loop.*

A do while loop always is executed at least once, because the test is made after the body of the loop has been executed. A for loop or a while loop, on the other hand, may be executed zero times, because the test is made before execution. You should restrict the use of do while loops to cases that require at least one iteration. For example, a password program could include a loop along these pseudocode lines:

```
do
{
    prompt for password
```

```
    read user input
} while (input not equal to password) ;
```

Avoid a `do while` structure of the type shown in the following pseudocode:

```
ask user if he or she wants to continue
do
some clever stuff
while (answer is yes)
```

Here, after the user answers "no," some clever stuff gets done anyway because the test comes too late.

Summary: The *do while* Statement

Keywords

```
do, while
```

General Comments

The `do while` statement creates a loop that repeats until the test *expression* becomes false or zero. The `do while` statement is an *exit-condition* loop—the decision to go through one more pass of the loop is made *after* the loop has been traversed. Thus, the loop must be executed at least once. The *statement* part of the form can be a simple statement or a compound statement.

Form

```
do
    statement
        while (expression);
```

The *statement* portion is repeated until the *expression* becomes false or zero.

Example

```
do
    scanf("%d", &number);
        while (number != 20);
```

Which Loop?

Once you decide you need a loop, which one should you use? First, decide whether you need an entry-condition loop or an exit-condition loop. Your answer should usually be an entry-condition loop. There are several reasons why computer scientists consider an entry-condition loop superior. One is the general principle that it is better to look *before* you leap (or loop) than after. A second is that a program is easier to read if the loop test is

189

found at the beginning of the loop. Finally, in many uses, it is important that the loop be skipped entirely if the test is not initially met.

Assume you need an entry-condition loop. Should it be a `for` or a `while`? This is partly a matter of taste, because what you can do with one, you can do with the other. To make a `for` loop like a `while`, you can omit the first and third expressions. For example,

```
for ( ;test; )
```

is the same as

```
while (test)
```

To make a `while` like a `for`, preface it with an initialization and include update statements. For example, initialize;

```
while (test)
{
  body;
  update;
}
```

is the same as

```
for (initialize; test; update)
    body;
```

In terms of style, a `for` loop is appropriate when the loop involves initializing and updating a variable, and a `while` loop is better when the conditions are otherwise. Thus, a `while` loop is natural for the following condition:

```
while (scanf("%ld", &num) == 1)
```

The `for` loop is a more natural choice for loops involving counting with an index.

```
for (count = 1; count <= 100; count++)
```

Nested Loops

A *nested loop* is one loop inside another loop. A common use for nested loops is to display data in rows and columns. One loop can handle, say, all the columns in a row, and the second loop handles the rows. Listing 6.15 shows a simple example.

Listing 6.15. `rows1.c`.

```
/* rows1.c -- uses nested loops */
#include <stdio.h>
#define ROWS  6
#define CHARS 6
int main(void)
```

```
{
    int row;
    char ch;

    for (row = 0; row < ROWS; row++)              /* line 10 */
    {
        for (ch = 'A'; ch < ('A' + CHARS); ch++)  /* line 12 */
            printf("%c", ch);
        printf("\n");
    }
    return 0;
}
```

Running the program produces this output:

```
ABCDEF
ABCDEF
ABCDEF
ABCDEF
ABCDEF
ABCDEF
```

Discussion

The for loop beginning on line 10 is called an *outer* loop, and the loop beginning on line 12 is called an *inner* loop because it is inside the other loop. The outer loop starts with row having a value of 0 and terminates when row reaches 6. Thus, the outer loop goes through six cycles, with row having the values 0 through 5. The first statement in each cycle is the inner for loop. This loop also goes through six cycles, printing the characters A through F on the same line. The second statement of the outer loop is printf("\n");. This statement starts a new line so that the next time the inner loop is run, the output is on a new line.

Note that, with a nested loop, the inner loop runs through its full range of iterations for each single iteration of the outer loop. In the last example, the inner loop prints six characters to a row, and the outer loop creates six rows.

A Nested Variation

In the last example, the inner loop did the same thing for each cycle of the outer loop. You can make the inner loop behave differently each cycle by making part of the inner loop depend on the outer loop. Listing 6.16, for example, alters the last program slightly by making the starting character of the inner loop depend on the cycle number of the outer loop.

Listing 6.16. `rows2.c.`

```
/* rows2.c -- using dependent nested loops */
#include <stdio.h>
#define ROWS  6
#define CHARS 6
int main(void)
{
    int row;
    char ch;

    for (row = 0; row < ROWS; row++)
    {
        for (ch = ('A' + row);  ch < ('A' + CHARS); ch++)
            printf("%c", ch);
        printf("\n");
    }
     return 0;
}
```

This time the output is as follows:

```
ABCDEF
BCDEF
CDEF
DEF
EF
F
```

Because row is added to A during each cycle of the outer loop, ch is initialized in each row to one character later in the alphabet. The test condition, however, is unaltered, so each row still ends on F. This results in one fewer character being printed in each row.

Arrays

Arrays are important features in many programs. They enable you to store several items of related information in a convenient fashion. We will devote all of Chapter 10, "Arrays and Pointers," to arrays, but because arrays often are used with loops, we want to introduce them now.

An *array* is a series of values of the same type, such as 10 chars or 15 ints, stored sequentially. The whole array bears a single name, and the individual items, or *elements*, are accessed by using an integer index. For instance, the declaration

```
float debts[20];
```

announces that debts is an array with 20 elements, each of which can hold a type float value. The first element of the array is called debts[0], the second element is called debts[1], etc., up to debts[19]. Note that the numbering of array elements starts with

0, not 1. Each element can be assigned a `float` value. For example, you can have the following:

```
debts[5] = 32.54;
debts[6] = 1.2e+21;
```

An array can be of any data type.

```
int nannies[22];    /* an array to hold 22 integers     */
char alpha[26];     /* an array to hold 26 characters    */
long big[500];      /* an array to hold 500 long integers */
```

Earlier, for example, we talked about strings, which are a special case of `char` arrays. (A char *array*, in general, is one whose elements are assigned `char` values. A *string* is a `char` array in which the null character, \0, is used to mark the end of the string. See Figure 6.6.)

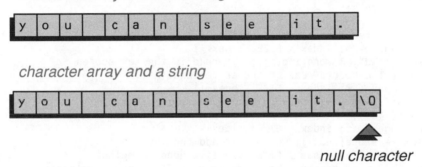

Figure 6.6. *Character arrays and strings.*

The numbers used to identify the array elements are called *subscripts*, *indices*, or *offsets*. The subscripts must be integers, and, as we mentioned, the subscripting begins with 0. The array elements are stored next to each other in memory, as shown in Figure 6.7.

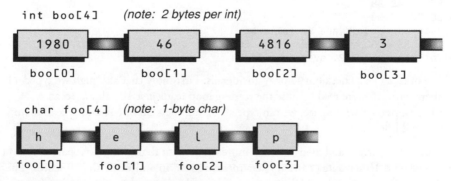

Figure 6.7. *The* char *and* int *arrays in memory.*

193

Using a *for* Loop with an Array

There are many, many uses for arrays. Listing 6.17 is a relatively simple one. It's a program that reads in ten scores, which will be processed later on. By using an array, we avoid inventing ten different variable names, one for each score. Also, we can use a `for` loop to do the reading. The program goes on to report the sum of the scores and their average.

Listing 6.17. `scores_in.c.`

```
/* scores_in.c -- uses loops for array processing */
#include <stdio.h>
#define SIZE 10
int main(void)
{
  int index, score[SIZE];
  int sum = 0;
  float average;

  printf("Enter %d scores:\n", SIZE);
  for (index = 0; index < SIZE; index++)
    scanf("%d", &score[index]);  /* read in the ten scores */
  printf("The scores read in are as follows:\n");
  for (index = 0; index < SIZE; index++)
    printf("%5d", score[index]); /* verify input           */
  printf("\n");
  for (index = 0; index < SIZE; index++)
    sum += score[index];         /* add them up            */
  average = (float) sum / SIZE;  /* time-honored method    */
  printf("Sum of scores = %d, average = %.2f\n", sum, average);
  return 0;
}
```

Let's see if Listing 6.17 works; then we can make a few comments. Here is the output:

```
Enter 10 scores:
76 85 62 48 98 71
66 89 70 77 99
The scores read in are as follows:
   76    85    62    48    98    71    66    89    70    77
Sum of scores = 742, average = 74.20
```

It works, so let's check out some of the details. First, note that although we typed 11 numbers, only 10 were read because the reading loop reads just 10 values. Because `scanf()` skips over whitespace, we can type all 10 numbers on one line or spread them over several lines.

Next, using arrays and loops is much more convenient than using 10 separate `scanf()` statements and 10 separate `printf()` statements to read in and verify the 10 scores. The `for` loop provides a simple and direct way to utilize the array subscripts. Notice that an element of a `int` array is handled like an `int` variable. To read the `int` variable `fue`, we would use scanf("%d", &fue). In Listing 6.17 we are reading the int element score[index], so we use scanf("%d", &score[index]).

This example illustrates several style points. First, we use a #define directive to create a manifest constant (SIZE) to specify the size of the array. We use this constant in defining the array and in setting the loop limits. If we later need to expand the program to handle 20 scores, we simply redefine SIZE to be 20. We don't have to change every part of the program that uses the array size.

Second, the idiom

```
for (index = 0; index < SIZE; index++)
```

is a handy one for processing an array of size SIZE. It's important to get the right array limits. The first element has index 0, and the loop starts by setting index to 0. Because the numbering starts with 0, the element index for the last element is SIZE - 1. That is, the tenth element is score[9]. Using the test condition index < SIZE accomplishes this, making the last value of index used in the loop SIZE - 1.

Third, a good practice is to have a program repeat or "echo" the values it has just read in. This helps ensure that the program is processing the data you think it is.

Finally, note that we used three separate for loops. You may wonder if this was really necessary. Could we have combined some of the operations in one loop? The answer is yes, we could have done so. That would have made the program more compact. However, we were swayed by the principle of *modularity*. The idea behind this term is that a program should be broken into separate units with each unit having one task to perform. This makes a program easier to read. Perhaps even more important, modularity makes it much easier to update or modify a program if different parts of the program are not intermingled. Once you know enough about functions, you could make each unit into a function, enhancing the modularity of the program.

A Loop Example Using a Function Return Value

For the last example in this chapter, we'll design a function that calculates the result of raising a number to an integer power. The three main tasks in this exercise are devising the algorithm for calculating the answer, expressing the algorithm in a function that returns the answer, and providing a convenient way of testing the function.

First, let's look at an algorithm. We'll keep the function simple by restricting it to positive integer powers. Then, if we want to raise a to the b power, we have to multiply a times itself b times. This is a natural task for a loop. We can set a variable pow to 1 and then multiply it by a repeatedly

```
for(i = 1; i <= b; i++)
    pow *= a;
```

Recall that the *= operator multiplies the left side by the right side. After the first loop cycle, pow is 1 times a, or a. After the second cycle, pow is its previous value (a) times a, or a squared, and so on. The `for` loop is natural in this context because the loop is executed a predetermined (once b is known) number of times.

Now that we have an algorithm, we should decide which data types to use. The exponent b, being an integer, should be type `int`. To allow maximum range in values for a and its power, we'll make a and pow type `double`.

Next, let's consider how to put the function together. We need to give the function two values, and the function should give back one. To get information to the function, we can use two arguments, one `double` and one `int`, specifying which number to raise to what power. How do we arrange for the function to return a value to the calling program? To write a function with a return value, do the following:

1. When you define a function, state the type of value it returns.

2. Use the keyword `return` to indicate the value to be returned.

For example, we can do this:

```
double power(double a, int b)   /* power() returns type double */
{
  double pow = 1.0;
  int i;

  for(i = 1; i <= b; i++)
      pow *= a;
  return pow;                   /* return the value of pow    */
}
```

To declare the function type, preface the function name with the type, just as you do when declaring a variable. The keyword `return` causes the function to return the following value to the calling function. Here we return the value of a variable, but you can return the value of expressions, too. For instance, the following is a valid statement:

```
return 2 * x + b;
```

The function would compute the value of the expression and return it. In the calling function, the return value can be assigned to another variable, can be used as a value in an expression, used as an argument to another function, as in `printf("%f", power(6.28, 3))`, or it can be ignored.

Now let's use the function in a program. To test the function, it would be convenient to be able to feed several values to the function to see how the function reacts. This suggests setting up an input loop. The natural choice is the `while` loop. We can use `scanf()` to read in two values at a time. If successful in reading two values, `scanf()` returns the value 2, so we can control the loop by comparing the `scanf()` return value to 2. One more point: to use the `power()` function in our program, we need to declare it, just as we declare variables that the program uses. Listing 6.18 shows the program.

Listing 6.18. power.c.

```
/* power.c -- raises numbers to integer powers */
#include <stdio.h>
double power(double a, int b);   /* ANSI prototype */
int main(void)
{
  double x, xpow;
     int n;

  printf("Enter a number and the positive integer power");
  printf(" to which\nthe number will be raised. Enter q");
  printf(" to quit.\n");
  while (scanf("%lf%d", &x, &n) == 2)
  {
      xpow = power(x,n);         /* function call            */
      printf("%.3e to the power %d is %.3e\n", x, n, xpow);
  }
  return 0;
}
double power(double a, int b)   /* function definition     */
{
  double pow = 1;
  int i;

  for(i = 1; i <= b; i++)
      pow *= a;
  return pow;                     /* return the value of pow  */
}
```

If your compiler doesn't recognize the ANSI forms, you can use the following declaration and function header:

```
double power();                 /* declaration */

double power(a,b);              /* header      */
double a;
int b;
```

Here is a sample run:

```
Enter a number and the positive integer power to which the number will
be raised. Enter q to quit.
2.2 5
2.200e+000 to the power 5 is 5.154e+001
8.0
8
8.000e+000 to the power 8 is 1.678e+007
144 2
1.440e+002 to the power 2 is 2.074e+004
q
```

Program Discussion

The `main()` program is an example of a *driver*, a short program designed to test a function.

The `while` loop is a generalization of a form we've used before. Entering `2.2 5` causes `scanf()` to return `2` and the loop continues. Because `scanf()` skips over whitespace, input can be spread over more than one line, as the sample output shows, but entering q produces a return value of `0` because q can't be read using the `%lf` specifier; this terminates the loop. Similarly, entering `2.8 q` would produce a return value of `1`; that, too, would terminate the loop.

Now let's look at the function-related matters. The `power()` function appears three times in this program. The first appearance is this:

```
double power(double a, int b);     /* ANSI prototype */
```

This statement announces, or declares, that the program will be using a function called `power()`. The initial keyword `double` indicates that the `power()` function returns a type `double` value. The compiler needs to know what kind of value `power()` returns so that it will know how many bytes of data to expect and how to interpret them; this is why we have to declare the function. The `double a, int b` within the parentheses means that `power()` takes two arguments. The first should be a type `double` value, and the second should be type `int`.

The second appearance is this:

```
xpow = power(x,n);    /* function call */
```

Here we call the function, passing it two values. The function calculates the *n*th power of x and returns it to the calling program, where the return value is assigned to the variable xpow.

The third appearance is in the head of the function definition.

```
double power(double a, int b)    /* function definition */
```

Here `power()` takes two arguments: a `double` and an `int` represented by the variables a and b. Note that `power()` is not followed by a semicolon when it appears in a function *definition*, but is followed by a semicolon when in a function *declaration*. After the function heading comes the code that specifies what `power()` does.

Recall that the function uses a `for` loop to calculate the value of a to the b power and assign it to pow. The following line makes the value of pow the function return value:

```
return pow;            /* return the value of pow */
```

Using Functions with Return Values

Declaring the function, calling the function, defining the function, using the `return` keyword: these are the basic elements in defining and using a function with a return value.

At this point, you may have some questions. For example, if you are supposed to declare functions before you use their return values, how come we used the return value of scanf() without declaring scanf()? Why do we have to declare power() separately when our definition of it says it is type double?

Let's take the second question first. The compiler needs to know what type power() is when it first encounters power() in the program. At this point, the compiler has not yet encountered the definition of power(), so it doesn't know that the definition says the return type is double. To help out the compiler, we previewed what is to come by using a *forward declaration*. This declaration informs the compiler that power() is defined elsewhere and that it will return type double. If we had placed the power() function definition ahead of main() in the file, we could have omitted the forward declaration because the compiler would have known all about power() before reaching main(). However, that is not standard C style. Because main() usually provides the overall framework for a program, it's best to show main() first. Also, functions often are kept in separate files, so a forward declaration is essential.

Next, why didn't we declare scanf()? Well, we did. The stdio.h header file has in it function declarations for scanf(), printf(), and several other I/O functions. The scanf() declaration states that it returns type int. However, if you forget to include stdio.h, the program still works. That's because C assumes that if you don't declare the type for a function, it is type int. Early C programming often relied heavily on this assumption, but modern practice is to declare the function type even if it is int.

Chapter Summary

The main topic of this chapter has been program control. C offers you many aids for structuring your programs. The while and the for statements provide *entry-condition* loops. The for statements are particularly suited for loops that involve initialization and updating. The *comma operator* enables you to initialize and update more than one variable in a for loop. For the rare occasion when an *exit-condition* loop is needed, C provides the do while statement.

All these loops use a test condition to determine if another loop cycle is to be executed. In general, the loop continues if the test expression evaluates to a nonzero value and terminates otherwise. Often, the test condition is a *relational expression*, which is an expression formed by using a relational operator. Such an expression has a value of 1 if the relation is true and a value of 0 otherwise.

In addition to relational operators, this chapter looked at several of C's arithmetic *assignment operators*, such as += and *=. These operators modify the value of the left-hand operand by performing an arithmetic operation upon it.

Arrays were the next subject. *Arrays* are declared in the same fashion as ordinary variables, but they have a number enclosed in brackets to indicate the number of elements.

The first element of an array is numbered 0; the second is numbered 1, etc. The subscripts used to number arrays can be manipulated conveniently by using loops.

Finally, the chapter showed how to write and use a function with a return value.

Review Questions

1. Find the value of quack after each line.

```
int quack = 2;
quack += 5;
quack *= 10;
quack -= 6;
quack /= 8;
quack %= 3;
```

2. Represent each of the following test conditions.

a. x is greater than 5.
b. scanf() attempts to read a single double and fails.
c. x has the value 5.

3. We suspect that the following program is not perfect. What errors can you find?

```
int main(void)
{                                       /* line 2  */
  int i, j, list(10);                   /* line 3  */

  for (i = 1, i <= 10,  i++)            /* line 5  */
  {                                     /* line 6  */
      list[i] = 2*i + 3;               /* line 7  */
      for (j = 1, j > = i, j++)         /* line 8  */
          printf("%d\n", list[j]);      /* line 9  */
}                                       /* line 10 */
```

4. What will each of the following programs print?

a.
```
#include <stdio.h>
int main(void)
{
    int i = 0;

    while (++i < 4)
        printf("Hi! ");
    do
        printf("Bye! ");
```

```
        while (i++ < 8);
        return 0;
    }
```

b.
```
    #include <stdio.h>
    int main(void)
    {
        int i;
        char ch;

        for (i = 0, ch = 'A'; i < 4; i++, ch += 2 * i)
                printf("%c", ch);
        return 0;
    }
```

5. What will the following program print?

```
    #include <stdio.h>
    int main(void)
    {
        int n, m;

        n = 10;
        while (++n <= 13)
                printf("%d",n);
        do
                printf("%d",n);
        while (++n <= 12);

        printf("\n***\n");

        for (n = 1; n*n < 60; n +=3)
                printf("%d\n", n);

        printf("\n***\n");

        for (n = 1, m = 5; n < m; n *= 2, m+= 2)
                printf("%d %d\n", n, m);

        printf("\n***\n");

        for (n = 4; n > 0; n--)
        {
            for (m = 0; m <= n; m++)
                    printf("+");
```

```
            printf("\n");
    }
    return 0;
}
```

6. Mr. Noah likes counting by twos, so he's written the following program to create an array and to fill it with the integers 2, 4, 6, 8, and so on. What, if anything, is wrong with this program?

```
#include <stdio.h>
#define SIZE 8
int main(void)
{
    int by_twos[SIZE];
    int index;

    for (index = 1; index <= SIZE; index++)
        by_twos[index] = 2 * index;
    for (index = 1; index <= SIZE; index++)
        printf("%d ", by_twos);
    printf("\n");
    return 0;
}
```

7. Define a function that takes an int argument and that returns, as a long, the square of that value.

Programming Exercises

1. Write a program that creates an array with 26 elements and stores the 26 lowercase letters in it. Also have it show the array contents.

2. Use nested loops to produce the following pattern:

```
$
$$
$$$
$$$$
$$$$$
```

3. Use nested loops to produce the following pattern:

```
F
FE
FED
FEDC
FEDCB
FEDCBA
```

4. Write a program that prints a table with each line giving an integer, its square, and its cube. Ask the user to input the lower and upper limits for the table. Use a `for` loop.

5. Write a program that reads a single word into a character array and then prints the word backwards. Hint: use `strlen()` (Chapter 4, "Characters Strings and Formatted Input/Output") to compute the index of the last character in the array.

6. Write a program that requests two floating-point numbers and prints the value of their difference divided by their product. Have the program loop through pairs of input values until the user enters nonnumeric input.

7. Modify Exercise 6 so that it uses a function to return the value of the calculation.

8. Write a program that reads eight integers into an array and then prints them in reverse order.

9. Daphne invests $100 at 10 percent simple interest. (That is, every year, the investment earns an interest equal to 10 percent of the original investment.) Deirdre invests $100 at 5 percent interest compounded annually. (That is, interest is 5 percent of the current balance, including previous addition of interest.) Write a program that finds how many years it takes for the value of Deirdre's investment to exceed the value of Daphne's investment. Also show the two values at that time.

C Control Statements: Branching and Jumps

Keywords
    if, else, switch, continue
    break, case, default, goto
Operators
    && ¦¦ ?:
Functions
    getchar(), putchar()

In this chapter you learn how to use the if and if else statements and how to nest them. You use logical operators to combine relational expressions into more involved test expressions. You encounter C's conditional operator, study the switch statement, learn about the break, continue, and goto jumps, and you use C's character I/O functions—getchar() and putchar().

As you grow more comfortable with C, you probably will want to tackle more complex tasks. When you do, you'll need ways to control and organize these projects. C has the tools to meet these needs. Already, you've learned to use loops to program repetitive tasks. In this chapter, you'll learn about branching structures, such as if and switch, that let a program base its actions on conditions that it checks. Also, you are introduced to C's logical operators, which enable you to test for more than one relationship in a while or if condition, and you look at C's jump statements, which shift the program flow to another part of a program. By the end of this chapter, you'll have all the basic information you need to design a program that behaves the way you want.

The *if* Statement

Let's start with a simple example of an if statement shown in Listing 7.1. This program reads in a list of daily low temperatures (in Celsius) and reports the total number of entries and the percentage that were below freezing. We use scanf() in a loop to read in the values. Once during each loop cycle we increment a counter to keep track of the number of entries. An if statement detects temperatures below freezing and keeps track of their number separately.

Listing 7.1. colddays.c.

```
/* colddays.c -- finds percentage of days below freezing */
#include <stdio.h>
#define SCALE "Celsius"
#define FREEZING 0
int main(void)
{
  float temperature;
  int freezing = 0;
  int days = 0;

  printf("Enter the list of daily low temperatures.\n");
  printf("Use %s, and enter q to quit.\n", SCALE);
  while (scanf("%f", &temperature) == 1)
  {
      days++;
      if (temperature < FREEZING)
          freezing++;
  }
  if (days != 0)
      printf("%d days total: %.1f%% were below freezing.\n",
              days, 100.0 * (float) freezing / days);
```

```
    if (days == 0)
        printf("No data entered!\n");
    return 0;
}
```

Here we follow the ANSI form of declaring `main()`'s type and giving `main()` a return value.

```
Enter the list of daily low temperatures.
Use Celsius, and enter q to quit.
20 11 3 -4 -6 -10 -2.5 10 8 -5 q
10 days total: 50.0% were below freezing.
```

The `while` loop test condition uses the return value of `scanf()` to terminate the loop when `scanf()` encounters nonnumeric input. By using `float` instead of `int` for `temperature`, the program is able to accept input like `-2.5` as well as `8`.

The new statement in the `while` block is this:

```
if (temperature < FREEZING)
  freezing++;
```

This `if` statement instructs the computer to increase `freezing` by 1 *if* the value just read (`temperature`) is less than zero. What happens if `temperature` is not less than zero? Then the `freezing++;` statement is skipped, and the `while` loop moves on to read the next temperature value.

We use the `if` statement two more times to control the output. If there is data, the program prints the results. If there is no data, the program reports that fact. (Soon you'll see a more elegant way to handle this part of the program.)

To avoid integer division, we used the cast to `float` when the percentage is being calculated. We don't really need the type cast, for in the expression `100.0 * freezing / days`, the subexpression `100.0 * freezing` is evaluated first and is forced into floating point by the automatic type conversion rules. Using the type cast documents our intent, however, and protects the program from faulty compilers.

if Basics

The `if` statement is called a *branching statement* because it provides a junction at which the program has to select which of two paths to follow. The general form is this:

```
if (expression)
     statement
```

If *expression* evaluates to true (nonzero), the *statement* is executed. Otherwise, it is skipped. As with a `while` loop, *statement* can be a single statement or a single block or compound statement. The structure is very similar to that of a `while` statement. The chief difference is that, in an if statement, the test and (possibly) the execution are done just once; but, in the while loop, the test and execution may be repeated several times.

Normally, *expression* is a relational expression; that is, it compares the magnitude of two quantities, as in the expressions x > y and c == 6. If *expression* is true (x is greater than y, or c does equal 6), then the statement is executed. Otherwise, the statement is ignored. More generally, any expression can be used, and an expression with a 0 value is taken to be false.

The statement portion can be a simple statement, as in our example, or it can be a compound statement or block, marked off by braces.

```
if (score > big)
    printf("Jackpot!\n");   /* simple statement    */

if (joe > ron)
{                            /* compound statement */
    joecash++;
    printf("You lose, Ron.\n");
}
```

Note that the entire if structure counts as a single statement, even when it uses a compound statement.

Adding *else* to the *if* Statement

The simple form of an if statement gives you the choice of executing a statement (possibly compound) or skipping it. C also enables you to choose between two statements by using the if else form. Let's use the if else form to fix an awkward segment from Listing 7.1.

```
if (days != 0)
  printf("%d days total: %.1f%% were below freezing.\n",
       days, 100.0 * (float) freezing / days);
if (days == 0)
  printf("No data entered!\n");
```

If the program finds that days is not unequal to 0, it should know that days must be 0 without retesting, and it does. With if else we can take advantage of that knowledge by rewriting the fragment this way:

```
if (days != 0)
  printf("%d days total: %.1f%% were below freezing.\n",
       days, 100.0 * (float) freezing / days);
else
  printf("No data entered!\n");
```

Only one test is made. If the if test expression is true, the temperature data is printed. If it's false, the warning message is printed.

Note the general form of the if else statement

```
if (expression)
    statement1
else
    statement2
```

If *expression* is true (nonzero), *statement1* is executed. If *expression* is false or zero, the single statement following the else is executed. The statements can be simple or compound. The indentation is not required by C, but it is the standard style. It shows at a glance those statements whose execution depends on a test.

If you want more than one statement between the if and the else, you must use braces to create a single block. The following construction violates C syntax, for the compiler expects just one statement (single or compound) between the if and the else. Instead, use this:

```
if (x > 0)
  printf("Incrementing x:\n");
  x++;
else
  printf("x <= 0 \n");
```

Instead, use this:

```
if (x > 0)
{
  printf("Incrementing x:\n");
  x++;
}
else
  printf("x <= 0 \n");
```

The if statement enables you to choose whether to do one action. The if else statement enables you to choose between two actions. Figure 7.1 compares the two statements.

Another Example: Introducing *getchar()* and *putchar()*

Most of our examples have used numeric input. To provide practice with other types, let's look at a character-oriented example. We can, of course, use scanf() and printf() with the %c specifier to read and write characters, but we won't. Instead, we'll use a pair of C functions specifically designed for character-oriented I/O: getchar() and putchar().

The getchar() function takes no arguments, and it returns the next character from input. For instance, the following statement reads the next input character and assigns its value to the variable ch:

```
ch = getchar();
```

This statement has the same effect as the following statement:

```
scanf("%c", &ch);
```

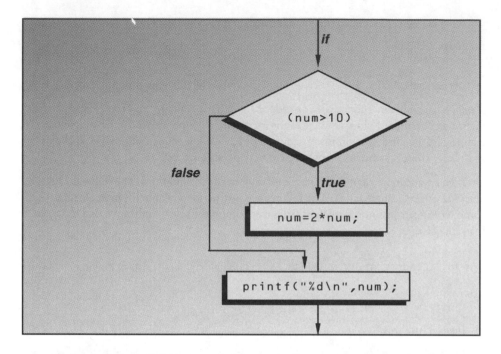

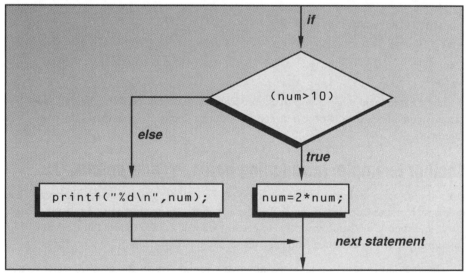

Figure 7.1. if *versus* if else.

The putchar() function prints its argument. For example, the next statement prints as a character the value previously assigned to ch:

```
putchar(ch);
```

This statement has the same effect as the following:

```
printf("%c", ch);
```

Because these functions deal only with characters, they are faster and more compact than the more general scanf() and printf() functions. Also, note that they don't need format specifiers. Both functions typically are defined in the stdio.h file. (Also, typically, they are preprocessor *macros* rather than true functions; we'll talk about function-like macros in Chapter 16, "The C Preprocessor and the C Library.")

Let's see how these functions work by writing a program that repeats an input line but replaces each nonspace character with the character that follows it in the ASCII code sequence. Spaces will be reproduced as spaces. We can state the desired response this way: if the character is a space, print it; else print the next character in the ASCII sequence. Our C code looks much like this statement, as you can see in Listing 7.2.

Listing 7.2. cypher1.c.

```
/* cypher1.c -- alters input, preserving spaces */
#include <stdio.h>
#define SPACE ' '              /* that's quote-space quote */
int main(void)
{
   char ch;

   ch = getchar();            /* read a character        */
   while (ch != '\n')         /* while not end of line   */
   {
       if (ch == SPACE)       /* leave the space         */
           putchar(ch);       /* character unchanged     */
       else
           putchar(ch + 1);   /* change other characters */
       ch = getchar();        /* get next character      */
   }
   return 0;
}
```

Here's a sample run:

```
CALL ME HAL.
DBMM NF IBM
```

Compare this loop to the one from Listing 7.1. Listing 7.1 uses the status returned by scanf() rather than the value of the input item to determine when to terminate the loop. Listing 7.2, however, uses the value of the input item itself to decide when to terminate the loop. This difference results in a slightly different loop structure, with one read statement before the loop, and one read statement at the end of each loop. C's flexible syntax, however, enables you to emulate Listing 7.1 by combining reading and testing into a single expression. Listing 7.3 presents Listing 7.2 rewritten in a more typically C style.

Listing 7.3. cypher2.c.

```
/* cypher2.c -- alters input, preserving spaces */
#include <stdio.h>
#define SPACE s' '              /* that's quote-space-quote */
int main(void)
{
   char ch;

   while ((ch = getchar()) != '\n')
   {
      if (ch == SPACE)        /*  leave the space        */
         putchar(ch);         /*  character unchanged     */
      else
         putchar(ch + 1);   /* change other characters  */
   }
   return 0;
}
```

The critical line is this:

```
while ((ch = getchar()) != '\n')
```

It demonstrates a characteristic C programming style: combining two actions in one expression. The actions are assigning a value to ch and comparing this value to the newline character. The parentheses around ch = getchar() make it the left operand of the != operator. To evaluate this expression, the computer must first call the getchar() function and then assign its return value to ch. Because the value of an assignment expression is the value of the left member, the value of ch = getchar() is just the new value of ch. Thus, after ch is read, the test condition boils down to ch != '\n', that is, to ch not being the newline character.

This particular idiom is very common in C programming. All the parentheses are necessary. Suppose we mistakenly used this:

```
while (ch = getchar() != '\n')
```

The != operator has higher precedence than =, so the first expression to be evaluated is getchar() != '\n'. Because this is a relational expression, its value is 1 or 0 (true or false). Then this value is assigned to ch. Omitting the parentheses means that ch is assigned 0 or 1 rather than the return value of getchar(); this is not desirable.

Multiple Choice: *else if*

Life often offers us more than two choices. We can extend the if else structure with else if to accommodate this fact. Let's look at a particular example. Utility companies often have charges that depend on the amount of energy the customer uses. Here are the rates that one company charges for electricity, based on kilowatt-hours (kWh):

first 240 kWh:	$0.11439 per kWh
next 300 kWh:	$0.13290 per kWh
over 540 kWh:	$0.14022 pcr kWh

If you worry about your energy management, you might wish to prepare a program to calculate your energy costs. The program in Listing 7.4 is a first step in that direction.

Listing 7.4. `electric.c`.

```
/* electric.c -- calculates electric bill */
#include <stdio.h>
#define RATE1 0.11439        /* rate for first 240 kwh     */
#define RATE2 0.12032        /* rate for next 300 kwh      */
#define RATE3 0.14022        /* rate for over 540 kwh      */
#define BREAK1 240.0         /* first breakpoint for rates */
#define BREAK2 540.0         /* second breakpoint for rates */
#define BASE1 (RATE1 * BREAK1)
                             /* cost for 240 kwh           */
#define BASE2 (BASE1 + (RATE2 * (BREAK2 - BREAK1)))
                             /* cost for 540 kwh           */
int main(void)
{
  float kwh;                 /* kilowatt-hours used        */
  float bill;                /* charges                    */

  printf("Please enter the kwh used.\n");
  scanf("%f", &kwh);
  if (kwh <= BREAK1)
      bill = RATE1 * kwh;
  else if (kwh <= BREAK2)    /* kwh between 240 and 540    */
      bill = BASE1 + (RATE2 * (kwh - BREAK1));
  else                       /* kwh above 540              */
      bill = BASE2 + (RATE3 * (kwh - BREAK2));
  printf("The charge for %.1f kwh is $%1.2f.\n", kwh, bill);
  return 0;
}
```

In Listing 7.4 we used symbolic constants for the rates so that the constants are conveniently gathered in one place. If the power company changes its rates (it's possible), having the rates in one place makes it easy to update them. We also expressed the rate breakpoints symbolically. They, too, are subject to change. BASE1 and BASE2 are expressed in terms of the rates and breakpoints. Then, if the rates or breakpoints change, the bases are updated automatically. You may recall that the preprocessor does not do calculations. Where BASE1 appears in the program, it will be replaced by `0.11439 * 240.0`. Don't worry; the compiler does evaluate this expression to its numerical value (27.4536) so that the final program code uses 27.4536 rather than a calculation.

The flow of the program is straightforward. The program selects one of three formulas, depending on the value of kwh. Figure 7.2 illustrates this flow. We should point out that the only way the program can reach the first else is if kwh is equal to or greater than 240. Thus, the else if (kwh <= BREAK2) line really is equivalent to demanding that kwh be between 240 and 540, as we noted in the program comment. Similarly, the final else can be reached only if kwh exceeds 540. Finally, note that BASE1 and BASE2 represent the total charges for the first 240 and 540 kilowatt-hours, respectively. Thus, we need add on only the additional charges for electricity in excess of those amounts.

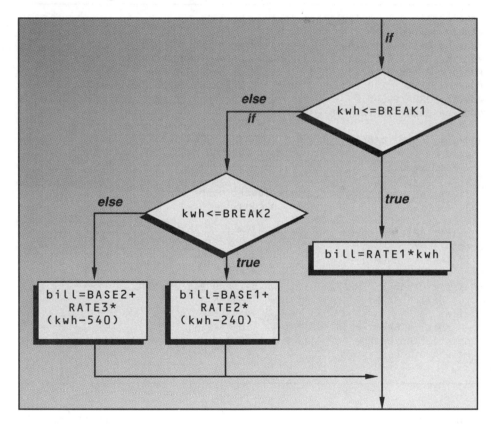

Figure 7.2. *Program flow for Listing 7.4,* electric.c.

Actually, the else if is a variation on what we already knew. For example, the core of our program is just another way of writing

```
if (kwh <=BREAK1)
    bill = RATE1 * kwh;
else
    if (kwh <=BREAK2)
        bill = BASE1 + RATE2 * (kwh - BREAK1);
```

```
else
    bill = BASE2 + RATE3 * (kwh - BREAK2);
```

That is, the program consists of an `if else` statement for which the statement part of the `else` is another `if else` statement. The second `if else` statement is said to be *nested* inside the first. Recall that the entire `if else` structure counts as a single statement, which is why we didn't have to enclose the nested `if else` in braces. However, using braces would clarify the intent of this particular format.

These two forms are perfectly equivalent. The only differences are in where we put spaces and newlines, and these differences are ignored by the compiler. Nonetheless, the first form is better because it shows more clearly that we are making a three-way choice. This form makes it easier to skim the program and see what the choices are. Save the nested forms of indentation for when they are needed, for instance, when you must test two separate quantities. An example of such a situation would be if there were a 10-percent surcharge for kilowatt-hours in excess of 540 during the summer only.

You may string together as many `else if` statements as you need (within compiler limits, of course), as illustrated by this fragment:

```
if (score < 1000)
    bonus = 0;
else if (score < 1500)
    bonus = 1;
else if (score < 2000)
    bonus = 2;
else if (score < 2500)
    bonus = 4;
else
    bonus = 6;
```

(This might be part of a game program, where `bonus` represents how many additional photon bombs or food pellets you get for the next round.)

Pairing *else* with *if*

When you have a lot of `if`s and `else`s, how does the computer decide which `if` goes with which `else`? For example, consider the following program fragment:

```
if (number > 6)
    if (number < 12)
        printf("You're close!\n");
else
    printf("Sorry, you lose a turn!\n");
```

When is `Sorry, you lose a turn!` printed? When `number` is less than or equal to 6, or when `number` is greater than 12? In other words, does the `else` go with the first `if` or the second? The answer is, the `else` goes with the second `if`. That is, you would get these responses:

Number	Response
5	none
10	You're close!
15	Sorry, you lose a turn!

The rule is that an `else` goes with the most recent `if` unless braces indicate otherwise. See Figure 7.3. We indented our example to make it look as if the `else` goes with the first `if`, but remember that the compiler ignores indentation. If we really want the `else` to go with the first `if`, we could write the fragment this way:

```
if (number > 6)
{
    if (number < 12)
        printf("You're close!\n");
}
else
    printf("Sorry, you lose a turn!\n");
```

Now we would get these responses:

Number	Response
5	Sorry, you lose a turn!
10	You're close!
15	none

More Nested *if*s

You've already seen that the `if...else if...else` sequence is a form of nested `if`, one that selects from a series of alternatives. Another kind of nested `if` is used when choosing a particular selection leads to an additional choice. For example, a program could use an `if else` to select between males and females. Each branch within the `if else` then could contain another `if else` to distinguish between different income groups.

Let's apply this form of nested `if` to the following problem. Given an integer, print all the integers that divide into it evenly; if there are no divisors, report that the number is prime.

This problem requires some forethought before we whip out the code. First, we need an overall design for the program. For convenience, the program should use a loop to enable us to input numbers to be tested. That way, we don't have to run the program again each time we want to examine a new number. We've already developed a model for this kind of loop:

```
prompt user
while the scanf() return value is 1
    analyze the number and report results
    prompt user
```

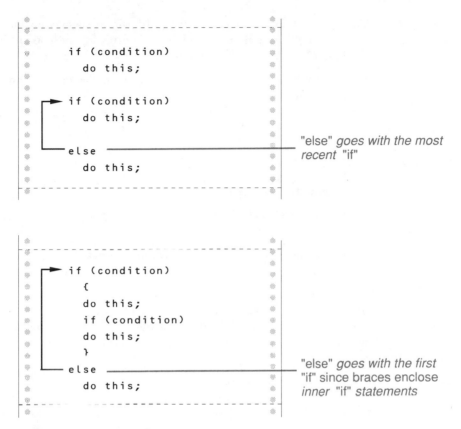

Figure 7.3. *The rule for* if else *pairings.*

Recall that by using scanf() in the loop test condition, the program attempts both to read a number and to check to see if the loop should be terminated.

Next, we need a plan for finding divisors. Perhaps the most obvious approach is something like this:

```
for (div = 2; div < num; div++)
  if (num % div == 0)
      printf("%d is divisible by %d\n", num, div);
```

The loop checks all the numbers between 2 and num to see if they divide evenly into num. Unfortunately, this approach is very wasteful of computer time. We can do much better. Consider, for example, finding the divisors of 144. We find that 144 % 2 is 0, meaning 2 goes into 144 evenly. If we then actually divide 2 into 144, we get 72, which also is a divisor, so we can get two divisors instead of one divisor out of a successful num % div test. The real payoff, however, comes in changing the limits of the loop test. To see how this works, look at the pairs of divisors we get as the loop continues: 2,72 3,48 4,36 6,24

217

8,18 9,16 12,12 16,9 18,8.... Ah! Once we get past the 12,12 pair, we start getting the same divisors (in reverse order) that we already found. Instead of running the loop to 143, we can stop after reaching 12. That saves a lot of cycles!

Generalizing this discovery, we see that we have to test only up to the square root of num instead of to num. For numbers like 9 this is not a big savings, but the difference is enormous for a number like 10000. Rather than messing with square roots, however, we can express the test condition as follows:

```
for (div = 2; (div * div) <= num; div++)
  if (num % div == 0)
        printf("%d is divisible by %d and %d.\n",
                 num, div, num / div);
```

If num is 144, the loop runs through div = 12. If num is 145, the loop runs through div = 13.

There are two reasons for using this test instead of a square root test. First, integer multiplication is much faster than extracting a square root. Second, the square root function hasn't been introduced yet.

We need to address just two more problems, and then we'll be ready to program. First, what if the test number is a perfect square? Reporting that 144 is divisible by 12 and 12 is a little clumsy, but we can use a nested if statement to test whether div equals num / div. If so, the program will print just one divisor instead of two.

```
for (div = 2; (div * div) <= num; div++)
{
  if (num % div == 0)
  {
    if (div * div != num)
      printf("%d is divisible by %d and %d.\n",
          num, div, num / div);
    else
      printf("%d is divisible by %d.\n", num, div);
  }
}
```

> **Note:** Technically, the if else statement counts as a single statement, so the braces around it are not needed. The outer if is a single statement also, so the braces around it are not needed. However, when statements get long, the braces make it easier to see what is happening, and they offer protection if later you add another statement to an if or to the loop.

Second, how do we know if a number is prime? If num is prime, then program flow never gets inside the if statement. To solve this problem, we can set a variable to some value, say 1, outside the loop and reset the variable to 0 inside the if statement. Then, after the loop is completed, we can check to see if the variable is still 1. If it is, the if statement was never entered, and the number is prime. Such a variable often is called a *flag*.

Listing 7.5 incorporates all the ideas we've discussed. To extend the range, we've switched to type long.

Listing 7.5. divisors.c.

```c
/* divisors.c -- nested ifs display divisors of a number */
#include <stdio.h>
#define NO 0
#define YES 1
int main(void)
{
    long num;                   /* number to be checked */
    long div;                   /* potential divisors   */
    int prime;

    printf("Please enter an integer for analysis; ");
    printf("Enter q to quit.\n");
    while (scanf("%ld", &num) == 1)
    {
        for (div = 2, prime = YES; (div * div) <= num; div++)
        {
            if (num % div == 0)
            {
                if ((div * div) != num)
                    printf("%ld is divisible by %ld and %ld.\n",
                        num, div, num / div);
                else
                    printf("%ld is divisible by %ld.\n", num, div);
                prime = NO;          /* number is not prime  */
            }
        }
        if (prime == YES)
            printf("%ld is prime.\n", num);
        printf("Please enter another integer for analysis; ");
        printf("Enter q to quit.\n");
    }
    return 0;
}
```

Note that we used the comma operator in the for loop control expression to enable us to initialize prime to YES for each new input number.

Here's a sample run:

```
Please enter an integer for analysis; Enter q to quit.
36
36 is divisible by 2 and 18.
36 is divisible by 3 and 12.
36 is divisible by 4 and 9.
36 is divisible by 6.
Please enter another integer for analysis; Enter q to quit.
149
149 is prime.
Please enter another integer for analysis; Enter q to quit.
30077
30077 is divisible by 19 and 1583.
Please enter another integer for analysis; Enter q to quit.
q
```

Summary: Using *if* Statements for Making Choices

Keywords

```
if, else
```

General Comments

In each of the following forms, the statement can be either a simple statement or a compound statement. A "true" expression means one with a nonzero value.

Form 1

```
if (expression)
    statement
```

The `statement` is executed if the `expression` is true.

Form 2

```
if (expression)
    statement1
  else
    statement2
```

If the `expression` is true, `statement1` is executed. Otherwise, `statement2` is executed.

Form 3

```
if (expression1)
    statement1
```

```
  else if (expression2)
    statement2
  else
    statement3
```

If *expression1* is true, then *statement1* is executed. If *expression1* is false but *expression2* is true, *statement2* is executed. Otherwise, if both expressions are false, *statement3* is executed.

Example

```
if (legs == 4)
    printf("It might be a horse.\n");
else if (legs > 4)
    printf("It is not a horse.\n");
else    /* case of legs < 4 */
{
    legs++;
    printf("Now it has one more leg.\n")
}
```

Let's Get Logical

You've seen how `if` and `while` statements often use relational expressions as tests. Sometimes you will find it useful to combine two or more relational expressions. For instance, suppose you want a program that counts only nonwhitespace characters (not counting the period) in an input sentence. That is, you wish to keep track of characters that are not spaces, not newline characters, and not tab characters. You can use *logical operators* to meet this need, and you can use the period character (.) to identify the end of a sentence. Listing 7.6 presents a short program illustrating the method.

Listing 7.6. chcount.c.

```
/* chcount.c -- counts nonwhitespace characters */
#include <stdio.h>
#define PERIOD '.'
int main(void)
{
  int ch;
  int charcount = 0;

  while ((ch = getchar()) != PERIOD)
  {
```

continues

Listing 7.6. continued

```
    if (ch != ' ' && ch != '\n' && ch != '\t')
            charcount++;
    }
    printf("There are %d nonwhitespace characters.\n", charcount);

    return 0;
}
```

Here's a sample run:

```
Logical operators
combine relationships.
There are 36 nonwhitespace characters.
```

The action begins as the program reads a character and checks to see whether it is a period, because the period marks the end of a sentence. Next comes something new, a statement using the logical AND operator &&. We can translate the if statement thus: If the character is not a blank AND if it is not a newline character AND if it is not a tab character, then increase charcount by 1.

All three conditions must be true if the whole expression is to be true. The logical operators have a lower precedence than the relational operators, so it was not necessary to use additional parentheses to group the subexpressions.

C has three logical operators

Operator	Meaning
&&	and
||	or
!	not

Suppose exp1 and exp2 are two simple relational expressions like cat > rat or debt == 1000. Then we can state the following:

1. exp1 && exp2 is true only if both exp1 and exp2 are true.

2. exp1 || exp2 is true if either exp1 or exp2 is true or if both are true.

3. !exp1 is true if exp1 is false and is false if exp1 is true.

Here are some concrete examples:

5 > 2 && 4 > 7 is false because only one subexpression is true.

5 > 2 || 4 > 7 is true because at least one of the subexpressions is true.

!(4 > 7) is true because 4 is not greater than 7.

The last expression, incidentally, is equivalent to the following:

```
4 <= 7
```

If you are unfamiliar or uncomfortable with logical operators, remember that

```
(practice && time) == perfection
```

Precedence

The ! operator has a very high precedence, higher than multiplication, the same as the increment operators, and just below that of parentheses. The && operator has higher precedence than ||, and both rank below the relational operators and above assignment in precedence. Thus, the expression

```
a > b && b > c || b > d
```

would be interpreted as

```
((a > b) && (b > c)) || (b > d)
```

That is, b is between a and c, or b is greater than d.

Order of Evaluation

Aside from those cases in which two operators share an operand, C ordinarily does not guarantee which parts of a complex expression will be evaluated first. For example, in the following statement the expression 5 + 3 might be evaluated before 9 + 6, or it might be evaluated afterwards:

```
apples = (5 + 3) * (9 + 6);
```

This ambiguity was left in the language to enable compiler designers to make the most efficient choice for a particular system. One exception to this rule (or lack of rule) is the treatment of logical operators. C guarantees that logical expressions are evaluated from left to right. The && and || operators are sequence points, so all side effects take place before a program moves from one operand to the next. Furthermore, it guarantees that as soon as an element is found that invalidates the expression as a whole, the evaluation stops. These guarantees make it possible to use constructions such as the following:

```
while ((c = getchar()) != ' ' && c != '\n')
```

This construction sets up a loop that reads characters up to the first space or newline character. The first subexpression gives a value to c, which then is used in the second subexpression. Without the order guarantee, the computer might try to test the second expression before finding out what value c had.

Another example is

```
if (number != 0 && 12/number == 2)
    printf("The number is 5 or 6.\n");
```

If number has the value 0, the first subexpression is false, and the relational expression is not evaluated any further. This spares the computer the trauma of trying to divide by zero. Many languages do not have this feature. After seeing that number is 0, they still plunge ahead to check the next condition.

Finally, consider this example:

```
while ( x++ < 10 && x + y < 20)
```

The fact that the && operator is a sequence point guarantees that x is incremented before the expression on the right is evaluated.

Summary: Logical Operators and Expressions

Logical Operators

Logical operators normally take relational expressions as operands. The ! operator takes one operand. The rest take two—one to the left, one to the right.

Operator	Meaning
&&	and
¦¦	or
!	not

Logical Expressions

expression1 && expression2 is true if and only if both expressions are true.
expression1 ¦¦ expression2 is true if either one or both expressions are true.
!expression is true if the expression is false, and vice versa.

Order of Evaluation

Logical expressions are evaluated from left to right. Evaluation stops as soon as something is discovered that renders the expression false.

Examples

6 > 2 && 3 == 3 is true.
! (6 > 2 && 3 == 3) is false.
x != 0 && (20 / x) < 5 The second expression is
evaluated only if x is nonzero.

A Word-Count Program

Now we have the tools to make a word-counting program, that is, a program that reads input and reports the number of words it finds. We may as well count characters and lines while we are at it. Let's see what such a program involves.

First, the program should read input character-by-character, and it should have some way of knowing when to stop. Second, it should be able to recognize and count the following units: characters, lines, words. Here's a pseudocode representation:

```
read a character
while there is more input
    increment character count
    if a line has been read, increment line count
    if a word has been read, increment word count
    read next character
```

We already have a model for the input loop:

```
while ((ch = getchar()) != STOP)
{
    ...
}
```

Here, STOP represents some value for ch that will signal the end of the input. So far we have used the newline character and a period for this purpose, but neither is satisfactory for a general word-counting program. For the present we'll choose a character (|) that is not common in text. In Chapter 8, "Character Input/Output and Redirection," we'll present a better solution that also allows the program to be used with text files as well as keyboard input.

Now let's consider the body of the loop. Because the program uses getchar() for input, it can count characters by incrementing a counter during each loop cycle. To count lines, the program can check for newline characters. If a character is a newline, then the program should increment the line count.

The trickiest part is identifying words. First, we have to define what we mean by a word. We will take a relatively simple approach and define a word as a sequence of characters that contains no whitespace. Thus, "glymxck" and "r2d2" are words. A word starts, then, when a program first encounters nonwhitespace, and it ends when the next whitespace character shows up. To keep track, we can set a flag (call it wordflag) to 1 when the first character in a word is read. We also can increment the word count at that point. Then, as long as wordflag remains 1, subsequent nonwhitespace characters don't mark the beginning of a word. At the next whitespace character, we must reset the flag to 0, and the program will be ready to find the next word. Let's put that into pseudocode.

```
if c is not whitespace and wordflag is 0
    set wordflag to 1 and count the word
if c is whitespace and wordflag is 1
    set wordflag to 0
```

This approach sets wordflag to 1 at the beginning of each word and to 0 at the end of each word. Words are counted only at the time the flag setting is changed from 0 to 1. Listing 7.7 translates these ideas into C.

Listing 7.7. wordcnt.c.

```c
/* wordcnt.c -- counts characters, words, lines */
#include <stdio.h>
#define STOP '|'
#define YES 1
#define NO 0
int main(void)
{
   char c;                  /* read in character      */
   long n_chars = 0L;       /* number of characters   */
   int n_lines = 0;         /* number of lines        */
   int n_words = 0;         /* number of words        */
   int wordflag = NO;       /* ==YES if c is in a word */

   while ((c = getchar()) != STOP)
   {
      n_chars++;                 /* count characters    */
      if (c == '\n')
         n_lines++;              /* count lines         */
      if (c != ' ' && c != '\n' && c != '\t' && wordflag == NO)
      {
         wordflag = YES;       /* starting a new word */
         n_words++;            /* count word          */
      }
      if ((c == ' ' || c == '\n' || c == '\t') &&
            wordflag == YES)
         wordflag = NO;        /* reached end of word */
   }
   printf("characters = %ld, words = %d, lines = %d\n",
         n_chars, n_words, n_lines);
   return 0;
}
```

Here is a sample run:

```
Reason is a
powerful servant but
an inadequate master.
|
characters = 55, words = 9, lines = 3
```

Because there are three different whitespace characters, we had to use the logical operators to check for all three possibilities. Consider the line:

```
if (c != ' ' && c != '\n' && c != '\t' && wordflag == NO)
```

It says, "If c is *not* a space and *not* a newline and *not* a tab, and if we are *not* in a word." (The first three conditions together ask if c is not whitespace.) If all four conditions are met, then we must be starting a new word, and n_words is incremented. If we are in the middle of a word, then the first three conditions hold, but wordflag will be YES, and n_words is not incremented. When we reach the next whitespace character, we set wordflag equal to NO again. Check the coding to see whether the program gets confused when there are several spaces between one word and the next. In Chapter 8, "Character Input/Output and Redirection," we'll show how to modify this program to count words in a file.

The Conditional Operator: *?:*

C offers a shorthand way to express one form of the if else statement. It is called a *conditional expression* and uses the ?: conditional operator. This is a two-part operator that has three operands. Here is an example that yields the absolute value of a number:

```
x = (y < 0) ? -y : y;
```

Everything between the = and the semicolon is the conditional expression. The meaning of the statement is this: If y is less than zero, then x = -y; otherwise, x = y. In if else terms, the statement can be expressed as

```
if (y < 0)
    x = -y;
else
    x = y;
```

The general form of the conditional expression is

```
expression1 ?expression2 : expression3
```

If *expression1* is true (nonzero), then the whole conditional expression has the same value as *expression2*. If *expression1* is false (zero), the whole conditional expression has the same value as *expression3*.

You can use the conditional expression when you have a variable to which you want to assign one of two possible values. A typical example is setting a variable equal to the maximum of two values.

```
max = (a > b) ? a : b;
```

This sets max to a if it is greater than b, and to b otherwise.

Usually, an if else statement can accomplish the same end as the conditional operator. The conditional operator version, however, is more compact and, depending on the compiler, may result in more compact program code.

Let's look at a paint program example, shown in Listing 7.8. The program calculates how many cans of paint are needed to paint a given number of square feet. The basic algorithm is simple: divide the square footage by the number of square feet covered per can. Suppose the answer is 1.7 cans, however. Stores sell whole cans, not fractional cans, so you would have to buy 2 cans. Therefore, the program should round up to the next integer when a fractional paint can is involved. We use the conditional operator to handle that situation. We also use the conditional operator to print cans or can, as appropriate.

Listing 7.8. `paint.c.`

```
/* paint.c -- uses conditional operator */
#include <stdio.h>
#define COVERAGE 200          /* square feet per paint can */
int main(void)
{
  int sq_feet;
  int cans;

  printf("Enter number of square feet to be painted:\n");
  while (scanf("%d", &sq_feet) == 1)
  {
      cans = sq_feet / COVERAGE;
      cans += ((sq_feet % COVERAGE == 0)) ? 0 : 1;
      printf("You need %d %s of paint.\n", cans,
             cans == 1 ? "can" : "cans");
  }
  return 0;
}
```

Here's a sample run:

```
Enter number of square feet to be painted:
200
You need 1 can of paint.
210
You need 2 cans of paint.
q
```

Because we're using type `int`, the division is truncated; that is, `210/200` becomes 1. Therefore, `cans` is rounded down to the integer part. If `sq_feet % COVERAGE` is 0, then `COVERAGE` divides evenly into `sq_feet` and `cans` is left unchanged. Otherwise, there is a remainder, so 1 is added. This is accomplished with the following statement:

```
cans += ((sq_feet % COVERAGE == 0)) ? 0 : 1;
```

It adds the value of the expression to the right of `+=` to `cans`. The expression to the right is a conditional expression having the value `0` or 1, depending on whether `COVERAGE` divides evenly into `sq_feet`.

The final argument to the `printf()` function also is a conditional expression.

```
cans == 1 ? "can" : "cans");
```

If the value of `cans` is 1, then the string "can" is used. Otherwise, "cans" is used. This demonstrates that the conditional operator can use strings for its second and third operands.

Summary: The Conditional Operator

The Conditional Operator

?:

General Comments

This operator takes three operands, each of which is an expression. They are arranged as follows:

expression1 ? *expression2* : *expression3*

The value of the whole expression equals the value of *expression2* if *expression1* is true. Otherwise, it equals the value of expression3.

Examples

```
(5 > 3) ? 1 : 2 has the value 1.
(3 > 5) ? 1 : 2 has the value 2.
(a > b) ? a : b has the value of the larger of a or b.
```

Loop Aids: *continue* and *break*

Normally, once the body of a loop has been entered, a program executes all the statements in the body before doing the next loop test. The continue and break statements enable you to skip part of a loop or even terminate it, depending on tests made in the body of the loop.

The *continue* Statement

This statement can be used in the three loop forms. When encountered, it causes the rest of an iteration to be skipped and the next iteration to be started. If the continue statement is inside nested structures, it affects only the innermost structure containing it. Let's try continue in the short program found in Listing 7.9.

Listing 7.9. skip.c.

```
/* skip.c  -- uses continue to skip part of loop */
#include <stdio.h>
#define MIN 0.0
#define MAX 100.0
int main(void)
{
```

continues

Listing 7.9. continued

```c
float score;
float total = 0.0;
int n = 0;
float min = MAX;
float max = MIN;

printf("Enter the scores:\n");
while (scanf("%f", &score) == 1)
{
    if (score < MIN || score > MAX)
    {
        printf("%0.1f is an invalid value.\n", score);
        continue;
    }
    printf("Accepting %0.1f:\n", score);
    min = (score < min)? score: min;
    max = (score > max)? score: max;
    total += score;
    n++;
}
if (n > 0)
{
    printf("Average of %d scores is %0.1f.\n", n, total / n);
    printf("Low = %0.1f, high = %0.1f\n", min, max);
}
else
    printf("No valid scores were entered.\n");
return 0;
}
```

In Listing 7.9 the while loop reads input until you enter nonnumeric data. The if statement within the loop screens out invalid score values. If, say, you enter 188, the program tells you that 188 is an invalid score. Then the continue statement causes the program to skip over the rest of the loop, which is devoted to processing valid input. Instead, the program starts the next loop cycle by attempting to read the next input value.

Note that there are two ways that we could have avoided using continue. One way would have been to omit the continue and to make the remaining part of the loop an else block.

```c
if (score < 0 || score > 100)
    /* printf() statement */
else
{
    /* statements */
}
```

We could have used this format instead:

```
if (score >= 0 && score <= 100)
{
    /* statements */
}
```

An advantage of using `continue` in this case is that we can eliminate one level of indentation in the main group of statements. This conciseness can be important for readability when the statements are long or are deeply nested already.

Another use for `continue` is as a placeholder. For example, the following loop reads and discards input up to, and including, the end of a line.

```
while (getchar() != '\n')
    ;
```

Such a technique is handy when a program already has read some input from a line and needs to skip to the beginning of the next line. The problem is that the lone semicolon is hard to spot. The code is much more readable if you use `continue`.

```
while (getchar() != '\n')
    continue;
```

Don't use `continue` if it complicates rather than simplifies the code. Consider the following fragment, for instance:

```
while ((ch = getchar() ) != '\n')
{
    if (ch == '\t')
        continue;
    putchar(ch);
}
```

This loop skips over the tabs and quits only when a newline character is encountered. The loop could have been expressed more economically as

```
while ((ch = getchar()) != '\n')
    if (ch != '\t')
        putchar(ch);
```

Often, as in this case, reversing an `if` test will eliminate the need for a `continue`.

You've seen that the `continue` statement causes the remaining body of a loop to be skipped. Where exactly does the loop resume? For the `while` and `do while` loops, the next action taken after the `continue` statement is to evaluate the loop test expression. For a `for` loop, the next actions are to evaluate the update expression, then the loop test expression.

The *break* Statement

A `break` statement in a loop causes the program to break free of the loop that encloses it and to proceed to the next stage of the program. In Listing 7.9, replacing `continue` with break would cause the loop to quit when, say, 188 is entered instead of just skipping to the next loop cycle. Figure 7.4 compares break and continue. If the break statement is inside nested loops, it affects only the innermost loop containing it.

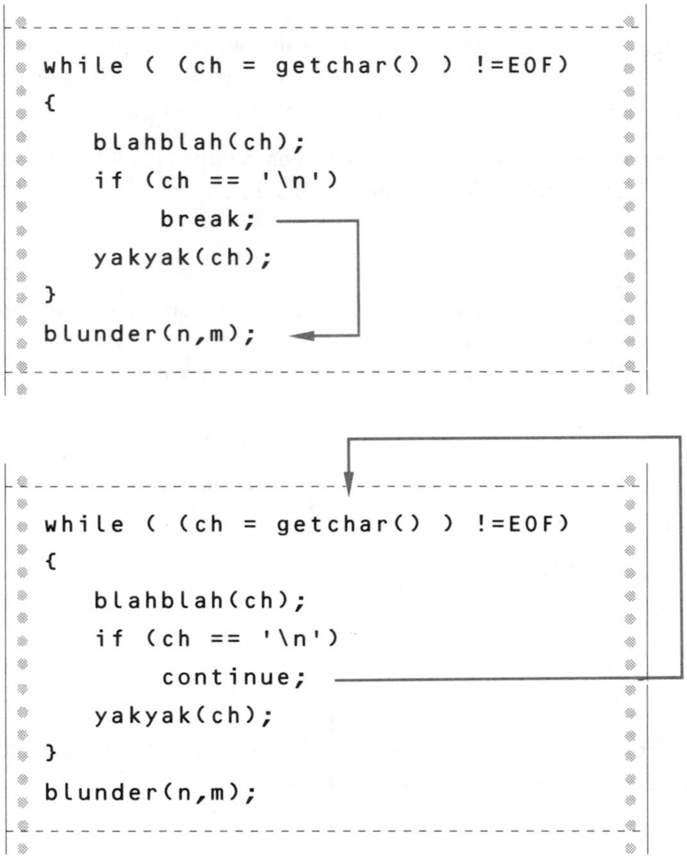

```
while ( (ch = getchar() ) !=EOF)
{
    blahblah(ch);
    if (ch == '\n')
        break;
    yakyak(ch);
}
blunder(n,m);
```

```
while ( (ch = getchar() ) !=EOF)
{
    blahblah(ch);
    if (ch == '\n')
        continue;
    yakyak(ch);
}
blunder(n,m);
```

Figure 7.4. break *and* continue.

Sometimes break is used to leave a loop when there are two separate reasons to leave. Listing 7.10 uses a loop that calculates the area of a rectangle. The loop terminates if you respond with nonnumeric input for the rectangle's length or width.

Listing 7.10. break.c.

```
/* break.c  -- uses break to exit a loop */
#include <stdio.h>
int main(void)
{
    float length, width;
```

```
    printf("Enter the length of the rectangle:\n");
    while (scanf("%f", &length) == 1)
    {
        printf("Length = %0.2f:\n", length);
        printf("Enter its width:\n");
        if (scanf("%f", &width) != 1)
            break;
        printf("Width = %0.2f:\n", width);
        printf("Area = %0.2f:\n", length * width);
        printf("Enter the length of the rectangle:\n");
    }
    return 0;
}
```

We could have controlled the loop this way:

```
while (scanf("%f %f", &length, &width) == 2)
```

However, using break makes it simple to echo each input value individually.

As with continue, don't use break when it complicates code. For instance, consider the following loop:

```
while ((ch = getchar()) != '\n')
{
    if (ch == '\t')
        break;
    putchar(ch);
}
```

The logic is clearer if both tests are in one place.

```
while ((ch = getchar() ) != '\n' && ch != '\t')
    putchar(ch);
```

The break statement is an essential adjunct to the switch statement, which we study next.

Multiple Choice: *switch* and *break*

The conditional operator and the if else construction make it easy to write programs that choose between *two* alternatives. Sometimes, however, a program needs to choose one of *several* alternatives. We can do this by using if else if...else, but in many cases it is more convenient to use the C switch statement. Listing 7.11 is an example showing how the switch statement works. This program reads in a letter and then responds by printing an animal name that begins with that letter.

Listing 7.11. animals.c.

```c
/* animals.c -- uses a switch statement */
#include <stdio.h>
int main(void)
{
  char ch;

  printf("Give me a letter of the alphabet, and I will give ");
  printf("an animal name\nbeginning with that letter.\n");
  printf("Please type in a letter; type # to end my act.\n");
  while ((ch = getchar()) != '#')
  {
    if (ch >= 'a' && ch <= 'z') /* lowercase only */
      switch (ch)
      {
        case 'a' :
                printf("argali, a wild sheep of Asia\n");
                break;
        case 'b' :
                printf("babirusa, a wild pig of Malay\n");
                break;
        case 'c' :
                printf("coati, racoonlike mammal\n");
                break;
        case 'd' :
                printf("desman, aquatic, molelike critter\n");
                break;
        case 'e' :
                printf("echidna, the spiny anteater\n");
                break;
        default :
                printf("That's a stumper!\n");
      }  /* end of switch */
    else
      printf("I recognize only lowercase letters.\n");
    while (getchar() != '\n')
      continue;                 /* skip rest of input line */
    printf("Please type another letter or a #.\n");
  }                             /* while loop end          */
  printf("Bye!\n");
  return 0;
}
```

We got a little lazy and stopped at e, but we could have continued in the same manner. Let's look at a sample run before explaining the program further.

```
Give me a letter of the alphabet, and I will give an animal name
beginning with that letter.
Please type in a letter; type # to end my act.
a [enter]
argali, a wild sheep of Asia
Please type another letter or a #.
dab [enter]
desman, aquatic, molelike critter
Please type another letter or a #.
r [enter]
That's a stumper!
Please type another letter or a #.
Q [enter]
I recognize only lowercase letters.
Please type another letter or a #.
# [enter]
Bye!
```

The program's two main features are its use of the switch statement and its handling of input. We'll look first at how switch works.

Using the *switch* Statement

The expression in the parentheses following the word switch is evaluated. In this case it has whatever value we last entered for ch. Then the program scans the list of *labels* (here, case 'a' :, case 'b' :, etc.) until it finds one matching that value. The program then jumps to that line. What if there is no match? If there is a line labeled default :, the program jumps there. Otherwise, the program proceeds to the statement following the switch.

What about the break statement? It causes the program to break out of the switch and skip to the next statement after the switch (see Figure 7.5). Without the break statement, every statement from the matched label to the end of the switch would be processed. For example, if we removed all the break statements from our program and then ran the program using the letter d, we would get this exchange:

```
Give me a letter of the alphabet, and I will give an animal name
beginning with that letter.
Please type in a letter; type # to end my act.
d [enter]
desman, aquatic, molelike critter
echidna, the spiny anteater
That's a stumper!
Please type another letter or a #.
# [enter]
Bye!
```

All the statements from case 'd' : to the end of the switch were executed.

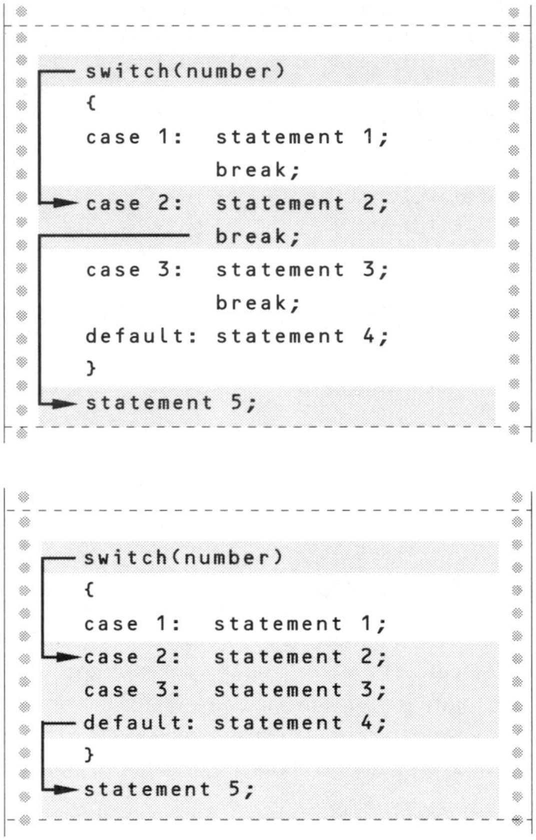

Figure 7.5. *Program flow in* switch*es, with and without* break*s.*

Incidentally, a break statement works with loops and with switch, but continue works just with loops. However, continue can be used as part of a switch statement if the statement is in a loop. In that situation, as with other loops, continue causes the program to skip over the rest of the loop, including other parts of the switch.

If you are familiar with Pascal, you will recognize the switch statement as being similar to the Pascal case statement. The most important difference is that the switch statement requires the use of a break if you want only the labeled statement to be processed.

The switch test expression in the parentheses should be one with an integer value (including type char). The case labels must be integer-type (including char) constants or integer constant expressions (expressions containing only integer constants). You can't use a variable for a case label. This, then, is the structure of a switch:

```
switch (integer expression)
    {
    case constant1:
            statements;                    →optional
    case constant2:
            statements;                    →optional
    default :                              →optional
            statements;                    →optional
    }
```

Reading Only the First Character of a Line

The other new feature incorporated into animals.c is how it reads input. As you may have noticed in the sample run, when dab was entered, only the first character was processed. Often this behavior is desirable in interactive programs looking for single-character responses. The code responsible for this behavior is the following:

```
while (getchar() != '\n')
    continue;          /* skip rest of input line */
```

This loop reads characters from input up to and including the newline character generated by the Enter key. Note that the function return value is not assigned to ch. Thus, the characters are merely read and discarded. Because the last character discarded is the newline character, the next character to be read will be the first character of the next line. It gets read by getchar() and assigned to ch in the outer while loop.

If you omit this loop, the program runs into a bit of trouble. Suppose, for instance, you respond with the letter a. Entering a involves pressing the Enter key, so you actually send the sequence a followed by the newline character. After the program processes the a, it reads the newline character and prints "I recognize only lowercase letters." Thus, each letter entered causes the program to run through the outer while loop twice, which is disconcerting to the user.

Another approach to the newline problem is to skip only newlines rather than the entire rest of the line. You can do that by using the following code as the first statement in the large while loop:

```
if (ch == '\n')
    continue;
```

Multiple Labels

You can use multiple case labels for a given statement, as shown in Listing 7.12.

Listing 7.12. `vowels.c.`

```c
/* vowels.c -- uses multiple labels */
#include <stdio.h>
int main(void)
{
  char ch;
  int a_ct, e_ct, i_ct, o_ct, u_ct;

  a_ct = e_ct = i_ct = o_ct = u_ct = 0;

  printf("Enter some text; enter # to quit.\n");
  while ((ch = getchar()) != '#')
  {
     switch (ch)
     {
       case 'a' :
       case 'A' :  a_ct++;
                   break;
       case 'e' :
       case 'E' :  e_ct++;
                   break;
       case 'i' :
       case 'I' :  i_ct++;
                   break;
       case 'o' :
       case 'O' :  o_ct++;
                   break;
       case 'u' :
       case 'U' :  u_ct++;
                   break;
       default :   break;
     }                                    /* end of switch  */
  }                                       /* while loop end */
  printf("number of vowels:   A    E    I    O    U\n");
  printf("                   %4d %4d %4d %4d %4d\n",
       a_ct, e_ct, i_ct, o_ct, u_ct);
  return 0;
}
```

If ch is, say, the letter i, the switch statement goes to the location labeled case 'i' :. Because there is no break associated with that label, program flow goes to the next statement, which is i_ct++;. If ch is I, program flow goes directly to that statement. In essence, both labels refer to the same statement.

Here's a sample run:

```
Enter some text; enter # to quit.
I see under the overseer.#
number of vowels:   A    E    I    O    U
                    0    7    1    1    1
```

Summary: Multiple Choice with *switch*

Keyword

`switch`

General Comments

Program control jumps to the `case` label bearing the value of *expression*. Program flow then proceeds through all the remaining statements unless redirected again with a `break` statement. Both *expression* and `case` labels must have integer values (type `char` is included), and the labels must be constants or expressions formed solely from constants. If no `case` label matches the expression value, control goes to the statement labeled `default`, if present. Otherwise, control passes to the next statement following the `switch` statement.

Form

```
switch (expression)
{
    case label1 : statement1
    case label2 : statement2
    default     : statement3
}
```

There can be more than two labeled statements, and the `default` case is optional.

Example

```
switch (choice)
    {
    case 1 :
    case 2 : printf("Darn tootin'!\n");  break;
    case 3 : printf("Quite right!\n");
    case 4 : printf("Good show!\n"); break;
    default  : printf("Have a nice day.\n");
    }
```

If `choice` has the integer value 1 or 2, the first message is printed. If it is 3, the second and third messages are printed. (Flow continues to the following statement because there is no `break` statement after `case 3`.) If it is 4, the third message is printed. Other values print only the last message.

---

switch and *if else*

When should you use a switch and when should you use the else-if construction? Often you don't have a choice. You can't use a switch if your choice is based on evaluating a float variable or expression. Nor can you conveniently use a switch if a variable must fall into a certain range. It is simple to write the following:

```
if (integer < 1000 && integer > 2)
```

Unhappily, covering this range with a switch would involve setting up case labels for each integer from 3 to 999. However, if you can use a switch, often your program will run a little faster and take less code.

The *goto* Statement

The goto statement, bulwark of the older versions of BASIC and FORTRAN, is available in C. However, C, unlike those two languages, can get along quite well without it. Kernighan and Ritchie refer to the goto statement as "infinitely abusable" and suggest that it "be used sparingly, if at all." First, we will show you how to use goto. Then, we will show why you usually don't need to.

The goto statement has two parts: the goto and a label name. The label is named following the same convention used in naming a variable. An example is

```
goto part2;
```

For the preceding statement to work, the function must contain another statement bearing the part2 label. This is done by beginning a statement with the label name followed by a colon.

```
part2: printf("Refined analysis:\n");
```

Avoiding *goto*

In principle, you never need to use the goto statement in a C program, but if you have a background in FORTRAN or BASIC, both of which require its use, you may have developed programming habits that depend on using the goto. To help you get over that dependence, we will outline some familiar goto situations and then show you a more C-like approach.

1. Handling an if situation that requires more than one statement:

```
if (size > 12)
    goto a;
goto b;
a: cost = cost * 1.05;
   flag = 2;
b: bill = cost * flag;
```

In old-style BASIC and FORTRAN, only the single statement immediately following the if condition is attached to the if. No provision is made for blocks or compound statements. We have translated that pattern into the equivalent C. The standard C approach of using a compound statement or block is much easier to follow:

```
if (size > 12)
{
     cost = cost * 1.05;
     flag = 2;
}
bill = cost * flag;
```

2. Choosing from two alternatives:

```
if (ibex > 14)
    goto a;
sheds = 2;
goto b;
a: sheds= 3;
b: help = 2 * sheds;
```

Having the if else structure available allows C to express this choice more cleanly:

```
if (ibex > 14)
     sheds = 3;
else
     sheds = 2;
help = 2 * sheds;
```

Indeed, newer versions of BASIC and FORTRAN have incorporated the else into their syntax.

3. Setting up an indefinite loop:

```
readin: scanf("%d", &score);
if (score < 0)
    goto stage2;
lots of statements;
goto readin;
stage2: more stuff;
```

Use a while loop instead:

```
scanf("%d", &score);
while (score <= 0)
{
     lots of statements;
     scanf("%d", &score);
}
more stuff;
```

4. Skipping to the end of a loop: use `continue` instead.

5. Leaving a loop: use `break` instead. Actually, `break` and `continue` are specialized forms of a `goto`. The advantages of using them are that their names tell you what they are supposed to do and that, because they don't use labels, there is no danger of putting a label in the wrong place.

6. Leaping madly about to different parts of a program: DON'T!

There is one use of `goto` that is tolerated by many C practitioners: getting out of a nested set of loops if trouble shows up. (A single `break` gets you out of the innermost loop only.)

```
while (funct > 0)
    {
    for (i = 1, i <= 100; i++)
        {
        for (j = 1; j <= 50; j++)
            {
            statements galore;
            if (bit trouble)
                goto help;
            statements;
            }
        more statements;
        }
    yet more statements;
    }
and more statements;
help : bail out;
```

As you can see from our other examples, the alternative forms are clearer than the `goto` forms. This difference grows even greater when you mix several of these situations. Which `gotos` are helping `ifs`, which are simulating `if elses`, which are controlling loops, which are just there because you have programmed yourself into a corner? By using `gotos` excessively you create a labyrinth of program flow. If you aren't familiar with `gotos`, keep it that way. If you are used to using them, try to train yourself not to. Ironically, C, which doesn't need a `goto`, has a better `goto` than most languages because it enables you to use descriptive words for labels instead of numbers.

Summary: Program Jumps

Keywords

`break, continue, goto`

General Comments

These three instructions cause program flow to jump from one location of a program to another location.

The *break* Command

The break command can be used with any of the three loop forms and with the switch statement. It causes program control to skip the rest of the loop or the switch containing it and to resume with the next command following the loop or switch.

Example

```
switch (number)
{
    case 4:  printf("That's a good choice.\n");
             break;
    case 5:  printf("That's a fair choice.\n");
             break
    default: printf("That's a poor choice.\n");
}
```

The *continue* Command

The continue command can be used with any of the three loop forms but not with a switch. It causes program control to skip the remaining statements in a loop. For a while or for loop, the next loop cycle is started. For a do while loop, the exit condition is tested and then, if necessary, the next loop cycle is started.

Example

```
while ((ch = getchar())   != EOF)
{
    if (ch == ' ')
        continue;
    putchar(ch);
    chcount++;
}
```

This fragment echoes and counts nonspace characters.

The *goto* Command

A goto statement causes program control to jump to a statement bearing the indicated label. A colon is used to separate a labeled statement from its label. Label names follow the rules for variable names. The labeled statement can come either before or after the goto.

continues

```
Form

goto label;
        .
        .
        .
label : statement
```

Example

```
top : ch = getchar();
        .
        .
        .
if (ch != 'y')
        goto top;
```

Chapter Summary

The `if` statement uses a test condition to control whether or not a program executes the single simple statement or block following the test condition. Execution occurs if the test expression has a nonzero value and doesn't occur if the value is zero. The `if else` statement enables you to select from two alternatives. If the test condition is nonzero, the statement before the `else` is executed. If the test expression evaluates to zero, the statement following the `else` is executed. By using another `if` statement to immediately follow the `else`, you can set up a structure that chooses between a series of alternatives.

The test condition often is a *relational expression*, that is, an expression formed by using one of the relational operators discussed in Chapter 6, "C Control Statements: Looping." By using C's logical operators, you can combine relational expressions. For example, you can test to see if x is greater than 0 and less than 20.

The *conditional operator* (`operand1 ? operand2 : operand3`) creates an expression whose value is governed by its first operand and is given by one of the next two operands. If the first operand is nonzero, the whole expression has the value of *operand2*; otherwise, the value that of *operand3*.

The `switch` statement enables you to select from a series of statements labeled with integer values. If the integer value of the test condition following the `switch` keyword matches a label, execution goes to the statement bearing that label. Execution then proceeds through the statements following the labeled statement unless you use a `break` statement.

The break, continue, and goto are *jump statements* that cause program flow to jump to another location in a program. A break statement causes the program to jump to the next statement following the end of the loop or switch containing the break. The continue statement causes the program or switch containing the break. The continue statement causes the program to skip the rest of the containing loop and to start the next cycle.

The control statements presented in these last two chapters will enable you to tackle programs much more powerful and ambitious than those you worked with before. As proof, just compare some of the examples in these chapters to those of the earlier chapters.

Review Questions

1. Determine which expressions are true and which are false.

   a. `100 > 3 && 'a'>'c'`

   b. `100 > 3 || 'a'>'c'`

   c. `!(100>3)`

2. The following program has unnecessarily complex relational expressions as well as some outright errors. Simplify and correct it.

```c
#include <stdio.h.
int main(void)                               /*  1  */
{                                            /*  2  */
  int weight, height;  /* weight in lbs, height in inches */
                                             /*  4  */
  scanf("%d, weight, height);                /*  5  */
  if (weight < 100)                          /*  6  */
    if (height >= 72)                        /*  7  */
      printf("You are very tall for your weight.\n");
    else if (height < 72 && > 64)            /*  9  */
      printf("You are tall for your weight.\n");
    else if (weight > 300 && ! (weight <= 300))    /* 11 */
    if (!(height >= 48)                      /* 12 */
       printf(" You are quite short for your weight.\n");
    else                                     /* 14 */
    printf("Your weight is ideaL.\n");       /* 15 */
                                             /* 16 */
  return 0;
}
```

3. What is the numerical value of each of the following expressions?

   a. 5 > 2
   b. 3 + 4 > 2 && 3 < 2
   c. x >= y ¦¦ y > x

4. What will the following program print?

```c
#include <stdio.h>
int main(void)
{
  int num;
  for (num = 1; num <= 11; num++)
  {
      if (num % 3 == 0)
          putchar('$');
      else
          putchar('*');
          putchar('#');
      putchar('%');
  }
  putchar('\n');
  return 0;
}
```

5. What's wrong with this program?

```c
#include <stdio.h>
int main(void)
{
  char ch;
  int lc = 0;     /* lowercase char count
  int uc = 0;     /* uppercase char count
  int oc = 0;     /* other char count

  while ((ch = getchar()) != '#')
  {
      if ('a' <= ch >= 'z')
          lc++;
      else if (!(ch < 'A') ¦¦ !(ch > 'Z')
          uc++;
      oc++;
  }
  printf(%d lowercase, %d uppercase, %d other, lc, uc, oc);
  return 0;
}
```

6. What will the following program print when given this input?

```
q
c
g
b
```

```c
#include <stdio.h>
int main(void)
{
  char ch;

  while ((ch = getchar()) != '#')
  {
      if (ch == '\n')
          continue;
      printf("Step 1\n");
      if (ch == 'c')
          continue;
      else if (ch == 'b')
          break;
      else if (ch == 'g')
          goto laststep;
      printf("Step 2\n");
  laststep:  printf("Step 3\n");
  }
  printf("Done\n");
  return 0;
}
```

Programming Exercises

1. Write a program that reads input until encountering the # character and then reports the number of spaces read, the number of newline characters read, and the number of all other characters read.

2. Write a program that reads input until encountering #. Have the program print each input character and its ASCII decimal code. Print eight character-code pairs per line. Suggestion: use a character count and the modulus operator (%) to print a newline character for every eight cycles of the loop.

3. Using if else statements, write a program that reads input up to #, replaces each period with an exclamation mark, replaces each exclamation mark initially present with two exclamation marks, and reports at the end the number of substitutions it has made.

4. Redo Exercise 3, but use a `switch`.

5. Write a program that reads input up to # and reports the number of times that the sequence ei occurs.

Note: The program will have to "remember" the preceding character as well as the current character. Test it with input like "Receive your eieio award."

---

6. Write a program that requests the hours worked in a week and then prints the gross pay, the taxes, and the net pay. Assume the following:

   a. Basic pay rate = $10.00/hr
   b. Overtime (in excess of 40 hours) = time and a half
   c. Tax rate = 15% of the first $300
                  20% of the next $150
                  25% of the rest

   Use `#define` constants, and don't worry if the example does not conform to current tax law.

7. Modify assumption a in Exercise 6 so that the program presents a menu of pay rates to choose from. Use a switch to select the pay rate. The beginning of a run should look something like this:

```
*****************************************************************
Enter the number corresponding to the desired pay rate or action:
1) $8.75/hr                        2) $9.33/hr
3) $10.00/hr                       4) $11.20/hr
5) quit
*****************************************************************
```

   If choices 1 through 4 are selected, then the program should request the hours worked. The program should recycle until 5 is entered. If something other than choices 1 through 5 is entered, the program should remind the user what the proper choices are and then recycle. Use `#defined` constants for the various earning rates and tax rates.

8. Write a program that accepts an integer as input and then displays all the prime numbers smaller than or equal to that number.

Character Input/Output and Redirection

In this chapter you learn more about input, output, and the differences between buffered and unbuffered input. You learn how to simulate the end-of-file condition from the keyboard and how to use redirection to connect your programs to files. Finally, you gain some experience in making the user interface friendlier.

In the computing world, we use the words *input* and *output* in several ways. We speak of input and output devices, such as keyboards, disk drives, and laser printers. We talk about the data used for input and output. We discuss the functions that perform input and output. This chapter concentrates on the functions used for input and output (*I/O* for short).

I/O functions transport information to and from your program; `printf()`, `scanf()`, `getchar()`, and `putchar()` are examples. You've seen these functions in previous chapters, and now you'll be able to look at their conceptual basis. Along the way, you'll see how to improve the program-user interface.

Originally, input/output functions were not part of the definition of C. Their development was left to the implementors of C. In practice, the UNIX implementation of C has served as a model for these functions. The ANSI C library, recognizing past practice, contains a large number of these UNIX I/O functions, including the ones we've used. Because such standard functions must work in a wide variety of computer environments, they seldom take advantage of features peculiar to a particular system. Thus, many C vendors supply additional I/O functions that do make use of special features, such as the 8086 microprocessor I/O ports or the Macintosh ROM routines. These specialized functions enable you to write programs that utilize a particular computer more effectively. Unfortunately, they often can't be used on other computer systems. Consequently, we'll concentrate on the standard I/O functions available on all systems, for they enable you to write portable programs that can be moved easily from one system to another.

Single-Character I/O: *getchar()* and *putchar()*

As you saw in Chapter 7, "C Control Statements: Branching and Jumps," `getchar()` and `putchar()` perform input and output one character at a time. That may strike you as a rather silly way of doing things. After all, you can easily read groupings larger than a single character, but this method does suit the capability of a computer. Furthermore, this approach is the heart of most programs that deal with text, that is, with ordinary words. To remind yourself of how these functions work, examine Listing 8.1, a very simple example. All it does is fetch characters from keyboard input and send them to the screen. We call this process *echoing the input*. We use a `while` loop that terminates when the `#` character is encountered.

Listing 8.1. `echo.c`.

```
/* echo.c -- repeats input */
#include <stdio.h>
int main(void)
{
  char ch;

  while ((ch = getchar()) != '#')
      putchar(ch);
  return 0;
}
```

On most systems the definitions of `getchar()` and `putchar()` are found in the system file `stdio.h`, which is why we have included that file in the program. (Typically, `getchar()` and `putchar()` are not true functions but are defined using preprocessor macros, a topic we'll cover in Chapter 16, "The C Preprocessor and the C Library.") Using this program produces exchanges like this:

```
Hello, there. I would[enter]
Hello, there. I would
like a #3 bag of potatoes.[enter]
like a
```

After watching this program run, you may wonder why you must type a whole line before the input is echoed. You also may wonder if there is a better way to terminate input. Using a particular character, such as #, to terminate input prevents you from using that character in the text. To answer these questions, we have to look at how C programs handle keyboard input. In particular, we need to examine buffering and the concept of a standard input file.

Buffers

When you run the previous program on some systems, the text that you input is echoed immediately. That is, a sample run would look like this:

```
HHeelllloo,,  tthheerree..  II  wwoouulldd[enter]

lliikkee  aa  #
```

The preceding behavior is the exception. On most systems, nothing happens until you press Enter, as in the first example. The immediate echoing of input characters is an instance of *unbuffered* (or *direct*) input, meaning that the character you type is immediately made available to the waiting program. The delayed echoing, on the other hand, illustrates *buffered* input, in which the characters you type are collected and stored in an area of temporary storage called a *buffer*. Pressing Enter causes the block of characters (or single character, if that is all you typed) to be made available to your program. Figure 8.1 compares these two kinds of input.

Why have buffers? First, it is less time-consuming to transmit several characters as a block than one by one. Second, if you mistype, you can use your keyboard correction facilities to fix your mistake. When you finally press Enter, the corrected version can be transmitted.

Unbuffered input, on the other hand, is desirable for some interactive programs. In a word processor, for instance, you would like each command to take place as soon as you press a key. Thus, both buffered and unbuffered input have their uses.

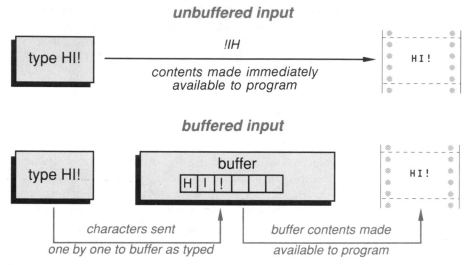

Figure 8.1. *Buffered versus unbuffered input.*

Buffering comes in two varieties: *fully buffered* I/O and *line-buffered* I/O. For fully buffered input, the buffer is flushed (the contents are sent to their destination) when the buffer is full. This kind of buffering usually occurs with file input. The buffer size depends on the system, but 512 bytes and 4096 bytes are common values. With line-buffered I/O, the buffer is flushed whenever a newline character shows up. Keyboard input normally is line-buffered so that pressing Enter flushes the buffer.

Which kind of input do you have: buffered or unbuffered? ANSI C specifies that input should be buffered, but K&R left the choice open to the compiler writer. You can find out by running the echo.c program and seeing which behavior results.

The reason ANSI C settled on buffered input as the standard is that some computer designs don't permit unbuffered input. If your particular computer does allow unbuffered input, most likely your C compiler will provide unbuffered input as an option. Compilers for IBM PC compatibles, for example, typically supply a special family of functions, supported by the conio.h header file, for unbuffered input. These functions include getche() for echoed unbuffered input and getch() for unechoed unbuffered input. (*Echoed input* means the character you type shows on screen, and *unechoed input* means the keystrokes don't show.) UNIX systems use a different approach, for there UNIX itself controls buffering. With UNIX, you use ioctl() function to specify the type of input that you want, and getchar() will behave accordingly. In ANSI C, the setbuf() and setvbuf() functions (Chapter 12, "File Input/Output") supply some control over buffering, but the inherent limitations of some systems can restrict the effectiveness of these functions. In short, there is no standard ANSI way of invoking unbuffered input; the means depend on the computer system. In this book, with apologies to our unbuffered friends, we assume that you are using buffered input.

Terminating Keyboard Input

Our program halts when # is entered, which is convenient as long as we exclude that character from normal input. As you've seen, however, # can show up in normal input. Ideally, we'd like a terminating character that normally does not show up in text. Such a character won't pop up accidentally in the middle of some input, stopping the program before we want it to stop. C has an answer to this need, but, to understand it, you need to know how C handles files.

Files, Streams, and Keyboard Input

A *file* is an area of memory in which information is stored. Normally a file would be kept in some sort of permanent memory, such as a floppy disk, a hard disk, or a tape. You doubtless are aware of the importance of files to computer systems. For instance, your C programs are kept in files, and the programs used to compile your programs are kept in files. This last example points out that some programs need to be able to access particular files. When you compile a program stored in a file called echo.c, the compiler opens the echo.c file and reads its contents. When the compiler finishes, it closes the file. Other programs, such as word processors, not only open, read, and close files, they also *write* to them.

C, being powerful, flexible, and so on, provides many library functions for opening, reading, writing, and closing files. On one level, it can deal with files using the basic file tools of the host operating system. This is called *low-level I/O*. Because of the many differences among computer systems, it is impossible to create a standard library of universal low-level I/O functions, and ANSI C does not attempt to do so, but C also deals with files on a second level called the *standard I/O package*. This involves creating a standard model and a standard set of I/O functions for dealing with files. At this higher level, differences between systems are handled by specific C implementations so that you deal with a uniform interface.

What sort of differences are we talking about? Different systems, for example, store files differently. Some store the file contents in one place and information about the file elsewhere. Some build a description of the file into the file itself. In dealing with text, some systems use a single newline character to mark the end of a line. Others may use the combination of the carriage return and linefeed characters to represent the end of a line. Some systems measure file sizes to the nearest byte; some measure in blocks of bytes.

When you use the standard I/O package, you are shielded from these differences. Thus, to check for a newline, you can use if (ch == '\n'). If the system actually uses the carriage-return/linefeed combination, the I/O functions automatically translate back and forth between the two representations.

Conceptually, the C program deals with a stream instead of directly with a file. A stream is an idealized flow of data to which the actual input or output is mapped. This means that various kinds of input with differing properties are represented by streams with more uniform properties. The process of opening a file then becomes one of associating a stream with the file, and reading and writing take place via the stream.

Chapter 12, "File Input/Output," discusses files in greater detail. For this chapter, simply note that C treats input and output devices the same as it treats regular files on storage devices. In particular, the keyboard and the display device are treated as files that are opened automatically by every C program. Keyboard input is represented by a stream called stdin, and output to the screen (or teletype, or other output device) is represented by a stream called stdout. The getchar(), putchar(), printf(), and scanf() functions all are members of the standard I/O package, and they deal with these two streams.

One implication of all this is that you can use the same techniques with keyboard input as you do with files. For example, a program reading a file needs a way to detect the end of the file so that it knows where to stop reading. Therefore, C input functions come equipped with a built-in end-of-file detector. Because keyboard input is treated like a file, you should be able to use that end-of-file detector to terminate keyboard input, too. Let's see how this is done, beginning with files.

The End of File

A computer operating system needs some way to tell where each file begins and ends. One method to detect the end of a file is to place a special character in the file to mark the end. This is the method used, for example, in CP/M, IBM-DOS, and MS-DOS text files. These operating systems use (or once used) the Control-Z character to mark the ends of files. (Control-Z is the character generated by holding down the Control key while typing the Z key.) Figure 8.2 illustrates this approach.

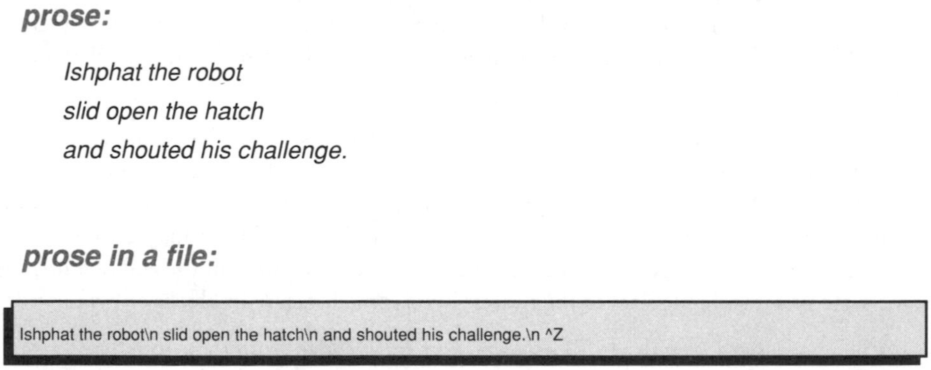

prose:

> *Ishphat the robot*
> *slid open the hatch*
> *and shouted his challenge.*

prose in a file:

```
Ishphat the robot\n slid open the hatch\n and shouted his challenge.\n ^Z
```

Figure 8.2. *A file with an end-of-file marker.*

A second approach is for the operating system to store information on the size of the file. If a file has 3000 bytes and a program has read 3000 bytes, then the program has reached the end. MS-DOS and its relatives use this approach for binary files, because this method allows the files to hold all characters, including Control-Z. Newer versions of DOS also use this approach for text files. UNIX uses this approach for all files.

C handles this variety of methods by having the `getchar()` function return a special value when the end of a file is reached, regardless of how the operating system actually detects the end of file. The name given to this value is EOF (end of file). Thus, the return value for `getchar()` when it detects an end of file is EOF. The `scanf()` function also returns EOF on detecting the end of a file. Typically, EOF is defined in the `stdio.h` file as follows:

```
#define EOF (-1)
```

Why -1? Normally, `getchar()` returns a value in the range 0 through 127, because those are values corresponding to the standard character set, but it might return values from 0 through 255 if the system recognizes an extended character set. In either case, the value -1 does not correspond to any character, so it can be used to signal the end of a file.

Some systems may define EOF to be a value other than -1, but the definition always will be different from a return value produced by a legitimate input character. If you include the `stdio.h` file and use the EOF symbol, you don't have to worry about the numeric definition. The important point is that EOF represents a value which signals that the end of a file was detected; it is not a symbol actually found in the file.

Okay, how can you use EOF in a program? Compare the return value of `getchar()` with EOF. If they are different, you have not yet reached the end of a file. In other words, you can use an expression like this:

```
while ((ch = getchar()) != EOF)
```

What if you are reading keyboard input and not a file? Most systems provide a way to simulate an end-of-file condition from the keyboard. Knowing that, we can rewrite our basic read and echo program as shown in Listing 8.2.

Listing 8.2. echo_eof.c.

```
/* echo_eof.c -- repeats input to end of file */
#include <stdio.h>
int main(void)
{
  int ch;

  while ((ch = getchar()) != EOF)
      putchar(ch);
  return 0;
}
```

Note these points:

- You don't have to define EOF because stdio.h takes care of that.

- You don't have to worry about the actual value of EOF because the #define statement in stdio.h enables you to use the symbolic representation EOF.

- The variable ch is changed from type char to type int because char variables may be represented by unsigned integers in the range 0 to 255, but EOF may have the numeric value -1. That is an impossible value for an unsigned char variable, but not for an int. Fortunately, getchar() is actually type int itself, so it can read the EOF character. Implementations that use a signed char type may get by with declaring ch as type char, but it is better to use the more general form.

- The fact that ch is an integer doesn't faze putchar(). It still prints the character equivalent.

- To use this program on keyboard input, you need a way to type the EOF character. No, you can't just type the letters *E-O-F*, and you can't just type –1. (Typing [ms]1 would transmit two characters: a hyphen and the digit 1.) Instead, you have to find out what your system requires. On most UNIX systems, for example, typing Control-D at the beginning of a line causes the end-of-file signal to be transmitted. Many microcomputing systems recognize a Control-Z typed anywhere on a line as an end-of-file signal.

Here is a buffered example of running echo_eof.c on a UNIX system:

```
She walks in beauty, like the night
She walks in beauty, like the night
  Of cloudless climes and starry skies...
  Of cloudless climes and starry skies...
                    Lord Byron
                    Lord Byron
[Control-D]
```

Each time you press Enter, the characters stored in the buffer are processed, and a copy of the line is printed. This continues until you simulate the end of file, UNIX-style. On a PC, you would type Control-Z instead.

Let's stop for a moment and think about the possibilities for echo_eof.c. It copies onto the screen whatever input you feed it. Suppose you could somehow feed a file to it. Then it would print the contents of the file onto the screen, stopping when it reached the end of the file, for it would find an EOF signal then. Suppose instead that you could find a way to direct the program's output to a file. Then you could enter data from the keyboard and use echo_eof.c to store in a file what you type. Suppose you could do both simultaneously: direct input from one file into echo_eof.c and send the output to another file. Then you could use echo_eof.c to copy files. Thus, our little program has the potential to look at the contents of files, to create new files, and to make copies of files—pretty good for such a short program! The key is to control the flow of input and output, and that is our next topic.

Redirection and Files

Input and output involve functions, data, and devices. Consider, for instance, our echo_eof.c program. It uses the input function getchar(). The input device (we have assumed) is a keyboard, and the input data stream consists of individual characters. Suppose you want to keep the same input function and the same kind of data, but wish to change where the program looks for data. A good question to ask (and to answer) is "How does a program know where to look for its input?"

By default, a C program using the standard I/O package looks to the standard input as its source for input. This is the stream identified earlier as stdin. It is whatever has been set up as the usual way for reading data into the computer. It could be magnetic tape, punched cards, a teletype, or (as we will continue to assume) your keyboard. A modern computer is a suggestible tool, however, and you can influence it to look elsewhere for input. In particular, you can tell a program to seek its input from a file instead of from a keyboard.

There are two ways to get a program to work with files. One way is to explicitly use special functions that open files, close files, read files, write in files, and so forth. That we'll save for Chapter 12, "File Input/Output." The second way is to use a program designed to work with keyboard and screen, but to *redirect* input and output along different channels, to and from files, for example. In other words, you reassign the stdin stream to file. The getchar() program continues to get its data from the stream, not really caring from where the stream gets its data. This approach is more limited in some respects than the first, but it is much simpler to use. It is the one that we will use now.

One major problem with redirection is that it is associated with the operating system, not C. but the most popular C environments (UNIX and DOS 2.0 and later) feature redirection, and some C implementations simulate it on systems lacking the feature. We'll look at the UNIX and DOS versions.

UNIX and DOS Redirection

UNIX and current DOS versions enable you to redirect both input and output. Redirecting input enables your program to use a file instead of the keyboard for input, and redirecting output enables it to use a file instead of the screen for output.

Redirecting Input

Suppose you have compiled our echo_eof.c program and placed the executable version in a file called echo_eof (or echo_eof.exe on DOS systems). To run the program, type the executable file's name

echo_eof

The program runs as we described earlier, taking its input from the keyboard. Now suppose that you wish to use the program on a text file called words. A *text file* is one containing text, that is, data stored as human-readable characters. It could be an essay or a program in C, for example. A file containing machine language instructions, such as the file holding the executable version of a program is not a text file. Because our program works with characters, it should be used with text files. All you need do is enter this command instead of the previous one:

```
echo_eof < words
```

The < symbol is a UNIX (and DOS) redirection operator. It causes the words file to be associated with the stdin stream, channeling the file contents into the echo_eof program. The echo_eof program itself doesn't know (or care) that the input is coming from a file instead of the keyboard. All it knows is that a stream of characters is being fed to it, so it reads them and prints them one character at a time until the end of file shows up. Because C puts files and I/O devices on the same footing, the file is now the I/O *device*. Try it!

Redirection Sidelights

With UNIX and DOS, the spaces on either side of the < are optional. Some systems, such as AmigaDOS, support redirection but don't allow a space between the redirection symbol and the filename. You can't use redirection from within some integrated environments. In such cases, you must create an executable file and run it in the standard environment.

Here is a sample run for one particular words file; the $ is one of the two standard UNIX prompts. On a DOS system, you would see the DOS prompt, perhaps an A> or C>.

```
$ echo_eof < words
The world is too much with us: late and soon,
Getting and spending, we lay waste our powers:
Little we see in Nature that is ours;
We have given our hearts away, a sordid boon!
$
```

Well, that time we got our words' worth.

Redirecting Output

Now suppose that you wish to have echo_eof send your keyboard input to a file called mywords. Then you can enter the following and begin typing

```
echo_eof > mywords
```

The > is a second redirection operator. It causes a new file called mywords to be created for your use, and then it redirects the output of echo_eof (that is, a copy of the characters you type) to that file. The redirection reassigns stdout from the display device (your screen) to the mywords file instead. If you already have a file with the name mywords, normally it would be erased and then replaced by the new one. (Some UNIX systems, however, give you the option of protecting existing files.) All that appears on your screen are the letters as you type them, and the copies go to the file instead. To end the program, type Control-D (UNIX) or Control-Z (DOS) at the beginning of a line. Try it. If you can't think of anything to type, just imitate the next example. In it we use the $ UNIX prompt. Remember to end each line by pressing Enter to send the buffer contents to the program.

```
$ echo_eof > mywords
```

```
You should have no problem recalling which redirection
operator does what. Just remember that each operator points
in the direction the information flows. Think of it as
a funnel.
[Control-D]
$
```

Once the Control-D or Control-Z is processed, the program terminates and your system prompt returns. Did the program work? The UNIX ls command or DOS dir command, which lists filenames, should show you that the file mywords now exists. You can use the UNIX cat or DOS type command to check the contents, or you can use echo_eof again, this time redirecting the file to the program.

```
$ echo_eof < mywords
You should have no problem recalling which redirection
operator does what. Just remember that each operator points
in the direction the information flows. Think of it as a
funnel.
$
```

Combined Redirection

Now suppose you want to make a copy of the file mywords and call it savewords. Just issue this next command

```
echo_eof < mywords > savewords
```

and the deed is done. The following command would have served as well, because the order of redirection operations doesn't matter:

```
echo_eof > savewords < mywords
```

Beware. Don't use the same file for both input and output to the same command.

```
echo_eof < mywords > mywords                    →WRONG
```

The reason is that > mywords causes the original mywords to be truncated to zero length before it is ever used as input.

In brief, here are the rules governing the use of the two redirection operators < and > with UNIX or DOS:

- A redirection operator connects an *executable* program (including standard UNIX commands) with a data file. It cannot be used to connect one data file to another, nor can it be used to connect one program to another program.

- Input cannot be taken from more than one file, nor can output be directed to more than one file using these operators.

- Normally, spaces between the names and operators are optional, except occasionally when some characters with special meaning to the UNIX shell or DOS are used. We could, for example, have used echo_eof<words.

You have already seen several proper examples. Here are some wrong examples, with a and count as executable programs and fish and beets as text files:

```
fish > beets                          →violates Rule 1
addup < count                         →violates Rule 1
addup < fish < beets                  →violates Rule 2
count > beets fish                    →violates Rule 2
```

UNIX and DOS also feature the >> operator, which enables you to add data to the end of an existing file, and the pipe operator (¦), which enables you to connect the output of one program to the input of a second program. See a UNIX book such as UNIX Primer Plus, Second Edition (Waite, Prata, and Martin, Indianapolis: Sams Publishing) for more information on all these operators.

Comment

Redirection enables you to use keyboard-input programs with files. For this to work, the program has to test for end of file. For example, Chapter 7, "C Control Statements: Branching and Jumps," presented a word-counting program that counted words up to the first ¦ character. Change ch from type char to type int, and replace '¦' with EOF in the loop test, and you can use the program to count words in text files.

Summary: How to Redirect Input and Output

With most C systems you can use redirection, either for all programs through the operating system or else just for C programs, courtesy of the C compiler. In the following, let prog be the name of the executable program and let file1 and file2 be names of files.

Redirecting Output to a File

```
>
```

```
prog >file1
```

> **Redirecting Input from a File**
>
> <
>
> prog <file2
>
> **Combined Redirection**
>
> prog <file2 >file1
> prog >file1 <file2
>
> Both forms use file2 for input and file1 for output.
>
> **Spacing**
>
> Some systems require a space to the left of the redirection operator and no space to the right. Other systems (UNIX, for example) will accept either spaces or no spaces on either side.

A Graphic Example

You can use getchar() and putchar() to produce geometric patterns using characters. Listing 8.3 shows such a program. It reads a character and then prints it a number of times, the number depending on the character's ASCII value. The program also prints a sufficient number of spaces to center each line.

Listing 8.3. patterns.c.

```
/* patterns.c -- produces a symmetric pattern of characters */
#include <stdio.h>
int main(void)
{
  int ch;                 /* read character                */
  int index;
  int chnum;

  while ((ch = getchar()) != '\n')
  {
    chnum = ch % 26;      /* produces a number from 0 to 25 */
    index = 0;
    while (index++ < (30 - chnum))
        putchar(' ');     /* spaces to center pattern      */
    index = 0;
    while (index++ < (2 * chnum + 1))
        putchar(ch);      /* print ch several times        */
```

continues

Listing 8.3. continued

```
putchar('\n');
    }
    return 0;

}
```

Listing 8.3 uses nested loops. The outer `while` loop gathers input characters. The first inner `while` loop prints leading spaces to center the text, and the second `while` loop prints the character multiple times. The number of characters printed is determined from the numeric value for the character. What you get depends on what you enter. If, for example, you type

```
What's up?
```

the response is

```
              WWWWWWWWWWWWWWWWWWWWW
                        h
aaaaaaaaaaaaaaaaaaaaaaaaaaaaaaaaaaaaaaa
              tttttttttttttttttttttttttt
                   ' ' ' ' ' ' ' ' ' ' ' '
              sssssssssssssssssssssss

              uuuuuuuuuuuuuuuuuuuuuuuuu
                ppppppppppppppppppp
              ?????????????????????????
```

What can you do with this program? You can ignore it. You can tinker with it to change the kinds of patterns it makes. You can try to find combinations of input characters that produce a pretty pattern. For example, the input

```
hijklmnopqrstuiii
```

produces

```
                    h
                   iii
                  jjjjj
                 kkkkkkk
                lllllllll
               mmmmmmmmmmm
              nnnnnnnnnnnnn
             ooooooooooooooo
            ppppppppppppppppp
           qqqqqqqqqqqqqqqqqqq
          rrrrrrrrrrrrrrrrrrrrr
         sssssssssssssssssssssss
        ttttttttttttttttttttttttt
       uuuuuuuuuuuuuuuuuuuuuuuuuuu
                   iii
                   iii
                   iii
```

Creating a Friendlier User Interface

Most of us have on occasion written programs that are awkward to use. Fortunately, C gives us the tools to make input a smoother, more pleasant process. Unfortunately, learning these tools may, at first, lead to new problems. Our goal in this section is to guide you through some of these problems to a friendlier user interface, one that eases data entry and smooths over the effects of faulty input.

Working with Buffered Input

Buffered input is often a convenience to the user, but it can be bothersome to the programmer when character input is used. The problem, as you've seen in some earlier examples, is that buffered input requires you to press the Enter key to transmit your input. This act also transmits a newline character which the program must handle. Let's examine this and other problems with a guessing program. You pick a number, and the computer tries to guess it. The computer uses a plodding method, but we are concentrating on I/O, not algorithms. See Listing 8.4 for the starting version of the program.

Listing 8.4. guess.c.

```
/* guess.c -- an inefficient number-guesser */
#include <stdio.h>
int main(void)
{
  int guess = 1;
  char response;

  printf("Pick an integer from 1 to 100. I will try to guess ");
  printf("it.\nRespond with a y if my guess is right and with");
  printf("\nan n if it is wrong.\n");
  printf("Uh...is your number %d?\n", guess);
  while ((response = getchar()) != 'y')       /* get response */
      printf("Well, then, is it %d?\n", ++guess);
  printf("I knew I could do it!\n");
  return 0;
}
```

Here's a sample run:

```
Pick an integer from 1 to 100. I will try to guess it.
Respond with a y if my guess is right and with
an n if it is wrong.
Uh...is your number 1?
n
Well, then, is it 2?
Well, then, is it 3?
n
```

```
Well, then, is it 4?
Well, then, is it 5?
y
I knew I could do it!
```

Out of consideration for the program's pathetic guessing algorithm, we chose a small number. Note that the program makes two guesses every time we enter n. What's happening is that the program reads our n response as a denial that the number is 1 and then reads the newline character as a denial that the number is 2.

One solution is to use a while loop to discard the rest of the input line, including the newline character. This has the additional merit of treating responses such as no or no way the same as a simple n. The version in Listing 8.4 treats no as two responses. Here is a revised loop that fixes the problem:

```c
while ((response = getchar()) != 'y')      /* get response */
{
    printf("Well, then, is it %d?\n", ++guess);
    while (getchar() != '\n')
        continue;               /* skip rest of input line     */
}
```

Using this loop produces responses like the following:

```
Pick an integer from 1 to 100. I will try to guess it.
Respond with a y if my guess is right and with
an n if it is wrong.
Uh...is your number 1?
n
Well, then, is it 2?
no
Well, then, is it 3?
no sir
Well, then, is it 4?
forget it
Well, then, is it 5?
y
I knew I could do it!
```

There are no more problems with the newline character. As a purist, you may not like f being treated as meaning the same as n. To eliminate that defect, we can use an if statement to screen out other responses. Change the loop to this:

```c
while ((response = getchar()) != 'y')       /* get response */
{
    if (response == 'n')
        printf("Well, then, is it %d?\n", ++guess);
    else
        printf("Sorry, I understand only y or n.\n");
    while (getchar() != '\n')
        continue;                  /* skip rest of input line */
}
```

Now the program's response looks like this:

```
Pick an integer from 1 to 100. I will try to guess it.
Respond with a y if my guess is right and with
an n if it is wrong.
Uh...is your number 1?
n
Well, then, is it 2?
no
Well, then, is it 3?
no sir
Well, then, is it 4?
forget it
Sorry, I understand only y or n.
n
Well, then, is it 5?
y
I knew I could do it?
```

When you write interactive programs, you should try to anticipate ways in which users will fail to follow instructions. Then you should design your program to handle user failures gracefully. Tell them when they are wrong, and give them another chance.

You should, of course, provide clear instructions to the user, but no matter how clear you make them, someone will always misinterpret them and then blame you for poor instructions.

Mixing Numeric and Character Input

Typically, you use getchar() to read input one character at a time and you use scanf() to read numbers or strings. This mixture can create problems because getchar() reads every character, including spaces, tabs, and newlines. In contrast, scanf(), when reading numbers, skips over spaces, tabs, and newlines. (However, when reading characters using the %c specifier, scanf() behaves like getchar().)

To illustrate a representative problem, Listing 8.5 presents a program that reads in a character and two numbers as input. It then prints the character using the number of rows and columns specified in the input.

Listing 8.5. showchar1.c.

```
/* showchar1.c -- program with an I/O problem */
#include <stdio.h>
void display(char c, int lines, int width);
int main(void)
{
    int ch;              /* character to be printed   */
    int rows, cols;      /* number of rows and columns */
```

continues

Listing 8.5. continued

```
printf("Enter a character and two integers:\n");
    while ((ch = getchar()) != EOF)
    {
      scanf("%d %d", &rows, &cols);
      display(ch, rows, cols);
      printf("Enter another character and two integers;\n");
      printf("Simulate eof to quit.\n");
    }
    return 0;
}

void display(char c, int lines, int width)
{
    int row, col;

    for (row = 1; row <= lines; row++)
    {
        for (col = 1; col <= width; col++)
            putchar;
        putchar('\n');   /* end line and start a new one */
    }
}
```

The program is set up so that main() gets the data, and the display() function does the printing. Let's look at a sample run to see what the problem is.

```
Enter a character and two integers:
a 2 3
aaa
aaa
Enter another character and two integers;
Simulate eof to quit.
b 1 2
```

```
Enter another character and two integers;
Simulate eof to quit.
bb
Enter another character and two integers;
Simulate eof to quit.
^Z
```

```
Enter another character and two integers;
Simulate eof to quit.
^Z
```

The program starts off fine. We enter a 2 3, and it prints two rows of three a characters, as expected. Then we enter b 1 2, and it prints one row with two b characters. In between it prints eight blank lines! What's wrong? It's that newline character again, this time the one immediately following the 3 on the first input line. Because getchar() doesn't skip over newline characters, this newline character is read by getchar() during the next cycle of the loop, becoming the character to be displayed.

Then scanf() has a turn at exposing our poor programming. Be cause getchar() reads the newline, the next input is the b character, so the scanf() function attempts to read it as an integer and fails. rows retains its previous value of 2. (At least, that is how our system behaves on a failed match; ANSI C doesn't require any particular behavior in that instance.) Then scanf() tries to read the cols value. Input is still stuck on the b, so that read fails, too, and cols remains at 3. The net result is that the program tells display() to print two rows of three newline characters. Each newline character generates a new line, giving a total of eight blank lines. Then the next loop cycle begins, and getchar() finally gets to read the b. This clears the way for scanf() to read the next two numbers. Similarly, the newline following this line forces us to enter Control-Z twice to end the program. (We're assuming the program is run on a DOS system.)

To clear up this problem, the program has to skip over any newlines or spaces between the last number typed for one cycle of input and the character typed at the beginning of the next line. Also, it would be nice if the program could be terminated at the scanf() stage in addition to the getchar() test. The next version, shown in Listing 8.6, accomplishes this.

Listing 8.6. showr2.c.

```
/* showchar2.c -- prints characters in rows and columns */
#include <stdio.h>
void display(char c, int lines, int width);
int main(void)
{
    int ch;          /* character to be printed   */
    int rows, cols;  /* number of rows and columns */

    printf("Enter a character and two integers:\n");
    while ((ch = getchar()) != EOF)
    {
        if (ch != '\n' && ch != ' ' && ch != '\t')
        {
            if (scanf("%d %d",&rows, &cols) != 2)
                break;
            display(ch, rows, cols);
```

continues

Listing 8.6. continued

```
printf("Enter another character and two integers;\n");
        printf("Simulate eof to quit.\n");
    }
  }
  return 0;
}

void display(char c, int lines, int width)
{
    int row, col;

    for (row = 1; row <= lines; row++)
    {
        for (col = 1; col <= width; col++)
            putchar(c);
        putchar('\n');   /* end line and start a new one */
    }
}
```

The if statement causes the program to skip over the scanf() and display() statements if ch is whitespace. This means we can enter data fairly freely

```
Enter a character and two integers:
a 2 3
aaa
aaa
Enter another character and two integers;
Simulate eof to quit.
b 1 2 c 3 5
bb
Enter another character and two integers;
Simulate eof to quit.
ccccc
ccccc
ccccc
Enter another character and two integers;
Simulate eof to quit.
[Control-Z]
```

By using an if statement with a break, we terminate the program if the return value of scanf() is not 2. This occurs if one or both input values are not integers or if end-of-file is encountered.

By using the if statement to skip spaces as well as newlines, the program can handle the second input line. If we omit the space skipping, the input line would have to look like this:

```
b 1 2c 3 5
```

Otherwise, a space between the 2 and c would be read into ch, and scanf() would try to read c as an integer.

Character Sketches

Now let's look at something a little more decorative. Our plan is to create a program that enables you to draw rough, filled-in figures using characters. Each line of output consists of an unbroken row of characters. You choose the character and the starting and stopping positions for printing the character in the row. The program, shown in Listing 8.7, keeps reading your choices until it finds EOF. This program illustrates several programming techniques, which, of course, we'll discuss soon.

Listing 8.7. sketcher.c.

```
/* sketcher.c  -- this program makes solid figures */
#include <stdio.h>
#define TRUE 1
#define FALSE 0
#define MAXLENGTH 80
int badlimits(int begin, int end, int limit);
void display(char c, int first, int last);
int main(void)
{
    int ch;                 /* character to be printed    */
    int start, stop;        /* starting and stopping points */
    int badlimits();        /* returns TRUE for bad limits  */

    while ((ch = getchar()) != EOF) /* read in character    */
    {
        if (ch == '\n' || ch == ' ' || ch == '\t')
            continue;       /* skip newlines, spaces */
        if (scanf("%d %d", &start, &stop) != 2)  /* read limits */
            break;
        if (badlimits(start, stop, MAXLENGTH) == TRUE)
            printf("Inappropriate limits were entered.\n");
        else
            display(ch, start, stop);
    }
    return 0;
}

int badlimits(int begin, int end, int limit)
{
    if (begin > end || begin < 1 || end > limit)
        return TRUE;
    else
```

continues

Listing 8.7. continued

```
return FALSE;
}

void display(char c, int first, int last)
{
   int column;

   for (column = 1; column < first; column++)
      putchar(' ');     /* print blanks to starting point */
   for (column = first; column <= last; column++)
      putchar(c);        /* print char to stopping point   */
   putchar('\n');        /* end line and start a new one    */
}
```

The general structure is similar to that of Listing 8.6. The three main differences are these:

- We use a `continue` statement to skip to the end of the loop if ch is whitespace, rather than isolating the relevant code with an `if` statement.

- The `display()` function has been rewritten to display the character in a different manner. Here `first` represents the first column and `last` represents the last column for displaying the character.

- We've added a `badlimits()` function to screen out bad input values.

Suppose we call the executable program `sketcher`. To run the program, we type its name. Then we enter a character and two numbers. The program responds, we enter another set of data, and the program responds again until we provide an `EOF` signal. On a UNIX system using the `%` prompt, an exchange could look like this:

```
% sketcher
B 10 20
         BBBBBBBBBBB
Y 12 18
           YYYYYYY
[Control-D]
%
```

The program printed the character B in columns 10 to 20, and it printed Y in columns 12 to 18. Unfortunately, when we use the program interactively, our commands are interspersed with the output. A more satisfactory way to use this program is to create a file containing suitable data and then use redirection to feed the file to the program. Suppose, for example, the file `fig` contains the following data:

```
 _  30 50
 ¦  30 50
 ¦  30 50
```

```
┊  30  50
┊  30  50
┊  30  50
=  20  60
:  31  49
:  30  49
:  29  49
:  27  49
:  25  49
:  30  49
:  30  49
/  30  49
:  35  48
:  35  48
```

The command `sketcher < fig` produces the output shown in Figure 8.3.

> **Note:** Printers and screens have different values for the vertical-to-horizontal ratio for characters. This difference causes figures of this sort to look more compressed vertically when printed than when displayed on a screen.

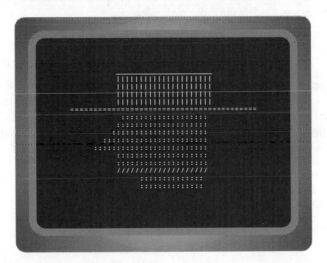

Figure 8.3. *Output of character sketch program.*

Analyzing the Program

The `sketcher.c` program is short, but it is more involved than the examples we have given before. Let's look at some of its elements.

Line Length

We limited the program to print no farther than the 80th column, because 80 characters is the standard width of many video monitors and of regular-width paper. However, you can redefine the value of MAXLENGTH if you wish to use the program with a device having a different output width.

Program Structure

We've followed a modular approach, using separate functions (modules) to verify input and to manage the display. The larger a program is, the more vital it is to use modular programming.

The main() function acquires the data

```
while ((ch = getchar()) != EOF)
{
    if (ch == '\n' || ch == ' ' || ch == '\t')
        continue;                   /* skip newlines, spaces */
    if (scanf("%d %d", &start, &stop) != 2)  /* read limits */
        break;
        }
```

With Listing 8.6, we discussed the rationale for skipping whitespace. Next the program checks to see whether the input makes sense.

```
if (badlimits(start, stop, MAXLENGTH) == TRUE)
    printf("Inappropriate limits were entered.\n");
else
```

The purpose of the if else statement is to let the program skirt any values of start and stop that would lead to trouble. We will discuss the details of the badlimits() function later. The important point here is that it returns a value of TRUE if the data fails to pass the testing procedure. In that case, the computer prints a message and skips over the else part, which is the display output.

The display() function uses one for loop to print spaces up to where the character is first to appear. The second for loop then prints the character from the start column to the end column. Finally, it prints a newline to end the line.

```
void display(char c, int first, int last)
{
    int column;

    for (column = 1; column < first; column++)
        putchar(' ');    /* print blanks to starting point */
    for (column = first; column <= last; column++)
        putchar(c);      /* print char to stopping point   */
    putchar('\n');       /* end line and start a new one   */
}
```

Error-Checking

Getting the user to provide data in a form that the computer can use properly is a pervasive problem. One technique is to use *error-checking*. In this technique the computer checks the data to see if it is okay before using it. We have included a beginning effort at error-checking in this program with the `badlimits()` function:

```
int badlimits(int begin, int end, int limit)
{
    if (begin > end ¦¦ begin < 1 ¦¦ end > limit)
        return TRUE;
    else
        return FALSE;
}
```

What is the `badlimits()` function protecting against? First, there's no sense having the starting position come after the final position. Terminals normally print from left to right, not vice versa, so the expression `begin > end` checks for that possible error. Second, the first column on a screen is column 1. We can't write to the left of the left margin. The `begin < 1` expression guards against making an error there. Finally, the expression `end > limit` checks to see that we don't try to print past the right margin.

Are there any other erroneous values we could give to `begin` and `end`? Well, we could try to make `begin` greater than `limit`. Would that pass our test? No. It's true we don't check for this error directly. However, suppose `begin` is greater than `limit`. Then, either `end` is also greater than `limit`—in which case that error is caught—or else `end` isn't greater than `limit`. If `end` is less than `limit`, it also must be less than `begin`. Thus, this case gets caught by the first test. Another possible error is that `end` is less than 1. We leave it to you to make sure that this error doesn't sneak through, either.

We kept the test pretty simple. If you design a program for serious use, you should put more effort than we did into this part of the program. For instance, you should put in error messages to identify which values are wrong and why, perhaps injecting your personality into the messages. Here are some possibilities:

```
Your value of 897654 for stop exceeds the screen width.
Oh my! Your START is bigger than your STOP. Please try again.
THE START VALUE SHOULD BE BIGGER THAN 0, HONORED USER.
```

The personality you inject, of course, is up to you.

Another input problem occurs if letters show up when `scanf()` expects numbers. As the program is set up, letters cause the program to terminate, which is preferable to it getting stuck or misinterpreting input. It's also possible to have `scanf()` skip over data it can't read; we'll show the technique later in the book.

Chapter Summary

Many programs use `getchar()` to read input character by character. Typically, systems use *line-buffered input,* meaning that input is transmitted to the program when you press

Enter. Pressing Enter also transmits a newline character that may require programming attention. ANSI C requires buffered input as the standard.

C features a family of functions, called the *standard I/O package,* that treats different file forms on different systems in a uniform manner. The `getchar()` and `scanf()` functions belong to this family. Both functions return the value EOF (defined in the `stdio.h` header) when they detect the end of a file. UNIX systems enable you to simulate the end-of-file condition from the keyboard by typing Control-D at the beginning of a line; DOS systems use Control-Z for the same purpose.

Many operating systems, including UNIX and DOS, feature *redirection,* which enables you to use files instead of the keyboard and screen for input and output. Programs that read input up to EOF can then be used either with keyboard input and simulated end-of-file signals or with redirected files.

Interspersing calls to `getchar()` with calls to `scanf()` can cause problems when `scanf()` leaves a newline character in the input just before a call to `getchar()`. By being aware of this problem, however, you can program around it.

When you are writing a program, plan the user interface thoughtfully. Try to anticipate the sort of errors that users are likely to make and then design your program to handle them.

Review Questions

1. `putchar(getchar())` is a valid expression; what does it do? Is `getchar(putchar())` also valid?

2. Suppose you have a program count that counts the characters in its input. Devise a command that counts the number of characters in the file `essay` and stores the result in a file named `essayct`.

3. What is EOF?

4. What is the output of each of the following fragments for the indicated input (assume that `ch` is type `int` and that the input is buffered):

   a. The input is as follows:

   ```
   If you quit, I will.[enter]
   ```

   The fragment is as follows:

   ```
   while ((ch = getchar()) != 'i')
       putchar(ch);
   ```

b. The input is as follows:

```
Harhar[enter]
```

The fragment is as follows:

```
while ((ch = getchar()) != '\n')
{
    putchar(ch++);
    putchar(++ch);
}
```

5. How does C deal with the fact that different computers systems have different file and newline conventions?

Programming Exercises

1. Devise a program that counts the number of characters in its input up to the end of file.

2. Modify the program in Exercise 1 so that it beeps each time that it counts a character. Insert a short delay loop (a loop that does nothing but increment a counter) to separate one beep from the next. Do not use it on long files.

3. Write a program that reads input until encountering EOF. Have the program print each input character and its ASCII decimal value. Note that characters preceding the space character in the ASCII sequence are nonprinting characters. Treat them specially. If the nonprinting character is a newline or tab, print \n or \t, respectively. Otherwise, use control-character notation. For instance, ASCII 1 is Control-A, which can be displayed as ^A. Note that the ASCII value for A is the value for Control-A plus 64. A similar relation holds for the other nonprinting characters. Print ten pairs per line, except start a fresh line each time that a newline character is encountered.

4. Write a program that reads input until encountering EOF. Have it report the number of uppercase letters and the number of lowercase letters in the input. Assume that the numeric values for the lowercase letters are sequential, and assume the same for uppercase.

5. Write a program that reads input until encountering EOF. Have it report the average number of letters per word. Don't count whitespace as being letters in a word. Actually, punctuation shouldn't be counted either, but don't worry about that now.

6. Modify the guessing program of Listing 8.4 so that it uses a more intelligent guessing strategy. For example, have the program initially guess 50, and have it ask

the user whether the guess is high, low, or correct. If, say, the guess is low, have the next guess be halfway between 50 and 100, that is, 75. If that guess is high, let the next guess be halfway between 75 and 50, and so on. Using this *binary search* strategy, the program quickly zeros in on the correct answer, at least if the user does not cheat.

Functions

Keyword
    return
Operators
    * (unary) & (unary)

In this chapter you learn about functions: how to define them, how to use arguments and return values, and how to use pointer variables as function arguments. You find out about function types, ANSI C prototypes, and recursion.

How do you organize a program? C's design philosophy is to use functions as building blocks. You've already relied on the standard C library for functions such as printf(), scanf(), getchar(), putchar(), and strlen(). Now you're ready for a more active role: creating your own functions. You've previewed several aspects of that process in earlier chapters, and this chapter consolidates your earlier information and expands on it.

Review

First, what is a function? A *function* is a self-contained unit of program code designed to accomplish a particular task. A function in C plays the same role that functions, subroutines, and procedures play in other languages, although the details may differ. Some functions cause action to take place. For example, `printf()` causes data to be printed on your screen. Some functions find a value for a program to use. For instance, `strlen()` tells a program how long a certain string is. In general, a function can both produce actions and provide values.

Why should you use functions? For one, they save you from repetitious programming. If you have to do a certain task several times in a program, you need to write an appropriate function only once. The program can then use that function wherever needed, or you can use the same function in different programs, just as you have used `putchar()` in many programs. Two, even if you do a task just once in just one program, using a function is worthwhile because functions make a program more modular, hence easier to read and easier to change or fix. Suppose, for example, you want to write a program that does the following:

```
Read in a list of numbers
Sort the numbers
Find their average
Print a bar graph
```

You could use this program

```c
#include <stdio.h>
#define SIZE 50
int main(void)
{
  float list[SIZE];

  readlist(list, SIZE);
  sort(list, SIZE);
  average(list, SIZE);
  bargraph(list, SIZE);
  return 0;
}
```

Of course, you would also have to write the four functions `readlist()`, `sort()`, `average()`, and `bargraph()`...mere details. Descriptive function names make it quite clear what the program does and how it is organized. You then can work with each function separately until it does its job right, and if you make the functions general enough, you can use them in other programs.

Many programmers like to think of a function as a "black box" defined in terms of the information that goes in (its input) and the value or action that it produces (its output). What goes on inside the black box is not our concern, unless we are the ones who have to write the function. For example, when you use `printf()`, you know that you have to give it a control string and, perhaps, some arguments. You also know what output `printf()` should produce. You never had to think about the programming that went into creating `printf()`. Thinking of functions in this manner helps you concentrate on the overall design of the program rather than on the details. Think carefully about what the function should do and how it relates to the program as a whole before worrying about writing the code.

What do you need to know about functions? You need to know how to define them properly, how to call them up for use, and how to set up communication between functions. To refresh your memory on these points, we will begin with a very simple example and then bring in more features until we have the full story.

Creating and Using a Simple Function

Our modest first goal is to create a function that types 65 asterisks in a row. To give our function a context, we will include it in a program that prints a simple letterhead. Listing 9.1 presents the complete program. It consists of the functions `main()` and `starbar()`.

Listing 9.1. `lethead1.c.`

```
/* lethead1.c */
#include <stdio.h>
#define NAME "MEGATHINK, INC."
#define ADDRESS "10 Megabuck Plaza"
#define PLACE "Megapolis, CA 94904"
#define LIMIT 65
void starbar(void);  /* prototype the function */

int main(void)
{
    starbar();
    printf("%s\n", NAME);
    printf("%s\n", ADDRESS);
    printf("%s\n", PLACE);
    starbar();              /* use the function */
    return 0;
}

void starbar(void)         /* define the function */
{
    int count;

    for (count = 1; count <= LIMIT; count++)
        putchar('*');
    putchar('\n');
}
```

Here is the output:

```
*******************************************************************
MEGATHINK, INC.
10 Megabuck Plaza
Megapolis, CA 94904
*******************************************************************
```

There are several major points to note about this program.

- We use the starbar identifier in three separate contexts: a function prototype that tells the compiler what sort of function starbar() is, a function call that causes the function to be executed, and a function definition that specifies exactly what the function does.

- Like variables, functions have types. Any program that uses a function should declare the type for that function before it is used. Therefore, this ANSI C prototype precedes the main() function definition:

```
void starbar(void);
```

The parentheses indicate that starbar is a function name. The first void is a function type; the void type indicates that the function does not return a value. The second void (the one in the parentheses) indicates that the function takes no arguments. The semicolon indicates that we are declaring the function, not defining it. That is, this line announces that the program uses a type void function called starbar() and that the compiler should expect to find the definition for this function elsewhere. For compilers that don't recognize ANSI C prototyping, just declare the type

```
void starbar();
```

Note that some very old compilers don't recognize the void type. In that case, use type int for functions that don't have return values.

- We placed the prototype before main(); instead, it can go inside main(), along with the variable declarations. Either way is fine.

- We called (invoked, summoned) the function starbar() from main() by using its name followed by parentheses and a semicolon, creating a statement

```
starbar();
```

This is one form for calling up a function, but it isn't the only one. Whenever the computer reaches a starbar(); statement, it looks for the starbar() function and follows the instructions there. When finished with the code within starbar(), the computer returns to the next line of the *calling function* — main(), in this case. See Figure 9.1.

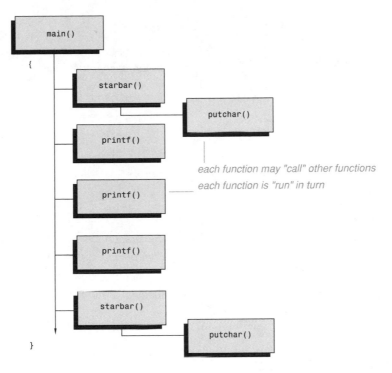

Figure 9.1. *Control flow for* `lethead1.c` *(Listing 9.1).*

- We followed the same form in defining `starbar()` as we did in defining `main()`. We started with the type, name, and parentheses. Then we supplied the opening brace, a declaration of variables used, the defining statements of the function, and then the closing brace. See Figure 9.2. Note that this instance of `starbar()` is not followed by a semicolon. The lack of a semicolon tells the compiler that we are *defining* `starbar()` rather than calling or prototyping it.

- We included `starbar()` and `main()` in the same file. We could have used two separate files. The single-file form is slightly easier to compile. Two separate files make it simpler to use the same function in different programs. If we do place the function in a separate file, then we would also place the necessary `#define` and `#include` directives in that file. We will discuss using two or more files later. For now, we will keep all our functions together. The closing brace of `main()` tells the compiler where that function ends, and the following `starbar()` header tells the compiler that `starbar()` is a function.

- The variable `count` in `starbar()` is a *local* variable. This means it is known only to `starbar()`. You can use the name `count` in other functions, including `main()`, and there will be no conflict. You simply wind up with separate, *independent* variables having the same name.

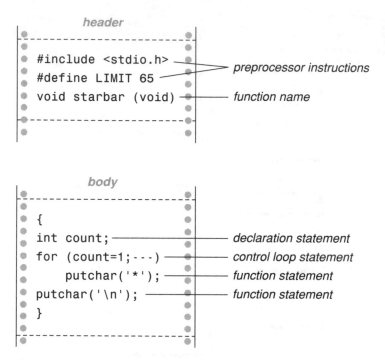

Figure 9.2. *Structure of a simple function.*

If you think of starbar() as a black box, its action is printing a line of stars. It doesn't have any input because it doesn't need to use any information from the calling function. It doesn't provide (return) any information to main(), so starbar() doesn't have a return value. In short, starbar() doesn't require any communication with the calling function.

Let's create a case where communication *is* needed.

Function Arguments

The letterhead shown earlier would look a little nicer if the text were centered. We can center text by printing the correct number of leading spaces before printing the text. This is similar to the starbar() function, which printed a certain number of asterisks, but now we want to print a certain number of spaces. Rather than writing separate functions for each task, we'll follow the C philosophy and write a single, more general function that does both. We'll call the new function n_chars(). Instead of having the display character and number of repetitions built into the function, we will use function arguments to convey those values.

Let's get more specific. Our bar of stars is 65 characters wide, and the function call n_chars('*', 65) should print that. What about spaces? MEGATHINK, INC. is 15 spaces wide. Thus, in our first version, there were 50 spaces following the heading. To center it, we should lead off with 25 spaces, which will result in 25 spaces on either side of the phrase. Therefore, we could use the call n_chars(' ', 25).

Aside from using arguments, the n_char() function will be quite similar to starbar(). One difference is that it won't add a newline the way starbar() does because we may want to print other text on the same line. Listing 9.2 shows the revised program. To emphasize how arguments work, the program uses a variety of argument forms.

Listing 9.2. `lethead2.c.`

```
/* lethead2.c */
#include <stdio.h>
#include <string.h>          /* for strlen() prototype       */
#define NAME "MEGATHINK, INC."
#define ADDRESS "10 Megabuck Plaza"
#define PLACE "Megapolis, CA 94904"
#define LIMIT 65
#define SPACE ' '
void n_char(char ch, int num);

int main(void)
{
  int spaces;

  n_char('*', LIMIT);         /* using constants as arguments */
  putchar('\n');
  n_char(SPACE, 25);          /* using constants as arguments */
  printf("%s\n", NAME);
  spaces = (65 - strlen(ADDRESS)) / 2;
                              /* we let the program calculate */
                              /* how many spaces to skip      */
  n_char(SPACE, spaces);      /* use a variable as argument   */
  printf("%s\n", ADDRESS);
  n_char(SPACE, (65 - strlen(PLACE)) / 2);
                              /* an expression as argument    */
  printf("%s\n", PLACE);
  n_char('*', LIMIT);
  putchar('\n');
  return 0;
}

/* here is n_char() */
void n_char(char ch, int num)
{
  int count;

  for (count = 1; count <= num; count++)
  putchar(ch);
}
```

Here is the result of running the program:

```
*********************************************************************
                        MEGATHINK, INC.
                        10 Megabuck Plaza
                        Megapolis, CA 94904
*********************************************************************
```

Now let's review how to set up a function that takes arguments. After that, we'll look at how the function is used.

Defining a Function with an Argument: Formal Arguments

Our function definition begins with this ANSI C declaration:

```
void n_char(char ch, int num)
```

This line informs the compiler that n_char() uses two arguments called ch and num, that ch is type char, and that num is type int. Both the ch and num variables are called *formal arguments*. Like variables defined inside the function, formal arguments are local variables, private to the function. This means that you don't have to worry about duplicating variable names used in other functions.

Note that the ANSI C form requires that each variable be preceded by its type. That is, unlike the case with regular declarations, you can't use a list of variables of the same type.

```
void dibs(int x, y, z)          /* invalid function header */
void dubs(int x, int y, int z)  /* valid function header   */
```

ANSI C also recognizes the pre-ANSI form

```
void n_char(ch, num)
char ch;
int num;
```

Here, the parentheses contain the list of argument names, but the types are declared afterwards. Note that the arguments are declared before the brace that marks the start of the function's body, but ordinary local variables are declared after the brace. This form does enable you to use comma-separated lists of variable names if the variables are of the same type.

```
void dibs(x, y, z)
int x, y, z;            /* valid */
```

Although the n_char() function accepts values from main(), it doesn't return a value. Thus, n_char() is type void.

Now let's see how this function is used.

Prototyping a Function with Arguments

We used an ANSI prototype to declare the function before it is used.

```
void n_char(char ch, int num);
```

When a function takes arguments, the prototype indicates their number and type by using a comma-separated list of the types. If you like, you can omit variable names in the prototype.

```
void n_char(char, int);
```

Using variable names in a prototype doesn't actually create variables. It merely clarifies the fact that char means a char variable, and so on.

Again, ANSI C also recognizes the older form of declaring a function, which is without an argument list.

```
void n_char();
```

Later, we'll look at the advantages of using the prototype format.

Calling a Function with an Argument: Actual Arguments

We give ch and num values by using *actual arguments* in the function call. Consider our first use of n_char():

```
n_char(SPACE, 25);
```

The actual arguments are the space character and 25. These *values* are assigned to the corresponding formal arguments in n_char()—the variables ch and num. In short, the formal argument is a variable in the *called* function, and the actual argument is the particular value assigned to the formal variable by the calling function. As we showed in the example, the actual argument can be a constant, a variable, or an even more elaborate expression. Regardless of which it is, the actual argument is evaluated, and its value is sent to the function. For instance, consider the final use of n_char():

```
n_char(SPACE, (65 - strlen(PLACE)) / 2);
```

The long expression forming the second actual argument is evaluated to 23. Then the value 23 is assigned to the variable num. The function neither knows nor cares whether that number came from a constant, a variable, or a more general expression. Again, the actual argument is a specific value that is assigned to the variable known as the formal argument (see Figure 9.3).

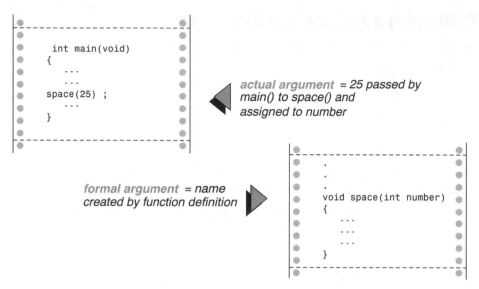

```
    int main(void)
    {
        ...
        ...
    space(25) ;
        ...
    }
```

actual argument = 25 passed by
main() to space() and
assigned to number

formal argument = name
created by function definition

```
        .
        .
        .
    void space(int number)
    {
        ...
        ...
        ...
    }
```

Figure 9.3. *Formal arguments and actual arguments.*

The Black Box Viewpoint

Taking a black box viewpoint of n_char(), the input is the character to be displayed and the number of spaces to be skipped. The resulting action is printing the character the specified number of times. The input is communicated to the function via arguments. This information is enough to tell you how to use the function in main(). Also, it serves as a design specification for writing the function.

The fact that ch, num, and count are local variables private to the n_char() function is an essential aspect of the black box approach. If we were to use variables with the same names in main(), they would be separate, independent variables. That is, if main() had a count variable, changing its value wouldn't change the value of count in n_char(), and vice versa. What goes on inside the black box is hidden from the calling function.

Returning a Value from a Function with *return*

You have seen how to communicate information from the calling function to the called function. To send information in the other direction, you use the function return value. To refresh your memory on how that works, we'll construct a function that returns the smaller of its two arguments. We'll call the function imin() because it's designed to handle int values. Also, we will create a simple main() whose sole purpose is to check to see if imin() works. A program designed to test functions this way sometimes is called a *driver*. The driver takes a function for a spin. If the function pans out, then it can be installed in a more noteworthy program. Listing 9.3 shows our driver and our minimum value function.

Listing 9.3. `lesser.c.`

```c
/* lesser.c -- finds the lesser of two evils */
#include <stdio.h>
int imin(int, int);

int main(void)
{
  int evil1, evil2;

  while (scanf("%d %d", &evil1, &evil2) == 2)
      printf("The lesser of %d and %d is %d.\n",
             evil1, evil2, imin(evil1,evil2));
  return 0;
}

int imin(int n,int m)
{
  int min;

  if (n < m)
      min = n;
  else
      min = m;
  return min;
}
```

Here is a sample run:

```
88 92
The lesser of 88 and 92 is 88.
q
```

The keyword `return` causes the value of the following expression to be the return value of the function. In this case, the function returns the value that was assigned to `min`. Because `min` is type `int`, so is the `imin()` function.

The variable `min` is private to `imin()`, but the value of `min` is communicated back to the calling function with `return`. The effect of a statement such as the next one is to assign the value of `min` to `lesser`:

```c
lesser = imin(n,m);
```

Could we say the following instead?

```c
imin(n,m);
lesser = min;
```

No, for the calling function doesn't even know that `min` exists. Remember that `imin()`'s variables are local to `imin()`. The function call `imin(evil1,evil2)` copies the values of one set of variables to another set.

Not only can the returned value be assigned to a variable, it can be used as part of an expression. You can do this, for example

```
answer = 2 * imin(z, zstar) + 25;
printf("%d\n", imin(-32 + answer, LIMIT));
```

The return value can be supplied by any expression, not just a variable. For example, we can shorten our program to the following:

```
/* minimum value function, second version */
imin(int n,int m)
{
    return (n < m) ? n : m;
}
```

The conditional expression is evaluated to either n or m, whichever is smaller, and that value is returned to the calling function. If you prefer for clarity or style to enclose the return value in parentheses, you may, though parentheses are not required.

Using return has one other effect. It terminates the function and returns control to the next statement in the calling function. This occurs even if the return statement is not the last in the function. Thus, we could have written imin() this way:

```
/* minimum value function, third version */
imin(int n,int m)
{
    if (n < m)
        return (n);
    else
        return (m);
}
```

Many, but not all, C practitioners deem it better to use return just once and at the end of a function in order to make it easier for someone to follow the control flow through the function. However, it's no great sin to use multiple returns in a function as short as this one. Anyway, to the user, all three versions are the same, because all take the same input and produce the same output. Just the innards are different. Even this version works the same:

```
/* minimum value function, fourth version */
imin(n, m)
int n, m;    /* pre-ANSI form for declaring arguments */
{
    if (n < m)
        return(n);
    else
        return(m);
    printf("Professor Fleppard is a fopdoodle.\n")
}
```

The return statements prevent the printf() statement from ever being reached. Professor Fleppard can use the compiled version of this function in his own programs and never learn the true feelings of his student programmer.

You can use a statement like this, too:

```
return;
```

It causes the function to terminate and return control to the calling function. Because no expression follows `return`, no value is returned, and this form should be used only in a type `void` function.

Function Types

Functions should be declared by type. A function with a return value should be declared the same type as the return value. Functions with no return value should be declared as type `void`. If no type is given for a function, C assumes that the function is type `int`. This convention stems from the early days of C when most functions were type `int` anyway.

The type declaration is part of the function definition. Keep in mind that it refers to the return value, not to the function arguments. For instance, the following function heading indicates that we are defining a function that takes two type `int` arguments but that returns a type `double` value:

```
double klink(int a, int b)
```

To use a function correctly, a program needs to know the function type before the function is used for the first time. One way to accomplish this is to place the complete function definition ahead of its first use. However, this may make the program harder to read. Also, the functions may be part of the C library or in some other file. Thus, we generally inform the compiler about functions by declaring them in advance. For example, the `main()` function in Listing 9.3 contains these lines:

```
#include <stdio.h>
int imin(int, int);
int main(void)
{
  int evil1, evil2, lesser;
```

The second line establishes that `imin` is the name of a function that returns a type `int` value. Now the compiler will know how to treat `imin()` when it appears later in the program.

We've placed the advance function declarations outside the function using them. They also can be placed inside the function. For example, we can rewrite the beginning of `lesser.c` as follows:

```
#include <stdio.h>
int main(void)
{
  int imin(int, int);      /* imin() declaration */
  int evil1, evil2, lesser;
```

In either case, your chief concern should be that the function declaration appear *before* the function is used.

In the ANSI C standard library, functions are grouped into families, each having its own *header file*. These header files contain, among other things, the declarations for the functions in the family. For instance, the `stdio.h` header contains function declarations for the standard I/O library functions, such as `printf()` and `scanf()`. The `math.h` header contains function declarations for a variety of mathematical functions. For example, it will contain

```
double sqrt(double);
```

(or a pre-ANSI equivalent) to tell the compiler that the `sqrt()` function returns a type `double` value. Don't confuse these declarations with definitions. A *function declaration* informs the compiler which type the function is, but the *function definition* supplies the actual code. Including the `math.h` header file tells the compiler that `sqrt()` returns type `double`, but the code for `sqrt()` resides in a separate file of library functions.

ANSI C Function Prototyping

The traditional, pre-ANSI C scheme for declaring functions was deficient in that it declared a function's return type but not its arguments. Let's look at the kinds of problems that arise when the old form of function declarations is used.

The following pre-ANSI declaration informs the compiler that `imin()` returns a type `int` value:

```
int imin();
```

However, it says nothing about the number or type of `imin()`'s arguments. Thus, if you use `imin()` with the wrong number or type of arguments, the compiler doesn't catch the error.

The Problem

Let's look at some examples involving `imax()`, a close relation to `imin()`. Listing 9.4 shows a program that declares `imax()` the old-fashioned way and then uses `imax()` incorrectly.

Listing 9.4. `misuse.c`

```
/* misuse.c -- uses a function incorrectly */
#include <stdio.h>
int imax();      /* old-style declaration */
int main(void)
{
  printf("The maximum of %d and %d is %d.\n",
      3, 5, imax(3));
  printf("The maximum of %d and %d is %d.\n",
      3, 5, imax(3.0, 5.0));
  return 0;
```

```
}

int imax(n, m)
int n, m;
{
  int max;

  if (n > m)
        max = n;
  else
        max = m;
  return max;
}
```

The first call to `printf()` omits an argument to `imax()`, and the second call uses floating-point arguments instead of integers. Despite these errors, the program compiles and runs.

Here's the output using Microsoft's QuickC compiler:

```
The maximum of 3 and 5 is 130.
The maximum of 3 and 5 is 0.
```

With Borland C, we got values of 3 and 0. The two compilers work fine; they merely are following the older C standards.

What's happening? The mechanics may differ among systems, but here's what goes on with a PC or VAX. The calling function places its arguments in a temporary storage area called the *stack*, and the called function reads those arguments off the stack. These two processes are *not* coordinated with one another. The calling function decides which type to pass based on the actual arguments in the call, and the called function reads values based on the types of its formal arguments. Thus, the call `imax(3)` places *one* integer on the stack. When the `imax()` function starts up, it reads *two* integers off the stack. Only one was actually placed on the stack, so the second value read is whatever value happened to be sitting in the stack at the time.

The second time we use `imax()` in the example, we pass it `float` values. This places two `double` values on the stack. (Recall that a `float` is promoted to `double` when passed as an argument.) On our system, that's two 8-byte values, so 16 bytes of data are placed on the stack. When `imax()` reads two `int`s from the stack, it reads the first 4 bytes on the stack. These happen to be all zeros, so `imax()` wound up with n and m set to 0.

The ANSI Solution

The ANSI Standard's solution to the problems of mismatched arguments is to permit the function declaration to declare the variable types, too. The result is a *function prototype*, a declaration that states the return type, the number of arguments, and the types of those arguments. To indicate that `imax()` requires two `int` arguments, we can declare it with either of the following prototypes:

291

```
int imax(int, int);
int imax(int a, int b);
```

The first form uses a comma-separated list of types. The second adds variable names to the types. Remember that the variable names are dummy names and don't have to match the names used in the function definition.

With this information at hand, the compiler can check to see if the function call matches the prototype. Are there the right number of arguments? Are they the correct type? If there is a type mismatch, the compiler does a type cast to convert the actual arguments to the same type as the formal arguments. For example, imax(3.0, 5.0) becomes imax ((int) 3.0, (int) 5.0). We've modified Listing 9.4 to use a function prototype. The result is shown in Listing 9.5.

Listing 9.5. proto1.c.

```
/* proto1.c -- uses a function prototype */
#include <stdio.h>
int imax(int, int);        /* prototype */
int main(void)
{
  printf("The maximum of %d and %d is %d.\n",
      3, 5, imax(3));
  printf("The maximum of %d and %d is %d.\n",
      3, 5, imax(3.0, 5.0));
  return 0;
}

int imax(int n, int m)
{
  int max;

  if (n > m)
      max = n;
  else
      max = m;
  return max;
}
```

When we tried to compile Listing 9.5, three compilers gave an error message stating that the call to imax() had too few parameters. A fourth compiler gave a warning to the same effect. (The difference between an error and a warning is that an error prevents compilation, and a warning permits compilation.) In all cases, the compiler now checked to see whether the correct number of arguments were present.

What about the type errors? To investigate those, we replaced imax(3) with imax(3, 5) and tried compilation again. This time there were no messages, and we ran the program. Here is the resulting output:

```
The maximum of 3 and 5 is 5.
The maximum of 3 and 5 is 5.
```

As promised, the 3.0 and 5.0 of the second call were converted to 3 and 5 so that the function could handle the input properly. One interesting point is that one compiler made this type cast without telling us. Most programmers object to this "silent" correction, but by resetting the warning level on that compiler, we got it to warn us about the type conversion. Many compilers enable you to select which warning you want made. However, the ANSI Standard does not require compilers to provide that feature.

No Arguments and Unspecified Arguments

Suppose you give a prototype like this:

```
void print_name();
```

An ANSI C compiler will assume that you have decided to forego function prototyping, and it will not check arguments. To indicate that a function really has no arguments, use the void keyword within the parentheses.

```
void print_name(void);
```

ANSI C interprets the preceding expression to mean that print_name() takes no arguments. It then will check to see that you, in fact, do not use arguments when calling this function.

A few functions, such as printf() and scanf(), take a variable number of arguments. In printf(), for instance, the first argument is a string, but the remaining arguments are fixed in neither type nor number. ANSI C allows partial prototyping for such cases. We could, for example, use this prototype for printf():

```
int printf(char *, ...);
```

This prototype says that the first argument is a string (Chapter 11, "Character Strings and String Functions," will elucidate that point) and that there may be further arguments of an unspecified nature.

Recursion

C permits a function to call itself. This process is termed *recursion*. Recursion is a sometimes tricky, sometimes convenient tool. It's tricky to get recursion to end, for a function that calls itself tends to do so indefinitely unless the programming includes a conditional test to terminate recursion.

Recursion Revealed

To see what's involved, let's look at an example. The function main() in Listing 9.6 calls the up_and_down() function. We'll term this the first level of recursion. Then up_and_down() calls itself; we'll term that the second level of recursion. The second level calls the third level, and so on. This example is set up to go four levels.

Listing 9.6. recur.c.

```
/* recur.c -- recursion illustration */
#include <stdio.h>
void up_and_down(int);
int main(void)
{
  up_and_down(1);
  return 0;
}

void up_and_down(int n)
{
  printf("Level %d\n", n);     /* print #1 */
  if (n < 4)
      up_and_down(n+1);
  printf("LEVEL %d\n", n);     /* print #2 */
}
```

The output looks like this:

```
Level 1
Level 2
Level 3
Level 4
LEVEL 4
LEVEL 3
LEVEL 2
LEVEL 1
```

Let's trace through the program to see how recursion works. First, main() calls up_and_down() with an argument of 1. As a result, the formal argument n in up_and_down() has the value 1, so print statement #1 prints Level 1. Then, because n is less than 4, up_and_down() (Level 1) calls up_and_down() (Level 2) with an argument of n + 1, or 2. This causes n in the Level 2 call to be assigned the value 2, so print statement #1 prints Level 2. Similarly, the next two calls lead to the printing of Level 3 and Level 4.

Once Level 4 is reached, n is 4, so the if test fails. The up_and_down() function is not called again. Instead, the Level 4 call proceeds to print statement #2, which prints LEVEL 4, because n is 4. Then it reaches the return statement. At this point, the Level 4 call ends, and control passes back to the function that called it, the Level 3 call. The last statement executed in the Level 3 call was the call to Level 4 in the if statement.

Therefore, Level 3 resumes with the following statement, which is print statement #2. This causes LEVEL 3 to be printed. Then Level 3 ends, passing control to Level 2, which prints LEVEL 2, and so on.

Recursion Fundamentals

Recursion can be confusing at first, so we'll look at a few basic points that will help you understand the process.

First, each level of function call has its own variables. That is, the n of Level 1 is a different variable from the n of Level 2, so our program created four separate variables, each called n, but each having a distinct value. When the program finally returned to the first level call of up_and_down(), the original n still had the value 1 it started with. See Figure 9.4.

variables:	*n*	*n*	*n*	*n*
after level 1 call	1			
after level 2 call	1	2		
after level 3 call	1	2	3	
after level 4 call	1	2	3	4
after return from level 4	1	2	3	
after return from level 3	1	2		
after return from level 2	1			
after return from level 1				
	(all gone)			

Figure 9.4. *Recursion variables.*

Second, each function call is balanced with a return. When program flow reaches the return at the end of the last recursion level, control passes to the previous recursion level. The program does not jump all the way back to the original call in main(). Instead, the program must move back through each recursion level, returning from one level of up_and_down() to the level of up_and_down() that called it.

Third, statements in a recursive function that come before the recursive call are executed in the same order that the functions are called. For instance, in Listing 9.6 print statement #1 comes before the recursive call. It was executed four times in the order of the recursive calls: Level 1, Level 2, Level 3, and Level 4.

Fourth, statements in a recursive function that come after the recursive call are executed in the opposite order from which the functions are called. For example, print statement #2 comes after the recursive call, and it was executed in this order: Level 4, Level 3, Level 2, Level 1. This feature of recursion is useful for programming problems involving reversals of order. We'll see an example soon.

Finally, although each level of recursion has its own set of variables, the code itself is not duplicated. The code is a sequence of instructions, and a function call is a command to go to the beginning of that set of instructions. Thus, a recursive call returns the program to the beginning of that instruction set. Aside from the fact that recursive calls create new variables on each call, they are much like a loop. Indeed, sometimes recursion can be used instead of loops, and vice versa.

Tail Recursion

In the simplest form of recursion, the recursive call is at the end of the function, just before the `return` statement. It is called *tail recursion*, or *end recursion*, because the recursive call comes at the end. Tail recursion is the simplest form because it acts like a loop.

Let's look at both a loop version and a tail recursion version of a function to calculate factorials. The factorial of an integer is the product of the integers from 1 through that number. For example, 3 factorial (written 3!) is 1*2*3. The 0! is taken to be 1, and factorials are not defined for negative numbers. Listing 9.7 presents a function that uses a `for` loop to calculate factorials.

Listing 9.7. factor.c.

```
/* factor.c -- uses loops to calculate factorials */
#include <stdio.h>
long fact(int n);
int main(void)
{
  int num;

  while (scanf("%d", &num) == 1)
  {
      if (num < 0)
          printf("No negative numbers, please.\n");
      else if (num > 15)
          printf("Keep input under 16.\n");
      else
          printf("%d factorial = %ld\n", num, fact(num));
  }
  return 0;
}
long fact(int n)            /* loop finds factorial */
{
  long ans;

  for (ans = 1; n > 1; n--)
```

```
    ans *= n;
  return ans;
}
```

The test driver program limits input to the integers 0\15. It turns out that 15! is slightly over 2 billion, which makes 16! much larger than `long` on our system. To go beyond 15!, we would have to use a type `double` function.

The loop initializes `ans` to 1 and then multiplies it by the integers from n down to 2. Technically, we should multiply by 1, but that doesn't change the value. Here's a sample run:

```
3
3 factorial = 6
10
10 factorial = 3628800
q
```

Now let's try a recursive version. The key is that `n! = n x (n-1)!`. This follows because `(n-1)!` is the product of all the positive integers through n-1. Thus, multiplying by n gives the product through n. This suggests a recursive approach. If we call the function `rfact()`, then `rfact(n)` is `n * rfact(n-1)`. We can thus evaluate `rfact(n)` by having it call `rfact(n 1)`, as in Listing 9.8. Of course, we have to end the recursion at some point, and we can do this by setting the return value to 1 when n is 0.

Listing 9.8. `rfactor.c.`

```
/* rfactor.c -- uses recursion to calculate factorials */
#include <stdio.h>
long rfact(int n);
int main(void)
{
  int num;

  while (scanf("%d", &num) == 1)
  {
      if (num < 0)
          printf("No negative numbers, please.\n");
      else if (num > 15)
          printf("Keep input under 16.\n");
      else
          printf("%d factorial = %ld\n", num, rfact(num));
  }
  return 0;
}
long rfact(int n)      /* recursive function */
{
  long ans;
```

continues

Listing 9.8. continued

```
    if (n > 0)
        ans= n * rfact(n-1);
    else
        ans = 1;
    return ans;
}
```

The recursive version of Listing 9.8 produces the same output as the previous version. Note that although the recursive call to rfact() is not the last line in the function, it is the last statement executed when n > 0, so it is tail recursion.

Recursion and Reversal

Now let's look at a problem in which recursion's ability to reverse order is handy. The problem is this: write a function that prints the binary equivalent of an integer. Binary notation represents numbers in terms of powers of 2. Just as 234 in decimal means 2 X 102 + 3 X 101 + 4 X 100, so 101 in binary means 1 X 22 + 0 X 21 + 1 X 20. Binary numbers use only the digits 0 and 1.

We need a method. How can we, say, find the binary equivalent of 5? Well, odd numbers must have a binary representation ending in 1. Even numbers end in 0, so we can determine if the last digit is a 1 or a 0 by evaluating 5 % 2. If the result is 1, then 5 is odd, and the last digit is 1. In general, if n is a number, the final digit is n % 2, so the first digit we find is the last digit we want to print. This suggests using a recursive function in which n % 2 is calculated before the recursive call but in which it is printed after the recursive call. That way, the first value calculated is the last value printed.

To get the next digit, divide the original number by 2. This is the binary equivalent to moving the decimal point one place to the left so that we can examine the next binary digit. If this value is even, the next binary digit is 0. If it is odd, the binary digit is 1. For example, 5/2 is 2 (integer division), so the next digit is 0. This gives 01 so far. Now repeat the process. Divide 2 by 2 to get 1. Evaluate 1 % 2 to get 1, so the next digit is 1. This gives 101. When do we stop? We stop when the result of dividing by 2 is less than 2 because as long as it is 2 or greater, there is one more binary digit. Each division by 2 lops off one more binary digit until we reach the end. (If this seems confusing to you, try working through the decimal analogy. The remainder of 628 divided by 10 is 8, so 8 is the last digit. Integer division by 10 yields 62, and the remainder from dividing 62 by 10 is 2, so that's the next digit, and so on.) Listing 9.9 implements this approach.

Listing 9.9. `binary.c.`

```c
/* binary.c -- prints integer in binary form */
#include <stdio.h>
void to_binary(int n);
int main(void)
{
  int number;

  while (scanf("%d", &number) == 1)
  {
      to_binary(number);
      putchar('\n');
  }
  return 0;
}
void to_binary(int n)    /* recursive function */
{
  int r;

  r = n % 2;
  if (n >= 2)
      to_binary(n / 2);
  putchar('0' + r);
  return;
}
```

In Listing 9.9 the expression '0' + r evaluates to the character '0' if r is 0 and to the character '1' if r is 1. This assumes that the numeric code for the '1' character is one greater than the code for the '0' character. Both the ASCII and the EBCDIC codes satisfy that assumption.

Here's a sample run:

```
5
101
255
1111111
256
10000000
q
```

All C Functions Are Created Equal

Each C function in a program is on equal footing with the others. Each can call any other function or be called by any other function. This makes the C function somewhat different from Pascal and Modula-2 procedures because those procedures can be nested within other procedures. Procedures in one nest will be ignorant of procedures in another nest.

Isn't the function main() special? Yes, it is a little special in that when a program of several functions is put together, execution starts with the first statement in main(), but that is the limit of its preference. Even main() can be called by itself recursively or by other functions, although this is rarely done.

Compiling Programs with Two or More Functions

The simplest approach to using several functions is to place them in the same file. Then just compile that file as you would a single-function file. Other approaches are more system dependent, as the next few sections illustrate.

UNIX

Suppose that file1.c and file2.c are two files containing C functions. Then the following command will compile both files and produce an executable file called a.out:

```
cc file1.c file2.c
```

In addition, two object files called file1.o and file2.o are produced. If you later change file1.c but not file2.c, you can compile the first and combine it with the object code version of the second file using the command

```
cc file1.c file2.o
```

Microsoft C Versions 4.0–7.0 (Command-Line)

If you're using the compiler as a command-line compiler, you should use the CL command to compile the two files.

```
cl file1.c file2.c
```

Compiling produces two object code files (file1.obj and file2.obj) and an executable file named file1.exe. The base name of the first file in the list is used for the executable file. If you reedit just file2.c, you can recompile using this command:

```
cl file1.obj file2.c
```

Microsoft C 6.0–7.0 (PWB)

If you're using Programmer's WorkBench (Microsoft's IDE), choose New Project from the Project menu. This opens a New Project dialog box. In it, select Set Project Template. This opens a new dialog box. In it, select C under Runtime Support and DOS EXE under Templates, then select OK. This returns you to the New Project dialog box, where you should again select OK. The Edit Project dialog now appears. From the File List box, select the names of the source code files (but not the header files) that constitute the program, then select Save List. Then use the Run menu to compile and run the program.

QuickC

Use the Set Program List ... entry from the File menu (version 1.0) or from the Make menu (version 2.0) to create a .mak file indicating which files belong to the program. Use the Edit Program List ... entry to modify this list. QuickC will compile the files in the current program list.

Turbo C/Borland C

From the Project menu, select Open Project. Enter a name for the project file, for example, file1.prj. Select OK. An empty project window appears. From the Project menu, select Add Item. You then can type the names of the source code files or select them from a displayed list of files. Clicking the Add button transfers a filename to the Project window. Continue until you've added all the source code files (but not header files), and click Done when you're finished. Then select the Run or Compile menu to compile and run the program.

Think C

Think C requires you to use a project file even for programs with a single source code file. If you have more than one source code file, add them all to the project file.

Using Header Files

Often you will have used the C preprocessor to define constants used in a program. Such definitions hold only for the file containing the #define directives. Thus, if you place the functions of a program into separate files, you also have to make the #define directives available to each file. The most direct way is to retype the directives for each file, but this is time-consuming and increases the possibility for error. Also, it poses a maintenance problem: if you revise a #define value, you have to remember to do so for each file.

A better solution is to place the #define directives in a header file and then use the #include directive in each source code file. Let's examine a programming example. Suppose you manage a chain of four hotels. Each hotel charges a different room rate, but all the rooms in a given hotel go for the same rate. For people who book multiple nights, the second night goes for 95 percent of the first night, the third night goes for 95 percent of the second night, and so on. (Don't worry about the economics of such a policy.) You want a program that enables you to specify the hotel and the number of nights and gives you the total charge. You'd like the program to have a menu that enables you to continue entering data until you choose to quit.

Listings 9.10, 9.11, and 9.12 show what you might come up with. The first listing contains the main() function, which provides the overall organization for the program. The second listing contains the supporting functions, which we assume are kept in a separate file. Finally, Listing 9.12 shows a header file that contains the defined constants and function prototypes for all the source files of the program. Recall that in UNIX and

DOS environments, the double quotes in the directive #include "hotels.h" indicate that the include file is in the current working directory (typically the directory containing the source code).

Listing 9.10. hotel1.c.

```
/* hotel1.c -- room rate program, continued in Listing 9.11 */
#include <stdio.h>
#include "hotels.h" /* defines constants, declares functions */
int main(void)
{
   int nights;
   double hotel;
   int code;

   while ((code = menu()) != QUIT)
   {
      switch(code)
      {
      case 1 : hotel = HOTEL1;
               break;
      case 2 : hotel = HOTEL2;
               break;
      case 3 : hotel = HOTEL3;
               break;
      case 4 : hotel = HOTEL4;
               break;
      default: hotel = 0.0;
               printf("Oops!\n");
               break;
      }
      nights = getnights();
      showprice(hotel, nights);
   }
   return 0;
}
```

Listing 9.11. hotel2.c.

```
/* hotel2.c -- rest of hotel program */
#include <stdio.h>
#include "hotels.h"
int menu(void)
{
   int code, status;

   printf("\n%s%s\n", STARS, STARS);
   printf("Enter the number of the desired hotel:\n");
```

```
   printf("1) Fairfield Arms          2) Hotel Olympic\n");
   printf("3) Chertworthy Plaza       4) The Stockton\n");
   printf("5) quit\n");
   printf("%s%s\n", STARS, STARS);
   while ((status = scanf("%d", &code)) != 1  ¦¦
           (code < 1 ¦¦ code > 5))
   {
       if (status != 1)
           scanf("%*s");
       printf("Enter an integer from 1 to 5, please.\n");
   }
   return code;
}
int getnights(void)
{
   int nights;

   printf("How many nights are needed? ");
   while (scanf("%d", &nights) != 1)
   {
       scanf("%*s");
       printf("Please enter an integer, such as 2.\n");
   }
   return nights;
}
void showprice(double hotel, int nights)
{
   int n;
   double total = 0.0;
   double factor = 1.0;

   for (n = 1; n <= nights; n++, factor *= DISCOUNT)
  total += hotel * factor;
   printf("The total cost will be $%0.2f.\n", total);
}
```

Listing 9.12. hotels.h.

```
/* hotels.h -- constants and declarations for hotel.c */
#define QUIT       5
#define HOTEL1     50.00
#define HOTEL2     55.00
#define HOTEL3     80.00
#define HOTEL4    100.00
#define DISCOUNT   0.95
#define STARS "********************************"

int menu(void);
int getnights(void);
void showprice(double, int);
```

Here's a sample run:

```
*********************************************************************
1) Fairfield Arms           2) Hotel Olympic
3) Chertworthy Plaza        4) The Stockton
5) quit
*********************************************************************
3
How many nights are needed? 1
The total cost will be $80.00.

*********************************************************************
Enter the number of the desired hotel:
1) Fairfield Arms           2) Hotel Olympic
3) Chertworthy Plaza        4) The Stockton
5) quit
*********************************************************************
4
How many nights are needed? 3
The total cost will be $285.25.
5) quit
*********************************************************************
Enter the number of the desired hotel:
1) Fairfield Arms           2) Hotel Olympic
3) Chertworthy Plaza        4) The Stockton
5) quit
*********************************************************************
5
```

Incidentally, the program itself has some interesting features. In particular, the menu()
and getnights() functions skip over nonnumeric data by testing the return value of
scanf() and by using the scanf("%*s") call to skip to the next whitespace. Note how
menu() checks for both nonnumeric input and out-of-limits numerical input.

```
while ((status = scanf("%d", &code)) != 1  ||
       (code < 1 || code > 5))
```

The preceding example uses C's guarantee that logical expressions are evaluated from
left to right and that evaluation ceases the moment the statement is clearly false. In this
instance, the values of code are checked only after it is determined that scanf() succeeded
in reading an integer value.

Assigning separate tasks to separate functions encourages this sort of refinement. A first
pass at menu() or getnights() might use a simple scanf() without the data verification
features we've added. Then, once the basic version works, you can begin improving each
module.

Finding Addresses: The & Operator

One of the most important C concepts (and sometimes one of the most perplexing) is the *pointer*. A pointer is a variable used to store an *address*. You've already seen that scanf() uses addresses for arguments. More generally, any C function that modifies a value in the calling function without using a return value uses addresses. We'll look at this topic next, beginning with the unary & operator.

The unary & operator gives you the address at which a variable is stored. If pooh is the name of a variable, then &pooh is the address of the variable. You can think of the address as a location in memory. Suppose you have the following statement:

```
pooh = 24;
```

Suppose that the address where pooh is stored is 0B76. (PC addresses often are given as four-digit hexadecimal values.) Then the statement

```
printf("%d %p\n", pooh, &pooh);
```

would produce this (%p is the specifier for addresses):

```
24 0B76
```

In Listing 9.13, let's use this operator to see where variables of the same name—but in different functions—are kept.

Listing 9.13. `loccheck.c.`

```
/* loccheck.c  -- checks to see where variables are stored */
#include <stdio.h>
void mikado(int);                    /* declare function */
int main(void)
{
    int pooh = 2, bah = 5;

    printf("In main(), pooh = %d and &pooh = %p\n",
         pooh, &pooh);
    printf("In main(), bah = %d and &bah = %p\n",
       bah, &bah);
    mikado(pooh);
    return 0;
}
void mikado(int bah)                 /* define function  */
{
    int pooh = 10;

    printf("In mikado(), pooh = %d and &pooh = %p\n",
       pooh, &pooh);
    printf("In mikado(), bah = %d and &bah = %p\n",
       bah, &bah);
}
```

Listing 9.13 used the %p format for printing the addresses. This format specifier is used for displaying addresses but is not available on some pre-ANSI systems. If your system lacks %p, try %u or, perhaps, %lu. On our system, the output of this little exercise is this:

```
In main(), pooh = 2 and &pooh = 0C06
In main(), bah = 5 and &bah = 0C04
In mikado(), pooh = 10 and &pooh = 0BF6
In mikado(), bah = 2 and &bah = 0BFE
```

The way that %p represents addresses varies between implementations. This one (Microsoft C 7.0 on a PC) displays the address in hexadecimal form.

What does this output show? First, the two poohs have different addresses. The same is true for the two bahs. Thus, as promised, the computer considers these to be four separate variables. Second, the call mikado(pooh) did convey the value (2) of the actual argument (pooh of main()) to the formal argument (bah of mikado()). Note that just the value was transferred. The two variables involved (pooh of main() and bah of mikado()) retain their distinct identities.

We raise the second point because it is not true for all languages. In a FORTRAN subroutine, for example, the subroutine affects the original variable in the calling routine. The subroutine's variable may have a different name, but the address is the same. C doesn't do this. Each function uses its own variables. This is preferable because it prevents the original variable from being altered mysteriously by some side effect of the called function. However, it can make for some difficulties, too, as the next section shows.

Altering Variables in the Calling Function

Sometimes you will want one function to make changes in the variables of a different function. For example, a common task in sorting problems is interchanging the values of two variables. Suppose you have two variables called x and y and you wish to swap their values. The simple sequence

```
x = y;
y = x;
```

does not work because, by the time the second line is reached, the original value of x has already been replaced by the original y value. An additional line is needed to store temporarily the original value of x.

```
temp = x;
x = y;
y = temp;
```

Now that the method works, you can put it into a function and construct a driver to test it. To make clear which variables belong to main() and which belong to the inter-change() function, Listing 9.14 uses x and y for the first, and u and v for the second.

```
/* swap1.c -- 1st attempt at a swapping function */
#include <stdio.h>
void interchange(int u, int v); /* declare function */
int main(void)
{
    int x = 5, y = 10;

    printf("Originally x = %d and y = %d.\n", x , y);
    interchange(x, y);
    printf("Now x = %d and y = %d.\n", x, y);
    return 0;
}
void interchange(int u, int v)  /* define function  */
{
    int temp;

    temp = u;
    u = v;
    v = temp;
}
```

Running the program gives these results:

```
Originally x = 5 and y = 10.
Now x = 5 and y = 10.
```

Oops! The values didn't get switched! Let's put some print statements into interchange() to see what's gone wrong (Listing 9.15).

Listing 9.15. swap2.c.

```
/* swap2.c -- researching swap1.c */
#include <stdio.h>
void interchange(int u, int v);
int main(void)
{
    int x = 5, y = 10;

    printf("Originally x = %d and y = %d.\n", x , y);
    interchange(x, y);
    printf("Now x = %d and y = %d.\n", x, y);
    return 0;
}
void interchange(int u, int v)
{
```

continues

Listing 9.15. continued

```
    int temp;

    printf("Originally u = %d and v = %d.\n", u , v);
    temp = u;
    u = v;
    v = temp;
    printf("Now u = %d and v = %d.\n", u, v);
}
```

Here is the new output:

```
Originally x = 5 and y = 10.
Originally u = 5 and v = 10.
Now u = 10 and v = 5.
Now x = 5 and y = 10.
```

Well, nothing is wrong with `interchange()`; it does swap the values of u and v. The problem is in communicating the results to `main()`. As we pointed out, `interchange()` uses different variables from `main()`, so interchanging the values of u and v has no effect on x and y! Can we somehow use `return`? Well, we could finish `interchange()` with the line

```
return(u);
```

and change the call in `main()` to

```
x = interchange(x,y);
```

This change gives x its new value, but it leaves y in the cold. With `return` you can send just *one* value back to the calling function, but we need to communicate *two* values. It can be done! All we have to do is use *pointers*.

Pointers: A First Look

Pointers? What are they? Basically, a *pointer* is a variable whose value is an address. Just as a `char` variable has a character as a value and an `int` variable has an integer as a value, the pointer variable has an address as a value. If we give a particular pointer variable the name `ptr`, then we can have statements like

```
ptr = &pooh;  /* assigns pooh's address to ptr */
```

We say that `ptr` "points to" pooh. The difference between `ptr` and `&pooh` is that `ptr` is a variable, and `&pooh` is a constant. If we wish, we can make `ptr` point elsewhere.

```
ptr = &bah;  /* make ptr point to bah instead of to pooh */
```

Now the value of `ptr` is the address of `bah`.

To create a pointer variable, you need to be able to declare its type. Suppose you want to declare `ptr` so that it can hold the address of an `int`. To make this declaration, you need to use a new operator. Let's examine that operator now.

The Indirection Operator: *

Suppose you know that `ptr` points to `bah`

```
ptr = &bah;
```

Then you can use the *indirection operator* * (also called the *dereferencing operator*) to find the value stored in `bah`. (Don't confuse this *unary* indirection operator with the *binary* * operator of multiplication.)

```
val = *ptr;   /* finding the value ptr points to */
```

The statements `ptr = &bah;` and `val = *ptr;` taken together amount to the following statements:

```
val = bah;
```

Using the address and indirection operators is a rather indirect way of accomplishing this result, hence the name "indirection operator."

Summary: Pointer-Related Operators

The Address Operator

&

General Comments

When followed by a variable name, & gives the address of that variable.

Example

&nurse is the address of the variable nurse.

The Indirection Operator

*

General Comments

When followed by a pointer name or an address, * gives the value stored at the pointed-to address.

continues

Example

```
nurse = 22;
ptr = &nurse;  /* pointer to nurse */
val = *ptr;
```

The net effect is to assign the value 22 to val.

Declaring Pointers

You already know how to declare int variables and other fundamental types. How do you declare a pointer variable? You might guess that the form is like this:

```
pointer ptr;      /* not the way to declare a pointer */
```

Why not? Because it is not enough to say that a variable is a pointer. You also have to say what kind of variable the pointer points to. The reason for this is that different variable types take up different amounts of storage, and some pointer operations require knowledge of that storage size. Also, the program has to know what kind of data is stored at the address. A long and a float may use the same amount of storage, but they store numbers quite differently. Here's how pointers are declared:

```
int * pi;         /* pi is a pointer to an integer variable  */
char * pc;        /* pc is a pointer to a character variable */
float * pf, * pg  /* pf, pg are pointers to float variables  */
```

The type specification identifies the type of variable pointed to, and the asterisk (*) identifies the variable itself as a pointer. The declaration int * pi; says that pi is a pointer and that *pi is type int. See Figure 9.5.

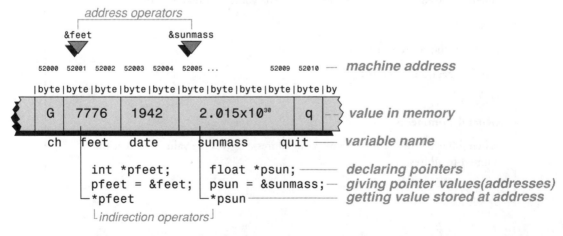

Figure 9.5. *Declaring and using pointers.*

The space between the * and the pointer name is optional. Often, programmers use the space in a declaration and omit it when dereferencing a variable.

The value (*pc) of what pc points to is of type char. What of pc itself? We describe it as being of type "pointer to char." Its value, being an address, is an unsigned integer on most systems. Thus, on most systems, you can use the %u format to print the value of pc. As we mentioned earlier, that need not hold true universally, so ANSI C provides the %p form specifically for pointers.

Using Pointers to Communicate Between Functions

We have touched only the surface of the rich and fascinating world of pointers, but our concern here is using pointers to solve our communication problem. Listing 9.16 shows a program that uses pointers to make the interchange() function work. Let's look at it, run it, and then try to understand how it works.

Listing 9.16. swap3.c.

```
/* swap3.c -- using pointers to make swapping work */
#include <stdio.h>
void interchange(int * u, int * v);
int main(void)
{
    int x = 5, y = 10;

    printf("Originally x = %d and y = %d.\n", x, y);
    interchange(&x, &y);  /* send addresses to function  */
    printf("Now x = %d and y = %d.\n", x, y);
    return 0;
}
void interchange(int * u, int * v)
{
    int temp;

    temp = *u;        /* temp gets value that u points to */
    *u = *v;
    *v = temp;
}
```

After all this trouble, does Listing 9.16 really work?

```
Originally x = 5 and y = 10.
Now x = 10 and y = 5.
```

Yes, it works.

Now, let's see how Listing 9.16 works. First, our function call looks like this:

```
interchange(&x, &y);
```

Instead of transmitting the *values* of x and y, we are transmitting their *addresses*. This means that the formal arguments u and v appearing in

```
void interchange(u, v)
```

will have addresses as their values. Therefore, they should be declared as pointers. Because x and y are integers, u and v are pointers to integers; so we declare them as follows:

```
void interchange (int * u, int * v)
```

Next, in the body of the function, we declare

```
int temp;
```

to provide the temporary storage we need. We want to store the value of x in temp. Therefore, we say

```
temp = *u;
```

Remember, u has the value &x, so u points to x. This means that *u gives us the value of x, which is what we want. We *don't* want to write

```
temp = u;    /* NO */
```

because that would assign temp the *address* of x rather than its *value*; and we are trying to interchange values, not addresses.

Similarly, to assign the *value* of y to x, we use

```
*u = *v;
```

which translates to

```
x = y;
```

Let's summarize what we did. We wanted a function that would alter the values x and y. By passing the function the addresses of x and y, we gave interchange() access to those variables. Using pointers and the * operator, the function could examine the values stored at those locations and change them.

There are a couple of variants that you should know about. The pre-ANSI form for the function heading is this:

```
void interchange(u, v)
int * u, * v;
```

You can omit the variable names in the ANSI prototype. Then the prototype declaration looks like this:

```
void interchange(int *, int *);
```

More generally, you can communicate two kinds of information about a variable to a function. If you use a call of the form

```
function1(x);
```

you transmit the *value* of x. If you use a call of the form

```
function2(&x);
```

you transmit the *address* of x. The first form requires that the function definition include a formal argument of the same type as x.

```
int function1(int num)
```

The second form requires that the function definition include a formal argument that is a pointer to the right type.

```
int function2(int * ptr)
```

Use the first form if the function needs a value for some calculation or action. Use the second form if the function needs to alter variables in the calling function. You have been doing this all along with the scanf() function. When you want to read in a value for a variable num, for example, you use scanf("%d", &num). That function reads a value and then uses the address you give it to store the value.

Pointers enable you to get around the fact that the variables of interchange() were local. They let that function reach out into main() and alter what was stored there.

Pascal and Modula-2 users may recognize the first form as being the same as Pascal's value parameter and the second form as being similar (but not identical) to Pascal's variable parameter. BASIC users may find the whole setup a bit unsettling. If this section seems strange to you, be assured that a little practice will make at least some uses of pointers seem simple, normal, and convenient. See Figure 9.6.

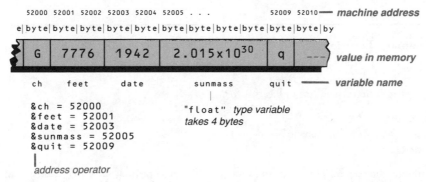

Figure 9.6. *Names, addresses, and values in a byte-addressable system, such as the IBM PC.*

Variables: Names, Addresses, and Values

The preceding discussion of pointers has hinged on the relationships between the names, addresses, and values of variables. Let's discuss these matters further.

When you write a program, you think of a variable as having two attributes: a name and a value. (There are other attributes, including type, but that's another matter.) After the program has been compiled and loaded, the computer also thinks of the same variable as having two attributes: an address and a value. An address is the computer's version of a name.

In many languages, the address is the computer's business, concealed from the programmer. In C, however, you can access the address through the & operator.

&barn is the address of the variable barn.

You can get the value from the name just by using the name.

printf("%d\n", barn) prints the value of barn.

You can get the value from the address by using the * operator.

Given pbarn = &barn;, then *pbarn is the value stored at address &barn.

In short, a regular variable makes the value the primary quantity and the address a derived quantity, via the & operator. A pointer variable makes the address the primary quantity and the value a derived quantity, via the * operator.

Although you can print an address to satisfy your curiosity, that is not the main use for the & operator. More important, using &, *, and pointers enables you to manipulate addresses and their contents symbolically, as in *swap3.c* (Listing 9.16).

Summary: Functions

Form

A typical function definition has this form:

```
name(argument list)
argument declarations
function body
```

The presence of the argument list and declarations is optional. Variables other than the arguments are declared within the body, which is bounded by braces.

ANSI C encourages the following form:

```
name(argument declaration list)
function body
```

The argument declaration list is a comma-separated list of variable declarations.

Examples

```
int diff(x,y)      /* function name and argument list */
int x,y;           /* declare arguments              */
{                  /* begin function body            */
  int z;           /* declare local variable         */

  z = x - y;
  return z;
}                  /* end function body              */

int diff(int x,int y)    /* ANSI version                  */
{                        /* begin function body           */
  int z;                 /* declare local variable        */

  z = x - y;
  return z;
}                        /* end function body             */
```

Communicating Values

Arguments are used to convey values from the calling function to the function. If variables a and b have the values 5 and 2, then the call

```
c = diff(a,b);
```

transmits 5 and 2 to the variables x and y. The values 5 and 2 are called *actual arguments*, and the diff() variables x and y are called *formal arguments*. The keyword return communicates one value from the function to the calling function. In our example, c receives the value of z, which is 3. A function ordinarily has no effect on the variables in a calling function. To directly affect variables in the calling function, use pointers as arguments. This may be necessary if you wish to communicate more than one value back to the calling function.

continues

Function Type

Functions must have the same type as the value they return. Functions are assumed to be type `int`. If a function is another type, it must be declared as such in the calling function and in the function definition.

Example

```
int main(void)
{
  double q, x, duff();  /* declare in calling function   */
  int n;
  .
  .
  .
   q = duff(x,n);
  .
  .
  .
 }
double duff(u, k)       /* declare in function definition */
double u;
int k;
{
  double tor;
   return tor;          /* returns a double value         */
}
```

Chapter Summary

Use *functions* as building blocks for larger programs. Each function should have a single, well-defined purpose. Use *arguments* to communicate values to a function, and use the keyword `return` to communicate back a value. If the function returns a value not of type `int`, then you must specify the function type in the function definition and in the declaration section of the calling function. If you want the function to affect variables in the calling function, use *addresses* and *pointers*.

ANSI C offers *function prototyping*, a powerful C enhancement that allows compilers to verify that the proper number and types of arguments are used in a function call.

A C function can call itself; this is called *recursion*.

Review Questions

1. What is the difference between an actual argument and a formal argument?

2. Write function headings (K&R style and the new ANSI C style) for the functions described below. Note that you need write only the headings, not the body.

   a. n_to_char() takes an int argument and returns a char.
   b. digits() takes a double argument and an int argument and returns an int.
   c. random() takes no argument and returns an int.

3. Devise a function that returns the sum of two double arguments.

4. Is anything wrong with this function definition?

```
void salami(num)
{
    int num, count;

    for (count = 1; count <= num; num++)
        printf(" O salami mio!\n");
}
```

5. Given the following output

```
Please choose one of the following:
1) copy files          2) move files
3) remove files        4) quit
Enter the number of your choice:
```

   a. Write a function that displays a menu of four numbered choices and asks you to choose one. (The output should look like the preceding.)

   b. Write a function that has two int arguments: a lower limit and an upper limit. The function should read an integer from input. If the integer is outside the limits, the function should print a menu (using the function from part a of this question) and get a new value. When an integer in the proper limits is entered, the function should return that value to the calling function.

   c. Write a minimal program using the functions from parts a and b of this question. By minimal, we mean it need not actually perform the actions promised by the menu; it should just show the choices and get a valid response.

Programming Exercises

1. Devise a function min(x,y) that returns the smaller of two double values, and test the function with a simple driver.

2. Devise a function `chline(ch,i,j)` that prints the requested character in columns `i` through `j`. Test it in a simple driver.

3. Write a function that takes three arguments: a character and two integers. The character is to be printed. The first integer specifies the number of times that the character is to be printed on a line, and the second integer specifies the number of lines that are to be printed. Write a program that makes use of this function.

4. The harmonic mean of two numbers is obtained by taking the inverses of the two numbers, averaging them, and taking the inverse of the result. Write a function that takes two `double` arguments and returns the harmonic mean of the two numbers.

5. Write a function that replaces the contents of two variables with two new values: the sum and the difference of the original contents.

6. Write a program that reads characters from the standard input to end-of-file. For each character, have the program report whether it is a letter. If it is a letter, also report its numerical location in the alphabet. For example, *c* and *C* would each be letter 3. Incorporate a function that takes a character as an argument and returns the numerical location if the character is a letter and that returns −1 otherwise.

7. In Chapter 6, "C Control Statements: Looping," (Listing 6.18) we wrote a `power()` function that returned the result of raising a type `double` number to a positive integer value. Improve the function so that it correctly handles negative powers. Also, build into the function that 0 to any power is 0 and that any number to the 0 power is 1. Use a loop. Test the function in a program.

8. Redo Exercise 7, but this time use a recursive function.

9. Generalize the `to_binary()` function of Listing 9.13 so that it takes a second argument in the range 2–10. It then prints the number that is its first argument to the number base given by the second argument.

10

Arrays and Pointers

Keyword
    static
Operators
    & *(unary)

In this chapter you learn how to create and initialize arrays. Along the way, you strengthen your knowledge of pointers and see how they relate to arrays. You write functions that process arrays and explore two-dimensional arrays.

People turn to computers for tasks like tracking monthly expenses or daily rainfall or quarterly sales or weekly weights. As a programmer, you inevitably will have to deal with large quantities of related data. Often, arrays offer the best way to handle such data in an efficient, convenient manner. Chapter 6, "C Control Statements: Looping," introduced arrays, and this chapter takes a more thorough look. In particular, it examines how to write array-processing functions. Such functions will enable you to extend the advantages of modular programming to arrays. In doing so, you'll see the intimate relationship between arrays and pointers.

Arrays

Recall that an *array* is composed of a series of elements of one data type. You use *declarations* to tell the compiler when you want an array. An *array declaration* tells the compiler how many elements the array contains and what the type is for these elements. Armed with this information, the compiler can set up the array properly. Array elements can have the same types as ordinary variables. Consider the following example of array declarations:

```
/* some array declarations */
int main(void)
{
    float candy[365];       /* array of 365 floats */
    char code[12];          /* array of 12 chars   */
    int states[50];         /* array of 50 ints    */
    ...
}
```

The brackets ([ ]) identify `candy` and the rest as arrays, and the number enclosed in the brackets indicates the number of elements in the array.

To access elements in an array, you identify an individual element by using its subscript number, also called an *index*. The numbering starts with 0. Hence, `candy[0]` is the first element of the `candy` array, and `candy[364]` is the 365th and last element.

This is rather old hat; let's learn something new.

Initialization and Storage Classes

Arrays are often used to store data needed for a program. For example, a 12-element array can store the number of days in each month. In cases such as these, it would be convenient to initialize the array at the beginning of a program. We can. Let's see how it is done.

You know that you can initialize single-valued variables (sometimes called *scalar* variables) in a declaration with expressions like

```
int fix = 1;
float flax = PI * 2;
```

where, we hope, `PI` was defined earlier as a macro. Can you do something similar with arrays? The answer is that old favorite, yes and maybe. It's yes for ANSI C and maybe for K&R C. If the array is an *external* array or a *static* array, it can be initialized. If it is an *automatic* array, it can be initialized under ANSI C but not under the older K&R definition of the language. We'll cover these new terms in Chapter 13, "Storage Classes and Program Development," but we'll preview them now.

The terms *external, static,* and *automatic* describe different *storage classes* that C allows. The storage class determines how widely known a data item is to various functions in a program and for how long it is kept in memory. Until now, we have used only automatic variables. Let's look at these three storage classes.

Automatic Variables and Arrays

An automatic variable or array is one defined *inside* a function (this includes formal arguments). As we've emphasized, a variable defined in a function is private to that function, even if it reuses a name appearing in another function. As we haven't mentioned, such a variable exists only for the duration of the function call. When a function finishes and returns to the calling function, the space used to hold its variables is freed.

ANSI C enables us to initialize automatic arrays.

```
int main(void)
{
  int powers[8] = {1,2,4,6,8,16,32,64}; /* ANSI only */
  ...
}
```

Because the array is defined inside main(), it is an automatic array. It is initialized by using a comma-separated list of values enclosed in braces. You can use spaces between the values and the commas, if you wish. The first element (powers[0]) is assigned the value 1, and so on.

K&R C, however, does not allow this. The only way to give values to an automatic array in K&R is to assign values to the elements individually, perhaps by using a loop.

External Variables and Arrays

An external variable or array is one defined *outside* a function. Here, for example, we define an external variable and an external array:

```
int report;
int sows[5] = {12, 10, 8, 9, 6};  /* ok in ANSI and K&R */
int feed(int n);   /* prototype */
int main(void)
{
  ...
}
int feed(int n)
{
  ...
}
```

External variables and arrays differ from their automatic cousins in three respects. First, they are known to all functions following them in a file. Thus, in our example, both main() and feed() can use and modify the int variable report and the array sows. Second, external variables and arrays persist as long as the program runs. Because they are not defined in a particular function, they don't expire when a particular function terminates. Third, external variables and arrays are initialized to zeros by default, so report is initialized to 0.

Static Variables and Arrays

You can define a static variable or array inside a function by beginning the definition with the keyword static.

```
int account(int n, int m)
{
  static int beans[2] = {343, 332}; /* ok in ANSI, K&R */
  ...
}
```

This creates an array that, like an automatic array, is local to the function account(). However, like an external array, a static array retains its values between function calls and is initialized to zeros by default.

Storage Classes: Comments

C offers multiple storage classes to meet different programming needs. In Chapter 13 we'll investigate the uses of each type. For most cases, automatic variables and arrays are the best choice. However, because K&R doesn't allow automatic arrays to be initialized, many programs use external or static arrays instead. We'll use external and static arrays so that our examples will work with pre-ANSI compilers as well as with ANSI compilers. That said, let's learn a bit more about array initialization.

More Array Initialization

Listing 10.1 presents a short program that prints the number of days per month.

Listing 10.1. day_mon1.c.

```
/* day_mon1.c -- prints the days for each month */
#include <stdio.h>
#define MONTHS 12
int days[MONTHS] = {31,28,31,30,31,30,31,31,30,31,30,31};
int main(void)
{
  int index;
  extern int days[];   /* optional declaration */

  for (index = 0; index < MONTHS; index++)
    printf("Month %d has %d days./n", index +1,
            days[index]);
  return 0;
}
```

The output looks like this:

```
Month 1 has 31 days.
Month 2 has 28 days.
Month 3 has 31 days.
Month 4 has 30 days.
Month 5 has 31 days.
Month 6 has 30 days.
Month 7 has 31 days.
Month 8 has 31 days.
Month 9 has 30 days.
Month 10 has 31 days.
Month 11 has 30 days.
Month 12 has 31 days.
```

Not quite a superb program, but it's wrong only one month in every four years. By defining days[] outside the function, we made it external. We initialized it with a list of comma-separated values enclosed in braces. Inside the function, the optional declaration

```
extern int days[];
```

uses the keyword extern to remind us that the days array is defined elsewhere in the program as an external array. Because the array is defined elsewhere, we needn't give its size here. (See Chapter 13, "Storage Classes and Program Development," for more about extern.) Omitting this entire declaration statement has no effect on how this program works. Indeed, it's a common practice to define external variables at the top of a file and to omit the optional extern declarations.

The number of items in the list should match the size of the array. What if we count wrong? Let's try the last example again, as shown in Listing 10.2, with a list that is two too short.

Listing 10.2. day_mon2.c.

```
/* day_mon2.c -- initializes 10 out of 12 elements */
#include <stdio.h>
#define MONTHS 12
int days[MONTHS] = {31,28,31,30,31,30,31,31,30,31};
int main(void)
{
  int index;
  extern int days[];   /* optional declaration */

  for (index = 0; index < MONTHS; index++)
    printf("Month %d has %d days.\n", index +1,
           days[index]);
  return 0;
}
```

This time the output looks like this:

```
Month 1 has 31 days.
Month 2 has 28 days.
Month 3 has 31 days.
Month 4 has 30 days.
Month 5 has 31 days.
Month 6 has 30 days.
Month 7 has 31 days.
Month 8 has 31 days.
Month 9 has 30 days.
Month 10 has 31 days.
Month 11 has 0 days.
Month 12 has 0 days.
```

As you can see, the compiler had no problem. When it ran out of values from the list, it initialized the remaining elements to 0. This initializing to 0 holds for external and static arrays.

If you don't initialize an automatic array at all, its elements, like uninitialized ordinary variables, get garbage values, but if you partially initialize an automatic array, the uninitialized elements are set to 0.

The compiler is not so forgiving if you have too many list values. This overgenerosity is considered an error. There is no need, however, to expose yourself to the ridicule of your compiler. Instead, you can let the compiler match the array size to the list by omitting the size from the braces (Listing 10.3).

Listing 10.3. day_mon3.c.

```
/* day_mon3.c -- initializes 10 out of 12 elements */
#include <stdio.h>
int days[] = {31,28,31,30,31,30,31,31,30,31};
int main(void)
{
  int index;
  extern int days[];   /* optional declaration */

  for (index = 0; index < sizeof days / sizeof (int); index++)
    printf("Month %d has %d days.\n", index +1,
            days[index]);
  return 0;
}
```

There are two main points to note in the program:

- When you use empty brackets to initialize an array, the compiler will count the number of items in the list and make the array that large.

- Notice what we did in the `for` loop control statement. Lacking faith (justifiably) in our ability to count correctly, we let the computer give us the size of the array. The `sizeof` operator gives the size, in bytes, of the object or type following it. On our system, each `int` element occupies 2 bytes, so we divide the total number of bytes by 2 to get the number of elements. Other systems may have a different size `int`. Therefore, to be general, we divide by `sizeof (int)`.

Here is the result of running this program:

```
Month 1 has 31 days.
Month 2 has 28 days.
Month 3 has 31 days.
Month 4 has 30 days.
Month 5 has 31 days.
Month 6 has 30 days.
Month 7 has 31 days.
Month 8 has 31 days.
Month 9 has 30 days.
Month 10 has 31 days.
```

Oops! We put in just ten values, but our method of letting the program find the array size kept us from trying to print past the end of the array. This points out a potential disadvantage of automatic counting: errors in the number of elements may pass unnoticed.

There is one more short method of initializing arrays. Because it works only for character strings, however, we will save it for the next chapter.

Assigning Array Values

You can *assign* values to array members, regardless of storage class. For example, the following fragment assigns even numbers to an automatic array:

```
/* array assignment */
#include <stdio.h>
#define SIZE 50
int main(void)
{
  int counter, evens[SIZE];

  for (counter = 0; counter < SIZE; counter++)
      evens[counter] = 2 * counter;
  ...
}
```

Note that this assignment is element by element. C doesn't let you assign one array to another as a unit. Nor can you use the list-in-braces form except when initializing.

```
/* nonvalid array assignment */
#define SIZE 5
int main(void)
{
```

```
int oxen[SIZE] = {5,3,2,8};      /* ok here      */
int yaks[SIZE];

yaks = oxen;                     /* not allowed  */
yaks[SIZE] = oxen[SIZE];         /* invalid      */
yaks[SIZE] = {5,3,2,8};          /* doesn't work */
```

Pointers to Arrays

Pointers, as you may recall from Chapter 9, "Functions," provide a symbolic way to use addresses. Because the hardware instructions of computing machines rely heavily on addresses, pointers enable you to express yourself in a way that is close to the way the machine expresses itself. This makes programs with pointers efficient. In particular, pointers offer an efficient way to deal with arrays. Indeed, as we shall see, array notation is simply a disguised use of pointers.

An example of this disguised use is that an array name is also the address of the first element of an array. That is, if flizny is an array, then the following is true:

```
flizny == &flizny[0]
```

Both flizny and &flizny represent the memory address of that first element. (Recall that & is the address operator). Both are *constants*, for they remain fixed for the duration of the program. However, they can be assigned as values to a pointer *variable*, and we can change the value of a variable, as Listing 10.4 shows. Notice what happens to the value of a pointer when we add a number to it. (Recall that %p specifier for the pointers typically displays hexadecimal values.)

Listing 10.4. pnt_add.c.

```
/* pnt_add.c -- pointer addition */
#include <stdio.h>
#define SIZE 4
int main(void)
{
  int dates [SIZE], * pti, index;
  float bills[SIZE], * ptf;

  pti = dates;     /* assign address of array to pointer */
  ptf = bills;
  for (index = 0; index < SIZE; index ++)
      printf("pointers + %d: %10p %10p\n",
              index, pti + index, ptf + index);
  return 0;
}
```

```
pointers + 0:      0B76       0B66
pointers + 1:      0B78       0B6A
pointers + 2:      0B7A       0B6E
pointers + 3:      0B7C       0B72
```

The first line prints the beginning addresses of the two arrays, and the next line gives the result of adding 1 to the address, and so on. Note that A is the hexadecimal digit for 10, C is the digit for 12, and E is the digit for 14. What?

```
0B76 + 1 = 0B78?
0B66 + 1 = 0B6A?
```

Pretty dumb? Like a fox! Our system is addressed by individual bytes, but type int uses 2 bytes and type float uses 4 bytes. What is happening here is that when you say "add 1 to a pointer," C adds one *storage unit*. For arrays, this means that the address is increased to the address of the next *element*, not just the next byte (see Figure 10.1). This is one reason we have to declare what sort of object a pointer points to. The address is not enough because the computer needs to know how many bytes are used to store the object. (This is true even for pointers to scalar variables; otherwise, the *pt operation to fetch the value wouldn't work correctly.)

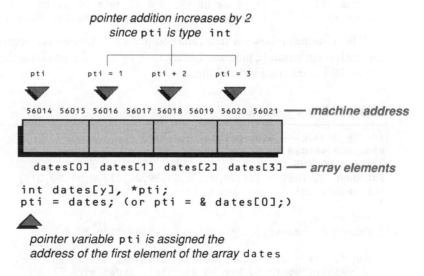

Figure 10.1. *An array and pointer addition.*

Now we can define more clearly what is meant by pointer-to-int or pointer-to-float or pointer to any other data object.

- The value of a pointer is the address of the object to which it points. How the address is represented internally is hardware dependent. Many computers, including

PCs and VAXs, are *byte addressable*, meaning that each byte in memory is numbered sequentially. Here, the address of a large object, such as type `double` variable, typically is the address of the first byte of the object.

- Applying the * operator to a pointer yields the value stored in the pointed-to object.

- Adding 1 to the pointer increases its value by the size, in bytes, of the pointed-to object.

As a result of this cleverness of C, we have the following equalities:

```
dates +2 == &date[2]        /* same address */
*(dates + 2) == dates[2]        /* same value   */
```

These relationships sum up the close connection between arrays and pointers. They mean that we can use a pointer to identify an individual element of an array and to get its value. In essence, we have two different notations for the same thing. Indeed, the C language standard describes array notation in terms of pointers, so the pointer approach is the more basic of the two.

Incidentally, don't confuse *(dates+2) with *dates+2. The indirection operator (*) binds more tightly (has higher precedence) than +, so the latter means (*dates)+2.

```
*(dates +2)        /* value of the 3rd element of dates        */
*dates +2        /* 2 added to the value of the 1st element */
```

The relationship between arrays and pointers means that we can often use either approach when writing a program. Listing 10.5, for instance, produces the same output as Listing 10.1 when compiled and run.

Listing 10.5. day_mon4.c.

```
/* day_mon4.c -- uses pointer notation */
#include <stdio.h>
#define MONTHS 12
int days[MONTHS] = {31,28,31,30,31,30,31,31,30,31,30,31};
int main(void)
{
  int index;
  extern int days[];   /* optional declaration */

  for (index = 0; index < MONTHS; index++)
    printf("Month %d has %d days.\n", index +1,
           *(days + index));
  return 0;
}
```

Here, days is the address of the first element of the array, days + index is the address of element days[index], and *(days + index) is the value of that element, just as `days[index]` is. The loop references each element of the array in turn and prints the contents of what it finds.

Is there an advantage to writing the program this way? Not really. The point to Listing 10.5 is that pointer notation and array notation are two equivalent methods. This example shows you can use pointer notation with arrays. The reverse also is true; you can use array notation with pointers. This turns out to be important when you have a function with an array as an argument.

Functions, Arrays, and Pointers

Suppose you wish to write a function that operates on an array. For instance, suppose you want a function that returns the sum of the elements of an array. Listing 10.6 shows a program that does this. To point out an interesting fact about array arguments, the program also prints the size of the relevant arrays. (Recall that some compilers, such as Think C for the Macintosh, require `%ld` for printing `sizeof` quantities.)

Listing 10.6. `sum_arr1.c.`

```
/* sum_arr1.c -- sums the elements of an array */
#include <stdio.h>
#define SIZE 10
long sum(int ar[], int n);
int main(void)
{
    static int marbles[SIZE] = {20,10,5,39,4,16,19,26,31,20};
    long answer;

    answer = sum(marbles, SIZE);
    printf("The total number of marbles is %ld.\n", answer);
    printf("The size of marbles is %d bytes.\n",
        sizeof marbles);
    return 0;
}

long sum(int ar[], int n)      /* how big an array? */
{
    int i;
    long total = 0;

    for( i = 0; i < n; i++)
        total += ar[i];
    printf("The size of ar is %d bytes.\n", sizeof ar);
    return total;

}
```

Recall that the += operator adds the value of the operand on its right to the operand on its left. Thus, `total` is a running sum of the array elements. The output on our system looks like this:

```
The size of ar is 2 bytes.
The total number of marbles is 190.
The size of marbles is 20 bytes.
```

Array Names as Arguments

Well, the function does successfully sum the number of marbles, but what is `ar`? From the function argument declarations, you might expect that `ar` is a new array into which are copied the values found in `marbles`—the actual argument to the function. After all, the formal argument `n` is assigned the value of its corresponding actual argument. Yet `ar` is only 2 bytes, so it couldn't be assigned the 20 bytes of data in `marbles`. Thus, `ar` is not an array of 10 `ints`.

The reason that `ar` is not an array is that C does not allow arrays to be passed as function arguments. Look at the function call

```
sum(marbles, SIZE);
```

The first argument is `marbles`, the name of an array, and the name of an array, recall, is the *address* of the first element of the array. That is, the identifier `marbles` is not an array; it is the address of an int, `marbles[0]`, so the function call `sum(marbles, SIZE)` passes two numbers: an address and an integer. This means that the formal arguments to `sum()` should be a pointer-to-int and an `int`. The function heading should look like this:

```
int sum(int *ar, int n)
```

Indeed, if you replace the heading in Listing 10.6 with this heading, the program works exactly the same as before. When you declare a formal argument (and *only* when you declare a formal argument) in C, the forms

```
int *ar;
```

and

```
int ar[];
```

are exactly equivalent. Both state that `ar` is a pointer-to-int. That is why `sizeof ar` is 2—our system uses 2-byte pointers.

If `ar` is a pointer, why can we use the expression `ar[i]` in `sum()`? In C, remember, `ar[i]` is the same as `*(ar + i)`. Both represent the value stored at address `ar +i`. This is true if `ar` is the name of an array, and it is true if `ar` is the name of a pointer variable. Thus, we can use pointer notation to process an array, and we can use array notation with a pointer variable. In this instance, `ar` starts out pointing to the first element of the `marbles` array. Increasing `i` then makes `ar + i` point to each element in turn. Because we also pass the size of the array, the `sum()` function knows when the end of the array is reached.

In short, when you use an array name as a function argument, you pass the address of the first element of the array to the function. The function then uses a pointer set to that address to access the original array in the calling program.

Incidentally, we designed the function to use an argument representing the array size, which enables us to use the same function for differently sized arrays. Note that the only way the function can know the array size is if we tell it. As the example shows, applying the `sizeof` operator to an array name yields the size of an array, but applying `sizeof` to a pointer variable yields the size of the pointer, not the size of the object that is pointed to. Another way to indicate the size is to build it into the function. That is, instead of using the n argument in `sum()`, we could have made the loop test be `i < 10`. However, such a function would be limited to working with 10-element arrays.

Using Pointer Arguments

The fact that ar is a variable offers an alternative way to write the `sum()` function. Rather than adding i to a fixed ar, we can alter the value of ar itself. Listing 10.7 illustrates this approach.

Listing 10.7. `sum_arr2.c.`

```
/* sum_arr2.c -- sums the elements of an array */
#include <stdio.h>
#define SIZE 10
long sump(int *ar, int n);
int main(void)
{
  static int marbles[SIZE] = {20,10,5,39,4,16,19,26,31,20};
  long answer;

  answer = sump(marbles, SIZE);
  printf("The total number of marbles is %ld.\n", answer);
  return 0;
}

long sump(int *ar, int n)      /* use pointer arithmetic   */
{
  int i;
  long total = 0;

  for (i = 0; i < n; i++)
  {
    total += *ar;      /* add value to total               */
    ar++;              /* advance pointer to next element */
  }
  return total;
}
```

Again, ar starts out pointing to the first element of marbles, so the assignment expression total +=*ar adds the value of the first element (20) to total. Then the expression ar++ increments the pointer variable ar so that it points to the next element in the array. Because ar points to type int, C increments the value of ar by the size of int.

Alternatively, we can condense the body of the loop to one line

```
total += *ar++;
```

The unary operators * and ++ have the same precedence but associate from right to left. This means the ++ applies to ar, not to *ar. That is, the pointer is incremented, not the value pointed to. The fact that we use the postfix form (ar++ rather than ++ar) means that the pointer is not incremented until after the pointed-to value is added to total. If we used *++ar, the order would be increment the pointer, then use the value pointed to. If we used (*ar)++, however, the program would use the value of ar and then increment the value, not the pointer. That would leave the pointer pointing to the same element, but the element would contain a new number. Although the *ar++ notation is commonly used, you may prefer to use *(ar++) for clarity. Listing 10.8 illustrates these niceties of precedence.

Listing 10.8. order.c.

```
/* order.c -- precedence in pointer operations */
#include <stdio.h>
int data[2] = {100, 300};
int moredata[2] = {200, 400};
int main(void)
{
  int * p1, * p2, * p3;

  p1 = p2 = data;
  p3 = moredata;
  printf("*p1++ = %d, *++p2 = %d, (*p3)++) = %d\n",
         *p1++, *++p2, (*p3)++);
  printf(" *p1 = %d, *p2 = %d, *p3 = %d\n",
         *p1, *p2, *p3);
  return 0;
}
```

Here is its output:

```
*p1++ = 100, *++p2 = 300, (*p3)++) = 200
  *p1 = 300,   *p2 = 300,      *p3 = 201
```

The only operation that altered an array value is (*p3)++. The other two operations caused p1 and p2 to advance to point to the next array element.

Comment: Pointers and Arrays

As you have seen, functions that process arrays actually use pointers as arguments, but you do have a choice between array notation and pointer notation for writing array-processing functions. Using array notation, as in Listing 10.6, makes it more obvious that the function is working with arrays. Also, array notation has a more familiar look to programmers versed in other languages, such as FORTRAN, Pascal, Modula-2, or BASIC. Other programmers may be more accustomed to working with pointers and may find the pointer notation more natural.

As far as C goes, the two notations are equivalent in meaning. Pointer notation, particularly when used with the increment operator, is closer to machine language and, with some compilers, leads to more efficient code. Many programmers, however, feel that the programmer's main concerns should be correctness and clarity and that code optimization should be left to the compiler.

Pointer Operations

Just what can you do with pointers? C offers five basic operations that you can perform on pointers, and the next program demonstrates these possibilities. To show the results of each operation, we will print the value of the pointer (which is the address it points to), the value stored in the pointed-to address, and the address of the pointer itself. (If your compiler doesn't support the %p specifier, try %u or perhaps %lu for printing the addresses.)

Listing 10.9 shows the five basic operations that can be performed with or on pointer variables.

Listing 10.9. pt_ops.c.

```
/* pt_ops.c -- pointer operations */
#include <stdio.h>
int main(void)
{
  static int urn[3] = {100,200,300};
  int * ptr1, * ptr2;

  ptr1 = urn;          /* assign an address to a pointer */
  ptr2 = &urn[2];      /* ditto                          */
  printf("ptr1 = %p, *ptr1 =%d, &ptr1 = %p\n",
      ptr1, *ptr1, &ptr1);
  ptr1++;              /* increment a pointer            */
  printf("ptr1 = %p, *ptr1 =%d, &ptr1 = %p\n",
      ptr1, *ptr1, &ptr1);
                       /* dereference a pointer and take */
                       /* the address of a pointer       */
```

continues

Listing 10.9. continued

```
printf("ptr2 = %p, *ptr2 =%d, &ptr2 = %p\n",
    ptr2, *ptr2, &ptr2);
++ptr2;    /* going past end of the array */
printf("ptr2 = %p, *ptr2 -%d, &ptr2 = %p\n",
    ptr2, *ptr2, &ptr2);
printf("ptr2 - ptr1 = %d\n", ptr2 - ptr1);
                        /* pointer subtraction          */
return 0;
}
```

Here is the output:

```
PTR1 = 00DC, *PTR1 =100, &PTR1 =   0C00
PTR1 = 00DE, *PTR1 =200, &PTR1 =   0C00
PTR2 = 00E0, *PTR2 =300, &PTR2 =   0BFE
PTR2 = 00E2, *PTR2 -3130, &PTR2 = 0BFE
PTR2 - PTR1 = 0002
```

The following list describes the five basic operations that can be performed with or on pointer variables:

- *Assignment.* You can assign an address to a pointer. Typically you do this by using an array name or by using the address operator (&). In the example, ptr1 is assigned the address of the beginning of the array urn. This address happens to be memory cell number 00DC. The variable ptr2 gets the address of the third and last element, urn[2].

- *Value-finding (dereferencing).* The * operator gives the value stored in the pointed-to location. Thus, *ptr1 initially is 100, the value stored at location 00DC.

- *Taking a pointer address.* Like all variables, pointer variables have an address and a value. The & operator tells us where the pointer itself is stored. In our example, ptr1 is stored in memory location 0C00. The content of that memory cell is 00DC, the address of urn.

- *Incrementing a pointer.* You can do this by regular addition or by using the increment operator. Incrementing a pointer to an array element makes it move to the next element of an array. Thus, ptr1++ increases the numerical value of ptr1 by 2 (2 bytes per int) and makes ptr1 point to urn[1] (see Figure 10.2). Now ptr1 has the value 00DE (the next array address) and *ptr1 has the value 200, the value of urn[1]. Note that the address of ptr1 itself remains 0C00. After all, a variable doesn't move around just because it changes value!

Of course, you can also decrement a pointer. There are some cautions to note when incrementing or decrementing a pointer, however. The computer does not keep track of whether a pointer still points to an array element. The operation ++ptr2 in our example caused ptr2 to move up another 2 bytes, and now it points to whatever happened to be stored after the array. Also, you can use the increment or decrement operators for pointer variables but not for address constants, such as array names, just as you can't use the increment operator on regular constants. However, you can use simple addition, as in urn + 2, for address constants.

Given

```
int urn[3];
int * ptr1, * ptr2;
int x, y;
```

Valid	Invalid
ptr1++;	urn++;
x++;	3++;
ptr2 = ptr1 + 2;	ptr2 = urn++;
ptr2 = urn + 1;	x = y + 3++;

* *Differencing.* You can find the difference between two pointers. Normally you do this for two pointers to elements that are in the same array to find out how far apart the elements are. The result is in the same units as the type size. For instance, in the output from Listing 10.9, ptr2 - prt1 has the value 2, meaning these pointers point to objects separated by 2 ints, not by 2 bytes.

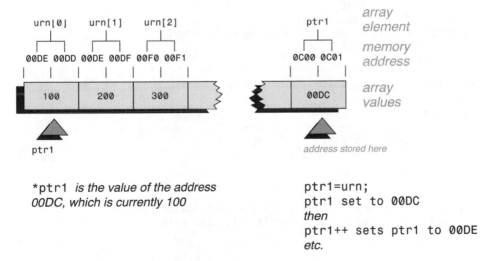

Figure 10.2. *Incrementing a type* int *pointer.*

These operations open many possibilities. C programmers create arrays of pointers, pointers to functions, arrays of pointers to pointers, arrays of pointers to functions, and so on. Relax, we'll stick to the basic uses we have already unveiled. The first basic use for pointers is to communicate information to and from functions. You already know that you must use pointers if you want a function to affect variables in the calling function. The second use is in functions designed to manipulate arrays. Let's look at a programming example using functions and arrays.

Another Example

In the program shown in Listing 10.10, one function displays an array and one function multiplies each element of an array by a given value. The second function emphasizes the fact that array functions operate on the original array, not on a copy. To provide some variety, we use array notation for one function and pointer notation for the other.

Listing 10.10. arf.c.

```
/* arf.c -- array functions */
#include <stdio.h>
#define SIZE 5
void show_array(double ar[], int n);
void mult_array(double mult, double ar[], int n);
int main(void)
{
  static double dip[SIZE] = {20.0, 17.66, 8.2, 15.3, 22.22};

  printf("The original dip array:\n");
  show_array(dip, SIZE);
  mult_array(2.5, dip, SIZE);
  printf("The dip array after calling mult_array():\n");
  show_array(dip, SIZE);
  return 0;
}
void show_array(double ar[], int n)
{
  int i;

  for (i = 0; i < n; i++)
      printf("%8.3f ", ar[i]);
  putchar('\n');
}

/* multiplies each array member by the same multiplier */
void mult_array(double mult, double ar[], int size)
{
  int i;

  for (i = 0; i < size; i++)
      *(ar++) *= mult;
}
```

Here is the output:

```
The original dip array:
  20.000   17.660    8.200   15.300   22.220
The dip array after calling mult_array():
  50.000   44.150   20.500   38.250   55.550
```

Note that both functions are type `void`. The `mult_array()` function does provide new values to the `dip` array, but not by using the `return` mechanism.

Multidimensional Arrays

Tempest Cloud, a weather person who takes her subject cirrusly, wants to analyze 5 years of monthly rainfall data. One of her first decisions is how to represent the data. One choice is to use 60 variables, one for each data item. (We mentioned this choice once before, and it is as senseless now as it was then.) Using an array with 60 elements would be an improvement, but it would be nicer still if she could keep each year's data separate. She could use 5 arrays, each with 12 elements, but that is clumsy and could get really awkward if Tempest decides to study 50 years' worth of rainfall instead of 5. She needs something better.

The better approach is to use an array of arrays. The master array would have 5 elements, one for each year. Each of those elements, in turn, would be a 12-element array, one for each month. This is how to declare such an array:

```
static float rain[5][12];
```

You also can visualize this `rain` array as a two-dimensional array consisting of 5 rows, each of 12 columns, as shown in Figure 10.3. By changing the second subscript, we move along a row, month by month. By changing the first subscript, we move vertically along a column, year by year.

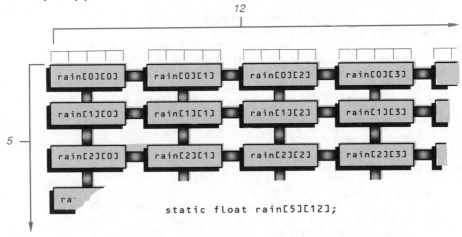

Figure 10.3. *Two-dimensional array.*

The two-dimensional view is merely a convenient way of visualizing an array with two indices. Internally, such an array is stored sequentially, beginning with the first 12-element array, followed by the second 12-element array, and so on.

Let's use this two-dimensional array in a weather program. Our program goal will be to find the total rainfall for each year, the average yearly rainfall, and the average rainfall for each month. To find the total rainfall for a year, we have to add all the data in a given row. To find the average rainfall for a given month, we have to add all the data in a given column. The two-dimensional array makes it easy to visualize and execute these activities. Listing 10.11 shows the program.

Listing 10.11. rain.c.

```
/* rain.c  -- finds yearly totals, yearly average, and monthly
               average for several years of rainfall data */
#include <stdio.h>
#define MONTHS 12    /* number of months in a year */
#define YRS    5     /* number of years of data     */
int main(void)
{
 /* initializing rainfall data for 1990 - 1994 */
 static float rain[YRS][MONTHS] = {
 {10.2, 8.1, 6.8, 4.2, 2.1, 1.8, 0.2, 0.3, 1.1, 2.3, 6.1, 7.4},
 {9.2, 9.8, 4.4, 3.3, 2.2, 0.8, 0.4, 0.0, 0.6, 1.7, 4.3, 5.2},
 {6.6, 5.5, 3.8, 2.8, 1.6, 0.2, 0.0, 0.0, 0.0, 1.3, 2.6, 4.2},
 {4.3, 4.3, 4.3, 3.0, 2.0, 1.0, 0.2, 0.2, 0.4, 2.4, 3.5, 6.6},
 {8.5, 8.2, 1.2, 1.6, 2.4, 0.0, 5.2, 0.9, 0.3, 0.9, 1.4, 7.2}
 };
 int year, month;
 float subtot, total;

 printf(" YEAR    RAINFALL  (inches)\n");
 for (year = 0, total = 0; year < YRS; year++)
 {            /* for each year, sum rainfall for each month */
    for (month = 0, subtot = 0; month < MONTHS; month++)
            subtot += rain[year][month];
    printf("%5d %15.1f\n", 1990 + year, subtot);
    total += subtot;                  /* total for all years */
 }
 printf("\nThe yearly average is %.1f inches.\n\n", total/YRS);
 printf("MONTHLY AVERAGES:\n\n");
 printf(" Jan Feb Mar Apr May Jun Jul Aug Sep Oct ");
 printf(" Nov  Dec\n");

 for (month = 0; month < MONTHS; month++)
 {              /* for each month, sum rainfall over years */
    for (year = 0, subtot =0; year < YRS; year++)
            subtot += rain[year][month];
```

```
        printf("%4.1f ", subtot/YRS);
    }
    printf("\n");
    return 0;
}
```

Here is the output:

```
YEAR     RAINFALL  (inches)
1990             50.6
1991             41.9
1992             28.6
1993             32.2
1994             37.8
```

```
The yearly average is 38.2 inches.
```

```
MONTHLY AVERAGES:
```

```
Jan  Feb  Mar  Apr  May  Jun  Jul  Aug  Sep  Oct  Nov  Dec
7.8  7.2  4.1  3.0  2.1  0.8  1.2  0.3  0.5  1.7  3.6  6.1
```

As you study this program, concentrate on the initialization and on the computation scheme. The initialization is the more involved of the two, so we will look at the computation first.

To find the total for a given year, we kept year constant and let month go over its full range. This is the inner for loop of the first part of the program. Then we repeated the process for the next value of year. This is the outer loop of the first part of the program. A nested loop structure like this is natural for handling a two-dimensional array. One loop handles the first subscript, and the other loop handles the second subscript.

The second part of the program has the same structure, but now we change year with the inner loop and month with the outer. Remember, each time the outer loop cycles once, the inner loop cycles its full allotment. Thus, this arrangement cycles through all the years before changing months. We get a five-year total for the first month, and so on.

Initializing a Two-Dimensional Array

For the initialization we included five embraced lists of numbers, all enclosed by one outer set of braces. The data in the first interior set of braces is assigned to the first row of the array, the data in the second interior set goes to the second row, and so on. The rules we discussed about mismatches between data and array sizes apply to each row. That is, if the first inner set of braces encloses 10 numbers, only the first 10 elements of the first row are affected. The last two elements in that row then are initialized by default to zero. If there are too many numbers, it is an error; the numbers do not get shoved into the next row.

We could have left out the interior braces and just retained the two outermost braces. As long as we have the right number of entries, the effect is the same. If we are short of entries, however, the array is filled sequentially row by row until the data runs out. Then the remaining elements are initialized to 0. Figure 10.4 shows both ways of initializing an array.

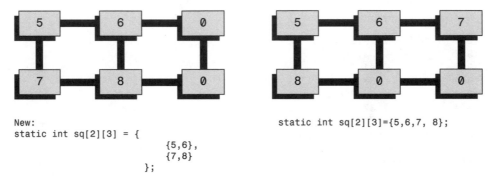

```
New:
static int sq[2][3] = {
                        {5,6},
                        {7,8}
            };
```

```
static int sq[2][3]={5,6,7, 8};
```

Figure 10.4. *Two methods of initializing an array.*

More Dimensions

Everything we have said about two-dimensional arrays can be generalized to three-dimensional arrays and further. You can declare a three-dimensional array this way:

```
int box[10][20][30]
```

You can visualize this array as 10 two-dimensional arrays (each 20 x 30) stacked atop each other, or you can think of it as an array of arrays of arrays. That is, it is a 10-element array, each element of which is a 20-element array. Each 20-element array then has elements that are 30-element arrays, or you can simply think of arrays in terms of the number of indices needed. We'll stick to two dimensions in our examples.

Pointers and Multidimensional Arrays

How do pointers relate to multidimensional arrays? We'll look at some examples now to find the answer. To simplify the discussion, we'll examine an array that is much smaller than rain. Suppose we have this declaration:

```
int zippo[4][2];   /* an array of arrays of ints */
```

Then zippo, being the name of an array, is the address of the first element of the array. In this case, the first element of zippo is itself an array of two ints, so zippo is the address of an array of two ints. Let's analyze that further in terms of pointer properties.

- Because zippo is the address of the array's first element, zippo equals &zippo[0]. Next, zippo[0] is itself an array of two integers, so zippo[0] equals &zippo[0][0], the address of its first element, an int. In short, zippo[0] is the address of an int-sized object, and zippo is the address of a two-int-sized object. Because both the integer and the array of two integers begin at the same location, both zippo and zippo[0] have the same numeric value.

- Adding 1 to a pointer or address yields a value larger by the size of the referred-to object. In this respect, zippo and zippo[0] differ, for zippo refers to an object two ints in size, and zippo[0] refers to an object one int in size. Thus, zippo + 1 and zippo[0] + 1 do not have the same value.

- Dereferencing a pointer or an address (applying the * operator) yields the value represented by the referred-to object. Because zippo[0] is the address of its first element zippo[0][0], *(zippo[0]) represents the value stored in zippo[0][0], an int value. Similarly, *zippo represents the value of its first element, zippo[0], but zippo[0] itself is the address of an int. It's the address &zippo[0][0], so *zippo is &zippo[0][0]. Applying the dereferencing operator to both expressions implies that **zippo equals *&zippo[0][0], which reduces to zippo[0][0], an int. In short, zippo is the address of an address and must be dereferenced twice to get an ordinary value. An address of an address or a pointer of a pointer is an example of *double indirection*.

Clearly, increasing the number of array dimensions increases the complexity of the pointer view. At this point, most students of C begin realizing why pointers are considered one of the more difficult aspects of the language. You may wish to study the preceding points carefully and see how they are borne out of the following examples. Listing 10.12 is a program that prints addresses.

Listing 10.12. zippo1.c.

```
/* zippo1.c -- addresses */
#include <stdio.h>
int main(void)
{

    int zippo[4][2];

    printf("zippo = %p, zippo[0] = %p, &zippo[0][0] = %p, ",
            zippo, zippo[0], &zippo[0][0]);
    printf("&zippo = %p\n", *zippo);
    return 0;
}
```

Here is the output:

```
zippo = 0B92, zippo[0] = 0B92, &zippo[0][0] = 0B92, *zippo = 0B92
```

The output shows that the address of the two-dimensional array `zippo` and the address of the one-dimensional array `zippo[0]` are the same. Each is the address of the corresponding array's first element, and this is the same numerically as `&zippo[0][0]`. Also, note that `zippo` and `*zippo` have the same value.

Nonetheless, there is a difference. On our system, `int` is 2 bytes. As discussed earlier, `zippo[0]` and `*zippo` point to a 2-byte data object. Adding 1 to either should produce a value larger by 2. The name `zippo` is the address of an array of two `ints`, so it identifies a 4-byte data object. Thus, adding 1 to `zippo` should produce an address 4 bytes larger. Let's modify the program, as shown in Listing 10.13, to check that.

Listing 10.13. `zippo2.c`.

```c
/* zippo2.c -- more zippo info */
#include <stdio.h>
int main(void)
{
    int zippo[4][2];
    printf("zippo = %p, zippo[0] = %p, &zippo[0][0] = %p\n",
    zippo, zippo[0], &zippo[0][0]);
    printf("*zippo = %p\n", *zippo);

    printf("zippo + 1 = %p, zippo[0] + 1 = %p\n",
    zippo + 1, zippo[0] + 1);
    printf("&zippo[0][0] + 1 = %p, *zippo + 1 = %p\n",
            &zippo[0][0] + 1, *zippo + 1);
    printf("*(zippo + 1) = %p\n", *(zippo + 1));
    return 0;
}
```

Here is the new output:

```
zippo = 0BF2, zippo[0] = 0BF2, &zippo[0][0] = 0BF2
*zippo = 0BF2
zippo + 1 = 0BF6, zippo[0] + 1 = 0BF4
&zippo[0][0] + 1 = 0BF4, *zippo + 1 = 0BF4
*(zippo + 1) = 0BF6
```

The results are as we predicted. Adding 1 to `zippo` moves us from one two-int array to the next array, and adding 1 to `zippo[0]` moves us from one `int` to the next. See Figure 10.5. Also, note what happens if we add 2 to `zippo[0]` (or, equivalently, to `*zippo`). We would go past the end of the first two-int array to the beginning of the next. The last two examples illustrate that `zippo[0]`, `&zippo[0][0]`, and `*zippo` are but three different notations for the same thing. All are addresses of the same `int`.

Note the difference between `*zippo + 1` and `*(zippo +1)`. The former applies the
`*` first and then adds, but the latter adds and then dereferences. In the first case, because
`*zippo` is the address of an `int`, adding 1 increases the value by 2 bytes on our system.
In the second case, because `zippo` is the address of a two-int object, 4 is added. This
means that `zippo + 1` is the address of the second two-int array element, and applying
the `*` operator yields the address of the first element of that array. Thus, `*(zippo + 1)`
is the address of an `int`. In particular, it's the address of the element `zippo[1][0]`.
The expression `*zippo + 1` also is the address of an `int`, but it's the address of
`zippo[0][1]`. In short, dereferencing, then adding, moves the address along a row
(changes the second index); adding, then dereferencing, moves the address along a column
(changes the first index).

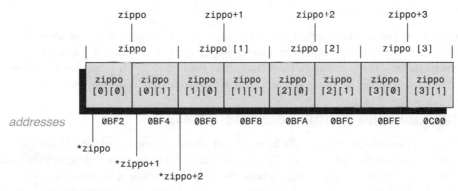

Figure 10.5. *An array of arrays.*

Another point to note is that *each* element of `zippo` is an array and hence the address
of a first element. Thus, we have these relationships:

```
zippo[0] == &zippo[0][0] == *zippo
zippo[1] == &zippo[1][0] == *(zippo + 1)
zippo[2] == &zippo[2][0] == *(zippo + 2)
zippo[3] == &zippo[3][0] == *(zippo + 3)
```

Applying the `*` operator to each gives the following results:

```
*zippo[0] == zippo[0][0] == **zippo
*zippo[1] == zippo[1][0] == *(*(zippo + 1)
*zippo[2] == zippo[2][0] == *(*(zippo + 2)
*zippo[3] == zippo[3][0] == *(*(zippo + 3)
```

More generally, we can represent individual elements using array notation and pointer
notation as follows:

```
zippo[m][n] == *(*(zippo + m) + n)
```

The value m, being the index associated with `zippo`, is added to `zippo`. The value n, being
the index associated with the subarray `zippo[m]`, is added to `zippo[m]`, which is `*(zippo`

+m) in array notation. This makes `*(zippo + m) + n` the address of element
`zippo[m][n]`, and applying the `*` operator yields the contents at that address.

Now suppose we want to declare a pointer variable `pz` that is compatible with `zippo`.
Such a pointer could be used, for example, in writing a function to deal with `zippo`-like
arrays. Will the type pointer-to-`int` suffice? No. That type is compatible with `zippo[0]`,
which points to a single `int`, but we want `pz` to point to an array of `int`s. Here is what we
can do:

```
int (* pz)[2];
```

This statement says that `pz` is a pointer to an array of two `int`s. Why the parentheses?
Well `[]` has a higher precedence than `*`. Thus, with a declaration like

```
int * pax[2];
```

we apply the brackets first, making `pax` an array of two somethings. Next, we apply the `*`,
making `pax` an array of two pointers. Finally, we use the `int`, making `pax` an array of two
pointers to `int`. Thus, this declaration creates two pointers, but our original version uses
parentheses to apply the `*` first, creating one pointer to an array of two `int`s.

Functions and Multidimensional Arrays

You may be wondering if you really have to learn about pointers to pointers. If you want
to write functions that process two-dimensional arrays, the answer is yes. Mainly you need
to understand pointers well enough to make the proper declarations for function arguments. In the function body itself, you usually can get by with array notation.

Suppose, then, that you want to write a function to deal with two-dimensional arrays.
You have several choices. You can use a function written for one-dimensional arrays on
each subarray, or you can use the same function on the whole array, but treat the whole
array as one-dimensional instead of two-dimensional, or you can write a function that
explicitly deals with two-dimensional arrays. To illustrate these three approaches, let's take
a small two-dimensional array and apply each of the approaches to double the magnitude
of each element.

Applying a One-Dimensional Function to Subarrays

To keep things simple, we'll declare `junk` to be a `static` array of arrays so that we can
initialize it. We'll write a function that takes an array address and an array size as arguments and doubles the indicated elements. We'll use a `for` loop to apply this function
to each subarray of `junk`, and we'll print the array contents. Listing 10.14 shows the
program.

Listing 10.14. dubarr1.c.

```c
/* dubarr1.c -- doubles array elements */
#include <stdio.h>
void dub(int ar[], int size);
int main(void)
{
    static int junk[3][4] = {
            {2,4,5,8},
            {3,5,6,9},
            {12,10,8,6}
    };
    int i, j;

    for (i = 0; i < 3 ; i++)
       dub(junk[i], 4);

    for (i = 0; i < 3; i++)
    {
       for (j = 0; j < 4; j++)
          printf("%5d", junk[i][j]);
       putchar('\n');
    }
    return 0;
}

void dub(int ar[], int size)    /* or int * ar */
{
    int i;

    for (i = 0; i < size; i++)
        ar[i] *= 2;
}
```

The first `for` loop in `main()` uses `dub()` to process the subarrays `junk[0]`, `junk[1]`, and so on. This approach works because `junk[0]`, `junk[1]`, etc., *are* each one-dimensional arrays. Note that we pass `dub()` a size parameter of 4, because that is the number of elements in each subarray. Here is the output:

```
 4    8   10   16
 6   10   12   18
24   20   16   12
```

Applying a One-Dimensional Function to a Two-Dimensional Array

In the preceding example, we looked at `junk` as being an array of 3 arrays of 4 `int`s. For most C implementations, we also can look at `junk` as being an array of 12 `int`s. Suppose, for instance, we pass `dub()` the value `junk[0]` as an argument. This act initializes the pointer `ar` in `dub()` to the address of `junk[0][0]`. As a result, `ar[0]` corresponds to junk[0][0], and ar[3] corresponds to junk[0][3]. What about ar[4]? It represents the element following junk[0][3], which is junk[1][0], the first element of the next subarray. In other words, we've finished one row and have gone to the beginning of the next. The program in Listing 10.15 continues in this fashion to cover the whole array, with ar[11] representing junk[2][3].

Listing 10.15. dubarr2.c.

```
/* dubarr2.c -- doubles array elements */
#include <stdio.h>
void dub(int ar[], int size);
int main(void)
{
    static int junk[3][4] = {
            {2,4,5,8},
            {3,5,6,9},
            {12,10,8,6}
    };
    int i, j;

    dub(junk[0], 3*4);

    for (i = 0; i < 3; i++)
    {
        for (j = 0; j < 4; j++)
            printf("%5d", junk[i][j]);
        putchar('\n');
    }
    return 0;
}

void dub(int ar[], int size)    /* or int * ar */
{
    int i;

    for (i = 0; i < size; i++)
        ar[i] *= 2;
}
```

In Listing 10.15, note that dub() is unchanged from Listing 10.14. We merely changed the limit to 3*4 (or 12) and used one call to dub() instead of three. (We wrote the limit as 3*4 to emphasize that it is the total number of elements calculated by multiplying the number of rows times the number of columns.) Does it work? Here is the output:

```
 4    8   10   16
 6   10   12   18
24   20   16   12
```

Because junk has the same numerical value as junk[0], could we use junk instead of junk[0] as the argument to dub()? K&R implementations let you, but ANSI C implementations point out that junk clashes with the prototype, which says the argument should be a pointer-to-int, not a pointer to a pointer.

Applying a Two-Dimensional Function

Both of the approaches so far lose track of the column-and-row information. In this application (doubling each element), that information is unimportant, but suppose each row represented a year and each column a month. Then you might want a function to, say, total up individual columns. In that case, the function should have the row and column information available. This can be accomplished by declaring the right kind of formal variable so that the function can pass the array properly. In this case, the array junk is an array of 3 arrays of 4 ints. As our earlier discussion has implied, this means that junk is a pointer to an array of four ints, and a variable of this type can be declared in this way:

```
int (* pj)[4];
```

Alternatively, if pj is a formal argument to a function, we can declare it this way:

```
int pj[][4];
```

Note that the first set of brackets is empty. The empty brackets identify pj as being a pointer. Such a variable can then be used in the same way as junk. That is what we have done in the next example, shown in Listing 10.16.

Listing 10.16. dubarr3.c.

```
/* dubarr3.c -- doubles array elements */
#include <stdio.h>
void dub2 (int ar[][4], int size);
int main(void)
{
    static int junk[3][4] = {
            {2,4,5,8},
            {3,5,6,9},
            {12,10,8,6}
    };
    int i, j;

    dub2(junk,3);
    for (i = 0; i < 3; i++)
    {
        for (j = 0; j < 4; j++)
            printf("%5d", junk[i][j]);
        putchar('\n');
    }
```

continues

Listing 10.16. continued

```
    return 0;
}

void dub2 (int ar[][4], int size)    /* or int (*ar)[4] */
{
    int i, j;

    for (i = 0; i < size; i++)
        for (j = 0; j < 4; j++)
            ar[i][j] *= 2;
}
```

In Listing 10.16 we pass as arguments junk, which is a pointer to the first array, and 3, the number of rows. The dub2() function then treats ar as an array of arrays of 4 ints. The number of columns is built into the function, but the number of rows is left open. The same function will work with, say, a 12-by-4 array if 12 is passed as the number of rows. That's because size is the number of elements; but, because each element is an array, or row, size becomes the number of rows.

Note that ar is used in the same fashion as junk is used in main(). This is possible because ar and junk are the same type: pointer to array-of-four-ints.

Here is the output:

```
 4    8   10   16
 6   10   12   18
24   20   16   12
```

Be aware that the following declaration will not work properly:

```
int ar[][]; /* faulty declaration */
```

Recall that the compiler converts array notation to pointer notation. This means, for example, that ar[1] will become ar+1. For the compiler to evaluate this, it needs to know what size of object ar points to. The declaration

```
int ar[][4];
```

says that ar points to an array of 4 ints, hence to an object 8 bytes long on our system, so ar+1 means "add 8 bytes to the address." With the empty-bracket version, the compiler would not know what to do.

You can also include a size in the other bracket pair, but it is ignored.

```
void dub2(ar, n)
int ar[3][4];    /* the 3 is ignored */
int n;
```

In general, to declare a pointer corresponding to an *N*-dimensional array, you must provide values for all but the left-most set of brackets.

Planning a Program

Now that you've seen the mechanics of writing array functions, let's try a more programming-oriented example. Our self-appointed task is to write a program that reads numbers into an array, prints the entered numbers, and reports the average. To make the program more realistic, we'll require that it enable the user to terminate input, if desired, before the array is filled. This will enable the program to process any number of items up to a maximum determined by the array size. Also, we'll want to avoid calculating the average if no numbers are entered.

General Plan

Conceptually, we expect the program to perform three major tasks: reading in a set of numbers, printing the set of numbers, and calculating the average. Now that you know how to process arrays with functions, let's use functions to modularize the work. As a first pass, we can visualize the program as shown in Listing 10.17.

Listing 10.17. `draft1.c.`

```
/* draft1.c -- first draft of program skeleton */
#include <stdio.h>
#define MAX 25
void read_array(double ar[]);
void show_array(double ar[]);
double mean(double ar[]);
int main(void)
{
  double data[MAX];

  read_array(data);
  show_array(data);
  printf("The average is %.2lf.\n", mean(data));
  return 0;
}
```

Now we have a modular program, but this draft doesn't handle data communication well. For instance, the `read_array()` function should know the maximum number of items that it is allowed to read. Thus, it should also take `MAX` as an argument. Incidentally, the fact that `data` is a pointer means that the `read_array()` function will modify the `data` array in `main()` directly, which is exactly what we want for this function.

Similarly, the `show_array()` and `mean()` functions should know how big an array they are using. Thus, they each need an additional argument. In general, this argument should not be `MAX`, because the user may enter fewer numbers. We can use a variable `size` to represent the actual number of items entered; it can be the second argument to these two functions.

This raises a new problem: How does main() know what size is? One solution is to have the read_array() function return that value. That is, it takes as arguments the array to be filled and the maximum number of values that the array holds. It then reads data into the array and returns the actual number of items read. If this number is zero, we can skip the rest of the program. This line of thought leads to a second draft for the skeleton, which we show in Listing 10.18.

Listing 10.18. draft2.c.

```
/* draft2.c -- second top-level draft for the program */
#include <stdio.h>
#define MAX 25
int read_array(double ar[], int limit);
void show_array(double ar[], int n);
double mean(double ar[], int n);
int main(void)
{
  double data[MAX];
  int size;
  double average;

  size = read_array(data, MAX);
  if (size == 0)
      printf("No data. Bye.\n");
  else
  {
      printf("The following numbers were entered:\n\n");
      show_array(data, size);
      printf("\nThe average of these values is %.2f.\n",
          mean(data, size));
  }
  return 0;
}
```

Note that we changed the prototype for read_array() to reflect that it now has a return value. Now we have the overall design for the program and its data flow, and we can turn to the individual functions.

The *read_array()* Function

The read_array() function is the most ambitious of the three. It should read in values until the array is filled or until the user wants to stop, whichever occurs first. The main question is how to let the user inform the program that he or she is finished. We can use the properties of scanf() to help here. Recall that scanf() returns the number of values successfully read. Nonnumeric input or end of file causes it to return 0 or EOF, respectively. Therefore, we can terminate input if scanf() doesn't return the value 1. Also, we can use a counter to keep track of the number of entries so that we can terminate input if the counter exceeds the size of the array. Here's one approach:

```c
int read_array(double ar[], int limit)
{
  int i = 0;

  printf("Enter up to %d numbers. To terminate\n", limit);
  printf("earlier, enter a letter or EOF.\n");
  while (i < limit && scanf("%lf", &ar[i]) == 1)
      i++;
  return i;
}
```

This approach looks simple enough, but there are two subtle points to note. The first is that the test i < limit comes first. Recall that the && operator guarantees that the second operand is not evaluated if the first operand is false. This means that if i equals limit, the expression scanf("%lf", &ar[i]) == 1 is not evaluated. This, in turn, means that the scanf() function is not called, which is good. Suppose that we had used the opposite order

```c
while ( scanf("%lf", &ar[i]) == 1 && i < limit)
```

In this case, scanf() reads a value into ar[limit] before finding out that it has gone too far. Remember, because array numbering begins with 0, ar[limit] is one position past the end of the array. You don't want to put data there!

The second subtle point is that the loop increments i after reading a value into ar[i]. This makes i one greater than the index of the last array element filled. Because indexing begins with 0, i at that point equals the number of array items, not the array index. This is convenient because the number of array items is the value we wish to return.

If you like, you can use pointers more explicitly. For instance, you could use the following input loop:

```c
while (i < limit && scanf("%lf", ar++) == 1)
    i++;
```

Recall that scanf() requires the address of the location that is to receive the data. Initially, ar holds the address of the first element of the array, so the first time through the loop scanf() places a number in the first element of the array. Then the increment operator increases ar so that it points to the next element of the array, thus preparing for the next loop cycle.

The *show_array()* Function

Next, we want a function to display the array values. We already have written one for Listing 10.10. A problem with that function, however, is that it prints everything on one line. Here we have more data, so we would like to insert some newline characters.

One scheme is to use a for loop as before and to print a newline after every sixth value. We can do this by using the modulus operator (%).

```c
void show_array(double ar[], int n)
{
  int i;

  for (i = 0; i < n; i++)
  {
      printf("%10.2f ", ar[i]);
      if (i % 6 == 5)
          putchar('\n');
  }
  if (i % 6 != 0)
      putchar('\n');
}
```

Because i starts at 0, i % 6 first becomes 5 after 6 values have been printed. The expression subsequently becomes 5 after each additional 6 values have been printed.

The if (i % 6 != 0) test causes a newline to be printed after all the values have been printed, unless the last value printed was already at the end of a line—in which case the loop itself prints a newline. If i % 6 is 5 inside the loop, the i++ operation at loop's end causes i % 6 to be 0 after leaving the loop.

The *mean()* Function

Finding the mean is a simple problem. We can use a for loop to sum the numbers and then divide by the total number of items to get the average.

```c
double mean(double ar[], int n)
{
  int i;
  double total = 0;

  for (i = 0; i < n ; i++)
      total += ar[i];
  return (total / n);
}
```

The only potential trouble spot is if n is 0 because dividing by 0 is a no-no. The main() function shields mean() from this possibility.

The Result

Putting the parts together results in the program shown in Listing 10.19.

Listing 10.19. mean.c.

```c
/* mean.c -- finds the mean of a set of numbers */
#include <stdio.h>
#define MAX 25
int read_array(double ar[], int limit);
void show_array(double ar[], int n);
double mean(double ar[], int n);
int main(void)
{
  double data[MAX];
  int size;
  double average;

  size = read_array(data, MAX);
  if (size == 0)
      printf("No data. Bye.\n");
  else
  {
      printf("The following numbers were entered:\n\n");
      show_array(data, size);
      printf("\nThe average of these values is %.2f.\n",
          mean(data, size));
  }
  return 0;
}
int read_array(double ar[], int limit)
{
  int i = 0;

  printf("Enter up to %d numbers. To terminate\n", limit);
  printf("earlier, enter a letter or EOF.\n");
  while (i < limit  && scanf("%lf", &ar[i]) == 1)
      i++;
  return i;
}
void show_array(double ar[], int n)
{
  int i;

  for (i = 0; i < n; i++)
  {
      printf("%10.2f ", ar[i]);
      if (i % 6 == 5)
          putchar('\n');
  }
  if (i % 6 != 0)
      putchar('\n');
}
double mean(double ar[], int n)
{
```

continues

Listing 10.19. continued

```
    int i;
    double total = 0;

    for (i = 0; i < n ; i++)
        total += ar[i];
    return (total/n);
}
```

Here's a sample run:

```
Enter up to 25 numbers. To terminate
earlier, enter a letter or EOF.
1 2 3 4 5 6 7 8 9 10 q
The following numbers were entered:
      1.00     2.00     3.00     4.00     5.00     6.00
      7.00     8.00     9.00    10.00

The average of these values is 5.50.
```

Chapter Summary

An *array* is a set of elements all having the same data type. Array elements are stored sequentially in memory and are accessed by using an integer index (or offset). In C, the first element of an array has an index of 0, so the final element in an array of n elements has an index of n - 1.

To declare a simple *one-dimensional array,* use this form:

```
type name[size];
```

Here, *type* is the data type for each and every element, *name* is the name of the array, and *size* is the number of elements.

C interprets the name of an array to be the address of the first element of the array. In other terms, the name of an array is equivalent to a pointer to the first element. In general, arrays and pointers are closely connected. If ar is an array, then the expressions ar[i] and *(ar + i) are equivalent.

C does not enable entire arrays to be passed as function arguments, but you can pass the address of an array. The function then can use this address to manipulate the original array. You can use either array notation or pointer notation in the called function. In either case, you're actually using a pointer variable.

Adding an integer to a pointer or incrementing a pointer changes the value of the pointer by the number of bytes of the object being pointed to. That is, if pd points to an

8-byte `double` value in an array, adding 1 to `pd` increases its value by 8 so that it will point to the next element of the array.

Two-dimensional arrays represent an array of arrays. For instance, the declaration

```
double sales[5][12];
```

creates an array `sales` having 5 elements, each of which is an array of 12 `double`s. The first of these one-dimensional arrays can be referred to as `sales[0]`, the second as `sales[1]`, and so on, with each being an array of 12 `int`s. Use a second index to access a particular element in these arrays. For instance, `sales[2][5]` is the sixth element of `sales[2]`, and `sales[2]` is the third element of `sales`.

We've used `int` arrays and `double` arrays in this discussion, but the same concepts apply to other types. Character strings, however, have many special rules. This stems from the fact that the terminal null character in a string provides a way for functions to detect the end of a string without being passed a size. We will look at character strings in detail in Chapter 11, "Character Strings and String Functions."

Review Questions

1. What will this program print?

   ```
   #include <stdio.h>
   char ref[] = { 'D', 'O', 'L', 'T'};
   int main(void)
   {
     char *ptr;
     int index;

     for (index = 0, ptr = ref; index < 4; index++, ptr++)
       printf("%c %c\n", ref[index], *ptr);
     return 0;
   }
   ```

2. In Question 1, of what is `ref` the address? What about `ref + 1`? What does `++ref` point to?

3. What is the value of `*ptr` and of `*(ptr + 2)` in each case?

   a.
   ```
   int *ptr;
   static int torf[2][2] = {12, 14, 16};
   ptr = torf[0];
   ```

b.
```
int * ptr;
static int fort[2][2] = { {12}, {14,16} };
ptr = fort[0];
```

4. Create an appropriate declaration for each of the following variables:

   a. digits is an array of 10 ints.
   b. rates is an array of 6 floats.
   c. mat is an array of 3 arrays of 5 integers.
   d. pstr is a pointer to an array of 20 chars.
   e. psa is an array of 20 pointers to char.

5. What is the index range for a 10-element array?

Programming Exercises

1. Modify the rain program in Listing 10.11 so that it does the calculations using pointers instead of subscripts. (You still have to declare and initialize the array.)

2. Write a program that initializes an array and then copies the contents of the array into two other arrays. (All three arrays should be declared in the main program.) To make the first copy, use a function with array notation. To make the second copy, use a function with pointer notation and pointer incrementing. Have each function take as arguments the name of the source array, the name of the target array, and the number of elements to be copied.

3. Write a function that returns the largest value stored in an array. Test the function in a simple program.

4. Write a function that returns the index of the largest value stored in an array. Test the function in a simple program.

5. Write a function that returns the difference between the largest and smallest elements of an array. Test the function in a simple program.

6. Write a program that initializes a two-dimensional array and uses one of the copy functions from Exercise 2 to copy it to a second two-dimensional array. (Because a two-dimensional array is an array of arrays, a one-dimensional copy function can be used with each subarray.)

7. Use a copy function from Exercise 2 to copy the 3rd through 5th elements of a 7-element array into a 3-element array. The function itself need not be altered; just choose the right actual arguments. (The actual arguments need not be an array name and array size. They only have to be the address of an array element and a number of elements to be processed.)

8. Write a function that sets each element in an array to the sum of the corresponding elements in two other arrays. That is, if array 1 has the values 2, 4, 5, 8 and array 2 has the values 1, 0, 4, 6, the function assigns array 3 the values 3, 4, 9, 12. The function should take three array names and an array size as arguments. Test the function in a simple program.

9. Write a program that declares a 3-by-5 array and initializes it to some values of your choice. Have the program print the values, double all the values, and then display the new values. Write a function to do the displaying and a second function to do the doubling. Have the functions take the array name and the number of rows as arguments.

10. Rewrite the rain program in Listing 10.11 so that the main tasks are performed by functions instead of in main().

11. Write a program that prompts the user to enter three sets of five double numbers each. The program should accomplish all of the following:

a. Store the information in a 3-by-5 array.
b. Compute the average of each set of 5 values.
c. Compute the average of the values.
d. Determine the largest value of the 15 values.
e. Report the results.

Each major task should be handled by a separate function.

Character Strings and String Functions

Functions

```
gets(), puts(), strcat(), strcmp()
strcpy(), sprint(), strchr(), isalnum()
isalpha(), iscntrl(), isdigit(), isgraph()
islower(), isprint(), ispunct(), isspace()
isupper(), isxdigit()
```

In this chapter you learn more about creating and using strings. You use several string and character functions from the C library and practice creating your own string functions. Also, you learn how to use command-line arguments.

Character strings are one of the most useful and important data types in C. You have been using character strings all along, but there still is much to learn about them. Of course, you already know the most basic fact: a *character string* is a char array terminated with a null character (\0). This chapter discusses the nature of strings, how to declare and initialize strings, how to get them into and out of programs, and how to manipulate strings.

Listing 11.1 presents a busy program that illustrates several ways to set up strings, read them, and print them. It uses two new functions: gets(), which reads a string, and puts(), which prints a string. (You probably notice a family resemblance to getchar() and putchar().) The rest of the program should look fairly familiar.

Listing 11.1. strings.c.

```
/* strings.c -- stringing the user along */
#include <stdio.h>
#define MSG "You must have many talents. Tell me some."
                        /* a symbolic string constant */
#define LIM  5
#define LINELEN 81       /* maximum string length + 1  */
char m1[] = "Just limit yourself to one line's worth.";
                        /* initializing an external   */
                        /* character array            */
char * m2 = "If you can't think of anything, fake it.";
                        /* initializing an external   */
                        /* character pointer          */
int main(void)
{
  char name[LINELEN];
  static char talents[LINELEN];
  int i;
  char *m3 = "\nEnough about me -- what's your name?";
                        /* initializing a pointer        */
  static char *mytal[LIM] = {  "Adding numbers swiftly",
          "Multiplying accurately", "Stashing data",
          "Following instructions to the letter",
          "Understanding the C language"};
                        /* initializing an array of    */
                        /* strings                     */

  printf("Hi! I'm Clyde the Computer. I have many talents.\n");

  printf("Let me tell you some of them.\n");
  puts("What were they? Ah, yes, here's a partial list.");
  for (i = 0; i < LIM; i++)
      puts(mytal[i]);  /* print list of computer talents */
  puts(m3);
  gets(name);
  printf("Well, %s, %s\n", name, MSG);
```

```
    printf("%s\n%s\n", m1, m2);
    gets(talents);
    puts("Let's see if I've got that list:");
    puts(talents);
    printf("Thanks for the information, %s.\n", name);
    return 0;
}
```

To show you what this program does, here is a sample run:

```
Hi! I'm Clyde the Computer. I have many talents.
Let me tell you some of them.
What were they? Ah, yes, here's a partial list.
Adding numbers swiftly
Multiplying accurately
Stashing data
Following instructions to the letter
Understanding the C language

Enough about me -- what's your name?
Nigel Barntwit
Well, Nigel Barntwit, You must have many talents. Tell me some.
Just limit yourself to one line's worth.
If you can't think of anything, fake it.
Fencing, yodeling, malingering, cheese tasting, and sighing.
Let's see if I've got that list:
Fencing, yodeling, malingering, cheese tasting, and sighing.
Thanks for the information, Nigel Barntwit.
```

Let's see how Listing 11.1 works. However, rather than go through it line by line, we will take a more encompassing approach. First, we will look at ways of defining a string within a program. Then we will see what is involved in reading a string into a program. Finally, we will study ways to output a string.

Defining Strings Within a Program

As you probably noticed when you read Listing 11.1, there are many ways to define a string. We are going to look at the principal ways now: using string constants, using char arrays, using char pointers, and using arrays of character strings. A program should make sure that there is a place to store a string, and we will take up that topic, too.

Character String Constants

A *string constant* is anything enclosed in double quotation marks. The enclosed characters, plus a terminating \0 character automatically provided by the compiler, are stored in memory as a character string. Our program uses several such character string constants, most often as arguments for the printf() and puts() functions. Note, too, that we can #define character string constants.

If you want to use a double quotation mark within a string, precede the quotation mark with a backslash.

```
printf("\"Run, Spot, run!\" exclaimed Dick.\n");
```

This produces the output

```
"Run, Spot, run!" exclaimed Dick.
```

Character string constants are placed in the *static storage* class. Static storage means that if you use a string constant in a function, the string is stored just once and lasts for the duration of the program, even if the function is called several times. The entire quoted phrase acts as a pointer to where the string is stored. This action is analogous to the name of an array acting as a pointer to the array's location. If this is true, what kind of output should the program in Listing 11.2 produce?

Listing 11.2. quotes.c.

```
/* quotes.c -- strings as pointers */
#include <stdio.h>
int main(void)
{
    printf(" %s, %p, %c\n", "We", "love", *"figs");
    return 0;
}
```

The %s format should print the string We. The %p format produces an address. Thus, if the phrase "love" is an address, then %u should print the address of the first character in the string. (Pre-ANSI implementations may have to use %u or %lu instead of %p.) Finally, *"figs" should produce the value of the address pointed to, which should be the first character of the string "figs". Does this really happen? Well, here is the output:

```
We, 00BA, f
```

Character String Arrays and Initialization

When you define a character string array, you must let the compiler know how much space is needed. One way to do this is to initialize the array with a string constant. Because automatic arrays cannot be initialized in older C implementations, you must use static or external arrays for this purpose. For example, the following declaration initializes the external array m1 to the characters of the indicated string:

```
char m1[] = "Just limit yourself to one line's worth.";
```

This form of initialization is short for the standard array initialization form:

```
char m1[] = { 'J', 'u', 's', 't', ' ', 'l', 'i', 'm', 'i',
't', ' ', 'y', 'o', 'u', 'r', 's', 'e', 'l',
'f', ' ', 't', 'o', ' ', 'o', 'n', 'e', ' ',
'l', 'i', 'n', 'e', '\"', 's', ' ', 'w', 'o', 'r',
't', 'h', '.', '\0'
};
```

Note the closing null character. Without it, you have a character array, but not a string. For either form (and we do recommend the first), the compiler counts the characters and sizes the array accordingly. Initializing character arrays is one case when it really does make sense to let the compiler determine the array size.

Just as for other arrays, so does the array name m1 yield the address of the first element of the array.

```
m1 == &m1[0] , *m1 == 'J', and *(m1+1) == m1[1] == 'u'
```

Indeed, you can use pointer notation to set up a string. For example, we used this declaration:

```
char *m3 = "\nEnough about me -- what's your name?";
```

This declaration is very nearly the same as

```
static char m3[] = "\nEnough about me -- what's your name?"
```

Both declarations amount to saying that m3 is a pointer to the indicated string. In both cases, the string itself determines the amount of storage set aside for the string. Nonetheless, the forms are not identical.

Array Versus Pointer

What is the difference, then, between an array and a pointer form? The array form (m3[]) causes an array of 38 elements (one for each character plus one for the terminating '\0') to be created in static storage. Each element is initialized to the corresponding character. Hereafter, the compiler will recognize the name m3 as a synonym for the address of the first array element, &m3[0]. One important point here is that in the array form, m3 is an address *constant*. You can't change m3 because that would mean changing the location (address) where the array is stored. You can use operations like m3+1 to identify the next element in an array, but ++m3 is not allowed. The increment operator can be used only with the names of variables, not with constants.

The pointer form (*m3) also causes 38 elements in static storage to be set aside for the string. In addition, it sets aside one more storage location for the pointer *variable* m3. This variable initially points to the first character of the string, but the value can be changed. Thus, you can use the increment operator. For instance, ++m3 would point to the second character (E). Note that *m3 does not have to be declared as static. The reason is that you are not initializing an array of 38 elements; rather, you are initializing a single pointer variable. There are no storage class restrictions for initializing ordinary, nonarray variables, either in K&R C or in ANSI C.

Are these differences important? Often they are not, but it depends on what you try to do. See the following discussion for some examples.

Array and Pointer Differences

Let's examine the differences between initializing a character array to hold a string and initializing a pointer to point to a string. (By "pointing to a string," we really mean pointing to the first character of a string.) For example, consider these two declarations:

```
static char heart[] = "I love Tillie!";
char *head = "I love Millie!";
```

The chief difference is that the array name heart is a constant, but the pointer head is a variable. What practical difference does this make?

First, both can use pointer addition.

```
for (i = 0; i < 6; i++)
    putchar(*(heart + i));
putchar('\n');
for (i = 0; i < 6; i++)
    putchar(*(head + i));
putchar('\n');
```

The output is

```
I love
I love
```

Only the pointer version, however, can use the increment operator.

```
while (*(head) != '\0') /* stop at end of string           */
    putchar(*(head++));  /* print character, advance pointer */
```

This produces

```
I love Millie!
```

Suppose you want head to agree with heart. You can say this:

```
head = heart;  /* head now points to the array heart */
```

However, you cannot say this:

```
heart = head;  /* illegal construction */
```

The situation is analogous to x = 3; versus 3 = x;. The left side of the assignment statement must be a variable or, more generally, an lvalue, such as *p_int. Incidentally, head = heart; does not make the Millie string vanish; it just changes the address stored in head. Unless you've saved the address of "I love Millie!" elsewhere, however, you won't be able to access that string once head points to another location.

There is a way to alter the `heart` message—go into the array itself.

```
heart[7]= 'M';
```

or

```
*(heart + 7) = 'M';
```

The *elements* of an array are variables, but the *name* is not a variable.

Specifying Storage Explicitly

Another way to set up storage is to be explicit. In the external declaration, we could have said

```
char m1[44] = "Just limit yourself to one line's worth.";
```

instead of

```
char m1[] = "Just limit yourself to one line's worth.";
```

Just be sure that the number of elements is at least one more (that null character again) than the string length. As with other static or external arrays, any unused elements are automatically initialized to 0 (which in `char` form is the null character, not the zero digit character). See Figure 11.1.

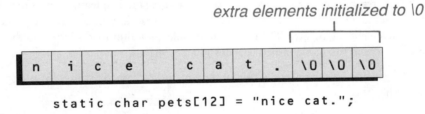

Figure 11.1. *Initializing an array.*

Note that in our program we had to assign a size for the array `name`.

```
char name[81];
```

Because the contents for `name` are to be read when the program runs, the compiler has no way of knowing in advance how much space to set aside unless we tell it. There is no string constant present whose characters the compiler can count, so we gambled that 80 characters would be enough to hold the user's name. When you declare an array, the array size must evaluate to an integer constant. You can't use a variable that gets set at runtime. The array size is locked into the program at compile time.

```
int n = 8;
char cakes[2 + 5];   /* valid, size is a constant expression */
char crumbs[n];      /* invalid, size is a variable */
```

Arrays of Character Strings

Often it is convenient to have an array of character strings. Then you can use a subscript to access several different strings. We used this example in Listing 11.1:

```
static char *mytal[LIM] = {"Adding numbers swiftly",
        "Multiplying accurately", "Stashing data",
        "Following instructions to the letter",
        "Understanding the C language"};
```

Let's study this declaration. Because LIM is 5, we can say that mytal is an array of 5 pointers-to-char. The first pointer is mytal[0], and it points to the first character of the first string. The second pointer is mytal[1], and it points to the beginning of the second string. In general, each pointer points to the first character of the corresponding string.

```
*mytal[0] == 'A', *mytal[1] == 'M', *mytal[2] == 'S'
```

and so on. You can think of mytal[0] as representing the first string and *mytal[0] as the first character of the first string. Because of the relationship between array notation and pointers, you also can use mytal[0][0] to represent the first character of the first string, even though mytal is not defined as a two-dimensional array.

The initialization follows the rules for arrays. The braced portion is equivalent to

```
{{...}, {...},...,{...} };
```

where the ellipses indicate the stuff we were too lazy to type in. The main point is that the first set of double quotation marks corresponds to a brace-pair and thus is used to initialize the first character string pointer. The next set of double quotation marks initializes the second pointer, and so on. A comma separates adjacent strings.

Again, we could have been explicit about the size of the character strings by using a declaration like this:

```
static char mytal_2[LIM][LINLIM];
```

One difference is that this second choice sets up a *rectangular* array with all the rows of the same length. The following choice, however, sets up a *ragged* array, with each row's length determined by the string it was initialized to:

```
static char *mytal[LIM];
```

This ragged array doesn't waste any storage space. Figure 11.2 shows the two kinds of arrays.

Another difference is that mytal and mytal_2 have different types; mytal is an array of pointers-to-char, but mytal_2 is an array of arrays of char. In short, mytal holds 5 addresses, but mytal_2 holds 5 complete character arrays.

Pointers and Strings

Perhaps you noticed an occasional reference to pointers in our discussion of strings. Most C operations for strings actually work with pointers. Consider, for example, the instructive program shown in Listing 11.3.

Listing 11.3. p_and_s.c.

```c
/* p_and_s.c -- pointers and strings */
#include <stdio.h>
int main(void)
{
  static char * mesg = "Don't be a fool!";
  static char * copy;

  copy = mesg;
  printf("%s\n", copy);
  printf("mesg = %s; &mesg = %p; value = %p\n",
      mesg, &mesg, mesg);
  printf("copy = %s; &copy = %p; value = %p\n",
      copy, &copy, copy);
  return 0;
}
```

> **Note:** Use %u or %lu instead of %p if your compiler doesn't support %p.

Looking at this program, you might think that it makes a copy of the string "Don't be a fool!", and your first glance at the output might seem to confirm this guess.

```
Don't be a fool!
mesg = Don't be a fool!; &mesg = 00AA; value = 00AC
copy = Don't be a fool!; &copy = 038E; value = 00AC
```

Study the printf() output. First, mesg and copy are printed as strings (%s). No surprises here; all the strings are "Don't be a fool!"

The next item on each line is the address of the specified pointer. The two pointers mesg and copy are stored in locations 00AA and 038E, respectively.

Now notice the final item, the one we called value. It is the value of the specified pointer. The value of the pointer is the address it contains. We see that mesg points to location 00AC, and so does copy. Thus, the string itself was never copied. All that copy = mesg; does is produce a second pointer pointing to the very same string.

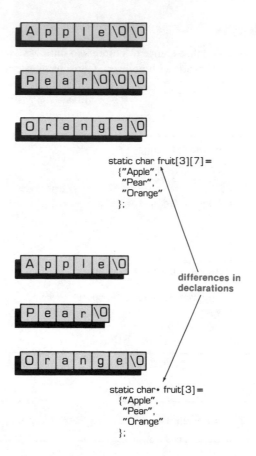

Figure 11.2. *Rectangular versus ragged array.*

Why all this pussyfooting around? Why not just copy the whole string? Well, ask yourself, which is more efficient: copying one address or copying, say, 50 separate elements? Often, the address is all that is needed to get the job done.

Now that we have discussed defining strings within a program, let's turn to strings that are read in.

String Input

If you wish to read a string into a program, you must first set aside space to store the string and then use an input function to fetch the string.

Creating Space

The first order of business is setting up a place to put the string once it is read. As we mentioned earlier, this means that you need to allot sufficient storage to hold whatever strings you expect to read. Don't expect the computer to count the string length as it is read and then allot space for it. The computer won't (unless you write a function to do so). For example, if you try something like this,

```
static char *name;

scanf("%s", name);
```

it probably will get by the compiler, but when the name is read, the name will be written over data or code in your program. Most programmers regard this as highly humorous, but only in other people's programs.

The simplest course is to include an explicit array size in the declaration.

```
char name[81];
```

Another possibility is to use the C library functions that allocate memory, and we'll touch on those in Chapter 16, "The C Preprocessor and the C Library." In our program, we used an automatic array for `name`. You can do that even under K&R C, because you don't have to initialize the array.

Once you have set aside space for the string, you can read the string. The C library provides a trio of functions that can read strings: `scanf()`, `gets()`, and `fgets()`. The last is file oriented, and we'll defer discussion of it until Chapter 12, "File Input/Output." The `scanf()` and `gets()` functions both can read strings. The more commonly used is `gets()`, which we discuss first.

The *gets()* Function

The `gets()` (*get* string) function is very handy for interactive programs. It gets a string from your system's standard input device, normally your keyboard. Because a string has no predetermined length, `gets()` needs a way to know when to stop. Its method is to read characters until it reaches a newline (\n) character, which you generate by pressing the Enter key. It takes all the characters up to (but not including) the newline, tacks on a null character (\0), and gives the string to the calling program. The newline character itself is read and discarded so that the next read will begin at the start of the next line. Listing 11.4 shows a simple means of using `gets()`.

Listing 11.4. name1.c.

```
/* name1.c -- reads a name */
#include <stdio.h>
#define MAX 81
```

continues

Listing 11.4. continued

```
int main(void)
{
    char name[MAX];              /* allot space              */

    printf("Hi, what's your name?\n");
    gets(name);                 /* place string into name array */
    printf("Nice name, %s.\n", name);
    return 0;
}
```

Listing 11.4 will accept any name (including spaces) up to 80 characters. (Remember to reserve one space for the \0.) Note that we want gets() to affect something (name) in the calling function. This means that we should use an address as an argument; and, of course, the name of an array *is* an address.

The gets() function is more sophisticated than this last example suggests. Look at Listing 11.5.

Listing 11.5. name2.c.

```
/* name2.c -- reads a name */
#include <stdio.h>
#define MAX 81
int main(void)
{
    char name[MAX];
    char * ptr;

    printf("Hi, what's your name?\n");
    ptr = gets(name);
    printf("%s? Ah! %s!\n", name, ptr);
    return 0;
}
```

Here is a sample exchange:

```
Hi, what's your name?
Tony de Tuna
Tony de Tuna? Ah! Tony de Tuna!
```

The gets() function gets input in two ways.

- It uses an address to feed the string into name.

- The code for gets() uses the return keyword to return the address of the string, and the program assigns that address to ptr. Notice that ptr is a pointer to char. This means that gets() must return a value that is a pointer to char.

ANSI C mandates that the `stdio.h` header file include a function prototype for `gets()`. Thus, with newer implementations, you need not declare the function yourself as long as you remember to include that header file. However, some older versions of C require that you provide your own function declaration for `gets()`.

The design of a `gets()` function could look something like this:

```
char *gets(char * s)
{
    ...
    return(s);
}
```

The function header indicates that `gets()` returns a pointer to a `char`. Note that `gets()` returns the same pointer that was passed to it. There is but one copy of the input string; the one placed at the address passed as a function argument, so `ptr` in Listing 11.5 winds up pointing to the name `array`. The actual design is slightly more complicated because `gets()` has two possible returns. If everything goes well, then it returns the address of the read string, as we have said. If something goes wrong or if `gets()` encounters EOF, it returns a null, or zero, address. This NULL address is called the *NULL pointer* and is represented in `stdio.h` by the defined constant NULL. Thus, `gets()` incorporates a bit of error-checking, making it convenient to use constructions like this:

```
while (gets(name) != NULL)
```

Such a construction enables you to both check for EOF and read a value. If EOF is encountered, nothing is read into `name`. This two-pronged approach is more compact than that of `getchar()`, which has a return value but no argument.

```
while ((ch = getchar()) != EOF)
```

By the way, don't confuse the NULL pointer with the null character. The NULL pointer is an address, and the null character is a type `char` data object with the value zero. Numerically, both can be represented by 0, but they differ conceptually from each other.

One weakness of `gets()` is that it doesn't check to see whether the input actually fits into the reserved storage area. Extra characters simply overflow into the adjoining memory. The `fgets()` function (Chapter 12, "File Input/Output") improves on this questionable behavior by enabling you to specify an upper limit for the number of characters to be read.

The *scanf()* Function

You've used `scanf()` with the `%s` format before to read a string. The chief difference between `scanf()` and `gets()` lies in how they decide when they have reached the end of the string: `scanf()` is more of a "get word" than a "get string" function. The `gets()` function, as you've seen, takes in all the characters up to the first newline. The `scanf()` function has two choices for terminating input. For either choice, the string starts at the first nonwhitespace character encountered. If you use the `%s` format, the string runs up to (but not including) the next whitespace character (blank, tab, or newline). If you specify a field width, as in %10s, the scanf() collects up to 10 characters or up to the first whitespace character, whichever comes first. See Figure 11.3.

Input Statement	Original Input Queue*	Name Contents	Remaining Queue
scanf("%s", name);	Fleebert □Hup	Fleebert	□ Hup
scanf("%5s", name);	Fleebert □Hup	Fleeb	ert □ Hup
scanf("%5s", name);	Ann □Ular	Ann	□Ular

the □ represents the space character

Figure 11.3. *Field widths and* scanf().

Recall that the scanf() function returns an integer value that equals the number of items successfully read or returns EOF if it encounters the end of file.

Listing 11.6 illustrates how scanf() works when you specify a field width.

Listing 11.6. scan_str.c.

```
/* scan_str.c -- using scanf() */
#include <stdio.h>
int main(void)
{
    static char name1[11], name2[11];
    int count;

    printf("Please enter 2 names.\n");
    count = scanf("%5s %10s",name1, name2);
    printf("I read the %d names %s and %s.\n",
            count, name1, name2);
    return 0;
}
```

Here are three runs:

```
Please enter 2 names.
Jesse Jukes
I read the 2 names Jesse and Jukes.

Please enter 2 names.
Liza Applebottham
I read the 2 names Liza and Applebotth.
```

```
Please enter 2 names.
Portensia Callowit
I read the 2 names Porte and nsia.
```

In the first example, both names fell within the allowed size limits. In the second example, only the first 10 characters of Applebottham were read because we used a %10s format. In the third example, the last four letters of Portensia went into name2 because the second call to scanf() resumed reading input where the first ended; in this case, that was still inside the word Portensia.

You are better off using gets() to read text from the keyboard. It is easier to use, faster, and more compact. The typical use for scanf() would be reading and converting a mixture of data types in some standard form. For example, if each input line contained the name of a tool, the number in stock, and the cost of the item, you might use scanf(), or you might throw together a function of your own that did some entry error-checking.

Now let's discuss how to print strings.

String Output

Again, we will use library functions. C recognizes three standard library functions for printing strings. One, fputs(), is file oriented, and we'll look at it in Chapter 12, "File Input/Output." The other two are puts() and printf().

The puts() Function

The puts() function is very easy to use. Just give it the address of a string for an argument. Listing 11.7 illustrates some of the many ways to do this.

Listing 11.7. put_out.c.

```
/* put_out.c -- using puts() */
#include <stdio.h>
#define DEF "I am a #defined string."
int main(void)
{
  static char str1[] = "An array was initialized to me.";
  char * str2 = "A pointer was initialized to me.";

  puts("I'm an argument to puts().");
  puts(DEF);
  puts(str1);
  puts(str2);
  puts(&str1[4]);
  puts(str2+4);
  return 0;
}
```

The output is

```
I'm an argument to puts().
I am a #defined string.
An array was initialized to me.
A pointer was initialized to me.
rray was initialized to me.
inter was initialized to me.
```

This example reminds us that phrases in double quotation marks are string constants and are treated as addresses. Also, the names of character array strings are treated as addresses. The expression &str1[4] is the address of the fifth element of the array str1. That element contains the character 'r', and that is what puts() uses for its starting point. Similarly, str2+4 points to the memory cell containing the 'i' of "pointer," and the printing starts there.

How does puts() know when to stop? It stops when it encounters the null character, so there had better be one. Don't try the program in Listing 11.8!

Listing 11.8. nono.c.

```
/* nono.c -- no! */
#include <stdio.h>
int main(void)
{
    static c1 = 'A';
    static char dont[] = {'W', 'O', 'W', '!', '!' };
    static c2 = 'B';

    puts(dont);    /* dont is not a string */
    return 0;
}
```

Because dont lacks a closing null character, it is not a string, so puts() won't know where to stop. It will just keep printing from memory following dont until it finds a null somewhere. There usually are lots of nulls in memory, and if you're lucky, puts() may find one soon, but don't count on it.

Notice that each string displayed by puts() begins a new line. When puts() finally finds the closing null character, it replaces it with a newline character.

The *printf()* Function

We discussed printf() pretty thoroughly in Chapter 4, "Character Strings and Formatted Input/Output." Like puts(), it takes a string address as an argument. The printf() function is less convenient to use than puts(), but it is more versatile because it formats various data types.

One difference is that `printf()` does not automatically print each string on a new line. Instead, you must indicate where you want new lines. Thus,

```
printf("%s\n", string);
```

has the same effect as

```
puts(string);
```

As you can see, the first form takes more typing. It also takes longer for the computer to execute. On the other hand, `printf()` makes it simple to combine strings for one line of printing. For example,

```
printf("Well, %s, %s\n", name, MSG);
```

combines `Well,` with the user's name and a `#defined` character string, all on one line.

The Do-It-Yourself Option

You aren't limited to the standard C library options for input and output. If you don't have these options or don't like them, you can prepare your own versions, building on `getchar()` and `putchar()`. Suppose you lack a `puts()` function or merely want to try your own hand at writing that function. Listing 11.9 shows one way to do it.

Listing 11.9. put1.c.

```
/* put1.c -- prints a string */
#include <stdio.h>
void put1(char * string)
{
    while (*string != '\0')
        putchar(*string++);
    putchar('\n');
}
```

The char pointer `string` initially points to the first element of the called argument. After the contents of that element are printed, the pointer increments and points to the next element. This goes on until the pointer points to an element containing the null character. Then a newline is tagged on at the end. Remember, the higher precedence of `++` compared to `*` means that `putchar(*string++)` prints the value pointed to by `string` but increments `string` itself, not the character it points to.

Many C programmers would use the following test for the `while` loop:

```
while (*string)
```

When `string` points to the null character, `*string` has the value 0, which terminates the loop. This approach certainly takes less typing than the previous version. If you are not familiar with C practice, it is less obvious. It may result in more efficient code, depending on the compiler. Regardless of its merits, this idiom is widespread.

Suppose you have a puts(), but you want a new function that also tells you how many characters are printed. As Listing 11.10 demonstrates, it's easy to add that feature.

Listing 11.10. put2.c.

```
/* put2.c -- prints a string and counts characters */
#include <stdio.h>
int put2(char * string)
{
    int count = 0;
    while (*string != '\0')
    {
        putchar(*string++);
        count++;
    }
    putchar('\n');              /* newline not counted */
    return(count);
}
```

The following call prints the string pizza:

```
put1("pizza");
```

The next call also returns a character count that is assigned to num, in this case, the value 5.

```
num = put2("pizza");
```

Listing 11.11 presents a driver using put1() and put2(), and showing nested functions.

Listing 11.11. put_put.c.

```
/* put_put.c -- nested functions */
#include <stdio.h>
void put1(char *);
int put2(char *);
int main(void)
{
    put1("If I'd as much money as I could spend,");
    printf("I count %d characters.\n",
        put2("I never would cry old chairs to mend."));
    return 0;
}
```

We assume that you'll place the put1() and put2() functions in the same file. Note that we used #include stdio.h because on our system putchar() is defined there, and our new functions use putchar().

Hmm, we are using printf() to print the value of put2(), but in the act of finding the value of put2() the computer first must execute that function, causing the string to be printed. Here's the output:

```
If I'd as much money as I could spend,
I never would cry old chairs to mend.
I count 37 characters.
```

String Functions

The C library supplies several string-handling functions. We'll look at five of the most useful and common ones: strlen(), strcat(), strcmp(), strcpy(), and sprintf().

The *strlen()* Function

The strlen() function, as you already know, finds the length of a string. We use it in the next example, a function that shortens lengthy strings:

```
/* fit.c -- procrustean function */
void fit(char * string, int size)
{
    if (strlen(string) > size)
        *(string + size) = '\0';
}
```

Try the fit() function in the test program of Listing 11.12.

Listing 11.12. test.c.

```
/* test.c -- try the string-shrinking function */
#include <stdio.h>
#include <string.h> /* contains string function declarations */
void fit(char *, int);
int main(void)
{
    static char mesg[] = "Hold on to your hats, hackers.";

    puts(mesg);
    fit(mesg,7);
    puts(mesg);
    return 0;
}
void fit(char *string, int size)
{
```

continues

Listing 11.12. continued

```
    if (strlen(string) > size)
        *(string + size) = '\0';
}
```

The output is this:

```
Hold on to your hats, hackers.
Hold on
```

Our `fit()` function placed a '\0' character in the eighth element of the array, replacing a blank. The rest of the array is still there, but `puts()` stops at the first null character and ignores the rest of the array.

The ANSI `string.h` file contains function prototypes for the C family of string functions, so we will include it in our examples.

> **Note:** Some pre-ANSI systems use `strings.h` instead, and others may lack a string header file entirely.

The *strcat()* Function

Listing 11.13 illustrates what `strcat()` can do.

Listing 11.13. `str_cat.c`.

```
/* str_cat.c -- joins two strings */
#include <stdio.h>
#include <string.h>  /* declares the strcat() function */
#define SIZE 80
int main(void)
{
    static char flower[SIZE];
    static char addon[] = "s smell like old shoes.";

    puts("What is your favorite flower?");
    gets(flower);
    strcat(flower, addon);
    puts(flower);
    puts(addon);
    return 0;
}
```

The output is

```
What is your favorite flower?
Rose
Roses smell like old shoes.
s smell like old shoes.
```

As you can see, strcat() (for *string* con*cate*nation) takes two strings for arguments. A copy of the second string is tacked onto the end of the first, and this combined version becomes the new first string. The second string is not altered. Function strcat() is type char *, that is, a pointer to char. It returns the value of its first argument—the address of the first character of the string to which the second string is appended.

> **Note:** This function does not check to see whether the second string will fit in the first array. If you fail to allot enough space for the first array, you will run into problems as excess characters overflow into adjacent memory locations. Of course, you can use strlen() to look before you leap, as shown in Listing 11.14. Note that we add 1 to the combined lengths to allow space for the null character.

Listing 11.14. join_chk.c.

```c
/* join_chk.c -- joins two strings, check size first */
#include <stdio.h>
#include <string.h>
#define SIZE 30
int main(void)
{
   static char flower[SIZE];
   static char addon[] = "s smell like old shoes.";

   puts("What is your favorite flower?");
   gets(flower);
   if ((strlen(addon) + strlen(flower) + 1) <= SIZE)
       strcat(flower, addon);
   puts(flower);
   return 0;
}
```

The *strcmp()* Function

Suppose you wish to compare someone's response to a stored string, as shown in Listing 11.15.

Listing 11.15. nogo.c.

```c
/* nogo.c -- will this work? */
#include <stdio.h>
#define ANSWER "Grant"
int main(void)
{
    char try[40];

    puts("Who is buried in Grant's tomb?");
    gets(try);
    while (try != ANSWER)
    {
        puts("No, that's wrong. Try again.");
        gets(try);
    }
    puts("That's right!");
    return 0;
}
```

As nice as this program may look, it will not work correctly. ANSWER and try really are pointers, so the comparison try != ANSWER doesn't check to see whether the two strings are the same. Rather, it checks to see whether the two strings have the same address. Because ANSWER and try are stored in different locations, the two addresses never are the same, and the user is forever told that he or she is wrong. Such programs tend to discourage people.

What we need is a function that compares string contents, not string addresses. We could devise one, but the job has been done for us with strcmp() (for *string comparison*). Our revised program is shown in Listing 11.16.

Listing 11.16. compare.c.

```c
/* compare.c -- this will work */
#include <stdio.h>
#include <string.h>   /* declares strcmp() */
#define ANSWER "Grant"
#define MAX 40
int main(void)
{
    char try[MAX];

    puts("Who is buried in Grant's tomb?");
    gets(try);
    while (strcmp(try,ANSWER) != 0))
```

```
    {
        puts("No, that's wrong. Try again.");
        gets(try);
    }
    puts("That's right!");
    return 0;
}
```

> **Note:** Because any nonzero value is "true," some programmers would abbreviate the
> `while` statement to `while (strcmp(try,ANSWER))`.

From Listing 11.16 you may correctly deduce that `strcmp()` takes two string pointers
as arguments and returns a value of `0` if the two strings are the same. Good for you for so
deducing.

One of the nice features of `strcmp()` is that it compares strings, not arrays. Thus,
although the array `try` occupies 40 memory cells and "Grant" only 6 (one for the null
character), the comparison looks only at the part of `try` up to its first null character. Thus,
`strcmp()` can be used to compare strings stored in arrays of different sizes.

What if the user answers "GRANT" or "grant" or "Ulysses S. Grant"? The user is told
that he or she is wrong. To make a friendlier program, you have to anticipate all possible
correct answers. There are some tricks. You can `#define` the answer as "GRANT" and
write a function that converts all input to uppercase. That eliminates the problem of
capitalization, but you still have the other forms to worry about. We leave that as an
exercise for you.

What value does `strcmp()` return if the strings are not the same? Listing 11.17 shows
a sample.

Listing 11.17. `compback.c.`

```
/* compback.c -- strcmp returns */
#include <stdio.h>
#include <string.h>
int main(void)
{
  printf("%d\n", strcmp("A", "A"));
  printf("%d\n", strcmp("A", "B"));
```

continues

Listing 11.17. continued

```
    printf("%d\n", strcmp("B", "A"));
    printf("%d\n", strcmp("C", "A"));
    printf("%d\n", strcmp("apples", "apple"));
    return 0;
}
```

Here is the output on one system:

```
0
-1
1
1
1
```

Comparing "A" to itself returns a 0. Comparing "A" to "B" gives a -1, and reversing the comparison gives a 1. These results suggest that strcmp() returns a negative number if the first string precedes the second alphabetically and that it returns a positive number if the order is the other way. Thus, comparing "C" to "A" gives a 1. Other systems may return 2—the difference in ASCII code values. The ANSI Standard says that strcmp() returns a negative number if the first string comes before the second alphabetically, returns a 0 if they are the same, and returns a positive number if the first string follows the second alphabetically. The exact numerical values, however, are left open to the implementation.

What if the initial characters are identical? In general, strcmp() moves along until it finds the first pair of disagreeing characters. It then returns the corresponding code. For instance, in the very last example, "apples" and "apple" agree until the final s of the first string. This matches up with the sixth character in "apple", which is the null character, ASCII 0. Because the null character is the very first character in the ASCII sequence, s comes after it, and the function returns a positive value.

The last comparison points out that strcmp() compares all characters, not just letters, so instead of saying the comparison is alphabetic, we should say that strcmp() goes by the machine *collating sequence*. This means that characters are compared according to their numeric representation, typically the ASCII values. In ASCII, the codes for uppercase letters precede those for lowercase letters. Thus, strcmp("A", "a") is negative.

Most often, you won't care about the exact value returned. You just want to know if it is zero or nonzero—that is, whether there is a match or not—or you may be trying to sort the strings alphabetically, in which case you want to know if the comparison is positive, negative, or zero.

In Listing 11.18, we can use the strcmp() function for checking to see whether a program should stop reading input.

Listing 11.18. `input.c.`

```
/* input.c -- beginning of some program */
#include <stdio.h>
#include <string.h>
#define SIZE 81
#define LIM 100
#define STOP "quit"
int main(void)
{
  static char input[LIM][SIZE];
  int ct = 0;

  while (ct < LIM && gets(input[ct]) != NULL &&
         strcmp(input[ct],STOP) != 0)
  {
          ct++;
  }
  printf("%d strings entered\n", ct);
  return 0;
}
```

This program quits reading input when it encounters an EOF character (`gets()` returns null in that case), or when you enter the word *quit,* or when you reach the limit `LIM`.

Incidentally, sometimes it is more convenient to terminate input by entering an empty line, that is, by pressing the Enter key or Return key without entering anything else. To do so, you can modify the `while` loop control statement so that it looks like this:

```
while (ct < LIM && gets(input[ct]) != NULL
                         && input[ct][0] != '\0')
```

Here `input[ct]` is the string just entered and `input[ct][0]` is the first character of that string. If the user enters an empty line, `gets()` places the null character in the first element, so the expression

```
input[ct][0] != '\0')
```

tests for an empty input line.

The *strcpy()* Function

We've said that if `pts1` and `pts2` are both pointers to strings, then the expression

```
pts2 = pts1;
```

copies only the address of a string, not the string itself. Suppose, though, that you do want to copy a string. Then you can use the `strcpy()` function. It works as shown in Listing 11.19.

Listing 11.19. copy1.c.

```
/* copy1.c -- strcpy() demo */
#include <stdio.h>
#include <string.h>  /* declares strcpy() */
#define WORDS  "Please reconsider your last entry."
#define SIZE 40
int main(void)
{
   static char * orig = WORDS;
   static char copy[SIZE] = "reserved space";

   puts(orig);
   puts(copy);
   strcpy(copy, orig);
   puts(orig);
   puts(copy);
   return 0;
}
```

Here is the output:

```
Please reconsider your last entry.
reserved space
Please reconsider your last entry.
Please reconsider your last entry.
```

You can see that the string pointed to by the second argument (orig) is copied into the array pointed to by the first argument (copy). The copy is called the *target*, and the original string is called the *source*. You can remember the order of the arguments by noting that it is the same as the order in an assignment statement: the target string is on the left. Note that strcpy() writes over any existing contents of the target string.

It is your responsibility to ensure that the destination array has enough room to copy the source. That is why we used the declaration

```
static char copy[SIZE];
```

and not

```
static char * copy;   /* allots no space for string */
```

In short, strcpy() takes two string pointers as arguments. The second pointer, which points to the original string, can be a declared pointer, an array name, or a string constant, but the first pointer, which points to the copy, should point to a data object, such as an array, roomy enough to hold the string.

The strcpy() function has two more properties that you may find useful. First, it is type char *. It returns the value of its first argument—the address of a character. Second, the first argument need not point to the beginning of an array. Listing 11.20 illustrates both these points.

Listing 11.20. copy2.c.

```c
/* copy2.c -- strcpy() demo */
#include <stdio.h>
#include <string.h>              /* declares strcpy() */
#define WORDS  "beast"
#define SIZE 40
int main(void)
{
    static char *o rig = WORDS;
    static char copy[SIZE] = "Be the best that you can be.";
    char * ps;

    puts(orig);
    puts(copy);
    ps = strcpy(copy + 7, orig);
    puts(copy);
    puts(ps);
    return 0;
}
```

Here is the output:

```
beast
Be the best that you can be.
Be the beast
beast
```

Note that `strcpy()` copies the null character from the source string. In this example, the null character overwrites the `t` in `that` in `copy` so that the new string ends with `beast`. See Figure 11.4. Also note that `ps` points to the eighth element (index of 7) of `copy` because the first argument is `copy + 7`. Therefore, `puts(ps)` prints the string starting at that point.

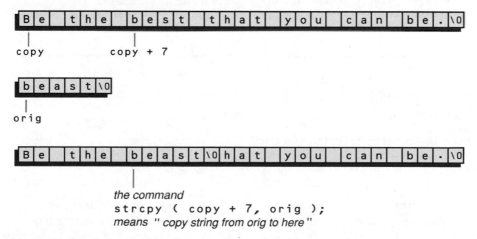

Figure 11.4. `strcpy()` *uses pointers.*

The *sprintf()* Function

The sprintf() function is declared in stdio.h instead of string.h. It works like printf(), but it writes to a string instead of writing to a display. Thus, it provides a way to combine several elements into a single string. The first argument to sprintf() is the address of the target string. The remaining arguments are the same as for printf()—a conversion specification string followed by a list of items to be written.

One use for sprintf() is to generate a system command. The C library has a system() function that allows a program to execute operating system commands. For example, you could have a program solicit information from the user about copying a file and then use the system() command to have the operating system do the copying. This command takes a string argument indicating which command to execute. Listing 11.21 is a simple example using the MS-DOS COPY command. Change copy to cp for UNIX.

Listing 11.21. command.c.

```
/* command.c -- generate a command string */
#include <stdio.h>
#include <stdlib.h> /* ANSI C: declares the system() function */
#define MAX 20
int main(void)
{
    char source[MAX];
    char target[MAX];
    char command[2 * MAX + 5];

    puts("Enter the name of the file you wish to copy:");
    gets(source);
    puts("Enter the desired name for the copy:");
    gets(target);
    sprintf(command, "copy %s %s", source, target);
    printf("Executing the following command: %s\n", command);
    system(command);
    return 0;
}
```

Here's a sample run:

```
Enter the name of the file you wish to copy:
taxing.c
Enter the desired name for the copy:
taxing1.c
Executing the following command: copy taxing.c taxing1.c
1 File(s) copied
```

The sprintf() command copied the string "copy taxing.c taxing1.c" into the command array. Next, the printf() command showed the contents of that string. Then the system() call executed the command specified by the string. The final line of output was produced by the operating system, not our program, after the operating system ran the COPY command.

Other String Functions

The ANSI C library has more than twenty string-handling functions, and the following list summarizes some of the more commonly used ones.

- char *strcpy(char * s1, const char * s2);

  This function copies the string (including the null character) pointed to by s2 to the location pointed to by s1. The return value is s1.

- char *strncpy(char * s1, const char * s2, size_t n);

  This function copies to the location pointed to by s1 no more than n characters from the string pointed to by s2. The return value is s1. No characters after a null character are copied, and if the source string is shorter than n characters, the target string is padded with null characters. If the source string has n or more characters, no null character is copied. The return value is s1.

- char *strcat(char * s1, const char * s2);

  The string pointed to by s2 is copied to the end of the string pointed to by s1. The first character of the s2 string is copied over the null character of the s1 string. The return value is s1.

- char *strncat(char * s1, const char * s2, size_t n);

  No more than the first n characters of the s2 string are appended to the s2 string, with the first character of the s2 string being copied over the null character of the s1 string. The null character and any characters following it in the s1 string are not copied, and a null character is appended to the result. The return value is s1.

- int strcmp(const char * s1, const char * s2);

  The function returns a positive value if the s1 string follows the s2 string in the machine collating sequence, the value 0 if the two strings are identical, and a negative value if the first string precedes the second string in the machine collating sequence.

- int strncmp(const char * s1, const char * s2, size_t n);

  This function works like strcmp() except that the comparison stops after n characters or when the first null character is encountered, whichever comes first.

- char *strchr(const char * s, int c);

  This function returns a pointer to the first location in the string s that holds the character c. (The terminating null character is part of the string, so it can be searched for.) The function returns the NULL pointer if the character is not found.

- `char *strpbrk(const char * s1, const char * s2);`

  This function returns a pointer to the first location in the string s1 that holds the character found in the s2 string. The function returns the NULL pointer if no character is found.

- `char *strrchr(const char * s, int c);`

  This function returns a pointer to the first occurrence of the character c in the string s. (The terminating null character is part of the string, so it can be searched for.) The function returns the NULL pointer if the character is not found.

- `char *strstr(const char * s1, const char * s2);`

  This function returns a pointer to the first occurrence of string s2 in string s1. The function returns the NULL pointer if the string is not found.

- `size_t strlen(const char * s);`

  This function returns the number of characters, not including the terminating null character, found in the string s.

Some of the terms in the preceding list need a little explanation. The const keyword, which we discuss in Chapter 13, "Storage Classes and Program Development," identifies variables that are not to be altered. Consider, for example, this prototype:

```
char *strcpy(char * s1, const char * s2);
```

It means s2 points to a string that can't be changed, at least not by the strcpy() function, but s1 points to a string that can be changed. The size_t type is whatever type the sizeof operator returns. C states that the sizeof operator returns an integer type, but it doesn't specify which integer type, so size_t can be unsigned int on one system and unsigned long on another. Your string.h file will define size_t for your particular system or else refer to another header file having the definition.

Many implementations provide additional functions beyond those required by the ANSI Standard. You should check the documentation for your implementation to see what is available.

Now that we have outlined some string functions, let's look at a full program that handles strings.

A String Example: Sorting Strings

Let's tackle the practical problem of sorting strings alphabetically. This task can show up in preparing name lists, in making up an index, and in many other situations. One of the main tools in such a program is strcmp(), because it can be used to determine the order of two strings. Our general plan will be to read an array of strings, sort them, and print them. A little while ago we presented a scheme for reading strings, and we will start the program that way. Printing the strings is no problem. We'll use a standard sorting algorithm that we'll explain later. We will do one slightly tricky thing; see whether you can spot it. Listing 11.22 presents the program.

Listing 11.22. sort_str.c.

```c
/* sort_str.c -- reads in strings and sorts them */
#include <stdio.h>
#include <string.h>
#define SIZE 81            /* string length limit, including \0  */
#define LIM 20             /* maximum number of lines to be read */
#define HALT ""            /* null string to stop input          */
void stsrt(char *strings[], int num);  /* string-sort function */
int main(void)
{
    static char input[LIM][SIZE];  /* array to store input       */
    char *ptstr[LIM];              /* array of pointer variables */
    int ct = 0;                    /* input count                */
    int k;                         /* output count               */

    printf("Input up to %d lines, and I will sort them.\n",LIM);
    printf("To stop, press the Enter key at a line's start.\n");
    while (ct < LIM && gets(input[ct]) != NULL
                        && input[ct][0] != '\0')
    {
        ptstr[ct] = input[ct];        /* set ptrs to strings     */
        ct++;
    }
    stsrt(ptstr, ct);                 /* string sorter           */
    puts("\nHere's the sorted list:\n");
    for (k = 0; k < ct; k++)
        puts(ptstr[k]) ;              /* sorted pointers         */
    return 0;
}
/* string-pointer-sorting function */
void stsrt(char *strings[], int num)
{
  char *temp;
  int top, seek;

  for (top = 0; top < num-1; top++)
     for (seek = top + 1; seek < num; seek++)
        if (strcmp(strings[top],strings[seek]) > 0)
        {
            temp = strings[top];
            strings[top] = strings[seek];
            strings[seek] = temp;
        }
}
```

We fed Listing 11.22 an obscure nursery rhyme to test it.

```
Input up to 20 lines, and I will sort them.
To stop, press the Enter key at a line's start.
O that I was where I would be,
Then would I be where I am not;
But where I am I must be,
And where I would be I can not.

Here's the sorted list:

And where I would be I can not.
But where I am I must be,
O that I was where I would be,
Then would I be where I am not;
```

Hmm, the nursery rhyme doesn't seem to suffer much from being alphabetized.

The tricky part of the program is that instead of rearranging the strings themselves, we just rearranged *pointers* to the strings. Let us explain. Originally, `ptrst[0]` is set to `input[0]`, and so on. This means that the pointer `ptrst[i]` points to the first character in the array `input[i]`. Each `input[i]` is an array of 81 elements, and each `ptrst[]` is a single variable. The sorting procedure rearranges `ptrst`, leaving `input` untouched. If, for example, `input[1]` comes before `input[0]` alphabetically, the program switches `ptrsts`, causing `ptrst[0]` to point to the beginning of `input[1]` and causing `ptrst[1]` to point to the beginning of `input[0]`. This is much easier than using, say, `strcpy()` to interchange the contents of the two `input` strings. See Figure 11.5 for another view of this process.

Sorting

To sort the pointers, we use the *selection sort* algorithm. The idea is to use a `for` loop to compare each element in turn with the first element. If the compared element precedes the current first element, the program swaps the two. Thus, by the time the program reaches the end of the loop, the first element contains a pointer to whichever string is first in the machine collating sequence. Then the outer `for` loop repeats the process, this time starting with the second element of `input`. When the inner loop completes, the pointer to the second-ranking string ends up in the second element of `ptrst`. The process continues until all the elements have been sorted. We'll take a more detailed look at this algorithm in Chapter 13, "Storage Classes and Program Development."

The *ctype.h* Character Functions

ANSI C, as well as many pre-ANSI implementations, provides a family of character-related functions declared in the `ctype.h` header file. Several of these functions analyze the nature of a character, returning a true (nonzero) value if the character belongs to a particular class, and false (zero) otherwise. Table 11.1 lists these functions.

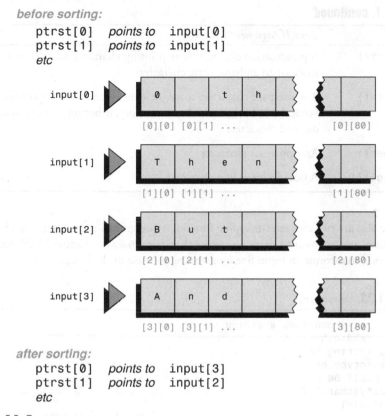

before sorting:

```
ptrst[0]  points to  input[0]
ptrst[1]  points to  input[1]
etc
```

input[0]

input[1]

input[2]

input[3]

after sorting:

```
ptrst[0]  points to  input[3]
ptrst[1]  points to  input[2]
etc
```

Figure 11.5. *Sorting string pointers.*

Table 11.1. Character-testing functions.

Name	True If Argument Is
isalnum()	Alphanumeric (alphabetic or numeric)
isalpha()	Alphabetic
iscntrl()	A control character, e.g., Control-B
isdigit()	A digit
isgraph()	Any printing character other than a space
islower()	A lowercase character
isprint()	A printing character

continues

Table 11.1. continued

Name	True If Argument Is
ispunct()	A punctuation character (any printing character other than a space or an alphanumeric character)
isspace()	A whitespace character: space, newline, formfeed, carriage return, vertical tab, horizontal tab, or, possibly, other implementation-defined characters
isupper()	An uppercase character
isxdigit()	A hexadecimal-digit character

There also are two character-mapping functions: toupper() maps lowercase characters to uppercase, and tolower() maps uppercase characters to lower. Listing 11.23 presents a program that transforms an input line by reversing the case of the letters.

Listing 11.23. invert.c.

```
/* invert.c -- modifies a string */
#include <stdio.h>
#include <string.h>
#include <ctype.h>
#define LIMIT 80
void modify(char *);
int main(void)
{
  char line[LIMIT];

  puts("Please enter a line:");
  gets(line);
  modify(line);
  puts(line);
  return 0;
}

void modify(char * str)
{
  while (*str != '\0')
  {
      if (isupper(*str))
          *str = tolower(*str);
      else if (islower(*str))
          *str = toupper(*str);
      str++;
  }
}
```

The while (*str != '\0') loop processes each character in the string pointed to by str until the null character is reached. Here is a sample run:

```
Please enter a line:
Hello, Mr. Potato Head!
hELLO, mR. pOTATO hEAD!
```

In modify(), we use isupper() to be sure that a character is uppercase before trying to convert it to lowercase. Under ANSI C, this isn't necessary because tolower() returns the original character if it is not uppercase to begin with. However, not all older implementations offer that protection, so for maximum portability we checked first.

Incidentally, the ctype.h functions usually are implemented as *macros*. These are C preprocessor constructions that act much like functions but have some important differences. We'll cover macros in Chapter 16, "The C Preprocessor and the C Library."

Next, let's try to fill an old emptiness in our lives, namely, the void between the parentheses in main().

Command-Line Arguments

The *command line* is the line you type to run your program. Suppose you have a program in a file named fuss. Then the command line to run it might look like this:

```
% fuss
```

or perhaps this:

```
A> fuss
```

Command-line arguments are additional items on the same line.

```
% fuss -r Ginger
```

A C program can read those additional items for its own use (see Figure 11.6).

A C program reads these items this by using arguments to main(). Listing 11.24 shows a typical example.

Listing 11.24. echo.c.

```c
/* echo.c -- main() with arguments */
#include <stdio.h>
int main(int argc, char *argv[])
{
    int count;

    for (count = 1; count < argc; count++)
        printf("%s ", argv[count]);  /* process each argument */
    printf("\n");
    return 0;
}
```

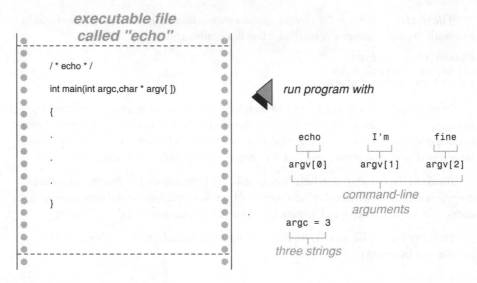

Figure 11.6. *Command-line arguments.*

Compile this program into an executable file called `echo`, and this is what happens when you run it:

```
A> echo I could use a little help.
I could use a little help.
```

You can see why it is called `echo`, but you may wonder how it works. We'll explain now.

C compilers allow `main()` to have no arguments or else to have two arguments. The first argument is the number of strings in the command line. By tradition (but not by necessity), this `int` argument is called `argc` for *arg*ument *c*ount. The system uses spaces to tell when one string ends and the next begins. Thus, our `echo` example has seven strings, including the command name, and our `fuss` example had three. The second argument is an array of pointers to strings. Each string on the command line is stored in memory and has a pointer assigned to point to it. By convention, this array of pointers is called `argv`, for *arg*ument *v*alues. When possible (some operating systems don't allow this), `argv[0]` is assigned the name of the program itself. Then `argv[1]` is assigned the first following string, and so on. For our example, we have the following relationships:

argv[0]	points to	echo (for most systems)
argv[1]	points to	I
argv[2]	points to	could
argv[3]	points to	use
argv[4]	points to	a
argv[5]	points to	little
argv[6]	points to	help

The program in Listing 11.24 uses a `for` loop to print each string in turn. Recall that the `printf()` `%s` specifier expects the address of a string to be provided as an argument. Each element, `argv[0]`, `argv[1]`, etc., is just such an address.

With pre-ANSI C, use the form

```
main(argc, argv)
int argc;
char *argv[];
```

to declare `argc` and `argv`. The form is the same as for any other function having formal arguments. Many programmers use a different declaration for `argv`.

```
int main(int argc, char **argv)
```

This alternative declaration for `argv` really is equivalent to `char *argv[]`. It says that `argv` is a pointer to a pointer to `char`. Our example comes down to the same thing. We had an array with seven elements. The name of the array is a pointer to the first element. Thus, `argv` points to `argv[0]`, and `argv[0]` is a pointer to `char`. Hence, even with the original definition, `argv` is a pointer to a pointer to `char`. You can use either form, but we think that the first more clearly suggests that `argv` represents a set of strings.

Incidentally, many environments, including UNIX, allow the use of quotation marks to lump several words into a single argument. For example, the command

```
echo "I am hungry" now
```

would assign the string "I am hungry" to `argv[1]` and the string "now" to `argv[2]`.

Command-Line Arguments in Integrated Environments

Integrated environments like QuickC, Borland C, and Turbo C don't use command lines to run programs. However, they have menu selections that enable you to specify a command-line argument. In QuickC 2.0, you open the Options menus, select Run/Debug, and enter the argument(s) into the Command Line box. With QuickC 1.0, you open the Run menu and select Set Runtime Options to get the Command Line box. In older versions of Turbo C, you open the Options menu, select Args, and enter the argument(s). In Borland C, select Arguments from the Run menu.

Command-Line Arguments with Think C

The Macintosh operating system doesn't use command lines, but Think C enables you to simulate a command-line environment with its `ccommand()` function. Use the `console.h` header file and start your programs like this:

```
#include <stdio.h>
#include <console.h>
int main(int argc, char *argv[])
{
```

```
...        /* variable declarations */
argc = ccommand(&argv);
...
}
```

When the program reaches the `ccommand()` function call, it puts a dialog box on screen and provides a box in which you can type a command line. The command then places the command-line words in the `argv` strings and returns the number of words. The current project name will appear as the first word in the command-line box, so you should type the command-line arguments after that name. The `ccommand()` function also enables you to simulate redirection.

String to Number Conversions

Numbers can be stored either as strings or in numeric form. Storing a number as a string means storing the digit characters. For instance, the number 213 can be stored in a character string array as the digits '2', '1', '3', '\0'. Storing 213 in numeric form means storing it as, say, an `int`.

C requires numeric forms for numeric operations, such as addition and comparison, but displaying numbers on your screen requires a string form because a screen displays characters. The `printf()` and `sprintf()` functions, through their `%d` and other specifiers, convert numeric forms to string forms. C also has functions whose sole purpose is to convert string forms to numeric forms.

Suppose, for example, we want our program to use a numeric command-line argument. Unfortunately, command-line arguments are read as strings. Therefore, to use the numeric value, we first must convert the string to a number. If the number is an integer, we can use the `atoi()` function (for *a*lphanumeric *to* *i*nteger). It takes a string as an argument and returns the corresponding integer value. Listing 11.25 shows a sample use.

Listing 11.25. `hello.c`.

```
/* hello.c -- converts command-line argument to number */
#include <stdio.h>
#include <stdlib.h>
int main(int argc, char *argv[])
{
  int i, times;
  if (argc < 2 || (times = atoi(argv[1])) < 1)
      printf("Usage: %s positive-number\n", argv[0]);
  else
      for (i = 0; i < times; i++)
           puts("Hello, good looking!");
  return 0;
}
```

Here's a sample run:

```
% hello 3
Hello, good looking!
Hello, good looking!
Hello, good looking!
```

The % is a UNIX prompt. The command-line argument of 3 was stored as the string '3"\0'. The atoi() function converted this string to the integer value 3, which was assigned to times. This then determined the number of for loop cycles executed.

If you run the program without a command-line argument, the argc < 2 test aborts the program and prints a usage message. The same thing happens if times is 0 or negative. C's order-of-evaluation rule for logical operators guarantees that if argc < 2, then atoi(argv[1]) is not evaluated.

What if the command line is something like hello what? On the implementations we've used, the atoi() function returns a value of 0 if its argument is not recognizable as a number. However, the ANSI Standard does not require that behavior.

We include the stdlib.h header because, under ANSI C, it contains the function declaration for atoi(). That header file also includes declarations for atof() and atol(). The atof() function converts a string to a type double value, and the atol() function converts a string to a type long value. They work analogously to atoi(), so they are type double and long, respectively.

Many implementations have itoa() and ftoa() functions for converting integers and floating-point values to strings. However, they are not part of the ANSI C library; use sprintf(), instead, for greater compatibility.

Chapter Summary

A C *string* is a series of chars terminated by the null character, '\0'. A string can be stored in a character array. A string also can be represented with a *string constant*, in which the characters, aside from the null character, are enclosed in double quotation marks. The compiler supplies the null character. Thus, "joy" is stored as the four characters j, o, y, and \0. The length of a string, as measured by strlen(), doesn't count the null character.

String constants can be used to initialize character arrays. In pre-ANSI C, only external and static arrays can be initialized, but ANSI C permits automatic arrays to be initialized, too. The array size should be at least one greater than the string length in order to accommodate the terminating null character. String constants also can be used to initialize pointers of type pointer-to-char.

Functions use pointers to the first character of a string to identify which string to act upon. Typically, the corresponding actual argument is an array name, a pointer variable, or a quoted string. In each case, the address of the first character is passed. In general, it is not necessary to pass the length of the string, because the function can use the terminating null character to locate the end of a string.

The gets() and puts() functions fetch a line of input and print a line of output, respectively. They are part of the stdio.h family of functions.

The C library includes several *string-handling* functions. Under ANSI C, these functions are declared in the string.h file. The library also has several *character-processing* functions; they are declared in the ctype.h file.

You can give a program access to *command-line arguments* by providing the proper two formal variables to the main() function. The first argument, traditionally called argc, is an int and is assigned the count of command-line words. The second argument, traditionally called argv, is a pointer to an array of pointers of char. Each pointer-to-char points to one of the command-line argument strings, with argv[0] pointing to the command name, argv[1] pointing to the first command-line argument, and so on.

The atoi(), atol(), and atof() functions convert string representations of numbers to type int, long, and double forms, respectively.

Review Questions

1. What's wrong with this attempted declaration of a character string?

```
int main(void)
{
    char name[] = {'F', 'e', 's', 's' };
    ...
}
```

2. What will this program print?

```
#include <stdio.h>
#include <string.h>
int main(void)
{
    static char food[] = "Yummy";
    char *ptr;

    ptr = food + strlen(food);
    while (--ptr >= food)
        puts(ptr);
    return 0;
}
```

3. Here is an exercise providing practice with strings, loops, pointers, and pointer incrementing. First, suppose you have this function definition:

```
#include <stdio.h>
char *pr (char *str);
{
  char *pc;

  pc = str;
  while (*pc)
     putchar(*pc++);
  do {
     putchar(*--pc);
     } while (pc - str);
  return (pc);
}
```

Consider the following function call:

```
x = pr("Ho Ho Ho!");
```

a. What is printed?

b. What type should x be?

c. What value does x get?

d. What does the expression *--pc mean, and how is it different from --*pc?

e. What would be printed if *--pc were replaced with *pc--?

f. What do the two while expressions test for?

g. What happens if pr() is supplied with a null string as an argument?

h. What must be done in the calling function so that pr() can be used as shown?

4. What does the following program print?

```
#include <stdio.h>
#include <string.h>
#define M1   "How are ya, sweetie? "
char M2[40] = "Beat the clock.";
char * M3  = "chat";
int main(void)
{
    char words[80];
    printf(M1);
    puts(M1);
    puts(M2);
    puts(M2 + 1);
    strcpy(words,M2);
    strcat(words, " Win a toy.");
    puts(words);
    words[4] = '\0';
```

```
            puts(words);
            while (*M3)
                puts(M3++);
            puts(--M3);
            puts(--M3);
            M3 = M1;
            puts(M3);
            return 0;
        }
```

5. The `strlen()` function takes a pointer to a string as an argument and returns the length of the string. Write your own version of this function.

6. Design a function that takes a string pointer as argument and returns a pointer to the first space character in the string on or after the pointed-to position. Have it return a NULL pointer if it finds no spaces.

7. Rewrite Listing 11.16 using `ctype.h` functions so that the program will recognize a correct answer regardless of the user's choice of uppercase and lowercase.

Programming Exercises

1. Design a function that fetches the next n characters from input, including blanks, tabs, and newlines.

2. Modify the function in Exercise 1 so that it stops after n characters or after the first blank, tab, or newline, whichever comes first. (Don't just use `scanf()`.)

3. Design a function that fetches the first word from a line of input and discards the rest of the line. Define a word as a sequence of characters with no blanks, tabs, or newlines in it.

4. Design a function that searches the specified string for the first occurrence of a specified character. Have the function return a pointer to the character if successful, and a null if the character is not found in the string. (This duplicates the way that the library `strchr()` function works.)

5. Write a function `is_within()` that takes a character and a string pointer as arguments. Have the function return a nonzero value (true) if the character is in the string and zero (false) otherwise.

6. The `strncpy(s1,s2,n)` function copies exactly n characters from s2 to s1, truncating s2 or padding it with extra null characters as necessary. The target string may not be null-terminated if the length of s2 is n or more. The function returns s1. Write your own version of this function.

7. Write a function `string_in()` that takes two string pointers as arguments. If the second string is contained in the first string, have the function return the address at which the contained string begins. For instance, `string_in("hats", "at)` would return the address of the `a` in `hats`. Otherwise, have the function return the NULL pointer.

8. Write a function that replaces the contents of a string with the string reversed.

9. Write a program that reads in up to 10 strings or to EOF, whichever comes first. Have it offer the user a menu with five choices: print the original list of strings, print the strings in ASCII collating sequence, print the strings in order of increasing length, print the strings in order of the length of the first word in the string, and quit. Have the menu recycle until the user enters the quit request. The program, of course, should actually perform the promised tasks.

10. Write a program that reads input up to EOF and reports the number of words, the number of uppercase letters, the number of lowercase letters, the number of punctuation characters, and the number of digits. Use the `ctype.h` family of functions.

11. Write a program that echoes the command-line arguments in reverse word order. That is, if the command-line arguments are `see you later`, the program should print `later you see`.

12. Write a power-law program that works on a command-line basis. The first command-line argument should be the type `double` number to be raised to a power, and the second argument should be the integer power.

13. Use the character classification functions to prepare an implementation of `atoi()`.

File Input/Output

Functions
```
fopen(), getc(), putc(), exit(), fclose()
fprintf(), fscanf(), fgets(), fputs()
rewind(), fseek(), ftell(), fflush()
ungetc(), setvbuf(), fread(), fwrite()
```

In this chapter you learn how to process files using C's standard I/O
family of functions. You learn about text modes and binary modes, text
and binary formats, and buffered and nonbuffered I/O. You practice using
functions that can access files both sequentially and randomly.

Files are essential to today's computer systems. They are used to store
programs, documents, data, correspondence, forms, graphics, and myriad
other kinds of information. As a programmer, you will have to write
programs that create files, write into files, and read from files. In this
chapter we show you how.

Communicating with Files

Often you need programs that can read information from files or can write results into a file. One such form of program-file communication is file redirection, as you saw in Chapter 8, "Character Input/Output and Redirection." This method is simple but limited. For instance, suppose you wish to write an interactive program that asks you for book titles and then saves the complete listing in a file. If you use redirection, as in

```
books > bklist
```

your interactive prompts are redirected into `bklist`. Not only does this put unwanted text into `bklist`, it prevents you from seeing the questions you are supposed to answer.

Fortunately, C offers more powerful methods of communicating with files. It enables you to open a file from within a program and then use special I/O functions to read from or write to that file. Before investigating these methods, however, let's review briefly the nature of a file.

What Is a File?

A *file* is a named section of storage, usually on a disk. We think of *stdio.h*, for instance, as the name of a file containing some useful information. To the operating system, however, a file is a bit more complicated. A large file, for example, may wind up stored in several scattered fragments, or it may contain additional data that allows the operating system to determine what kind of file it is, but these are the operating system's concerns, not ours (unless we are writing operating systems). Our concern is how files appear to a C program.

C views a file as a continuous sequence of bytes, each of which can be read individually. This corresponds to the file structure in the UNIX environment, where C grew up. Because other environments may not correspond exactly to this model, ANSI C provides two ways to view files.

The Text View and the Binary View

The two ANSI-mandated views of a file are *binary* and *text*. In the binary view, each and every byte of the file is accessible to a program. In the text view, what the program sees can differ from what is in the file. With the text view, the local environment's representation of such things as the end of a line are mapped to the C view when a file is read. Similarly, the C view is mapped to the local representation of output. For example, MS-DOS text files represent the end of a line with the carriage-return, linefeed combination: \r\n. Macintosh text files represent the end of a line with just a carriage-return \r. C programs represent the end of a line with just \n. Thus, when a C program takes the text view of an MS-DOS text file, it converts \r\n to \n when reading from a file, and it converts \n to \r\n when writing to a file. When a C program takes the text view of a Macintosh text file, it converts the \r to \n when reading from a file, and it converts \n to \r when writing to a file.

You aren't restricted to using only the text view for an MS-DOS text file. You can also use the binary view of the same file. If you do, your program sees both the \r and the \n characters in the file; no mapping takes place. See Figure 12.1. MS-DOS distinguishes between text and binary *files*, but C provides for text and binary *views*. Normally, you use the text view for text files, and the binary view for binary files. However, you can use either view of either type of file, although a text view of a binary file works poorly.

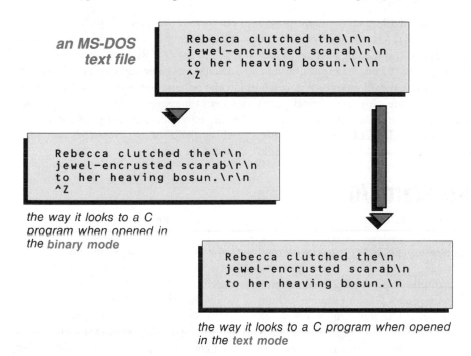

Figure 12.1. *Binary view and text view.*

Although ANSI C provides for both a binary and a text view, these views can be implemented identically. For instance, because UNIX uses just one file structure, both views are the same for UNIX implementations.

Levels of I/O

In addition to selecting the view of a file, you can, in most cases, choose between two levels of I/O, that is, between two levels of handling access to files. *Low-level I/O* uses the fundamental I/O services provided by the operating system. *Standard high-level I/O* uses a standard package of C library functions and stdio.h header file definitions. ANSI C supports only the standard I/O package because there is no way to guarantee that all operating systems can be represented by the same low-level I/O model. Because ANSI C establishes the portability of the standard I/O model, we will concentrate on it.

Standard Files

C programs automatically open three files on your behalf. They are termed the *standard input*, the *standard output*, and the *standard error output*. The standard input, by default, is the normal input device for your system, usually your keyboard. Both the standard output and the standard error output, by default, are the normal output device for your system, usually your display screen.

The standard input, naturally, provides input to your program. It's the file that is read by getchar(), gets(), and scanf(). The standard output is where normal program output goes. It is used by putchar(), puts(), and printf(). Redirection, as you learned in Chapter 8, "Character Input/Output and Redirection," causes other files to be recognized as the standard input or standard output. The purpose of the standard error output file is to provide a logically distinct place to send error messages. If, for example, you use redirection to send output to a file instead of to the screen, output sent to the standard error output still goes to the screen. This is good because if the error messages were routed to the file, you would not see them until you viewed the file.

Standard I/O

The standard I/O package has two advantages, besides portability, over low-level I/O. First, it has many specialized functions that simplify the handling of various I/O problems. For instance, printf() converts various forms of data to string output suitable for terminals. Second, input and output are *buffered*. That is, information is transferred in large chunks (typically 512 bytes at a time or more) instead of a byte at a time. When a program reads a file, for example, a chunk of data is copied to a buffer—an intermediate storage area. This buffering greatly increases the data transfer rate. The program then can examine individual bytes in the buffer. The buffering is handled behind the scenes, so you have the illusion of character-by-character access. (You can also buffer low-level I/O, but you have to do much of the work yourself.) Listing 12.1 shows how to use standard I/O to read a file and count the number of characters in the file. We'll discuss the features of Listing 12.1 in the next several sections. (Think C users should use console.h and the ccommand() function as described in Chapter 11, "Characters Strings and String Functions," and in the Think C documentation.)

Listing 12.1. count.c.

```
/* count.c -- using standard I/O */
#include <stdio.h>
#include <stdlib.h> /* ANSI C exit() prototype              */
int main(int argc, char *argv[])
{
    int ch;         /* place to store each character as read */
    FILE *fp;       /* "file pointer"                        */
    long count = 0;
```

```
    if (argc != 2)
    {
        printf("Usage: %s filename\n", argv[0]);
        exit(1);
    }
    if ((fp = fopen(argv[1], "r")) == NULL)
    {
        printf("Can't open %s\n", argv[1]);
        exit(1);
    }
    while ((ch = getc(fp)) != EOF)
    {
        putc(ch,stdout);
        count++;
    }
    fclose(fp);
    printf("File %s has %ld characters\n", argv[1], count);
    return 0;
}
```

Checking for Command-Line Arguments

First, the program in Listing 12.1 checks the value of argc to see if there is a command-line argument. If there isn't, the program prints a usage message and exits. The string argv[0] is the name of the program. Using argv[0] instead of the program name explicitly causes the error message to change automatically if you change the name of the executable file. This feature also is handy in environments like UNIX that permit multiple names for a single file, but beware, some operating systems, such as pre MS-DOS 3.0, don't recognize argv[0], so this usage is not completely portable.

The exit() function causes the program to terminate, closing any open files. The argument to exit() is passed on to some operating systems, including UNIX and PC DOS, where it can be used by other programs. The usual convention is to pass a value of 0 for programs that terminate normally and to pass nonzero values for abnormal termination. Different exit values can be used to distinguish between different causes of failure.

Under ANSI C, using return in the initial call to main() has the same effect as calling exit(). Thus, the following statement

```
return 0;
```

which we've been using all along, is equivalent in effect to

```
exit(0);
```

Note, however, the qualifying phrase "the initial call." If you make main() into a recursive program, exit() still terminates the program, but return passes control to the previous level of recursion until the original level is reached. Then return terminates the program.

Another difference between `return` and `exit()` is that `exit()` terminates the program even if called in a function other than `main()`.

Under ANSI C, the `stdlib.h` header file contains the prototype for `exit()`. You can omit this file on pre-ANSI systems.

The *fopen()* Function

Next, the program uses `fopen()` to open the file. This function is declared in `stdio.h`. Its first argument is the name of the file to be opened; more exactly, it is the address of a string containing that name. The second argument is a string identifying the mode in which the file is to be opened. The C library provides for several possibilities, as shown in Table 12.1.

Table 12.1. Mode strings for `fopen()`.

Mode String	Meaning
`"r"`	Open a text file for reading
`"w"`	Open a text file for writing, truncating an existing file to zero length, or creating the file if it does not exist
`"a"`	Open a text file for writing, appending to the end of an existing file, or creating the file if it does not exist
`"r+"`	Open a text file for update, i.e., for both reading and writing
`"w+"`	Open a text file for update (reading and writing), first truncating the file to zero length if it exists or creating the file if it does not exist
`"a+"`	Open a text file for update (reading and writing), appending to the end of an existing file, or creating the file if it does not yet exist; the whole file can be read, but writing can only be appended
`"rb"`, `"wb"`, `"ab"`, `"ab+"`, `"a+b"`, `"wb+"`, `w+b"`, `"ab+"`, `"a+b"`	Like the preceding modes, except using binary mode instead of text mode

For systems like UNIX, which have just one file type, the modes with the `b` are equivalent to the corresponding modes lacking the `b`.

> **Caution!** If you use any of the "w" modes for an existing file, the file contents are truncated so that your program can start with a clean slate.

Once your program successfully opens a file, fopen() returns a *file pointer*, which the other I/O functions then can use to specify the file. The file pointer, fp in our example, is of type pointer-to-FILE, where FILE is a derived type defined in stdio.h. The pointer fp doesn't point to the actual file. Instead, it points to a data package containing information about the file, including information about the buffer used for the file's I/O. Because the I/O functions in the standard library use a buffer, they need to know where the buffer is. They also need to know how full the buffer is and which file is being used. This enables the functions to refill or empty the buffer when necessary. The data package pointed to by fp has all that information. (This data package is an example of a C structure, a topic we discuss in Chapter 14, "Structures and Other Data Forms.")

The fopen() function returns the NULL pointer (also defined in stdio.h) if it cannot open the file. Our program exits if fp is NULL. The fopen() function can fail because the disk is full, because the name is illegal, because access is restricted, or because of a hardware problem, to name just a few reasons, so check for trouble; a little error-trapping can go a long way.

The *getc()* and *putc()* Functions

The two functions getc() and putc() work very much like getchar() and putchar(). The difference is that you must tell these newcomers which file to use. Thus, our old standby

```
ch = getchar();
```

means get a character from the standard input, but

```
ch = getc(fp);
```

means get a character from the file identified by fp.

Similarly,

```
putc(ch, fpout);
```

means put the character ch into the file identified by the FILE pointer fpout. In the putc() argument list, the character comes first, then the file pointer.

In Listing 12.1, we use stdout for the second argument of putc(). It is defined in stdio.h as being the file pointer associated with the standard output, so putc(ch,stdout) is the same as putchar(ch). Indeed, the latter function normally is defined as being the former. Similarly, getchar() is defined as being getc() using the standard input.

The *fclose()* Function

The fclose(fp) closes the file identified by fp, flushing buffers as needed. For a program less casual than this one, we would check to see if the file had been closed successfully. The function fclose() returns a value of 0 if successful, and EOF if not.

```
if (fclose(fp) != 0)
  printf("Error in closing file %s\n", argv[1]);
```

The fclose() function can fail, for example, if the disk is full, if the diskette has been removed, or if there has been an I/O error.

Standard Files

The stdio.h file associates three file pointers with the three standard files automatically opened by C programs.

Standard File	File Pointer	Normally
Standard input	stdin	Your keyboard
Standard output	stdout	Your screen
Standard error	stderr	Your screen

These pointers are all type pointer-to-FILE, so they can be used as arguments to the standard I/O functions, just as fp was in our example. Let's move on to an example that creates a new file and writes to it.

A Simple-Minded File-Condensing Program

In this next program we'll copy selected data from one file to another. Thus, we'll open two files simultaneously, using the "r" mode for one and the "w" mode for the other. The program (Listing 12.2) condenses the contents of the first file by the brutal expedient of retaining only every third character. Finally, it places the condensed text into the second file. The name for the second file is the old name with .red (for reduced) appended. Command-line arguments, opening more than one file simultaneously, and filename appending are quite useful techniques generally. This particular form of condensing is of more limited appeal, but it can have its uses, as you will see.

Listing 12.2. reducto.c.

```
/* reducto.c -- reduces your files by two-thirds ! */
#include <stdio.h>
#include <stdlib.h>
#include <string.h>        /* for strcpy(), strcat() */
int main(int argc, char *argv[])
{
    FILE  *in, *out;   /* declare two FILE pointers        */
    int ch;
```

```
    char name[40];      /* storage for output filename   */
    int count = 0;

    if (argc < 2)       /* check for an input file        */
    {
        fprintf(stderr, "Usage: %s filename\n", argv[0]);
        exit(1);
    }
    if ((in = fopen(argv[1], "r")) == NULL)
    {
        fprintf(stderr, "I couldn't open the file \"%s\"\n",
                argv[1]);
        exit(2);
    }
    strcpy(name,argv[1]);   /* copy filename into array   */
    strcat(name,".red");    /* append .red to name        */
    if ((out = fopen(name, "w")) == NULL)
    {                           /* open file for writing   */
        fprintf(stderr,"Can't create output file.\n");
        exit(3);
    }
    while ((ch = getc(in)) != EOF)
        if (count++ % 3 == 0)
            putc(ch, out);  /* print every 3rd char       */
    if (fclose(in) != 0 || fclose(out) != 0)
        fprintf(stderr,"Error in closing files\n");
    return 0;
}
```

Our executable file is called reducto. We applied it to a file called eddy, which contained the single line

So even Eddy came oven ready.

The command was

reducto eddy

and the output was written to a file called eddy.red. The program doesn't produce any onscreen output, but displaying the eddy.red file revealed the following:

Send money

Here are some program notes.

The fprintf() function is like printf() except that it requires a file pointer as its first argument. We've used the stderr pointer to send our error messages to the standard error; this is a standard C practice.

To construct the new name for the output file, we used strcpy() to copy the name eddy into the array name. Then we used the strcat() function to combine that name with .red, producing eddy.red. We also checked to see if the program succeeded in opening a file by that name. This is particularly important in the DOS environment because a filename like, say, strange.c.red is invalid; you can't add extensions to extensions under DOS. (The proper MS-DOS approach would be to replace any existing extension with .red, so that the reduced version of strange.c would be strange.red.)

This program had two files open simultaneously, so we declared two FILE pointers. Note that each file is opened and closed independently of the other. There are limits to how many files you can have open at one time. The limit depends on your system and implementation; the range is often 10 to 20. You can use the same file pointer for different files, providing those files are not open at the same time.

File I/O: *fprintf(), fscanf(), fgets(),* and *fputs()*

For each of the I/O functions in the preceding chapters, there is a similar file I/O function. The main distinction is that you need to use a FILE pointer to tell the new functions which file to work with. Like getc() and putc(), these functions require that you identify a file by using a pointer-to-FILE such as stdout or that you use the return value of fopen().

The *fprintf()* and *fscanf()* Functions

The file I/O functions fprintf() and fscanf() work just like printf() and scanf(), except that they require an additional first argument to identify the proper file. We've already used fprintf(). Listing 12.3 illustrates both of these file I/O functions along with the rewind() function.

Listing 12.3. addaword.c.

```
/* addaword.c -- uses fprintf(), fscanf(), and rewind() */
#include <stdio.h>
#include <stdlib.h>
#define MAX 20
int main(void)
{
    FILE *fp;
    char words[MAX];

    if ((fp = fopen("wordy", "a+")) == NULL)
    {
        fprintf(stdin,"Can't open \"words\" file.\n");
        exit(1);
    }
    puts("Enter words to add to the file; press the Enter");
    puts("key at the beginning of a line to terminate.");
    while (gets(words) != NULL  && words[0] != '\0')
        fprintf(fp, "%s ", words);
```

```
    puts("File contents:");
    rewind(fp);              /* go back to beginning of file */
    while (fscanf(fp,"%s",words) == 1)
        puts(words);
    if (fclose(fp) != 0)
        fprintf(stderr,"Error closing file\n");
    return 0;
}
```

This program enables you to add words to a file. By using the "a+" mode, the program can both read and write in the file. The first time the program is used, it creates the words file and enables you to place words in it. When you use the program subsequently, it enables you to add (append) words to the prior contents. The append modes only enables you to add material to the end of the file, but the "a+" mode does enable you to read the whole file. The rewind() command takes the program to the file beginning so that the final while loop can print the file contents. Note that rewind() takes a file pointer argument.

If you enter an empty line, gets() places a null character in the first element of the array. We use that fact to terminate the loop.

Here's a sample run from a DOS environment:

```
C>addaword
Enter words to add to the file; press the Enter
key at the beginning of a line to terminate.
See the canoes[enter]
[enter]
File contents:
See
the
canoes
C>addaword
Enter words to add to the file; press the Enter
key at the beginning of a line to terminate.
on the[enter]
sea[enter]
[enter]
File contents:
See
the
canoes
on
the
sea
```

As you can see, fprintf() and fscanf() work like printf() and scanf(). Unlike putc(), the fprintf() and fscanf() functions take the FILE pointer as the first argument instead of as the last argument.

The *fgets()* and *fputs()* Functions

The fgets() function takes three arguments to gets()'s one. The first argument, as with gets(), is the address (type char *) where input should be stored. The second argument is an integer representing the maximum size of the input string. The final argument is the file pointer identifying the file to be read. Thus, a function call looks like this:

```
fgets(buf, MAX, fp);
```

Here, buf is the name of a char array, MAX is the maximum size of the string, and fp is the pointer-to-FILE.

The fgets() function reads input through the first newline character or until one fewer than the upper limit of characters is read or until the end of file is found; fgets() then adds a terminating null character to form a string. Thus, the upper limit represents the maximum number of characters plus the null character. If fgets() reads in a whole line before running into the character limit, it adds the newline character marking the end of the line into the string, just before the null character. Here it differs from gets(), which reads the newline but discards it.

Like gets(), fgets() returns the value NULL when it encounters EOF. You can use this to check for the end of a file. Otherwise, it returns the address passed to it.

The fputs() function takes two arguments: first, an address of a string, then a file pointer. It writes the string found at the pointed-to location into the indicated file. Unlike puts(), fputs() does not append a newline when it prints. A function call looks like this:

```
fputs(buf, fp);
```

Here, buf is the string address, and fp identifies the target file.

Because fgets() keeps the newline and fputs() doesn't add one, they work well in tandem. Listing 12.4 shows an echo program using these two functions.

Listing 12.4. echo.c.

```
/* echo.c -- using fgets() and fputs() */
#include <stdio.h>
#define MAXLINE 20
int main(void)
{
    char line[MAXLINE];

    while (fgets(line, MAXLINE, stdin) != NULL &&
        line[0] != '\n')
    fputs(line, stdout);
    return 0;
}
```

When you press the Enter key at the beginning of a line, `fgets()` reads the newline and places it into the first element of the array `line`. We use that fact to terminate the input loop. Encountering end of file also terminates it. (In Listing 12.3 we tested for '\0' instead of '\n' because `gets()` discards the newline.)

Here is a sample run. Do you notice anything odd?

```
It is Spring.
It is Spring.
The hills are green and the sea is sparkling.
The hills are green and the sea is sparkling.
[enter]
```

The program works fine. This should seem surprising because the second line we entered contains 45 characters, and the `line` array holds only 20, including the newline character! What happened? When `fgets()` read the second line, it read just the first 19 characters, through the n in green. These were copied into `line`, which `fputs()` printed. Because `fgets()` hadn't reached the end of a line, `line` did not contain a newline character, so `fputs()` didn't print a newline. The third call to `fgets()` resumed where the second call left off. Thus, it read the next 19 characters into `line` beginning with the space after the n in green. This next block replaced the previous contents of `line` and, in turn, was printed on the same line as the output. Remember, the last output didn't have a newline. In short, `fgets()` read the second line in chunks of 19 characters, and `fputs()` printed it in the same-size chunks.

This program also terminates input if a line has exactly 19 characters. In that case, `fgets()` stops reading input after the 19 characters, so the next call to `fgets()` starts with the newline at the end of the line. This newline becomes the first character read, thus terminating the loop.

You may be wondering why the program didn't print the first 19 characters of the second line as soon as we typed them. That is where screen buffering comes in. The second line wasn't sent to the screen until the newline character had been reached.

Commentary: *gets()* and *fgets()*

Because `fgets()` can be used to prevent storage overflow, it is a better function than `gets()` for serious programming. Because it does read a newline into a string and because `puts()` appends a newline to output, `fgets()` should be used in conjunction with `fputs()`, not `puts()`. Otherwise, one newline in input can become two on output.

The six I/O functions we have just discussed should give you tools aplenty for reading and writing text files. So far, we have used them only for *sequential access*, that is, processing the file contents in order. Next, we look at *random access*, that is, accessing the contents in any desired order.

Adventures in Random Access:
fseek() and *ftell()*

The fseek() function enables you to treat a file like an array and move directly to any particular byte in a file opened by fopen(). To see how it works, let's create a program (Listing 12.5) that displays a file in reverse order. Borrowing from our earlier examples, it uses a command-line argument to obtain the name of the file that it will read. Note that fseek() has three arguments and returns an int value. The ftell() function returns the current position in a file as a long value.

Listing 12.5. reverse.c.

```
/* reverse.c -- displays a file in reverse order */
#include <stdio.h>
#include <stdlib.h>
#define CNTL_Z '\032'    /* eof marker in DOS text files */
int main(int argc, char *argv[])
{
    char ch;
    FILE *fp;
    long count, last;

    if (argc != 2)
    {
    printf("Usage: reverse file\n");
        exit(1);
    }
    if ((fp = fopen(argv[1],"rb")) == NULL)
    {                           /* read-only and binary modes */
        printf("reverse can't open %s\n", argv[1]);
        exit(1);
    }
    fseek(fp, 0L, SEEK_END);        /* go to end of file */
    last = ftell(fp);
    for (count = 1L; count <= last; count++)
    {
    fseek(fp, -count, SEEK_END);     /* go backward      */
        ch = getc(fp);
        if (ch != CNTL_Z && ch != '\r')
            putchar(ch);
    }
    fclose(fp);
    return 0;
}
```

Here is the output for a sample file:

```
.C ni eno naht ylevol erom margorp a
ees reven llahs I taht kniht I
```

We need to discuss three topics: how `fseek()` and `ftell()` work, how to use a binary stream, and how to make the program portable.

How *fseek()* and *ftell()* Work

The first of the three arguments to `fseek()` is a `FILE` pointer to the file being searched. The file should have been opened by using `fopen()`.

The second argument to `fseek()` is called the *offset*. This argument tells how far to move from the starting point (see the following list of mode starting points). The argument must be a `long` value. It can be positive (move forward) or negative (move backward) or zero (stay put).

The third argument is the *mode*, and it identifies the starting point. Under ANSI, the `stdio.h` header file specifies the following manifest constants for the mode:

Mode	Measure Offset from
SEEK_SET	Beginning of file
SEEK_CUR	Current position
SEEK_END	End of file

Older implementations may lack these definitions and, instead, use the numeric values `0L`, `1L`, and `2L`, respectively, for these modes. Recall that the `L` suffix identifies type `long` values, or the implementation may have the constants defined in a different header file. When in doubt, consult your usage manual or the online manual.

The value returned by `fseek()` is `0` if everything is okay, and `-1` if there is an error, such as attempting to move past the bounds of the file.

The `ftell()` function is type `long`, and it returns the current file location. Under ANSI, it is declared in `stdio.h`. As originally implemented in UNIX, `ftell()` specifies the file position by returning the number of bytes from the beginning, with the first byte being byte 0, and so on. Under ANSI C, this definition applies to files opened in the binary mode, but not necessarily to files opened in the text mode. That is one reason why we used the binary mode for Listing 12.5.

Now we can explain the basic elements of Listing 12.5. First, the statement

```
fseek(fp, 0L, SEEK_END);
```

takes us to an offset of 0 bytes from the file end. That is, it takes us to the end of the file. Next, the statement

```
last = ftell(fp);
```

assigns to `last` the number of bytes from the beginning to the end of the file.

Then, we have this loop:

```
for (count = 1L; count <= last; count++)
{
```

417

```
    fseek(fp, -count, SEEK_END);      /* go backward */
      ch = getc(fp);
}
```

The first cycle positions the program at the first character before the end of the file, that is, at the final character of the file. Then the program prints that character. The next loop positions the program at the preceding character and prints it. This continues until the first character is reached and printed.

Binary Versus Text Mode

We designed Listing 12.5 to work in both the UNIX and the MS-DOS environments. UNIX has only one file format, so no special adjustments are needed. MS-DOS, however, does require extra attention. Many MS-DOS editors mark the end of a text file with the character Control-Z. When such a file is opened in the text mode, C recognizes this character as marking the end of the file. When the same file is opened in the binary mode, however, the Control-Z character is just another character in the file, and the actual end-of-file comes later. It may come immediately after the Control-Z, or the file may be padded with null characters to make the size a multiple of, say, 256. Null characters don't print under DOS, and we included code to prevent the program from trying to print the Control-Z character.

Another difference is one we've mentioned before: MS-DOS represents a text file newline with the \r\n combination. A C program opening the same file in a text mode "sees" \r\n as a simple \n, but, when using the binary mode, the program sees both characters. Thus, we included coding to suppress the printing of \r. (Different coding would be needed for Macintosh text files, because they use the \r as the end-of-line marker.)

Because a UNIX text file normally contains neither Control-Z nor \r, this extra coding does not affect most UNIX text files.

The ftell() function may work differently in the text mode than in the binary mode. Many systems have text file formats that are sufficiently different from the UNIX model that a byte count from the beginning of the file is not a meaningful quantity. ANSI C states that, for the text mode, ftell() returns a value that can be used as the second argument to fseek(). For MS-DOS, for example, ftell() can return a count that sees \r\n as a single byte.

Portability

Ideally, fseek() and ftell() should conform to the UNIX model. However, differences in real systems sometimes make this impossible. Therefore, ANSI provides lowered expectations for these functions. Here are some limitations:

- In the binary mode, implementations need not support the SEEK_END mode. (Thus, Listing 12.5 is not guaranteed to be portable.)

- In the text mode, the only calls to fseek() that are guaranteed to work are these:

fseek(*file*, 0L, SEEK_SET)	Go to beginning of file
fseek(*file*, 0L, SEEK_CUR)	Stay at current position
fseek(*file*, 0L, SEEK_END)	Go to file end
fseek(*file*,*ftell-pos*, SEEK_SET)	Go to position *ftell-pos* from the beginning, where *ftell-pos* is a value returned by ftell()

Fortunately, many common environments allow stronger implementations of these functions. Let's look at a text mode example.

Using Random-Access in a Text Mode

Our goal is to write a program that takes a list of filenames from the command line and prints the name of each file followed by the last line of that file. Lest we get too rusty, let's use the modular approach to structure the program. Listing 12.6 shows the result.

Listing 12.6. lastline.c.

```
/* lastline.c -- prints last lines of files */
#include <stdio.h>
#include <stdlib.h>
void show_end(char *name, FILE *file);
int main(int argc, char *argv[])
{
    FILE *fp;
    int file;

    if (argc < 2)
    {
        printf("Usage: %s file(s)\n", argv[0]);
        exit(1);
    }
    for (file = 1; file < argc; file++)
    {
        if ((fp = fopen(argv[file],"r")) == NULL)
            fprintf(stderr,"%s can't open %s\n", argv[0],
                argv[file]);
        else
        {
            show_end(argv[file],fp);
            fclose(fp);
        }
    }
    return 0;
}
```

Listing 12.6. continued

```c
void show_end(char *name, FILE *file)
{
    int ch;
    int newlines = 0;
    long count, start, last;

    printf("%s:\n", name);
    start = ftell(file);
    fseek(file, 0L, SEEK_END);              /* go to end of file */
    last = ftell(file);
    for (count = 1L; count <= last; count++)
    {
        fseek(file, -count, SEEK_END);   /* go backward      */
        ch = getc(file);
        if (ch == '\n')
            newlines++;
        if (newlines == 2)                  /* or maybe 3       */
        {
            start = ftell(file);
                             /* or maybe ftell(file) - 1     */
            break;
        }
    }
    fseek(file, start, SEEK_SET);
    while ((ch = getc(file)) != EOF)
        putchar(ch);
}
```

We let main() handle the command-line arguments and the opening and closing of files. The show_end() function takes care of finding and displaying the final line.

The program does expect the final line in each text file to be terminated with a newline character. Most, but not all, text editors do so. Here is a sample run from the MS-DOS environment:

```
C>lastline prose prod produce
prose:
a program more lovely than one in C.
lastline can't open prod
produce:
red potatoes
C>
```

The main() program contains a loop for processing the command-line arguments. Recall that argc includes the command name in the count, so it is one greater than the number of command-line arguments. Also, because argv[0] is the command name, argv[count-1] is the last argument. Thus, the loop cycles through all the arguments. If the argument is the name of a file that the program can open, the file is processed.

Otherwise, the loop prints an error message and goes to the next argument. You can use this form for any program that is expected to handle a list of files.

The `show_last()` function assumes that the text file ends with a newline. It searches backward from the end of the file until it finds a second newline character. This would mark the end of the next-to-last line. By reading the character, we move to the next character, which would be the first character on the final line. The fragment

```
if (newlines == 2)                    /* or maybe 3  */
{
  start = ftell(file);
                        /* or maybe ftell(file) - 1 */
  break;
}
```

saves the location of this character and breaks the `for` loop. The file may have only one line, causing the test `newlines == 2` to never become true. In that case, the loop runs to completion, examining all the characters in the file. Then the program prints the entire file, using the value of `start` that was set before the loop was entered.

Portability

In testing this program in diverse environments, we found that the era of complete portability has not yet arrived. Each of the three environments required some changes.

The files are opened in text mode, so we shouldn't have to worry about detecting the \r character. However, with Turbo C 2.0, we had to use 3 instead of 2 for the number of newlines. The reason is that although this version of Turbo C correctly transforms \r\n to \n when moving forward through a file, it transforms \r\n to \n \n when moving backward. Apparently the \n is passed as \n. Then the \r is detected. Turbo C notes that it is immediately followed by a \n, so it maps the combination to a second \n. Borland C 3.1, on the other hand, works with a value of 2, not 3.

With Microsoft C and QuickC, we sometimes had to subtract 1 from `start`; otherwise, the first letter of the final line was omitted. Sometimes? Yes, the behavior depended on which text editor created the files! If the file had a terminal Control-Z, the subtraction of 1 was needed; otherwise, it wasn't.

The UNIX system we use is not yet ANSI compliant. Therefore, to run the program on UNIX, we had to define `SEEK_END`, etc., to be the corresponding numeric values. Also, we couldn't use the ANSI C prototypes and function declarations.

With some modifications, therefore, the program works in the UNIX and MS-DOS environments, but it does go beyond the ANSI guarantees for `fseek()`. For example, we use offsets from the file end, and the offsets are not values returned by `ftell()`. All in all, you'll be better off using the binary mode rather than the text mode for random-access programs.

Behind the Scenes with Standard I/O

Now that you've seen some of the features of the standard I/O package, let's examine a representative conceptual model to see how standard I/O works.

Normally, the first step in using standard I/O is to use `fopen()` to open a file. (Recall, however, that the `stdin`, `stdout`, and `stderr` files are opened automatically.) The `fopen()` function not only opens a file but sets up a buffer (two buffers for read-write modes), and it sets up a data structure containing data about the file and about the buffer. Also, `fopen()` returns a pointer to this structure so that other functions will know where to find it. We'll assume that this value is assigned to a pointer variable named `fp`. The `fopen()` function is said to open a *stream*. If the file is opened in the text mode, we get a text stream, and if the file is opened in the binary mode, we get a binary stream.

The data structure typically includes a *file position indicator* to specify the current position in the stream. It also has indicators for errors and end-of-file, a pointer to the beginning of the buffer, a file identifier, and a count for the number of bytes actually copied into the buffer.

Let's concentrate on file input. Usually, the next step is to call upon one of the input functions declared in `stdio.h`, such as `fscanf()`, `getc()`, or `fgets()`. Calling any one of these functions causes a chunk of data to be copied from the file to the buffer. The buffer size is implementation dependent, but it typically is 512 bytes or some multiple thereof. In addition to filling the buffer, the initial function call sets values in the structure pointed to by `fp`. In particular, the current position in the stream, and the number of bytes copied into the buffer are set. Usually the current position starts at byte 0.

Once the data structure and buffer are initialized, the input function reads the requested data from the buffer. As it does so, the file position indicator is set to point to the character following the last character read. Because all the input functions from the `stdio.h` family use the same buffer, a call to any one function resumes where the previous call to any of the functions stopped.

When an input function finds that it has read all the characters in the buffer, it requests that the next buffer-sized chunk of data be copied from the file into the buffer. In this manner, the input functions can read all the file contents up to the end of the file. After a function reads the last character of the final buffer's worth of data, it sets the end-of-file indicator to true. The next call to an input function then returns EOF.

In a similar manner, output functions write to a buffer. When the buffer is filled, the data is copied to the file.

Other Standard I/O Functions

The ANSI standard library contains over three dozen functions in the standard I/O family. Although we don't cover them all here, we will briefly describe a few more to give you a better idea of what is available. We'll list each function by its ANSI C prototype to indicate its arguments and return values. Of those functions we discuss here, all but setvbuf() are also available in pre-ANSI implementations. Appendix F, "Standard I/O Functions (ANSI C)," lists the full ANSI C standard I/O package.

int ungetc(int c, FILE *fp)

The int ungetc(int c, FILE *fp) function pushes the character specified by c back onto the input stream. If you push a character onto the input stream, the next call to a standard input function will read that character. See Figure 12.2. Suppose, for example, you want a function to read characters up to, but not including, the next colon. You can use getchar() or getc() to read characters until a colon is read and then use ungetc() to place the colon back in the input stream. The ANSI C Standard guarantees only one pushback at a time. If an implementation permits you to push back several characters in a row, the input functions will read them in the reversed order of pushing.

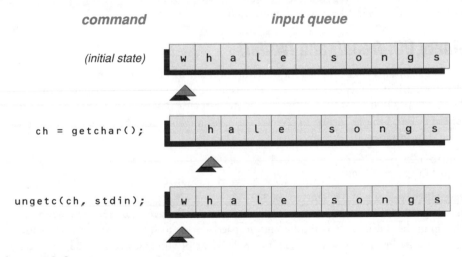

Figure 12.2. *The* ungetc() *function.*

int fflush(FILE *fp)

Calling the int fflush(FILE *fp) function causes any unwritten data in the buffer to be sent to the output file identified by fp. This process is called *flushing a buffer*. If fp is the NULL pointer, all output buffers are flushed.

int setvbuf(FILE *fp, char *buf, int mode, size_t size)

The int setvbuf(FILE *fp, char *buf, int mode, size_t size) function sets up an alternative buffer to be used by the standard I/O functions. It is called after the file has been opened and before any other operations have been performed on the stream. The pointer fp identifies the stream, and buf points to the storage to be used. If the value of buf is not NULL, you must create the buffer. For instance, you could declare an array of 1024 chars and pass the address of that array. However, if you use NULL for the value of buf, the function allocates a buffer itself. The size variable tells setvbuf() how big the array is. (The size_t type is a derived integer type; see Chapters 11, "Character Strings and String Functions," and 16, "The C Preprocessor and the C Library.") The mode is selected from the following choices: _IOFBF means fully buffered, _IOLBF means line-buffered, and _IONBF means nonbuffered. The function returns zero if successful, nonzero otherwise.

Suppose you had a program that worked with stored data objects having, say, a size of 3000 bytes each. You could use setvbuf() to create a buffer whose size matched that of the data object. Many pre-ANSI implementations use setbuf() instead. It takes two arguments. The first is a pointer-to-FILE to identify the file to be buffered. The second is the desired buffer size in bytes. The setbuf() function does not select among different buffering modes, nor does it have a return value.

Binary I/O: *fread()* and *fwrite()*

The fread() and fwrite() functions are next on our list, but first some background. The standard I/O functions we've used to this point are text oriented, dealing with characters and strings. What if you want to save numeric data in a file? True, you can use fprintf() and the %f format to save a floating-point value, but then you are saving it as a string. For instance, the sequence

```
double num = 1./3.;
fprintf(fp,"%f", num);
```

saves num as a string of 8 characters: 0.333333. Using a %.2f specifier saves it as 4 characters: 0.33. Using a %.12f specifier saves it as 14 characters: 0.333333333333. Changing the specifier alters the amount of space needed to store the value; it also can result in different values being stored. Once the value of num is stored as 0.33, there is no way to get back the full precision when reading the file. In general, fprintf() converts numeric values to strings, possibly altering the value.

The most accurate and consistent way to store a number is to use the same pattern of bits that the program does. Thus, a double value should be stored in a size double container. When data is stored in a file using the same representation that the program uses, we say that the data is stored in binary form. There is no conversion from numeric forms to strings. For standard I/O, the fread() and fwrite() functions provide this binary service. See Figure 12.3.

Actually, all data is stored in binary form. Even characters are stored using the binary representation of the character code. However, if all data in the file is interpreted as character codes, we say that the file contains text data. If some or all of the data is interpreted as numeric data in binary form, we say that the file contains binary data. (Also, files in which the data represents machine language instructions are binary files.)

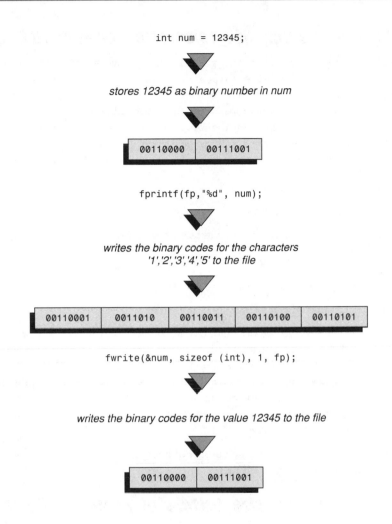

```
int num = 12345;
```

stores 12345 as binary number in num

00110000	00111001

```
fprintf(fp,"%d", num);
```

writes the binary codes for the characters
'1','2','3','4','5' to the file

00110001	0011010	00110011	00110100	00110101

```
fwrite(&num, sizeof (int), 1, fp);
```

writes the binary codes for the value 12345 to the file

00110000	00111001

(this figure assumes an integer size of 16 bits)

Figure 12.3. *Binary and text output.*

The uses of the terms *binary* and *text* can get confusing. ANSI C recognizes two modes for opening files: binary and text. Many operating systems recognize two file formats: binary and text. Information can be stored or read as binary data or as text data. These are all related, but not identical. You can open a text format file in the binary mode. You can store text in a binary format file. You can use getc() to copy files containing binary data. In general, however, you would use the binary mode to store binary data in a binary format file. Similarly, you most often would use text data in text files opened in the text format.

size_t fwrite(void *ptr, size_t size, size_t nmemb, FILE *fp)

The `size_t fwrite(void *ptr, size_t size, size_t nmemb, FILE *fp)` function writes binary data to a file. The `size_t` type is defined in terms of the standard C types. It is the type returned by the `sizeof` operator. Typically it is `unsigned int`, but an implementation can choose another type. The pointer `ptr` is the address of the chunk of data to be written. The `size` represents the size, in bytes, of the chunks to be written, and the `nmemb` represents the number of chunks to be written. As usual, `fp` identifies the file to be written to. For instance, to save a data object (such as an array) that is 256 bytes in size, you can do this:

```
char buffer[256];
   fwrite(buffer, 256, 1, fp);
```

This call writes one chunk of 256 bytes from `buffer` to the file, or to save an array of 10 `double` values, you can do this:

```
double earnings[10];
  fwrite(earnings, sizeof (double), 10, fp);
```

This call writes data from the `earnings` array to the file in 10 chunks, each of size `double`.

You probably noticed the odd declaration of `void *ptr` in the `fwrite()` prototype. One problem with `fwrite()` is that its first argument is not a fixed type. For instance, our first example used `buffer`, which is type pointer-to-`char`, and the second example used `earnings`, which is type pointer-to-double. Under ANSI C function prototyping, these actual arguments are converted to the pointer-to-`void` type, which acts as a sort of catchall type for pointers. (Pre-ANSI C uses type `char *` for this argument, requiring you to typecast actual arguments to that type.)

The `fwrite()` function returns the number of items successfully written. Normally, this equals `nmemb`, but it can be less if there is a write error.

size_t fread(void *ptr, size_t size, size_t nmemb, FILE *fp)

The `size_t fread(void *ptr, size_t size, size_t nmemb, FILE *fp)` function takes the same set of arguments that `fwrite()` does. This time `ptr` is the address of the memory storage into which file data is read, and `fp` identifies the file to be read. Use this function to read data that was written to a file using `fwrite()`. For example, to recover the array of 10 `double`s saved in the last example, use this call:

```
double earnings[10];
  fread(earnings, sizeof (double), 10, fp);
```

This call copies 10 size `double` values into the `earnings` array.

The `fread()` function returns the number of items successfully read. Normally, this equals `nmemb`, but it can be less if there is a read error or if the end of file is reached.

*int feof(FILE *fp)* and *int ferror(FILE *fp)*

When the standard input functions return EOF, it usually means that they have reached the end of a file. However, it also can indicate that a read error has occurred. The feof() and ferror() functions enable you to distinguish between the two possibilities. The feof() function returns a nonzero value if the last input call detected the end of file and returns zero otherwise. The ferror() function returns a nonzero value if a read or write error has occurred and zero otherwise.

An Example

Let's use some of these functions in a program that will append the contents from a list of files to the end of another file. One problem is passing the file information to the program. This can be done interactively or by using command-line arguments. We'll take the second approach, letting the final command-line argument represent the name of the append file. That is, a command like

```
append file1 file2 file3
```

will append file1 and file2 to file3. This suggests a plan along the following lines:

- If there are fewer than three words on the command-line, quit.

- Otherwise, open the final command line file in the append mode.

- Open each of the remaining command-line files in turn in the read mode and add it to the append file.

To illustrate setvbuf(), we'll use it to specify a different buffer size. The next stage of refinement examines the opening of the append file. We will use the following steps:

- Open the final command-line file in the append mode.

- If this cannot be done, quit.

- Establish a 1024-byte buffer for this file.

- If this cannot be done, quit.

Similarly, we can refine the copying portion in this way:

For each remaining file in the command-line list

- If it is the same as the append file, skip to the next file.

- If it cannot be opened in the read mode, skip to the next file.

- Add the contents of the file to the append file.

For practice, we'll use fread() and fwrite() for the copying. Listing 12.7 shows the result.

Listing 12.7. append.c.

```
/* append.c -- appends files to a file */
#include <stdio.h>
#include <stdlib.h>
#include <string.h>
#define BUFSIZE 1024
char temp[BUFSIZE];
void append(FILE *source, FILE *dest);

int main(int argc, char *argv[])
{
    FILE *fa, *fr;
    int file;

    if (argc < 3)
    {
        fprintf(stderr,
         "Usage: %s source-file(s) destination-file\n", argv[0]);
        exit(1);
    }
    if ((fa = fopen(argv[argc - 1], "a")) == NULL)
    {
        fprintf(stderr, "Can't open %s\n", argv[argc - 1]);
        exit(2);
    }
    if (setvbuf(fa, NULL, _IOFBF, BUFSIZE) != 0)
    {
        fputs("Can't create output buffer\n", stderr);
        exit(3);
    }
    for (file = 1; file < argc - 1; file++)
    {
        if (strcmp(argv[argc - 1], argv[file]) == 0)
            fputs("Can't append file to itself\n",stderr);
        else if ((fr = fopen(argv[file], "r")) == NULL)
            fprintf(stderr, "Can't open %s\n", argv[file]);
        else
        {
            if (setvbuf(fr, NULL, _IOFBF, BUFSIZE) != 0)
            {
                fputs("Can't create output buffer\n",stderr);
                continue;
            }
            append(fr, fa);
            if (ferror(fr) != 0)
                fprintf(stderr,"Error in reading file %s.\n",
                        argv[file]);
            if (ferror(fa) != 0)
                fprintf(stderr,"Error in writing file %s.\n",
                        argv[argc - 1]);
            fclose(fr);
        }
```

```
    }
    fclose(fa);
    return 0;
}

void append(FILE *source, FILE *dest)
{
    size_t bytes;
    extern char temp[]; /* use the external temp array */

    while ((bytes = fread(temp,sizeof(char),BUFSIZE,source)) > 0)
        fwrite(temp, sizeof (char), bytes, dest);
}
```

The following code creates a buffer 1024 bytes in size to be used with the append file:

```
if (setvbuf(fa, NULL, _IOFBF, BUFSIZE) != 0)
{
    fputs("Can't create output buffer\n", stderr);
    exit(3);
}
```

If setvbuf() is unable to create the buffer, it returns a nonzero value, and the code then terminates the program. Similar coding establishes a 1024-byte buffer for the file currently being copied. By using NULL as the second argument to setvbuf(), we let that function allocate storage for the buffer.

This code prevents the program from trying to append a file to itself:

```
if (strcmp(argv[argc - 1], argv[file]) == 0)
    fputs("Can't append file to itself\n",stderr);
```

The argument argv[argc - 1] represents the name of the final file in the command line, but argv[file] represents the name of the file currently being processed.

The append() function does the copying. Instead of copying a byte at a time, it uses fread() and fwrite() to copy 1024 bytes at a time.

```
void append(source, dest)
FILE *source, *dest;
{
    size_t bytes;
    extern char temp[];

    while ((bytes = fread(temp,sizeof(char),BUFSIZE,source)) > 0)
        fwrite(temp, sizeof (char), bytes, dest);
}
```

Because the file specified by dest is opened in the append mode, each source file is added to the end of the destination file, one after the other.

Chapter Summary

Writing to and reading from files is essential for most C programs. Most C implementations offer both *low-level* I/O services and *standard high-level* I/O services for these purposes. Because the ANSI C library includes the standard I/O services but not the low-level services, the standard package is more portable.

The standard I/O package automatically creates input and output buffers to speed up data transfer. The `fopen()` function opens a file for standard I/O and creates a data structure designed to hold information about the file and the buffer. The `fopen()` function returns a pointer to that data structure, and this pointer is used by other functions to identify the file to be processed.

ANSI C provides two file-opening modes: *binary* and *text*. When a file is opened in binary mode, it can be read byte-for-byte. When a file is opened in text mode, its contents may be mapped from the system representation of text to the C representation. For UNIX systems the two modes are identical because the C model for text files is derived from the UNIX file model.

The input functions `getc()`, `fgets()`, `fscanf()`, and `fread()` normally read a file sequentially, starting at the beginning of the file. However, the `fseek()` and `ftell()` functions let a program move to an arbitrary position in a file, enabling random access. Random access works better in the binary than in the text mode.

Review Questions

1. What's wrong with this program?

```
int main(void)
{
   int * fp;
   int k;

   fp = fopen("gelatin");
   for (k = 0; k < 30; k++)
       fputs(fp, "Nanette eats gelatin.");
   fclose("gelatin");
   return 0;
}
```

2. Suppose you have these statements in a program:

```
#include <stdio.h>
FILE * fp1,* fp2;
char ch;
```

```
fp1 = fopen("terky", "r");
fp2 = fopen("jerky", "w");
```

Also, suppose that both files were opened successfully. Supply the missing arguments in the following function calls:

```
a. ch = getc();
b. fprintf( ,"%c\n", );
c. putc( , );
d. fclose(); /* close the terky file */
```

3. Write a program that takes two command-line arguments. The first is a character, and the second is a filename. The program should print only those lines in the file containing the given character.

> **Note:** Lines in a file are identified by a terminating '\n'. Assume that no line is more than 256 characters long. You may wish to use `fgets()`.

4. What is the difference between

   a. Saving 8238201 using `fprintf()` and saving it using `fwrite()`?
   b. Saving the character S using `putc()` and saving it using `fwrite()`?

5. The "a+", "r+", and "w+" modes all open files for both reading and writing. Which one is best suited for altering material already present in a file?

Programming Exercises

1. Write a file copy program that takes the original filename and the copy file from the command line. Use standard I/O and the binary mode, if possible.

2. Write a program that sequentially displays on screen all the files listed in the command line. Use `argc` to control a loop.

3. Modify the program in Listing 12.6 so that it recognizes an optional flag command-line argument of the form -n, where n is an integer. Have the program print the last n lines of listed file(s). Use the binary mode.

4. Write a program that opens two files whose names are provided by command-line arguments.

   a. Have the program print line 1 of the first file, line 1 of the second file, line 2 of the first file, line 2 of the second file, and so on, until the last line of the longer file (in terms of lines) is printed.
   b. Modify the program so that lines with the same line number are printed on the same line.

5. Write a program that takes as command-line arguments a character and zero or more filenames. If no arguments follow the character, have the program read the standard input. Otherwise, have it open each file in turn and report how many times the character appears in each file. The filename and the character itself should be reported along with the count. Include error-checking to see if the number of arguments is correct and to see if the files can be opened. If a file can't be opened, have the program report that fact and go on to the next file.

6. Modify the program in Listing 12.3 so that each word is numbered according to the order in which it was added to the list, starting with 1. Make sure that, when the program is run a second time, new word numbering resumes where the previous numbering left off.

7. Write a program that opens a text file whose name is obtained interactively. Set up a loop that asks the user to enter a file position. The program then prints the part of the file starting at that position and proceeding to the next newline character. Let nonnumeric input terminate the user-input loop.

8. Write a program that takes two command-line arguments. The first is a string; the second is the name of a file. The program then should search the file, printing all lines containing the string. Because this task is line-oriented rather than character-oriented, use `fgets()` rather than `getc()`. Use a function like `string_in()` from Exercise 7, Chapter 11, "Character Strings and String Functions," to search each line for the string.

9. Write a function that reads one word from a file, leaving the boundary character (a tab, space, or newline) in the input buffer. Don't use `scanf()` or `fscanf()`.

10. Programs using command-line arguments rely on the user's memory of how to use them correctly. Rewrite the program in Listing 12.7 so that, instead of using command-line arguments, it prompts the user for the required information.

Storage Classes and Program Development

Keywords
    auto, extern, static
    register, const, volatile
Function
    rand()

In this chapter you learn how C enables you to determine the scope of a variable (how widely known it is) and the lifetime of a variable (how long it remains in existence). Also, you gain experience in designing more complex programs.

One of C's strengths is that it enables you to control the fine points of a program. C's storage classes exemplify that control by enabling you to determine which functions know which variables and for how long a variable persists in a program. Using storage classes is one more element of program design. There is more to programming than just knowing the rules of the language, just as there is more to writing a novel (or even a memo) than knowing the rules of English. We will reinforce some of the general principles and concepts of program design introduced earlier. We will also develop several useful functions. As we do so, we will try to demonstrate some of the general considerations that go into designing a function. In particular, we will emphasize the value of a *modular* approach—the division of a job into smaller, more manageable tasks.

Storage Classes and Scope

We gave storage classes a passing mention in Chapter 10, "Arrays and Pointers." We'll take a longer look now. As we mentioned in Chapter 10, *local variables* are known only to the functions containing them. However, C also offers the possibility of *global variables*, those known to several functions. Suppose you want both main() and critic() to have access to the variable Units. You can do this by declaring Units so that it belongs to the external storage class, as shown in Listing 13.1. (Here we follow a common, but not universal, convention of uppercasing the first character of a global variable name.)

Listing 13.1. global.c.

```c
/* global.c  -- uses an external variable */
#include <stdio.h>
int Units;                 /* an external variable */
void critic(void);
int main(void)
{
   extern int Units;

   printf("How many pounds to a firkin of butter?\n");
   scanf("%d", &Units);
   while ( Units != 56)
       critic();
   printf("You must have looked it up!\n");
   return 0;
}
void critic(void)
{
   extern int Units;

   printf("No luck, chummy. Try again.\n");
   scanf("%d", &Units);
}
```

Here is a sample output:

```
How many pounds to a firkin of butter?
14
No luck, chummy. Try again.
56
You must have looked it up!
```

(We did.)

Note how the second value for Units was read by the critic() function, yet main() also knew the new value when it finished the while loop. We made Units an external variable by defining it outside of (external to) any function definition. That's all you need to do to make Units available to all the following functions in the file.

There are three ways to treat Units within the functions. The simplest is to have no further declarations. In that case, the functions will use the externally defined Units by default.

The second way, and the one we took, is to place the following declaration in each function:

```
extern int Units;
```

In our example, inserting this declaration is mainly a matter of documentation. It tells the compiler that any mention of Units in this particular function refers to a variable defined outside the function, perhaps even outside the file. Again, both functions use the externally defined Units.

The third way, and one quite different in meaning, is to use this declaration in the functions:

```
int Units;
```

Suppose we do this for main() but not for critic(). Omitting the keyword extern causes the compiler to create a separate variable private to main(), but also named Units. The new Units would be *visible* while main() is running, but when control passes to critic(), the program would interpret Units as the externally defined one, and the value assigned to Units in main() would *not* affect the value of Units in critic().

Each variable, as you know, has a type. In addition, each variable has a *storage class*. There are four keywords used to describe storage classes: extern (for external), auto (for automatic), static, and register. Variables declared within a function are considered to be class auto unless declared otherwise. The formal arguments to functions normally are class auto, but they can be made class register.

The storage class of a variable is determined by where it is defined and by what keyword, if any, is used. The storage class determines three things. First, it controls which functions in a file have access to a variable. If a section of code can use a particular variable, we say the variable is visible in that section. The visibility of a variable to the various parts of a program is its *scope*. Second, the storage class determines in how many places the same variable can be declared; this is described by a variable's linkage. Finally, the storage class determines how long the variable persists in memory—its storage duration. Let's look at each of these terms briefly, then see how they relate to the various storage types.

Scope, Linkage, and Storage Duration

A C variable has one of the following three scopes: *file scope, block scope,* or *function prototype scope.* A variable with file scope is visible from the point it is defined to the end of the file containing the definition. For instance, the variable Units in Listing 13.1 has file scope, and it's visible to all the functions following its definition.

A variable with block scope is visible from the point it is defined until the end of the block containing the definition. (A block, recall, is marked by braces.) The local variables we've used to date, including formal function arguments, have block scope. Indeed, block scope is what makes them local, confining them to the functions in which they are defined. The function body is considered to be the block containing the formal function arguments. Thus, the variables jim and sandy in the following code both have block scope extending to the closing brace:

```
double blocky(double jim)
{
    double sandy = 0.0;
    ...
    return sandy;
}
```

Function prototype scope applies to variable names used in function prototypes, as in the following:

```
int mighty(int mouse, double large);
```

Function prototype scope runs from the point the variable is defined to the end of the prototype declaration. What this means is that all the compiler cares about when handling a function prototype arguments are the types; the names you use, if any, don't matter.

A C variable has one of the following linkages: *external linkage, internal linkage,* or *no linkage.* A variable with external linkage can be used anywhere in a multifile program. A variable with internal linkage can be used anywhere in a single file, and a variable with no linkage can be used only in the block in which it is defined. Variables with internal or external linkage can appear in more than one declaration, but variables with no linkage can be declared only once.

As you may have noticed, the concepts of linkage and scope are related. Variables with block scope or function prototype scope have no linkage, which is why the descriptions of no linkage and block scope are similar. As you'll see later, the concepts of internal and external linkage enable you to divide variables with file scope into two groups.

A C variable has one of the following two storage durations: *static storage duration* or *automatic storage duration.* If a variable has static storage duration, it exists throughout program execution. External variables like Units from Listing 13.1 have static storage duration. A variable with automatic storage duration is guaranteed to exist only while the program is executing the block in which the variable is defined. The local variables we've used to date fall into this category. For instance, in the following code, the variables number and index come into being each time the bore() function is called and pass away each time the function completes:

```
void bore(int number)
{
    int index;
    for (index = 0; index < number; index++)
        puts("They don't make them the way they used to.\n");
    return 0;
}
```

Now let's discuss C's storage classes in more detail.

Automatic Variables

By default, variables declared in a function are automatic. You can, however, make your intentions perfectly clear by explicitly using the keyword auto.

```
int main(void)
{
  auto int plox;
```

You might do this, for example, to document that you intentionally are overriding an external function definition or that it is important not to change the variable to another storage class.

An automatic variable has block scope. Only the function in which the variable is defined can access that variable by name. (Of course, arguments can be used to communicate the value and the address of the variable to another function, but that is indirect knowledge.) Another function can use a variable with the same name, but it will be an independent variable stored in a different memory location.

An automatic variable has no linkage. You can't declare it twice in the same block. You can declare variables having the same name but existing in different blocks, but these would be separate, independent variables with no links between them.

An automatic variable has automatic storage duration. It comes into existence when the function that contains it is called. When the function finishes its task and returns control to its caller, the automatic variable disappears. Its memory location can now be used for something else.

One more point about the scope of an automatic variable: its scope is confined to the block (paired braces) in which the variable is declared. We have always declared our variables at the beginning of the function block, so the scope is the whole function, but in principle you could declare a variable within a sub-block. Then that variable would be known only to that subsection of the function. Here's an example:

```
int loop(int n)
{
    int m;
    scanf("%d", &m);
    {
        int i;    /* local to this sub-block */
        for (i = m; i < n; i++)
                puts("i is local to a sub-block\n");
    }
    return m;
}
```

In this code, *i* is visible only within the inner braces. You'd get a compiler error if you tried to use it before or after the inner block. Normally, you wouldn't use this feature when designing a program. Sometimes, however, it is useful to define a variable in a sub-block if it is not used elsewhere. In that way, you can document the meaning of a variable close to the location at which it is used. The variable also doesn't sit unused, occuping memory when it no longer is needed.

Initialization of Automatic Variables

Automatic variables are not initialized unless you do so explicitly. Consider the following declarations:

```
int main(void)
{
  int repid;
  int tents = 5;
```

The `tents` variable is initialized to 5, but the `repid` variable winds up with whatever value happened to previously occupy the space assigned to `repid`. You cannot rely on this value being 0.

External Variables

A variable defined outside a function is external. As a matter of documentation, an external variable also can be declared inside a function that uses it by using the `extern` keyword. If the variable is defined in *another* file, declaring the variable with `extern` is mandatory. Declarations look like this:

```
int Errupt;            /* externally defined variable   */
double Up[100];        /* externally defined array      */
extern char Coal;      /* mandatory declaration         */
                       /* Coal defined in another file  */
void next(void);
int main(void)
{
  extern int Errupt;   /* optional declaration          */

  extern double Up[]; /* optional declaration           */
  ...
```

```
}
void next(void)
{
  ...
}
```

The two declarations of Errupt are examples of linkage, for they both refer to the same variable. External variables have external linkage, a point we'll return to later.

Note that we don't have to give the array size in the optional declaration of double_Up. That's because the original declaration already supplied that information. The group of extern declarations inside main() may be omitted entirely because external variables have file scope and thus are known from the point of declaration to the end of the file.

If only the extern is omitted from the declaration inside a function, then a separate automatic variable is set up. That is, replacing

```
extern int Errupt;
```

with

```
int Errupt;
```

in main() would cause the compiler to create an automatic variable named Errupt. This would be a separate, local variable, distinct from the original Errupt. The local variable would be in scope while the program executes main(), but the external Errupt would be in scope for other functions, such as next(), in the same file. In short, a variable in block scope "hides" a variable of the same name in file scope while the program executes statements in the block.

External variables have static storage duration. Thus, the array double_Up maintains its existence and values regardless of whether the program is executing main(), next(), or some other function.

The following three examples show four possible combinations of external and automatic variables. In Example 1, there is one external variable: Hocus. It is known to both main() and magic().

```
/* Example 1 */
int Hocus;
int magic();
int main(void)
{
    extern int Hocus;  /* Hocus declared external */
    ...
}}
int magic()
{
    extern int Hocus;
    ...
}
```

Example 2 has one external variable, Hocus, known to both functions. This time, magic() knows it by default.

```
/* Example 2 */
int Hocus;
int magic();
int main(void)
{
    extern int Hocus;   /* Hocus declared external */
    ...
}}
int magic()
{
                        /* Hocus not declared at all */
    ...
}}
```

In Example 3, four separate variables are created. The Hocus in main() is automatic by default and is local to main. The Hocus in magic() is automatic explicitly and is known only to magic(). The external Hocus is not known to main() or magic() but would be known to any other function in the file that did not have its own local Hocus. Finally, Pocus is an external variable known to magic() but not to main() because Pocus follows main().

```
/* Example 3 */
int Hocus;
int magic();
int main(void)
{
  int Hocus;         /* Hocus declared, is auto by default */
    ...
}}
int Pocus;
int magic()
{
    auto int Hocus;  /* Hocus declared automatic         */
    ...
}
```

These examples illustrate the scope of external variables. They also illustrate the lifetimes of variables. The external Hocus and Pocus variables persist as long as the program runs, and, because they aren't confined to any one function, they don't fade away when a particular function returns.

> **Note:** If you use the keyword extern without a type, the compiler interprets it as being extern int.

Initializing External Variables

Like automatic variables, external variables can be initialized explicitly. Unlike automatic variables, external variables automatically are initialized to zero if you don't initialize them. This applies to elements of an externally defined array, too.

External Names

The rules for names of external variables are more restrictive than for local variables. The reason is that external names need to comply with the rules of the local environment, which may be more limiting. For local names, the ANSI C Standard requires that a compiler distinguish between upper- and lowercase and that it recognize the first 31 characters in a name. For external variables, the compiler need not distinguish between upper- and lowercase, and it need recognize only the first 6 characters in a name. These rules apply to function names, too. The preceding limitations stem from the desire to make C programs compatible with some of the older, more limited operating systems and languages.

Definitions and Declarations

There is a difference between defining a variable and declaring it. Consider this example:

```
int tern;
main()
{
      external int tern;
```

Here tern is declared twice. The first declaration causes storage to be set aside for the variable. It constitutes a *definition* of the variable. The second declaration merely tells the compiler to use the tern variable that previously has been created; thus, it is not a definition. The first declaration is called a *defining declaration*, and the second is called a *referencing declaration*. The keyword extern *always* indicates that a declaration is not a definition, because it instructs the compiler to look elsewhere.

Suppose you do this:

```
extern int tern;
int main(void)
{
```

Then the compiler would assume that the actual definition of tern is somewhere else in your program, perhaps in another file. This declaration will not cause space to be allocated. Therefore, don't use the keyword extern to create an external definition; use it only to *refer* to an existing external definition.

An external variable can be initialized only once, and that must occur when the variable is defined. A statement like

```
extern char permis = 'Y';    /* error */
```

is in error because the presence of the keyword `extern` signifies a referencing declaration, not a defining declaration.

Static Variables

The name *static variable* sounds like a contradiction, like a variable that can't vary. Actually, "static" means that the variable stays put. These variables have the same scope as automatic variables, but they don't vanish when the containing function ends its job. That is, static storage class variables have block scope but static storage duration. The computer remembers their values from one function call to the next. The example in Listing 13.2 illustrates this point and shows how to declare a static variable.

Listing 13.2. static.c.

```
/* static.c -- using a static variable */
#include <stdio.h>
void trystat(void);
int main(void)
{
    int count;

    for (count = 1; count <= 3; count++)
    {
        printf("Here comes iteration %d:\n", count);
        trystat();
    }
    return 0;
}
void trystat(void)
{
    int fade = 1;
    static int stay = 1;

    printf("fade = %d and stay = %d\n", fade++, stay++);
}
```

Note that `trystat()` increments each variable after printing its value. Running the program gives this output:

```
Here comes iteration 1:
fade = 1 and stay = 1
Here comes iteration 2:
fade = 1 and stay = 2
Here comes iteration 3:
fade = 1 and stay = 3
```

The static variable `stay` remembers that its value was increased by 1, whereas the `fade` variable starts anew each time. This points out a difference in initialization: `fade` is initialized each time `trystat()` is called, but `stay` is initialized just once, when `trystat()` is compiled. Like external variables, static variables are initialized to zero if you don't explicitly initialize them to some other value.

External Static Variables

You can also declare a `static` variable outside all functions. This creates an *external static* function. The difference between an ordinary external variable and an external static variable lies in its linkage (see Figure 13.1). The ordinary external variable can be used by functions in any file, but the external static variable can be used only by functions in the same file. In other words, an ordinary external variable has external linkage, but a static external variable has internal linkage. You set up an external static variable by placing the definition outside all functions and by using the keyword static in that definition.

```
static int randx = 1;
int rand()
{
```

Later on, Listing 13.3 shows an example with a static variable.

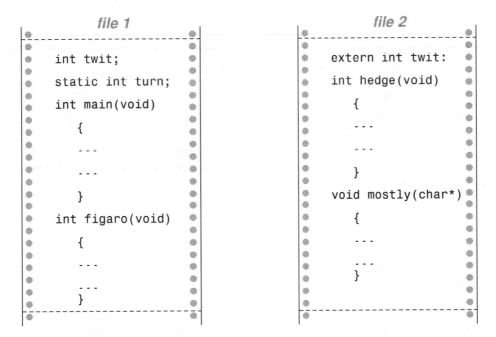

```
                 file 1                          file 2

    int twit;                           extern int twit:

    static int turn;                    int hedge(void)

    int main(void)                         {

       {                                    ...

       ...                                  ...

       ...                                  }

       }                                 void mostly(char*)

    int figaro(void)                       {

       {                                    ...

       ...                                  ...

       ...                                  }

       }
```

Figure 13.1. *External variable versus external static variable.*

Multiple Files

Complex C programs often use several separate files of code. Sometimes these files may need to share an external variable. The ANSI C way to do this is to have a defining declaration in one file and referencing declarations in the other files. That is, all but one declaration (the defining declaration) should use the `extern` keyword, and only the defining declaration can be used to initialize the variable.

Note that an external variable defined in one file is not available to a second file unless it is also declared (using `extern`) in the second file. An external declaration by itself only makes a variable *potentially* available to other files.

Historically, however, many compilers have followed different rules in this regard. Many UNIX systems, for example, enable you to declare a variable in several files without using the `extern` keyword, providing that no more than one declaration includes an initialization. If there is a declaration with an initialization, it is taken to be the definition.

Scope and Functions

Functions, too, have storage classes. A function can be either external (the default) or static. An *external function* can be accessed by functions in other files, but a *static function* can be used only within the defining file. Consider, for example, a file containing these function declarations:

```
double gamma();          /* external by default */
static double beta();
extern double delta();
```

The functions `gamma()` and `delta()` can be used by functions in other files that are part of the program, but `beta()` cannot. Because this `beta()` is restricted to one file, you can use a different function having the same name in the other files. One reason to use the `static` storage class is to create functions that are private to a particular module, thereby avoiding the possibility of name conflicts.

We recommend that you use the `extern` keyword when declaring functions that are defined in other files. This is mostly a matter of clarity, because a function declaration is assumed to be `extern` unless the keyword `static` is used.

Register Variables

Variables normally are stored in computer memory. With luck, *register variables* are stored in the CPU registers or, more generally, in the fastest memory available, where they can be accessed and manipulated more rapidly than regular variables. In other respects, register variables are the same as automatic variables. They are declared this way:

```
int main(void)
{
   register int quick;
```

We say "with luck" because declaring a variable as register class is more a request than a direct order. The compiler has to weigh your demands against the number of registers or amount of fast memory available, so you may not get your wish. In that case, the variable becomes an ordinary automatic variable.

You can request that formal parameters be `register` variables. Just use the keyword in the function heading.

```
void macho(register int n)
```

The types that can be declared `register` may be restricted. For example, the registers in a processor may not be large enough to hold type `double`. Also, the & operator will not work with `register` variables.

Summary: Scopes

Automatic variables have block scope, no linking, and automatic storage duration. They are local and private to the block (typically a function) in which they are defined. When a variable is declared external to any function in a file, it's an external variable and has file scope, external linking, and static storage duration. An external variable will be known to all functions following it in that file, whether or not those functions explicitly declare the variable as `extern`. If you want a function in a second file to access an external variable in the first file, you must declare the variable in the second file using the keyword `extern`.

A static variable is defined inside a function by using the keyword `static`. It is local to that function. It has block scope, no linkage, and static storage duration. A static external variable is defined outside a function by using the keyword `static`. It has file scope, internal linking, and static storage duration. A static external variable is local to its file.

Which Storage Class?

The answer to the question "Which storage class?" most often is "automatic." After all, why else was *automatic* selected as the default? Yes, we know that at first glance external storage is quite alluring. Just make all your variables external, and you'll never have to worry about using arguments and pointers to communicate between functions. There is a subtle pitfall, however. You will have to worry about function A() sneakily altering the variables used in function B(), despite your intentions to the contrary. The unquestionable evidence of untold years of collective computer experience is that this one subtle danger far outweighs the superficial attraction of using external storage indiscriminately.

One of the golden rules of protective programming is the "need to know" principle. Keep the inner workings of each function as private to that function as possible, sharing only those variables that need to be shared. The other classes are useful, and they are available. Before using one, though, ask yourself if it is necessary.

Summary: Storage Classes

Keywords

`auto`, `extern`, `static`, `register`

General Comments

The storage class of a variable determines its scope, its linkage, and its storage duration. Storage class is determined both by where the variable is defined and by its associated keyword. Variables defined outside all functions are external, have file scope, external linkage, and static storage duration. Variables declared inside a function are automatic unless one of the other keywords is used. They have block scope, no linkage, and automatic storage duration. Variables defined with the keyword `static` inside a function have block scope, no linkage, and static storage duration. Variables defined with the keyword `static` outside a function have file scope, internal linkage, and static storage duration.

Properties

In the following list, those variables in storage classes above the dotted line are declared inside a function; those below the line are defined outside a function.

Storage Class	Keyword	Duration	Scope and Linkage
automatic	`auto`	temporary	local
register	`register`	temporary	local
static	`static`	persistent	local
external	`extern*`	persistent	global (all files)
external static	`static`	persistent	global (one file)

*The keyword `extern` is used only to redeclare variables that have been defined externally elsewhere. The act of defining the variable outside of a function makes it external.

A Random Number Function

Now let's look at a function that makes use of an external static variable: a *random number function*. The ANSI C library provides the `rand()` function to generate random numbers.

There are a variety of algorithms for generating random numbers, and ANSI C enables implementors to choose the best algorithm for a particular machine, but the ANSI C standard also supplies a standard, portable algorithm that will produce the same random numbers on different systems. Actually, rand() is a "pseudorandom number generator." This means that the actual sequence of numbers is predictable (computers are not known for their spontaneity) but that the numbers are spread pretty uniformly over the possible range of values.

Rather than use your compiler's built-in rand() function, we'll use the portable ANSI version so that you can see what goes on inside. The scheme starts with a number called the *seed.* The function uses the seed to produce a new number, which becomes the new seed. Then the new seed can be used to produce a newer seed, and so on. For this scheme to work, the random number function must remember the seed it used the last time it was called. Aha! This calls for a static variable. Listing 13.3 is version 0. (Yes, version 1 comes soon.)

Listing 13.3. rand0.c.

```
/* rand0.c -- produces random numbers          */
/*               uses ANSI C portable algorithm */
static unsigned long int next = 1;  / * the seed */
int rand0(void)
{
    /* magic formula to generate pseudorandom number */
    next = next * 1103515245 + 12345;
    return (unsigned int) (next/65536) % 32768;
}
```

In Listing 13.3 the static variable next starts with the value 1 and is altered by the magic formula each time that the function is called. The result is a return value somewhere in the range of 0 to 32767

Let's try the rand0() function with the simple driver in Listing 13.4.

Listing 13.4. r_drive1.c.

```
/* r_drive1.c */
#include <stdio.h>
extern int rand0(void);
int main(void)
{
    int count;

    for (count = 0; count < 5; count++)
        printf("%hd\n", rand0());
    return 0;
}
```

447

Here's a good chance to practice using multiple files. Use one file for Listing 13.3 and one for Listing 13.4. (See Chapter 9, "Functions," or your compiler manual for guidance.) The extern keyword reminds us that rand0() is defined in a separate file.

The output is

```
16838
5758
10113
17515
31051
```

The output looks random, but let's run it again. This time the result is as follows:

```
16838
5758
10113
17515
31051
```

Hmmm, that looks familiar; this is the "pseudo" aspect. Each time the main program is run, we start with the same seed of 1. We can get around this problem by introducing a second function srand1() that enables us to reset the seed. The trick is to make next an external static variable known only to rand1() and srand1(). (The C library equivalent to srand1() is called srand().) Keep rand1() and srand1() in their own file and compile that file separately. Listing 13.5 is the modification.

Listing 13.5. s_and_r.c.

```
/* s_and_r.c -- file for rand1() and srand1() */
/*              uses ANSI C portable algorithm */
static unsigned long int next = 1;  / * the seed */
int rand1(void)
{
    /* magic formula to generate pseudorandom number */
    next = next * 1103515245 + 12345;
    return (unsigned int) (next/65536) % 32768;
}

void srand1(unsigned int seed)
{
    next = seed;
}
```

Notice that next is an external static variable. This means that it can be used by both rand1() and srand1(), but not by functions in other files. To test these functions, use the driver in Listing 13.6.

Listing 13.6. `r_drive2.c`

```
/* r_drive2.c */
#include <stdio.h>
extern void srand1(unsigned int x);
extern int rand1(void);
int main(void)
{
    int count;
    unsigned seed;

    printf("Please enter your choice for seed.\n");
    scanf("%u", &seed);
    srand1(seed);    /* reset seed */
    for (count = 0; count < 5; count++)
        printf("%hd\n", rand1());
    return 0;
}
```

Again, use two files. Run the program once.

```
Please enter your choice for seed.
1
16838
5758
10113
17515
31051
```

Using a value of 1 for seed yields the same values as before. Now let's try a value of 3.

```
Please enter your choice for seed.
3
17747
7107
10365
8312
20622
```

Very good! We get a different set of numbers.

Automated Reseeding

If your C implementation gives you access to some changing quantity, such as the system clock, you can use that value (possibly truncated) to initialize the seed value. For instance, ANSI C has a `clock()` function that returns the system time. The time units are system dependent, but what matters here is that the return value is an

continues

> integer type and that its value changes with time. The exact integer type also is system dependent, but you can use a type cast. Here's the basic setup:
>
> ```
> #include <time.h>   /* ANSI prototype for clock() */
>         srand1((unsigned) clock());   /* initialize seed */
> ```

(You can use the same technique with the standard ANSI C functions `srand()` and `rand()`. If you do use these functions, include the `stdlib.h` header file.) Now let's develop a use for our set of functions.

Roll 'Em

We are going to simulate that very popular random activity, dice-rolling. The most popular form of dice-rolling uses two 6-sided dice, but there are other possibilities. Many adventure-fantasy games use all of the five geometrically possible dice: 4, 6, 8, 12, and 20 sides. Those clever ancient Greeks proved that there are but five regular solids having all faces the same shape and size, and these solids are the basis for the dice varieties. One could make dice with other numbers of sides, but the faces would not all be the same, so they wouldn't all have equal odds of turning up.)

Computer calculations aren't limited by these geometric considerations, so we can devise an electronic die that has any number of sides. Let's start with 6 sides and then generalize.

We want a random number from 1 to 6, but because `rand1()` produces the range 0 to 32767, we have some adjustments to make. Here's one approach.

1. Take the random number modulus 6. This produces an integer in the range 0 through 5.

2. Add 1. The new number is in the range 1 through 6.

3. To generalize, just replace the number 6 in step 1 by the number of sides.

Listing 13.7 shows a function that does these steps for a general number of sides. The listing includes some explicit type casts to emphasize where type conversions take place.

Listing 13.7. `diceroll.c.`

```
/* diceroll.c */
extern int rand1(void);
int rollem(int sides)
{
    int roll;
```

```
    roll = rand1() % sides + 1.0;
    return roll;
}
```

Listing 13.8 shows a program that uses the rand1(), srand1(), and rollem()
functions.

Listing 13.8. manydice.c.

```
/* manydice.c -- multiple dice roll */
#include <stdio.h>
extern void srand1(unsigned);
extern int rollem(int);
int main(void)
{
  int dice, count, roll;
  short seed;
  int sides;

  printf("Enter a seed value.\n");
  scanf("%hd", &seed);
  srand1(seed);
  printf("Enter the number of sides per die, 0 to stop.\n");
  while (scanf("%d", &sides) == 1 && sides > 0)
  {
      printf("How many dice?\n");
      scanf("%d", &dice);
      for (roll = 0, count = 0; count < dice; count++)
          roll += rollem(sides);
          /* running total of dice pips */
      printf("You have rolled a %d using %d %d-sided dice.\n",
              roll, dice, sides);
      printf("How many sides? Enter 0 to stop.\n");
  }
  printf("GOOD FORTUNE TO YOU!\n");
  return 0;
}
```

Compile Listing 13.8 with the files containing Listings 13.5 and 13.7. Then use it.

```
Enter a seed value.
1
Enter the number of sides per die, 0 to stop.
6
How many dice?
2
You have rolled a 8 using 2 6-sided dice.
How many sides? Enter 0 to stop.
6
```

```
How many dice?
2
You have rolled a 6 using 2 6-sided dice.
How many sides? Enter 0 to stop.
0
GOOD FORTUNE TO YOU!
```

You can use `rollem()` in many ways. With `sides` equal to 2, the program simulates a coin toss with "heads" - 2 and "tails" - 1 (or vice versa if you really prefer it). You can easily modify the program to show the individual results as well as the total, or you can construct a craps simulator. If you require a large number of rolls, as may occur in some role-playing games, you can easily modify the program to produce output like this:

```
Enter a seed value.
10
Enter the number of sets; enter q to stop.
18
How many sides and how many dice?
6 3
Here are 18 sets of 3 6-sided throws.
   12  10   6   9   8  14   8  15   9  14  12  17  11   7  10
   13   8  14
How many sets? Enter q to stop.
q
```

Another use for `rand1()` or `rand()` (but not of `rollem()`) would be to create a number-guessing program so that the computer chooses and you guess. You can try that yourself.

Now let's develop some more functions. Our first project will be to design a program that reads in a list of integers and sorts them.

Sorting Numbers

One of the most common tasks for a computer is sorting. Here we'll develop a program to sort integers. We'll take a black box approach and think in terms of input and output. Our overall plan, shown in Figure 13.2, is pretty simple.

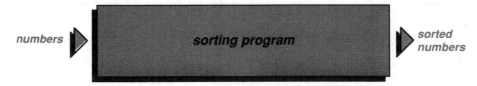

Figure 13.2. *Sorting program: a black box view.*

At this point, the program is still too vaguely defined for us to begin writing code. The next step is to identify the main tasks that the program must do to accomplish our goals. We can break down our example to three such tasks.

1. Read the numbers.

2. Sort them.

3. Print the sorted numbers.

Figure 13.3 shows this breakdown as we descend from the top level of organization to a more detailed level.

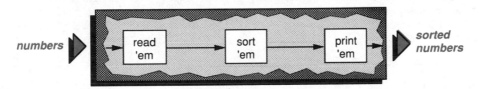

Figure 13.3. *Sorting program: peeking inside.*

Global Decisions

Before designing the individual modules, we need to make some global decisions. We need to choose a data form and to decide what information will be passed to the individual modules.

Data Form

How do we represent a collection of numbers? We could use a collection of variables, one for each number. That is just too much trouble to even think about. An immensely superior approach is to use an array.

What kind of an array? Type int? Type double? We need to know how the program is going to be used. Let's assume it is to be used with modestly sized integers. We will use an array of ints to store the numbers we read.

Information Flow

The first module gathers input. It should know where to place the values it reads. It also should know the maximum number of values it can accept, and it should report the actual number of items read. The sorting module should know which array to sort and how many elements are present. The printing module should know which array to use and how many elements to print. These considerations suggest the main() function shown in Listing 13.9.

Listing 13.9. sort_int.c.

```
/* sort_int.c -- sorts integers */
#define MAXSIZE  100    /* limit to number of integers to sort */
extern int getarray(int ar[], int n);
extern void sort(int ar[], int n);
extern void print(int ar[], int n);
int main(void)
{
  int numbers[MAXSIZE];               /* array to hold input    */
  int size;                           /* number of input items  */

  size = getarray(numbers, MAXSIZE); /* put input into array    */
  sort(numbers, size);               /* sort the array          */
  print(numbers, size);              /* print the sorted array  */
  return 0;
}
```

Here we have the skeleton of our program. The function `getarray()` places the values read into the array `numbers` and reports how many values were read. That value is assigned to `size`. Then `sort()` sorts the array, and `print()` prints the sorted results.

Now that we have refined our picture of the information flow, we should modify our black box sketch. As Figure 13.4 shows, we now have three black boxes, each with its own input and output. Because we are emphasizing modularity, we have broken the original problem into three smaller, more manageable pieces. We can assign each part to a different programming team, provided that the numbers output by "read 'em" are in the same form that "sort 'em" uses for input.

We will apply our efforts to each of the three boxes separately, breaking them down to simpler units until we reach a point at which the code is obvious. As we do this, we must pay attention to these important points: data-form choice, error-trapping, and information flow. Let's continue with our example, tackling the reading portion first (see Figure 13.5).

Reading Numeric Data

Many programs read numbers, so the ideas we develop here will be useful elsewhere. The general form for this part of the program is clear: Use a loop to read in numbers until all the numbers are read, but there is more to reading numbers than you might think!

Ending Input

How will the function know when to quit reading numbers? We faced a similar problem in Chapter 10, "Arrays and Pointers." There we had a `read_array()` function that quit reading numbers when the user either simulated EOF or entered a nonnumeric value. This time we'll take a different tack. Our main change is how we handle nonnumeric input. We'll design the function so that it alerts the user when the input is nonnumeric and then lets the user try again.

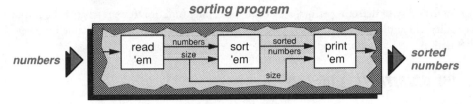

Figure 13.4. *Sorting program: adding details.*

Figure 13.5. *Sorting program: the first task.*

Why this change? Suppose you are entering data at the keyboard and accidentally enter 1o instead of 10. Would you rather have the program terminate, forcing you to reenter all the data or have it just reject that one entry and let you continue? It is simpler to rely on the "perfect user theory," which states that the user makes no entry errors. However, we recognize that this theory may not apply to users other than ourselves. Therefore, we opt for the second choice. This checking of input for suitability is termed *data validation*.

Here is one approach:

1. Read a word

2. While not EOF

3. If the word is an integer, assign it to an array

4. Else skip that word and request numeric input again

5. Read the next word if the array isn't full

Note that there are two separate conditions that bring this portion of the program to a close: an EOF signal or filling the array.

Further Considerations

Before we translate this approach into C code, we still have decisions to make. The data validation to which we've committed ourselves has two aspects: detecting an error and reporting that error to the user. We can try to code all this directly into getarray(), or we can put the code into an input function called by getarray(). We'll adopt an intermediate approach that follows a common C style: we'll give the input function the responsibility of detecting errors, and leave the calling function (getarray()) the responsibility of handling the error. This provides greater flexibility because the same input function can be used in programs that process errors differently.

The *getarray()* Function

Now let's look at getarray() shown in Listing 13.10.

Listing 13.10. getarray.c.

```
/* getarray.c -- reads in an array */
#include <stdio.h>
#include "getint.h"      /* declares getint(), constants */
int getarray(int array[], int limit)
{
  int num, status;
  int index = 0;                              /* array index */

  printf("This program stops reading numbers after %d ",
         limit);
  printf("values\nor if EOF is encountered.\n");
  while (index < limit && (status = getint(&num)) != EOF )
  {
    if (status == YESNUM)
    {
      array[index++] = num;
      printf("The number %d has been accepted.\n", num);
    }
    else if (status == NONUM)
      printf("That was no integer! Try again.\n");
    else
      printf("This can't happen! Something's very wrong.\n");
  }
  if (index == limit )    /* report if array gets filled */
  printf("All %d elements of the array were filled.\n",
        limit);
  return(index);
}
```

This is a not a simple function, and we have quite a few points to note.

Explanation

The getarray() function is premised on the existence of a getint() function with the following properties:

- The getint() function returns YESNUM if it has read an integer. It places the value of that integer into the location pointed to by its argument, an address of an int.

- It returns NONUM if it reads a noninteger. It discards the invalid input.

- It returns EOF if it encounters the end of file.

- The getint.h file contains the function declaration and definitions of the getint() return values. The implementation of this function will come after we finish discussing getarray().

We set up getarray() to handle each of the possible return values. An EOF return causes the while loop to end. A YESNUM return results in a valid entry being stored in the awaiting array. Also, that number is echoed back to the user showing that it was accepted. A NONUM return sends the user back for another try.

There is one more else statement. Logically, the only way that statement can be reached is if getint() returns a value other than YESNUM, NONUM, or EOF, but those are the only values that can be returned, so this seems to be a useless statement. We included it as an example of *defensive programming*, the art of protecting a program from future fiddling. Someday, we, or someone else, may decide to rewrite getint(), adding a few more possible return values to its repertoire. Most likely we will by then have forgotten, and they may never have known, that getarray() assumes that there are just three possible responses. Therefore, to assist in future debugging, we include this final else to trap any new responses that show up.

We use the keyword return to communicate the number of items read. Thus, our function call

```
size = getarray(numbers, MAXSIZE);
```

assigns a value to size and puts values into the numbers array.

In functions involving counters and limits, like this one, the most likely place to find an error is at the *boundary conditions*, where counts reach their limits. Are we going to read a maximum of MAXSIZE numbers, or are we going to be off by 1? We need to pay attention to details such as ++index versus index++ and < versus <=. We also have to keep in mind that arrays start their subscripting with 0, not 1. Take a moment to check our code and see if it works as it should. The easiest way to do that is to imagine that limit is 1 and then walk through the procedure step by step.

Finally, the function informs the user when the array is full so that he or she is not taken by surprise.

The *getint()* Function

Now we need to supply a getint() function. We'll take the easy way and use existing library functions. Listing 13.11 shows an implementation based on scanf().

Listing 13.11. getint.c.

```
/* getint.c */
#include <stdio.h>
#include "getint.h"
int getint(int * ptint)
{
  int status;

  status = scanf("%d", ptint);
  if (status == NONUM)
      scanf("%*s");
  return status;
}
```

Also, we need a getint.h file.

```
/* getint.h -- definitions used by getint() */
#define NONUM 0
#define YESNUM 1
extern int getint(int * pt);
```

Recall that scanf() returns the number of items successfully read. If it finds an int, it returns 1, or YESNUM. If it finds a noninteger, it returns 0, or NONUM, and if it finds the end of file, it returns EOF. The getint() function merely passes along these return values. If the return value of scanf() is 0, the getint() function skips over the invalid input. Recall that the %*s specifier causes scanf() to skip over the next word. If status is 0, then the word is not an integer, so we want to skip it. Otherwise, scanf() will remain stuck on that word forever.

Getting a program to interact in a convenient, dependable manner with the user is often the most difficult part of writing code. That is the case with this part of the program. You'll find sort() and print() easier. Let's move on to sort() now.

Sorting the Data

Let's look at main() again from Listing 13.9.

```
/* sort_int.c -- sorts integers */
#define MAXSIZE  100    /* limit to number of integers to sort */
extern int getarray(int ar[], int n);
extern void sort(int ar[], int n);
extern void print(int ar[], int n);
int main(void)
{
  int numbers[MAXSIZE];                 /* array to hold input    */
  int size;                             /* number of input items  */

  size = getarray(numbers, MAXSIZE); /* put input into array    */
  sort(numbers, size);                  /* sort the array         */
```

```
    print(numbers, size);              /* print the sorted array */
    return 0;
}
```

We see that the two arguments to sort() are an array of integers to be sorted and a count of the number of elements to be sorted. The function sorts the numbers but has no return value. We still haven't decided how to do the sorting, so we need to refine this description further.

One obvious point to decide is the direction of the sort. Are we going to sort from largest to smallest or vice versa? Again, we'll be arbitrary and say that we'll sort from largest to smallest. (We could design a function to do either, but then we would have to develop a way to tell the function which choice we want.) See Figure 13.6.

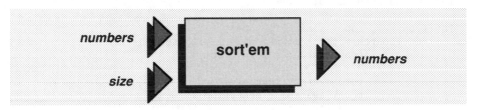

Figure 13.6. *Sorting function: the second task.*

Now let's consider the method we will use to sort. Many sorting algorithms have been developed for computers. We'll use one of the simplest—the *selection sort*.

Here is our plan in pseudocode:

```
for n = first to n = next-to-last element,
    find largest remaining number and place it in the nth element
```

The plan works like this. First, start with n = 1. Scan the entire array, find the largest number, and swap it with the first element. Next, set n = 2, and scan all but the first element of the array. Find the largest remaining number, and swap it with the second element. Continue this process until reaching the next-to-last element. Now only two elements are left. Compare them and place the larger in the next-to-last position. This leaves the smallest element of all in the final position.

It looks like a for loop task, but we still have to describe the "find and place" process in more detail. Here is one way to select the largest remaining value. Compare the first and second elements of the remaining array. If the second is larger, swap the two values. Now compare the first element with the third. If the third is larger, swap those two. Each swap moves a larger element to the top. Continue this way until you have compared the first with the last element. When you finish, the largest number is now in the first element of the remaining array. You have sorted the array for the first element, but the rest of the array is in a jumble. Here is the procedure in pseudocode:

```
for n - second element to last element,
  compare nth element with first element; if nth is greater, swap values
```

This looks like another for loop. It will be nested in the first for loop. The outer loop indicates which array element is to be filled, and the inner loop finds the value to put there. Putting the two parts of the pseudocode together and translating into C, we get the function in Listing 13.12.

Listing 13.12. sort.c.

```c
/* sort.c -- sorts an integer array in decreasing order */
void sort(int array[], int limit)
{
   int top, search, temp;

   for (top = 0; top < limit -1; top++)
       for (search = top + 1; search < limit; search++)
           if (array[search] > array[top])
           {
                temp = array[search];
                array[search] = array[top];
                array[top] = temp;
           }
}
```

In Listing 13.12 we were clever enough to remember that the first element has 0 for a subscript. Also, we used the swapping technique discussed in Chapter 9, "Functions." We used top as the subscript for the array element that is to be filled, because it is at the top of the unsorted part of the array. The search index roams over the array below the current top element. Now we just have print() left to write.

Printing the Data

Our last task is to write the function that will print the sorted numbers (see Figure 13.7). This function, as shown in Listing 13.13, is pretty simple.

Listing 13.13. print.c.

```c
/* print.c -- prints an array */
#include <stdio.h>
void print(int array[], int limit)
{
   int index;

   for (index = 0; index < limit; index++)
     printf("%d\n", array[index]);
}
```

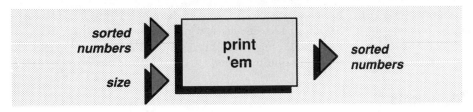

Figure 13.7. *Printing results: the third task.*

If we want something a little different, such as printing in rows instead of in one column, we can always change this function, leaving the other functions untouched. Similarly, if we found a sorting algorithm that we liked better, we could replace the sort() module. That is one of the nice features about a modular program.

Results

Let's compile and test this package. To make checking the boundary conditions simpler, we'll temporarily change MAXSIZE to 5. For our first test, we will feed numbers to the program until it refuses to take more.

```
This program stops reading numbers after 5 values
or if EOF is encountered.
12 34 54 23 67 232[enter]
All 5 elements of the array were filled.
67
54
34
23
12
```

Good, it stopped when five numbers were read, and it sorted the results. Now we test to see if it stops when the end of file is encountered.

```
This program stops reading numbers after 5 values
or if EOF is encountered.
456 928
MCMLXXXIX
That's no integer! Try again.
-23 +16
[Control-D]          →(transmits EOF on UNIX system)
928
456
16
-23
```

Faster than you can say "oikology is the science of housekeeping," the whole enormous array is sorted. Recall that Control-Z transmits EOF on MS-DOS systems.

Success wasn't easy, but it was possible. By breaking the problem into smaller parts and by thinking about what information should flow into and out of each part, we reduced the problem to manageable proportions. Furthermore, the individual modules we produced could be used as parts of similar programs.

Comments

One major advantage of the modular design is that it makes it simpler to tinker with the program. For instance, consider the sorting module. After thinking about it, you might decide that you can improve the efficiency by changing the algorithm slightly. As the program moves through the inner loop, instead of immediately promoting each new claimant to the top ranking to the top, just keep track of the index of the claimant. Then, when the inner loop finishes, just swap the current top claimant with the current top position, or you might want to modify the printing module to print six numbers to a line. With a modular approach, you can fix just that module and leave the rest of the program unchanged. If each function has its own file, you need only recompile the altered one, then link it to the compiled versions of the other files. Integrated environments do this automatically when you have a project file. That is, they keep track of which files need to be recompiled and which have been unaltered.

ANSI C Type Qualifiers

You've seen that a variable is characterized by both its type and its storage class. ANSI C adds two more properties: constancy and volatility. These properties are declared with the keywords const and volatile. These keywords create *qualified types*.

The *const* Type Qualifier

The const keyword in a declaration establishes a variable whose value cannot be modified by assignment or by incrementing or decrementing. On an ANSI-compliant compiler, the code

```
const int nochange;    /* qualifies m as being constant */
nochange = 12;         /* not allowed                    */
```

should produce an error message. You can, however, initialize a const variable. Thus, the following is fine:

```
const int nochange = 12;   /* ok */
```

The preceding declaration makes nochange a read-only variable. Once initialized, it cannot be changed.

You can use the const keyword, for example, to create an array of data that the program can't alter.

```
const int days1[12] = {31,28,31,30,31,30,31,31,30,31,30,31};
```

Using the const keyword when declaring a simple variable and an array is pretty easy. Pointers are more complicated because you have to distinguish between making the pointer itself const and making the value that is pointed to const. The declaration

```
const float * pf;  /* pf points to a constant float value */
```

establishes that pf points to a value that must remain constant. The value of pf itself can be changed. For example, it can be set to point at another const value. In contrast, the declaration

```
float * const pt;     /* pt is a const pointer */
```

says that the pointer pt itself cannot have its value changed. It must always point to the same address, but the pointed-to value can change. Finally, the declaration

```
const float * const ptr;
```

means both that ptr must always point to the same location and that the value stored at the location must not change.

One common use for this new keyword is declaring pointers that serve as formal function parameters. For example, consider the function strlen(). We pass it a pointer to the beginning of the string, and the function returns the length of the string. In general, passing a pointer to a function enables that function to alter data in the calling function, but as we mentioned in Chapter 11, "Character Strings and String Functions," the following declaration prevents that from happening:

```
int strlen(const char * str)  /* ANSI form */
```

This declaration says that the data to which str points cannot be changed, but str itself can be altered, so the program can use str++ in its code. It just can't do stuff like *str = '!'.

The ANSI C library follows this practice. If a pointer is used only to give a function access to values, the pointer is declared as a pointer to a const-qualified type. If the pointer is used to alter data in the calling function, then the const keyword isn't used. For instance, the ANSI C declaration for strcat() is this:

```
char *strcat(char *, const char *);
```

Recall that strcat() adds a copy of the second string to the end of the first string. This modifies the first string but leaves the second string unchanged. The declaration reflects this.

The *volatile* Type Qualifier

The volatile qualifier tells the compiler that a variable can have its value altered by agencies other than the program. It typically is used for hardware addresses. For instance, an address may hold the current clock time. The value at that address changes as time changes regardless of what your program is doing, or the address may be used to receive information transmitted from, say, another computer.

The syntax is the same as for `const`.

```
volatile int loc1;   /* loc1 is a volatile location    */
volatile int * ploc; /* ploc points to a volatile location */
```

These statements declare `loc1` to be a `volatile` value and `ploc` to point to a `volatile` value.

You may think that `volatile` is an interesting concept, but you may be wondering why the ANSI committee felt it necessary to make `volatile` a keyword. The reason is that it facilitates compiler optimization. Suppose, for example, you have code like this:

```
val1 = x;
 /* some code not using x */
val2 = x;
```

A smart (optimizing) compiler might notice that you use x twice without changing its value. It would temporarily store the x value in a register. Then, when x is needed for `val2`, it can save time by reading the value from a register instead of from the original memory location. This is called *caching*. Ordinarily, caching is a good optimization, but not if x is changed between the two statements by some other agency. If there were no `volatile` keyword, a compiler would have no way of knowing whether this might happen. Therefore, to be safe, the compiler couldn't cache. That was the pre-ANSI situation. Now, however, if the `volatile` keyword is not used in the declaration, the compiler can assume that a value hasn't changed between uses, and it then can attempt to optimize the code.

A value can be both `const` and `volatile`. For instance, the hardware clock setting normally should not be changed by the program, making it `const`; and it is changed by an agency other than the program, making it `volatile`. Just use both qualifiers in the declaration; the order doesn't matter.

```
volatile const int loc;
const volatile int * ploc;
```

Chapter Summary

What have we accomplished? On the practical side we developed a random-number generator and an integer-sorting program. In the process we developed `getint()` and `sort()` functions that we can use in other programs. On the educational side we illustrated some general principles and concepts useful in designing complex programs.

Programs should be *designed* rather than allowed to evolve through some random process of growth, trial, and error. You should think carefully about the form and content of input and output for a program. You should break the program into well-defined tasks and then write the code for these tasks separately, keeping in mind how they interface with one another. The idea is to achieve modularity. When necessary, break a module into smaller modules. Use functions to enhance the modularity and clarity of the program.

When designing a program, try to anticipate what might go wrong and then write the program accordingly. Use error-trapping to circumvent potential problems or, at least, to alert the user if a problem shows up. It's much better to give the user a second chance to enter data than to let the program crash in ignominy.

When designing a function, first decide how it will interact with the calling function. Decide what information flows in and what information flows out. What will the arguments be? Will you use pointers, or return, or both? Once you have these design parameters in mind, you can turn your attention to the mechanics of the function.

As you put these ideas to use, you'll produce programs with greater reliability. You may acquire a body of functions that you can use in other programs. If so, your programming will take less time.

Don't forget about storage classes. Variables can be defined outside of functions, in which case they are external (or global) and are available to more than one function. Variables defined within a function are local to that function and are not known to other functions. When possible, use local variables. This keeps variables in one function from being contaminated by the actions of other functions.

Review Questions

1. Which storage classes create variables local to the function containing them?

2. Which storage class creates variables that can be used across several files? restricted to just one file?

3. How would you change our sorting routine to make it sort in increasing order instead of decreasing order?

4. Which functions know each variable in the following? Are there any errors?

```
/* file 1 */
int daisy;
int main(void)
{
  int lily;
  ...;
}
int petal()
{
  extern int daisy, lily;
  ...;
}
```

```
/* file 2 */
extern int daisy;
static int lily;
int rose;
int stem()
{
  int rose;
  ...;
}
void root()
{
  ...;
}
```

5. A file begins with the following declarations:

```
static int plink;
int value_ct(const int arr[], int value, int n);
```

a. What do these declarations tell you about the intent of the programmer?
b. Will replacing int value and int n with const int value and const int n enhance the protection of values in the calling program?

Programming Exercises

1. Some users might be daunted by being asked to enter an EOF character. Modify getarray() and getint() so that a # character also terminates input.

2. Create a program that sorts float numbers in increasing order.

3. Modify Listing 13.10 so that it uses the suggestion given in the Comments section following the sample output for Listing 13.14.

4. Write and test in a loop a function that returns the number of times it has been called.

5. Write a program that generates a list of 100 random numbers in the range 1–10 in sorted decreasing order.

6. Write a program that generates 1000 random numbers in the range 1–10. Don't save or print the numbers, but do print how many times each number was produced. Have the program do this for 10 different seed values. Do the numbers appear in equal amounts? You can use the functions from this chapter or ANSI C rand() and srand() functions, which follow the same format that our functions do. This is one way to test the randomness of a particular random-number generator.

7. Write a program that behaves like the modification of Listing 13.9, which we discussed after showing the output of Listing 13.9. That is, have the program produce the output shown on page 518.

8. Write an interactive program that lets the user enter as many as 20 words. Have the program display the words in sorted order (recall the string sorting example from Chapter 11, "Character Strings and String Functions") and then ask the user if the words should be saved in a file. If the user responds with a yes, have the program request a name for the file and then write the words into a file by that name.

9. Write a function that skips over input until encountering a digit. It then stores that digit and subsequent digits in a string until encountering a nondigit. The nondigit is placed back in the input, and the function converts the digit string to a numeric value. The function should use a pointer argument to provide the numeric value to the calling program. Use the function return value to return EOF if the function encounters end of file; have it return 1 otherwise. Use getc() and ungetc(). In short, this function finds the next integer in output, whether it be isolated or embedded in text, as in be22again.

10. Modify Exercise 8 so that the function recognizes an optional minus sign. That is, confronted with an input of be-22now, it extracts the value -22.

11. Construct a text file containing 10 lines, each composed of a name, a colon, and three integers. Write a program that reads the file and prints the lines in order of increasing average value of the integers in the line. That is, the line

```
Shalla Booger: 80 70 84
```

would precede the line

```
Hagar Joe Plinty: 70 90 80
```

because the average of its three values is less than the second average. Also have the program append the average to each line when it is printed. Note that the name part of the input need not consist of exactly two names.

Structures
and Other
Data Forms

Keywords
struct, union, typedef
Operators
. ->

In this chapter you learn what C structures are and how to create structure templates and variables. Then you learn how to access the members of a structure and how to write functions to handle structures. A short look at C's typedef facility and at unions and pointers to functions concludes the chapter.

One of the most important steps in designing a program is choosing a good way to represent the data. In many cases, a simple variable or even an array is not enough. C takes your ability to represent data a step further with the C *structure variables*. The C structure is flexible enough in its basic form to represent a diversity of data, and it enables you to invent new forms. If you are familiar with the "records" of Pascal, you should be comfortable with structures. If not, this chapter will introduce you to C structures. Let's study a concrete example to see why a C structure might be needed and how to create and use one.

Example Problem: Creating an Inventory of Books

Gwen Glenn wishes to print an inventory of her books. She would like to print a variety of information for each book: title, author, publisher, copyright date, the number of pages, the number of copies, and the dollar value. Some of these items, such as the titles, can be stored in an array of strings. Other items require an array of int or an array of float. With seven different arrays, keeping track of everything can get complicated, especially if Gwen wishes to generate several complete lists, one sorted by title, one sorted by author, one sorted by value, and so on. A better solution would be to use one array, in which each member contained all the information about one book.

Gwen needs a data form, then, that can contain both strings and numbers and somehow keep the information separate. The C structure meets this need. To see how a structure is set up and how it works, we'll start with a limited example. To simplify the problem, we will impose two restrictions. First, we'll include only title, author, and current market value. Second, we'll limit the inventory to one book. If you have more books than that, don't worry; we'll extend the program soon.

Look at the program in Listing 14.1 and its output. Then read our explanation of the main points.

Listing 14.1. book.c.

```
/* book.c -- one-book inventory */
#include <stdio.h>
#define MAXTIT   41      /* maximum length of title + 1         */
#define MAXAUT   31      /* maximum length of author's name + 1 */
struct book {            /* structure template: tag is book     */
    char title[MAXTIT];
    char author[MAXAUT];
    float value;
};                       /* end of structure template           */
int main(void)
{
    struct book libry; /* declare libry as book-type variable */
    printf("Please enter the book title.\n");
    gets(libry.title);           /* access to the title portion */
    printf("Now enter the author.\n");
    gets(libry.author);
```

```
    printf("Now enter the value.\n");
    scanf("%f", &libry.value);
    printf("%s by %s: $%.2f\n",libry.title,
        libry.author, libry.value);
    printf("%s: \"%s\" \($%.2f\)\n", libry.author,
        libry.title, libry.value);
    return 0;
}
```

Here is a sample run:

```
Please enter the book title.
Chicken of the Alps
Now enter the author.
Bismo Lapoult
Now enter the value.
12.95
Chicken of the Alps by Bismo Lapoult: $12.95
Bismo Lapoult: "Chicken of the Alps" ($12.95)
```

The structure created in Listing 14.1 has three parts (called *members* or *fields*): one to store the title, one to store the author, and one to store the value. The three main points we will study are

- How to set up a format or *template* for a structure

- How to declare a variable to fit that template

- How to gain access to the individual components of a structure variable

Setting Up the Structure Template

A *structure template* is the master plan that describes how a structure is put together. Our template looked like this:

```
struct book {
    char title[MAXTIT];
    char author[MAXAUT];
    float value;
};
```

This template describes a structure made up of two character arrays and one float variable. Let's look at the details. First comes the keyword struct. This identifies what comes next as a structure. Next comes an optional *tag*, the word book. The tag book is a shorthand label that we can use to refer to this structure. Thus, later on we have this declaration:

```
struct book libry;
```

It declares libry to be a structure variable using the book structure template.

Next in the structure definition, we find the list of structure members enclosed in a pair of braces. Each member is described by its own declaration, complete with terminating semicolon. For instance, the `title` portion is a `char` array with `MAXTIT` elements. A member can be any C data type. That includes other structures!

A semicolon after the closing brace ends our definition of the template. You can place this template outside any function (externally), as we have done, or inside a function definition. If the template is defined inside a function, then its tag can be used only inside that function. If the template is external, it is available to all the functions following the definition in the file. For example, in a second function, you could define

```
struct book dickens;
```

and that function would have a variable `dickens` that followed the form of our `book` template.

The tag name is optional, but you must use one when you set up structures as we did, with the template defined one place and the actual variables defined elsewhere. We will return to this point soon, after we look at defining structure variables.

Defining a Structure Variable

The word *structure* is used in two senses. One is the sense "structure template," which is what we just discussed. The template is a plan; it tells the compiler how to represent the data, but it doesn't make the computer allocate space for the data. The next step is to create a "structure variable" the second sense of the word. The line in our program that causes a structure variable to be created is this:

```
struct book libry;
```

Seeing this instruction, the compiler creates the variable `libry`. Using the `book` template, the compiler allots space for a `char` array of `MAXTIT` elements, for a `char` array of `MAXAUT` elements, and for a `float` variable. This storage is lumped together under the single name `libry` (see Figure 14.1). (In the next section we explain how to unlump it as needed.)

In declaring a structure variable, `struct book` plays the same role that `int` or `float` does in simpler declarations. For example, we could declare two variables of the `struct book` type or even a pointer to that kind of structure.

```
struct book doyle, panshin, * ptbook;
```

The structure variables `doyle` and `panshin` would each have the parts `title`, `author`, and `value`. The pointer `ptbook` could point to `doyle`, `panshin`, or any other `book` structure.

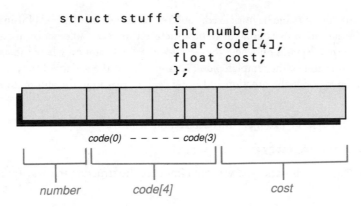

```
struct stuff {
              int number;
              char code[4];
              float cost;
              };
```

code(0) – – – – – code(3)

number   code[4]   cost

Figure 14.1. *Memory allocation for a structure.*

As far as the computer is concerned, the following declaration

```
struct book libry;
```

is short for

```
struct book {
   char title[MAXTIT];
   char author[AXAUT];
   float value;
} libry;    /* follow template with variable name */
```

In other words, the process of defining a structure template and the process of defining a structure variable can be combined into one step. Combining the template and the variable definitions is the one circumstance in which a tag need not be used.

```
struct {            /* no tag */
   char title[MAXTIT];
   char author[MAXAUT];
   float value;
} libry;
```

Use the tag form, however, if you plan to use a structure template more than once.

There is one aspect of defining a structure variable that did not come up in our example: initialization. We'll look at that now.

Initializing a Structure

You've seen how to initialize variables and arrays.

```
int count = 0;
static int fibo[] = {0,1,1,2,3,5,8};
```

Can a structure variable be initialized, too? Yes, although many pre-ANSI implementations limit initialization to external or static structure variables. Whether or not a structure variable is external depends on where the *variable* is defined, not on where the *template* is defined. In our example, the template book is external, but the variable libry is not because it is defined inside the function and is, by default, placed in the automatic storage class.

Suppose, though, we had made this declaration:

```
static struct book libry;
```

Then the storage class is static, and we could initialize the structure this way (pre-ANSI or ANSI):

```
static struct book libry = {
    "The Pirate and the Damsel",
    "Renee Vivotte",
    1.95
};
```

In short, you use a comma-separated list of initializers enclosed in braces. Each initializer should match the type of structure member being initialized. Thus, we can initialize the title member to a string and the value member to a number. To make the associations more obvious, we gave each member its own line of initialization, but all the compiler needs are commas to separate one member's initialization from the next.

Now, let's continue with structure properties.

Gaining Access to Structure Members

A structure is like a "superarray" in which one element can be char, the next element float, and the next an int array. We can access the individual elements of an array by using a subscript. How do we access individual members of a structure? We use a dot (.), the structure member operator. For example, libry.value is the value portion of libry. You can use libry.value exactly as you would use any other float variable. Similarly, you can use libry.title exactly as you would use a char array. Thus, we used expressions like

```
gets(libry.title);
```

and

```
scanf("%f", &libry.value);
```

In essence, .title, .author, and .value play the role of subscripts for a book structure.

Note that although libry is a structure, libry.value is a float type and is used like any other float type. For example, scanf("%f",...) requires the address of a float location, and that is what &libry.float is. The dot has higher precedence than the & here, so the expression is the same as &(libry.float).

If we had a second structure variable of the same type, we would use the same method:

```
struct book spiro, gerald;

gets(spiro.title);
gets(gerald.title);
```

The .title refers to the first member of book structure. Notice how in our initial program we printed the contents of the structure libry in two different formats. This illustrates the freedom we have in using the members of a structure.

Now that you have these basics in hand, you're ready to expand your horizons and look at several ramifications of structures. You'll see arrays of structures, structures of structures, pointers to structures, and functions that process structures.

Arrays of Structures

Let's extend our book program to handle a greater number of books. Clearly each book can be described by one structure variable of the book type. To describe two books, we need to use two such variables, and so on. To handle several books, we can use an array of such structures, and that is what we have created in the next program, shown in Listing 14.2. (If you're using Borland C/C++, read the box about Borland C and Floating-Point.)

Structures and Memory

The manybook.c program uses an array of 100 structures. Such a large array requires a good-sized chunk of memory, which can cause problems. For example, Microsoft C places automatic variables in the stack and uses a default stack size of 2048, much too small for this program. You can set the stack size to 10000 to accommodate the array of structures, however, or make the array static or external (so that it isn't placed in the stack), or reduce the array size to 16.

Borland C and Floating-Point

The Borland C compilers attempt to make programs more compact by using a small version of scanf() if the program doesn't use floating-point values. However, the compilers (at least through version 3.1) are fooled if the only floating point values are in an array of structures, as in the case for Listing 14.2. As a result, you get a message like this:

continues

```
  scanf : floating point formats not linked
Abnormal program termination
```

One workaround is to add this code to your program:

```
#include <math.h>
double dummy = sin(0.0);
```

This forces the compiler to load the floating point version of scanf().

Listing 14.2. manybook.c.

```c
/* manybook.c -- multiple book inventory */
#include <stdio.h>
#define MAXTIT   40
#define MAXAUT   40
#define MAXBKS   100            /* maximum number of books  */
struct book {                   /* set up book template     */
    char title[MAXTIT];
    char author[MAXAUT];
    float value;
};
int main(void)
{
    struct book libry[MAXBKS]; /* array of book structures */
    int count = 0;
    int index;

    printf("Please enter the book title.\n");
    printf("Press [enter] at the start of a line to stop.\n");
    while (count < MAXBKS && gets(libry[count].title) != NULL
                     && libry[count].title[0] != '\0')
    {
        printf("Now enter the author.\n");
        gets(libry[count].author);
        printf("Now enter the value.\n");
        scanf("%f", &libry[count++].value);
        while (getchar() != '\n')
            continue;                  /* clear input line */
        if (count < MAXBKS)
        printf("Enter the next title.\n");
    }
    printf("Here is the list of your books:\n");
    for (index = 0; index < count; index++)
    printf("%s by %s: $%.2f\n", libry[index].title,
        libry[index].author, libry[index].value);
    return 0;
}
```

Here is a sample program run:

```
Please enter the book title.
Press [enter] at the start of a line to stop.
My Life as a Budgie
Now enter the author.
Mack Zackles
Now enter the value.
12.95
Enter the next title.
    ...more entries...
Here is the list of your books:
My Life as a Budgie by Mack Zackles: $12.95
Thought and Unthought by Kindra Schlagmeyer: $33.50
The Anatomy of an Ant by Salome Deschamps: $9.99
Power Tiddlywinks by Jack Deltoids: $13.25
Artificial Life Playhouse by Stephen Prata: $24.95
Coping with Coping by Dr. Rubin Thonkwacker: $0.00
Delicate Frivolity by Neda McFey: $29.99
Fate Wore a Bikini by Mickey Splats: $8.95
A History of Buvania by Prince Nikoli Buvan: $50.00
Mastering Your Digital Watch by Miklos Mysz: $13.95
A Foregone Confusion by Phalty Reasoner: $25.66
```

First we'll describe how to declare arrays of structures and how to access individual members. Then we will highlight two aspects of the program.

Declaring an Array of Structures

Declaring an array of structures is like declaring any other kind of array.

```
struct book libry[MAXBKS];
```

This declares libry to be an array with MAXBKS elements. Each element of this array is a structure of book type. Thus, libry[0] is one book structure, libry[1] is a second book structure, and so on. Figure 14.2 may help you visualize this. The name libry itself is not a structure name; it is the name of the array holding the structures.

Identifying Members of an Array of Structures

To identify members of an array of structures, you apply the same rule that we used for individual structures: follow the structure name with the dot operator and then with the member name.

```
libry[0].value   /* the value associated with the first array element */

libry[4].title   /* the title associated with the fifth array element */
```

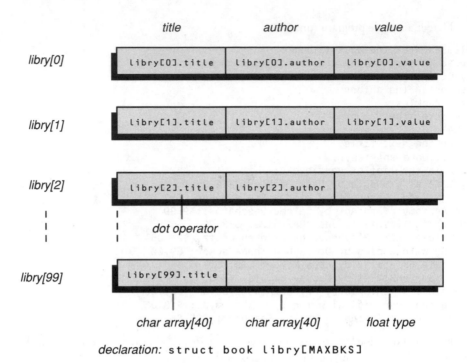

Figure 14.2. *An array of structures.*

Note that the array subscript is attached to libry, not to the end of the name.

```
libry.value[2]     /* WRONG */
libry[2].value     /* RIGHT */
```

The reason we use libry[2].value is that libry[2] *is* the structure variable name, just as libry[1] is another structure variable name.

By the way, what do you suppose the following represents?

```
libry[2].title[4]
```

It's the fifth character in the title (the title[4] part) of the book described by the third structure (the libry[2] part). In our example, this would be the character A. This example points out that subscripts found to the right of the dot operator apply to individual members, but subscripts to the left of the dot operator apply to arrays of structures.

Let's finish the program now.

Program Details

The main change from our first program is that we inserted a loop to read multiple entries. We begin the loop with this `while` condition:

```
while (count < MAXBKS && gets(libry[count].title) != NULL
               && libry[count].title[0] != '\0')
```

The expression `gets(libry[count].title)` reads a string for the title of a book. The expression `libry[count].title[0] != '\0'` tests if the first character in the string is the null character, that is, if the string is empty. If the user presses the Enter key at the beginning of a line, the empty string is transmitted, and the loop ends. We also have a check to keep the number of books entered from exceeding the size limit of the array.

Then we have these lines:

```
while (getchar() != '\n')
  continue;                 /* clear input line */
```

As you may recall from earlier chapters, this code overcomes the fact that the `scanf()` function ignores spaces and newlines. When you respond to the request for the book's value, you type something like

```
12.50[enter]
```

which transmits the sequence of characters

```
12.50\n
```

The `scanf()` function collects the 1, the 2, the ., the 5, and the 0, but it leaves the \n sitting there, awaiting whatever read statement comes next. If our precautionary code were missing, the next read statement, `gets(libry[count].title)`, would read the leftover newline character as an empty line, and the program would think we had sent a stop signal. The code we inserted will eat up characters until it finds and disposes of the newline. It doesn't do anything with the characters except remove them from the input queue. This gives `gets()` a fresh start.

Now let's return to exploring structures.

Nested Structures

Sometimes it is convenient for one structure to contain, or *nest*, another. For example, Shalala Pirosky is building a structure of information about her friends. One member of the structure, naturally enough, is the friend's name. The name, however, can be represented by a structure itself, with separate entries for first and last name members. Listing 14.3 is a condensed example of Shalala's work.

Listing 14.3. friend.c.

```c
/* friend.c -- example of a nested structure */
#include <stdio.h>
#define LEN 20
#define M1 "    Thank you for the wonderful evening, "
#define M2 "You certainly prove that a "
#define M3 "is a special kind of guy. We must get together"
#define M4 "over a delicious "
#define M5 " and have a few laughs."
struct names {                      /* first template       */
    char first[LEN];
    char last[LEN];
};
struct guy {                        /* second template      */
    struct names handle;            /* nested structure     */
    char favfood[LEN];
    char job[LEN];
    float income;
};
int main(void)
{
    static struct guy fellow = {    /* initialize a variable */
        { "Egbert", "Snivley" },
        "eggplant",
        "harddisk eraser",
         25435.00
    };

    printf("Dear %s, \n\n", fellow.handle.first);
    printf("%s%s.\n", M1, fellow.handle.first);
    printf("%s%s\n", M2, fellow.job);
    printf("%s\n", M3);
    printf("%s%s%s\n\n", M4, fellow.favfood, M5);
    printf("%40s%s\n", " ", "See you soon,");
    printf("%40s%s\n", " ", "Shalala");
    return 0;
}
```

Here is the output:

```
Dear Egbert,

    Thank you for the wonderful evening, Egbert.
You certainly prove that a harddisk eraser
is a special kind of guy. We must get together
over a delicious eggplant and have a few laughs.

                                       See you soon,
                                       Shalala
```

First, note how the nested structure is set up in the template. It is simply declared, just as an `int` variable would be.

```
struct names handle;
```

This declaration says that `handle` is a variable of the `struct names` type. Of course, the file should also include the template for the `names` structure.

Second, note how we gain access to a member of a nested structure. We merely use the dot operator twice.

```
fellow.handle.first == "Egbert"
```

The construction is interpreted this way, going from left to right:

```
(fellow.handle).first
```

That is, find `fellow`, then find the `handle` member of `fellow`, and then find the `first` member of that.

Pointers to Structures

Pointer lovers will be glad to know that you can have pointers to structures. There are at least three reasons why having pointers to structures is a good idea. First, just as pointers to arrays are easier to manipulate (in a sorting problem, say) than the arrays themselves, so pointers to structures are often easier to manipulate than structures themselves. Second, in some older implementations, a structure can't be passed as an argument to a function, but a pointer to a structure can. Third, many wondrous data representations use structures containing pointers to other structures.

The next short example (Listing 14.4) shows how to define a pointer to a structure and how to use it to access the members of a structure.

Listing 14.4. `friends.c`

```
/* friends.c -- uses pointer to a structure */
#include <stdio.h>
#define LEN 20
struct names {
    char first[LEN];
    char last[LEN];
};
struct guy {
    struct names handle;
    char favfood[LEN];
    char job[LEN];
    float income;
};
```

continues

Listing 14.4. continued

```
int main(void)
{
    static struct guy fellow[2] = {
        {{ "Egbert", "Snivley"},
         "eggplant",
         "harddisk eraser",
         25435.00
         },
        {{"Rodney", "Swillbelly"},
         "salmon mousse",
         "interior decorator",
         35000.00
         }
    };
    struct guy * him;    /* here is a pointer to a structure */
    printf("address #1: %p #2: %p\n", &fellow[0], &fellow[1]);
    him = &fellow[0];    /* tell the pointer where to point  */
    printf("pointer #1: %p #2: %p\n", him, him + 1);
    printf("him->income is $%.2f: (*him).income is $%.2f\n",
        him->income, (*him).income);
    him++;                    /* point to the next structure      */
    printf("him->favfood is %s:  him->handle.last is %s\n",
        him->favfood, him->handle.last);
    return 0;
}
```

The output, please:

```
address #1: 00AA  #2: 00FE
pointer #1: 00AA  #2: 00FE
him->income is $25435.00: (*him).income is $25435.00
him->favfood is salmon mousse:  him->handle.last is Swillbelly
```

Let's look first at how we created a pointer to a guy structure. Then we'll study how to specify individual structure members by using the pointer.

Declaring and Initializing a Structure Pointer

Declaration is as easy as can be.

```
struct guy * him;
```

First is the keyword struct, then the template tag guy, and then an * followed by the pointer name. The syntax is the same as for the other pointer declarations you have seen.

The pointer him can now be made to point to any structures of the guy type. We initialize him by making it point to fellow[0]. Note that we use the address operator

```
him = &fellow[0];
```

The first two output lines show the success of this assignment. Comparing the two lines, we see that him points to fellow[0], and him + 1 points to fellow[1]. Note that adding 1 to him adds 84 to the address. In hexadecimal, FE − AA = 54 (hex) = 84 (base 10). This is because each guy structure occupies 84 bytes of memory: names.first is 20, names.last is 20, favfood is 20, job is 20, and income is—4 the size of float on our system. Incidentally, on some systems the size of a structure may be greater than the sum of its parts. That's because those systems may align individual numbers on, for example, only even addresses or on addresses that are multiples of four. Such structures may wind up with unused "holes" in them.

Member Access by Pointer

The pointer him is pointing to the *structure* fellow[0]. How can we use him to get a value of a *member* of fellow[0]? The third output line shows two methods.

The first method, and the most common, uses a new operator, ->. This operator is formed by typing a hyphen (-) followed by the greater-than symbol (>). The example helps to make the meaning clear.

```
him->income  is  fellow[0].income  if  him == &fellow[0]
```

In other words, a structure *pointer* followed by the -> operator works the same way as a structure *name* followed by the . (dot) operator. (We can't properly say him.income because him is not a structure name.)

It is important to note that him is a *pointer* but him->income is a *member* of the pointed-to structure. Thus, in this case, him->income is a float variable.

The second method for specifying the value of a structure member follows from this sequence: If him == &fellow[0], then *him == fellow[0]. This is because & and * are reciprocal operators. Hence, by substitution

```
fellow[0].income == (*him).income
```

The parentheses are required because the . operator has higher precedence than *.

In summary, if him is a pointer to the structure fellow[0], the following are all equivalent:

```
fellow[0].income == (*him).income == him->income
```

Now let's look at the interaction between structures and functions.

Telling Functions About Structures

Recall that function arguments pass *values* to the function. Each value is a number, perhaps int, perhaps float, perhaps ASCII character code, or perhaps an address. A structure is a bit more complicated than a single value, so it is not surprising that older implementations do not allow a structure to be used as an argument for a function. This limitation has been removed in newer implementations, and ANSI C allows structures to be used as arguments. Thus, modern implementations give you a choice between passing structures as arguments or passing pointers to structures as arguments, or if you are concerned with just part of a structure, you can pass structure members as arguments. We'll examine all three methods, beginning with passing structure members as arguments.

Passing Structure Members

As long as a structure member is a data type with a single value (i.e., an int or one of its relatives, a char, a float, a double, or a pointer), it can be passed as a function argument. The primitive financial analysis program of Listing 14.5, which adds the client's bank account to his or her savings and loan account, illustrates this point. Note, incidentally, that we combined the template definition, the variable declaration, and the initialization into one statement.

Listing 14.5. funds1.c.

```
/* funds1.c -- passing structure members as arguments */
#include <stdio.h>
struct funds {
    char * bank;
    float bankfund;
    char * save;
    float savefund;
} stan = {
    "Garlic-Melon Bank",
    1023.43,
    "Snoopy's Savings and Loan",
    4239.87
    };
float sum(float, float);
int main(void)
{
    float total;
    extern struct funds stan;   /* optional declaration */

    printf("Stan has a total of $%.2f.\n",
            sum(stan.bankfund, stan.savefund) );
    return 0;
}
/* adds two float numbers */
float sum(float x, float y)
{
    return(x + y);
}
```

The result of running this program is

```
Stan has a total of $5263.30.
```

Ah, it works. Notice that the function `sum()` neither knows nor cares whether the actual arguments are members of a structure; it requires only that they be type `float`.

Of course, if you want a called function to affect the value of a member in the calling function, you can transmit the address of the member

```
modify(&stan.bankfund);
```

and this would be a function that altered Stan's bank account.

The next approach to telling a function about a structure involves letting the called function know that it is dealing with a structure.

Using the Structure Address

We will solve the same problem as before, but this time we will use the address of the structure as an argument. Because the function will have to work with the `funds` structure, it, too, will have to make use of the `funds` template. See Listing 14.6 for the program.

Listing 14.6. `funds2.c.`

```
/* funds2.c -- passing a pointer to a structure */
#include <stdio.h>
struct funds  {
    char * bank;
    float bankfund;
    char * save;
    float savefund;
} stan = {
    "Garlic-Melon Bank",
    1023.43,
    "Snoopy's Savings and Loan",
    4239.87
    };
float sum(struct funds *);   /* argument is a pointer */
int main(void)
{
  printf("Stan has a total of $%.2f.\n", sum(&stan));
  return 0;
}
float sum(struct funds * money)
{
  return(money->bankfund + money->savefund);
}
```

This, too, produces the output

```
Stan has a total of $5263.30.
```

The sum() function use a pointer (money) to a fund structure for its single argument. Passing the address &stan to the function causes the pointer money to point to the structure stan. We then use the -> operator to gain the values of stan.bankfund and stan.savefund.

This function also has access to the institution names, although it doesn't use them. Note that we must use the & operator to get the structure's address. Unlike the array name, the structure name alone is *not* a synonym for its address.

Passing a Structure as an Argument

For compilers that permit passing structures as arguments, the last example can be rewritten as shown in Listing 14.7.

Listing 14.7. funds3.c.

```
/* funds3.c -- passing a pointer to a structure */
#include <stdio.h>
struct funds  {
    char * bank;
    float bankfund;
    char * save;
    float savefund;
} stan = {
    "Garlic-Melon Bank",
    1023.43,
    "Snoopy's Savings and Loan",
    4239.87
    };
float sum(struct funds);   /* structure argument */
int main(void)
{
    printf("Stan has a total of $%.2f.\n", sum(stan));
    return 0;
}
float sum(struct funds moolah)
{
    return(moolah.bankfund + moolah.savefund);
}
```

Again, the output is this:

```
Stan has a total of $5263.30.
```

We replaced money, which was a pointer to struct funds, with moolah, which is a struct funds variable. When sum() is called, an automatic variable moolah is created according to the funds template. The members of this structure are then initialized to be copies of the values held in the corresponding members of the structure stan. Thus, the computations are done using a copy of the original structure, whereas the preceding program used the original structure itself. Because moolah is a structure, we use moolah.bankfund, not moolah->bankfund. In Listing 14.6, we used money->bankfund because money is a pointer, not a structure.

More on the New, Improved Structure Status

Under modern C, including ANSI C, not only can structures be passed as function arguments, they also can be returned as function return values. To make this return mechanism workable, the values in one structure can be assigned to another. That is, if n_data and o_data are both structures of the same type, you can do the following:

```
o_data = n_data;    /* assigning one structure to another */
```

This causes each member of o_data to be assigned the value of the corresponding member of n_data.

The fact that structures can be used as function arguments enables you to convey structure information to a function. The fact that functions can return structures enables you to convey structure information from a called function to the calling function. Structure pointers also allow two-way communication. Thus, you can often use either approach to solve programming problems. Let's look at another set of examples illustrating these two approaches.

To contrast the two approaches, we'll write a simple program that handles structures by using pointers; then we'll rewrite it by using structure-passing and structure returns. The program itself asks for your first and last names and reports the total number of letters in them. This project hardly requires structures, but it provides a simple framework for seeing how they work. Listing 14.8 presents the pointer form.

Listing 14.8. nameln1.c.

```
/* nameln1.c -- uses pointers to a structure */
#include <stdio.h>
#include <string.h>
struct namect {
    char fname[20];
    char lname[20];
    int letters;
};
void getinfo(struct namect *);
void makeinfo(struct namect *);
```

continues

Listing 14.8. continued

```c
void showinfo(struct namect *);
int main(void)
{
    struct namect person;

    getinfo(&person);
    makeinfo(&person);
    showinfo(&person);
    return 0;
}

void getinfo (struct namect * pst)
{
    printf("Please enter your first name.\n");
    gets(pst->fname);
    printf("Please enter your last name.\n");
    gets(pst->lname);
}

void makeinfo (struct namect * pst)
{
    pst->letters = strlen(pst->fname) +
                   strlen(pst->lname);
}

void showinfo (struct namect * pst)
{
    printf("%s %s, your name contains %d letters.\n",
        pst->fname, pst->lname, pst->letters);
}
```

Compiling and running the program produces results like the following:

```
Please enter your first name:
Nathan
Please enter your last name:
Hale
Nathan Hale, your name contains 10 letters.
```

We've allocated the work of the program to three functions called from main(). In each case, we pass the address of the person structure to the function.

The getinfo() function transfers information from itself to main(). In particular, it obtains names from the user and places them in the person structure, using the pst pointer to locate it. Recall that pst->lname means the lname member of the structure pointed to by pst. This makes pst->lname equivalent to the name of a char array, hence a suitable argument for gets(). Note that although getinfo() feeds information to the main program, it does not use the return mechanism, so it is type void.

The makeinfo() function performs a two-way transfer of information. By using a pointer to person, it locates the two names stored in the structure. It uses the C library function strlen() to calculate the total number of letters in each name and then uses the address of person to stow away the sum. Again, the type is void. Finally, the showinfo() function uses a pointer to locate the information to be printed.

In all of these operations, there has been but one structure variable, person, and each of the functions used the structure address to access it. One function transferred information from itself to the calling program, one transferred information from the calling program to itself, and one did both.

Now let's see how we can program the same task using structure arguments and return values. First, to pass the structure itself, we use the argument person rather than &person. The corresponding formal argument, then, is declared type struct namect instead of being a pointer to that type. Second, to provide structure values to main(), we can return a structure. Listing 14.9 presents the nonpointer version.

Listing 14.9. nameln2.c.

```
/* nameln2.c -- passes and returns structures */
#include <stdio.h>
#include <string.h>
struct namect {
    char fname[20];
    char lname[20];
    int letters;
};
struct namect getinfo(void);
struct namect makeinfo(struct namect);
void showinfo(struct namect);
int main(void)
{
    struct namect person;

    person = getinfo();
    person = makeinfo(person);
    showinfo(person);
    return 0;
}

struct namect getinfo(void)
{
    struct namect temp;
    printf("Please enter your first name.\n");
    gets(temp.fname);
    printf("Please enter your last name.\n");
    gets(temp.lname);
    return temp;
}
```

Listing 14.9. continued

```
struct namect makeinfo(struct namect info)
{
    info.letters = strlen(info.fname) + strlen(info.lname);
    return info;
}

void showinfo(struct namect info)
{
    printf("%s %s, your name contains %d letters.\n",
        info.fname, info.lname, info.letters);
}
```

This version produces the same final result as the preceding one, but it proceeds in a different manner. Each of the three functions creates its own copy of person, so this program uses four distinct structures instead of just one.

Consider the makeinfo() function, for example. In the first program, the address of person was passed, and the function fiddled with the actual person values. In this second version, a new structure called info is created. The values stored in person are copied to info, and the function works with the copy, so when the number of letters is calculated, it is stored in info, but not in person. The return mechanism, however, fixes that. By having the line

```
return info;
```

and the line

```
person = makeinfo(person);
```

we copy the values stored in info into person. Note that the makeinfo() function had to be declared type struct namect because it returns a structure.

Structures or Pointer to Structures?

Suppose you have to write a structure-related function. Should you use structure pointers as arguments, or should you use structure arguments and return values? Each approach has its strengths and weaknesses.

The two advantages of the pointer argument method are that it works on older as well as newer C implementations and that it is quick; you just pass a single address. The disadvantage is that you have less protection for your data. Some operations in the called function may inadvertently affect data in the original structure.

The ANSI C addition of the `const` qualifier (Chapter 13, "Storage Classes and Program Development") offers the means to protect against accidental changes. For example, the pointer version of `showinfo()` (Listing 14.8) prints the structure contents and should not alter them. Therefore, you should use this function heading:

```
void showinfo(const struct namect * pst)
```

It states that `pst` points to a structure whose values cannot be changed. If you place code in `showinfo()` to modify, say, `pst->letters`, the compiler will generate an error message.

One advantage of passing structures as arguments is that the function works with copies of the original data, which is safer than working with the original data. Also, the programming style tends to be clearer. Suppose you define the following structure type:

```
struct vector = {double x; double y;};
```

You want to set the vector `ans` to the sum of the vectors `a` and `b`. You could write a structure-passing and returning function that would make the program like this:

```
struct vector ans, a, b, sum_vect();
...
ans = sum_vect(a,b);
```

The preceding version is more natural-looking to an engineer than a pointer version, which might look like this:

```
struct vector ans, a, b;
void sum_vect();
...
sum_vect(&a, &b, &ans);
```

Also, in the pointer version the user has to remember whether the address for the sum should be the first or the last argument.

The two main disadvantages to passing structures are that older implementations may not handle the code and that it wastes time and space. It's especially wasteful to pass large structures to a function that uses only one or two members of the structure. In that case, passing a pointer or passing just the required members as individual arguments makes more sense.

Functions Using an Array of Structures

Suppose you have an array of structures that you wish to process with a function. The name of an array *is* a synonym for its address, so it can be passed to a function. Again, the function will need access to the structure template. To show how this works, in Listing 14.10 we expand our monetary program to two people so that we have an array of two `funds` structures.

Listing 14.10. funds4.c.

```c
/* funds4.c -- passing an array of structures to a function */
#include <stdio.h>
#define N 2
struct funds {
    char * bank;
    float bankfund;
    char * save;
    float savefund;
} jones[N] = {
    {
    "Garlic-Melon Bank",
    1023.43,
    "Snoopy's Savings and Loan",
    4239.87
    },
    {
    "Honest Jack's Bank",
    976.57,
    "First Draft Savings",
    1760.13
    }
};
float sum(const struct funds *, int);
int main(void)
{
    printf("The Joneses have a total of $%.2f.\n",
            sum(jones,N));
    return 0;
}

float sum(const struct funds *money, int n)
{
    float total;
    int i;

    for (i = 0, total = 0; i < n; i++, money++)
        total += money->bankfund + money->savefund;
    return(total);
}
```

The output is

```
The Joneses have a total of $8000.00.
```

(What an even sum! One would almost think the figures were invented.)

The array name jones is the address of the array. In particular, it is the address of the first element of the array, which is the structure jones[0]. Thus, initially the pointer money is given by this expression:

```
money = &jones[0];
```

Then the -> operator enables us to add the two funds for the first Jones. This is very much like Listing 14.6. Next, the for loop increments the pointer money by 1. Now it points to the next structure, jones[1], and the rest of the funds can be added to total.

These are the main points:

- You can use the array name to pass the address of the first structure in the array to a function.

- You then can use pointer arithmetic to move the pointer to successive structures in the array. Note that the function call

    ```
    sum(&jones[0],N)
    ```

    would have the same effect as using the array name, because both refer to the same address. Using the array name is just an indirect way of passing the structure address.

- Because the sum() function isn't supposed to alter the original data, we used the ANSI C const qualifier.

Saving the Structure Contents in a File

Because structures can hold a wide variety of information, they are an important tool for constructing databases. For example, you could use a structure to hold all the pertinent information about an employee or an auto part. Ultimately, you would want to be able to save this information in, and retrieve it from, a file. A database file could contain an arbitrary number of such data objects. The entire set of information held in a structure is termed a *record*, and the individual items are *fields*. Let's investigate these topics.

What is perhaps the most obvious way to save a record is the least efficient way, and that is to use fprintf(). For example, recall the book structure introduced in Listing 14.1.

```
#define MAXTIT    40
#define MAXAUT    40
struct book {
    char title[MAXTIT];
    char author[MAXAUT];
    float value;
};
```

If pbooks identified a file stream, you could save the information in a struct book variable called primer with the following statement:

```
fprintf(pbooks, "%s %s %.2f\n", primer.title,
        primer.author,primer.value);
```

This setup becomes unwieldy for structures with, say, 30 members. Also, it poses a retrieval problem because the program would need some way of telling where one field ends and another begins. This problem can be fixed by using a format with fixed-size fields, for example, "%39s%39s%8.2f", but the awkwardness remains.

A better solution is to use fread() and fwrite() to read and write structure-sized units. Recall that these functions read and write using the same binary representation that the program uses. For example,

```
fwrite(&primer, sizeof (struct book), 1, pbooks);
```

goes to the beginning address of the primer structure and copies all the bytes of the structure to the file associated with pbooks. The sizeof (struct book) term tells the function how large a block to copy, and the 1 indicates that it should copy just one block. The fread() function with the same arguments copies a structure-sized chunk of data from the file to the location pointed to by &primer. In short, these functions read and write one whole record at a time instead of a field at a time.

To show how these functions can be used in a program, we've modified the program in Listing 14.2 so that the book titles are saved in a file called book.dat. If the file already exists, the program shows you its current contents and then enables you to add to the file. Listing 14.11 presents the new version. (If you're using a Borland compiler, review the *Borland C and Floating-Point* discussion near Listing 14.2.)

Listing 14.11. booksave.c.

```
/* booksave.c -- saves structure contents in a file */
#include <stdio.h>
#include <stdlib.h>
#define MAXTIT   40
#define MAXAUT   40
#define MAXBKS   10             /* maximum number of books */
struct book {                   /* set up book template    */
    char title[MAXTIT];
    char author[MAXAUT];
    float value;
};
int main(void)
{
    struct book libry[MAXBKS]; /* array of structures      */
    int count = 0;
```

```
    int index, filecount;
    FILE * pbooks;
    int size = sizeof (struct book);

    if ((pbooks = fopen("book.dat", "a+b")) == NULL)
    {
        fputs("Can't open book.dat file\n",stderr);
        exit(1);
    }
    rewind(pbooks);                  /* go to start of file     */
    while (count < MAXBKS &&  fread(&libry[count], size,
                1, pbooks) == 1)
    {
        if (count == 0)
            puts("Current contents of book.dat:");
        printf("%s by %s: $%.2f\n",libry[count].title,
            libry[count].author, libry[count].value);
        count++;
    }
    filecount = count;
    if (count == MAXBKS)
    {
        fputs("The book.dat file is full.", stderr);
        exit(2);
    }
    puts("Please add new book titles.");
    puts("Press [enter] at the start of a line to stop.");
    while (count < MAXBKS && gets(libry[count].title) != NULL
                    && libry[count].title[0] != '\0')
    {
        puts("Now enter the author.");
        gets(libry[count].author);
        puts("Now enter the value.");
        scanf("%f", &libry[count++].value);
        while (getchar() != '\n')
            continue;                    /* clear input line  */
        if (count < MAXBKS)
            puts("Enter the next title.");
    }
    puts("Here is the list of your books:");
    for (index = 0; index < count; index++)
        printf("%s by %s: $%.2f\n",libry[index].title,
            libry[index].author, libry[index].value);
    fseek(pbooks, 0L, SEEK_END);      /* go to end of file */
    fwrite(&libry[filecount], size, count - filecount,
            pbooks);
    fclose(pbooks);
    return 0;
}
```

We'll look at a couple sample runs and then discuss the main programming points.

```
% booksave
Please add new book titles.
Press [enter] at the start of a line to stop.
Metric Merriment
Now enter the author.
Polly Poetica
Now enter the value.
18.99
Enter the next title.
Epicurean Dreams
Now enter the author.
Waldo Snid
Now enter the value.
15.99
Enter the next title.
[enter]
Here is the list of your books:
Metric Merriment by Polly Poetica: $18.99
Epicurean Dreams by Waldo Snid: $15.99
% booksave
Current contents of book.dat:
Metric Merriment by Polly Poetica: $18.99
Epicurean Dreams by Waldo Snid: $15.99
Please add new book titles.
Nit for Gnat
Now enter the author.
Nellie Nicely
Now enter the value.
21.99
Enter the next title.
[enter]
Here is the list of your books:
Metric Merriment by Polly Poetica: $18.99
Epicurean Dreams by Waldo Snid: $15.99
Nit for Gnat by Nellie Nicely: $21.99
%
```

Running the `booksave` program again would show all three books as current file records.

Program Points

First, we use the `"a+b"` mode for opening the file. The a+ part lets the program read the whole file and append data to the end of the file. The b is the ANSI way of signifying that the program will use the binary file format. For UNIX systems that don't accept the b, you can omit it, because UNIX has only one file form anyway. For other pre-ANSI implementations, you may need to find the local equivalent to using b.

We chose the binary mode because `fread()` and `fwrite()` are intended for binary files. True, some of the structure contents are text, but the `.value` member is not. If you use a text editor to look at `book.dat`, the text part will show up okay, but the numeric part will be unreadable and may even cause your text editor to barf.

The `rewind()` command ensures that the file position pointer is situated at the start of the file, ready for the first read.

The initial `while` loop reads one structure at a time into the array of structures, stopping when the array is full or when the file is exhausted. The variable `filecount` keeps track of how many structures were read.

The next `while` loop prompts for, and takes, user input. As in Listing 14.2, this loop quits when the array is full or when the user presses the Enter key at the beginning of a line. Notice that the `count` variable starts with the value it had after the preceding loop. This causes the new entries to be added to the end of the array.

The `for` loop then prints the data both from the file and from the user. The `fseek()` call places the file position pointer at the end of the file, ready to append new data. Note that ANSI C specifies that `SEEK_END` is defined in `stdio.h`. If you are on a pre-ANSI system, you may have to use the numerical value `2` instead or include a different system header file.

We could have used a loop to add one structure at a time to the end of the file. However, we decided to utilize the ability of `fwrite()` to write more than one block at a time. The expression `count - filecount` yields the number of new book titles to be added, and the call to `fwrite()` writes that number of structure-sized blocks to the file. The expression `&libry[filecount]` is the address of the first new structure in the array, so copying begins from that point.

This example is, perhaps, the simplest way to write structures to a file and to retrieve them but it can waste space because the unused parts of a structure are saved, too. The size of this structure is `2 x 40 x sizeof (char) + sizeof (float)`, which totals 84 bytes on our system. None of our entries actually needed all that space. However, the fact that each data chunk is the same size makes retrieving the data easy.

Another approach is to use variably sized records. To facilitate reading such records from a file, each record can begin with a numerical field specifying the record size. This is a bit more complex than what we have done. Normally this method involves "linked structures," which we describe next, and dynamic memory allocation, which we discuss in Chapter 16, "The C Preprocessor and the C Library."

Structures: What Next?

Before we end our explanation of structures, we would like to mention one of the more important uses of structures: creating new data forms. Computer users have developed data forms much more efficient for certain problems than the arrays and simple structures we have presented. These forms have names such as *queues, binary trees, heaps, hash tables,* and *graphs*. Many such forms are built from *linked* structures. Typically, each structure will contain one or two items of data plus one or two pointers to other structures of the same type. Those pointers link one structure to another and furnish a path to enable you to search through the overall tree of structures. For example, Figure 14.3 shows a binary tree structure, with each individual structure (or *node*) connected to the two below it.

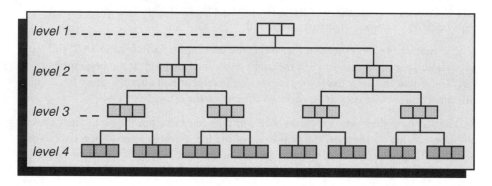

Figure 14.3. *A binary tree structure.*

Is the hierarchical, or tree, structure shown in Figure 14.3 more efficient than an array? Consider the case of a tree with ten levels of nodes. It has $2^{10}-1$, or 1023, nodes in which you could store up to 1023 words. If the words were arranged according to some sensible plan, you could start at the top level and find any word in at most nine moves as your search moved down one level to the next. If you had the words in an array, you might have to search all 1023 elements before finding the word you sought.

If you are interested in more advanced concepts such as this, you can consult any number of computer science texts on data structures. With the C structures, you will be able to create and use virtually every form presented in these texts. Also, Chapter 17, "Advanced Data Representation," will investigate some of these advanced forms.

That's our final word on structures for this chapter, but we will present examples of linked structures in Chapter 17. Next, we'll look at two other C features for dealing with data: the union and typedef.

Unions—A Quick Look

A *union* is a type that enables you to store different data types in the same memory space (but not simultaneously). A typical use would be a table designed to hold a mixture of types in some order which is neither regular nor known in advance. With a union you can create an array of equal-sized units, each of which can hold a variety of data types.

Unions are set up in much the same way as structures. There is a union template and a union variable. They can be defined in one step or, by using a union tag, in two. Here is an example of a union template with a tag:

```
union hold {
    int digit;
    double bigfl;
    char letter;
};
```

Here is an example of defining three union variables of the hold type:

```
union hold fit;       /* union variable of hold type       */
union hold save[10]; /* array of 10 union variables        */
union hold * pu;      /* pointer to a variable of hold type */
```

The first declaration creates a single variable fit. The compiler allots enough space so that it can hold the largest of the described possibilities. In this case, the biggest possibility listed is double, which requires 64 bits, or 8 bytes, on our system. The second declaration creates an array save with 10 elements, each 8 bytes in size. The third declaration creates a pointer that can hold the address of a hold union.

You can use the -> operator with pointers to unions in the same fashion that you use the operator with pointers to structures:

```
pu = &fit;
x = pu->digit;  /* same as x = fit.digit */
```

Here is how a union is used:

```
fit.digit = 23;    /* 23 is stored in fit; 2 bytes used     */
fit.bigfl = 2.0;   /* 23 cleared, 2.0 stored; 8 bytes used */
fit.letter = 'h'; /* 2.0 cleared, h stored; 1 byte used    */
```

The dot operator shows which data type is being used. Only one value is stored at a time. You can't store a char and an int at the same time, even though there is enough space to do so. It is your responsibility to keep track of the data type currently being stored in a union.

You can use the -> operator with pointers to unions in the same fashion that you use the operator with pointers to structures:

```
pu = &fit;
x = pu->digit;  /* same as x = fit.digit */
```

The next sequence shows what not to do.

```
fit.letter = 'A';
flnum = 3.02*fit.bigfl;   /* ERROR ERROR ERROR */
```

This sequence is wrong because a char type is stored, but the next line assumes that the content of fit is a double type.

However, sometimes it can be useful to use one member to place values into a union and to then use a different member for viewing the contents. Listing 15.4 in the next chapter will show an example.

Another place you might use a union is in a structure for which the stored information depends on one of the members. For instance, suppose you have a structure representing an automobile. If the automobile is owned by the user, you want a structure member describing the owner. If the automobile is leased, you want the member to describe the leasing company. Then you can do something along the following lines:

```
struct owner {
    char socsecurity[12];
    ...
};
struct leasecompany  {
    char name[40];
    char headquarters[40];
    ...
}
union data {
    struct owner owncar;
    struct leasecompany leasecar;
};
struct car_data {
    char make[15];
    int status; /* 0 = owned, 1 = leased */
    union data ownerinfo;
    ...
};
```

Suppose `flits` is a `car_data` structure. Then if `flits.status` were 0, the program would use `flits.status.ownerinfo.owncar`, and if `flits.status` were 1, the program would use `flits.status.ownerinfo.leasecar`.

Summary: Structure and Union Operators

The Membership Operator

.

General Comments

The . operator is used with a structure or union name to specify a member of that structure or union. If name is the name of a structure and member is a member specified by the structure template, then

```
name.member
```

identifies that member of the structure. The type of name.member is the type specified for member. The membership operator can also be used in the same fashion with unions.

Example

```
struct {
      int code;
      float cost;
} item;

item.code = 1265;
```

The last statement assigns a value to the code member of the structure item.

The Indirect Membership Operator

```
->
```

General Comments

This operator is used with a pointer to a structure or union to identify a member of that structure or union. Suppose that ptrstr is a pointer to a structure and that member is a member specified by the structure template. Then…

```
ptrstr->member
```

identifies that member of the pointed-to structure. The indirect membership operator can be used in the same fashion with unions.

Example

```
struct {
      int code;
      float cost;
} item, * ptrst;
ptrst = &item;
ptrst->code = 3451;
```

The last statement assigns an int value to the code member of item. The following three expressions are equivalent:

```
ptrst->code    item.code    (*ptrst).code
```

typedef—A Quick Look

The typedef function is an advanced data feature that enables you to create your own name for a type. It is similar to #define in that respect, but with three differences.

- Unlike `#define`, `typedef` is limited to giving symbolic names to data types only.

- The `typedef` function is performed by the compiler, not the preprocessor.

- Within its limits, `typedef` is more flexible than `#define`.

Let's see how `typedef` works. Suppose you want to use the term `real` for `float` numbers. You simply define `real` as if it were a `float` variable and precede the definition by the keyword `typedef`.

```
typedef float real;
```

From then on, you can use `real` to define variables.

```
real x, y[10], * z;
```

The scope of this definition depends on the location of the `typedef` statement. If the definition is inside a function, then the scope is local, confined to that function. If the definition is outside a function, then the scope is global.

Sometimes, uppercase letters are used for these definitions to remind the user that the type name is really a symbolic abbreviation.

```
typedef float REAL;
```

This example can be duplicated with a `#define`.

```
#define REAL float
```

Here is one that can't be duplicated with a `#define`:

```
typedef char * STRING;
```

Without the keyword `typedef`, this example would identify `STRING` itself as a pointer to `char`. With the keyword, it makes `STRING` an *identifier* for pointers to `char`. Thus,

```
STRING name, sign;
```

means

```
char * name, * sign;
```

Suppose, instead, we did this:

```
#define STRING char *
```

Then

```
STRING name, sign;
```

would translate to the following:

```
char * name, sign;
```

In this case, only `name` would be a pointer.

You can use `typedef` with structures, too.

```
typedef struct {
        float real;
        float imag;
} COMPLEX;
```

You then can use the type `COMPLEX` to represent complex numbers. One reason to use `typedef` is to create convenient, recognizable names for types that turn up often. For instance, many people prefer to use `STRING` or its equivalent, as in our earlier example.

A second reason for using `typedef` is that `typedef` names are often used for complicated types. For example, the declaration

```
typedef char (* FRPTC ()) [5];
```

makes `FRPTC` announce a type that is a function that returns a pointer to a five-element array of `char`. (See the upcoming discussion on fancy declarations.)

A third reason for using `typedef` is to make programs more portable. Suppose that your program needs to use 32-bit numbers. On some systems, that would be type `int`. On others it might be type `long`. If you used only `long` or `int` in your declarations, you would have to alter all the declarations when you moved from one system to the other. Instead, you can do the following. In an `#include` file you have this definition.

```
typedef int FOURBYTE;
```

Use `FOURBYTE` in your programming for those `int` variables that must be 32 bits. Then when you move the program to a machine where type `long` is needed, just change the single definition in your `#include` file.

```
typedef long FOURBYTE;
```

Some programmers prefer using `#define` for this purpose. Either way is an example of what makes C such a portable language.

ANSI C implementations often use `typedef`s for implementation-dependent definitions. We've mentioned the `size_t` type as representing the type of value produced by the `sizeof` operator. It's used, for example, in the prototypes for `fread()` and `fwrite()`. Borland C, for example, uses this `typedef`:

```
typedef unsigned int size_t;
```

When using `typedef`, bear in mind that it does not create new types; it just creates convenient labels. This means, for example, that variables using the `STRING` type we created can be used as arguments for functions expecting type pointer-to-`char`.

With structures, unions, and `typedef`, C gives you the tools for efficient and portable data handling.

Fancy Declarations

C enables you to create elaborate data forms. Although we are sticking to simpler forms, we feel it is our duty to point out the potentialities. When you make a declaration, the name (or identifier) that you use can be modified by tacking on a modifier.

Modifier	Significance
*	Indicates a pointer
( )	Indicates a function
[ ]	Indicates an array

C enables you to use more than one modifier at a time, and that enables you to create a variety of types.

```
int board[8][8];    /* an array of arrays of int          */
int ** ptr;         /* a pointer to a pointer to int       */
int * risks[10];    /* a 10-element array of pointers to int */
int (* rusks)[10];  /* a pointer to an array of 10 ints     */
int * oof[3][4];    /* a 3 x 4 array of pointers to int     */
int (* uuf)[3][4];  /* a pointer to a 3 x 4 array of ints   */
int (* uof[3])[4];  /* a 3-element array of pointers to
                       4-element arrays of int              */
```

The trick to unravelling these declarations is figuring out the order in which to apply the modifiers. These rules should get you through:

1. The [ ], which indicates an array, and the ( ), which indicates a function, have the same precedence. This precedence is higher than that of the * indirection operator, which means that the following declaration makes risks an array of pointers rather than a pointer to an array:

   ```
   int * risks[10];
   ```

2. The [ ] and ( ) associate from left to right. This next declaration makes goods an array of 12 arrays of 50 ints, not an array of 50 arrays of 12 ints.

   ```
   int goods[12][50];
   ```

3. The [ ] and ( ) have the same precedence, but because they associate from left to right, the following declaration groups the * and rusks together before applying the brackets. This means that the following declaration makes rusks a pointer to an array of 10 ints:

   ```
   int (* rusks)[10];
   ```

Let's apply these rules to this declaration:

```
int * oof[3][4];
```

The [3] has higher precedence than the *, and, because of the left-to-right rule, it has higher precedence than the [4]. Hence, oof is an array with three elements. Next in order is [4], so the elements of oof are arrays of four elements. The * tells us that these elements are pointers. The int completes the picture: oof is a three-element array of four-element arrays of pointers to int, or, for short, a 3 x 4 array of pointers to int. Storage is set aside for 12 pointers.

Now look at this declaration:

```
int (* uuf)[3][4];
```

The parentheses cause the * modifier to have first priority, making uuf a pointer to a 3 x 4 array of ints. Storage is set aside for a single pointer.

These rules also yield the following types:

```
char * fump();        /* function returning pointer to char   */
char (* frump)();     /* pointer to a function that returns
                              type char                       */
char (* flump[3])();/* array of 3 pointers to functions that
                          return type char                    */
```

When you bring structures into the picture, the possibilities for declarations truly grow baroque. And the applications—well, we'll leave that for more advanced texts.

Functions and Pointers

As the discussion on declarations illustrated, it's possible to declare pointers to functions. You may wonder if such a beast has any usefulness. Typically, a function pointer is used as an argument to another function, telling the second function which function to use. For instance, the qsort() function from the C library takes a pointer to a function as one of its arguments. We've used one sorting function for integers and another for strings. The algorithm was the same, but we used > for comparing integers and strcmp() for strings. The qsort() function takes a more general approach. You pass it a pointer to a comparison function appropriate to the type you wish to sort, and qsort() then uses that function to sort the type, whether it be integer, string, or structure.

To show the essential ideas, the program in Listing 14.12 uses function pointers to print a command-line argument in normal and reverse order. We use ANSI prototyping not only for the program's functions but also for describing the characteristics of the pointed-to functions.

Listing 14.12. func_ptr.c.

```
/* func_ptr.c -- uses function pointers */
#include <stdio.h>
#include <stdlib.h>
int rputs(const char *);
```

continues

Listing 14.12. continued

```
void show(int (* fp)(const char * ps), char * str);
int main(int argc, char * argv[])
{
  if (argc < 2)
     exit(1);
  show(puts, argv[1]);     /* use puts()              */
  show(rputs, argv[1]);    /* use rputs()             */
  return 0;
}
int rputs(const char * str)
{
   const char * start = str;

   while (*str != '\0')
      str++;                /* go to end of string      */
   while (str != start)
      putchar(*--str);
   return putchar('\n');
}
void show(int (* fp)(const char * ps), char * str)
                /* fp points to function returning int */
{
   (*fp)(str); /* pass str to the pointed-to function    */
}
```

Here are two sample runs:

```
C>funct_ptr pretty polly
pretty
ytterp
C>funct_ptr "fabulous duo"
fabulous duo
oud suolubaf
```

As we mentioned in an earlier chapter, some operating systems enable you to use quotes to group several words into a single command-line argument.

The first point to observe in Listing 14.12 is that the name of a function used without parentheses yields the address of that function, so the function call show(puts,argv[1]) passes the address of the puts() function, and show(rputs,argv[1]) passes the address of the rputs() function. Both also pass the address of a string.

Incidentally, you can use function names in assignment statements. For instance, if pfun is declared to be a pointer to a function that returns double, you can do this:

```
pfun = atof;
```

Then pfun is assigned the address of the library function atof(), providing the atof() declaration appears prior to this statement.

Second, the show() function definition must declare its argument types. Both puts() and rputs() return an int, so the proper declaration for fp is this:

```
int (*fp)();
```

In ANSI C, you also can (and should) indicate what type of arguments the pointed-to function takes.

```
int (*fp)(conts char * ps);    /* ANSI C prototyping */
```

That is, fp points to a function that takes a pointer to a char as an argument and that returns an int. Note that we defined rputs() so that it has the same type arguments and return value as puts(). Passing addresses of different types of functions can cause problems. The ANSI C function prototyping helps catch that sort of error.

Third, the example shows how to use a function pointer. Because fp points to a function, the expression *fp represents the function that is pointed to, and (*fp)(str) is a call to that function, passing str as an argument to it. Similarly, given the definition

```
pfun = atof;
```

you can use this call to invoke the atof() function:

```
(*pfun)(string);
```

Some C compilers have also allowed the following usage when pfun is a pointer:

```
pfun(string);   /* alternative usage */
```

ANSI C allows this form, but K&R C does not.

Note the difference between the following two function calls:

```
function1(sqrt);       /* passes address of sqrt function      */
function2(sqrt(4.0)); /* passes return value of sqrt function */
```

The first passes the address of the sqrt() function and presumably, will use that function in its code. The second statement initially calls the sqrt() function, evaluates it, and then passes the return value (2.0, in this case) to function2().

You've now seen all four ways in which a function name can be used: in defining a function, in declaring a function, in calling a function, and as a pointer. Figure 14.4 sums up the uses.

Chapter Summary

A C *structure* provides the means to store several data items, usually of different types, in the same data object. You can use a *tag* to identify a specific structure template and to declare variables of that type. The *membership dot operator* (.) enables you to access the individual members of a structure by using labels from the structure template.

```
function name used in a prototype declaration: int comp(int x, int y);
       function name used in a function call: status = comp(q,r);
   function name used in a function definition: int comp(x,y)
                                                int x,y;
                                                { ...
function name used as a pointer in assignment: pfunct = comp;
     function name used as pointer argument: slowsort(arr,n,comp);
```

Figure 14.4. *Uses for a function name.*

If you have a pointer to a structure, you can use the pointer and the *indirect membership operator* (->) instead of a name and the dot operator to access individual members. To obtain the address of a structure, use the & operator. Unlike arrays, the name of a structure does not serve as the address of the structure.

Traditionally, structure-related functions have used pointers to structures as arguments. Modern C, including ANSI C, permits structures to be passed as arguments, used as return values, and assigned to structures of the same type.

Unions use the same syntax as structures. However, with unions, the members share a common storage space. Instead of storing several data types simultaneously in the manner of a structure, the union stores a single data item type from a list of choices. That is, a structure can hold, say, an int and a double and a char, and the corresponding union can hold an int or a double or a char.

The typedef facility enables you to establish aliases or shorthand representations of standard C types.

The name of a function yields the address of that function. Such addresses can be passed as arguments to functions, which then use the pointed-to function.

Review Questions

1. What's wrong with this template?

```
structure {
        char itable;
        int  num[20];
        char * togs
}
```

2. Devise a structure template that will hold the name of a month, a three-letter abbreviation for the month, the number of days in the month, and the month number.

3. Write a function that, when given the month number, returns the total days in the year up to and including that month. Assume that the structure template of Question 2 and an appropriate array of such structures are declared externally.

4. Consider the following programming fragment:

```
struct name {
        char first[20];
        char last[20];
};
struct bem {
        int limbs;
        struct name title;
        char type[30];
};
struct bem * pb;
struct bem deb = {
        6,
        {"Berbnazel", "Gwolkapwolk"},
        "Arcturan"

};

pb = &deb;
```

a. What would each of the following statements print?

```
printf("%d", deb.limbs);
printf("%s", pb->type);
printf("%s", pb->type + 2);
```

b. How could you represent "Gwolkapwolk" in structure notation (two ways)?
c. Write a function that takes the address of a bem structure as its argument and prints the contents of that structure in the form shown below. Assume that the structure template is in a file called starfolk.h.

```
Berbnazel Gwolkapwolk is a 6-limbed Arcturan.
```

5. Define a structure template suitable for holding the following items: the name of an automobile, its horsepower, its EPA city-driving mpg rating, its wheelbase, and its year. Use car as the template tag.

6. Suppose you have this structure:

```
struct gas {
    float distance;
    float gals;
    float mpg;
};
```

509

Devise a function that takes a `struct gas` argument. Assume that the passed structure contains the `distance` and `gals` information. Have the function calculate the correct value for the `mpg` member and return the now completed structure.

7. Declare a pointer to a function that returns a pointer to `char` and which takes a pointer to `char` and a `char` as arguments.

Programming Exercises

1. Redo Review Question 3, but make the argument the spelled-out name of the month instead of the month number. (Don't forget about `strcmp()`.)

2. Write a program that prompts the user to enter the day, month, and year. The month can be a month number, a month name, or a month abbreviation. The program then returns the total number of days in the year up through the given day.

3. Revise our book-listing program in Listing 14.2 so that it prints both the book descriptions alphabetized by title and the total value of the books.

4. Write a program that creates a structure template with two members according to the following criteria:

   a. The first member is a social security number. The second member is a structure with three members. Its first member contains a first name, its second member contains a middle name, and its final member contains a last name. Create and initialize an array of five such structures. Have the program print the data in this form:

   ```
   Dribble, Flossie M. -- 302039823
   ```

   Only the initial of the middle name is printed, and a period is added. Neither the initial (of course) nor the period should be printed if the middle name member is empty. Write a function to do the printing; pass the structure array to the function.

   b. Modify part a by passing the structure value instead of the address.

5. Write a program that fits the following recipe:

   a. Externally define a `name` structure template with two members: a string to hold the first name, and a string to hold the second name.

   b. Externally define a `student` structure template with three members: a `name` structure, a `grade` array to hold floating-point scores, and a variable to hold the average of those three scores.

   c. Have the `main()` function declare an array of CSIZE (with CSIZE = 4) student structures and initialize the name portions to names of your choice. Use functions to perform the tasks described in parts d, e, f, and g.

d. Interactively acquire scores for each student by prompting the user with a student name and a request for scores. Place the scores in the grade array portion of the appropriate structure. The required looping may be done in main() or in the function, as you prefer.

e. Calculate the average score value for each structure and assign it to the proper member.

f. Print the information in each structure.

g. Print the class average for each of the numeric structure members.

6. Modify Listing 14.11 so that as each record is read from the file and shown to you, you are given the chance to delete the record or to modify its contents. If you delete the record, use the vacated array position for the next record to be read.

7. The Colossus Airlines fleet consists of one plane with a seating capacity of 12. It makes one flight daily. Write a seating reservation program with the following features:

a. The program uses an array of 12 structures. Each structure should hold a seat identification number, a marker that indicates whether the seat is assigned, the last name of the seat holder, and the first name of the seat holder.

b. The program displays the following menu:

```
To choose a function, enter its letter label:

a) Show number of empty seats
b) Show list of empty seats
c) Show alphabetical list of seats
d) Assign a customer to a seat assignment
e) Delete a seat assignment
f) Quit
```

c. The program successfully executes the promises of its menu. Choices d) and e) will require additional input, and each should enable the user to abort entry.

d. After executing a particular function, the program shows the menu again, except for choice f).

e. Data is saved in a file between runs. When the program is restarted, it first loads in the data, if any, from the file.

8. Write a program that implements a menu by using an array of pointers to functions. For instance, choosing a from the menu would activate the function pointed to by the first element of the array.

Bit Fiddling

Operators
~   &   ¦ ^
>>   <<
&=   ¦=   ^=   >>=   <<=

In this chapter you review binary, octal, and hexadecimal number notations. Then you learn about two C facilities for handling the individual bits in a value: bitwise operators and bit fields.

With C, you can manipulate the individual bits in a variable. Perhaps you are wondering why anyone would want to. Be assured that sometimes this ability is necessary, or at least useful. For example, a hardware device often is controlled by sending it a byte in which each bit has a particular meaning. Also, operating system information about files often is stored by using particular bits to indicate particular items.

We'll investigate C's bit powers in this chapter after we supply you with some background about bits, bytes, binary notation, and other number bases.

Binary Numbers, Bits, and Bytes

Our usual way to write numbers is based on the number 10. For instance, 2157 has a 2 in the thousands place, a 1 in the hundreds place, a 5 in the tens place, and a 7 in the ones place. This means that we can think of 2157 as being

```
2 x 1000 + 1 x 100 + 5 x 10 + 7 x 1
```

However, 1000 is 10 cubed, 100 is 10 squared, 10 is 10 to the first power, and, by convention, 1 is 10 (or any positive number) to the zero power. Thus, we also can write 2157 as

```
2 x 10³ + 1 x 10² + 5 x 10¹ + 7 x 10⁰
```

Because our system of writing numbers is based on powers of ten, we say that 2157 is written in *base 10.*

Presumably, the decimal system evolved because we have ten fingers. A computer bit, in a sense, has only two fingers because it can be set only to 0 or 1, off or on. Therefore, a *base 2* system is natural for a computer. It uses powers of two instead of powers of ten. Numbers expressed in base 2 are termed *binary* numbers. For example, a binary number such as 1101 would mean

```
1 x 2³ + 1 x 2² + 0 x 2¹ + 1 x 2⁰
```

In decimal numbers this becomes

```
1 x 8 + 1 x 4 + 0 x 2 + 1 x 1 = 13
```

You can use the binary system to express any number (if you have enough bits) as a combination of 1s and 0s. This system is very convenient for digital computers, which express information in combinations of on and off states that can be interpreted as 1s and 0s. Let's see how the binary system works for a 1-byte integer.

Binary Integers

By modern definition, a byte contains 8 bits. (A few, rare, older systems use a bigger byte.) You can think of these 8 bits as being numbered from 7 to 0, left to right. Bit 7 is called the *high-order* bit, and bit 0 is the *low-order* bit in the byte. Each bit number corresponds to a particular exponent of 2. Imagine the byte as looking like Figure 15.1.

Here, 128 is 2 to the 7th power, and so on. The largest number this byte can hold is 1, with all bits set to 1: 11111111. The value of this binary number is

```
128 + 64 + 32 + 16 + 8 + 4 + 2 + 1 = 255
```

The smallest binary number would be 00000000, or a simple 0. A byte can store numbers from 0 to 255, for a total of 256 possible values. By changing the interpretation, a byte can store numbers from −128 to +127, again a total of 256 values.

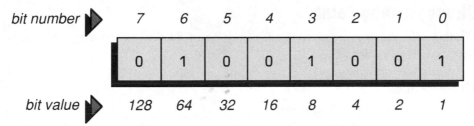

This example shows bits 6, 3, and 0 set to 1.
The value of this byte is 64 + 8 + 1 or 73.

Figure 15.1. *Bit numbers and bit values.*

Signed Integers

The representation of signed numbers is determined by the hardware, not by C. Probably the simplest way to represent signed numbers is to reserve 1 bit, such as the high-order bit, to represent the sign. In a 1-byte value, this leaves 7 bits for the number itself. In such a *sign-magnitude* representation, 10000001 is –1 and 00000001 is 1. The total range, then, is –127 to +127.

One disadvantage of this approach is that it has two zeros: +0 and –0. This is confusing, and it also uses up two bit patterns for just one value.

The *two's-complement* method avoids that problem and is the most common system used today. We'll discuss this method as it applies to a 1-byte value. In that context, the values 0 through 127 are represented by the last 7 bits, with the high-order bit set to 0. So far, that's the same as the sign-magnitude method. Also, if the high-order bit is 1, the value is negative. The difference comes in determining the value of that negative number. Subtract the bit-pattern from the 9-bit pattern 100000000 (256 in binary), and the result is the magnitude of value. For example, suppose the pattern is 10000000. As an unsigned byte, this would be 128. As a signed value, it is negative (bit 7 is 1) and has a value of 100000000 – 10000000, or 10000000 (128). Thus, the number is –128. Similarly, 10000001 is –127, and 11111111 is –1. Thus, the method represents numbers in the range –128 to +127.

The simplest method for reversing the sign of a two's-complement binary number is to invert each bit (convert 0s to 1s and 1s to 0s) and then add 1. Because 1 is 00000001, –1 is 11111110 + 1, or 11111111, just as you saw earlier.

The *one's-complement* method forms the negative of a number by inverting each bit in the pattern. For instance, 00000001 is 1 and 11111110 is –1. This method also has a –0: 11111111. Its range (for a 1-byte value) is –127 to +127.

Binary Floating Point

Floating-point numbers are stored in two parts: a binary fraction and a binary exponent. Let's see how this is done.

Binary Fractions

The ordinary fraction 0.527 represents

```
5/10 + 2/100 + 7/1000
```

with the denominators representing increasing powers of ten. In a binary fraction, we use powers of two for denominators. Thus, the binary fraction .101 represents

```
1/2 + 0/4 + 1/8
```

which in decimal notation is

```
0.50 + 0.00 + 0.125
```

or 0.625.

Many fractions, such as 1/3, cannot be represented exactly in decimal notation. Similarly, many fractions cannot be represented exactly in binary notation. Indeed, the only fractions that can be represented exactly are combinations of multiples of powers of 1/2. Thus, 3/4 and 7/8 can be represented exactly as binary fractions, but 1/3 and 2/5 cannot be.

Floating-Point Representation

To represent a floating-point number in a computer, a certain number (system-dependent) of bits are set aside to hold a binary fraction. Additional bits hold an exponent. In general terms, the actual value of the number consists of the binary fraction times 2 to the indicated exponent. Thus, multiplying a floating-point number by, say, 4, increases the exponent by 2 and leaves the binary fraction unchanged. Multiplying by a number that is not a power of 2 will change the binary fraction and, if necessary, the exponent.

Other Bases

Computer workers often use number systems based on 8 and on 16. Because 8 and 16 are powers of 2, these systems are more closely related to a computer's binary system than the decimal system is.

Octal

Octal refers to a base 8 system. In this system, the different places in a number represent powers of 8. We use the digits 0 to 7. For example, the octal number 451 (written 0451 in C) represents

$$4 \times 8^2 + 5 \times 8^1 + 1 \times 8^0 = 297 \text{ (base 10)}$$

A handy thing to know about octal is that each octal digit corresponds to three binary digits. Table 15.1 shows the correspondence. This correspondence makes it simple to translate between the two systems. For example, the octal number 0377 is 11111111 in binary. We replaced the 3 with 011, dropped the leading 0, and then replaced each 7 with 111. The only awkward part is that a 3-digit octal number may take up to 9 bits in binary form, so an octal value larger than 0377 requires more than a byte. Note that internal 0s are not dropped: 0173 is 01 111 011, not 01 111 11.

Table 15.1. Binary equivalents for octal digits.

Octal Digit	Binary Equivalent
0	000
1	001
2	010
3	011
4	100
5	101
6	110
7	111

Hexadecimal

Hexadecimal (or "hex") refers to a base 16 system. Here we use powers of 16 and the digits 0 to 15, but because we don't have single digits to represent the values 10 to 15, we use the letters *A* to *F* for that purpose. For instance, the hex number A3F (written 0xA3F in C) represents

```
10 x 16² + 3 x 16¹ + 15 x 16⁰ = 2623 (base 10)
```

because *A* represents 10 and *F* represents 15. In C, you can use either lowercase or uppercase letters for the additional hex digits. Thus, you also can write 2623 as 0xa3f.

Each hexadecimal digit corresponds to a 4-digit binary number. Thus, two hexadecimal digits correspond exactly to an 8-bit byte. The first digit represents the upper 4 bits, and the second digit the last 4 bits. This makes hexadecimal a natural choice for representing byte values. Table 15.2 shows the correspondence. For example, the hex value 0xC2 translates to 11000010.

Table 15.2. Decimal, hexadecimal, and binary equivalents.

Decimal Digit	Hexadecimal Digit	Binary Equivalent	Decimal Digit	Hexadecimal Digit	Binary Equivalent
0	0	0000	8	8	1000
1	1	0001	9	9	1001
2	2	0010	10	A	1010
3	3	0011	11	B	1011
4	4	0100	12	C	1100
5	5	0101	13	D	1101
6	6	0110	14	E	1110
7	7	0111	15	F	1111

Now that you've seen what bits and bytes are, let's examine what C can do with them. C has two facilities to help you manipulate bits. The first is a set of six *bitwise* operators that act on bits. The second is the `field` data form, which gives you access to bits within an `int`. The following discussion will outline these C features.

C's Bitwise Operators

C offers bitwise logical operators and shift operators. In the following examples, we will write out values in binary notation so that you can see what happens to the bits. In an actual program, you would use integer variables or constants written in the usual forms. For instance, instead of `00011001`, you would use `25` or `031` or `0x19`. For our examples, we will use 8-bit numbers, with the bits numbered 7 to 0, left to right.

Bitwise Logical Operators

The four bitwise logical operators work on integer-type data, including `char`. They are termed bitwise because they operate on each bit independently of the bit to the left or right. Don't confuse them with the regular logical operators (`&&`, `||`, and `!`), which operate on values as a whole.

One's Complement, or Bitwise Negation: ~

The unary operator `~` changes each 1 to a 0 and each 0 to a 1, as in the following example:

`~(10011010) == (01100101)`

Suppose that `val` is an `unsigned char` assigned the value 2. In binary, 2 is `00000010`. Then `~val` has the value `11111101`, or 253. Note that the operator does not *change* the value of val, just as 3 * val does not change the value of val; val is still 2, but it does create a new value that can be used or assigned elsewhere.

```
newval = ~val;
printf("%d", ~val);
```

If you want to change the value of val to ~val, use simple assignment.

```
val = ~val;
```

Bitwise AND: &

The binary operator & produces a new value by making a bit-by-bit comparison between two operands. For each bit position, the resulting bit is 1 only if both corresponding bits in the operands are 1. (In terms of true-false, the result is true only if each of the two bit operands is true.) Thus,

```
(10010011) & (00111101) == (00010001)
```

because only bits 4 and 0 are 1 in both operands.

C also has a combined bitwise AND-assignment operator: &=. The statement

```
val &= 0377;
```

produces the same final result as the following:

```
val = val & 0377;
```

Bitwise OR: /

The binary operator ¦ produces a new value by making a bit-by-bit comparison between two operands. For each bit position, the resulting bit is 1 if either of the corresponding bits in the operands is 1. (In terms of true-false, the result is true if one or the other bit operands are true or if both are true.) Thus,

```
(10010011) ¦ (00111101) == (101111111)
```

because all bit positions but bit 6 have the value 1 in one or the other operands.

C also has a combined bitwise OR-assignment operator: ¦=. The statement

```
val ¦= 0377;
```

produces the same final result as

```
val = val ¦ 0377;
```

Bitwise EXCLUSIVE OR: ^

The binary operator ^ makes a bit-by-bit comparison between two operands. For each bit position, the resulting bit is 1 if one or the other (but not both) of the corresponding bits in the operands is 1. (In terms of true-false, the result is true if one or the other bit operands—but not both—are true.) Thus,

```
(10010011) ^ (00111101) == (10101110)
```

Note that because bit position 0 has the value 1 in both operands, the resulting 0 bit has value 0.

C also has a combined bitwise OR-assignment operator: ^=. The statement

```
val ^= 0377;
```

produces the same final result as

```
val = val ^ 0377;
```

Usage: Masks

The bitwise AND operator often is used with a *mask*. A mask is a bit pattern with some bits that are set to ON (1) and some bits to OFF (0). To see why a mask is called a mask, let's see what happens when a quantity is ANDed with a mask. For example, suppose you #define MASK to be 2, i.e., binary 00000010, with only bit number 1 being nonzero. Then the statement

```
flags = flags & MASK;
```

would cause all the bits of flags (except bit 1) to be set to 0, because any bit combined with 0 via the & operator yields 0. Bit number 1 will be left unchanged. (If the bit is 1, then 1 & 1 is 1; if the bit is 0, then 0 & 1 is 0.) This process is called using a *mask* because the zeros in the mask hide the corresponding bits in flags.

Extending the analogy, you can think of the 0s in the mask as being opaque and the 1s as being transparent. The expression flags & MASK is like covering the flags bit pattern with the mask; only the bits under MASK's 1s are visible. See Figure 15.2.

You can shorten the code by using the AND-assignment operator.

```
flags &= MASK;
```

One common C usage is this:

```
ch &= 0377;
```

The value 0377, recall, is 11111111 in binary. This mask leaves the final 8 bits of ch alone and sets the rest to 0. Thus, regardless of whether the original ch is 8 bits, 16 bits, or more, the final value is trimmed to something that fits into a single byte.

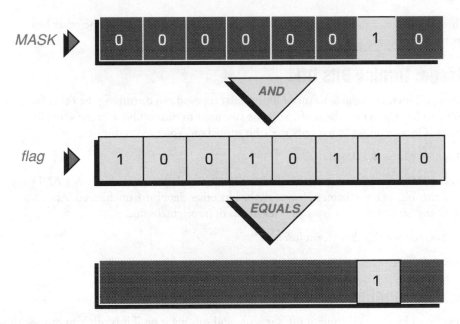

Figure 15.2. *A mask.*

Usage: Turning Bits On

Sometimes you may need to turn on particular bits in a value while leaving the remaining bits unchanged. For instance, an IBM PC controls hardware through values sent to *ports*. To turn on, say, the speaker, you may have to turn on 1 bit while leaving the others unchanged. This can be done with the bitwise OR operator.

For example, consider our MASK, which has bit 1 set to 1. The statement

```
flags = flags | MASK;
```

will set bit number 1 in flags to 1 and leave all the other bits unchanged. This follows because any bit combined with 0 via the ¦ operator is itself, and any bit combined with 1 via the ¦ operator is 1.

For short, you can use the bitwise OR-assignment operator.

```
flags |= MASK;
```

This, too, sets to 1 those bits in `flags` that also are on in `MASK`, leaving the other bits unchanged.

Usage: Turning Bits Off

Just as it's useful to be able to turn on particular bits without disturbing the other bits, it's useful to be able to turn them off. Suppose you want to turn off bit 1 in the variable `flags`. Once again, `MASK` has only the 1 bit turned on. You can do this:

```
flags = flags & ~MASK;
```

Because `MASK` is all 0s except for bit 1, then `~MASK` is all 1s except for bit 1. A 1 AND any bit is that bit, so our statement leaves all the bits other than bit 1 unchanged. Also, a 0 AND any bit is 0, so bit 1 is set to 0 regardless of its original value.

You can use this short form instead:

```
flags &= ~MASK;
```

Usage: Toggling Bits

Toggling a bit means turning it off if it is on, and turning it on if it is off. You can use the bitwise EXCLUSIVE OR operator to toggle a bit. The idea is that if b is a bit setting (1 or 0), then 1 ^ b is 0 if b is 1 and is 1 if b is 0. Also 0 ^ b is b, regardless of its value. Thus, if you EXCLUSIVE OR a value with a mask, values corresponding to 1s in the mask are toggled, and values corresponding to 0s in the mask are unaltered. To toggle bit 1 in `flag`, you can do either of the following:

```
flag = flag ^ MASK;
flag ^= MASK;
```

Usage: Checking the Value of a Bit

You've seen how to change the values of bits. Suppose, instead, that you want to check the value of a bit. For example, does `flag` have bit 1 set to 1? You shouldn't simply compare `flag` to `MASK`.

```
if (flag == MASK)
  puts("Wow!");      /* doesn't work right */
```

Even if bit 1 in `flag` is set to 1, the other bit setting in `flag` can make the comparison untrue. Instead, you must first mask the other bits in `flag` so that you compare only bit 1 of `flag` with `MASK`.

```
if ((flag & MASK) == MASK)
  puts("Wow!");
```

The bitwise operators have lower precedence than ==, so the parentheses around flag & MASK are needed.

Bitwise Shift Operators

Now let's look at C's shift operators. The bitwise shift operators shift bits to the left or right. Again, we will write binary numbers explicitly to show the mechanics.

Left Shift: <<

The << left shift operator shifts the bits of the value of the left operand to the left by the number of places given by the right operand. The vacated positions are filled with 0s, and bits moved past the end of the left operand are lost. Thus,

```
(10001010) << 2 == (00101000)
```

where each bit is moved two places to the left.

This operation produces a new bit value, but it doesn't change its operands. For example, suppose stonk is 1. Then stonk<<2 is 4, but stonk still is 1. You can use the left-shift assignment operator (<<=) to actually change a variable's value. This operator shifts the bit in the variable to its left by the number of places given by the righthand value.

```
int stonk = 1;
int onkoo;
onkoo = stonk << 2;    /* assigns 4 to onkoo */
stonk <<= 2;           /* changes stonk to 4 */
```

Right Shift: >>

The >> right shift operator shifts the bits of the value of the left operand to the right by the number of places given by the right operand. Bits moved past the right end of the left operand are lost. For unsigned types, the places vacated at the left end are replaced by 0s. For signed types, the result is machine dependent. The vacated places may be filled with 0s, or they may be filled with copies of the sign (leftmost) bit. For an unsigned value, we have

```
(10001010) >> 2 == (00100010)
```

where each bit is moved two places to the right.

The right-shift assignment operator (>>=) shifts the bits in the lefthand variable to the right by the indicated number of places.

```
int sweet = 16;
int ooosw;

ooosw = sweet >> 3;   /* ooosw = 2, sweet still 16 */
sweet >>=3;           /* sweet changed to 2         */
```

Usage

The bitwise shift operators can provide swift, efficient (depending on the hardware) multiplication and division by powers of 2.

number << n   Multiplies number by 2 to the nth power.

number >> n   Divides number by 2 to the nth power if number is not negative.

These shift operations are analogous to the decimal system procedure of shifting the decimal point to multiply or divide by 10.

Programming Example

In Chapter 9, "Functions," we used recursion to write a program to convert numbers to a binary representation. Now we'll solve the same problem using the bitwise operators. The program in Listing 15.1 reads an integer from the keyboard and passes it and a string address to a function called itobs() (for integer to binary string, of course). This function then uses the bitwise operators to figure out the correct pattern of 1s and 0s to put into the string.

Listing 15.1. binary.c.

```
/* binary.c -- using bit operations to display binary */
#include <stdio.h>
char * itobs(int, char *);
int main(void)
{
   char bin_str[8 * sizeof(int) + 1];
   int number;

   puts("Enter integers and see them in binary.\n");
   puts("Nonnumeric input terminates program.");
   while (scanf("%d", &number) == 1)
       printf("%d is %s\n", number, itobs(number,bin_str));
   return 0;
}

char * itobs(int n, char * ps)
{
   int i;
   static int size = 8 * sizeof(int);
```

```
    for (i = size - 1; i >= 0; i--, n >>= 1)
        ps[i] = (01 & n) + '0';
    ps[size] = '\0';
    return ps;
}
```

Listing 15.1 assumes that the system uses 8 bits to a byte. Thus, the expression `8 * sizeof(int)` is the number of bits in an `int`. The `bin_str` array has that many elements plus 1 to allow for the terminating null character.

The `itobs()` function returns the same address passed to it. Thus, you can use the function as, say, an argument to `printf()`. The first time through the `for` loop, the function evaluates the quantity `01 & n`. The term `01` is the octal representation of a mask with all but the zero bit set to 0. Therefore, `01 & n` is just the value of the final bit in `n`. This value is a `0` or a `1`, but for the array we need the *character* '0' or the *character* '1'. Adding the ASCII code for '0' accomplishes that conversion. The result is placed in the next-to-last element of the array. (The last element is reserved for the null character.)

By the way, you can just as well use `1 & n` as `01 & n`. Using octal 1 instead of decimal 1 just makes the mood a bit more computerish.

Then the loop executes the statements `i--` and `n >>= 1`. The first statement moves us one element earlier in the array, and the second shifts the bits in `n` over one position to the right. Thus, the next time through the loop we find the value of the new rightmost bit. The corresponding digit character then is placed in the element preceding the final digit. In this fashion, the function fills the array from right to left.

Here is a sample run:

```
Enter integers and see them in binary.
Nonnumeric input terminates program.
7
7 is 0000000000000111
255
255 is 0000000011111111
30000
30000 is 0111010100110000
-1
-1 is 1111111111111111
q
```

Another Example

Let's work through one more example. Our goal this time is to write a function that inverts the last `n` bits in a value, where both `n` and the value are function arguments.

The `~` operator inverts bits, but it inverts all the bits in a byte, not just a select few. However, the EXCLUSIVE OR operator, as you saw, can be used to toggle individual bits. Suppose you create a mask with the last n bits set to 1 and the remaining bits set to 0. Then EXCLUSIVE ORing that mask with a value will toggle, or invert, the last n bits, leaving the other bits unchanged. That's the approach used here:

```
int invert_end(int num, int bits)
{
    int mask = 0;
    int bitval = 1;

    while (bits-- > 0)
    {
        mask |= bitval;
        bitval <<= 1;
    }
    return num ^ mask;
}
```

The while loop creates the mask. Initially, mask has all its bits set to 0. The first pass through the loop sets bit 0 to 1 and then increases the value of bitval to 2; that is, it sets bit 0 to 0 and bit 1 to 1. The next pass through then sets bit 1 of mask to 1, and so on. Finally, the num ^ mask operation produces the desired result.

To test the function, we can slip it into the preceding program. See Listing 15.2.

Listing 15.2. invert4.c.

```
/*  invert4.c -- inverts last 4 bits of integers */
#include <stdio.h>
char * itobs(int n, char * ps);
int invert_end(int num, int bits);
int main(void)
{
    char bin_str[8 * sizeof(int) + 1];

    int number;

    puts("Enter integers and see them in binary.");
    puts("Nonnumeric input terminates program.");
    while (scanf("%d", &number) == 1)
    {
        printf("%d is %s\n", number, itobs(number,bin_str));
        printf("Inverting the last 4 bits gives %s\n",
                    itobs(invert_end(number,4),bin_str));
    }
    return 0;
}
char * itobs(int n, char * ps)
{
    int i;
    static int size = 8 * sizeof(int);
```

```
        for (i = size - 1; i >= 0; i--, n >>= 1)
            ps[i] = (01 & n) + '0';
        ps[size] = '\0';
        return ps;
}
int invert_end(int num, int bits)
{
    int mask = 0;
    int bitval = 1;

    while (bits-- > 0)
    {
        mask |= bitval;
        bitval <<= 1;
    }
    return num ^ mask;
}
```

Here's a sample run:

```
Enter integers and see them in binary.
Nonnumeric input terminates program.
7
7 is 0000000000000111
Inverting the last 4 bits gives 000000000001000
255
255 is 0000000011111111
Inverting the last 4 bits gives 0000000011110000
q
```

Bit Fields

The second method of manipulating bits is to use a bit field. A *bit field* is just a set of neighboring bits within an `unsigned int`. A bit field is set up with a structure definition that labels each field and determines its width. For instance, the following definition sets up four 1-bit fields:

```
struct    {
          unsigned autfd    : 1;
          unsigned bldfc    : 1;
          unsigned undln    : 1;
          unsigned itals    : 1;
} prnt;
```

This definition causes `prnt` to contain four 1-bit fields. Now you can use the usual structure membership operator to assign values to individual fields.

```
prnt.itals = 0;
prnt.undln = 1;
```

Because each field is just 1 bit, 1 and 0 are the only values you can use for assignment. The variable prnt is stored in an int-sized memory cell, but only 4 bits are used in this example.

Fields aren't limited to 1-bit sizes. You also can do this:

```
struct {
        unsigned code1 : 2;
        unsigned code2 : 2;
        unsigned code3 : 8;
} prcode;
```

This creates two 2-bit fields and one 8-bit field. You can now make assignments such as

```
prcode.code1 = 0;
prcode.code2 = 3;
prcode.code3 = 102;
```

Just make sure that the value doesn't exceed the capacity of the field.

What if the total number of bits you declare exceeds the size of an int? Then the next int storage location is used. A single field is not allowed to overlap the boundary between two ints. The compiler automatically shifts an overlapping field definition so that the field is aligned with the int boundary. When this occurs, it leaves an unnamed hole in the first int.

You can "pad" a field structure with unnamed holes by using unnamed field widths. Using an unnamed field width of 0 forces the next field to align with the next integer.

```
struct {
        field1 : 1;
               : 2;
        field2 : 1;
               : 0;
        field3 : 1;
} stuff;
```

Here, there is a 2-bit gap between stuff.field1 and stuff.field2; and stuff.field3 is stored in the next int.

One important machine dependency is the order in which fields are placed into an int. On some machines the order is left to right, and on others it is right to left. Also, machines differ in the location of boundaries between fields. For these reasons, bit fields tend not to be very portable. Typically, however, they are used for nonportable purposes, such as putting data in the exact form used by a particular hardware device.

Bit-Field Example

As we mentioned, bit fields typically are used in programs dedicated to a particular piece of hardware. Our example will be IBM PC-based, but if you aren't using that platform, you still can read through the example to see how it works.

The original IBM PC had various configuration switches that had to be set on the motherboard. When the computer was turned on, it copied information from these switch settings to a 2-byte memory location. Within that 2-byte word, the bits have the meaning shown in Table 15.3.

Table 15.3. Equipment word.

Bit(s)	Meaning	Value
0	Diskette drive	1 if present
1	Not used	
2–3	Motherboard memory	00 = 16k, 01 = 32k, 10 = 48k, 11 = 64k
4–5	Initial video setup	01 = 40x25, 10 = 80x25, 11 = mono
6–7	Number of drives	Number of diskette drives – 1
8	Not used	
9–11	Number of comm. cards	Number of cards
12	Game port	1 if present
13	Not used	
14–15	Number of printers	Number of printers

You can use a structure with bit fields to represent this data:

```
struct equip_word { unsigned has_drive  : 1;
                    unsigned            : 1;
                    unsigned mother_bd  : 2;
                    unsigned vid_setup  : 2;
                    unsigned num_drives : 2;
                    unsigned            : 1;
                    unsigned num_comcds : 3;
                    unsigned gameio     : 1;
                    unsigned            : 1;
                    unsigned num_ptrs   : 2;
};
```

Note that the unnamed bit fields represent the unused bits in the equipment word.

To determine whether a game I/O card, for example, is present, you can test whether the gameio member is 1. The tricky part is getting the correct values into the structure. Listing 15.3 shows one way.

Listing 15.3. ibmchk.c.

```c
/* ibmchk.c -- checks IBM PC equipment word */
#include <stdio.h>
#include <dos.h>               /* MS-DOS specific declarations  */
#define DSKTE    0x0001        /* diskette drives are present   */
#define DRV_MASK 0x00C0        /* drive count bits              */
#define DRV_SHFT 6             /* shift drive bits to right end */
#define GAMES    0x1000        /* game I/O?                     */
#define PRN_SHFT 14            /* printer count shift           */
#define EQCK 0x11              /* equipment check interrupt     */
struct equip_word {
        unsigned has_drive  : 1;
        unsigned            : 1;
        unsigned mother_bd  : 2;
        unsigned vid_setup  : 2;
        unsigned num_drives : 2;
        unsigned            : 1;
        unsigned num_comcds : 3;
        unsigned gameio     : 1;
        unsigned            : 1;
        unsigned num_ptrs   : 2;
};
int main(void)
{
    union REGS rin, rout;
    unsigned int equip;
    union {
          struct equip_word s_view;
          unsigned int    i_view;
     } eq_data;

    equip = int86 (EQCK, &rin, &rout);
    eq_data.i_view = equip;
    if (equip & DSKTE != DSKTE)
        printf("No disk drives\n");
    else
    {
        printf("Bit operations: %u floppy drive(s)\n",
               ((equip & DRV_MASK) >> DRV_SHFT) + 1);
        printf("Bit fields: %u floppy drive(s)\n",
               eq_data.s_view.num_drives + 1);
    }
    printf("Bit operations: %u printer(s) attached\n",
           equip >> PRN_SHFT);
    printf("Bit fields: %u printer(s) attached\n",
           eq_data.s_view.num_ptrs);
    return 0;
}
```

The `int86()` function, found both in MS C and Turbo C, uses *interrupts* to obtain information. Interrupts, more or less, are subroutines built into the PC. The `int86()` function, then, is quite implementation specific and is not part of any general C library. The particular interrupt we used, represented by `EQCK`, causes `int86()` to return the value of the equipment word in integer form.

To convert this integer to a structure, we used a trick. The union `eq_data` has two members: an `equip_word` structure and an unsigned integer.

```
union {
        struct equip_word s_view;
        unsigned int    i_view;
} eq_data;
```

Both, on a PC, are 16-bit data objects. We make the following assignment:

```
eq_data.i_view = equip;
```

The `i_view` member views the union as an unsigned `int`, and we read in the equipment word in that form. Then, by using `eq_data.s_view`, we can look at the same data as a bit-field structure. That is, bit 0 of the integer `eq_data.i_view` also is the `has_drive` member of the structure `eq_data.s_view`. Thus, we can use the `eq_data` union to view the equipment word two ways: as a bit-field structure and as an `unsigned int`. This correspondence depends on the implementation-dependent feature that structures are loaded into memory from the low-bit end to the high-bit end of a byte. That is, the first bit field in the structure goes into bit 0 of the word. See Figure 15.3.

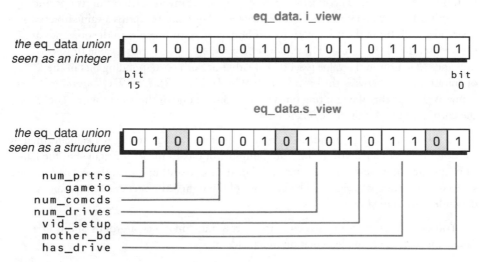

Figure 15.3. *A union as an integer and as a structure.*

Incidentally, the type REGS union (defined in dos.h) uses a similar approach to provide both a word-view and a byte-view of the CPU registers.

The program then proceeds to use both the bit-wise operator approach and the bit-field method for examining the contents of the equipment word. Once the bit fields are set up, they are easier to use. For example, eq_data.s_view.num_drives represents the value stored in the 2 bits representing the number of floppy drives. Compare that to what we have to do using bit operations. First we evaluate equip & DRV_MASK to turn off all other bits. At this point we have a value in the form 00000000bb000000. Then we do a right shift to move these 2 bits to the low end of the word: 00000000000000bb. Now we can evaluate the expression numerically to determine the number of drives.

Chapter Summary

Computing hardware is closely tied to the *binary number system* because the 1s and 0s of binary numbers can be used to represent the on and off states of bits in computer memory and registers. Although C does not allow you to write numbers in binary form, it does recognize the related octal and hexadecimal notations. Just as each binary digit represents 1 bit, each octal digit represents 3 bits, and each hexadecimal digit represents 4 bits. This relationship makes it relatively simple to convert binary numbers to octal or hexadecimal form.

C features several *bit-wise operators*, so called because they operate independently on each bit within a value. The *bitwise negation operator* (~) inverts each bit in its operand, converting 1s to 0s and vice versa. The *bitwise AND operator* (&) forms a value from two operands. Each bit in the value is set to 1 if both corresponding bits in the operands are 1. Otherwise, the bit is set to 0. The *bitwise OR operator* (¦) also forms a value from two operands. Each bit in the value is set to 1 if either or both corresponding bits in the operands are 1; otherwise, the bit is set to 0. The *bitwise EXCLUSIVE OR operator* (^) acts similarly, except that the resulting bit is set to 1 only if one or the other, but not both, of the corresponding bits in the operands is 1.

C also has *left-shift* (<<) and *right-shift* (>>) operators. Each produces a value formed by shifting the bits in a pattern the indicated number of bits to the left or right. For the left-shift operator, the vacated bits are set to 0. For the right-shift operator, the vacated bits are set to 0 if the value is unsigned. The behavior of the right-shift operator is implementation dependent for signed values.

You can use *bit fields* in a structure to address individual bits or groups of bits in a value. The details are implementation independent.

These bit tools assist C programs in dealing with various hardware matters, so they most often appear in implementation-dependent contexts.

Review Questions

1. Convert the following decimal values to binary.

   a. 3
   b. 13
   c. 59
   d. 119

2. Convert the following binary values to decimal, octal, and hexadecimal.

   a. 00010101
   b. 01010101
   c. 01001100
   d. 10011101

3. Evaluate the following expressions; assume each value is 1 byte.

   a. ~3
   b. 3 & 6
   c. 3 ¦ 6
   d. 1 ¦ 6
   e. 3 ^ 6
   f. 7 >> 1
   g. 7 << 2

4. Evaluate the following expressions; assume each value is 1 byte.

   a. ~0
   b. !0
   c. 2 & 4
   d. 2 && 4
   e. 2 ¦ 4
   f. 2 ¦¦ 4
   g. 5 << 3

5. Because the ASCII code uses only the final 7 bits, sometimes it is desirable to mask off the other bits. What's the appropriate mask in binary? In decimal? In octal? In hexadecimal?

6. In Listing 15.3, we masked `equip` with `drive_mask` before doing the right shift to get the drive number, but we didn't mask `equip` before doing the right shift to get the number of printers? Why didn't this omission cause problems?

Programming Exercises

1. Write a function that converts a binary string to a numeric value. That is, if you have

   ```
   char * pbin = "01001001";
   ```

   then you can pass pbin as an argument to the function and have the function return an int value of 25.

2. Write a program that reads two binary strings as command-line arguments and prints the results of applying the ~ operator to each number and the results of applying the &, ¦, and ^ operators to the pair. Show the results as binary strings.

3. Write a function that takes an int argument and returns the number of ON bits in the argument.

4. Write a function that takes two int arguments: a value and a bit position. Have the function return 1 if that particular bit position is 1, and have it return 0 otherwise.

5. Write a function that rotates the bits of an unsigned int by a specified number of bits to the left. For instance, rotate_1(x,4) would move the bits in x four places to the left, and the bits lost off the left end would reappear at the right end. That is, the bit moved out of the high-order position is placed in the low-order position.

The C Preprocessor and the C Library

Keywords

    #define, #include, #ifdef
    #else, #endif, #ifndef
    #if, #elif, enum

Functions

    sqrt(), atan(), atan2()
    exit(), atexit(), malloc()

In this chapter you investigate further the capabilities of the C pre-processor, learning about macro "functions" and conditional compilation.

Also, you are introduced to the enum facility and you learn more about the C library and dynamic memory allocation.

The ANSI C Standard encompasses more than just the C language. The Standard also describes how the C preprocessor should perform, establishes which functions form the standard C library, and details how these functions work. We'll explore the C preprocessor and the C library in this chapter, beginning with the preprocessor.

The preprocesor looks at your program before it is compiled (hence the term *prepro-cessor*). Following your preprocessor directives, the preprocessor replaces the symbolic abbreviations in your program with the directions they represent. The preprocessor can include other files at your request. It can select which code the compiler sees. This description does not do justice to the true utility and value of the preprocessor, so let's turn to examples. With #define and #include, we have provided examples all along. Now we can gather what we have learned in one place and add to it.

Manifest Constants: *#define*

The #define preprocessor directive, like all preprocessor directives, begins with a # symbol. The ANSI Standard permits the # symbol to be preceded by spaces or tabs, and it allows for space between the # and the remainder of the directive. Older versions of C, however, typically require that the directive begin in the leftmost column and that there be no spaces between the # and the remainder of the directive. A directive can appear anywhere in the source file, and the definition holds from its place of appearance to the end of the file. We have used directives heavily to define symbolic, or manifest, constants in our programs, but they have more range than that, as we will show. Listing 16.1 illustrates some of the possibilities and properties of the #define directive.

Preprocessor directives run until the first newline following the #. That is, a directive is limited to one line in length. However, the combination backslash-newline is treated as a space, so the one *logical* line can use more than one physical line in the file.

Listing 16.1. preproc.c.

```
/* preproc.c -- simple preprocessor examples */
#include <stdio.h>
#define TWO 2        /* you can use comments if you like    */
#define MSG "The old grey cat sang a merry \
song."           /* a backslash continues a definition */
                 /* to the next line                   */
#define FOUR  TWO*TWO
#define PX printf("X is %d.\n", x)
#define FMT  "X is %d.\n"
int main(void)
{
   int x = TWO;
```

```
    PX;
    x = FOUR;
    printf(FMT, x);
    printf("%s\n", MSG);
    printf("TWO: MSG\n");
    return 0;
}
```

Each #define line has three parts. The first part is the #define directive itself. The second part is your chosen abbreviation, known as a *macro* or *alias* in the computer world. (Some programmers reserve the term "macro" for the macro functions we discuss later and use the term "alias" for the symbolic constants we are discussing now.) The macro name must have no spaces in it. Its name must conform to the same rules that C variables follow: only letters, digits, and the underscore (_) character can be used, and the first character cannot be a digit. The third part (the remainder of the line) is termed the *body*. When the preprocessor finds an example of one of your aliases within your program, it almost always replaces it with the body. (There is one exception as we will show you in just a moment.) This process of going from a macro to a final replacement is called *macro expansion*. Note that you can use standard C comments on a #define line; they will be ignored by the preprocessor. Also, in most systems (and the ANSI C standard) you can use the backslash (\) to extend a definition over more than one line. See Figure 16.1.

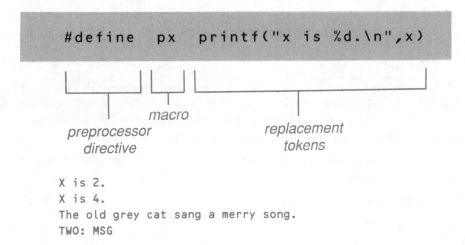

```
X is 2.
X is 4.
The old grey cat sang a merry song.
TWO: MSG
```

Figure 16.1. *Parts of a macro definition.*

Let's run our example and see how it works.

```
X is 2.
X is 4.
The old grey cat sang a merry song.
TWO: MSG
```

Here's what happened. The statement

```
int x = TWO;
```

becomes

```
int x = 2;
```

as 2 is substituted for TWO. Then the statement

```
PX;
```

becomes

```
printf("X is %d.\n", x);
```

as that wholesale substitution is made. This is a new wrinkle, because up to now we've used macros only to represent constants. Here you see that a macro can express any string, even a whole C expression. Note, though, that this is a constant string; PX will print only a variable named x.

The next line also represents something new. You might think that FOUR is replaced by 4, but the actual process is this:

```
x = FOUR;
```

becomes

```
x = TWO*TWO;
```

which then becomes

```
x = 2*2;
```

The macro expansion process ends there. The actual multiplication takes place, not while the preprocessor works, but during compilation, because the C compiler evaluates all *constant expressions* (expressions with just constants) at compile time. The preprocessor does no calculation; it just makes the suggested substitutions very literally.

Note that a macro definition can include other macros. (Some compilers do not support this nesting feature.)

In the next line

```
printf (FMT, x);
```

becomes

```
printf("X is %d.\n",x);
```

as FMT is replaced by the corresponding string. This approach could be handy if you had a lengthy control string that you had to use several times. Alternatively, you can do the following:

```
char * fmt = "X is %d.\n";
```

Then you can use `fmt` as the `printf()` control string.

In the next line `MSG` is replaced by the corresponding string. The double quotation marks make the replacement string a character string constant. The compiler will store it in an array terminated with a null character. Thus,

```
#define HAL 'Z'
```

defines a character constant, but

```
#define HAP "Z"
```

defines a character string: Z\O.

In the example, we used a backslash immediately before the end of the line to extend the string to the next line.

```
#define MSG "The old grey cat sang a merry \
            song."
```

The space between the `y` and the `\` prevents us from getting the word `merrysong`. Note that `song` is flush left. Suppose, instead, we did this:

```
#define MSG "The old grey cat sang a merry \
            song."
```

Then the output would be this:

```
The old grey cat sang a merry            song.
```

The space between the beginning of the line and `song` counts as part of the string.

In general, wherever the preprocessor finds one of your macros in your program, it literally replaces it with the equivalent replacement text. If that string also contains macros, they, too, are replaced. The one exception to replacement is a macro found within double quotation marks. Thus,

```
printf("TWO: MSG");
```

prints `TWO: MSG` literally instead of printing

```
2: The old grey cat sang a merry song.
```

To print this last line, you would use this:

```
printf("%d: %s\n", TWO, MSG);
```

Here, the macros are outside the double quotation marks.

When should you use symbolic constants? You should use them for most numbers. If the number is some constant used in a calculation, a symbolic name makes its meaning clearer. If the number is an array size, a symbolic name makes it simpler to change the array size and loop limits later. If the number is a system code for, say, EOF, a symbolic representation makes your program much more portable; just change one EOF definition. Mnemonic value, easy alterability, portability. These all make symbolic constants worthwhile.

Tokens

Technically, the body of a macro is considered to be a string of *tokens* rather than a string of characters. C preprocessor tokens are the separate "words" in the body of a macro definition. They are separated from one another by whitespace. For example, the definition

```
#define FOUR 2*2
```

has one token: the sequence `2*2`, but the definition

```
#define SIX 2 * 3
```

has three tokens in it: `2`, `*`, and `3`.

Character strings and token strings differ in how multiple spaces in a body are treated. Consider this definition:

```
#define EIGHT 4    *     8
```

A preprocessor that interpreted the body as a character string would replace `EIGHT` with `4    *     8`. That is, the extra spaces would be part of the replacement, but a preprocessor that interprets the body as tokens will replace `EIGHT` with three tokens separated by single spaces: `4 * 8`. In other words, the character string interpretation views the spaces as *part* of the body, whereas the token interpretation views the spaces as *separators* between the tokens of the body. In practice, some C compilers have viewed macro bodies as strings rather than tokens. The difference is of practical importance only for usages more intricate than what we will attempt.

Incidentally, the C compiler takes a more complex view of tokens than does the preprocessor. The compiler understands the rules of C and doesn't necessarily require spaces to separate tokens. For instance, the C compiler would view `2*2` as three tokens because it recognizes that the 2's are constants and the `*` is an operator.

Redefining Constants

Suppose you define `LIMIT` to be 20; then later in the same file you define it again to be 25. This is called *redefining a constant*. Implementations differ on redefinition policy. Some consider it an error unless the new definition is the same as the old. Others allow redefinition, perhaps issuing a warning. The ANSI Standard takes the first view, allowing redefinition only if the new definition duplicates the old.

Having the same definition means the bodies must have the same tokens in the same order. Thus, these two definitions agree:

```
#define SIX 2 * 3
#define SIX 2       *     3
```

Both have the same three tokens, and the extra spaces are not part of the body. The next definition is considered different.

```
#define SIX 2*3
```

It has just one token, not three, so it doesn't match. If you want to redefine a macro, use the #undef directive, which we discuss later.

Using Arguments with *#define*

By using arguments, you can create macros that look and act much like functions. A macro with arguments looks very much like a function, because the arguments are enclosed within parentheses. Listing 16.2 provides some examples that illustrate how such a *macro function* is defined and used. Some of the examples also point out possible pitfalls, so read them carefully.

Listing 16.2. mac_arg.c.

```
/* mac_arg.c -- macros with arguments */
#include <stdio.h>
#define SQUARE(X) X*X
#define PR(X)    printf("The result is %d.\n", X)
int main(void)
{
    int x = 4;
    int z;

    z = SQUARE(x);
    PR(z);
    z = SQUARE(2);
    PR(z);
    PR(SQUARE(x+2));
    PR(100/SQUARE(2));
    PR(SQUARE(++x));
    return 0;
}
```

Wherever SQUARE(x) appears in Listing 16.2, it is replaced by x*x. This differs from our earlier examples in that we are free to use symbols other than x when we use this macro. The x in the macro definition is replaced by the symbol used in the macro call in the program. Thus, SQUARE(2) is replaced by 2*2, so the x really does act as an argument.

However, as you shall soon see, a macro argument does not work exactly like a function argument. Here are the results of running the program. Note that some of the answers are different from what you might expect. Indeed, your compiler may not even give the same answer as shown here for the last line.

```
The result is 16.
The result is 4.
The result is 14.
The result is 100.
The result is 30.
```

The first two lines are predictable, but then we come to some peculiar results. Recall that x has the value 4. This might lead you to expect that SQUARE(x+2) would be 6*6, or 36, but the printout says it is 14, which sure doesn't look like a square to us! The simple reason for this misleading output is the one we have already stated: the preprocessor doesn't make calculations; it just substitutes strings. Wherever our definition shows an x, the preprocessor will substitute the string x+2. Thus,

x*x

becomes

x+2*x+2

The only multiplication is 2*x. If x is 4, then the value of this expression is

4+2*4+2 = 4 + 8 + 2 = 14

This example pinpoints a very important difference between a function call and a macro call. A function call passes the *value* of the argument to the function while the program is running. A macro call passes the argument *token* to the program before compilation; it's a different process at a different time. Can our definition be fixed to make SQUARE(x+2) yield 36? Sure. We simply need more parentheses.

```
#define SQUARE(x)  (x)*(x)
```

Then SQUARE(x+2) becomes (x+2)*(x+2), and we get our desired multiplication as the parentheses carry over in the replacement string.

This doesn't solve all our problems, however. Consider the events leading to the next output line:

100/SQUARE(2)

becomes

100/2*2

By the laws of precedence, the expression is evaluated from left to right.

(100/2)*2   or   50*2   or   100

This mix-up can be cured by defining SQUARE(x) as

```
#define SQUARE(x)  (x*x)
```

This produces 100/(2*2), which eventually evaluates to 100/4, or 25.

To handle both of the last two examples, we need the definition

```
#define SQUARE(x)  ((x)*(x))
```

The lesson here is to use as many parentheses as necessary to ensure that operations and associations are done in the right order.

Even these precautions fail to save the final example from grief.

```
SQUARE(++x)
```

becomes

```
++x*++x
```

and x gets incremented twice, once before the multiplication and once afterwards.

```
++x*++x = 5*6 = 30
```

Because the order of operations is left open, some compilers will render the product 6*5. Yet other compilers might increment both terms before multiplication, yielding 6*6.

The only remedy for this problem is to avoid using ++x as a macro argument. In general, *don't* use increment or decrement operators with macros. Note that ++x would work as a *function* argument, for it would be evaluated to 6 and then the value 6 would be sent to the function.

Including the Macro Argument in a String

Under K&R C you could define macros like the following:

```
#define PSQR(X)  printf("The square of X is %d.\n", ((X)*(X)));
```

Suppose you used the preceding macro like this:

```
PSQR(8);
PSQR(2 + 3);
```

Then the output would be this:

```
The square of 8 is 64.
The square of 2 + 3 is 25.
```

That is, the macro argument inside the double quotes would be replaced by the actual argument, contrary to the normal rule that tokens inside double quotes are left unaltered. ANSI C disallows this substitution within quotes. Running the same code under ANSI C produces the following output:

```
The square of X is 64.
The square of X is 25.
```

The X in the quoted string is treated as ordinary text, not as a token that can be replaced.

Suppose you do want to include the macro argument in a string? A new feature of ANSI C enables you to do that. If, say, x is a macro parameter, then #x is that parameter converted to a string. Listing 16.3 illustrates how this works.

Listing 16.3. subst.c.

```
/* subst.c -- substitute in string */
#include <stdio.h>
#define PSQR(x) printf("The square of " #x " is %d.\n",((x)*(x)))
int main(void)
{
    int y = 5;

    PSQR(y);
    PSQR(2 + 4);
    return 0;
}
```

Here's the output:

```
The square of y is 25.
The square of 2 + 4 is 36.
```

In the first call to the macro, #x was replaced by "y", and in the second call it was replaced by "2 + 4". ANSI C string concatenation then combined these strings with the other strings in the printf() statement to produce the final strings that were used.

Macro or Function?

Many tasks can be done by using a macro with arguments or by using a function. Which one should you use? There is no hard and fast rule, but here are some considerations.

Macros are somewhat trickier to use than regular functions because they can have odd side effects if you are unwary. Some compilers limit the macro definition to one line, and it is probably best to observe that limit even if your compiler does not.

The macro-versus-function choice represents a trade-off between time and space. A macro produces *in-line* code; that is, you get a statement in your program. If you use the macro 20 times, then you get 20 lines of code inserted into your program. If you use a function 20 times, you have just one copy of the function statements in your program, so less space is used. On the other hand, program control must shift to where the function is and then return to the calling program, and this takes longer than in-line code.

Macros have an advantage in that they don't worry about variable types. (This is because they deal with character strings, not with actual values.) Thus, our SQUARE(x) macro can be used equally well with int or float.

Programmers typically use macros for simple functions like the following:

```
#define MAX(X,Y)    ((X) > (Y) ? (X) : (Y))
#define ABS(X)      ((X) < 0 ? -(X) : (X))
#define ISSIGN(X)   ((X) == '+' ¦¦ (X) == '-' ? 1 : 0)
```

(The last macro has the value 1—true—if x is an algebraic sign character.)

Here are some points to note:

* Remember that there are no spaces in the macro name, but that spaces can appear in the replacement string. With K&R C, there can be no spaces in the argument list. The preprocessor thinks the macro ends at the first space, so anything after that space is lumped into the replacement string, as shown in Figure 16.2. ANSI C, however, does permit spaces in the argument list.

* Use parentheses around each argument and around the definition as a whole. This ensures that the enclosed terms are grouped properly in an expression like
  `forks = 2 * MAX(guests + 3, last);`

* Use capital letters for macro function names. This convention is not as widespread as that of using capitals for macro constants. However, one good reason for using capitals is to remind yourself to be alert to possible macro side effects.

* If you intend to use a macro instead of a function primarily to speed up a program, try to first determine if it is likely to make a significant difference. A macro that is used once in a program most likely will make no noticeable improvement in running time. A macro inside a nested loop is a much better candidate for speed improvements. Many systems offer program profilers to help you pin down where a program spends the most time.

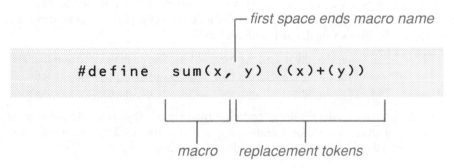

Figure 16.2. *Faulty spacing in a macro definition.*

Suppose you have developed some macro functions that you like. Do you have to retype them each time you write a new program? Not if you remember the #include directive. We will review that now.

File Inclusion: *#include*

When the preprocessor spots an #include directive, it looks for the following filename and includes the contents of that file within the current file. The #include directive in your source code file is replaced with the text from the included file. It's as if you sat down and typed in the entire contents of the included file at that particular location in your source file. The #include directive comes in two varieties.

```
#include <stdio.h>          →filename in angle brackets

#include "mystuff.h"        →filename in double quotation marks
```

On a UNIX system, the angle brackets tell the preprocessor to look for the file in one or more standard system directories. The double quotation marks tell it to first look in your current directory (or some other directory that you have specified in the filename) and then look in the standard places.

```
#include <stdio.h>          →searches system directories

#include "hot.h"            →searches your current working directory

#include "/usr/biff/p.h"    →searches the /usr/biff directory
```

Microsoft C uses an environmental variable called INCLUDE to identify the directory with the system include files. Borland C and Turbo C have you use their menu systems to specify default locations for the include files. Open the Options menu and select Directories.

ANSI C doesn't demand adherence to the directory model for files because not all computer systems are organized similarly. In general, the method used to name files is system dependent, but the use of the angle brackets and double quotation marks is not.

Why include files? Because they have information that the compiler needs. The stdio.h file, for example, typically includes definitions of EOF, NULL, getchar(), and putchar(). The last two are defined as macro functions.

The .h suffix conventionally is used for *header* files—files with information that are placed at the head of your program. Header files usually consist of preprocessor statements. Some, like stdio.h, come with the system, but you are free to create your own.

Including a large header file doesn't necessarily add much to the size of your program. The content of include files, for the most part, is information used by the compiler to generate the final code, not material to be added to the final code.

Header Files: An Example

Suppose that you like using Boolean values. That is, instead of having 1 be true and 0 be false, you prefer using the words TRUE and FALSE. You could create a file called, say, bool.h that contains these definitions:

```
/* bool.h file */
#define BOOLEAN int
#define TRUE 1
#define FALSE 0
```

Listing 16.4 is an example of a program using this header.

Listing 16.4. `cnt_sp.c`.

```c
/* cnt_sp.c -- counts whitespace characters */
#include <stdio.h>
#include "bool.h"
BOOLEAN whitesp(char);
int main(void)
{
    int ch;
    int count = 0;

    while ((ch = getchar() ) != EOF)
        if (whitesp(ch) == TRUE)
                count++;
    printf("There are %d whitespace characters.\n", count);
    return 0;
}
BOOLEAN whitesp(char c)
{
    if (c == ' ' || c == '\n'  || c == '\t')
        return(TRUE);
    else
        return(FALSE);
}
```

Note the following points about this program:

- If the two functions in this program, `main()` and `whitesp()`, were to be compiled separately, you would use the `#include "bool.h"` directive with each.

- We have not created a new type `BOOLEAN`, because `BOOLEAN` is just `int`. The purpose of labeling the function `BOOLEAN` is to remind the programmer that the function is being used for a logical (as opposed to arithmetic) calculation.

- Using a function for involved logical comparisons can make a program clearer. It also can save effort if the comparison is made in more than one place in a program.

- We could have used a macro instead of a function to define `whitesp()`, in which case we would use all uppercase for the macro name.

Uses for Header Files

A look through any of the standard header files will give you a good idea of the sort of information found in them. Typical header contents include the following:

- *Manifest constants.* A typical `stdio.h` file, for instance, defines EOF, NULL, and BUFSIZE (the size of the standard I/O buffer).

- *Macro functions.* For example, `getchar()` usually is defined as `getc(stdin)`, `getc()` usually is defined as a rather complex macro, and the `ctype.h` header typically contains macro definitions for the `ctype` functions.

- *Function declarations.* The string.h header (strings.h on some older systems), for instance, contains function declarations for the family of string functions. Under ANSI C, the declarations are in function prototype form.

- *Structure template definitions.* The standard I/O functions make use of a structure containing information about a file and its associated buffer. The stdio.h file contains the template for this structure.

- *Type definitions.* You may recall that the standard I/O functions use a pointer-to-FILE argument. Typically, stdio.h uses a #define or a typedef to make FILE represent a pointer to a structure.

Many programmers develop their own standard header files to use with their programs. Some files might be for special purposes; others might be used with almost every program. Because included files can incorporate #include directives, you can create concise, well-organized header files if you like.

Consider this example:

```
/* header file mystuff.h */
#include <stdio.h>
#include "bool.h"
#include "funct.h"
#define YES 1
#define NO 0
```

First, it's a good idea to use a comment to identify the name of the header file. Second, we have included three files. Presumably the third one contains some macro functions or function prototypes that we use often. Third, we have defined YES to be 1, whereas in bool.h we defined TRUE to be 1. There is no conflict here. We can use YES and TRUE in the same program. Each will be replaced by a 1.

Also, you can use header files to declare external variables to be shared by several files. Some programmers think it's okay to do so. Others think it is poor style, because you have to check another file to see whether a variable is declared.

The #include and #define directives are the most heavily used C preprocessor features. We'll look at the other directives in less detail.

Other Directives

The #undef directive cancels an earlier #define definition. The #if, #ifdef, #ifndef, #else, #elif, and #endif directives are typically used to produce files that can be compiled in more than one way.

The *#undef* Directive

The #undef directive *undefines* a given #define. That is, suppose you have this definition:

#define LIMIT 400

Then the directive

```
#undef LIMIT
```

removes that definition. Now, if you like, you can redefine LIMIT so that it has a new value. Even if LIMIT is not defined in the first place, it still is valid to undefine it. Thus, if you want to use a particular name and you are unsure whether it has been used previously, you can undefine it to be on the safe side.

With some compilers you can redefine a defined name and to nest #defines and #undefs so that undefining a name causes it to revert to its original value. This is not, however, the standard practice, and it is not part of the ANSI Standard. More typically, you'll get a warning or error message if you redefine a name, so use #undef first if you wish to redefine.

Conditional Compilation

You can use the other directives we mentioned to set up conditional compilations. That is, you can use them to tell the compiler to accept or ignore blocks of information or code according to conditions at the time of compilation.

The *#ifdef*, *#else*, and *#endif* Directives

A short example will clarify what conditional compilation does. Consider the following:

```
#ifdef MAVIS
     #include "horse.h"   /* gets done if MAVIS is #defined    */
     #define  STABLES    5
#else
     #include "cow.h"     /* gets done if MAVIS isn't #defined */
     #define  STABLES   15
#endif
```

Here we've used the indentation allowed by newer implementations and by the ANSI Standard. If you have an older implementation, you may have to move all the directives, or at least the # symbols (see the next example), to flush left.

```
#ifdef MAVIS
#    include "horse.h"   /* gets done if MAVIS is #defined    */
#    define  STABLES    5
#else
#    include "cow.h"     /* gets done if MAVIS isn't #defined */
#    define  STABLES   15
#endif
```

The #ifdef directive says that if the following identifier (MAVIS) has been defined by the preprocessor, then follow all the directives and compile all the C code up to the next #else or #endif, whichever comes first. If there is an #else, then everything from the #else to the #endif is done if the identifier isn't defined.

Incidentally, an "empty" definition like

```
#define MAVIS
```

is sufficient to define MAVIS for the purposes of #ifdef.

The form #ifdef #else is much like that of the C if else. The main difference is that the preprocessor doesn't recognize the braces ({}) method of marking a block, so it uses the #else (if any) and the #endif (which must be present) to mark blocks of directives. These conditional structures can be nested. You can use these directives to mark blocks of C statements, too, as Listing 16.5 illustrates.

Listing 16.5. ifdef.c.

```
/* ifdef.c -- uses conditional compilation */
#include <stdio.h>
#define JUST_CHECKING
#define LIMIT 4
int main(void)
{
    int i;
    int total = 0;

    for (i = 1; i <= LIMIT; i++)
    {
        total += 2*i*i + 1;
#ifdef JUST_CHECKING
        printf("i=%d, running total = %d\n", i, total);
#endif
    }
    printf("Grand total = %d\n", total);
    return 0;
}
```

Compiling and running the program as shown produces this output:

```
i=1, running total = 3
i=2, running total = 12
i=3, running total = 31
i=4, running total = 64
Grand total = 64
```

If you omit the JUST_CHECKING definition (or enclose it inside a C comment) and recompile the program, only the final line is displayed. You can use this approach, for instance, to help in program debugging. Define JUST_CHECKING and use a judicious selection of #ifdefs, and the compiler will include program code for printing intermediate values for debugging. Once everything is working, you can remove the definition and recompile. If, later, you find that you need the information again, you can reinsert the definition and avoid having to retype all the extra print statements. Another possibility is using #ifdef to select among alternative chunks of codes suited for different C implementations.

The *#ifndef* Directive

The #ifndef directive can be used with #else and #endif in the same way that #ifdef is. The #ifndef asks if the following identifier is *not* defined; #ifndef is the negative of #ifdef. This directive often is used to define a constant if it is not already defined.

```
#ifndef SIZE
    #define SIZE 100
#endif
```

Again, older implementations may not permit indenting the #define directive. Suppose this directive were in an include file called arrays.h. Placing the line

```
#include "arrays.h"
```

at the head of a file would result in SIZE being defined as 100, but placing

```
#define SIZE 10
#include "arrays.h"
```

at the head would set SIZE to 10. Here, SIZE is defined by the time the lines in arrays.h are processed, so the #define SIZE 100 line is skipped. You might do this, for example, to test a program using a smaller array size. Once it works to your satisfaction, you can remove the #define SIZE 10 statement and recompile. That way you never have to worry about modifying the header array itself.

The #ifndef directive commonly is used to prevent multiple inclusions of a file. That is, an include file may be set up along the following lines:

```
/* things.h */
#ifndef __THINGS__
    #define __THINGS__
    /* rest of include file */
#endif
```

Suppose this file somehow got included several times. The first time the preprocessor encounters this include file, __THINGS__ is undefined, so the program proceeds to define __THINGS__ and to process the rest of the file. The next time the preprocessor encounters this file, __THINGS__ is defined, so the preprocessor skips the rest of the file.

The *#if* and *#elif* Directives

The #if directive is more like the regular C if. It is followed by a constant integer expression that is considered true if nonzero, and you can use C's relational and logical operators with it.

```
#if SYS == 1
#include "ibm.h"
#endif
```

551

You can use the #elif (not available in some older implementations) directive to extend an if-else sequence. For example, you could do this:

```
#if SYS == 1
     #include "ibmpc.h"
#elif SYS == 2
     #include "vax.h"
#elif SYS == 3
     #include "mac.h"
#else
     #include "general.h"
#endif
```

Many newer implementations offer a second way to test whether a name is defined. Instead of using

```
#ifdef VAX
```

you can use this form:

```
#if defined (VAX)
```

Here, defined is a preprocessor operator that returns 1 if its argument is #defined and 0 otherwise. The advantage of this newer form is that it can be used with #elif. Using it, we can rewrite the last example this way:

```
#if defined (IBMPC)
     #include "ibmpc.h"
#elif defined (VAX)
     #include "vax.h"
#elif defined (MAC)
     #include "mac.h"
#else
     #include "general.h"
#endif
```

If you were using these lines on, say, a VAX, you would have defined VAX somewhere earlier in the file with this line:

```
#define VAX
```

One use for these conditional compilation features is to make a program more portable. By changing a few key definitions at the beginning of a file, you can set up different values and include different files for different systems. We'll show you some examples when we discuss the library.

Enumerated Types

You can use the *enumerated type* to declare symbolic names to represent integer constants. It is a common C extension that has been incorporated into the ANSI C Standard. By using the enum keyword, you can create a new "type" and specify the values it may have.

(Actually, enum is type int, so you really create a new name for an existing type.) The purpose of enumerated types is to enhance the readability of a program. The syntax is similar to that used for structures. For example, you can make these declarations:

```
enum spectrum {red, orange, yellow, green, blue, violet};
enum spectrum color;
```

The first declaration establishes spectrum as a type name, and the second declaration makes color a variable of that type. The identifiers within the braces enumerate the possible values that a spectrum variable can have. Thus, the possible values for color are red, orange, yellow, and so on. Then, you can use statements like the following:

```
color = blue;
if (color == yellow)
    ...;
for (color = red; color <= violet; color++)
    ...;
```

enum Constants

Just what are blue and red? Technically, they are integer type constants. (Which integer type? That depends on the implementation.) For instance, given the preceding enumeration declaration, you can try this:

```
printf("red = %d, orange = %d\n", red, orange);
```

Here is the output:

```
red = 0, orange = 1
```

What has happened is that red has become a *named constant* representing the integer 0. Similarly, the other identifiers are named constants representing the integers 1 through 5. The process is similar to using defined constants, except that these definitions are set up by the compiler rather than the preprocessor.

Default Values

By default, the constants in the enumeration list are assigned the integer values 0, 1, 2, etc. Thus, the declaration

```
enum kids {nippy, slats, skippy, nina, liz};
```

results in nina having the value 3.

Assigned Values

You can choose the integer values that you want the constants to have. Just include the desired values in the declaration.

```
enum levels {low = 100, medium = 500, high = 2000};
```

If you assign a value to one constant but not to the following constants, the following constants will be numbered sequentially. For example, suppose you have this declaration:

```
enum feline {cat, lynx = 10, puma, tiger};
```

Then cat is 0, by default, and lynx, puma, and tiger are 10, 11, and 12, respectively.

Usage

Recall that the purpose of enumerated types is to enhance the readability of a program. If you are dealing with colors, using red and blue is much more obvious than using 0 and 1. Note that the enumerated types are for internal use. If you want to enter a value of orange for color, you have to enter a 1, not the word orange, or you can read in the string "orange" and have the program convert it to the value orange.

Because the enumerated type is an integer type, enum variables can be used in expressions in the same manner as integer variables.

Listing 16.6 shows a short example using enum. The example relies on the default value-assignment scheme. This gives red the value 0, which makes it the index for the pointer to the string "red".

Listing 16.6. enum.c.

```
/* enum.c -- uses enumerated values */
#include <stdio.h>
#include <string.h>
#include "bool.h"
enum spectrum {red, orange, yellow, green, blue, violet};
char * colors[] = {"red", "orange", "yellow", "green",
                   "blue", "violet"};
#define LEN 30
int main(void)
{
    char choice[LEN];
    enum spectrum color;
    BOOLEAN found = FALSE;

    puts("Enter a color:");
    while (gets(choice) != NULL && choice[0] != '\0')
    {
        for (color = red; color <= violet; color++)
        {
            if (strcmp(choice, colors[color]) == 0)
            {
                found = TRUE;
                break;
            }
        }
        if (found == TRUE)
```

```
        printf("%s is in my color list.\n", choice);
     else
        printf("I don't know about the color %s.\n", choice);
     found = FALSE;
     puts("Next color, please:");
   }
   return 0;
}
```

This example uses the *bool.h* header file presented earlier in this chapter. By the way, you can rewrite the bool.h file using enum instead of #define.

```
/* bool.h -- enum version */
typedef enum {FALSE, TRUE} BOOLEAN;
```

> **Note:** Think C predefines FALSE and TRUE, so you would have to use, say, False and True instead in this enum definition.

Many programs use a single enum statement instead of several #define directives to create named constants.

The C Library

Originally, there was no official C library. Later, a de facto standard emerged based on the UNIX implementation of C. The ANSI C committee, in turn, developed an official standard library, largely based on the de facto standard. Recognizing the expanded C universe, the committee then sought to redefine the library so that it could be implemented on a wide variety of systems.

We've already discussed some I/O functions and string functions from the library. In this chapter we'll browse through several more. First, however, let's talk about how to use a library.

Gaining Access to the C Library

How you gain access to a C library depends on your implementation. Thus, you need to see how our more general statements apply to your system. First, there are often several different places to find library functions. For example, getchar() is usually defined as a macro in the file stdio.h, but strlen() is usually kept in a library file. Second, different systems have different ways to reach these functions. Here are three possibilities.

Automatic Access

On many systems, you just compile the program and the more common library functions are made available automatically.

Keep in mind that you should declare the function type for functions you use. Usually you can do this by including the appropriate header file. User manuals describing library functions will tell you which files to include. On some older systems, however, you may have to enter the function declarations yourself. Again, the user manual will indicate the function type.

In the past, header filenames have not been consistent among different implementations. The ANSI C Standard groups the library functions into families, with each family having a specific header file for its function prototypes.

File Inclusion

If a function is defined as a macro, then you can #include the file containing its definition. Often, similar macros will be collected in an appropriately named header file. For example, many systems have a ctype.h file containing several macros that determine the nature of a character: uppercase, digit, etc.

Library Inclusion

At some stage in compiling or linking a program, you may have to specify a library option. Even a system that automatically checks its standard library may have other libraries of functions less frequently used. These libraries will have to be requested explicitly by using a compile-time option. Note that this process is distinct from including a header file. A header file provides a function declaration or prototype. The library option tells the system where to find the function code. Clearly, we can't go through all the specifics for all systems, but these discussions should alert you to what you should look for.

Using the Library Descriptions

We haven't the space to discuss the complete library, but we will look at some representative examples. First, though, let's take a look at documentation.

You can find function documentation in a number of places. Your system may have an online manual, and integrated environments often have online help. C implementors supply printed user's guides describing library functions. Several publishers have issued reference manuals for C library functions. Some are generic in nature; some targeted towards specific implementations.

The key skill you need in reading the documentation is that of interpreting function headings. The idiom has changed with time. Here, for instance, is how fread() is listed in older UNIX documentation:

```
#include <stdio.h>

fread(ptr, sizeof(*ptr), nitems, stream)
FILE *stream;
```

First, the proper `include` file is given. No type is given for `fread()`, `ptr`, `sizeof(*ptr)`, or `nitems`. By default, then, these are taken to be type `int`, but the context makes it clear that `ptr` is a pointer. (In C's early days, pointers were handled as integers.) The `stream` argument is declared as a pointer to `FILE`. The declaration makes it look as if you are supposed to use the `sizeof` operator as the second argument. Actually, it's saying that the value of this argument should be the size of the object pointed to by `ptr`. Often, you would use `sizeof` as illustrated, but any type `int` value satisfies the syntax.

Later, the form changed to this:

```
#include <stdio.h>

int fread(ptr, size, nitems, stream;)
char *ptr;
int size, nitems;
FILE *stream;
```

Now all types are given explicitly, and `ptr` is treated as a pointer to `char`.

The ANSI C Standard provides the following description:

```
#include <stdio.h>
size_t fread(void *ptr, size_t size, size_t nmemb, FILE *stream);
```

First, it uses the new prototype format. Second, it changes some types. The `size_t` type is defined to be the unsigned integer type that the `sizeof` operator returns. Usually this is either `unsigned int` or `unsigned long`. The `stddef.h` file contains a `typedef` or a `#define` for `size_t`, as do several other files, including `stdio.h`. Many functions, including `fread()`, often incorporate the `sizeof` operator as part of an actual argument. The `size_t` type makes that formal argument match this common usage.

Also, ANSI C uses pointer-to-`void` as a kind of generic pointer for situations in which pointers to different types may be used. For instance, the actual first argument to `fread()` may be a pointer to an array of `double` or to a structure of some sort. If the actual argument is, say, a pointer-to-array-of-20-`double` and the formal argument is pointer-to-`void`, the compiler will make the appropriate type version without complaining about type clashes.

Now let's turn to some specific functions.

The Math Library

The math library contains many useful mathematical functions. The `math.h` header file provides the function declarations or prototypes for these functions.

We'll use the math library to solve a common problem: converting from *x-y* coordinates to magnitudes and angles. For example, suppose that you draw, on a gridwork, a line that transverses 4 units horizontally (the *x* value), and 3 units vertically (the *y* value). What is the length (magnitude) of the line and what is its direction? Trigonometry tells us the following:

```
magnitude = square root (x2 + y2)
```

and

```
angle = arctangent (y/x)
```

The math library provides a square root function and a couple of arctangent functions, so we can express this solution in a C program. The square root function is called `sqrt()`. This function takes a `double` argument and returns the argument's square root, also as a type `double` value.

The `atan()` function takes a double argument—the tangent—and returns the angle having that value as its tangent. Unfortunately, the `atan()` function is confused by, say, a line with *x* and *y* values of –5 and –5. Because (–5)/(–5) is 1, `atan()` would report 45<DEG>, the same as it does for a line with *x* and *y* of 5 and 5. In other words, `atan()` doesn't distinguish between a line of a given angle and one 180<DEG> in the opposite direction. (Actually, `atan()` reports in radians, not degrees; we'll discuss that conversion soon.)

Fortunately, the C library also provides the `atan2()` function. It takes two arguments: the *x* value and the *y* value. That way, it can examine the signs of *x* and *y* and figure out the correct angle. Like `atan()`, `atan2()` returns the angle in radians. To convert to degrees, multiply the resulting angle by 180 and divide by pi. Listing 16.7 illustrates these steps. It also gives you a chance to use structures and the `typedef` facility.

Listing 16.7. `convert.c.`

```c
/* convert.c -- converts rectangular coordinates to polar */
#include <stdio.h>
#include <math.h>
#define RAD_TO_DEG (180/3.141592654)
typedef struct polar_v {
    double magnitude;
    double angle;
} POLAR_V;
typedef struct rect_v {
    double x;
    double y;
} RECT_V;
POLAR_V rect_to_polar(RECT_V);
int main(void)
{
    RECT_V input;
    POLAR_V result;

    puts("Enter x,y coordinates; enter q to quit:");
```

```
    while (scanf("%lf %lf", &input.x, &input.y) == 2)
    {
        result = rect_to_polar(input);
        printf("magnitude = %0.2f, angle = %0.2f\n",
                result.magnitude, result.angle);
    }
    return 0;
}
POLAR_V rect_to_polar(RECT_V rv)
{
    POLAR_V pv;

    pv.magnitude = sqrt(rv.x * rv.x + rv.y * rv.y);
    if (pv.magnitude == 0)
        pv.angle = 0.0;
    else
        pv.angle = RAD_TO_DEG * atan2(rv.y, rv.x);
    return pv;
}
```

Here's a sample run:

```
Enter x,y coordinates; enter q to quit:
10 10
magnitude = 14.14, angle = 45.00
-12 -5
magnitude = 13.00, angle = -157.38
q
```

If, when you compile, you get a message like this:

```
Undefined:      _sqrt
```

or this:

```
'sqrt': unresolved external
```

or something similar, then your compiler-linker is not finding the math library. UNIX systems require that you instruct the linker to search the math library by using the -lm flag.

```
cc spring.c -lm
```

The General Utilities Library

The general utilities library contains a grab bag of functions, including a random number generator, searching and sorting functions, conversion functions, and memory management functions. Under ANSI C, prototypes for these functions exist in the stdlib.h header file.

The exit() and atexit() Functions

We've already used `exit()` in several examples, but the ANSI Standard has added a couple of nice features that we haven't used yet. The most important addition is that you can specify particular functions to be called when a program exits. The `atexit()` function provides this feature by *registering* the functions to be called on exit. Listing 16.8 shows how this works. It also uses the C preprocessor to make the code a bit more portable between ANSI and non-ANSI implementations.

Listing 16.8. byebye.c.

```
/* byebye.c -- atexit() example */
#include <stdio.h>
#define ANSI             /* omit for non-ANSI implementations      */

#if defined (ANSI)    /* or use __STDC__ (see text)               */
#include <stdlib.h>
#define ATEXIT(X) atexit(X)
#define VOID void
#else
void exit();
void sign_off();
#define ATEXIT(X)
#define VOID
#endif

#ifndef EXIT_SUCCESS
#define EXIT_SUCCESS 0
#endif

#ifndef EXIT_FAILURE
#define EXIT_FAILURE 1
#endif

void sign_off(VOID);
int main(VOID)
{
    int n;

    ATEXIT(sign_off);
    puts("Enter an integer:");
    if (scanf("%d",&n) != 1)
    {
        puts("That's no integer!");
        exit(EXIT_FAILURE);
    }
    printf("%d is %s.\n", n,  (n % 2 == 0)? "even" : "odd");
    exit(EXIT_SUCCESS);
    return 0;
```

```
}
void sign_off(VOID)
{
    puts("Thus terminates another magnificent program from");
    puts("SeeSaw Software!");
}
```

Here's a sample run:

```
Enter an integer:
212
212 is even.
Thus terminates another magnificent program from
SeeSaw Software!
```

Let's look at three main areas: the use of atexit(), the exit() arguments, and the ANSI, pre-ANSI adjustment.

Using *atexit()*

Here's a function that uses function pointers! To use the atexit() function, simply pass it the address of the function that you want called on exit. Because the name of a function acts as an address when used as a function argument, you use sign_off as the argument. Then atexit() registers that function in a list of functions to be executed when exit() is called. ANSI guarantees that you can place at least 32 functions on the list. Each function is added with a separate call to atexit(). When the exit() function is finally called, it executes these functions, with the last function added being executed first.

The functions registered by atexit() should, like sign_off(), be type void functions taking no arguments. Typically, they would perform housekeeping tasks such as updating a program-monitoring file or resetting environmental variables.

Using *exit()*

After exit() executes the functions specified by atexit(), it does some tidying of its own. It flushes all output streams, closes all open streams, and closes temporary files created by calls to the standard I/O function tmpfile(). Then exit() returns control to the host environment and, if possible, reports a termination status to the environment. Traditionally, UNIX programs have used 0 to indicate successful termination and nonzero to report failure. ANSI C uses the macros EXIT_SUCCESS and EXIT_FAILURE for that purpose. Thus, it may be possible to define them meaningfully on systems for which 0 and 1 make no sense as termination report values. Under ANSI C, using the exit() function in a nonrecursive main() function is equivalent to using the keyword return. However, exit() also terminates programs when used in functions other than main().

ANSI Differences

The exit() function has a prototype in the stdlib.h file, but older implementations don't have that file. Therefore, if ANSI is not defined, Listing 16.8 provides an old-fashioned function declaration for exit(). If ANSI is defined, then the program uses the prototypes in stdlib.h. Also, pre-ANSI implementations don't recognize void as an indication of no arguments. Therefore, we define VOID as void for the ANSI case and as a blank for the non-ANSI case. Similarly, we define ATEXIT(x) to be atexit(x) for the ANSI case and a blank for the non-ANSI case. We use the #if defined() #else directive to set up these cases.

Also, to give an example of #ifndef, we set up definitions for the exit value macros to be used if they hadn't been defined.

The listing shows ANSI being defined, so that version can be used in an ANSI implementation. Remove the definition, and you can compile the program on an older implementation. (However, because atexit() isn't supported in that case, the sign_off() function isn't called.)

Another possibility is to test whether __STDC__ is defined. The ANSI C Standard stipulates that implementations conforming to the Standard predefine the name __STDC__. Thus, you can use the test

```
#if defined (__STDC__)
```

without having to define that name yourself. Our method, on the other hand, also works with compilers that are not strictly conforming but that support the features used in the program.

Memory Allocation: *malloc()* and *free()*

All programs have to set aside enough memory to store the data they use. Some of this memory allocation is done automatically. For example, you can declare

```
char place[] = "Pork Liver Creek";
```

and enough memory to store that string is set aside, or you can be more explicit and ask for a certain amount of memory.

```
int plates[100];
```

This declaration sets aside 100 memory locations, each fit to store an int value.

C goes beyond this. you can allot more memory as a program runs. The main tool is the malloc() function. This function takes one argument: the number of bytes of memory desired. Then malloc() finds a suitable block of free memory and returns the address of the first byte of that block. Because char represents a byte, malloc() traditionally has been defined as type pointer-to-char. The ANSI C Standard, however, uses a new type: pointer-to-void. This type is intended to be a "generic pointer." The malloc() function can be used to return pointers to arrays, structures, etc., so normally the return value is type-cast to the proper value. Under ANSI C you still should type-cast for clarity, but assigning a pointer-to-`void` value to a pointer of another type is not considered a type clash. If `malloc()` fails to find the required space, it returns a NULL pointer.

Let's apply `malloc()` to the task of creating an array. We can use `malloc()` to request a block of storage. We also will need a pointer to keep track of where the block is in memory. For example, consider this code:

```
double * ptd;
ptd = (double *) malloc(30 * sizeof(double));
```

Here we've requested space for 30 type `double` values and have set `ptd` to point to the location. Note that we've declared `ptd` to be a pointer to a single `double` and not to a block of 30 `double` values. Remember that the name of an array is the address of its first element. Therefore, if we make `ptd` point to the first element of the block, we can use it just like an array name. That is, we can use the expression `ptd[0]` to access the first element of the block, `ptd[1]` to access the second element, and so on. As you've learned earlier, you can use pointer notation with array names, and you can use array notation with pointers.

We now have two ways to create an array.

- Declare an array and use the array name to access elements.

- Declare a pointer, call `malloc()`, and use the pointer to access elements.

You can use the second method to do something you can't do with a declared array—create a dynamic array. A dynamic array is an array allocated while the program runs and for which you can choose a size while the program runs. Suppose, for example, that n is an integer variable. You can't do the following:

```
double item[n];        /* not allowed if n is a variable */
```

You can do the following, however:

```
ptd = (double *) malloc(n * sizeof(double));   /* okay */
```

By using `malloc()` then, a program can decide what size array is needed and create it while the program runs. Listing 16.9 illustrates this possibility. It assigns the address of block of memory to the pointer `ptd`, then it uses `ptd` in the same fashion you would use an array name.

Listing 16.9. `dyn_arr.c`.

```
 /* dyn_arr.c -- dynamically allocated arr
ay */
#include <stdio.h>

#include <stdlib.h>
int main(void)
```

Listing 16.9. continued

```
{
    double * ptd;
    int max;
    int number;
    int i = 0;

    puts("What is the maximum number of entries?");
    scanf("%d", &max);
    ptd = (double *) malloc(max * sizeof (double));
    if (ptd == NULL)
    {
        puts("Memory allocation failed. Goodbye.");
        exit(EXIT_FAILURE);
    }
    /* ptd now points to an array of max elements */
    puts("Enter the values (q to quit):");
    while (i < max && scanf("%lf", &ptd[i]) == 1)
        ++i;
    printf("Here are your %d entries:\n", number = i);
    for (i = 0; i < number; i++)
    {
        printf("%7.2f ", ptd[i]);
        if (i % 7 == 6)
            putchar('\n');
    }
    if (i % 7 != 0)
        putchar('\n');
    puts("Done.");
    free(ptd);
    return 0;
}
```

Here's a sample run. In it, we entered six numbers, but the program processes just five of them because we limited the array size to 5.

```
What is the maximum number of entries?
5
Enter the values (q to quit):
20 30 35 25 40 80
Here are your 5 entries:
  20.00   30.00   35.00   25.00   40.00
Done.
```

Let's look at the code. The program finds the desired array size with the following lines:

```
puts("What is the maximum number of entries?");
scanf("%d", &max);
```

Next, the following line allocates enough space to hold the requested number of entries and then assigns the address of the block to the pointer ptd:

```
ptd = (double *) malloc(max * sizeof (double));
```

It's possible that malloc() can fail to procure the desired amount of memory. In that case, the function returns the NULL pointer, and our program terminates.

```
if (ptd == NULL)
{
    puts("Memory allocation failed. Goodbye.");
    exit(EXIT_FAILURE);
}
```

If the program clears this hurdle, then it can treat ptd as if it were the name of an array of max elements, and so it does.

Note the free() function near the end of the program. It frees memory allocated by malloc(). Think of malloc() and free() as managing a pool of memory. Each call to malloc() allocates memory for program use, and each call to free() restores memory to the pool so it can be reused. The free() function frees only the block of memory that its argument points to. The argument to free() should be a pointer to a block of memory allocated by malloc(); you can't use free() to free memory allocated by other means, such as declaring a structure or array. In this particular example, using free() isn't really necessary, for any allocated memory automatically is freed when the program terminates. In a more complex program, however, the ability to free and reuse memory can be important.

What have we gained by using a dynamic array? Primarily, we've gained program flexibility. Suppose you know that most of the time the program will need no more than 100 elements but that sometimes it would need 10,000 elements. If you declared an array, you would have to allow for the worst case and declare an array with 10,000 elements. Most of the time, that program would be wasting memory. Then, the one time you need 10,001 elements, the program will fail. You can use a dynamic array to adjust the program to fit the circumstances.

The *calloc()* Function

Another option for memory allotment is to use calloc(). A typical use would look like this:

```
long * newmem;

newmem = (long *)calloc(100, sizeof (long));
```

Like malloc(), calloc() returns a pointer-to-char in its pre-ANSI version and a pointer-to-void under ANSI. You should use the cast operator if you want to store a different type. This new function takes two arguments, both of which should be unsigned integers (type size_t under ANSI). The first argument is the number of memory cells desired. The second argument is the size of each cell in bytes. In our case, `long` uses 4 bytes, so this instruction would set up one hundred 4-byte units, using 400 bytes in all for storage.

By using `sizeof (long)` instead of 4, we made this coding more portable. It will work on those rare systems where `long` is some size other than 4.

The `calloc()` function throws in one more feature: it sets all the bits in the block to zero. (Note, however, that on some hardware systems, a floating-point value of 0 is not represented by all bits set to 0.)

The `free()` function also can be used to free memory allocated by `calloc()`.

Dynamic memory allocation is the key to many advanced programming techniques. We'll examine some in Chapter 17, "Advanced Data Representation." Your own C library probably offers several other memory-management functions, some portable, some not. You may wish to take a moment to look them over.

Storage Classes and Dynamic Memory Allocation

You may be wondering about the connect between storage classes and dynamic memory allocation. Let's look at an idealized model. You can think of a program as dividing its available memory into three separate sections: one for external, static and static external variables, one for automatic variables, and one for dynamically allocated memory.

The amount of memory needed for the external, static, and external static storage classes is known at compile time, and the data stored in this section is available as long as the program runs. Each variable of these classes comes into being when the program starts and expires when the program ends.

An automatic variable, however, comes into existence when a program enters the block of code containing the variable's definition and expires when its block of code is exited. Thus, as a program calls functions and as functions terminate, the amount of memory used by automatic variables grows and shrinks. This section of memory typically is handled as a *stack*. That means new variables are added sequentially in memory as they are created and then are removed in the opposite order as the pass away.

Dynamically allocated memory comes into existence when `malloc()` or a related function is called, and is freed when `free()` is called. Memory persistence is controlled by the programmer, not by a set of rigid rules. Thus, a memory block can be created in one function and disposed of in another function. Because of this, the section of memory used for dynamic memory allocation can wind up fragmented, that is, having unused chunks interspersed among active blocks of memory.

Chapter Summary

The C preprocessor and the C library are two important adjuncts to the C language. The *C preprocessor*, following preprocessor directives, adjusts your source code before it is compiled. The *C library* provides many functions designed to help with tasks such as input, output, file handling, memory management, sorting and searching, mathematical calculations, and string processing, to name a few.

Review Questions

1. Here are groups of one or more macros followed by a source code line that uses them. What code results in each case? Is it valid code?

   a. `#define FPM  5280      /* feet per mile */`
   `   dist = FPM * miles;`

   b. `#define FEET 4`
   `   #define POD FEET + FEET`
   `   plort = FEET * POD;`

   c. `#define SIX = 6;`
   `   nex = SIX;`

   d. `#define NEW(X) X + 5`
   `   y = NEW(y);`
   `   berg = NEW(berg) * lob;`
   `   est = NEW(berg) / NEW(y);`
   `   nilp = lob * NEW(-berg);`

2. Define a macro function that returns the minimum of two values.

3. Define a macro function that prints the representations and the values of two integer expressions. For example, it might print

   `3+4 is 7 and 4*12 is 48`

   if its arguments are 3+4 and 4*12.

4. Define a macro that prints the name, value, and address of an `int` variable in the following format:

   `name: fop;  value: 23;  address: 4016`

5. a. How would you create an enumerated type `days` that makes the abbreviations `sun`, `mon`, `tue`, `wed`, `thu`, `fri`, and `sat` stand for the integers 0–6? for the integers 1–7?

   b. How would you create a variable `visit` of that type?

6. How could you dynamically allot space to hold an array of structures?

Programming Exercises

1. Start developing a header file of preprocessor definitions that you wish to use.

2. The harmonic mean of two numbers is obtained by taking the inverses of the two numbers, averaging them, and taking the inverse of the result. Use a `#define` directive to define a macro "function" that performs this operation.

3. Polar coordinates describe a vector in terms of magnitude and the counterclockwise angle from the x-axis to the vector. Rectangular coordinates describe the same vector in terms of x and y components. See Figure 16.3. Write a program that reads the magnitude and angle (in degrees) of a vector and then displays the x and y components. The relevant equations are these:

$x = r \cos A \quad y = r \sin A$

To do the conversion, use a function that takes a structure containing the polar coordinates and returns a structure containing the rectangular coordinates (or use pointers to such structures, if you prefer).

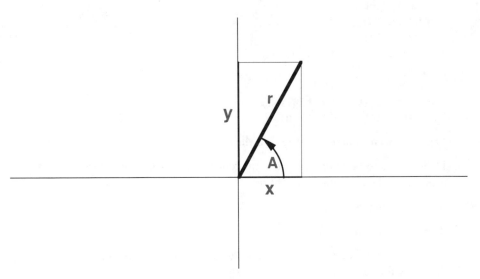

Figure 16.3. *Rectangular and polar coordinates.*

4. Modify the program in Listing 16.9 so that it processes TV show names instead of numbers and so that it saves the strings in a file. If the file already exists when the program is run, have it first load the contents into memory and then display them. Use a fixed size record for storing each string, and use `fread()` and `fwrite()`.

5. This exercise is the same as Exercise 4 except that you should use variable-sized records to store the strings. Each string should be preceded in storage by a byte

holding the length of the string. On input, the program will first read the number byte and then use that information to determine the number of bytes to read for the string.

6. The ANSI library features a `clock()` function with this description:

```
#include <time.h>
clock_t clock (void);
```

Here `clock_t` is a type defined in `time.h`. The function returns the processor time, which is given in some implementation-dependent units. (If the processor time is unavailable or cannot be represented, the function returns a value of -1.) However, `CLOCKS_PER_SEC`, also defined in `time.h`, is the number of processor time units per second. Thus, dividing the difference between two return values of `clock()` by `time.h` provides the number of seconds elapsed between the two calls. Type-casting the values to `double` before division enables you to obtain fractions of a second. Write a function that takes a `double` argument representing a desired time delay and then runs a loop until that amount of time has passed.

Advanced Data Representation

Functions
> more *malloc()*

In this chapter you learn more about using C to represent a variety of data types. You'll encounter new algorithms and increase your ability to develop programs conceptually. Also, you'll learn about abstract data types (ADTs).

Learning a computer language is like learning music, carpentry, or engineering. At first, you work with the tools of the trade, playing scales, learning which end of the hammer to hold and which end to avoid, solving countless problems involving falling, sliding, and balanced objects. Acquiring and practicing skills is what you've been doing so far in this book, learning to create variables, structures, functions, and the like.

Eventually, however, you move to a higher level in which using the tools is second nature and the real challenge is designing and creating a project. You develop an ability to see the project as a coherent whole. This chapter concentrates on that higher level. You may find the material covered here a little more challenging than the preceding chapters, but you also may find it more rewarding as it helps you move from the role of apprentice to the role of craftsperson.

We'll start by examining a vital aspect of program design: the way a program represents data. Often the most important aspect of program development is finding a good representation of the data manipulated by that program. Getting data representation right can make writing the rest of the program simple. By now you've seen C's built-in data types: simple variables, arrays, pointers, structures, and unions. However, finding the right data representation often has more to it than simply selecting one of these types. You also should think about what operations will be necessary. That is, you should decide how to store the data, and you should define what operations are valid for the data type.

This dual task of specifying how data is stored and how it can be used is something the C compiler does for basic C types. For instance, C implementations typically store both the C int type and the C pointer type as integers, but the two types have different sets of valid operations. You can multiply one integer by another, but you can't multiply a pointer by a pointer. Alternatively, you can use the * operator to dereference a pointer, but that operation is meaningless for an integer. The C language defines the valid operations for its fundamental types, and it won't let you do things like multiply two pointers.

When you design a scheme to represent data, for instance, by using a structure, you may need to define the valid operations yourself. In C you can do so by designing C functions to represent the desired operations. In short, designing a data type consists of deciding two matters: how to store the data and how to manipulate the data.

The reason is that defining a type has two parts. The first part is deciding how to store the data, and the second part is defining what operations are valid for the data type. For instance, C implementations typically store both the C int type and the C pointer type as integers, but the two types have different sets of valid operations. For example, you can multiply one integer by another, but you can't multiply a pointer by a pointer. You can use the * operator to dereference a pointer, but that operation is meaningless for an integer. The C language defines the valid operations for its fundamental types. However, when you design a scheme to represent data, you may need to define the valid operations yourself. In C you can do so by designing C functions to represent the desired operations. In short then, designing a data type consists of deciding on how to store the data and of designing a set of functions to manage the data.

You also will look at some *algorithms*, recipes for manipulating data. As a programmer, you will acquire a repertoire of such recipes that you'll apply over and over again to similar problems.

This chapter looks into the process of designing data types, a process that matches algorithms to data representations. In it, you'll meet some common data forms such as the queue, the list, and the binary search tree.

You'll also be introduced to the concept of the abstract data type (ADT). An ADT packages methods and data representations together in a way that is problem-oriented rather than language-oriented. Once you've designed an ADT, you easily can reuse it in different circumstances. Understanding ADTs prepares you conceptually for entering the world of object-oriented programming (OOP) and the C++ language.

Exploring Data Representation

Let's begin by thinking about data. Suppose you had to create an address book program. What data form would you use to store information? Because there's a variety of information associated with each entry, it makes sense to represent each entry with a structure. How do you represent several entries? With a standard array of structures? With a dynamic array? With some other form? Should the entries be alphabetized? Should you be able to search through the entries by zip code? by area code? The actions you want to perform might affect how you decide to store the information. In short, you have a lot of design decisions to make before plunging into coding.

How would you represent a bit-mapped graphics image that you wish to store in memory? A bit-mapped image is one in which each pixel on the screen is set individually. In the days of black-and-white screens, you could use one computer bit (1 or 0) to represent one pixel (on or off), hence the name *bit-mapped*. With color monitors, it takes more than one bit to describe a single pixel. For instance, you can get 256 colors if you dedicate 8 bits to each pixel. Now the industry is moving toward 65536 colors (16 bits per pixel) and 16,777,216 colors (24 bits per pixel). If you have 16 million colors and if your monitor has a resolution of 1024 x 768, you'll need 18.9 million bits (2.25 Mb) to represent a single screen of bit-mapped graphics. Is this the way to go, or can you develop a way of compressing the information? Should this compression be *lossless* (no data lost) or *lossy* (relatively unimportant data lost)? Again, you have a lot of design decisions to make before plunging into coding.

Let's tackle a particular case of representing data. Suppose you want to write a program that enables you to enter a list of all the movies (including videotapes) you've seen in a year. For each movie, you'd like to record a variety of information, such as the title, the year it was released, the director, the lead actors, the length, the kind of film (comedy, science fiction, romance, drivel, etc.), your evaluation, and so on. That suggests using a structure for each film and an array of structures for the list. To simplify matters, let's limit the structure to two members: the film title and your evaluation, a ranking on a 0 to 10 scale. Listing 17.1 shows a bare-bones implementation using this approach.

Listing 17.1. `films1.c.`

```
/* films1.c -- using an array of structures */
#include <stdio.h>
#define TSIZE      45      /* size of array to hold title   */
#define FMAX        5      /* maximum number of film titles */
struct film {
   char title[TSIZE];
   int rating;
};
int main(void)
{
   struct film movies[FMAX];
   int i = 0;
   int j;

   puts("Enter first movie title:");
   while (i < FMAX && gets(movies[i].title) != NULL &&
      movies[i].title[0] != '\0')
   {
      puts("Enter your rating <0-10>:");
      scanf("%d", &movies[i++].rating);
      while(getchar() != '\n')
         continue;
      puts("Enter next movie title (empty line to stop):");
   }
   if (i == 0)
      printf("No data entered. ");
   else
      printf ("Here is the movie list:\n");

   for (j = 0; j < i; j++)
      printf("Movie: %s  Rating: %d\n", movies[j].title,
         movies[j].rating);
   printf("Bye!\n");
   return 0;
}
```

The program creates an array of structures and proceeds to fill the array with data entered by the user. Entry continues until the array is full (the FMAX test), until end of file (the NULL test) is reached, or until the user presses the Enter key at the beginning of a line (the '\0' test).

This formulation has some problems. First, the program most likely will waste a lot of space, for most movies don't have titles 40 characters long, but some movies do have long titles, titles like *The Discreet Charm of the Bourgeoisie* and *Won Ton Ton, The Dog Who Saved Hollywood.* Second, many people will find the limit of 5 movies a year too restrictive. Of course, we can increase that limit, but what would be a good value? Some people see 500 movies a year, so we could increase FMAX to 500, but that still might be too small for some, yet it might waste enormous amounts of memory for others. Also, some compilers set a default limit for the amount of memory available for automatic storage class variables such as `movies`, and such a large array may exceed that value. You can fix that by making the array a static or external array or by instructing the compiler to use a larger stack, but that's not fixing the real problem.

The real problem here is that our data representation is too inflexible. We have to make decisions at compile time that are better made at runtime. This suggests switching to a data representation that uses dynamic memory allocation. We could try something like this:

```
#define TSIZE  45          /* size of array to hold title  */
struct film {
    char title[TSIZE];
    int rating;
};
...
int n, i;
struct film * movies;      /* pointer to a structure       */
...
printf("Enter the maximum number of movies you'll enter:\n");
scanf("%d", &n);
movies = (struct film *) malloc(n * sizeof(struct film));
```

Here, as in the preceding chapter, we can use the pointer `movies` just as if it were an array name:

```
while (i < FMAX && gets(movies[i].title) != NULL &&
        movies[i].title[0] != '\0')
```

By using `malloc()`, we can postpone determining the number of elements until the program runs. Thus the program need not allocate 500 elements if only 20 are needed. However, it puts the burden on the user to supply a correct value for the number of entries.

Beyond the Array to the Linked List

Ideally, we'd like to be able to add data indefinitely (or until the program runs out of memory) without specifying in advance how many entries we'll make and without committing the program to allocating huge chunks of memory unnecessarily. We can do this by calling `malloc()` after each entry and allocating just enough space to hold the new entry. If the user enters 3 films, the program calls `malloc()` 3 times. If the user enters 300 films, the program calls `malloc()` 300 times.

This fine idea raises a new problem. To see what it is, compare calling `malloc()` once, asking for enough space for 300 `film` structures, and calling `malloc()` 300 times, each time asking for enough space for 1 `film` structure. The first case allocates the memory as one contiguous memory block and all we need to keep track of the contents is a single pointer-to-`struct film` variable that points to the first structure in the block. Simple array notation lets the pointer access each structure in the block, as shown in the preceding code segment. The problem with the second approach is that there is no guarantee that consecutive calls to `malloc()` yield adjacent blocks of memory. This means the structures won't necessarily be stored contiguously. (See Figure 17.1.) Thus, instead of storing one pointer to a block of 300 structures, we need to store 300 pointers, one for each independently allocated structure!

```
struct film * movie;

movie = (struct film *) malloc(5*sizeof(struct film);
```

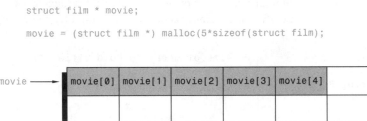

```
int i;
struct film * movies[s];

for (i = 0; i << 5; itt)
movies[i] = (struct films *) malloc(sizeof(struct films));
```

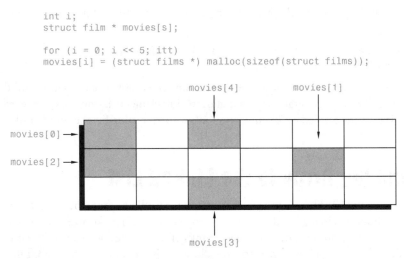

Figure 17.1. *Allocating structures in a block versus allocating them individually.*

One solution, which we won't use, is to create a large array of pointers and assign values to the pointers one by one as new structures are allocated.

```
#define TSIZE   45          /* size of array to hold titles    */
#define FMAX    500         /* maximum number of film titles   */
struct film {
```

```
    char title[TSIZE];
    int rating;
};
...
struct film * movies[FMAX];    /* array of pointers to structures */
int i;
...
movies[i] = (struct film *) malloc (sizeof (struct film));
```

This approach saves a lot of memory if you don't use the full allotment of pointers, because an array of 500 pointers takes much less memory than an array of 500 structures. It still wastes the space occupied by unused pointers, however, and it still imposes a 500-structure limit.

There's a better way. Each time we use malloc() to allocate space for a new structure, we can also allocate space for a new pointer. "But," you say, "then I need another pointer to keep track of the newly allocated pointer, and that needs a pointer to keep track of it, and so on." The trick to avoiding this potential problem is to redefine the structure so that each structure includes a pointer to the next structure. Then, each time we create a new structure, we can store its address in the preceding structure. In short, we need to redefine the film structure this way:

```
#define TSIZE  45       /* size of array to hold titles  */
struct film {
    char title[TSIZE];
    int rating;
    struct film * next;
};
```

True, a structure can't contain in itself a structure of the same type, but it can contain a pointer to a structure of the same type. Such a definition is the basis for defining a *linked list*, which is a list in which each item contains information describing where to find the next item.

Before looking at C code for a linked list, let's take a conceptual walk through such a list. Suppose that a user enters Modern Times as a title and 10 as a rating. The program would allocate space for a film structure, copy the string Modern Times into the title member, and set the rating member to 10. To indicate that no structure follows this one, the program would set the next member pointer to NULL. (NULL, recall, is a symbolic constant defined in the *stdio.h* file and representing the null pointer.) Of course, we need to keep track of where the first structure is stored. We can do this by assigning its address to a separate pointer that we'll refer to as the head pointer. The head pointer points to the first item in a linked list of items. Figure 17.2 represents how this structure looks. (The empty space in the title member is suppressed to save space in the figure.)

```
#define TSIZE 45
struct film {
    char title[TSIZE];
    int rating;
    struct film * next;
};
struct film * head;
```

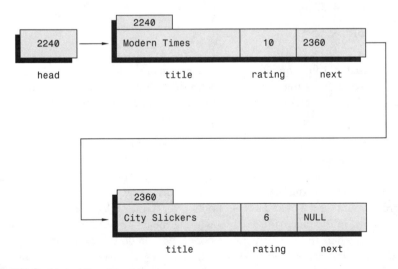

Figure 17.2. *First item in a linked list.*

Now suppose the user enters a second movie and rating, for example, `City Slickers` and 6. The program allocates space for a second `film` structure, storing the address of the new structure in the `next` member of the first structure (overwriting the NULL previously stored there) so that the `next` pointer of one structure points to the following structure in the linked list. Then the program copies `City Slickers` and 6 to the new structure and sets its `next` member to NULL, indicating that this is now the last structure in the list. Figure 17.3 represents this list of two items.

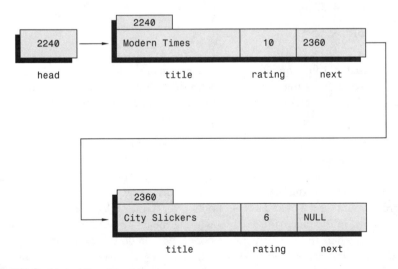

Figure 17.3. *Linked list with two items.*

Each new movie will be handled the same way. Its address will be stored in the preceding structure, the new information goes into the new structure, and its `next` member is set to NULL, setting up a linked list like that shown in Figure 17.4.

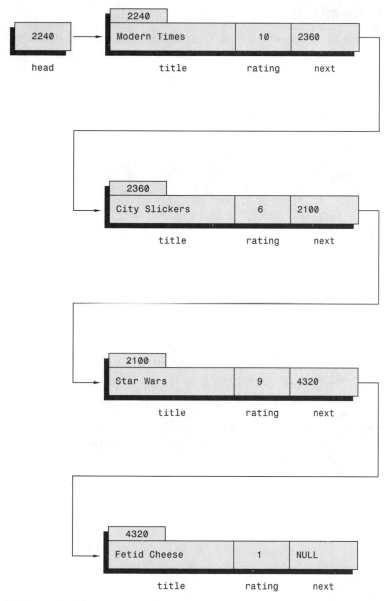

Figure 17.4. *Linked list with several items.*

Suppose you want to display the list. Each time you display an item, you can use the address stored in the corresponding structure to locate the next item to be displayed. For this scheme to work, however, you need a pointer to keep track of the very first item in the list, because no structure in the list stores the address of the first item. Fortunately, we've already accomplished this with the head pointer.

579

Using a Linked List

Now that you have a picture of how a linked list works, let's implement it. Listing 17.2 modifies Listing 17.1 so that it uses a linked list instead of an array to hold the movie information.

Listing 17.2. films2.c.

```
/* films2.c -- using a linked list of structures */
#include <stdio.h>
#include <stdlib.h>          /* has the malloc prototype    */
#include <string.h>          /* has the strcpy prototype    */
#define TSIZE    45          /* size of array to hold title */
struct film {
   char title[TSIZE];
   int rating;
   struct film * next;
};

int main(void)
{
   struct film * head = NULL;
   struct film * prev, * current;
   char input[TSIZE];

   puts("Enter first movie title:");
   while (gets(input) != NULL && input[0] != '\0')
   {
      current = (struct film *) malloc(sizeof(struct film));
      if (head == NULL)        /* first structure      */
         head = current;
      else                     /* subsequent structures */
         prev->next = current;
      current->next = NULL;
      strcpy(current->title, input);
      puts("Enter your rating <0-10>:");
      scanf("%d", &current->rating);
      while(getchar() != '\n')
         continue;
      puts("Enter next movie title (empty line to stop):");
      prev = current;
   }
   if (head == NULL)
      printf("No data entered. ");
   else
      printf ("Here is the movie list:\n");
   current = head;
   while (current != NULL)
   {
      printf("Movie: %s  Rating: %d\n", current->title, current->rating);
```

```
        current = current->next;
    }
    printf("Bye!\n");
    return 0;
}
```

The program performs two tasks using the linked list. First, it constructs the list and fills it with the incoming data. Second, it displays the list. This is the simpler task, so let's look at it first.

Displaying a List

The idea is to begin by setting a pointer (call it current) to point to the first structure. Because the head pointer (call it head) already points there, this code suffices:

```
current = head;
```

Then we can use pointer notation to access the members of that structure.

```
printf("Movie: %s  Rating: %d\n", current->title, current->rating);
```

The next step is to reset the current pointer to point to the next structure in the list. That information is stored in the next member of the structure, so this code accomplishes the task:

```
current = current->next;
```

Once this is accomplished, repeat the whole process. When the last item in the list is displayed, current will be set to NULL, for that's the value of the next member of the final structure. We can use that fact to terminate the printing. Here's all the code *films2.c* uses to display the list:

```
while (current != NULL)
{
    printf("Movie: %s  Rating: %d\n", current->title, current->rating);
    current = current->next;
}
```

Why not just use head instead of creating a new pointer current to march through the list? Because using head would change the value of head, and the program no longer would have a way to find the beginning of the list.

Creating the List

Creating the list involves three steps:

1. Use malloc() to allocate enough space for a structure.

2. Store the address of the structure.

3. Copy the correct information into the structure.

There's no point in creating a structure if none is needed, so the program uses temporary storage (the `input` array) to get the user's choice for a movie name. If the user simulates EOF from the keyboard or enters an empty line, the input loop quits.

```
while (gets(input) != NULL && input[0] != '\0')
```

If there is input, the program requests space for a structure and assigns its address to the pointer variable `current`.

```
current = (struct film *) malloc(sizeof(struct film));
```

The address of the very first structure should be stored in the pointer variable `head`. The address of each subsequent structure should be stored in the `next` member of the structure that precedes it. Thus, the program needs a way to know whether it's dealing with the first structure or not. A simple way is to initialize the `head` pointer to NULL when the program starts. Then the program can use the value of `head` to decide what to do.

```
if (head == NULL)        /* first structure       */
    head = current;
else                     /* subsequent structures */
    prev->next = current;
```

Here `prev` is a pointer that points to the structure allocated the previous time.

Next, we have to set the structure members to the proper values. In particular, we should set the `next` member to NULL to indicate that the current structure is the last one in the list. We should copy the film title from the `input` array to the `title` member, and we should get a value for the `rating` member. The following code does these things:

```
current->next = NULL;
strcpy(current->title, input);
puts("Enter your rating <0-10>:");
scanf("%d", &current->rating);
```

Finally, we should prepare the program for the next cycle of the input loop. In particular, we need to set `prev` to point to the current structure, for that will become the previous structure after the next movie name is entered and the next structure is allocated. The program sets this pointer at the end of the loop:

```
prev = current;
```

Does it work? Here is a sample run:

```
Enter first movie title:
Desperately Seeking Susan
Enter your rating <0-10>:
7
Enter next movie title (empty line to stop):
The Duelists
Enter your rating <0-10>:
8
```

```
Enter next movie title (empty line to stop):
Devil Dog: The Hound of Hell
Enter your rating <0-10>:
1
Enter next movie title (empty line to stop):

Here is the movie list:
Movie: Desperately Seeking Susan   Rating: 7
Movie: The Duelists   Rating: 8
Movie: Devil Dog: The Hound of Hell   Rating: 1
Bye!
```

Afterthoughts

The *films2.c* program is a bit skimpy. For example, it fails to check whether malloc()
finds the requested memory. It doesn't have any provisions for deleting items from the list.
These failings are fixable. For instance, we can add code that checks whether malloc()'s
return value is NULL (the sign it failed to obtain the desired memory). If the program
needs to delete entries, we can write some more code to do that. This approach to solving
problems and adding features as the need arises isn't the best programming method. In
particular, it tends to intermingle coding details and the conceptual model. For instance,
in our example program, the conceptual model is that we add items to a list. The program
obscures that interface by pushing details such as malloc() and the current->next
pointer into the foreground. It would be nice if we could write a program in a way that
made it obvious that we're adding something to a list and in which bookkeeping details
like calling memory-management functions and setting pointers were hidden. By making a
fresh start, we can meet these goals. Let's see how.

Abstract Data Types (ADTs)

In programming, you try to match the data type to the needs of a programming problem.
For instance, you would use the int type to represent the number of shoes you own and
the float or double type to represent your average cost per pair of shoes. In the movie
examples, the data formed a list of items, each of which consisted of a movie name (a C
string) and rating (an int). No basic C type matches that description, so we defined a
structure to represent individual items, and then we devised a couple methods for tying
together a series of structures to form a list. In essence, we used C capabilities to design a
new data type that matched our needs, but we did so in an unsystematic fashion. Now
we'll take a more systematic approach to defining types.

What constitutes a type? A type specifies two kinds of information: a set of properties
and a set of operations. For instance, the int type's property is that it represents an integer
value and thus shares the properties of integers. The allowed arithmetic operations are
changing the sign, adding two ints, subtracting two ints, multiplying two ints, dividing
one int by another, and taking the modulus of one int with respect to another. When
you declare a variable to be an int, you're saying that these and only these operations can
affect it.

> **Integer Properties**
>
> Behind the C int type is a more abstract concept, that of the integer. Mathematicians can, and do, define the properties of integers in a formal abstract manner. For instance, if N and M are integers, then N + M = M + N, or for every two integers N and M there is an integer S such that N + M = S. If N + M = S and if N + Q = S, M = Q. We can think of mathematics as supplying the abstract concept of the integer and of C as providing an implementation of that concept. For example, C provides a means of storing an integer and of performing integer operations such as addition and multiplication. Note that providing support for arithmetic operations is an essential part of representing integers. The int type would be much less useful if all you could do was store a value but not use it in arithmetic expressions. Note also that the implementation doesn't do a perfect job of representing integers. For instance, there are an infinity of integers, but a two-byte int can represent only 65,536 of them; don't confuse the abstract idea with a particular implementation.

Suppose you want to define a new data type. First, you have to provide a way to store the data, perhaps by designing a structure. Second, you have to provide ways of manipulating the data. For instance, consider the *films2.c* program (Listing 17.2). It provides a linked set of structures to hold the information and provides code for adding information and displaying information. This program, however, doesn't do these things in a way that makes it clear that we were creating a new type. What should we have done?

Computer science has developed a very successful way to define new data types. It's a three-step process that moves from the abstract to the concrete.

1. Provide an abstract description of the type's properties and of the operations you can perform on the type. This description shouldn't be tied to any particular implementation. It shouldn't even be tied to a particular programming language. Such a formal abstract description is called an *abstract data type* (ADT).

2. Develop a programming interface that implements the ADT. That is, indicate how to store the data and describe a set of functions that perform the desired operations. In C, for instance, you might provide a structure definition along with prototypes for functions to manipulate the structures. These functions play the same role for the user-defined type that C's built-in operators play for the fundamental C types. Someone who wants to use the new type will use this interface for her or his programming.

3. Write code to implement the interface. This step is essential, of course, but the programmer using the new type need not be aware of the details of the implementation.

Let's work through an example to see how this process works. Because we've already invested some effort into the movie listing example, let's redo it using the new approach.

Getting Abstract

Basically, all we need for the movie project is a list of items. Each item contains a movie name and a rating. We need to be able to add new items to the end of the list, and we need to be able to display the contents of the list. Let's call the abstract type that will handle these needs a *list*. What properties should a list have? Clearly, a list should be able to hold a sequence of items. That is, a list can hold several items, and these items are arranged in some kind of order, so we can speak of the first item in a list or of the second item or of the last item. Next, the list type should support operations such as adding an item to the list. Here are some useful operations:

- Initializing a list to empty
- Adding an item to the end of a list
- Determining whether the list is empty
- Determining whether the list is full
- Determining how many items are in the list
- Visiting each item in a list in order to perform some action, such as displaying the item

We don't need any further operations for our project, but a more general list of operations for lists might include the following:

- Inserting an item anywhere in the list
- Removing an item from the list
- Retrieving an item from the list (list left unaltered)
- Replacing one item in the list with another
- Searching for an item in the list

Our informal, but abstract, definition of a list, then, is that it is a data object capable of holding a sequence of items and to which one can apply any of the preceding operations. This definition doesn't state what kind of items can be stored in the list. It doesn't specify whether an array or a linked set of structures or some other data form be used to hold the items. It doesn't dictate what method to use, for example, to find the number of elements in a list. These matters are all details left to the implementation.

To keep the example simple, we'll adopt a simplified list as our abstract data type, one that embodies only the features needed for the movie project. Here's a summary of the type:

Type Name:	Simple List
Type Properties:	Can hold a sequence of items

Type Operations:	Initialize list to empty
	Determine if list is empty
	Determine if list is full
	Determine number of items in the list
	Add item to end of list
	Traverse list, processing each item in list

The next step is develop a C-language interface for the simple list ADT.

Building an Interface

The interface for the simple list has two parts. The first part describes how the data will be represented. The second part describes functions that implement the ADT operations. For instance, there will be functions for adding an item to a list and for reporting the number of items in the list. The interface design should parallel the ADT description as closely as possible. Thus, it should be expressed in terms of some general Item type instead of in terms of some specific type, such as int or struct film. One way to do this is to use C's typedef facility to define Item as the needed type.

```
#define TSIZE    45      /* size of array to hold title   */
struct film
{
   char title[TSIZE];
   int rating;
};

typedef struct film Item;
```

Then we can use the Item type for the rest of our definitions. If we later want a list of some other form of data, we can redefine the Item type and leave the rest of the interface definition unchanged.

Having defined Item, we now have to decide how to store items of that type. This step really belongs to the implementation stage, but making a decision now will make the example easier to follow. The linked structure approach worked pretty well in the *films2.c* program, so let's adapt it.

```
typedef struct node
{
   Item item;
   struct node * next;
} Node;
typedef Node * List;
```

In a linked list implementation, each link is called a *node*. Each node contains information that forms the contents of the list along with a pointer to the next node. To emphasize this terminology, we've used the tag name node for a node structure, and we've used typedef to make Node the type name for a struct node structure. Finally, to manage a linked list, we need a pointer to its beginning, and we've used typedef to make List the name for a pointer of this type. Thus, the declaration

```
List movies;
```

establishes movies as a pointer suitable for referring to a linked list.

Is this the only way to define the List type? No. For instance, we could incorporate a variable to keep track of the number of entries.

```
typedef struct list
{
   Node * head;    /* pointer to head of list      */
   int size;       /* number of entries in list    */
} List;            /* alternative definition of list */
```

We could add a second pointer to keep track of the end of the list. Later, we'll look at an example that does that. For now, let's stick to the first definition of a List type. The important point is that you should think of the declaration

```
List movies;
```

as establishing a list, not as establishing a pointer to a node or as establishing a structure. The exact data representation of movies is an implementation detail that should be invisible at the interface level.

For example, a program should initialize the head pointer to NULL when starting out, but you should not use code like this:

```
movies = NULL;
```

Why not? Because later you may find you like the structure implementation of a List type better, and that would require the following initializations:

```
movies.next = NULL;
movies.size = 0;
```

Anyone using the List type shouldn't have to worry about such details. Instead, they should be able do something along the following lines:

```
InitializeList(movies);
```

Programmers only need to know that they should use the InitializeList() function to initialize a list. They don't have to know the exact data implementation of a List variable. This is an example of *data hiding*, the art of concealing details of data representation from the higher levels of programming.

To guide the user, we can provide a function prototype along these lines:

```
/* operation:      initialize a list                  */
/* preconditions:  plist points to a list             */
/* postconditions: the list is initialized to empty   */
void InitializeList(List * plist);
```

There are three points you should notice. First, the comments outline preconditions, that is, conditions that should hold before the function is called. Here, for instance, you need a list to initialize. Second, the comments outline postconditions, that is, conditions that should hold after the function executes. Finally, the function uses a pointer to a list instead of a list as its argument. Thus, the function call would be this:

```
InitializeList(&movies);
```

The reason is that C passes arguments by value, so the only way a C function can alter a variable in the calling program is by using a pointer to that variable. Here the restrictions of the language make the interface deviate slightly from the abstract description.

The C way to tie all the type and function information into a single package is to place the type definitions and function prototypes (including precondition and postcondition comments) in a header file. This file should provide all the information a programmer needs to use the type. Listing 17.3 shows a header file for our simple list type. It defines a particular structure as the Item type, then defines Node in terms of Item and List in terms of Node. The functions representing list operations then use Item types and List types as arguments. If the function needs to modify an argument, it uses a pointer to the corresponding type instead of using the type directly. We capitalized each function name as a way of marking them as part of an interface package.

Listing 17.3. list.h.

```
/* list.h -- header file for a simple list type */

/* program-specific declarations */

#define TSIZE       45    /* size of array to hold title  */
struct film
{
   char title[TSIZE];
   int rating;
};

/* general type definitions */

typedef struct film Item;
typedef enum boolean {False, True} BOOLEAN;
typedef struct node
{
   Item item;
   struct node * next;
} Node;
typedef Node * List;

/* function prototypes */

/* operation:       initialize a list                              */
```

```
/* preconditions:      plist points to a list                      */
/* postconditions:     the list is initialized to empty            */
void InitializeList(List * plist);

/* operation:          determine if list is empty                  */
/* preconditions:      l is an initialized list                    */
/* postconditions:     function returns True if list is empty      */
/*                     and returns False otherwise                 */
BOOLEAN EmptyList(List l);

/* operation:          determine if list is full                   */
/* preconditions:      l is an initialized list                    */
/* postconditions:     function returns True if list is full       */
/*                     and returns False otherwise                 */
BOOLEAN FullList(List l);

/* operation:          determine number of items in list           */
/* preconditions:      l is an initialized list                    */
/* postconditions:     function returns number of items in list    */
unsigned int ListItems(List l);

/* operation:          add item to end of list                     */
/* preconditions:      item is an item to be added to list         */
/*                     plist points to an initialized list         */
/* postconditions:     if possible, function adds item to end      */
/*                     of list and returns True; otherwise the     */
/*                     function returns False                      */
BOOLEAN AddItem(Item item, List * plist);

/* operation:          apply a function to each item in list       */
/* preconditions:      l is an initialized list                    */
/*                     pfun points to a function that takes an     */
/*                     Item argument and has no return value       */
/* postcondition:      the function pointed to by pfun is          */
/*                     executed once for each item in the list     */
void Traverse (List l, void (* pfun)(Item item) );
```

One of the prototypes in the header file is a bit more complex than the others.

```
/* operation:          apply a function to each item in list       */
/* preconditions:      l is an initialized list                    */
/*                     pfun points to a function that takes an     */
/*                     Item argument and has no return value       */
/* postcondition:      the function pointed to by pfun is          */
/*                     executed once for each item in the list     */
void Traverse (List l, void (* pfun)(Item item) );
```

The argument pfun is a pointer to a function. In particular, it is a pointer to a function that takes an item as an argument and which has no return value. As you may recall from Chapter 14, "Structures and Other Data Forms," you can pass a pointer to a function as an argument to a second function, and the second function then can use the pointed-to function. Here, for instance, we can let pfun point to a function that displays an item. The Traverse() function then would apply this function to each item in the list, thus displaying the whole list.

It would have been more stylistically consistent to use

```
typedef enum boolean {FALSE, TRUE} Boolean;
```

instead of the following:

```
typedef enum boolean {False, True} BOOLEAN;
```

However, the use of capitalized FALSE and TRUE conflicted with predefined terms used by the Think C compiler.

Using the Interface

Our claim is that you should be able to use this interface to write a program without knowing any further details, for example, without knowing how the various functions are written. Let's write a new version of the movie program right now before we write the supporting functions. Because the interface is in terms of List and Item types, the program should be phrased in those terms. Here's one possible plan:

> create a List variable
> create an Item variable
> initialize the list to empty
> while the list isn't full and while there's more input
>   read the input into the Item variable
>   add the item to the end of the list
> visit each item in the list and display it

The program shown in Listing 17.4 follows this basic plan, with some error-checking. Note how it makes use of the interface described in the list.h file (Listing 17.3). Also note that the listing provides code for a showmovies() function that conforms to the prototype required by Traverse(). Thus, the program can pass the pointer showmovies to Traverse() so that Traverse() can apply the showmovies() function to each item in the list. (Recall that the name of a function is a pointer to the function.)

Listing 17.4. films3.c.

```
/* films3.c -- using and ADT-style linked list */
#include <stdio.h>
#include <stdlib.h>     /* prototype for exit() */
#include "list.h"
void showmovies(Item item);

int main(void)
```

```
{
    List movies;
    Item temp;

    InitializeList(&movies);
    if (FullList(movies))
    {
        fprintf(stderr,"No memory available! Bye!\n");
        exit(1);
    }
    puts("Enter first movie title:");
    while (gets(temp.title) != NULL && temp.title[0] != '\0')
    {
        puts("Enter your rating <0-10>:");
        scanf("%d", &temp.rating);
        while(getchar() != '\n')
            continue;
        if (AddItem(temp, &movies)== False)
        {
            fprintf(stderr,"Problem allocating memory\n");
            break;
        }
        if (FullList(movies))
        {
            puts("The list is now full.");
            break;
        }
        puts("Enter next movie title (empty line to stop):");
    }
    if (EmptyList(movies))
        printf("No data entered. ");
    else
    {
        printf ("Here is the movie list:\n");
        Traverse(movies, showmovies);
    }
    printf("Bye!\n");
    return 0;
}

void showmovies(Item item)
{
        printf("Movie: %s  Rating: %d\n", item.title,
            item.rating);
}
```

Implementing the Interface

Of course, we still have to implement the List interface. The C approach is to collect the function definitions in a file called *list.c*. Thus, the complete program consists of three files: *list.h*, which defines the data structures and provides prototypes for the user interface, *list.c*, which provides the function code to implement the interface, and *films3.c*, which is a source code file that applies the list interface to a particular programming problem. Listing 17.5 shows one possible implementation of *list.c*. To run the program, you must compile both *films3.c* and *list.c* and link them. (You may wish to review the discussion in Chapter 9, "Functions," on compiling multiple-file programs.) Together, the files *list.h*, *list.c*, and *films3.c* constitute a complete program. See Figure 7.5.

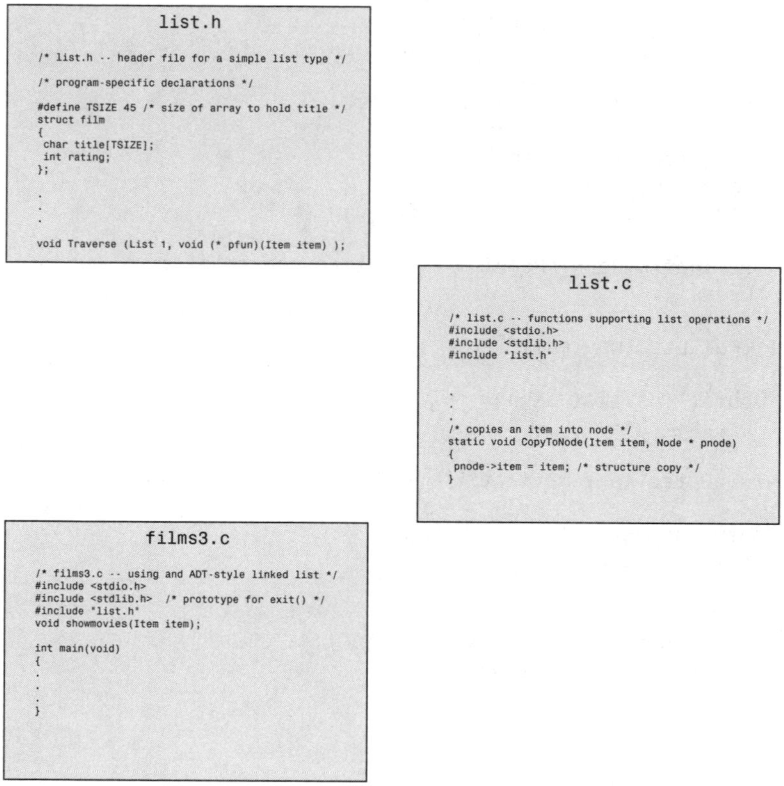

```
                       list.h

/* list.h -- header file for a simple list type */

/* program-specific declarations */

#define TSIZE 45 /* size of array to hold title */
struct film
{
 char title[TSIZE];
 int rating;
};
   .
   .
   .
void Traverse (List 1, void (* pfun)(Item item) );
```

```
                          list.c

/* list.c -- functions supporting list operations */
#include <stdio.h>
#include <stdlib.h>
#include "list.h"

   .
   .
   .
/* copies an item into node */
static void CopyToNode(Item item, Node * pnode)
{
  pnode->item = item; /* structure copy */
}
```

```
                      films3.c

/* films3.c -- using and ADT-style linked list */
#include <stdio.h>
#include <stdlib.h>  /* prototype for exit() */
#include "list.h"
void showmovies(Item item);

int main(void)
{
   .
   .
   .
}
```

Figure 7.5. *The three parts of a program package.*

Listing 17.5. `list.c`.

```
/* list.c -- functions supporting list operations */
#include <stdio.h>
#include <stdlib.h>
#include "list.h"

/* local functions */
```

```c
static void CopyToNode(Item item, Node * pnode);

/* interface functions */
/* set the list to empty    */
void InitializeList(List * plist)
{
    * plist = NULL;
}

/* returns true if list is empty */
BOOLEAN EmptyList(List l)
{
    if (l == NULL)
        return True;
    else
        return False;
}

/* returns true if list is full */
BOOLEAN FullList(List l)
{
    Node * pt;
    BOOLEAN full;

    pt = (Node *) malloc(sizeof(Node));
    if (pt == NULL)
        full = True;
    else
        full = False;
    free(pt);
    return full;
}

/* returns number of nodes */
unsigned int ListItems(List l)
{
    unsigned int count = 0;

    while (l != NULL)
    {
        ++count;
        l = l->next;    /* set l to next node */
    }
     return count;
}

/* creates node to hold item and adds it to the end of */
/* the list pointed to by plist (slow implementation)  */
BOOLEAN AddItem(Item item, List * plist)
{
    Node * pnew;
```

continues

Listing 17.5. continued

```c
    Node * scan = *plist;

    pnew = (Node *) malloc(sizeof(Node));
    if (pnew == NULL)
        return False;  /* quit function on failure  */

    CopyToNode(item, pnew);
    pnew->next = NULL;
    if (scan == NULL)      /* empty list, so place */
        * plist = pnew;    /* pnew at head of list */
    else
    {
        while (scan->next != NULL)
            scan = scan->next;  /* find end of list  */
        scan->next = pnew;      /* add pnew to end    */
    }
    return True;
}

/* visit each node and execute function pointed to by pfun */
void Traverse (List l, void (* pfun)(Item item) )
{
    while (l != NULL)
    {
        (*pfun)(l->item);   /* apply function to item in list */
        l = l->next;
    }
}

/* copies an item into a node */
static void CopyToNode(Item item, Node * pnode)
{
    pnode->item = item;  /* structure copy */
}
```

Program Notes

The *list.c* file has many interesting points. For one, it illustrates when you might use static storage class functions. As described in Chapter 13, "Storage Classes and Program Development," static functions are known only in the file in which they are defined. When implementing an interface, sometimes you may find it convenient to write auxiliary functions that aren't part of the official interface. For instance, our example uses a function CopyToNode() to copy a type Item value to a type Item variable. Because this function is part of the implementation but not part of the interface, we hid it in the *list.c* file by making it static. Now, examine the other functions.

The `InitializeList()` function initializes a list to empty. In our implementation, that means setting a type `List` variable to NULL. As mentioned earlier, this requires passing a pointer to the `List` variable to the function.

The `EmptyList()` function is quite simple, but it does depend on the list variable being set to NULL when the list is empty. Thus, it's important to initialize a list before first using the `EmptyList()` function. Also, if you were to extend the interface to include deleting items, you should make sure that the deletion function resets the list to empty when the last item is deleted. Because this function doesn't alter the list, we don't need to pass a pointer as argument, so the argument is a `List` instead of a pointer to a `List`.

With a linked list, the size of the list is limited by the amount of memory available. The `FullList()` function attempts to allocate enough space for a new item. If it fails, the list is full. If it succeeds, it has to free the memory it just allocated so that it will be available for a real item.

The `ListItems()` function uses the usual linked-list algorithm to transverse the list, counting items as it goes.

```c
unsigned int ListItems(List l)
{
    unsigned int count = 0;

    while (l != NULL)
    {
       ++count;
       l = l->next;    /* set l to next node */
    }
     return count;
}
```

The `AddItem()` function is the most elaborate of the group.

```c
BOOLEAN AddItem(Item item, List * plist)
{
    Node * pnew;
    Node * scan = *plist;

    pnew = (Node *) malloc(sizeof(Node));
    if (pnew == NULL)
        return False;          /* quit function on failure */

    CopyToNode(item, pnew);
    pnew->next = NULL;
    if (scan == NULL)          /* empty list, so place    */
       * plist = pnew;         /* pnew at head of list     */
    else
    {
       while (scan->next != NULL)
          scan = scan->next;   /* find end of list         */
```

```
        scan->next = pnew;      /* add pnew to end        */
    }
    return True;
}
```

The first thing the AddItem() function does is allocate space for a new node. If this succeeds, the function uses CopyToNode() to copy the item to the node. Then it sets the next member of the node to NULL. This, recall, indicates that the node is the last node in the linked list. Finally, after creating the node and assigning the correct values to its members, the function attaches the node to the end of the list. If the item is the first item added to the list, the program sets the head pointer to the first item. (Remember, AddItem() is called with the address of the head pointer as its second argument, so * plist is the value of the head pointer.) Otherwise, the code marches through the linked list until it finds the item having its next member set to NULL. That node is currently the last node, so the function resets its next member to point to the new node.

Good programming practice would dictate that you call FullList() before attempting to add an item to the list. However, a user may fail to observe this dictate, so AddItem() checks for itself whether malloc() has succeeded. Also, it's possible that a user might do something else to allocate memory between calling FullList() and calling AddItem(), so it's best to check whether malloc() worked.

Finally, the Traverse() function is similar to the ListItems() function with the addition of applying a function to each item in the list.

```
void Traverse (List l, void (* pfun)(Item item) )
{
    while (l != NULL)
    {
        (*pfun)(l->item);       /* apply function to item in list */
        l = l->next;
    }
}
```

Recall that l->item represents the data stored in a node, and the l->next identifies the next node in the linked list. For example, the function call

```
Traverse(movies, showmovies);
```

applies the showmovies() function to each item in the list.

Contemplating Our Work

Take a little time now to evaluate what the ADT approach has done for us. First, compare Listing 17.2 with Listing 17.4. Both programs use the same fundamental method (dynamic allocation of linked structures) to solve the movie listing problem, but Listing 17.2 exposes all the programming plumbing, putting malloc() and prev->next in public view. Listing 17.4, on the other hand, hides these details and expresses the program in a language that relates directly to the tasks. That is, it talks about creating a list and adding items to the list, not about calling memory functions or resetting pointers. In short, Listing

17.4 expresses the program in terms of the problem to be solved, not in terms of the low-level tools needed to solve the problem. The ADT version is oriented to the concerns of the end user and is much easier to read.

Next, the *list.h* and *list.c* files together constitute a reusable resource. If you need another simple list, just haul out these files. Suppose you need to store an inventory of your relatives: names, relationships, addresses, and phone numbers. First, you would go to the *list.h* file and redefine the Item type.

```
typedef struct itemtag
{
    char fname[14];
    char lname [24];
    char relationship[36];
    char address [60];
    char phonenum[20];
}   Item;
```

Next...well, that's all you have to do in this case, for all the simple list functions are defined in terms of the Item type. In some cases, you would also have to redefine the CopyToNode() function. For example, if an item were an array, you couldn't copy it by assignment.

Another important point is that the user interface is defined in terms of abstract list operations, not in terms of some particular set of data representation and algorithms. This leaves you free to fiddle with the implementation without having to redo the final program. For instance, the current AddItem() function is a bit inefficient because it always starts at the beginning of the list, then searches for the end. You can fix this by keeping track of the end of the list. For instance, you can redefine the List type this way:

```
typedef struct list
{
    Node * head;      /* points to head of list */
    Node * end;       /* points to end of list  */
} List;
```

Of course, you then would have to rewrite the list-processing functions using this new definition, but you wouldn't have to change a thing in Listing 17.4. This sort of isolation of implementation from final interface is particularly useful for large programming projects. It's called *data hiding*, for the detailed data representation is hidden from the final user.

Note that our particular ADT doesn't even force you to implement the simple list as a linked list. Here's another possibility:

```
#define MAXSIZE 100
typedef struct list
{
    Item entries[MAXSIZE];  /* array of items          */
    int items;              /* number of items in list */
} List;
```

Again, this would require rewriting the *list.c* file, but the program using the list need not be changed.

Getting Queued with an ADT

The abstract data type approach to programming in C, as you've seen, involves the following three steps:

1. Describing a type, including its operations, in an abstract, general fashion

2. Devising a function interface to represent the new type

3. Writing detailed code to implement the interface

You've seen this approach applied to a simple list. Now, apply it to something slightly more complex, the queue.

Defining the Queue Abstract Data Type

A queue is a list with two special properties. First, new items can be added only to the end of the list. In this respect the queue is like our simple list. Second, items can be removed from the list only at the beginning. You can visualize a queue as a line of people buying tickets to a theater. You join the line at the end, and you leave the line at the front, after purchasing your tickets. A queue is a *first in, first out* (FIFO) data form, just the way a movie line is (if no one cuts into the line). Once again, let's frame an informal, abstract definition, as shown here:

Type Name:	queue
Type Properties:	Can hold an ordered sequence of items
Type Operations:	Initialize queue to empty
	Determine whether queue is empty
	Determine whether queue if full
	Determine number of items in the queue
	Add item to rear of queue
	Remove and recover item from front of queue

Defining an Interface

The interface definition will go into a file called *queue.h*. We'll use C's `typedef` facility to create names for two types: `Item` and `Queue`. The exact implementation for the corresponding structures should be part of the *queue.h* file, but conceptually, designing the structures is part of the detailed implementation stage. For the moment, just assume that the types have been defined and concentrate on the function prototypes.

First, consider initialization. This will involve altering a `Queue` type, so the function should take the address of a `Queue` as an argument.

```
void InitializeQueue (Queue * pq);
```

Next, determining if the queue is empty or full involves a function that should return a true or false value. Because the function doesn't alter the queue, it can take a `Queue` argument. On the other hand, it can be faster and less memory intensive to just pass the address of a `Queue`, depending on how large a `Queue`-type object is. Try that approach this time. To indicate that these functions don't change a queue, we can use the `const` qualifier.

```
BOOLEAN FullQueue(const Queue * pq);
BOOLEAN EmptyQueue(const Queue * pq);
```

Paraphrasing, the pointer `pq` points to a `Queue` data object that cannot be altered through the agency of `pq`. We can define a similar prototype for a function that returns the number of items in a queue.

```
int QueueItems(const Queue * pq);
```

Adding an item to the end of the queue involves identifying the item and the queue. This time the queue is altered, so using a pointer is necessary, not optional. The function could be type `void`, or we can use the return value to indicate whether or not the operation of adding an item succeeded. Let's take the second approach.

```
BOOLEAN EnQueue(Item item, Queue * pq);
```

Finally, removing an item can be done several ways. If the item is defined as a structure or as one of the fundamental types, it could be returned by the function. The function argument could be either a `Queue` or a pointer to a `Queue`. Thus, one possible prototype is this:

```
Item DeQueue(Queue q);
```

However, the following prototype is a bit more general.

```
BOOLEAN DeQueue(Item * pitem, Queue * pq);
```

The item removed from the queue goes to the location pointed to by the `pitem` pointer, and the return value indicates whether the operation succeeded.

Implementing the Interface Data Representation

The first step is deciding what C data form to use for a queue. One possibility is an array. The advantages to arrays are that they're easy to use and that adding an item to end of an array's filled portion is easy. The problem comes with removing an item from the front of the queue. In the analogy of people in a ticket line, removing an item from the front of the queue consists of copying the value of the first element of the array (simple), then moving each item left in the array one element towards the front. That is easy to program, but it wastes a lot of computer time. See Figure 17.6.

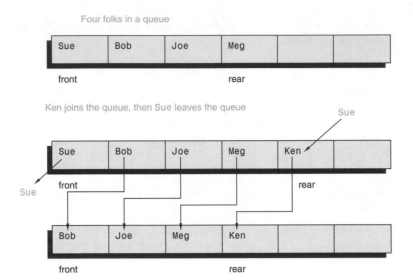

Figure 17.6. *Using an array as a queue.*

A second way to handle the removal problem in an array implementation is to leave the remaining elements where they are and, instead, change which element we call the front. See Figure 17.7. This method's problem is that the vacated elements become dead space and so the available space in the queue keeps decreasing.

A clever solution to the dead space problem is to make the queue *circular*. This means wrapping around from the end of the array to the beginning. That is, consider the first element of the array as immediately following the last element so that when you reach the end of the array, you can start adding items to the beginning elements if they have been vacated. See Figure 17.8. You can imagine drawing the array on a strip of paper, then pasting one end of the array to the other to form a band. Of course, you now have to do some fancy bookkeeping to make sure the end of the queue doesn't pass the front.

Yet another solution is to use a linked list. This has the advantage that removing the front item doesn't require moving all the other items. Instead, you just reset the front pointer to point to the new first element. Because we've already been working with linked lists, we'll take this tack. To test our ideas, we'll start with a queue of integers.

```
typedef int Item;
```

A linked list is built from nodes, so let's define a node next.

```
typedef struct node
{
   Item item;
   struct node * next;
} Node;
```

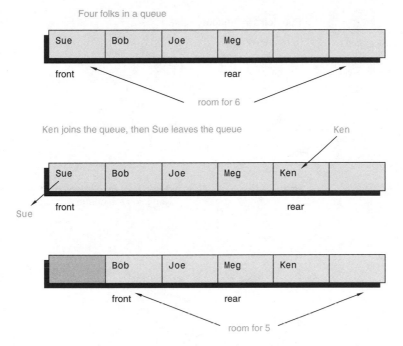

Four folks in a queue

Ken joins the queue, then Sue leaves the queue

Figure 17.7. *Redefining the front element.*

For the queue, we need to keep track of the front and rear items. We can use pointers to do this. Also, we can use a counter to keep track of the number of items in a queue.

```
typedef struct queue
{
    Node * front;    /* pointer to front of queue */
    Node * rear;     /* pointer to rear of queue  */
    int items;       /* number of items in queue  */
} Queue;
```

Note that a Queue is a structure with three members, so our earlier decision to use pointers to queues rather than entire queues as arguments is a time and space saver.

Next, let's think about the size of a queue. With a linked list, the amount of available memory sets the limit, but often a much smaller size is more appropriate. For example, you might use a queue to simulate airplanes waiting to land at an airport. If the number of waiting planes gets too large, new arrivals might be rerouted to other airports. We'll set a maximum queue size of 10. Listing 17.6 contains the various definitions and prototypes for the queue interface. It leaves open the exact definition of the Item type. When using the interface, you would insert the appropriate definition for your particular program.

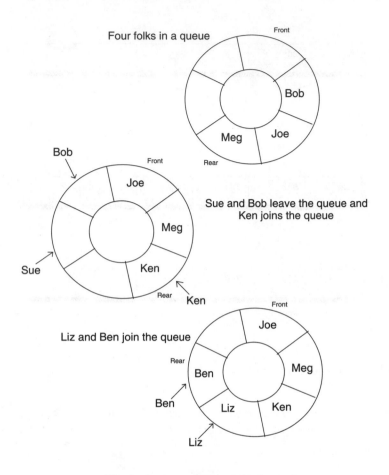

Figure 17.8. *A circular queue.*

Listing 17.6. queue.h.

```
/* queue.h -- interface for a queue */

/* INSERT ITEM TYPE HERE */
/* FOR EXAMPLE, typedef int Item; */
/* OR typedef struct item {int gumption; int charisma;} Item; */

#define MAXQUEUE 10

typedef enum boolean {False, True} BOOLEAN;

typedef struct node
```

```
{
   Item item;
   struct node * next;
} Node;

typedef struct queue
{
   Node * front;  /* pointer to front of queue   */
   Node * rear;   /* pointer to rear of queue    */
   int items;     /* number of items in queue    */
} Queue;

/* operation:      initialize the queue                     */
/* precondition:   pq points to a queue                     */
/* postcondition:  queue is initialized to being empty      */
void InitializeQueue(Queue * pq);

/* operation:      check if queue is full                   */
/* precondition:   pq points to previously initialized queue */
/* postcondition:  returns True if queue is full, else False */
BOOLEAN FullQueue(const Queue * pq);

/* operation:      check if queue is empty                  */
/* precondition:   pq points to previously initialized queue */
/* postcondition:  returns True if queue is empty, else False */
BOOLEAN EmptyQueue(const Queue *pq);

/* operation:      determine number of items in queue       */
/* precondition:   pq points to previously initialized queue */
/* postcondition:  returns number of items in queue         */
int QueueItems(const Queue * pq);

/* operation:      add item to rear of queue                */
/* precondition:   pq points to  previously initialized queue */
/*                 item is to be placed at rear of queue     */
/* postcondition:  if queue is not empty, item is placed at  */
/*                 rear of queue and function returns         */
/*                 True; otherwise, queue is unchanged and    */
/*                 function returns False                     */
BOOLEAN EnQueue(Item item, Queue * pq);

/* operation:      remove item from front of queue          */
/* precondition:   pq points to previously initialized queue */
/* postcondition:  if queue is not empty, item at head of    */
/*                 queue is copied to *pitem and deleted from */
/*                 queue, and function returns True; if the   */
/*                 operation empties the queue, the queue is  */
/*                 reset to empty. If the queue is empty to   */
/*                 begin with, queue is unchanged and the     */
/*                 function returns False                     */
BOOLEAN DeQueue(Item *pitem, Queue * pq);
```

Implementing the Interface Functions

Now we can get down to writing the interface code. First, initializing a queue to empty means setting the front and rear pointers to NULL and setting the item count (the `items` member) to 0.

```
void InitializeQueue(Queue * pq)
{
    pq->front = pq->rear = NULL;
    pq->items = 0;
}
```

Next, the `items` member makes it easy to check for a full queue or empty queue and to return the number of items in a queue.

```
BOOLEAN FullQueue(const Queue * pq)
{
    return pq->items == MAXQUEUE;
}

BOOLEAN EmptyQueue(const Queue * pq)
{
    return pq->items == 0;
}

int QueueItems(const Queue * pq)
{
    return pq->items;
}
```

Adding an item to the queue involves the following steps:

1. Creating a new node

2. Copying the item to the node

3. Setting the node's `next` pointer to NULL, identifying the node as the last in the list

4. Setting the current rear node's `next` pointer to point to the new node, linking the new node to the queue

5. Setting the `rear` pointer to the new node, making it easy to find the last node

6. Adding 1 to the item count

Also, the function has to handle two special cases. First, if the queue is empty, the `front` pointer should be set to point to the new node. That's because when there is just one node, that node is both the front and the rear of the queue. Second, if the function is unable to obtain memory for the node, it should do something. Because we envision using small queues, such failure should be rare, so we'll simply have the function terminate the program if the program runs out of memory.

```
BOOLEAN EnQueue(Item item, Queue * pq)
{
    Node * pnew;

    if (FullQueue(pq))
        return False;
    pnew = (Node *) malloc( sizeof(Node));
    if (pnew == NULL)
    {
        fprintf(stderr,"Unable to allocate memory!\n");
        exit(1);
    }
    CopyToNode(item, pnew);
    pnew->next = NULL;
    if (EmptyQueue(pq))
        pq->front = pnew;              /* item goes to front      */
    else
        pq->rear->next = pnew;        /* link at end of queue    */
    pq->rear = pnew;                  /* record location of end */
    pq->items++;                      /* one more item in queue */
    return True;
}
```

The `CopyToNode()` function is a static function to handle copying the item to a node.

```
static void CopyToNode(Item item, Node * pn)
{
    pn->item = item;
}
```

Removing an item from the front of the queue involves the following steps:

1. Copying the item to a waiting variable

2. Freeing the memory used by the vacated node

3. Resetting the front pointer to the next item in the queue

4. Resetting the front and rear pointers to NULL if the last item is removed

5. Decrementing the item count

Here's code that does these things:

```
BOOLEAN DeQueue(Item * pitem, Queue * pq)
{
    Node * pt;

    if (EmptyQueue(pq))
        return False;
    CopyToItem(pq->front, pitem);
    pt = pq->front;
    pq->front = pq->front->next;
    free(pt);
```

```
    pq->items--;
    if (pq->items == 0)
        pq->rear = NULL;
    return True;
}
```

There are a couple of pointer facts you should note. First, the code doesn't explicitly set the front pointer to NULL when the last item is deleted. That's because it already sets the front pointer to the next pointer of the node being deleted. If that node is the last node, its next pointer is NULL, so the front pointer gets set to NULL. Second, the code uses a temporary pointer pt to keep track of the deleted node's location. That's because the official pointer to the first node (pq->front) gets reset to point to the next node, so without the temporary pointer, the program would lose track of which block of memory to free.

Keeping Your ADT Pure

Once you've defined an ADT interface, you should use only the functions of the interface to handle the data type. Note, for instance, that Dequeue() depends on the EnQueue() function doing its job of setting pointers correctly and setting the next pointer of the rear node to NULL. If, in a program using the ADT, you decided to manipulate parts of the queue directly, you might mess up the coordination between the functions in the interface package.

Listing 17.7 shows all the functions of the interface, including the CopyToItem() function used in EnQueue().

Listing 17.7. queue.c.

```c
/* queue.c -- the Queue type implementation*/
#include <stdio.h>
#include <stdlib.h>
#include "queue.h"

/* local functions */
static void CopyToNode(Item item, Node * pn);
static void CopyToItem(Node * pn, Item * pi);

void InitializeQueue(Queue * pq)
{
    pq->front = pq->rear = NULL;
    pq->items = 0;
}

BOOLEAN FullQueue(const Queue * pq)
{
```

```
      return pq->items == MAXQUEUE;
}

BOOLEAN EmptyQueue(const Queue * pq)
{
    return pq->items == 0;
}

int QueueItems(const Queue * pq)
{
    return pq->items;
}

BOOLEAN EnQueue(Item item, Queue * pq)
{
    Node * pnew;

    if (FullQueue(pq))
        return False;
    pnew = (Node *) malloc( sizeof(Node));
    if (pnew == NULL)
    {
        fprintf(stderr,"Unable to allocate memory!\n");
        exit(1);
    }
    CopyToNode(item, pnew);
    pnew->next = NULL;
    if (EmptyQueue(pq))
        pq->front = pnew;
    else
        pq->rear->next = pnew;
    pq->rear = pnew;
    pq->items++;
    return True;
}

BOOLEAN DeQueue(Item * pitem, Queue * pq)
{
    Node * pt;

    if (EmptyQueue(pq))
        return False;
    CopyToItem(pq->front, pitem);
    pt = pq->front;
    pq->front = pq->front->next;
    free(pt);
    pq->items--;
    if (pq->items == 0)
        pq->rear = NULL;
    return True;
}
```

continues

Listing 17.7. continued

```
static void CopyToNode(Item item, Node * pn)
{
    pn->item = item;
}

static void CopyToItem(Node * pn, Item * pi)
{
    *pi = pn->item;
}
```

Testing the Queue

It's a good idea to test a new design, like our queue package, before inserting it into a critical program. One approach to testing is writing a short program, sometimes called a *driver*, whose sole purpose is to test the package. For instance, Listing 17.8 uses a queue that enables you to add and delete integers. Before using the program, add the following line to *queue.h*:

```
typedef int item;    /* place in queue.h file */
```

Remember, too, that you have to link *queue.c* and *use_q.c*.

Listing 17.8. use.qc.

```
/* use_q.c -- driver testing the Queue interface */
#include <stdio.h>
#include "queue.h"

int main(void)
{
    Queue line;
    Item temp;
    char ch;

    InitializeQueue(&line);
    puts("Testing the Queue interface. Type a to add a value,");
    puts("type d to delete a value, and type q to quit.");
    while ((ch = getchar()) != 'q')
    {
        if (ch != 'a' && ch != 'd')    /* ignore other input */
            continue;
        if ( ch == 'a')
        {
            printf("Integer to add: ");
            scanf("%d", &temp);
            if (!FullQueue(&line))
            {
```

```
            printf("Putting %d into queue\n", temp);
            EnQueue(temp,&line);
        }
        else
            puts("Queue is full!");
    }
    else
    {
        if (EmptyQueue(&line))
            puts("Nothing to delete!");
        else
        {
            DeQueue(&temp,&line);
            printf("Removing %d from queue\n", temp);
        }
    }
    printf("%d items in queue\n", QueueItems(&line));
    puts("Type a to add, d to delete, q to quit:");
    }
    puts("Bye!");

    return 0;
}
```

Here is a sample run. You should also test to see that the implementation behaves correctly when the queue is full.

```
Testing the Queue interface. Type a to add a value,
type d to delete a value, and type q to quit.
a
Integer to add: 40
Putting 40 into queue
1 items in queue
Type a to add, d to delete, q to quit:
a
Integer to add: 20
Putting 20 into queue
2 items in queue
Type a to add, d to delete, q to quit:
a
Integer to add: 55
Putting 55 into queue
3 items in queue
Type a to add, d to delete, q to quit:
d
Removing 40 from queue
2 items in queue
Type a to add, d to delete, q to quit:
d
Removing 20 from queue
1 items in queue
```

```
Type a to add, d to delete, q to quit:
d
Removing 55 from queue
0 items in queue
Type a to add, d to delete, q to quit:
d
Nothing to delete!
0 items in queue
Type a to add, d to delete, q to quit:
q
Bye!
```

Simulating with a Queue

Well, the queue works! Now let's do something more interesting with it. Many real-life situations involve queues. For instance, customers queue in banks and in supermarkets, airplanes queue at airports, and tasks queue in multitasking computer systems. We can use our queue package to simulate such situations.

Suppose, for example, that Sigmund Landers has set up an advice booth in a mall. Customers can purchase one, two, or three minutes of advice. To ensure a free flow of foot traffic, mall regulations limit the number of customers waiting in line to ten (conveniently equal to our maximum queue size.) Suppose people show up randomly and that the time they wish to spend in consultation is spread randomly over the three choices (one, two, or three minutes). How many customers, on average, will Sigmund handle an hour? How long, on average, will customers have to wait? How long, on average, will the line be? These are the sort of questions a queue simulation can answer.

First, let's decide on what to put in the queue. We can describe each customer in terms of the time at which he or she joins the queue and in terms of how many minutes of consultation he or she wants. This suggests the following definition for the `Item` type:

```
typedef struct item
{
    long arrive;       /* the time when a customer joins the queue   */
    int processtime;   /* the number of consultation minutes desired */
} Item;
```

To convert the queue package to handle this structure, rather than the `int` type the last example used, all you have to do is replace the former `typedef` for `Item` with the one shown here. Once that's done, you don't have to worry about the detailed mechanics of a queue. Instead, you can proceed to the real problem—simulating Sigmund's waiting line.

Here's one approach. Let time move in one-minute increments. Each minute check to see whether a new customer has arrived. If a customer arrives and the queue isn't full, add the customer to the queue. This involves recording in an `Item` structure the customer's arrival time and the amount of consultation time the customer wants, then adding the item to the queue. If the queue is full, however, turn the customer away. For bookkeeping, keep track of the total number of customers and the total number of turnaways (people who can't get in line because it is full).

Next, process the front of the queue. That is, if the queue isn't empty and if Sigmund isn't occupied with a previous customer, remove the item at the front of the queue. The item, recall, contains the time when the customer joined the queue. By comparing this time with the current time, we get the number of minutes the customer has been in the queue. The item also contains the number of consultation minutes the customer wants, and this determines how long Sigmund will be occupied with the new customer. Use a variable to keep track of this waiting time. If Sigmund is busy, no one is "dequeued." However, the variable keeping track of the waiting time should be decremented.

The core code can look like this, where each cycle corresponds to one minute of activity:

```
for (cycle = 0; cycle < cyclelimit; cycle++)
{
    if (newcustomer(min_per_cust))
    {
        if (FullQueue(&line))
            turnaways++;
        else
        {
            customers++;
            temp = customertime(cycle);
            EnQueue(temp, &line);
        }
    }
    if (wait_time <= 0 && !EmptyQueue(&line))
    {
        DeQueue (&temp, &line);
        wait_time = temp.processtime;
        line_wait += cycle - temp.arrive;
        served++;
    }
    if (wait_time > 0)
        wait_time--;
    sum_line += QueueItems(&line);
}
```

Here are the meanings of some of the variables and functions:

* min_per_customer is the average number of minutes between customer arrivals

* newcustomer() uses the C rand() function to determine whether a customer shows up during this particular minute

* turnaways is the number of arrivals turned away

* customers is the number of arrivals who join the queue

* temp is an Item variable describing the new customer

- customertime() sets the arrive and processtime members of the temp structure

- wait_time is the number of minutes remaining until Sigmund finishes with the current client

- line_wait is the cumulative time spent in line by all customers to date

- served is the number of clients actually served

- sum_line is the cumulative length of the line to date

Think of how much messier and more obscure this code would look if it were sprinkled with malloc() and free() functions and pointers to nodes. Having the queue package enables us to concentrate on the simulation problem, not on programming details.

Listing 17.9 shows the complete code for the mall advice booth simulation. It uses the standard rand(), srand(), and clock() functions to generate random values, following the method suggested in Chapter 13, "Storage Classes and Program Development." To use the program, remember to update the Item definition in *queue.h* with the following:

```
typedef struct item
{
    long arrive;        /* the time when a customer joins the queue  */
    int processtime;    /* the number of consultation minutes desired */
} Item;
```

Also remember to link the code for *mall.c* with *queue.c*.

Listing 17.9. mall.c.

```
/* mall.c -- use the Queue interface */
#include <stdio.h>
#include <stdlib.h>     /* for rand() and srand() */
#include <time.h>       /* for clock()            */
#include "queue.h"
#define MIN_PER_HR 60.0

BOOLEAN newcustomer(double x);   /* is there a new customer? */
Item customertime(long when);    /* set customer parameters  */

int main(void)
{
    Queue line;
    Item temp;                   /* new customer data                */
    int hours;                   /* hours of simulation              */
    int perhour;                 /* average # of arrival per hour    */
    long cycle, cyclelimit;      /* loop counter, limit              */
    long turnaways = 0;          /* turned away by full queue        */
    long customers = 0;          /* joined the queue                 */
    long served = 0;             /* served during the simulation     */
    long sum_line = 0;           /* cumulative line length           */
    int wait_time = 0;           /* time until Sigmund is free       */
```

```
double min_per_cust;      /* average time between arrivals */
long line_wait = 0;       /* cumulative time in line       */

InitializeQueue(&line);
srand(clock());           /* random initializing of rand() */
puts("Case Study: Sigmund Lander's Advice Booth");
puts("Enter the number of simulation hours:");
scanf("%d", &hours);
cyclelimit = MIN_PER_HR * hours;
puts("Enter the average number of customers per hour:");
scanf("%d", &perhour);
min_per_cust = MIN_PER_HR / perhour;

for (cycle = 0; cycle < cyclelimit; cycle++)
{
    if (newcustomer(min_per_cust))
    {
        if (FullQueue(&line))
            turnaways++;
        else
        {
            customers++;
            temp = customertime(cycle);
            EnQueue(temp, &line);
        }
    }
    if (wait_time <= 0 && !EmptyQueue(&line))
    {
        DeQueue (&temp, &line);
        wait_time = temp.processtime;
        line_wait += cycle - temp.arrive;
        served++;
    }
    if (wait_time > 0)
        wait_time--;
    sum_line += QueueItems(&line);
}

if (customers > 0)
{
    printf("customers accepted: %ld\n", customers);
    printf("  customers served: %ld\n", served);
    printf("         turnaways: %ld\n", turnaways);
    printf("average queue size: %.2f\n",
        (double) sum_line / cyclelimit);
    printf(" average wait time: %.2f minutes\n",
        (double) line_wait / served);
}
else
    puts("No customers!");
```

continues

Listing 17.9. continued

```c
    return 0;
}

/* x = average time, in minutes, between customers     */
/* return value is true if customer shows up this minute */
BOOLEAN newcustomer(double x)
{
    if (rand() * x / RAND_MAX < 1)
        return True;
    else
        return False;
}

/* when is the time at which the customer arrives      */
/* function returns an Item structure with the arrival time */
/* set to when and the processing time set to a random value */
/* in the range 1 - 3                                  */
Item customertime(long when)
{
    Item cust;

    cust.processtime = rand() % 3 + 1;
    cust.arrive = when;
    return cust;
}
```

The program enables you to specify the number of hours to simulate and the average number of customers per hour. Choosing a large number of hours gives good average values, and choosing a small number of hours shows the sort of random variation you can get from hour to hour. The following runs illustrate these points. Note that the average queue sizes and wait times for 80 hours are about the same as for 800 hours, but that the two one-hour samples differ quite a bit from each other and from the long-term averages. That's because smaller statistical samples tend to have larger relative variations.

```
Case Study: Sigmund Lander's Advice Booth
Enter the number of simulation hours:
80
Enter the average number of customers per hour:
20
customers accepted: 1635
  customers served: 1635
        turnaways: 0
average queue size: 0.48
 average wait time: 1.42 minutes
Case Study: Sigmund Lander's Advice Booth
Enter the number of simulation hours:
800
```

```
Enter the number of customers per hour:
20
customers accepted: 16015
  customers served: 16015
       turnaways: 1
average queue size: 0.45
 average wait time: 1.35 minutes
Case Study: Sigmund Lander's Advice Booth
Enter the number of simulation hours:
1
Enter the average number of customers per hour:
20
customers accepted: 20
  customers served: 20
       turnaways: 0
average queue size: 0.23
 average wait time: 0.70 minutes
Case Study: Sigmund Lander's Advice Booth
Enter the number of simulation hours:
1
Enter the average number of customers per hour:
20
customers accepted: 22
  customers served: 22
       turnaways: 0
average queue size: 0.75
 average wait time: 2.05 minutes
```

Another way to use the program is to keep the numbers of hours constant but to try different average numbers of customers per hour. Here a few sample runs exploring this variation:

```
Case Study: Sigmund Lander's Advice Booth
Enter the number of simulation hours:
80
Enter the average number of customers per hour:
25
customers accepted: 1964
  customers served: 1964
       turnaways: 5
average queue size: 1.34
 average wait time: 3.27 minutes
Case Study: Sigmund Lander's Advice Booth
Enter the number of simulation hours:
80
Enter the average number of customers per hour:
30
customers accepted: 2376
  customers served: 2373
       turnaways: 94
average queue size: 5.85
 average wait time: 11.83 minutes
```

Note how the average wait time takes a sharp upturn as the frequency of customers increases. The average wait for 20 customers per hour (80-hour simulation) was 1.42 minutes. It climbs to 3.27 minutes at 25 customers per hour and soars to 11.83 minutes at 30 customers an hour. Also, the number of turnaways climbs from 0 to 5 to 94. Sigmund could use this sort of analysis to decide whether he needs a second booth.

The Linked List Versus the Array

Many programming problems, such as creating a list or a queue, can be handled with a linked list—by which we mean a linked sequence of dynamically allocated structures—or with an array. Each form has its strengths and weaknesses, so the choice of which to use depends on the particular requirements of a problem. The following list summarizes the qualities of linked lists and arrays:

Table 17.1. Comparing arrays to linked lists.

Data Form	Pros	Cons
Array	Directly supported by C Provides random	Size determined at compile time Inserting and deleting elements is time-consuming
Linked List	Size determined during runtime Inserting and deleting elements is quick	No random access user Must provide programming support

Take a closer look at the process of inserting and deleting elements. To insert an element in an array, you have to move elements to make way for the new element, as shown in Figure 17.9. The closer to the front the new element goes, the more elements have to be moved. To insert a node in a linked list, however, you just have to assign values to two pointers, as shown in Figure 17.10. Similarly, removing an element from an array involves a wholesale relocation of elements, but removing a node from a linked list involves resetting a pointer and freeing the memory used by the deleted node.

Next, consider how to access the members of a list. With an array, you can use the array index to access any element immediately. This is called *random access*. With a linked list, you have to start at the top of the list, and then move from node to node until you get to the node you want, which is termed *sequential access*. You can have sequential access with an array, too. Just increment the array index by one step each to move through the array in order. For some situations, sequential access is sufficient. For instance, if you want to display every item in a list, sequential access is fine. Other situations greatly favor random access, as you will see next.

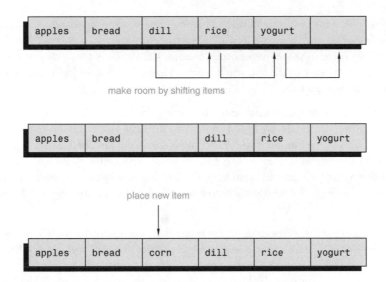

make room by shifting items

place new item

Figure 17.9. *Inserting an element into an array.*

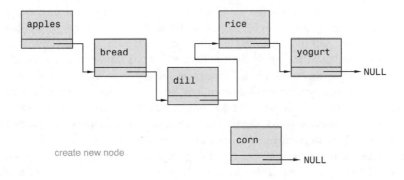

create new node

reset pointers

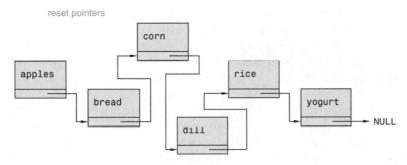

Figure 17.10. *Inserting an element into a linked list.*

Suppose you want to search a list for a particular item. One algorithm is to start at the beginning of list and to search through it in sequence, called a *sequential search*. If the items aren't arranged in some sort of order, a sequential search is about all you can do. If the sought-for item isn't in the list, you'll have to look at every item in the list before concluding the item isn't there.

You can improve the sequential search by sorting the list first. That way, you can terminate a search if you haven't found an item by the time you reach an item that would come later. For instance, suppose you're seeking *Susan* in an alphabetical list. Starting from the top of the list, you look at each item and eventually encounter *Sylvia* without finding *Susan*. At that point you can quit searching because *Susan*, if in the list, would precede *Sylvia*. On the average, this would cut search times in half for attempting to find items not in the list.

With an ordered list, you can do much better than a sequential search by using the *binary search* method. Here's how it works. First, call the list item you want to find the *goal* and assume the list is in alphabetical order. Next, pick the item halfway down the list and compare it to the goal. If the two are the same, the search is over. If the list item comes before the goal alphabetically, the goal, if it's in the list, must be in the second half. If the list item follows the goal alphabetically, the goal must be in the first half. Either way, the comparison rules out half the list as a place to search. Next, apply the method again. That is, choose an item midway in the half of the list that remains. Again, this either finds the item or rules out half the remaining list. Proceed in this fashion until you find the item or until you've eliminated the whole list. See Figure 17.11. This method is quite efficient. Suppose, for example, that the list is 127 items long. A sequential search, on the average, would take 64 comparisons before finding an item or ruling out its presence. The binary search method, on the other hand, will take at most 7 comparisons. The first comparison prunes the possible matches to 63, the second comparison cuts the possible matches to 31, and so on, until the sixth comparison cuts down the possibilities to 1. The seventh comparison then determines if the one remaining choice is the goal or not. In general, n comparisons let you process an array with $2\ n - 1$ members, so the advantage of a binary search over a sequential search gets greater the longer the list is.

It's simple to implement a binary search with an array, for you can use the array index to determine the midpoint of any list or subdivision of a list. Add the subscripts of the initial and final elements of the subdivision and divide by 2. For instance, in a list of 100 elements, the first index is 0, the final index is 99, and our initial guess would be (0 + 99) / 2, or 49 (integer division). If the element having index 49 were too far down the alphabet, the correct choice must be in the range 0–48, so the next guess would be (0 + 48) / 2, or 24. If element 24 were too early in the alphabet, the next guess would be (25 + 48) / 2, or 36. This is where the random access feature of the array comes into play. It enables us to jump from one location to another without visiting every location in between. Linked lists, which only support sequential access, don't provide a means to jump to the midpoint of a list, so you can't use the binary search technique with linked lists.

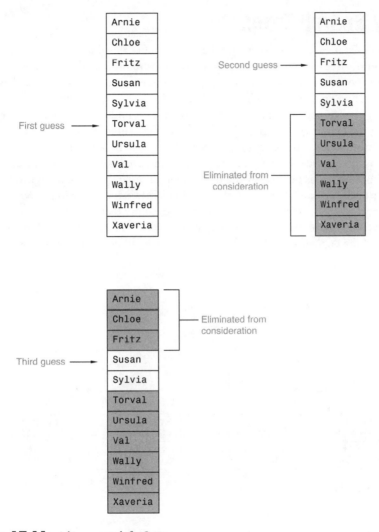

Figure 17.11. *A binary search for Susan.*

You can see, then, that the choice of data type depends on the problem. If the situation calls for a list that is continuously resized with frequent insertions and deletions but that isn't searched often, the linked list is the better choice. If the situation calls for a stable list with only occasional insertions and deletions but that has to be searched often, an array is the better choice.

What if you need a data form that supports frequent insertions and deletions and frequent searches? Neither a linked list nor an array is ideal for that need. Another form, the binary search tree, may be just what you need.

Binary Search Trees

The *binary search tree* is a linked structure that incorporates the binary search strategy. Each node in the tree contains an item and two pointers to other nodes, called *child nodes*. Figure 17.12 shows how the nodes in a binary search tree are linked. The idea is that each node has two child nodes, a left node and a right node. The ordering comes from the fact that the item in a left node precedes the item in the parent node, and the item in the right node follows the item in the parent node. This relationship holds for every node with children. Furthermore, all items that can trace their ancestry back to a left node of a parent contain items that precede the parent item in order, and every item descended from the right node contains items that follow the parent item in order. The tree in Figure 17.12 stores words in this fashion. The top of the tree, in an interesting inversion of botany, is called the root. A tree is a *hierarchical* organization, meaning that the data are organized in ranks, or levels, with each rank, in general, having ranks above and below it. If a binary search tree is fully populated, each level has twice as many nodes as the level above it.

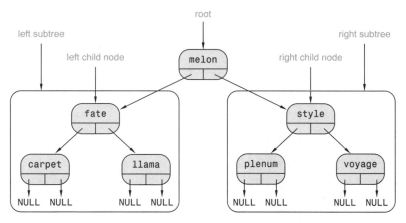

Figure 17.12. *A binary search tree storing words.*

Each node in the binary search tree is itself the root of the nodes descending from it, making the node and its descendants a *subtree*. In Figure 17.12, for example, the nodes containing the words *fate*, *carpet*, and *llama* form the left subtree of the whole tree, and the word *voyage* is the right subtree of the *style-plenum-voyage* subtree.

Suppose you want to find an item, call it the *goal*, in such a tree. If the item precedes the root item, you need search only the left half of the tree, and if the goal follows the root item, you need search only the right subtree of the root node. Thus one comparison eliminates half the tree. Suppose you proceed to search the left half. That means comparing the goal with the item in the left child. If the goal precedes the left-child item, you need search only the left half of its descendants, and so on. As with the binary search, each comparison cuts the number of potential matches in half.

Apply this method to see whether the word *puppy* is in the tree shown in Figure 17.12. Comparing *puppy* to *melon* (the root node item), you see that *puppy*, if present, must be in the right half of the tree. Thus you go to the right child and compare *puppy* to *style*. In this case, *puppy* precedes the node item, so you must follow the link to the left node. There you find *plenum*, which precedes *puppy*. You now have to follow the right branch, but it is empty. Hence three comparisons show that *puppy* isn't in the tree.

A binary search tree, then, combines a linked structure with binary search efficiency. The programming price is that putting a tree together is more involved than creating a linked list. Let's make a binary tree our next, and final, ADT project.

A Binary Tree ADT

As usual, we'll start by defining a binary tree in general terms. Table 17.1 summarizes the ADT. The following summary assumes the tree contains no duplicate items. Many of the operations are the same as list operations. The difference is in the hierarchical arrangement of data. ADT is summarized as follows:

Type Name	binary search tree
Type Properties	A binary tree is either an empty set of nodes (an empty tree) or a set of nodes with one node designated the *root.*
	Each node has exactly two trees, called the *left subtree* and the *right subtree,* descending from it.
	Each subtree is itself a binary tree, which includes the possibility of being an empty tree.
	A binary search tree is an ordered binary tree in which each node contains an item, in which all items in the left subtree precede the root item, and in which the root item precedes all items in the right subtree.
Type Operations	Determining if the tree is empty
	Determining if the tree is full
	Determining the number of items in the tree
	Adding an item to the tree
	Removing an item from the tree
	Searching the tree for an item
	Visiting each item in the tree

The Binary Search Tree Interface

In principle, you can implement a binary search tree in a variety of ways. You can even implement one as an array by manipulating array indices. The most direct way to implement a binary search tree is by using dynamically allocated nodes linked by using pointers. We'll start with definitions like these:

```
typedef SOMETHING Item;
typedef struct node
{
    Item item;
    struct node * left;
    struct node * right;
} Node;
typedef struct tree
{
    Node * root;
    int size;
} Tree;
```

Each node contains an item, a pointer to the left child node, and a pointer to the right child node. We could have defined a Tree to be type pointer-to-Node, for you only need know the location of the root node to access the entire tree. Using a structure with a size member makes it simpler to keep track of the size of the tree.

The example we'll be developing is maintaining the roster of the Nerfville Pet Club, with each item consisting of a pet name and a pet kind. With that in mind, we can set up the interface shown in Listing 17.10. One point to note is that there's no function to remove a node from a tree. The reason for this omission is that removing a node from a tree is much more complex than adding a node, and we didn't want this book to lose its Primer status. A second point is that we've limited the tree size to 10. The small size makes it easier to test whether the program behaves correctly when the tree fills. You can always set MAXITEMS to a larger value, if necessary.

Listing 17.10. tree.h.

```
/* tree.h -- binary search tree */
/*          no duplicate items are allowed in this tree */

/* redefine Item as appropriate */
typedef struct item
{
    char petname[20];
    char petkind[20];
} Item;

#define MAXITEMS 10
```

```
typedef enum boolean {False, True} BOOLEAN;

typedef struct node
{
   Item item;
   struct node * left;         /* pointer to right branch    */
   struct node * right;        /* pointer to left branch     */
} Node;

typedef struct tree
{
   Node * root;                /* pointer to root of tree    */
   int size;                   /* number of items in tree    */
} Tree;

/* function prototypes */

/* operation:        initialize a tree to empty             */
/* preconditions:    ptree points to a tree                 */
/* postconditions:   the tree is initialized to empty        */
void InitializeTree(Tree * ptree);

/* operation:        determine if tree is empty             */
/* preconditions:    ptree points to a tree                 */
/* postconditions:   function returns True if tree is empty */
/*                   and returns False otherwise            */
BOOLEAN EmptyTree(const Tree * ptree);

/* operation:        determine if tree is full              */
/* preconditions:    ptree points to a tree                 */
/* postconditions:   function returns True if tree is full  */
/*                   and returns False otherwise            */
BOOLEAN FullTree(const Tree * ptree);

/* operation:        determine number of items in tree      */
/* preconditions:    ptree points to a tree                 */
/* postconditions:   function returns number of items in tree */
int TreeItems(const Tree * ptree);

/* operation:        add an item to a tree                  */
/* preconditions:    pi is address of item to be added      */
/*                   ptree points to an initialized tree     */
/* postconditions:   if possible, function adds item to tree */
/*                   and returns True; otherwise the        */
/*                   function returns False                 */
BOOLEAN AddItem(const Item * pi, Tree * ptree);

/* operation:        find an item in a tree                 */
/* preconditions:    pi points to an item                   */
/*                   ptree points to an initialized tree     */
/* postconditions:   function returns True if item is in tree */
```

continues

Listing 17.10. continued

```
/*                       and returns False otherwise         */
BOOLEAN SeekItem(const Item * pi, const Tree * ptree);

/* operation:           apply a function to each item in tree  */
/* preconditions:       ptree points to a tree                 */
/*                      pfun points to a function that takes an */
/*                      Item argument and has no return value   */
/* postcondition:       the function pointed to by pfun is      */
/*                      executed once for each item in the tree */
void Traverse (const Tree * ptree, void (* pfun)(Item item) );
```

The Binary Tree Implementation

Next, we proceed to the task of implementing the splendid functions outlined in *tree.h*. The InitializeTree(), EmptyTree(), FullTree(), and TreeItems() functions are pretty simple, working like their counterparts for the list and queue ADTs, so we'll concentrate on the remaining ones.

Consider the process of adding an item to the tree. First, we check whether the tree has room for a new node. Then, because the binary search tree is defined so that it has no duplicate items, we check that the item isn't already in the tree. If the new item clears these first two hurdles, we create a new node, copy the item to the node, and set the node's left and right pointers to NULL. This indicates that the node has no children. Then we update the size member of the Tree structure to mark the adding of a new item. Next, we have to find where the node should be located in the tree. If the tree is empty, we set the root pointer to point to the new node. Otherwise, we look through the tree for a place to add the node. The AddItem() function follows this recipe, offloading some of the work to functions we have not yet defined: MakeNode() and AddNode().

```
BOOLEAN AddItem(const Item * pi, Tree * ptree)
{
   Node * new;

   if (FullTree(ptree))
   {
      fprintf(stderr,"Tree is full\n");
      return False;                   /* early return */
   }
   if (SeekItem(pi, ptree))
   {
      fprintf(stderr, "Attempted to add duplicate item\n");
      return False;                   /* early return */
   }
   new = MakeNode(pi);            /* new points to new node */
   if (new == NULL)
   {
```

```
        fprintf(stderr, "Couldn't create node\n");
        return False;                  /* early return */
    }
    /* succeeded in creating a new node */
    ptree->size++;

    if (ptree->root == NULL)        /* case 1: tree is empty */
        ptree->root = new;          /* new node is tree root */
    else                            /* case 2: not empty      */
        AddNode(new,ptree->root);   /* add new node to tree   */
    return True;
}
```

The MakeNode() and AddNode() functions aren't part of the public interface for our Tree type. Instead, they're static functions hidden in the *tree.c* file. The MakeNode() function is pretty simple. It handles the dynamic memory allocation and the initialization of the node. The function argument is a pointer to the new item, and the function's return value is a pointer to the new node. Recall that malloc() returns the NULL pointer if it can't make the requested allocation. The MakeNode() function initializes the new node only if memory allocation succeeds.

```
static Node * MakeNode(const Item * pi)
{
    Node * new;

    new = (Node *) malloc(sizeof(Node));
    if (new != NULL)
    {
        new->item = *pi;
        new->left = NULL;
        new->right = NULL;
    }
    return new;
}
```

The AddNode() function is the most difficult function in our binary search tree package. It has to determine where the new node goes, then it has to add it. In particular, it needs to compare the new item with the root item to see if the new item goes into the left subtree or the right subtree. If the item were a number, we could use < and > to make comparisons. If the item were a string, we could use strcmp() to make comparisons. The item is a structure containing two strings, so we have to define our own functions for making comparisons. The ToLeft() function, to be defined later, returns True if the new item should be in the left subtree, and the ToRight() function returns True if the new item should be in the right subtree. These two functions are analogous to < and >, respectively. Suppose the new item goes to the left subtree. It could be that the left subtree is empty. In that case, the function just makes the left child pointer point to the new node. What if the left subtree isn't empty? Then the function should compare the new item to the item in the left child node, deciding whether the new item should go in the left subtree or right subtree of the child node. This process should continue until the function arrives at an empty subtree, at which point the new node can be added. One way to implement this search is to use recursion, that is, apply the AddNode() function to a child node instead of to the root node. The recursive series of function calls ends when a left or right subtree is empty, that is, when root->left or root->right is NULL. Keep in mind that root is a pointer to the top of the current subtree, so it points to a new, and lower level, subtree each recursive call. (You may wish to review the discussion of recursion in Chapter 9, "Functions.")

```
static void AddNode (Node * new, Node * root)
{
   if (ToLeft(&new->item, &root->item))
   {
      if (root->left == NULL)                /* empty subtree           */
         root->left = new;                   /* so add node here        */
      else
         AddNode(new, root->left);           /* else process subtree    */
   }
   else if (ToRight(&new->item, &root->item))
   {
      if (root->right == NULL)
         root->right = new;
      else
         AddNode(new, root->right);
   }
   else                                      /* should be no duplicates */
   {
      fprintf(stderr,"location error in AddNode()\n");
      exit(1);
   }
}
```

The ToLeft() and ToRight() functions depend on the nature of the Item type. We'll order the members of the Nerfville Pet Club alphabetically by name. If two pets have the same name, we'll order them by kind. If they also are the same kind, the two items are duplicates, which aren't allowed in our basic search tree. Recall that the standard C library function strcmp() returns a negative number if the string represented by the first argument precedes the second string, returns zero if the two strings are the same, and returns a positive number if the first string follows the second. The ToRight() function has similar code. Using these two functions instead of making comparisons directly in AddNode() makes the code easier to adapt to new requirements. Rather than rewriting AddNode() when a different form of comparison is needed, you rewrite ToLeft() and ToRight().

```
static BOOLEAN ToLeft(const Item * i1, const Item * i2)
{
   int comp1;

   if ((comp1 = strcmp(i1->petname, i2->petname)) < 0)
      return True;
   else if (comp1 == 0 &&
```

```
                  strcmp(i1->petkind, i2->petkind) < 0 )
        return True;
    else
        return False;
}
```

The SeekItem() function also has to search through the tree. This function, too, can be implemented recursively. However, in order to expose you to a variety of programming techniques, we'll use a while loop to handle descending through the tree. Like AddNode(), SeekItem() uses ToLeft() and ToRight() to navigate through the tree. AddNode() initially sets the root pointer to point to the root of the tree, then resets root to successive subtrees as it traces the path to where the item should be found.

```
BOOLEAN SeekItem(const Item * pi, const Tree * ptree)
{
    Node * root;
    BOOLEAN found = False;

    if (ptree->root == NULL)
        return False;
    root = ptree->root;
    while (root != NULL)
    {
        if (ToLeft(pi, &root->item))
            root = root->left;
        else if (ToRight(pi, &root->item))
            root = root->right;
        else                    /* must be same if not to left or right */
        {
            found = True;
            break;
        }
    }

    return found;
}
```

Traversing a tree is more involved than traversing a linked list because each node has two branches to follow. This branching nature makes recursion a natural choice for handling the problem. At each node, the function should do the following:

- Process the item in the node

- Process the left subtree (a recursive call)

- Process the right subtree (a recursive call)

We can break down this process into two functions: Traverse() and InOrder(). Note that the InOrder() function processes the left subtree, then processes the item, then processes the right subtree. This order results in traversing the tree in alphabetic order. If you have the time, you might want to see what happens if you use different orders, such as item-left-right and left-right-item.

```
void Traverse (const Tree * ptree, void (* pfun)(Item item))
{

   if (ptree != NULL)
      InOrder(ptree->root, pfun);
}

static void InOrder(const Node * root, void (* pfun)(Item item))
{
   if (root != NULL)
   {
      InOrder(root->left, pfun);
      (*pfun)(root->item);
      InOrder(root->right, pfun);
   }
}
```

Listing 17.11 shows the entire *tree.c* code. Together, *tree.h* and *tree.c* constitute a tree programming package.

Listing 17.11. tree.c.

```
#include <string.h>
#include <stdio.h>
#include <stdlib.h>
#include "tree.h"

/* prototypes for local functions */
static Node * MakeNode(const Item * pi);
static BOOLEAN ToLeft(const Item * i1, const Item * i2);
static BOOLEAN ToRight(const Item * i1, const Item * i2);
static void AddNode (Node * new, Node * root);
static void InOrder(const Node * root, void (* pfun)(Item item));

/* function definitions */

void InitializeTree(Tree * ptree)
{
   ptree->root = NULL;
   ptree->size = 0;
}

BOOLEAN EmptyTree(const Tree * ptree)
{
   if (ptree->root == NULL)
      return True;
   else
      return False;
}


BOOLEAN FullTree(const Tree * ptree)
```

```
{
    if (ptree->size == MAXITEMS)
        return True;
    else
        return False;
}

int TreeItems(const Tree * ptree)
{
    return ptree->size;
}

BOOLEAN AddItem(const Item * pi, Tree * ptree)
{
    Node * new;

    if (FullTree(ptree))
    {
        fprintf(stderr,"Tree is full\n");
        return False;                    /* early return */
    }
    if (SeekItem(pi, ptree))
    {
        fprintf(stderr, "Attempted to add duplicate item\n");
        return False;                    /* early return */
    }
    new = MakeNode(pi);          /* new points to new node */
    if (new == NULL)
    {
        fprintf(stderr, "Couldn't create node\n");
        return False;                    /* early return */
    }
    /* succeeded in creating a new node */
    ptree->size++;

    if (ptree->root == NULL)          /* case 1: tree is empty */
        ptree->root = new;            /* new node is tree root */
    else                              /* case 2: not empty     */
        AddNode(new,ptree->root);     /* add new node to tree  */
    return True;
}

BOOLEAN SeekItem(const Item * pi, const Tree * ptree)
{
    Node * root;
    BOOLEAN found = False;

    if (ptree->root == NULL)
        return False;
    root = ptree->root;
    while (root != NULL)
    {
```

Listing 17.11. continued

```
         if (ToLeft(pi, &root->item))
            root = root->left;
         else if (ToRight(pi, &root->item))
            root = root->right;
         else                    /* must be same if not to left or right */
         {
            found = True;
            break;
         }
      }
   }

   return found;
}

void Traverse (const Tree * ptree, void (* pfun)(Item item))
{

   if (ptree != NULL)
      InOrder(ptree->root, pfun);
}

static void InOrder(const Node * root, void (* pfun)(Item item))
{
   if (root != NULL)
   {
      InOrder(root->left, pfun);
      (*pfun)(root->item);
      InOrder(root->right, pfun);
   }
}

static void AddNode (Node * new, Node * root)
{
   if (ToLeft(&new->item, &root->item))
   {
      if (root->left == NULL)            /* empty subtree      */
         root->left = new;               /* so add node here   */
      else
         AddNode(new, root->left);       /* else process subtree */
   }
   else if (ToRight(&new->item, &root->item))
   {
      if (root->right == NULL)
         root->right = new;
      else
         AddNode(new, root->right);
   }
   else                                  /* should be no duplicates */
   {
      fprintf(stderr,"location error in AddNode()\n");
      exit(1);
```

```
      }
}

static BOOLEAN ToLeft(const Item * i1, const Item * i2)
{
   int comp1;

   if ((comp1 = strcmp(i1->petname, i2->petname)) < 0)
      return True;
   else if (comp1 == 0 &&
              strcmp(i1->petkind, i2->petkind) < 0 )
      return True;
   else
      return False;
}

static BOOLEAN ToRight(const Item * i1, const Item * i2)
{
   int comp1;

   if ((comp1 = strcmp(i1->petname, i2->petname)) > 0)
      return True;
   else if (comp1 == 0 &&
              strcmp(i1->petkind, i2->petkind) > 0 )
      return True;
   else
      return False;
}

static Node * MakeNode(const Item * pi)
{
   Node * new;

   new = (Node *) malloc(sizeof(Node));
   if (new != NULL)
   {
      new->item = *pi;
      new->left = NULL;
      new->right = NULL;
   }
   return new;
}
```

Trying the Tree

Now that we have the interface and the function implementations, let's use them. The program in Listing 17.12 uses a menu to offer a choice of adding pets to the club membership roster, listing members, reporting the number of members, checking for membership, and quitting. The brief main() function concentrates on the essential program outline. Supporting functions do most of the work.

Listing 17.12. petclub.c.

```c
/* petclub.c -- use a binary search tree */
#include <stdio.h>
#include <string.h>
#include <ctype.h>
#include "tree.h"

char menu(void);
void addpet(Tree * pt);
void showpets(const Tree * pt);
void findpet(const Tree * pt);
void printitem(Item item);
void uppercase(char * str);

int main(void)
{
    Tree pets;
    char choice;

    InitializeTree(&pets);
    while ((choice = menu()) != 'q')
    {
        switch (choice)
        {
            case 'a' :    addpet(&pets);
                        break;
            case 'l' :    showpets(&pets);
                        break;
            case 'f' :    findpet(&pets);
                        break;
            case 'n' :    printf("%d pets in club\n", TreeItems(&pets));
                        break;
            default  :    puts("Switching error");
        }
    }
    puts("Bye.");
    return 0;
}

char menu(void)
{
    int ch;

    puts("Nerfville Pet Club Membership Program");
    puts("Enter the letter corresponding to your choice:");
    puts("a) add a pet      l) show list of pets");
    puts("n) number of pets   f) find pets");
    puts("q) quit");
    while ((ch = getchar()) != EOF)
    {
        while (getchar() != '\n')  /* discard rest of line */
```

```
                continue;
        ch = tolower(ch);
        if (strchr("alrfnq",ch) == NULL)
            puts("Please enter an a, l, f, n, or q:");
        else
            break;
    }
    if (ch == EOF)      /* make EOF cause program to quit */
        ch = 'q';

    return ch;
}

void addpet(Tree * pt)
{
    Item temp;

    if (FullTree(pt))
        puts("No room in the club!");
    else
    {
        puts("Please enter name of pet:");
        gets(temp.petname);
        puts("Please enter pet kind:");
        gets(temp.petkind);
        uppercase(temp.petname);
        uppercase(temp.petkind);
        AddItem(&temp, pt);
    }
}

void showpets(const Tree * pt)
{
    if (EmptyTree(pt))
        puts("No entries!");
    else
        Traverse(pt, printitem);
}

void printitem(Item item)
{
    printf("Pet: %-19s  Kind: %-19s\n", item.petname,
            item.petkind);
}

void findpet(const Tree * pt)
{
    Item temp;

    if (EmptyTree(pt))
    {
        puts("No entries!");
```

Listing 17.12. continued

```
        return;     /* quit function if tree is empty */
    }

    puts("Please enter name of pet you wish to find:");
    gets(temp.petname);
    puts("Please enter pet kind:");
    gets(temp.petkind);
    uppercase(temp.petname);
    uppercase(temp.petkind);
    printf("%s the %s ", temp.petname, temp.petkind);
    if (SeekItem(&temp, pt))
        printf("is a member.\n");
    else
        printf("is not a member.\n");
}

void uppercase(char * str)
{
    while (*str != '\0')
    {
        *str = toupper(*str);
        str++;
    }
}
```

The program converts all letters to uppercase so that *SNUFFY*, *Snuffy*, and *snuffy* aren't considered distinct names. Here is a sample run:

```
Nerfville Pet Club Membership Program
Enter the letter corresponding to your choice:
a) add a pet      l) show list of pets
n) number of pets   f) find pets
q) quit
a
Please enter name of pet:
Quincy
Please enter pet kind:
pig
Nerfville Pet Club Membership Program
Enter the letter corresponding to your choice:
a) add a pet      l) show list of pets
n) number of pets   f) find pets
q) quit
a
Please enter name of pet:
Betty
Please enter pet kind:
Boa
Nerfville Pet Club Membership Program
```

```
Enter the letter corresponding to your choice:
a) add a pet      l) show list of pets
n) number of pets   f) find pets
q) quit
a
Please enter name of pet:
Hiram Jinx
Please enter pet kind:
domestic cat
Nerfville Pet Club Membership Program
Enter the letter corresponding to your choice:
a) add a pet      l) show list of pets
n) number of pets   f) find pets
q) quit
n
3 pets in club
Nerfville Pet Club Membership Program
Enter the letter corresponding to your choice:
a) add a pet      l) show list of pets
n) number of pets   f) find pets
q) quit
l
Pet: BETTY         Kind: BOA
Pet: HIRAM JINX    Kind: DOMESTIC CAT
Pet: QUINCY        Kind: PIG
Nerfville Pet Club Membership Program
Enter the letter corresponding to your choice:
a) add a pet      l) show list of pets
n) number of pets   f) find pets
q) quit
q
Bye.
```

Tree Thoughts

The binary search tree has some drawbacks. For instance, it's efficient only if it is fully populated, or *balanced*. Suppose we're storing words and the words are entered randomly. The chances are the tree will have a fairly bushy look, as in Figure 17.12. Now suppose we enter data in alphabetical order. Then each new node would be added to the right, and the tree might look like Figure 17.13. The Figure 17.12 tree is said to be *balanced*, but the Figure 17.13 tree is *unbalanced*. Searching this tree is no more effective than sequentially searching a linked list.

One way to avoid stringy trees is use more care when building a tree. If a tree or subtree begins to get too unbalanced on one side or the other, rearrange the nodes to restore a better balance. The Russian mathematicians Adel'son-Vel'skii and Landis developed an algorithm to do this. Trees built with their method are called AVL trees. It takes longer to build a balanced tree because of the extra restructuring, but you ensure maximum, or nearly maximum, search efficiency.

635

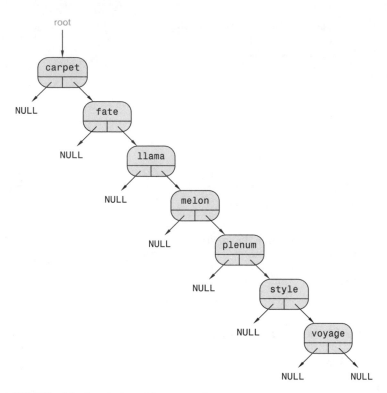

Figure 17.13. *A badly unbalanced binary search tree.*

You might want a binary search tree that allows duplicate items. Suppose, for example, you wanted to analyze some text by tracking how many times each word in the text appears. One approach is to define `Item` as a structure that holds one word and a number. The first time a word is encountered, it's added to the tree, and the number is set to 1. The next time the same word is encountered, the program finds the node containing the word and increments the number. It doesn't take much work to modify the basic binary search tree to behave in this fashion.

For another possible variation, consider the Nerfville Pet Club. Our example ordered the tree by both name and kind. Thus, it could hold Sam the cat in one node, Sam the dog in another node, and Sam the goat in a third node. You couldn't have two cats called Sam. Another approach is to order the tree just by name. Making that change alone would allow for only one Sam regardless of kind. You then could define `Item` to be a list of structures instead of being a single structure. The first time a Sally shows up, the program would create a new node, then create a new list, then add Sally and her kind to the list. The next Sally that shows up would be directed to the same node and added to the list.

Other Directions

In this book we've covered the essential features of C, but we've only touched on the library. The ANSI C library contains scores of useful functions. Most implementations additionally offer extensive libraries of functions specific to particular systems. Microsoft C, Turbo C, and Borland C, for instance, offer functions to facilitate hardware control, keyboard input, and the generation of graphics for IBM PCs and clones. Think C provides functions to access the Macintosh toolbox to facilitate producing programs with the standard Macintosh interface. Take the time to explore what your system has to offer. If it doesn't have what you want, make your own functions. That's part of C. If you think you can do a better job on, say, an input function, do it! As you refine and polish your programming technique, you will go from C to shining C.

If you've found the concepts of lists, queues, and trees exciting and useful, you may wish to read a book or take a course on advanced programming techniques. Computer scientists have invested a lot of energy and talent into developing and analyzing algorithms and ways of representing data. You may find that someone already has developed exactly the tool you need.

Once you are comfortable with C, you may wish to investigate C++ or Objective C. These *object-oriented* languages have their roots in C. C already has data objects ranging in complexity from a simple char variable to large and intricate structures. C++ and Objective C carry the idea of the object even further. Object-oriented programming (OOP) goes beyond that, for instance, the properties of an object include not only what kinds of information it can hold but also what kinds of operations can be performed on it. The ADTs in this chapter follow that pattern, but OOP languages provide formal mechanisms for tying together the data representation and the allowed operations is one definition of an object. Also, objects can inherit properties from other objects. OOP carries modularizing to a higher level of abstraction than does C, and it facilitates the writing of large programs.

You may wish to check the bibliography in Appendix A, "Additional Reading," for books that might further your interests.

Chapter Summary

A data type is characterized by how the data is structured and stored and also by what operations are possible. An abstract data type (ADT) specifies in an abstract manner the properties and operations characterizing a type. Conceptually, you can translate an ADT to a particular programming language in two steps. The first step is defining the programming interface. In C, you can do this by using a header file to define type names and to provide function prototypes that correspond to the allowed operations. The second step is implementing the interface. In C, you can do this with a source code file that provides the function definitions corresponding to the prototypes.

The list, the queue, and the binary tree are examples of ADTs commonly used in computer programming. Often they are implemented using dynamic memory allocation and linked structures, but sometimes implementing them with an array is a better choice.

When you program using a particular type, say a queue or a tree, you should write the program in terms of the type interface. That way, you can modify and improve the implementation without having to alter programs using the interface.

Review Questions

1. What's involved in defining a data type?

2. Why can the linked list in Listing 17.2 be traversed only in one direction? How could you modify the `struct film` definition so that the list could be traversed in both directions?

3. What's an ADT?

4. The `EmptyList()` function took a list as an argument, but the `EmptyQueue()` function took a pointer to a queue as an argument. What are the advantages and disadvantages of each approach?

5. The *stack* is another data form from the list family. In a stack, additions and deletions can be made only from one end of the list. Items are said to be pushed onto the top of the stack and to be popped off the stack. Thus, the stack is LIFO structure, that is, Last In, First Out.

    a. Devise an ADT for a stack
    b. Devise a C programming interface for a stack.

6. What is the maximum number of comparisons a sequential search and a binary search would need to determine that a particular item isn't in a sorted list of 3 items? 1023 items? 65,535 items?

7. Suppose a program constructs a binary search tree of words using the algorithm developed in this chapter. Draw the tree assuming words are entered in the following order:

    a. nice food roam dodge gate office wave
    b. wave roam office nice gate food dodge
    c. food dodge roam wave office gate nice
    d. nice roam office food wave gate dodge

Programming Exercises

1. Modify Listing 17.2 so that it displays the movie list both in the original order and in reverse order. One approach is to modify the linked-list definition so that the list can be traversed in both directions. Another approach is to use recursion.

2. Suppose *list.h* (Listing 17.3) uses the following definition of a list:

```
typedef struct list
{
    Node * head;    /* points to head of list */
    Node * end;     /* points to end of list  */
} List;
```

Rewrite the *list.c* (Listing 17.5) functions to fit this definition and test the resulting code with the *films3.c* (Listing 17.4) program.

3. Suppose *list.h* (Listing 17.3) uses the following definition of a list:

```
#define MAXSIZE 100
typedef struct list
{
    Item entries[MAXSIZE];    /* array of items          */
    int items;                /* number of items in list */
} List;
```

Rewrite the *list.c* (Listing 17.5) functions to fit this definition and test the resulting code with the *films3.c* (Listing 17.4) program.

4. Rewrite *mall.c* (Listing 17.7) so that it simulates a double booth having two queues.

5. Write a program that enables you to input a string. The program then pushes the characters of the string onto a stack one by one (see Review Question 5), then pops the characters from the stack and displays them. This results in displaying the string in reverse order.

6. Write a function that takes three arguments: the name of an array of sorted integers, the number of elements of the array, and an integer to seek. The function returns the value 1 if the integer is in the array and 0 if it isn't. Have the function use the binary search technique.

7. Write a program that opens and reads a text file and records how many times each word occurs in the file. Use a binary search tree modified to store both a word and the number of times it occurs. After the program has read the file, it offers a menu with three choices. The first is to list all the words along with the number of occurrences. The second enables you to enter a word, and the program reports how many times the word occurred in the file. The third choice is to quit.

8. Modify the Pet Club program so that all pets with the same name are stored in a list in the same node. When the user chooses to find a pet, the program requests the pet name and then lists all pets (along with their kinds) having that name.

Additional Reading

If you wish to learn more about C and programming, you will find the following references useful.

C Language

BYTE, 8, no. 8 (August 1983).

This issue of *BYTE* magazine is devoted to C. It includes articles discussing the history, philosophy, and uses of C. Also included is an extensive bibliography of books and articles on C. Each bibliographic entry has a short summary of the book or article.

Feuer, Alan R. *The C Puzzle Book.* **Englewood Cliffs, NJ: Prentice Hall, 1982.**

This book contains a large number of programs whose output you are supposed to predict. Predicting the output gives you a good opportunity to test and expand your understanding of C. The book includes answers and explanations.

Kernighan, Brian W., and Dennis M. Ritchie. *The C Programming Language.* **Englewood Cliffs, NJ: Prentice Hall, 1978.**

This is the first book on C. (Note that the creator of C, Dennis Ritchie, is one of the authors.) It constitutes the definition of "K&R" C, the unofficial standard for many years. The book includes many interesting examples. It does, however, assume that the reader is familiar with systems programming.

Kernighan, Brian W., and Dennis M. Ritchie. *The C Programming Language.* **second edition. Englewood Cliffs, NJ: Prentice Hall, 1988.**

This edition incorporates ANSI changes based on the ANSI draft that was standard at the time the book was written.

Koenig, Andrew. *C Traps and Pitfalls.* **Reading, MA: Addison-Wesley, 1988.**

The title says it all.

Ritchie, Dennis M., S.C. Johnson, M.E. Lesk, and Brian W. Kernighan. **"The C Programming Language," The Bell System Technical Journal 57, no. 6 (July/August 1978).**

This article discusses the history of C and provides an overview of its design features.

Stroustrup, Bjarne. *The C++ Programming Language,* **second edition**. **Reading, MA: Addison-Wesley, 1991.**

This book, by the creator of C+, presents the C++ language and includes the Reference Manual for C++.

Prata, Stephen. *C++ Primer Plus.* **Corte Madera, CA: Waite Group Press, 1991.**

This book introduces you to the C++ language and to the philosophy of object-oriented programming.

Programming

Kernighan, Brian W., and P.J. Plauger. *The Elements of Programming Style.* **second edition. New York: McGraw-Hill, 1978.**

This slim classic draws on examples from other texts to illustrate the dos and don'ts of clear, effective programming.

Knuth, Donald E. *The Art of Computer Programming,* **Volume 1 (Fundamental Algorithms), second edition. Reading, MA: Addison-Wesley, 1973.**

This standard reference examines data representation and algorithm analysis in great detail. Volume 2 (Seminumerical Algorithms, 1980) includes an extensive discussion of pseudorandom numbers. Volume 3 (Sorting and Searching, 1973), as the name suggests, examines sorting and searching. Examples are given in pseudocode and assembly language.

Kruse, Robert L., Leung, Bruce P., and Tondo, Clovis L. *Data Structures and Program Design in C.* **Englewood Cliffs, NJ: Prentice Hall, 1991.**

This textbook covers advanced topics such as software engineering, linked lists, searching, sorting, trees, and graphs. The examples, although in C, show their Pascal heritage.

Reference

Barkakati, Naba. *The Waite Group's Essential Guide to ANSI C.* **Indianapolis, IN: SAMS, 1989.**

This is a compact summary of the C language and its standard library. Also available are *The Waite Group's Essential Guide to Turbo C* and *The Waite Group's Essential Guide to Microsoft C*; these volumes additionally describe the Turbo C and Microsoft C additions to the standard library.

Harbison, Samuel P. and Steele, Guy L. *C: A Reference Manual.,* **third edition. Englewood Cliffs, NJ: Prentice Hall, 1991.**

This reference manual presents the rules of the C language and describes most of the standard library functions. It points out differences between K&R C and ANSI C and provides many examples.

Plauger, P.J. *The Standard C Library.* **Englewood Cliffs, NJ: Prentice Hall, 1992.**

This large reference manual describes the standard library functions, providing more description than you would find in a typical compiler manual.

C Operators

C is rich in operators. Table B.1 lists the C operators in order of decreasing precedence and indicates how they associate. All operators are binary (two operands) unless otherwise indicated. Note that some binary and unary operators, such as * (multiplication) and * (indirection), share the same symbol but have different precedence. Following the table are summaries of each operator.

Table B.1. The C operators.

Operators (from high to low precedence)	Associativity
++ (postfix) −− (postfix) ( ) [ ] . ->	L–R
++ (prefix) −− (prefix) - + ~ ! sizeof * (dereference) & (address) (*type*) (all unary)	R–L
* / %	L–R
+ - (both binary)	L–R

continues

Table B.1. continued

Operators (from high to low precedence)	Associativity
<< >>	L–R
< > <= >=	L–R
== !=	L–R
&	L–R
^	L–R
¦	L–R
&&	L–R
¦¦	L–R
? : (trinary operator)	L–R
= *= /= %= += -= <<= >>= &= ¦= ^=	R–L
, (comma operator)	L–R

Arithmetic Operators

+ adds the value at its right to the value at its left.

- subtracts the value at its right from the value at its left.

-, as a unary operator, changes the sign of the value at its right.

* multiplies the value at its right by the value at its left.

/ divides the value at its left by the value at its right. Answer is truncated if both operands are integers.

% yields the remainder when the value at its left is divided by the value to its right (integers only).

++ adds 1 to the value of the variable to its *right* (prefixmode) or adds 1 to the value of the variable to its *left* (postfixmode).

-- is like ++, but subtracts 1.

Relational Operators

Each operator compares the value at its left to the value at its right.

< Less than
<= Less than or equal to
== Equal to
>= Greater than or equal to
> Greater than
!= Unequal to

Relational Expressions

A simple relational expression consists of a relational operator with an operand on each side. If the relation is true, the relational expression has the value 1. If the relation is false, the relational expression has the value 0.

5 > 2 is true and has the value 1.
(2 + a) == a is false and has the value 0.

Assignment Operators

= assigns the value at its right to the lvalue on its left.

Each of the following assignment operators updates the lvalue at its left by the value at its right, using the indicated operation. We use R–H for righthand, and L–H for lefthand.

+= adds the R–H quantity to the L–H variable.

-= subtracts the R–H quantity from the L–H variable.

*= multiplies the L–H variable by the R–H quantity.

/= divides the L–H variable by the R–H quantity.

%= gives the remainder from dividing the L–H quantity by the R–H quantity.

&= assigns L–H & R–H to the L–H quantity.

¦= assigns L–H ¦ R–H to the L–H quantity.

^= assigns L–H ^ R–H to the L–H quantity.

>>= assigns L–H >> R–H to the L–H quantity.

<<= assigns L–H << R–H to the L–H quantity.

Example

rabbits *= 1.6; is the same as rabbits = rabbits * 1.6;

Logical Operators

Logical operators normally take relational expressions as operands. The ! operator takes one operand. The rest take two: one to the left, one to the right.

&& AND
¦¦ OR
! NOT

Logical Expressions

`expression1 && expression2` is true if and only if both expressions are true.

`expression1 ¦¦ expression2` is true if either one or both expressions are true.

`!expression` is true if the expression is false, and vice versa.

Order of Evaluation for Logical Expressions

Logical expressions are evaluated from left to right. Evaluation stops as soon as something is discovered that renders the expression false.

Examples

`6 > 2 && 3 == 3` is true.

`! ( 6 > 2 && 3 == 3 )` is false.

`x != 0 && 20/x < 5` the second expression is evaluated only if x is nonzero.

The Conditional Operator

`? :` takes three operands, each of which is an expression. They are arranged this way: *expression1* ? *expression2* : *expression3*. The value of the whole expression equals the value of *expression2* if *expression1* is true, and equals the value of *expression3* otherwise.

Examples

`( 5 > 3 ) ? 1 : 2` has the value 1.
`( 3 > 5 ) ? 1 : 2` has the value 2.
`( a > b ) ? a : b` has the value of the larger of a or b.

Pointer-Related Operators

`&` is the address operator. When followed by a variable name, & gives the address of that variable.

* is the indirection or dereferencing operator. When followed by a pointer, * gives the value stored at the pointed-to address.

Example

&nurse is the address of the variable nurse.

```
nurse = 22;
ptr = &nurse; /* pointer to nurse */
val = *ptr;
```

The net effect is to assign the value 22 to val.

Sign Operators

– is the minus sign which reverses the sign of the operand.
+ is the plus sign, which leaves the sign unchanged.

Structure and Union Operators

The Membership Operator

. is used with a structure or union name to specify a member of that structure or union. If name is the name of a structure and member is a member specified by the structure template, then name.member identifies that member of the structure. The type of name.member is the type specified for member. The membership operator can also be used in the same fashion with unions.

Example

```
struct {
        int code;
        float cost;
} item;

item.code = 1265;
```

This statement assigns a value to the code member of the structure item.

The Indirect Membership Operator

-> is used with a pointer to a structure or union to identify a member of that structure or union. Suppose that ptrstr is a pointer to a structure and that member is a member specified by the structure template. Then ptrstr->member identifies that member of the pointed-to structure. The indirect membership operator can be used in the same fashion with unions.

Example

```
struct {
        int code;
        float cost;
} item, * ptrst;
ptrst = &item;
ptrst->code = 3451;
```

This program fragment assigns a value to the code member of item. The following three expressions are equivalent:

```
ptrst->code   item.code   (*ptrst).code
```

Bitwise Operators

All of the following bitwise operators except ~ are binary operators.

~ is the unary operator and produces a value with each bit of the operand inverted.

& is AND and produces a value in which each bit is set to 1 only if both corresponding bits in the two operands are 1.

¦ is OR and produces a value in which each bit is set to 1 if either, or both, corresponding bits of the two operands are 1.

^ is EXCLUSIVE OR and produces a value in which each bit is set to 1 only if one or the other (but not both) of the corresponding bits of the two operands is 1.

<< is left-shift and produces a value obtained by shifting the bits of the lefthand operand to the left by the number of places given by the righthand operand. Vacated slots are filled with zeros.

>> is right-shift and produces a value obtained by shifting the bits of the lefthand operand to the right by the number of places given by the righthand operand. For unsigned integers, the vacated slots are filled with zeros. The behavior for signed values is implementation dependent.

Examples

Suppose you have the following:

```
int x = 2;
int y = 3;
```

Then x & y has the value 2, since only bit 1 is ON for both x and y. Also, y<<x has the value 12 because that is the value obtained when the bit pattern for 3 is shifted two bits to the left.

Miscellaneous Operators

sizeof yields the size, in units the size of a char value, of the operand to its right. Typically, a char value is one byte in size. The operand can be a type-specifier in parentheses, as in sizeof (float), or it can be the name of a particular variable or array, etc., as in sizeof foo. A sizeof expression is of type size_t.

(type) is the cast operator and converts the following value to the type specified by the enclosed keyword(s). For example, (float) 9 converts the integer 9 to the floating-point number 9.0.

, is the comma operator and links two expressions into one and guarantees that the leftmost expression is evaluated first. The value of the whole expression is the value of the righthand expression. This operator is typically used to include more information in a for loop control expression.

Example

```
for (step = 2, fargo = 0; fargo < 1000; step *= 2)
        fargo += step;
```

Basic Types and Storage Classes

Summary: The Basic Data Types

Keywords

The basic data types are set up using the following eight keywords: int, long, short, unsigned, char, float, double, and signed (ANSI C).

Signed Integers

Signed integers can have positive or negative values.

`int` is the basic integer type for a given system.

`long` or `long int` can hold an integer at least as large as the largest `int` and possibly larger.

`short` or `short int` is the largest `short` integer, is no larger than the largest `int`, and may be smaller. Typically, `long` will be bigger than `short`, and `int` will be the same as one of the two. For example, Turbo C and Microsoft C for the PC provide 16-bit `short` and `int` and 32-bit `long`. It all depends on the system.

Unsigned Integers

Unsigned integers have zero or positive values only, which extends the range of the largest possible positive number. Use the keyword `unsigned` before the desired type: `unsigned int`, `unsigned long`, `unsigned short`. A lone `unsigned` is the same as `unsigned int`.

Characters

Characters are typographic symbols such as A, &, and +. Typically, just 1 byte of memory is used.

`char` is the keyword for this type.

Some implementations use a signed `char`, but others use an unsigned `char`. ANSI C allows you to use the keywords `signed` and `unsigned` to specify which form you want.

Floating Point

Floating-point numbers can have positive or negative values.

`float` is the basic floating-point type for the system.

`double` is a (possibly) larger unit for holding floating-point numbers. It may allow more-significant figures and perhaps larger exponents than `float`.

`long double` is a (possibly) even larger unit for holding floating-point numbers. It may allow more-significant figures and perhaps larger exponents than `double`.

Summary: How to Declare a Simple Variable

1. Choose the type you need.

2. Choose a name for the variable.

3. Use this format for a declaration statement: *type-specifier variable-name;*.
   The *type-specifier* is formed from one or more of the type keywords. Here are some examples:

```
int erest;
unsigned short cash;
```

4. To declare more than one variable of the same type, separate the variable names with commas:

```
char ch, init, ans;
```

5. You can initialize a variable in a declaration statement:

```
float mass = 6.0E24;
```

Summary: Storage Classes

Keywords

`auto, extern, static, register.`

General Comments

The storage class of a variable determines its scope, its linkage, and its storage duration. Storage class is determined both by where the variable is defined and by its associated keyword. Variables defined outside all functions are external, have file scope, external linkage, and static storage duration. Variables declared inside a function are automatic unless one of the other keywords is used. They have block scope, no linkage, and automatic storage duration. Variables defined with the keyword `static` inside a function have block scope, no linkage, and static storage duration. Variables defined with the keyword `static` outside a function have file scope, internal linkage, and static storage duration.

Properties

In the following list, those variables in storage classes above the dotted line are declared inside a function; those below the line are defined outside a function.

Storage Class	Keyword	Duration	Scope and Linkage
automatic	auto	temporary	local
register	register	temporary	local
static	static	persistent	local
external	extern*	persistent	global (all files)
external static	static	persistent	global (one file)

*The keyword `extern` is used only to redeclare variables that have been defined externally elsewhere. The act of defining the variable outside a function makes it external.

Summary: Qualifiers

Keywords

Use the following keywords to qualify variables:

```
const, volatile
```

General Comments

A qualifier constrains the modifiability of a variable. A const variable, once initialized, can't be altered. The compiler can't assume that volatile variable hasn't been changed by some outside agency, such as a hardware update.

Properties

The declaration

```
const int joy = 101;
```

establishes that the value of joy is fixed at 101.

The declaration

```
volatile unsigned int incoming;
```

establishes that the value of incoming might change between one occurrence of incoming in a program and its next occurrence.

The declaration

```
const int * ptr = &joy;
```

establishes that the pointer ptr can't be used to alter the value of the variable joy. The pointer can, however, be made to point to another location.

The declaration

```
int * const ptr = &joy;
```

establishes that the pointer ptr can't have its value changed; that is, it can only point to joy. However, it can be used to alter joy.

The prototype

```
void simple (const char * s);
```

establishes that once the formal argument s is initialized to whatever value is passed to simple() in a function call, sample() may not alter the value to which s points.

Expressions, Statements, and Program Flow

Summary: Expressions and Statements

Expressions

An *expression* is a combination of operators and operands. The simplest expression is just a constant or a variable with no operator, such as 22 or beebop. More complex examples are 55 + 22 and vap = 2 * (vip + (vup = 4)).

Statements

A *statement* is a command to the computer. Any expression followed by a semicolon forms a statement, albeit not necessarily a meaningful one. Statements can be simple or compound. *Simple statements* terminate in a semicolon. Examples are

Declaration statement	`int toes;`
Assignment statement	`toes = 12;`
Function call statement	`printf("%d\n", toes);`
Control statement	`while (toes < 20) toes = toes + 2;`
Null statement	`; /* does nothing */`

Compound statements, or *blocks*, consist of one or more statements (which themselves can be compound) enclosed in braces. The following `while` statement contains an example:

```
while (years < 100)
{
    wisdom = wisdom + 1;
    printf("%d %d\n", years, wisdom);
    years = years + 1;
}
```

Summary: The *while* Statement

Keyword

The keyword for the `while` statement is `while`.

General Comments

The `while` statement creates a loop that repeats until the test *expression* becomes false, or zero. The `while` statement is an *entry-condition* loop; the decision to go through one more pass of the loop is made *before* the loop has been traversed. Thus, it is possible that the loop is never traversed. The *statement* part of the form can be a simple statement or a compound statement.

Form

```
while (expression)
      statement
```

The *statement* portion is repeated until the *expression* becomes false or zero.

Examples

```
while (n++ < 100)
      printf(" %d %d\n",n, 2*n+1);
```

```
while (fargo < 1000)
{
      fargo = fargo + step;
      step = 2 * step;
}
```

Summary: The *for* Statement

Keyword

The for statement keyword is for.

General Comments

The for statement uses three control expressions, separated by semicolons, to control a looping process. The *initialize* expression is executed once, before any of the loop statements are executed. If the *test* expression is true (or nonzero), the loop is cycled through once. Then the *update* expression is evaluated, and it is time to check the *test* expression again. The for statement is an *entry-condition* loop; the decision to go through one more pass of the loop is made *before* the loop has been traversed. Thus, it is possible that the loop is never traversed. The *statement* part of the form can be a simple statement or a compound statement.

Form

```
for (initialize ; test ; update)
      statement
```

The loop is repeated until *test* becomes false or zero.

Example

```
for (n = 0;  n < 10 ; n++)
      printf("%d %d\n", n, 2 * n+1);
```

Summary: The *do while* Statement

Keywords

The keywords for the do while statement are do and while.

General Comments

The do while statement creates a loop that repeats until the test *expression* becomes false or zero. The do while statement is an *exit-condition* loop; the decision to go through one more pass of the loop is made *after* the loop has been traversed. Thus, the loop must be executed at least once. The `statement` part of the form can be a simple statement or a compound statement.

Form

```
do
    statement
while (expression);
```

The `statement` portion is repeated until the `expression` becomes false or zero.

Example

```
do
    scanf("%d", &number)
while(number != 20);
```

Summary: Using *if* Statements for Making Choices

Keywords

The keywords for `if` statements are `if` and `else`.

General Comments

In each of the following forms, the `statement` can be either a simple statement or a compound statement. A "true" expression, more generally, means one with a nonzero value.

Form 1

```
if (expression)
    statement
```

The `statement` is executed if the `expression` is true.

Form 2

```
if (expression)
    statement1
  else
      statement2
```

If the `expression` is true, `statement1` is executed. Otherwise, `statement2` is executed.

Form 3

```
if (expression1)
    statement1
 else if (expression2)
    statement2
 else
     statement3
```

If *expression1* is true, *statement1* is executed. If *expression1* is false but *expression2* is true, *statement2* is executed. Otherwise, if both expressions are false, *statement3* is executed.

Example

```
if (legs == 4)
    printf("It might be a horse.\n");
 else if (legs > 4)
     printf("It is not a horse.\n");
 else    /* case of legs < 4 */
 {
     legs++;
     printf("Now it has one more leg.\n")
 }
```

Summary: Multiple Choice with *switch*

Keyword

The keyword for the switch statement is switch.

General Comments

Program control jumps to the statement bearing the value of *expression* as a label. Program flow then proceeds through the remaining statements unless redirected again. Both *expression* and labels must have integer values (type char is included), and the labels must be constants or expressions formed solely from constants. If no label matches the expression value, control goes to the statement labeled default, if present. Otherwise, control passes to the next statement following the switch statement. Once control goes to a particular label, all the subsequent statements in the switch are executed until the end of the switch, or a break statement, is encountered, whichever comes first.

Form

```
switch (expression)
{
    case label1 : statement1
    case label2 : statement2
    default     : statement3
}
```

There can be more than two labeled statements, and the `default` case is optional.

Examples

```
switch (value)
    case 1  : find_sum(ar, n);
              break;
    case 2  : show_array(ar, n);
              break;
    case 3  : puts("Goodbye!");
              break;
    default : puts("Invalid choice, try again.");
              break;
}

switch (letter)
{
    case 'a' :
    case 'e' : printf("%d is a vowel\n", letter);
    case 'c' :
    case 'n' : printf("%d is in \"cane\"\n", letter);
    default  : printf("Have a nice day.\n");
}
```

If `letter` has the value 'a' or 'e', all three messages are printed; 'c' and 'n' cause the last two to be printed. Other values print only the last message.

Summary: Program Jumps

Keywords

The keywords for program jumps are `break`, `continue`, and `goto`.

General Comments

The three instructions `break`, `continue`, and `goto` cause program flow to jump from one location of a program to another location.

The *break* Command

The `break` command can be used with any of the three loop forms and with the `switch` statement. It causes program control to skip the rest of the loop or `switch` containing it and to resume with the next command following the loop or `switch`.

Example

```
switch (number)
{
    case  4:  printf("That's a good choice.\n");
              break;
    case  5:  printf("That's a fair choice.\n");
              break;
    default:  printf("That's a poor choice.\n");
}
```

The *continue* Command

The continue command can be used with any of the three loop forms but not with a switch. It causes program control to skip the remaining statements in a loop. For a while or for loop, the next loop cycle is started. For a do while loop, the exit condition is tested and then, if necessary, the next loop cycle is started.

Example

```
while ((ch = getchar())  != EOF)
{
    if (ch == ' ')
         continue;
    putchar(ch);
    chcount++;
}
```

This fragment echoes and counts nonspace characters.

The *goto* Command

A goto statement causes program control to jump to a statement bearing the indicated label. A colon is used to separate a labeled statement from its label. Label names follow the rules for variable names. The labeled statement can come either before or after the goto.

Form

```
goto label;
    label : statement
```

Example

```
top : ch = getchar();
      if (ch != 'y')
        goto top;
```

ASCII Table

DEC X_{10}	HEX X_{16}	OCT X_8	Binary X_2	ASCII	Key
0	00	00	000 0000	NUL	Ctrl/1
1	01	01	000 0001	SOH	Ctrl/A
2	02	02	000 0010	STX	Ctrl/B
3	03	03	000 0011	ETX	Ctrl/C
4	04	04	000 0100	EOT	Ctrl/D
5	05	05	000 0101	ENQ	Ctrl/E
6	06	06	000 0110	ACK	Ctrl/F
7	07	07	000 0111	BEL	Ctrl/G
8	08	10	000 1000	BS	Ctrl/H, Backspace
9	09	11	000 1001	HT	Ctrl/I, Tab
10	0A	12	000 1010	LF	Ctrl/J, Line Feed
11	0B	13	000 1011	VT	Ctrl/K
12	0C	14	000 1100	FF	Ctrl/L
13	0D	15	000 1101	CR	Ctrl/M, Return
14	0E	16	000 1110	SO	Ctrl/N
15	0F	17	000 1111	SI	Ctrl/O
16	10	20	001 0000	DLE	Ctrl/P
17	11	21	001 0001	DC1	Ctrl/Q
18	12	22	001 0010	DC2	Ctrl/R

DEC X_{10}	HEX X_{16}	OCT X_8	Binary X_2	ASCII	Key
19	13	23	001 0011	DC3	Ctrl/S
20	14	24	001 0100	DC4	Ctrl/T
21	15	25	001 0101	NAK	Ctrl/U
22	16	26	001 0110	SYN	Ctrl/V
23	17	27	001 0111	ETB	Ctrl/W
24	18	30	001 1000	CAN	Ctrl/X
25	19	31	001 1001	EM	Ctrl/Y
26	1A	32	001 1010	SUB	Ctrl/Z
27	1B	33	001 1011	ESC	Esc, Escape
28	1C	34	001 1100	FS	Ctrl/\
29	1D	35	001 1101	GS	Ctrl/]
30	1E	36	001 1110	RS	Ctrl/=
31	1F	37	001 1111	US	Ctrl/-
32	20	40	010 0000	SP	Spacebar
33	21	41	010 0001	!	!
34	22	42	010 0010	"	"
35	23	43	010 0011	#	#
36	24	44	010 0100	$	$
37	25	45	010 0101	%	%
38	26	46	010 0110	&	&
39	27	47	010 0111	'	'
40	28	50	010 1000	(	(
41	29	51	010 1001	)	)
42	2A	52	010 1010	*	*
43	2B	53	010 1011	+	+
44	2C	54	010 1100	,	,
45	2D	55	010 1101	-	-
46	2E	56	010 1110	.	.
47	2F	57	010 1111	/	/
48	30	60	011 0000	0	0
49	31	61	011 0001	1	1
50	32	62	011 0010	2	2
51	33	63	011 0011	3	3
52	34	64	011 0100	4	4
53	35	65	011 0101	5	5

DEC X_{10}	HEX X_{16}	OCT X_8	Binary X_2	ASCII	Key
54	36	66	011 0110	6	6
55	37	67	011 0111	7	7
56	38	70	011 1000	8	8
57	39	71	011 1001	9	9
58	3A	72	011 1010	:	:
59	3B	73	011 1011	;	;
60	3C	74	011 1100	⟨	⟨
61	3D	75	011 1101	=	=
62	3E	76	011 1110	⟩	⟩
63	3F	77	011 1111	?	?
64	40	100	100 0000	@	@
65	41	101	100 0001	A	A
66	42	102	100 0010	B	B
67	43	103	100 0011	C	C
68	44	104	100 0100	D	D
69	45	105	100 0101	E	E
70	46	106	100 0110	F	F
71	47	107	100 0111	G	G
72	48	110	100 1000	H	H
73	49	111	100 1001	I	I
74	4A	112	100 1010	J	J
75	4B	113	100 1011	K	K
76	4C	114	100 1100	L	L
77	4D	115	100 1101	M	M
78	4E	116	100 1110	N	N
79	4F	117	100 1111	O	O
80	50	120	101 0000	P	P
81	51	121	101 0001	Q	Q
82	52	122	101 0010	R	R
83	53	123	101 0011	S	S
84	54	124	101 0100	T	T
85	55	125	101 0101	U	U
86	56	126	101 0110	V	V
87	57	127	101 0111	W	W
88	58	130	101 1000	X	X

DEC X_{10}	HEX X_{16}	OCT X_8	Binary X_2	ASCII	Key
89	59	131	101 1001	Y	Y
90	5A	132	101 1010	Z	Z
91	5B	133	101 1011	[	[
92	5C	134	101 1100	\	\
93	5D	135	101 1101	]	]
94	5E	136	101 1110	^	^
95	5F	137	101 1111	–	–
96	60	140	110 0000	'	'
97	61	141	110 0001	a	a
98	62	142	110 0010	b	b
99	63	143	110 0011	c	c
100	64	144	110 0100	d	d
101	65	145	110 0101	e	e
102	66	146	110 0110	f	f
103	67	147	110 0111	g	g
104	68	150	110 1000	h	h
105	69	151	110 1001	i	i
106	6A	152	110 1010	j	j
107	6B	153	110 1011	k	k
108	6C	154	110 1100	l	l
109	6D	155	110 1101	m	m
110	6E	156	110 1110	n	n
111	6F	157	110 1111	o	o
112	70	160	111 0000	p	p
113	71	161	111 0001	q	q
114	72	162	111 0010	r	r
115	73	163	111 0011	s	s
116	74	164	111 0100	t	t
117	75	165	111 0101	u	u
118	76	166	111 0110	v	v
119	77	167	111 0111	w	w
120	78	170	111 1000	x	x
121	79	171	111 1001	y	y
122	7A	172	111 1010	z	z
123	7B	173	111 1011	{	{

DEC X_{10}	HEX X_{16}	OCT X_8	Binary X_2	ASCII	Key
124	7C	174	111 1100	|	|
125	7D	175	111 1101	}	}
126	7E	176	111 1110	~	~
127	7F	177	111 1111	Del	Del, Rubout

Standard I/O Functions (ANSI C)

The ANSI C standard library includes several standard I/O functions associated with streams and the stdio.h file. Table F.1 presents the ANSI prototypes for these functions along with a brief explanation of what they do. For complete descriptions, consult the documentation for your implementation or a reference manual.

Table F.1. ANSI C standard I/O functions.

Prototype	Description
`void clearerr(FILE *)`	Clears end-of-file and error indicators
`int fclose(FILE *)`	Closes the indicated file
`int feof(FILE *)`	Tests for end of file
`int ferror(FILE *)`	Tests error indicator
`int fflush(FILE *)`	Flushes the indicated file
`int fgetc(FILE *)`	Gets the next character from the indicated input stream
`int fgetpos(FILE *,` `  fpos_t *)`	Stores the current value of the file position indicator
`char * fgets(char *,` `  int, FILE *)`	Gets the next line (or indicated number of characters) from the indicated stream
`FILE * fopen(const char *,` `  const char *)`	Opens the indicated file
`int fprintf(FILE *,` `  const char *, ...)`	Writes the formatted output to the indicated stream
`int fputc(int, FILE *)`	Writes the indicated character to the indicated stream
`int fputs(const char *,` `  FILE *)`	Writes the indicated character to the indicated stream
`size_t fread(void *, size_t,` `  size_t, FILE *)`	Reads binary data from the indicated stream
`FILE * freopen(const char *,` `  const char *, FILE *)`	Opens the indicated file and associates it with the indicated stream
`int fscanf(FILE *,` `  const char *, ...)`	Reads formatted input from the indicated stream
`int fsetpos(FILE *,` `  const fpos_t *)`	Sets the file-position pointer to the indicated value
`int fseek(FILE *, long, int)`	Sets the file-position pointer to the indicated value

Prototype	Description
`long ftell(FILE *)`	Gets the current file position
`size_t fwrite(const void *, size_t, size_t, FILE *)`	Writes binary data to the indicated stream
`int getc(FILE *)`	Reads the next character from the indicated input
`int getchar()`	Reads the next character from the standard input
`char * gets(char *)`	Gets the next line from the standard input
`void perror(const char *)`	Writes system error messages to the standard error
`int printf(const char *, ...)`	Writes formatted output to the standard output
`int putc(int, FILE *)`	Writes the indicated character to the indicated output
`int putchar(int)`	Writes the indicated character to the standard output
`int puts(const char *)`	Writes the string to the standard output
`int remove(const char *)`	Removes the named file
`int rename(const char *, constchar *)`	Renames the named file
`void rewind(FILE *)`	Sets the file-position pointer to the start of the file
`int scanf(const char *, ...)`	Reads formatted input from the standard input
`void setbuf(FILE *, char *)`	Sets the buffer size and location
`int setvbuf(FILE *, char *, int, size_t)`	Sets the buffer size, location, and mode
`int sprintf(char *, const char *, ...)`	Writes formatted output to the indicated string
`int sscanf(const char *, const char *, ...)`	Reads formatted input from the indicated string
`FILE * tmpfile(void)`	Creates a temporary file

continues

Table F.1. continued

Prototype	Description
`char * tmpnam(char *)`	Generates a unique name for a temporary file
`int ungetc(int, FILE *)`	Pushes the indicated character back onto the input stream
`int vfprintf(FILE *, const char *, va_list)`	Like `fprintf()`, except uses a single list-argument instead of a variable argument list
`int vprintf(const char *, va_list)`	Like `printf()`, except uses a single list-argument instead of a variable argument list
`int vsprintf(char *, const char *, va_list)`	Like `sprintf()`, except uses a single list-argument instead of a variable argument list

Answers to the Review Questions

Chapter 1

1. A perfectly portable program is one whose source code can, without modification, be compiled to a successful program on a variety of different computer systems.

2. A source code file contains code as written in whatever language the programmer is using. An object code file contains machine language code; it need not be the code for a complete program. An executable file contains the complete code, in machine language, constituting an executable program.

3. a. Defining program objectives.
   b. Designing the program.
   c. Coding the program.
   d. Compiling the program.
   e. Running the program.
   f. Testing and debugging the program.
   g. Maintaining and modifying the program.

4. A compiler converts source code, such as code in the C language, to machine language code.

5. A linker combines object code from several sources, such as compiled source code and compiled library code, into a single, executable program.

Chapter 2

1. They are called functions.

2. A syntax error is a violation of the rules governing how sentences or programs are put together. Here's an example in English: "Me speak English good." Here's an example in C:

```
printf"Where are the parentheses?";.
```

3. A semantic error is one of meaning. Here's an example in English: "This sentence is excellent Italian." Here's a C example: thrice_n = 3 + n;.

4. Line 1: Begin the line with a #; spell the file stdio.h; place the filename within angle brackets.
   Line 2: Use (), not {}; end comment with */, not /*.
   Line 3: Use {, not (.
   Line 4: Complete the statement with a semicolon.
   Line 5: Mr. IBM got this one (the blank line) right!
   Line 6: Use =, not := for assignment. (Apparently Mr. IBM knows a little Pascal.) Use 52, not 56, weeks per year.
   Line 7: Should be

```
printf("There are %d weeks in a year.\n",s);
```

   Line 9: There isn't a line 9, but there should be, and it should consist of the closing brace, }.

5. a. Baa Baa Black Sheep.Have you any wool?

   (Note that there is no space after the period. We could have had a space by using " Have instead of "Have.)

   b. Begone!
      O creature of lard!

(Note that the cursor is left at the end of the second line.)

c. `What?`
    `No/nBonzo?`

(Note that the slash (/) does not have the same effect as the backslash \.)

d. `2 + 2 = 4`

(Note how each `%d` is replaced by the corresponding variable value from the list. Note, too, that + means addition and that calculation can be done inside a `printf()` statement.)

6. `int` and `char`

7. `printf`("There were %d words and %d lines.\n", words, lines);

8. After line 7, `a` is 5 and `b` is 2. After line 8, both `a` and `b` are 5. After line 9, both `a` and `b` are 5. Note that `a` can't be 2 because by the time you say `a = b;`, `b` already has been changed to 5.

Chapter 3

1. a. `int`, possibly `short` or `unsigned` or `unsigned short`; population is a whole number.

   b. `float`; it's unlikely the average will be an exact integer.

   c. `char`

   d. `int`, possibly `unsigned`

2. Line 1: Should be #include <stdio.h>.
   Line 2: Should have a pair of parentheses following `main`; i.e., `main()`.
   Line 3: Use {, not (.
   Line 4: Should be a comma, not a semicolon, between g and h.
   Line 5: Fine.
   Line 6: (blank) Fine.
   Line 7: There should be at least one digit before the e. Either `1e21` or `1.0e21` is okay.
   Line 8: Fine.
   Line 9: Use }, not). Missing Lines: First, `rate` is never assigned a value. Second, the variable h is never used. Also, the program never informs us of the results of its calculation. Neither of these errors will stop the program from running (although you may be given a warning about the unused variable), but they do detract from its already limited usefulness. Also, there should be a return statement at the end.

3. a. `int, %o`
   b. `long double, %Lf`
   c. `char, %c`
   d. `long, %ld`
   e. `char, %c`
   f. `float, %f`
   g. `int, %x%`

4. Line 0: It's better form to have `#include <stdio.h>`.
   Line 1: Use `/*` and `*/`.
   Line 3: `int cows, legs;`
   Line 5: `count?\n");`
   Line 6: `%d`, not `%c`
   Line 6: `&legs`
   Line 8: `%d`, not `%f`

Chapter 4

1. The program bombs. The first `scanf()` statement reads just your first name, leaving your last name untouched but still stored in the input "buffer." (This buffer is just a temporary storage area used to store the input.) When the next `scanf()` statement comes along looking for your weight, it picks up where the last reading attempt ended, and attempts to read your last name as your weight. This frustrates `scanf()`. On the other hand, if you respond to the name request with something like `Lasha 144`, it will use `144` as your weight even though you typed it before your weight was requested.

2. a. `He sold the painting for $234.50.`

   b. `Hi!` (Note: The first character is a character constant, the second is a decimal integer converted to a character, and the third is an ASCII representation of a character constant.)

   c. `His Hamlet was funny without being vulgar.`
   `has 41 characters.`

   d. `Is 1.20e+003 the same as 1201.00?`

3. Recall the `%%` construction for printing `%`.

   ```
   printf("This copy of \"%s\" sells for $%0.2f.\n", BOOK, cost);
   printf("That is %0.0f%% of list.\n", percent);
   ```

4. a. `%15lu`
   b. `%#4x`
   c. `%-12.2E`
   d. `%+10.3f`
   e. `%8.8s`

5. a. `int dalmations;`
     `scanf("%d", &dalmations);`

   b. `float kgs, share;`
     `scanf("%f%f", &kgs, &share);`

   Note: For input, e, f, and g can be used interchangeably. Also, for all but `%c`, it makes no difference if you leave spaces between the conversion specifiers.

   c. `char name[20];`
     `scanf("%s", name);`

   d. `char action[20];`
     `int value;`
     `scanf("%s %d", action, &value);`

   e. `int value;`
     `coanf("%*s %d", &value);`

6. The substitutions would take place. Unfortunately, the preprocessor cannot discriminate between those parentheses that should be replaced with braces and those that should not. Thus,

   ```
   int main(void)

       printf("Hello, O Great One!\n");
   )
   ```

   becomes

   ```
    int main{void}
        {
            printf{"Hello, O Great One!\n"};
        }
   ```

Chapter 5

1. a. `30`
   b. `27` (not 3). `(12 + 6)/(2*3)` would give 3.
   c. `x = 1, y = 1` (integer division)
   d. `x = 3` (integer division) and `y = 9`

2. Line 4: Should end in a semicolon, not a comma.

   Line 8: The `while` statement sets up an infinite loop because the value of `i` remains 1 and is always less than 30. Presumably we meant to write `while(i++ < 30)`.

   Lines 8, 10: The indentation implies that we wanted lines 9 and 10 to form a block, but the lack of braces means that the `while` loop includes only line 9. Braces should be added.

   Line 9: Since 1 and `i` are both integers, the result of the division will be 1 when `i` is 1, and 0 for all larger values. Using `n = 1.0/i;` would cause `i` to be converted to floating-point before division and would yield nonzero answers.

   Line 10: We omitted a newline character (\n) in the control statement. This will cause the numbers to be printed on one line, if possible.

   Line 12: should be `return 0;`

3. The main problem lies in the relationship between the test statement (is `sec` greater than 0?) and the `scanf()` statement that fetches the value of `sec`. In particular, the first time the test is made, the program hasn't had a chance to even get a value for `sec`, and the comparison will be made to some garbage value that happens to be at that memory location. One solution, albeit an inelegant one, is to initialize `sec` to, say, 1 so that the test is passed the first time through. This uncovers a second problem. When we finally type 0 to halt the program, `sec` doesn't get checked until after the loop is finished, and the results for 0 seconds are printed out. What we really want is to have a `scanf()` statement just before the `while` test is made. We can accomplish that by altering the central part of the program to read this way:

```
scanf("%d", &sec);
while ( sec > 0 ) {
  min = sec/SM;
  left = sec % SM;
  printf("%d sec is %d min, %d sec. \n", sec, min, left);
  printf("Next input?\n");
  scanf("%d", &sec);
  }
```

   The first time through, the `scanf()` outside the loop is used. Thereafter, the `scanf()` at the end of the loop (and hence just before the loop begins again) is used. This is a common method for handling problems of this sort.

4. Here is the output:

```
%s is a string
is a string
1
1
2
1
```

Let us explain. The first `printf()` statement is the same as:

```
printf("%s is a string\n","%s is a string\n");
```

The second print statement first increments num to 1 and then prints the value. The third print statement prints num, which is 1, and then increments it to 2. The fourth print statement prints the current value of n, which still is 2, and then decrements n to 1. The final print statement prints the current value of n, 1.

5. It prints on one line the digits 1 through 10 in fields that are five columns wide and then starts a new line:

```
1    2    3    4    5    6    7    8    9    10
```

6. Here is the output for each example:

a. `1    2`

Note that x is incremented and then compared. The cursor is left on the same line.

b.
```
101
102
103
104
```

Note that this time x is compared and then incremented. In both this case and in example *a.*, x is incremented before printing takes place. Note, too, that indenting the second `printf()` statement does not make it part of the `while` loop. Thus, it is called only once, after the `while` loop ends.

c. `stuvw`

Here, there is no incrementing until after the first `printf()`.

7. a. `x = x + 10;`
   b. `x++;`
   c. `c = 2 * (a + b);`
   d. `c = a + 2* b;`

Chapter 6

1. 2, 7, 70, 64, 8, 2

2. a. `x > 5`
   b. `scanf("%lf",&dnum) != 1`
   c. `x == 5`

3. For style, should start with `#include <stdio.h>`.
   Line 3: Should be `list[10]`.
   Line 5: Commas should be semicolons.
   Line 5: Range for i should be from 0 to 9, not 1 to 10.

Line 8: Commas should be semicolons.

Line 8: >= should be <=. Otherwise, when *i* is 1, the loop never ends.

Line 10: There should be another closing brace between lines 9 and 10. One brace closes the compound statement, and one closes the program. In between should be a `return 0;` line.

4. a. `Hi! Hi! Hi! Bye! Bye! Bye! Bye! Bye!`
   b. `ACGM`

5. Here is the output we get:

```
11121314
***
1
4
7

***
1 5
2 7
4 9
8 11

***
+++++
++++
+++
++
```

6. Because the first element has index `0`, the loop range should be 1 to `SIZE` - 1, not 1 to `SIZE`. Making that change, however, causes the first element to be assigned the value `0` instead of `2`. So rewrite the loop this way:

```c
for (index = 0; index < SIZE; index++)
    by_twos[index] = 2 * (index + 1);
```

Similarly, the limits for the second loop should be changed. Also, an array index should be used with the array name:

```c
for( index = 0; index < SIZE; index++)
    printf("%d ", by_twos[index]);
```

7.
```c
long square(int num)
{
    return ((long) num) * num;
}
```

Chapter 7

1. True: b

2. Line 5: Should be scanf("%d %d", &weight, &height);. Don't forget those &s for scanf(). Also, this line should be preceded by a line prompting input.

   Line 9: What is meant is (height > 72 && height > 64). However, the first part of the expression is unnecessary, since height must be less than 72 for the else if to be reached in the first place. Thus, a simple (height > 64) will serve.

   Line 11: The condition is redundant; the second subexpression (weight not less than or equal to 300) means the same as the first. A simple (weight > 300) is all that is needed. But there is more trouble. Line 11 gets attached to the wrong if!. Clearly this else is meant to go along with line 6. By the most recent if not rule, however, it will be associated with the if of line 9. Thus, line 11 is reached when weight is less than 100 and height is 64 or under. This makes it impossible for weight to exceed 300 when this statement is reached.

   Lines 7 through 9: Should be enclosed in braces. Then line 11 will become an alternative to line 6, not to line 9.

   Line 12: Simplify the expression to height > 48).

   Line 14: This else associates with the last if, the one on line 12. Enclose lines 12 and 13 in braces to force this else to associate with the if of line 11. Note that the final message is printed only for those weighing between 100 and 300 pounds.

3. a. 1. The assertion is true, which numerically is a 1.
   b. 0. 3 is not less than 2.
   c. 1. If the first expression is false, the second is true, and vice versa; just one true expression is needed.

4. The program prints the following:

   ```
   *#%*#%$#%*#%*#%$#%*#%*#%$#%*#%*#%
   ```

   Despite what the indentation suggests, the # is printed during every loop, since it is not part of a compound statement.

5. The comments on lines 5 through 7 should be terminated with */. The expression 'a' <= ch >= 'z' should be replaced with

   ```
   ch >= 'a' && ch <= 'z'
   ```

   Incidentally, 'a' <= ch >= 'z' is valid C; it just doesn't have the right meaning. Since relational operators associate left to right, the expression is interpreted as ('a' <= ch) >= 'z'. The expression in parentheses has the value 1 or 0 (true or false), and this value is checked to see whether it is equal to or greater than the numeric code for 'z'. Neither 0 nor 1 satisfies that test, so the whole expression always evaluates to 0 (false). In the second test expression, |¦| should be &&. Also, while !(ch < 'A') is both valid and correct in meaning, ch >= 'A' is simpler. The 'Z' should be followed by two closing parentheses, not one. The `oc++;` statement should be preceded by an `else`. Otherwise, it is incremented every character. The control expression in the `printf()` call should be enclosed in double quotes.

6. Here is the resulting run using the given input:

```
q
Step 1
Step 2
Step 3
c
Step 1
g
Step 1
Step 3
b
Step 1
Done
```

Note that both `b` and `#` terminate the loop, but that entering `b` elicits the printing of `Step 1`, while entering `#` doesn't.

Chapter 8

1. The statement `putchar(getchar());` causes the program to read the next input character and to print it; the return value from `getchar()` is the argument to `putchar()`. No, `getchar(putchar())` is invalid because `getchar()` doesn't use an argument and `putchar()` needs one.

2. `count <essay >essayct` or else `count >essayct <essay`

3. It's a signal (a special value) returned by `getchar()` and `scanf()` to indicate that they have detected the end of a file.

4. a. The output is as follows:

```
If you qu
```

Note that the character `I` is distinct from the character `i`. Also note that the `i` is not printed because the loop quits upon detecting it.

b. The output is as follows:

```
HJacrthjacrt
```

The first time through, `ch` has the value `H`. The `ch++` causes the value to be used (printed) and then incremented (to `I`). Then the `++ch` causes the value to be incremented (to `J`) and then used (printed). After that, the next character (a) is read, and the process is repeated. An important point to note here is that the incrementations affect the value of ch after it has been assigned a value; they don't somehow cause the program to move through the input queue.

5. C's standard I/O library maps diverse file forms to uniform streams that can be handled equivalently.

Chapter 9

1. A formal argument is a variable that is defined in the function being called. The actual argument is the value appearing in the function call; this value is assigned to the formal argument.

2. a.

```
char n_to_ char(n)
int n;
```

or

```
char n_to_char( int n)
```

b.

```
int digits(x, n)
double x;
int n;
```

or

```
int digits(double x, int n)
```

c.

```
int random()
```

or

```
int random(void)
```

3.

```
  double sum(double a, double b)
  {
      return a + b;
  }
```

4. Yes; num should be declared before the first brace, not after or else in the salami() argument list. Also, it should be count++, not num++.

5. Here is the minimal program; the showmenu() and getchoice() functions are possible solutions to parts a. and b.

```
#include <stdio.h>
void showmenu(void);   /* declare functions used */
int getchoice(int, int);
main()
{
    int res;

    showmenu();
    while ((res = getchoice(1,4)) != 4)
        printf("I like choice %d.\n", res);
    printf("Bye!\n");
}
void showmenu(void)
{
    printf("Please choose one of the following:\n");
    printf("1) copy files        2) move files\n");
    printf("3) remove files      4) quit\n");
    printf("Enter the number of your choice:\n");
}

int getchoice(int low, int high)
{
    int ans;
    scanf("%d", &ans);
    while (ans < low || ans  > high)
    {
        printf("%d is not a valid choice; try again\n", ans);
        showmenu();
        scanf("%d", &ans);
    }
    return ans;
}
```

Chapter 10

1. The printout is

   D D
   O O
   L L
   T T

2. The array name ref points to the first element of the array, the character D. The
   expression ref + 1 points to the second element, the character O. The construction
   ++ref is not a valid C expression; ref is a constant, not a variable.

3. a. 12 and 16
   b. 12 and 14 (just the 12 goes in the first row
      because of the braces)

4. a. int digits[10];
   b. float rates[6];
   c. int mat[3][5];
   d. char (*pstr)[20];

> **Note:** char (*pstr)[20]; is incorrect. This would make pstr a constant pointer
> (not a variable) to a single char, the first member of the array; pstr + 1 would
> point to the next byte. With the correct declaration, pstr is a variable, and pstr +
> 1 points 20 bytes beyond the initial byte.

   e. char * psa[20];. Note that the [] have higher precedence than *, so in the absence
      of parentheses, the array descriptor is applied first, then the pointer descriptor.
      Hence, this declaration is the same as char *(psa[20]);.

5. 0 through 9

Chapter 11

1. Storage class should be external or static for pre-ANSI implementations; initialization should include a '\0'.

2. y
   my
   mmy
   ummy
   Yummy

3. a. Ho Ho Ho!!oH oH oH
   b. pointer-to-char
   c. The address of the initial H
   d. *--pc means to decrement the pointer by 1 and use the value found there.
      --*pc means to take the value pointed to by pc and decrement that value by 1.
      (For example, H becomes G.)
   e. Ho Ho Ho!!oH oH o

> **Note:** A null character comes between ! and !, but it produces no printing effect.

f. while(*pc). Check to see that pc does not point to a null character (i.e., to the end of the string). The expression uses the value at the pointed-to location, while(pc - str). Check to see that pc does not point to the same location that str does (the beginning of the string). The expression uses the values of the pointers themselves.

g. After the first while loop, pc points to the null character. Upon entering the second loop, it is made to point to the storage location before the null character, i.e., to the location just before the one that str points to. That byte is interpreted as a character and is printed. The pointer then backs up to the preceding byte. The terminating condition (pc == str) never occurs, and the process continues until you or the system tire.

h. pr() must be declared in the calling program: char *pr();

4. Here is what you get:

```
How are ya, sweetie? How are ya, sweetie?
Beat the clock.
eat the clock.
Beat the clock. Win a toy.
Beat
chat
hat
at
t
t
at
How are ya, sweetie?
```

5. Here is one solution:

```
int strlen(char * s)
{
  int ct = 0;

  while (*s++ != '\0')      /* or while (*s++) */
      ct++;
  return(ct);
}
```

6.

```
#include <stdio.h>
char * strblk(string)
char * string;
{
```

```
    while (*string != ' ' && *string != '\0')
      string++;             /* stops at first blank or null */
    if (*string == '\0')
      return NULL;          /* NULL is the null pointer     */
    else
      return string;
  }
```

Chapter 12

1. It should have `#include <stdio.h>` for its file definitions. It should declare `fp` a file pointer: `FILE *fp;`. The function `fopen()` requires a mode: `fopen("gelatin", "w")` or perhaps the `"a"` mode. The order of the arguments to `fputs()` should be reversed. The `fclose()` function requires a file pointer, not a filename: `fclose(fp);`.

2. a. `ch = getc(fp1);`
   b. `fprintf(fp2,"%c"\n",ch);`
   c. `putc(ch,fp2);`
   d. `fclose(fp1); /* close the terky file */`

> **Note:** `fp1` is used for input operations, because it identifies the file opened in the read mode. Similarly, `fp2` was opened in the write mode, so it is used with output functions.

3. Here is one approach:

   Macintosh C users remember to use `console.h` and `ccommand()`.

```
#include <stdio.h>
#define BUF 256
int has_ch(char ch, char * line);
int main(int argc,char * argv[])
{
   FILE * fp;
   char ch;
   char line [BUF];
   char * fgets();
```

```
        if (argc != 3)
        {
           printf("Usage: %s character filename\n", argv[0]);
           exit(1);
        }
        ch = argv[1][0];
        if ((fp = fopen(argv[2], "r")) == NULL)
        {
           printf("Can't open %s\n", argv[2]);
           exit(1);
        }
        while (fgets(line,BUF,fp) != NULL)
        {
           if (has_ch(ch,line))
              fputs(line,stdout);
        }
        fclose(fp);
        return 0;
     }


     int has_ch(char ch, char * line)
     {
        while (*line)
           if (ch == *line++)
              return(1);
        return 0;
     }
```

The fgets() and fputs() functions work together because fgets() leaves the \n produced by Enter in the string, and fputs() does not add a \n the way that puts() does.

4. a. When 8238201 is saved using fprintf(), it's saved as seven characters stored in 7 bytes. When saved using fwrite(), it's saved as a 4-byte integer using the binary representation of that numeric value.
   b. No difference; in each case it's saved as a 1-byte binary code.

5. The "r+" mode lets you read and write anywhere in a file, so it's best suited. The "a+" only lets you append material to the end of the file, and the "w+" starts with a clean slate, discarding prior file contents.

Chapter 13

1. The automatic and the static storage classes.

2. The external storage class; the external static storage class.

3. Replace `array[search] > array[top]` with `array[search] < array[top]`.

4. `daisy` is known to `main()` by default, and to `petal()`, `stem()`, and `root()` because of the `extern` declaration. The `extern int daisy;` declaration in file 2 makes `daisy` known to all the functions in file 2. The first `lily` is local to `main()`: the reference to `lily` in `petal()` is an error because there is no external `lily` in either file. There is an external static `lily`, but it is known just to functions in the second file. The first external `rose` is known to `root()`, but `stem()` has overridden it with its own local `rose`.

5. a. It tells us that the program will use a variable `plink` that is local to the file containing the function. The first argument to `value_ct()` is a pointer to an integer, presumably the first element of an array of n members. The important point here is that the program will not be allowed to use the pointer `arr` to modify values in the original array.
   b. No. Already `value` and n are copies of original data, so there is no way for the function to alter the corresponding values in the calling program. What these declarations do accomplish is to prevent the function from altering `value` and n within the function. For example, the function couldn't use the expression n++ if n were qualified as `const`.

Chapter 14

1. The proper keyword is `struct`, not `structure`. The template requires either a tag before the opening brace or a variable name after the closing brace. Also, there should be a semicolon after `* togs` and at the end of the template.

2.
```
struct month {
        char name[10];
        char abbrev[4];
        int days;
        int monumb;
};
```

3.
```
extern struct month months[];
int days(int month)
{
    int index, total;

    if (month < 1 || month > 12)
        return(-1);   /* error signal */
    else
    {
        for (index = 0, total = 0; index < month; index ++)
                total += months[index].days;
        return( total);
    }
}
```

Note that `index` is one less than month number, since arrays start with subscript 0. Hence, we use `index < month` instead of `index <= month`.

4. a. 6
   Arcturan
   cturan
   b. Use the structure name and use the pointer.

```
deb.title.last
pb->title.last
```
   c. Here is one version:

```
#include <stdio.h>
#include "starfolk.h"    /* make struct defs available */
void prbem ( pbem )
struct bem * pbem;
{
    printf("%s %s is a %d-limbed %s.\n", pbem->title.first,
            pbem->title.last, pbem->limbs, pbem->type);
}
```

5. Here is one possibility:

```
struct car {
        char name[20];
        float hp;
        float epampg;
        float wbase;
        int year;
};
```

6. The function could be set up like this:

```
        struct gas {
    float distance;
    float gals;
    float mpg;
};
struct gas mpgs(struct gas trip)
{
  if (trip.gals > 0)
    trip.mpg = trip.distance / trip.gals ;
  else
    trip.mpg = -1.0;
  return trip;
}
```

Note that this function cannot directly alter values in the calling program, so we must use the return value to convey the information:

```
struct gas idaho;

idaho = mpgs(idaho);
```

7. `char * (*pfun)(char *, char);`

Chapter 15

1. a. 00000011
   b. 00001101
   c. 00111011
   d. 01110111

2. a. 21, 025, 0x15
   b. 85, 0125, 0x55
   c. 76, 0114, 0x4C
   d. 157, 0235, 0x9D

3. a. 252
   b. 2
   c. 7
   d. 7
   e. 5
   f. 3
   g. 28

4. a. 255
   b. 1 (not false is true)
   c. 0

d. 1 (true and true is true)

e. 6

f. 1 (true or true is true)

g. 8

5. In binary, the mask is 1111111. In decimal, it's 127. In octal, it's 0177. In hexadecimal, it's 0xFF.

6. The two printer-number bits are the left-most bits of an unsigned quantity. When they are right-shifted to bit positions 1 and 0, all the vacated bits are replaced with 0s, so there is no need for further masking.

Chapter 16

1. a. `dist = 5280 * miles;` is valid.

   b. `plort = 4 * 4 + 4;` is valid. But if the user really wanted `4 * (4 + 4)`, he or she should have used `#define POD (FEET + FEET)`.

   c. `nex = = 6;;` valid, but not meaningful. Apparently the user forgot that he or she was writing for the preprocessor, not writing in C.

   d. `y = y + 5;` is valid.

   `berg = berg + 5 * lob;` is valid, but this is probably not the desired result.

   `est = berg + 5/ y + 5;` is valid, but this is probably not the desired result.

   `nilp = lob *-berg + 5;` is valid, but this is probably not the desired result.

2. `#define MIN(X,Y) ( (X) < (Y) ? (X) : (Y)`

3. `#define PR(X,Y) printf(#X " is %d and " #Y " is %d\n", X,Y)`
   Since X and Y are never exposed to any other operations (such as multiplication) in this macro, we don't have to cocoon everything in parentheses.

4. Try this:

   ```
   #define P(X) printf("name: "#X"; value: %d; address: %u\n",\
           X, &X)
   ```

   Or, if your implementation allows, use the `%p` specification for the address.

5. a. `enum days {sun, mon, tue, wed, thu, fri, sat};`
      `enum days {sun = 1, mon, tue, wed, thu, fri, sat};`
   b. `enum days visit;`

6. The program should include the `stdlib.h` file, if available, or else declare `malloc()` or `calloc()`.

```
struct wine * ptrwine;

ptrwine = (struct wine *) calloc(100, sizeof (struct wine));

or

ptrwine = (struct wine *)
             malloc(100 * sizeof (struct wine));
```

Chapter 17

1. Defining a data type consists of deciding how to store the data and of designing a set of functions to manage the data.

2. The list can be traversed in only one direction because each structure contains the address of the next structure but not of the preceding structure. You could modify the structure definition so that each structure contains two pointers, one to the preceding structure and one to the next structure. The program, of course, would have to assign proper addresses to these pointers each time a new structure is added.

3. An ADT is an abstract data type, a formal definition of the properties of a type and of the operations that can be performed with the type. An ADT should be expressed in general terms, not in terms of some specific computer language or implementation details.

4. Advantages of passing a variable directly: These functions inspect a list or queue but should not alter them. Passing a list or queue variable directly means the function works with a copy of the original, guaranteeing that the function will not alter the original data. When passing a variable directly, you don't have to remember to use the address operator or a pointer. Disadvantages of passing a variable directly: The program has to allocate enough space to hold the variable, then copy information from the original to the copy. If the variable is a large structure, using it has a time and space penalty. Advantages of passing the address of a variable: passing an address and accessing the original data is faster and requires less memory than passing a variable if the variable is a large structure. Disadvantages of passing the address of a variable: You have to remember to use the address operator or a pointer. Under K&R C the function could inadvertently alter the original data, but you can overcome this objection with the ANSI C `const` qualifier.

5. a.

Type Name:	stack
Type Properties:	Can hold an ordered sequence of items

Type Operations:	Initialize stack to empty
	Determine whether stack is empty
	Determine whether stack is full
	Add item to top of stack (pushing an item)
	Remove and recover item from top of stack
	(popping an item)

b.

```
/* stack.h -- interface for a stack */

/* INSERT ITEM TYPE HERE */
/* FOR EXAMPLE, typedef int Item; */

#define MAXSTACK 100

typedef enum boolean {False, True} BOOLEAN;

typedef struct node

{
    Item item;
    struct node * next;
} Node;

typedef struct stack

{
    Node * top;      /* pointer to top of stack */
    Node * base;     /* pointer to base of stack */
    int items;       /* number of items in stack */
} Stack;

/* operation:       initialize the stack */
/* precondition:    ps points to a stack */
/* postcondition:   stack is initialized to being empty */
void InitializeStack(Stack * ps);

/* operation:       check if stack is full */
/* precondition:    ps points to previously initialized stack */
```

```
/* postcondition:   returns True if stack is full, else False */
BOOLEAN FullStack(const Stack * ps);

/* operation:       check if stack is empty */
/* precondition:    ps points to previously initialized stack */
/* postcondition:   returns True if stack is empty, else False  */
BOOLEAN EmptyStack(const Stack *ps);

/* operation:       push item onto top of stack  */
/* precondition:    ps points to previously initialized stack  */
/*                  item is to be placed on top of stack  */
/* postcondition:   if stack is not empty, item is placed at  */
/*                  top of stack and function returns  */
/*                  True; otherwise, stack is unchanged and  */
/*                  function returns False  */
BOOLEAN Push(Item item, Stack * ps);

/* operation:       remove item from top of stack  */
/* precondition:    ps points to previously initialized stack  */
/* postcondition:   if stack is not empty, item at top of  */
/*                  stack is copied to *pitem and deleted from  */
/*                  stack, and function returns True; if the  */
/*                  operation empties the stack, the stack is  */
/*                  reset to empty. If the stack is empty to  */
/*                  begin with, stack is unchanged and the  */
/*                  function returns False  */
BOOLEAN Pop(Item *pitem, Stack * ps);
```

6. Maximum number of comparisons required:

Items	Sequential Search	Binary Search
3	3	2
1023	1023	10
65535	65535	16

7. See Figure G.1

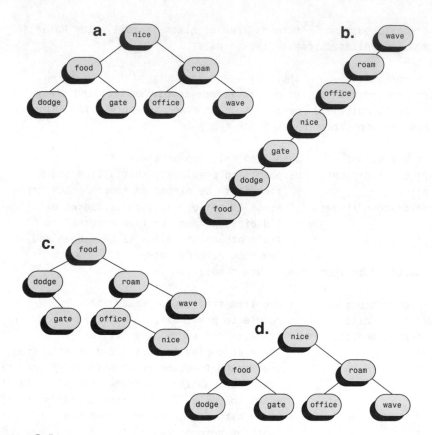

Figure G.1. *Binary search tree of words*

I

Index

Symbols

! character, 152
! NOT operator, 222-223
!= operator, 212
flag, 97
preprocessor symbol, 27
% modulus operator, 134, 352, 646
% placeholder symbol, 32
%% specifier, 93, 109
& address operator, 648
& AND operator, 650
& binary operator, 519
& operator, 305-306
&& AND operator, 222-223
&= bitwise logical operator, 519
, comma operator, 219, 651
-> structure pointer operator, 483-484
. member operator, 474-475
{ } braces, 122
} closing brace, 122
* dereferencing operator, 334, 649
* Indirection operator, 309-310
* modifier, 112
* multiplication operator, 126-128, 646
*= operator, 195-200
+ addition operator, 125, 646
+ flag, 97
++ increment operator, 135-138, 646
++ postfix mode, 135
++ prefix mode, 135
+= operators, 200
- decrement operator, 138-139
- flag, 97
- subtraction operator, 125, 646
-> indirect membership operator, 649-650
-1 end of file (EOF) signal, 255-257
< (less than) symbol, 121

<, redirection operator, 259-260
= assignment operator, 122-125, 647
> redirection operator, 259-260
>> add data operator, 260
?: conditional operator, 227-229, 648
\\ (backslash) escape sequence, 61-62
\ (backslash) escape sequence symbol, 61
\" (double quote) escape sequence, 61-62
\' (single quote) escape sequence, 61-62
/ division operator, 128-129, 646
^ binary operator, 519-520
^ EXCLUSIVE OR operator, 650
^= bitwise logical operator, 520
{ } (braces), 26-28
| binary operator, 519
| pipe operator, 260
| OR operator, 650
|= bitwise logical operator, 519
|| OR operator, 222-223
~ bitwise logical operator, 518-519, 525
\0 (octal value) escape sequence, 61-62
0 flag, 97

A

\a (alert) escape sequence, 61
abstract data types (ADTs), 571-573, 583-598
accessing
    array elements, 320
    libraries, 555-556
    members by pointers, 483
    structure members, 474-475
    user interface, 263-269
activating functions with return values, 198-203

actual arguments, 152, 285-286
add_one.c file (listing 5.10), 135
addemup.c file (listing 5.13), 143
adding items to queues, 599, 604-606
AddItem( ) function, 595-597, 624-625
addition (+) operator, 646
AddNode( ) function, 624-627
address (&) operator, 648
address operators, 482-483
addresses, 314
    assigning to pointer, 334
    of structures, 485-486
    used by functions, 305-306
    variables, 305
ADTs (abstract data types), 571-573, 583-598
    binary tree, 621-636
algorithms, 572
    selection sort alogrithm, 390
alias.c file (listing 4.5), 90
aliases, creating, 89
allocating
    memory, 562-565
        dynamic memory allocation, 575
        for structures, 472-473
        storage classes, 566
    structures, 575-579
American National Standards
    Institute, see ANSI
American Standard Code for
    Information Interchange, see ASCII
AmigaDOS, redirection, 258-260
AND (&) operator, 650
animals.c file (listing 7.11), 234
ANSI
    committee X3J11, 18
    forms recognition by compilers, 197

ANSI C, 18
    ctype.h character functions, 390-393
    function library, 84, 290, 637
        string-handling functions, 387-388
    function prototype, 153, 285, 290-293
    keywords, 49-52
    naming standards, 29
    standard input/output functions, 92
    structure, 33
append( ) function, 429
append.c file (listing 12.7), 428-429
appending file contents, 427-429
applications
    entry-condition loop, 189-190
    exit-condition loop, 189-190
arf.c file (listing 10.10), 336
argc (argument count), 394-395
argument values, see argv
arguments, 588
    array names as, 330-331
    calling functions with, 285-286
    command-line, 393-396, 407-408
    #define directive, 541-544
    float data type, 96
    forms, 285
    functions, 73, 282-284
    macro, 541-543
        in strings, 543-544
    passing, 104
    pointer, 331-332
argv (argument values), 394-395
arithmetic
    operators, 199-200, 646
    with bitwise shift operators, 524-534
array forms
    constant addresses, 363
    elements, 365

name, 365
  versus pointer form, 363-365
array notation, 333, 343
arrays, 82
  addresses of, 491-496
  and loops, 192-195
  as queue data forms, 599-603
  automatic, 321
  binary searches, implementing,
    618-619
  char, 81-82
  declarations, 320, 477
  dynamic, creating, 563-564
  elements, 192-195
    accessing, 320
    indices, 193
    inserting, 616
    numbering, 193-195
    offsets, 193
    subscripts, 193
  external, 321-322
  first elements, as structures,
    493-496
  identification in structures,
    477-478
  initializing, 320-325, 364-365
  multidimensional, 337-340
    and functions, 344-348
    and pointers, 340-348
    initializing, 339-340
  names
    as function argument, 330-331
    see also addresses
  of strings, 366
  of structures, 491-496
  pointers to, 326-329
  ragged, 366-368
  rectangular, 366-368
  size, 195-197, 365
  static, 322

structures, 475-479
  subscripts, 478
  values
    assigning, 325-326
    displaying, 351-352
  versus linked lists, 616-619
  with for loops, 194-197
ASCII code, 168, 665-668
  initializing constants, 60
  nonprinting characters, 60
  standard, 59
  values in for loops, 178-182
assigning
  addresses to pointers, 334
  array values, 325-326
assignment (=) operator, 123, 647
assignment operators, 182, 647
  priorities, 182
  updating variables, 185-186
assignment statement, 30-31, 143
  type conversions, 148
association rule, 132
atan( ) function, 558
atan2( ) function, 558-559
atexit( ) function, 560-562
atof( ) function, 397
atoi( ) function, 396-397
atol( ) function, 397
auto keyword, 437
automatic arrays, 321, 362
  assigning values, 325
automatic storage duration, 436
automatic type conversions, 149
automatic variables, 321, 437-438
  initializing, 438
  linkage, 437
  scope, 437
  storage duration, 437
AVL trees, 635

B

\b (backspace) escape sequence, 32, 61-62
backslash character (\\), 32
badcount.c file (listing 3.8), 73
badlimits( ) function, 270-273
balanced trees, 635
base 2 numbering system, 514
bases.c file (listing 3.3), 55
BASIC programming language, 2
begin/end function symbol { }, 26-28
beta( ) function, 444
binary
    decimal equivalents, 518
    fractions, 516
    hexadecimal equivalents, 518
    notation, 298-299
    numbers
        floating-point, 516-518
        maximum, 514
        minimum, 514
    octal equivalents, 517
    operators, 125
    searches, 618-619
    system, 514-516
binary data
    reading, 426
    writing, 426
binary files, 404-405, 496-511
    end-marking, 254-257
binary search tree interface, 620-624
binary trees, 621-636
    data forms, 497-511
    drawbacks, 635-636
    implementing, 624-631
binary.c file file
    listing 9.9, 299
    listing 15.1, 524-525
bit fields, 527-532
    creating, 527-528
    example, 528-532

exceding size of, 528
    hardware dedication, 529
    placement order, 528
    unnamed, 529
bit-mapped images, 573
bits, 50, 514, 573
    bit fields, 527-532
    checking values of, 522-523
    high-order, 514
    low-order, 514
    toggling, 522
    turning off, 522
    turning on, 521-522
bitwise logical operators, 518-527
    data types, 518-520
    masks, 520-521
    precedence, 523
bitwise operators, 650
    programming with, 524-527
bitwise shift operators, 518-527
    arithmetic with, 524-534
black box viewpoint, 286
block scope, 436
blocks, 122, 145, 658
book structures
    subscripts, 474-475
    templates, 471-472
book.c file (listing 14.1), 470-471
booksave.c file (listing 14.11), 494-506
Borland C
    compiling programs, 301
    floating-point values, 475-479
bottles.c file (listing 5.12), 138-139
braces ({ }), 28, 122
    in if else statements, 218
branching statements, 207
break statement, 243, 662-663
    avoiding, 233
    echoing input value, 233
    in nested loops, 232
    loops, 231-233

break.c file (listing 7.10), 232-233
buffered
    functions, 252
    input, 251-252
        programming problems,
        263-269
buffering I/O functions, 252
buffers
    advantages, 251-252
    flushing, 423
building interfaces, 586-590
butler( ) function, 37
byebye.c file (listing 16.8), 560-561
bytes, 50, 514

C

%c specifier, 92, 109, 265-271
%c variable code, 47
C compiler, 572
C language
    advantages, 2-5
    comments within, 26-28, 35
    conventions, 19
    creators, 2
    files, naming, 10, 15-17
    function library, 84
    IBM PC systems, 13-17
    Macintosh systems, 17-18
    publications, 641-642
    standards, 18-19
    Unix systems, 11-13
    writing programs, 6
calloc( ) function, 565-566
case labels, multiple, 237-238
cast operators
    type conversions, 149-150
casts, 149
char (character variable type), 47
    array, 81-82
    declaring variables, 60

char keyword, 49, 59, 64, 70
character arrays
    initializing, 363
    templates, 471-472
character data type, 29
character strings, see strings
character variable type (char), 47
character-mapping functions, 392
character-testing functions, 391-392
characters, 654
    input, 249-250
    nonprinting, 60-63
    null, 81-82
    output, 249-250
    printing, 63-64
    redirection, 249-250
charcode.c file (listing 3.5), 64
chcount.c file (listing 7.6), 221-222
child nodes, 620
circular queues, 600-603
classes, storage, 321
    automatic variables, 321
    choosing, 445-446
    comments, 322
    dynamic memory allocation, 566
    external variables, 321-322,
       438-441
    properties, 655
    scope, 434-446
    static variables, 322, 442-443
clock( ) function, 612
closing files, 410
closing brace (}), 122
cnt_sp.c file (listing 16.4), 547
code
    library, 11
    source
        compiling, 7
        debugging, 8
        files, 10
        testing, 8

coding programs, 169-170
colddays.c file (listing 7.1), 206-207
collating sequence, 382
combined redirection, 259-260
combining template/variable
  definition, 473
comma (,) operator, 651
  solving problems, 185-191
comma operators
  as separators, 184-186
  as sequence pointer, 183
  expression linking, 185
  for loop extension, 183-186
  initialize expression, 183-186
  multiple use, 186
  update expression, 183-186
command-line, 13-15, 393
  arguments, 393-396, 407-408
  integrated enviroments, 395
  Think C, 395-401
command.c file (listing 11.21), 386
comments
  in C programs, 26-28, 35
  storage classes, 322
compare.c file (listing 11.16),
  380-381
comparing
  arrays to linked lists, 616
  do while loop to while loop,
    187-189
  while loop to do while loop,
    187-189
comparison expressions, 167-168
compback.c file (listing 11.17),
  381-382
compile time substitution, 86
compilers, 10
  ANSI forms recognition, 197
  command-line, 13-15

compiling programs, 7
  on IBM PC systems, 13-19
  on UNIX systems, 12-13
  with multiple functions,
    300-304
compound statements, 145-149, 658
compression
  lossless, 573
  lossy, 573
condensing files, 410-412
conditional (?:) operator, 648
conditional expressions, 227-229
  layout, 227
  setting variables, 227
conditional operators, 244
const keyword, 462-463
const qualifiers, 491
constants, 48, 85
  DBL_DIG, 91
  defining, 551
  enumerated type, 553
  floating-point, 66
  FLT_DIG, 91
  INT_MAX, 91
  INT_MIN, 91
  integer
    int, 53-54
    long, 58
  symbolic
    defining, 86
    naming, 88
    NULL, 577
continue statement, 230-231, 243,
  270-273, 663
  loops, 229-231
control expressions, 180-182
control statement, 175
Control-D, UNIX end of file signal,
  256-257

Control-Z
  end-marking files, 254-257
  PCs end-of file signal, 256-257
conventions, C language, 19-20
conversion
  I/O files to devices, 258
  scanf( ) function modifiers, 109
  specification, 92-95, 101
convert.c file file
  listing 5.14, 148
  listing 16.7, 558-559
converting
  for loop to while, 190
  while loop to for, 190
copy1.c file (listing 11.19), 384
copy2.c file (listing 11.20), 385
copying files, 256
CopyToItem( ) function, 606
CopyToNode( ) function, 594-597, 605
count.c file (listing 12.1), 406-407
counting loops, 174-175
CP/M files, end marking, 254-257
creating
  aliases, 89
  bit fields, 527-528
  functions, 279-282
    with ANSI prototypes, 285
    with arguments, 284
  pointer variables, 309
ctype.h header file, 390-393
customertime( ) function, 612
cypher1.c file (listing 7.2), 211
cypher2.c file (listing 7.3), 212

D

#define directive, 86-89, 301, 536-541
  arguments, 541-544
  redefining constants, 540-541
  tokens, 540

%d notation, 54
%d print specifier, 59
%d specifier, 92, 109
data, 48-49
  forms, 497-511
  hiding, 587
  I/O streams, 253-256
  representation, 572-575
data objects, 123
data types, 29, 49, 52-72
  characters, 29, 654
  defining, 584-598
  floating point, 29, 654
  integers, 29
  keywords, 49-52
  signed integers, 653-654
  unsigned integers, 654
day_mon1.c file (listing 10.1), 322
day_mon2.c file (listing 10.2), 323
day_mon3.c file (listing 10.3), 324
day_mon4.c file (listing 10.5), 328
DBL_DIG constant, 91
debugger program, 41
debugging programs, 8, 38-41
decimal number systems, binary equivalents, 518
declaration statement, 29, 35, 143
declaring
  arrays in structures, 477
  functions
    ANSI, 291-293
    pre-ANSI, 290-291
  nested structures in templates, 481
  pointers, 310-311
  static variables, 442
  structure pointers, 482-483
  variables, 29-30, 47, 71, 441-442, 654
    char, 60
    floating-point numbers, 66
    int, 52-53

decrement operators, 140-141
decrementing
    operators, 138-139
    pointers, 334-335
defining
    constants, 551
    interfaces, 598-599
    pointers to structures, 481-482
    string arrays, 362-368
    string constants, 361-362
    strings, 360-362
    symbolic constants, 86
    types, 583-584
        queue, 598
    variables, 441-442
delayed input, *see* buffered input
deleting items from queues, 599
delta( ) function, 444
dcmotion type conversion, 148
Dequeue( ) function, 606
dereferencing (*) operator, 309, 334, 649
designing
    operations, types, 585-586
    programs, 583
    queues, 610-616
devices
    input, 19-21
    output, 19-21
diceroll.c file (listing 13.7), 450-451
differencing pointers, 335
direct input, *see* unbuffered input
directives
    #define, 536-541
        arguments, 541-544
        redefining constants, 540-541
        tokens, 540
    #elif, 551-552
    #else, 549-551

#endif, 549-551
#if, 551-552
#ifdef, 549-551
#ifndef, 551
#include, 27, 545-548
    header files, 546-547
#undef, 548-549
conditional compilations,
    549-553
discarding newline input, 264-265
display ( ) function, 270-273
divide.c file (listing 5.6), 129
division (/) operator, 646
divisors.c file (listing 7.5), 219
do keyword, 659
do while loop, 187-189
    comparisons to while loop,
        187-189
    in password programs, 188-189
    loop structures, 159-160
    structure, 188-189
    test conditions, 189
do while statement, 659-660
DOS
    files, end marking, 254-257
    input redirection, 257-260
    output redirection, 257-260
    redirection operators, 258-260
double indirection, 341
double keyword data type, 49, 65-67,
    70
dowhile.c file (listing 6.13), 187
draft1.c file (listing 10.17), 349
draft2.c file (listing 10.18), 350
driver programs, 198
drivers, 608
dubarr1.c file (listing 10.13), 345
dubarr2.c file (listing 10.15), 346

dubarr3.c file (listing 10.16), 347-348
dyadic operators, *see* binary operators
dyn_arr.c file (listing 16.9), 563-564
dynamic arrays, creating, 563-564
dynamic memory allocation, 575

E

#elif directive, 551-552
#else directive, 549-551
#endif directive, 549-551
%e specifier (conversion), 92, 109
echo.c file
   listing 8.1, 250
   listing 11.24, 393
   listing 12.4, 414
echo_eof.c file (listing 8.2), 255
echoed input, 252
echoing input, 250
editors
   emacs, 15
   vi, 15
electric.c file (listing 7.4), 212-214
elements, array, 192-195
   accessing, 320
   indices, 193
   inserting, 616
   offsets, 193
   subscripts, 193
   structures in arrays, 493-496
else if elements, 215
   in if else statements, 212-215
   regulation, 215-216
else keyword, 660
emacs editor, 15
empty queues, checking, 604
EmptyList( ) function, 595
EmptyTree( ) function, 624

end marking
   binary files, 254-257
   Control-Z files, 254-257
   CP/M files, 254-257
   IBM-DOS files, 254-257
   MS-DOS files, 254-257
   text files, 255-257
end of file signal
   Control-D, 256-257
   PCs, 256-257
   test conditions, 260-263
end-of-file detector, 254
EnQueue( ) function, 606
entry-condition loops
   applications, 189-190
   while statement, 162-165, 173-174
entry.c file. (listing 6.14), 187-188
enum keyword, 552
enum.c file (listing 16.6), 554-555
enumerated type, 552-555
   assigned values, 553-554
   constants, 553
   default values, 553
   uses, 554-555
EOF (end of file) value, 255-257
EOF symbol
   end of file (-1), 255-257
   system requirements, 256-257
   typing, 256-257
EQCK, 531
equality operator, 161-162
error-checking, 273
errors
   symantic, 39-40
   syntax, 38-39
   values identification, 273
escape sequences, 32, 61-63
escape.c file (listing 3.9), 74

EXCLUSIVE OR (^) operator, 650
exit( ) function, 407-408, 560-562
exit-condition loops
    applications, 189-190
    do while, 187-189
exiting programs, 407-408
exponential growth operators,
  127-128
exponential notation, 65
expression linking, comma
  operators, 185
expression trees, 130-131
expressions, 141-142, 147, 657
    comparison, 167-168
    full, 144-145
    logical, 648
    parameters, loops, 181-203
    relational, 647
      values, 168-169
    subexpressions, 141
    values, 141-142
extern keyword, 438
external
    arrays, 321-322, 362
    function placement templates,
     472
    functions, 444
    linkage, 436
    static variables, 443
    variables, 321-322, 438-441
      in structures, 474-477
      initializing, 441
      names, 441
      scope, 439-440
      storage duration, 439

F

%f specifier, 92, 109
%f variable code, 47
\f (form feed) escape sequence, 61-62

factor.c file (listing 9.7), 296-297
fathm_ft.c file (listing 2.2), 35
fclose( ) function, 410
feof( ) function, 427
ferror( ) function, 427
fflush( ) function, 423
fgets( ) function, 369-371, 414-415
field width specifier, 112
FIFO (first in, first out) data
  forms, 598
file pointers, 410
file scope, 436
files, 404
    add_one.c, 135
    addaword.c, 412-413
    addemup.c, 143
    alias.c, 90
    animals.c, 234
    append.c, 428-429
    appending contents, 427-429
    associating with streams, 254
    arf.c, 336
    badcount.c, 73
    bases.c, 55
    binary, 496-511
      end-marking, 254-257
    binary mode, 418
    binary view, 404-405
    binary.c, 299, 524-525
    book.c, 470-471
    booksave.c, 494-506
    bottles.c, 138-139
    break.c, 232-233
    byebye.c, 560-561
    charcode.c, 64
    chcount.c, 221-222
    closing, 410
    cnt_sp.c, 547
    colddays.c, 206-207
    command.c, 386
    compare.c, 380-381

compback.c, 381-382
condensing, 410-412
convert.c, 148, 558-559
copy1.c, 384
copy2.c, 385
copying, 256
count.c, 406-407
cypher1.c, 211
cypher2.c, 212
day_mon1.c, 322
day_mon2.c, 323
day_mon3.c, 324
day_mon4.c, 328
diceroll.c, 450-451
divide.c, 129
divisors.c, 219
dowhile.c, 187
draft1.c, 349
draft2.c, 350
dubarr1.c, 345
dubarr2.c, 346
dubarr3.c, 347-348
dyn_arr.c, 563-564
echo_eof.c, 255
echo.c, 250, 393, 414
electric.c, 213
end marking
    Control-Z, 254-257
    CP/M, 254-257
    IBM-DOS, 254-257
    MS-DOS, 254-257
end-of-file detector, 254
entry.c, 187-188
enum.c, 554-555
escape.c, 74
invert.c, 392
factor.c, 296-297
feeding to programs, 270-273
getarray.c, 456
getint.c, 458
fathm_ft.c, 35

films1.c, 574
films2.c, 580-581, 596-597
films3.c, 590-591, 596-597
flags.c, 99
floatcnv.c, 103
floats.c, 98
for_cube.c, 176-177
friend.c, 480
friends.c, 481-482
func_ptr.c, 505
funds 1.c, 484
funds2.c, 485
funds3.c, 486-487
funds4.c, 492-496
global.c, 434
goldyou.c, 46
golf.c, 124
guess.c, 263-266
header, 588
    float.h, 91
    in include files, 546-547
    limits.h, 91
    list.h, 592
    math.h, 557
    stdio.h, 25-27, 410
    stdlib.h, 559
    string.h, 84
    uses, 547-548
hello.c, 396
hotel1.c, 302
hotel2.c, 302-303
ibmchk.c, 530
ifdef.c, 550
input.c, 108, 383
intconv.c, 101
invert4.c, 526-527
I/O device conversion, 258
join_chk.c, 379
lastline.c, 419-420
lethead1.c, 279
lethead2.c, 283

lesser.c, 287
list.c, 592-594
loccheck.c, 305
longstrg.c, 107
low-level I/O, 253-256
mac_arg.c, 541
mall.c, 612-614
manybook.c, 476-479
manydice.c, 451
mean.c, 353-354
min_sec.c, 134
misuse.c, 290-291
name1.c, 369-370
name2.c, 370
nameln 1.c, 487-488
nameln2.c, 489-490
naming, 10, 15-17
nogo.c, 380
nogood.c, 38
nono.c, 374
opening, 408-409, 422
order.c, 332
p_and_s.c, 367
paint.c, 228
patterns.c, 261-262
petclub.c, 632-634
pizza.c, 88
pnt_add.c, 326
post_pre.c, 137
postage.c, 183
pound.c, 151
power.c, 197
praise1.c, 82
praise2.c, 84
preproc.c, 536-537
print1.c, 54
print2.c, 58
print.c, 460
printout.c, 93
prntval.c, 106
proto1.c, 292

pt_ops.c, 333-334
put_out.c, 373
put_put.c, 376
put1.c, 375
put2.c, 376
queue.c, 606-608
quotes.c, 362
r_drive1.c, 447
r_drive2.c, 449
rain.c, 338-339
rand0.c, 447
random access, 416-419
    in text mode, 419-421
recur.c, 294
redirection symbols, spacing,
    258-260
reducto.c, 410-411
reusing, 597
reversc.c, 416
rfactor.c, 297-298
rows 1.c, 190-191
rows2.c, 192
rules.c, 132
running.c, 153-154
saving structure contents,
    493-496
scan_str.c, 372
scores_in.c, 194
shoes1.c, 120
shoe2.c, 121
showchar1.c, 265-268
showfpt.c, 67
showr2.c, 267-270
sizeof.c, 133
sketcher.c, 269-270
skip.c, 229-230
skip2.c, 113
sort_int.c, 454
sort_str.c, 389
sort.c, 460
source code, 10
squares.c, 127

standard error output, 406
standard I/O package, 253-256
standard input, 406
standard output, 406
static.c, 442
stillbad.c, 39
storage differences, 253-256
str_cat.c, 378
strings.c, 100, 360-361
subst.c, 544
sum_arr1.c, 329
sum_arr2.c, 331
summing.c, 160-161
swap1.c, 307
swap2.c, 307-308
swap3.c, 311
sweetie 1.c, 174-175
sweetie2.c., 175-182
talkback.c, 80
test.c, 377-378
text, 257-260
    end-marking, 255-257
    word counts, 260-263
text mode, 418
text view, 404-405
two_func.c, 36
t_and_f.c, 168
tree.c, 628-631
trouble.c, 170
truth.c, 169
use.qc, 609-610
varwid.c, 113
vowels.c, 238
wheat.c, 127-128
when.c, 164
while 1.c, 165-168
while2.c, 166-168
width.c, 97
wordcnt.c, 226
zeno.c, 186
zippo1.c, 341
zippo2.c, 342

films1.c file (listing 17.1), 574
films2.c file (listing 17.2), 580-581,
    596-597
films3.c file (listing 17.4), 590-592,
    596-597
first in, first out (FIFO) data form,
    598
flags, 219
    printf( ) function, 97-101
flags.c file (listing 4.9), 99
float (floating-point variable type),
    47
    templates, 471-472
float keyword, 49, 65-67, 70-71
float.h header file, 91
floatcnv.c file (listing 4.12), 103
floating point data type, 29, 50, 654
    constants, 66
floating-point numbers, 51-52, 65,
    70
    binary, 516-518
    declaring variables, 66
    initializing variables, 66
    overflow, 68
    printing, 67-78
    relational operators, 168
    rounding errors, 69
    underflow, 68
floating-point values, 475-479
floats.c file (listing 4.8), 98
FLT_DIG constants, 91
flushing buffers, 423
fopen( ) function, 408-409, 422
for keyword, 659
for loop, 175-182, 272
    control expressions, 180-182
    conversion to while, 190
    first expression, 180-182
    flexibility, 177-185
    initialization expression, 176
    selecting, 190

solving problems, 185-191
structure, 159-160, 176
termination, 180-182
test conditions, 176
updating, 179-182
values of ASCII, 178-182
with arrays, 194-197
for statement, 181-182, 659
for_cube.c file. (listing 6.10),
176-177
formal arguments, 152, 284
ANSI C requirements, 284
formats, structures, 475
forms
data, 497-511
first in, first out (FIFO), 598
fprintf( ) function, 411-413,
493-496
fputs( ) function, 414-415
fractions, binary, 516
fread( ) function, 424-426, 494-496
free( ) function, 562-565, 612
friend.c file (listing 14.3), 480
friends.c file (listing 14.4), 481-482
fscanf( ) function, 412-413
fseek( ) function, 416-419, 497-511
ftell( ) function, 416-419
ftoa( ) function, 397
full expressions, 144-145
FullList( ) function, 595-596
FullTree( ) function, 624
fully buffered I/O, 252
func_ptr.c file (listing 14.12), 505
function prototype scope, 436
function return value, 286-289
with while loops, 195-199
function statement, 143
functions, 278-290, 299-300,
671 674
AddItem( ), 595-597, 624-625
AddNode( ), 624-627
addresses, 305-306

advantages, 278
and multidimensional arrays,
344-348
ANSI C library, 387-388
ANSI C prototyping, 153,
290-293
append( ), 429
applying
one-dimensional to
two-dimensional, 345-347
to subarrays, 344-345
two-dimensional arrays,
347-348
arguments, 73, 151-153, 282-284
array names as, 330-331
passing structures as, 484-485
assigning tasks, 304
atan( ), 558
atan2( ), 558-559
atexit( ), 560-562
atof( ), 397
atoi( ), 396
atol( ), 397
badlimits( ), 270-273
begin/end symbol { }, 26-28
beta( ), 444
black box viewpoint, 286
buffered compilations, 252
butler( ), 37
calling, 152, 280, 542
altering variables, 306-308
with arguments, 285-286
calloc( ), 565-566
character-mapping, 392
character-testing, 391-392
clock( ), 612
communicating
with arguments, 315
with pointers, 311 318
CopyToItem( ), 606
CopyToNode( ), 594-597, 605

creating, 279-282
ctype.h character functions, 390-393
custom input/output, 375-377
customertime( ), 612
declaring, 196-199, 289
   no return value, 289
   pre-ANSI, 290-291
   type errors, 292
   with ANSI, 291-293
   with return values, 289
   with semicolons, 280-281
definitions, placement, 289
delta( ), 444
Dequeue( ), 606
display ( ), 270-273
documentation, 556
EmptyList( ), 595
EmptyTree( ), 624
EnQueue( ), 606
exit( ), 407-408, 560-562
external, 444
fclose( ), 410
feof( ), 427
ferror( ), 427
fflush( ), 423
fgets( ), 369-371, 414-415
fopen( ), 408-409, 422
for string storage, 369
fprintf( ), 411-413, 493-496
fputs( ), 414-415
fread( ), 424-426, 494-496
free( ), 562-565, 612
fscanf( ), 412-413
fseek( ), 416-419, 497-511
ftell( ), 416-419
ftoa( ), 397
FullList( ), 595-596
FullTree( ), 624
function return value, 286-289

fwrite( ), 424-426, 494-496
gamma( ), 444
getarray( ), 454-457
getc( ), 409
getchar( ), 209, 250-251, 267-271
getinfo( ), 488-490
getint( ), 457-458
gets( ), 360, 369, 488-490
header files, 301-304
headings
   pre-ANSI form, 312
   selecting, 313
   with ANSI, 312
in ANSI C standard library, 290
in different programs, 281
indicating no arguments, 293
InitializeList( ), 587, 595
InitializeTree( ), 624
InOrder( ), 627-628
input, 249-250
int86( ), 531
interchange( ), 306
interface, implementing, 604-620
itoa( ), 397
itobs( ), 524-525
K&R function declaration, 152-153
ListItems( ), 595
main( ), 26-28, 32, 301, 306, 394-396, 488-490
makeinfo( ), 489-490
MakeNode( ), 624-625
malloc( ), 562-565, 596, 612
mean( ), 352
multiple, 36-38
   compiling programs with, 300-304
naming, 151, 278
newcustomer( ), 611
output, 249-250

parentheses, 280
power ( ), 198
printf( ), 26-27, 31-32, 47, 83,
    91-114, 143, 191, 250, 278,
    374-375
prototypes, 152, 291-293
putc( ), 409
putchar( ), 210, 250-251
puts( ), 360, 373-374
rand( ), 446-452, 611-612
rand1( ), 451-452
read_array( ), 349-351
recursion, 293-299
returning values, 286
rewind( ), 412-413, 497-511
rollem( ), 451-452
scanf( ), 47, 73, 83, 91-114,
    160-162, 206-207, 217, 250,
    267-273, 305, 369-373
scope, 444
SeekItem( ), 627
setvbuf( ), 427
show_array( ), 351-352
show_last( ), 421
showinfo( ), 489-491
showmovies( ), 590
sort( ), 458-460
sprintf( ), 386-387, 397
sqrt( ), 558
srand( ), 612
srand1( ), 451
static, 444, 594
strcat( ), 378-379, 387
strchr( ), 387
strcmp( ), 379-383, 387
strcpy( ), 383-387
string reading, 369-371
string-handling, 377-388
strlen( ), 81-89, 278, 377-378,
    388, 489-490

strncat( ), 387
strncmp( ), 387
strncpy( ), 387
strpbrk( ), 388
strrchr( ), 388
strstr( ), 388
structures
    arrays of, 491-496
    as return values of, 487-490
    identification, 483-484
sum( ), 485, 493-496
testing, 196-199
ToLeft( ), 625-627
tolower( ), 392
ToRight( ), 625-627
toupper( ), 392
Traverse( ), 590, 596, 627-628
TreeItems( ), 624
type cast, 152
types, 280, 316
ungetc( ), 423
variables, 472
versus macros, 544-545
with arguments, creating, 284
with count variables, 286
with return values, 196-199
    activating, 198-203
without return values, 280
writing, 151-153
    for arrays, 329-330
funds templates, 487
funds 1.c file (listing 14.5), 484
funds2.c file (listing 14.6), 485-486
funds3.c file (listing 14.7), 486-487
funds4.c file (listing 14.10), 492-496
fwrite( ) function, 424-426, 494-496

G

%G specifier (conversion), 92, 109
%g specifier (conversion), 92, 109
gamma( ) function, 444
general utilities library, 559-566
geometric character patterns, 261-262
getarray( ) function, 454-457
getarray.c file (listing 13.10), 456
getc( ) function, 409
getchar( ) function, 209, 257, 267
    format specifiers, 211
    in word-couting program, 225
    replaced with preprocessor macro, 251
    single-character I/O, 250
getinfo( ) functions, 488-490
getint( ) function, 457-458
getint.c file (listing 13.11), 458
gets( ) function, 360, 369-371, 488-490
global.c file (listing 13.1), 434
goldyou.c file (listing 3.1), 46
golf.c file (listing 5.3), 124
goto statement, 240-248, 663
graphs, 497-511
guess.c file (listing 8.4), 263-266
guy structures, 483

H

%hd print specifier, 59
hardware, bit field dedication, 529
hash tables, 497-511
header files, 301-304, 588
    float.h, 91
    gets( ) function, 371
    in include files, 546-547
    limits.h, 91
    math.h, 557

stdio.h, 410
stdlib.h, 397, 559
strings, 378
uses, 547-548
with #define directives, 301
with #include directive, 301
heaps, 497-511
hello.c file (listing 11.25), 396
hexadecimal numbers, 54-55
    printing, 55-56
hexadecimal number systems, 517-518
hiding data, 587, 597
hierarchical organizations, 620
high-order bit, 514
hotel1.c file (listing 9.10), 302
hotel2.c file (listing 9.11), 302-303
hotels.h (listing 9.12), 303

I

#if directive, 551-552
#ifdef directive, 549-551
#ifndef directive, 551
#include directive, 27, 86-89, 545-548
    header files, 301, 546-547
%i specifier (conversion), 92, 109
I/O
    files
        appending contents, 427-429
        binary mode, 418
        condensing, 410-412
        text mode, 418
    files to device conversion, 258
    low-level, 253-256, 405
    redirection, 257, 260-261
    standard I/O package, 253-256, 405-410
        command-line arguments, 407-408
    streams, 253-256

I/O functions, 91
    availability on all systems, 250
    buffering availability, 252
    custom functions, 375-377
    exit( ), 407-408
    fclose( ), 410
    feof( ), 427
    ferror( ), 427
    fflush( ), 423
    fgets( ), 414-415
    fopen( ), 408-409, 422
    fprintf( ), 411-413
    fputs( ), 414-415
    fread( ), 424-426
    fscanf( ), 412-413
    fseek( ), 416-419
    ftell( ), 416-419
    fully buffered, 252
    fwrite( ), 424-426
    getc( ), 409
    line-buffered, 252
    putc( ), 409
    rewind( ), 412-413
    setvbuf( ), 427
    ungetc( ), 423
IBM PC Systems, 13-19
ibmchk.c file (listing 15.3), 530
IDE (Integrated Development
    Environments), 17
identifying
    errors in values, 273
    members of structure arrays,
        477-478
    structures to functions, 483-484
if else statements, 208-221, 272-273
    braces in, 218
    else if elements, regulation,
        215-216
    multiple statements in, 209

    nesting, 215-221
    versus switch statements, 239-240
    with else if elements, 212-215
if keyword, 660
if statement, 206-208, 264-265,
    660-661
    making choices with, 220-221
    test and execution, 208
ifdef.c file (listing 16.5), 550
images, bit-mapped, 573
implementing
    binary trees, 624-631
    functions, 604-620
    interface data representations,
        599-608
    interfaces, 591-594
    linked lists, 580-587
increment (++) operator, 646
increment operators, 135-138, 175
    precautions, 140-141
    suggestions, 141
incrementing pointers, 334
indefinite loops, 174-175, 241
indices, array elements, 193
indirect membership (->) operator,
    649-650
infinite failure loops, 171-172
infinite loops, 137, 166
initialization expression, 176
InitializeList( ) function, 587, 595
initializer structure, 474
InitializeTree( ) function, 624
initializing
    arrays, 320-325, 364-365
        character arrays, 363
        multidimensional arrays,
            339-340
        string arrays, 362
    pointers, 364-365
        structure pointers, 482-483

structures, 473-477
sum to 0 (type int zero), 161
sum to 0L (type long zero), 161
variables
    automatic variables, 438
    char, 60
    external variables, 441
    floating-point numbers, 66
    int, 53
    scalar variables, 320
inner loop, *see* nested loops
InOrder( ) function, 627-628
input
    buffered (delayed), 251-252
    buffering problems, 263-269
    characters, 249-250
    devices, 19-21
    echoed, 252
    functions, 84, 249-252
    keyboard stream, 254
    newline discarding, 264-265
    numeric and character, 265-269
    reading, 110
    redirection (UNIX), 257-260
    standard, 257
    strings, 368-373
    terminating keyed, 253-256
    termination, 160
        with specific values, 268-271
    unbuffered (direct), 251-252
    unechoed, 252
    see also I/O
input.c file
    listing 4.15, 108
    listing 11.18, 383
int (integer variable type), 47
    declaring variables, 52-53
    integer constants, 53-54
int keyword , 49-59, 70
INT_MAX constant, 91

INT_MIN constant, 91
int86( ) function, 531
intconv.c file listing 4.11., 101
integer data type, 29, 50
integer variable type (int), 47
integers, 50-52
    constants
        int, 53-54
        long, 58
    overflow, 57
    properties, 584
    signed, 70, 653-654
    unsigned, 70, 654
    values, printing, 54, 58-59
Integrated Development
    Environments (IDEs), 17
integrated enviroments, 395
inter-loop dependency, nested
    loops, 191-193
interactive programs, user
    failure, 265
interchange( ) function, 306
interfaces
    binary search tree, 622-624
    building, 586-590
    data representations,
        implementing, 599-608
    defining, 598-599
    functions, implementing,
        604-620
    implementing, 591-594
internal
    function definition templates, 472
    linkage, 436
International Standards Organization
    (ISO), 18
interrupts, 531
inventory uses for structures,
    470-471
invert.c file (listing 11.23), 392

invert4.c file (listing 15.2), 526-527
is statement, 207-208
ISO (International Standards
  Organization), 18
iterations, while loop, 163
itoa( ) function, 397
itobs( ) function, 524-525

J-K

join_chk.c file (listing 11.14), 379
jump statements, 243-245

K&R function declaration, 152-153
keyboard input, 254
keywords, 29, 41, 49-52
  auto, 437
  char, 49, 59, 64, 70
  const, 462-463
  do, 659
  double, 49, 65 67, 70
  else, 660
  enum, 552
  extern, 438
  float, 49, 65-67, 70-71
  for, 659
  if, 660
  int, 49, 52-59, 70
  long, 49, 56-58, 70
  long double, 49
  short, 49, 56-57, 70
  static, 445
  switch, 661
  unsigned, 49, 56, 70
  volatile, 463-464
  while, 658-659

L

%ld specifier, 80
%lx notation, 58
languages, 637

lastline.c file (listing 12.6), 419-420
lesser.c file (listing 9.3), 287
lethead1.c file (listing 9.1), 279
lethead2.c file (listing 9.2), 283
libraries, 84
  accessing, 555-556
  ANSI C, 637
  documentation, 556-557
  general utilities, 559-566
  math, 557-559
library code, 11
library routines, *see* functions
limits.h header file, 91
line length of programs, 271-273
line-buffered I/O, 252
linked lists
  as queue data form, 600-601
  creating, 581-583
  displaying, 577-583
  implementing, 580-583, 586-587
  nodes, inserting, 616
  versus arrays, 616-619
linkers, 7, 10
linking structures, 498-511
list.c file (listing 17.5), 592-594
list.h (listing 17.3), 588-592
listings
  2.1. A simple C program, 24
  2.2. fathm_ft.c file, 35
  2.3. two_func.c file, 36
  2.4. nogood.c file, 38
  2.5. stillbad.c file, 39
  3.1. goldyou.c file, 46
  3.2. print1.c file, 54
  3.3. bases.c file, 55
  3.4. print2.c file, 58
  3.5. charcode.c file, 64
  3.6. showfpt.c file, 67
  3.8. badcount.c file, 73
  3.9. escape.c file, 74
  4.1. talkback.c file, 80

4.2. praise1.c file, 82
4.3. praise2.c file, 84
4.4. pizza.c file, 88
4.5. alias.c file, 90
4.6. printout.c file, 93
4.7. width.c file, 97
4.8. floats.c file, 98
4.9. flags.c file, 99
4.10. strings.c file, 100
4.11. intconv.c file, 101
4.12. floatcnv.c file, 103
4.13. prntval.c file, 106
4.14. longstrg.c file, 107
4.15. input.c file, 108
4.16. varwid.c file, 113
4.17. skip2.c file, 113
5.1. shoes1.c file, 120
5.2. shoe2.c file, 121
5.3. golf.c file, 124
5.4. squares.c file, 127
5.5. wheat.c file, 127-128
5.6. divide.c file, 129
5.7. rules.c file, 132
5.8. sizeof.c file, 133
5.9. min_sec.c file, 134
5.10. add_one.c file, 135
5.11. post_pre.c file, 137
5.12. bottles.c file, 138-139
5.13. addemup.c file, 143
5.14. convert.c file, 148
5.15. pound.c file, 151
5.16. running.c file, 153-154
6.1. summing.c file, 160-161
6.2. when.c file, 164
6.3. while 1.c file, 165-168
6.4. while2.c file, 166-168
6.5. t_and_f.c file, 168
6.6. truth.c file, 169
6.7. trouble.c file, 170
6.8. sweetie 1.c file, 174-175
6.9. sweetie2.c file., 175-182

6.10. for_cube.c file, 176-177
6.11. postage.c file, 183
6.12. zeno.c file, 186
6.13. dowhile.c file, 187
6.14. entry.c file, 187-188
6.15. rows 1.c file, 190-191
6.16. rows2.c file, 192
6.17. scores_in.c file, 194
6.18. power.c file, 197
7.1. colddays.c file, 206-207
7.2. cypher1.c file, 211
7.3. cypher2.c file, 212
7.4. electric.c file, 213
7.5. divisors.c file, 219
7.6. chcount.c file, 221-222
7.7. wordcnt.c file, 226
7.8. paint.c file, 228
7.9. skip.c file, 229-230
7.10. break.c file, 232-233
7.11. animals.c file, 234
7.12. vowels.c file, 238
8.1. echo.c file, 250
8.2. echo_eof.c file, 255
8.3. patterns.c file, 261-262
8.4. guess.c file, 263-266
8.5. showchar1.c file, 265-268
8.6. showr2.c file, 267-270
8.7. sketcher.c file, 269-270
9.1. lethead1.c file, 279
9.2. lethead2.c file, 283
9.3. lesser.c file, 287
9.4. misuse.c file, 290-291
9.5. proto1.c file, 292
9.6. recur.c file, 294
9.7. factor.c file, 296-297
9.8. rfactor.c file, 297-298
9.9. binary.c file, 299
9.10. hotel1.c file, 302
9.11. hotel2.c file, 302-303
9.12. hotels.h, 303
9.13. loccheck.c file, 305

9.14. swap1.c file, 307
9.15. swap2.c file, 307-308
9.16. swap3.c file, 311
10.1. day_mon1.c file, 322
10.2. day_mon2.c file, 323
10.3. day_mon3.c file, 324
10.4. pnt_add.c file, 326
10.5. day_mon4.c file, 328
10.6. sum_arr1.c file, 329
10.7. sum_arr2.c file, 331
10.8. order.c file, 332
10.9. pt_ops.c file, 333-334
10.10. arf.c file, 336
10.11. rain.c file, 338-339
10.12. zippo1.c file, 341
10.13. zippo2.c file, 342
10.14. dubarr1.c file, 345
10.15. dubarr2.c file, 346
10.16. dubarr3.c file, 347-348
10.17. draft1.c file, 349
10.18. draft2.c file, 350
10.19. mean.c file, 353-354
11.1. strings.c file, 360-361
11.2. quotes.c file, 362
11.3. p_and_s.c file, 367
11.4. name1.c file, 369-370
11.5. name2.c file, 370
11.6. scan_str.c file, 372
11.7. put_out.c file, 373
11.8. nono.c file, 374
11.9. put1.c file, 375
11.10. put2.c file, 376
11.11. put_put.c file, 376
11.12. test.c file, 377-378
11.13. str_cat.c file, 378
11.14. join_chk.c file, 379
11.15. nogo.c file, 380
11.16. compare.c file, 380-381
11.17. compback.c file, 381-382
11.18. input.c file, 383
11.19. copy1.c file, 384

11.20. copy2.c file, 385
11.21. command.c file, 386
11.22. sort_str.c file, 389
11.23. invert.c file, 392
11.24. echo.c file, 393
11.25. hello.c file, 396
12.1. count.c file, 406-407
12.2. reducto.c file, 410-411
12.3. addaword.c file, 412-413
12.4. echo.c file, 414
12.5. reverse.c file, 416
12.6. lastline.c file, 419-420
12.7. append.c file, 428-429
13.1. global.c file, 434
13.2. static.c file, 442
13.3. rand0.c file, 447
13.4. r_drive1.c file, 447
13.5. s_and_r.c file, 448
13.6. r_drive2.c file, 449
13.7. diceroll.c file, 450-451
13.8. manydice.c file, 451
13.9. sort_int.c file, 454
13.10. getarray.c file, 456
13.11. getint.c file, 458
13.12. sort.c file, 460
13.13. print.c file, 460
14.1. book.c file, 470-471
14.2. manybook.c file, 476-479
14.3. friend.c file, 480
14.4. friends.c file, 481-482
14.5. funds1.c file, 484
14.6. funds2.c file, 485
14.7. funds3.c file, 486-487
14.8. nameln1.c file, 487-488
14.9. nameln2.c file, 489-490
14.10. funds4.c file, 492-496
14.11. booksave.c file, 494-506
14.12. func_ptr.c file, 505
15.1. binary.c file, 524-525
15.2. invert4.c file, 526-527
15.3. ibmchk.c file, 530

16.1. preproc.c file, 536-537
16.2. mac_arg.c file, 541
16.3. subst.c file, 544
16.4. cnt_sp.c file, 547
16.5. ifdef.c file, 550
16.6. enum.c file, 554-555
16.7. convert.c file, 558-559
16.8. byebye.c file, 560-561
16.9. dyn_arr.c file, 563-564
17.1. films1.c file, 574
17.2. films2.c file, 580-581,
596-597
17.3. list.h, 588-589
17.4 films3.c file, 590-591,
596-597
17.5. list.c file, 592-594
17.6. A circular queue, 602-603
17.7. queue.c file, 606-608
17.8. use.qc, 609-610
17.9. mall.c file, 612-614
17.10 tree.h, 622-624
17.11. tree.c file, 628-631
17.12. petclub.c file, 632-634

ListItems( ) function, 595
lists, linked, 577-579
    as queue data form, 600-601
    creating, 581-583
    displaying, 581-583
    implementing, 580-583, 586-587
    nodes, inserting, 616
    versus arrays, 616-619
loccheck.c file (listing 9.13), 305
logical expressions, 224, 648
    order of evaluation, 223
logical operators, 221-224, 648
long
    character strings, printing,
        106-110
    integer constants, 58
long double keyword, 49
long keyword, 49, 56-58, 70

longstrg.c file (listing 4.14), 107
loops, 120-122, 211, 216-221,
229-233
    , (comma operator), 219
    and arrays, 192-195
    break statements, 231-233, 243
    continue statement, 229-231, 243
    counting, 174-175
    do while, 159-160, 187-189
    entry-condition, 162
        while statement, 173-174
    exiting, 242
    expression parameters, 181-203
    for, 159-160, 175-182
    in word-counting program, 225
    indefinite, 174-175, 241
    infinite, 137, 166
    infinite failure, 171-172
    nested, 190-192, 262-263
    nesting
        break statements in, 232
        exiting, 242
    reading, 162, 194-197, 237
    scanf( ) function, 217
    skipping to end, 242
    statements in, 143
    switch statements in, 236
    terminating, 161-162
    versus tail recursion, 296-298
    while, 121-122, 159-160, 163,
        375
    while counting, 174-175
lossless compression, 573
lossy compression, 573
low-level I/O, 253, 405
low-order bit, 514
lvalues, 123-124

M

mac_arg.c file (listing 16.2), 541
Macintosh systems, 17-18
macros
    arguments, 541-543
        in strings, 543-544
    calls, 542
    ctype.h character functions, 393
    versus functions, 544-545
main( ) function, 26-28, 32, 301,
    394-396, 488-490
makeinfo( ) function, 489-490
MakeNode( ) function, 624-625
mall.c file (listing 17.9), 612-614
malloc( ) function, 562-565,
    575-579, 596, 612
manybook.c file (listing 14.2),
    476-479
manydice.c file (listing 13.8), 451
masks
    bitwise AND operator, 520-522
    bitwise logical operators, 520-522
math library, 557-559
math.h header file, 557
mean( ) function, 352
mean.c file (listing 10.19), 353-354
member operators (.), 474-475
members of structures, accessing,
    483-484
membership operators, 500-501
memory
    allocating, 562-565
        dynamic memory allocation,
        575
        for structures, 472-473
        storage classes, 566
    storing data types as unions,
    498-511
    structure stack sizes, 475-479

Microsoft C WorkBench, compiling
    programs, 300
min_sec.c file (listing 5.9), 134
misuse.c file (listing 9.4), 290-291
modifiable lvalue, 123-124
modifiers
    conversion, 109
    printf( ) function, 95
modifying programs, 195-197
modulus (%) operator, 352, 646
MS-DOS, see DOS
multidimensional arrays, 337-340
    and functions, 344-348
    and pointers, 340-348
    initializing, 339-340
multiple
    case labels, 237-238
    functions, 36-38
    program entries with while loops,
    479-482
multiplication (*) operator, 646

N

\n (newline) escape sequence, 32,
    61-62, 369
name1.c file (listing 11.4), 369-370
name2.c file (listing 11.5), 370
nameln 1.c file (listing 14.8),
    487-488
nameln2.c file (listing 14.9), 489-490
names
    array, as function arguments,
        330-331
    external variables, 441
    files, 10, 15-17
    symbolic constants, 88
    variables, 29-30
nested loops, 190-192, 262-263
    inner loop, 191
    inter-loop dependency, 191-192

outer loop, 191
variations, 191-193
nested structures, 479-482
template declaration, 481
nesting, 216-221
in if else statements, 215
using braces, 215
newcustomer( ) function, 611
newline (\n) character, 32, 237, 369
newline input, discarding, 264-265
nodes, 586
child, 620
inserting in linked lists, 616
removing from trees, 622
nogo.c file (listing 11.15), 380
nogood.c file (listing 2.4), 38
nono.c file (listing 11.8), 374
nonprinting characters, 60-63
nonzero values, 169-170
notation
exponential, 65
scientific, 65
null character, 81-82
NULL pointer, 371
NULL statement, 166-167
NULL symbolic constant, 577
number systems
binary, 514-516
one's complement method,
515
sign-magnitude method, 515
signed numbers, 515
two's complement method,
515
hexadecimal, 54-55, 517-518
octal, 54-55, 516-517
numbering array elements, 193-195
numbers
calculating average, 349-354
floating-point, 51-52, 65, 70
hexadecimal (base 16), 54-55
integers, 50-52
octal (base 8), 54-55
printing, 55-56, 349-354
random, 446-450
reading, 349-354
sorting, 452-462
getarray( ) function, 456-457
getint( ) function, 457-458
global decisions, 453-454
printing sorted numbers,
460-461
reading numeric data, 454-456
sort( ) function, 458-460
testing sort, 461-462
numeric input, with characters,
265-269

O

%o specifier (conversion), 92, 109
object code (UNIX), 13
object code file, 15
object files, 10
object-oriented programming
(OOP), 637
Objective C programming language,
637
octal (base 8) numbers, 54-55,
516-517
printing, 55-56
offsets, array elements, 193
one's complement method, 515
OOP (object-oriented programming), 637
opening files, 408-409, 422
operands, 123-124
operators, 122-141
, comma, 183-186, 219, 651
! NOT, 222
!=, 212
% modulus, 134, 352, 646

& address, 648
& AND, 305-306, 650
& binary operator, 519
&& AND operator, 222
* dereferencing, 334, 649
* Indirection operator, 309-310
* multiplication, 126-128, 646
*= arithmetic, 195-199
+ addition, 125, 646
++ increment, 646
- subtraction, 125, 646
-> structure pointer, 483-484
/ division, 128-129, 646
< redirection, 139, 259-260
= assignment, 122-125, 647
> redirection, 139, 259-260
?: conditional operator, 227-229
^ binary operator, 519-520
^ EXCLUSIVE OR, 650
^= bitwise logical operator, 520
| binary operator, 519
| OR, 650
|= bitwise logical operator, 519
|| OR operator, 222
~ bitwise logical operator,
    518-519
address, 482-483
arithmetic, 199-200, 646
assignment, 182, 647
association rule, 132
binary, 125
bitwise, 650
bitwise << left shift operator, 523
bitwise >> right shift, 523-524
bitwise logical operators, 518
bitwise shift operators, 518-527
cast operators, 149-150
data objects, 124
decrement operators, 140-141
decrementing, 138-139
DOS, 260

equality, 161-162
exponential growth, 127-128
expression trees, 130-131
increment, 135-141, 175
incrementing process, 136
logical, 221-224, 648
lvalue, 124
membership, 500-501
miscellaneous, 651
modifiable lvalue, 124
operands, 124
order of evaluation, 131-133,
    223-224
pointer-related, 648-649
precedence, 129-131, 139-140,
    172-177, 223
priorities, 172
reciprocal, 483-484
redirection, 258
    DOS, 258-260
    executable program
      connection, 260
    UNIX, 258-260
relational, 139, 159-160,
    167-168, 646-647
    floating-point numbers, 168
    values comparison, 174
rvalue, 124
sign, 125-126, 649
sizcof, 133
structure, 649-650
unary, 125
union, 649-650
OR (|) operator, 650
order of evaluation
    logical expressions, 223
    operators, 131-133, 223-224
order.c file (listing 10.8), 332
organizations, hierarchical, 620
outer loop, *see* nested loops

output
   characters, 249-250
   devices, 19-21
   functions, 84, 249-250
   redirection, 258-260
      DOS, 257-260
      UNIX, 257-260
   screen stream, 254
   strings, 373-375
   see also I/O
overflow
   floating-point numbers, 68
   integer, 57

P

%p format, 306, 362
%p specifier, 92, 109
paint.c file (listing 7.8), 228
parameters
   loop expressions, 181-203
   reading loop, 194-197
parentheses, 280
Pascal programming language, 2
passing
   arguments, 104
   structures as arguments, 484-487
password programs, 188-189
patterns.c file (listing 8.3), 261-262
petclub.c file (listing 17.12), 632-634
pipe (|), 260
pixels, 573
pizza.c file (listing 4.4), 88
pnt_add.c file (listing 10.4), 326
pointer form
   changing variables, 363
   increment operator, 364
   versus array form, 363-365
pointer notation, 333, 343, 363
pointer operators, 483-484

pointers, 305-316, 333-337
   accessing members, 483-484
   addresses, 334
   and multidimensional arrays,
     340-348
   arguments, 331-332
   creating, 309
   declaring, 310-311
   decrementing, 334-335
   differencing, 335
   in function communication,
     311-318
   incrementing, 334
   initializing, 364-365
   storing, 575-579
   structure, 487-490
   temporary, 606
   to arrays, 326-329
   to structures, 481-482
     declaring, 482-483
     defining, 481-482
     initializing, 482-483
     vs. structures, 490-491
   values, finding, 334
   with strings, 367-368
portability of programming
  languages, 2-3
post_pre.c file (listing 5.11), 137
postage.c file. (listing 6.11), 183
pound.c file (listing 5.15), 151
power( ) function, 198
power.c file (listing 6.18), 197
praise1.c file (listing 4.2), 82
praise2.c file (listing 4.3), 84
precedence, operators, 139-140,
  172-177
   bitwise logical operators, 523
   of relational operators, 172-177
preproc.c file (listing 16.1), 536-537
preprocessor, 90
   directives, *see* directives

preprocessor macro, 251
preprocessor symbol (#), 27
print( ) function, 73
print.c file (listing 13.13), 460
print1.c file (listing 3.2), 54
print2.c file (listing 3.4), 58
printf( ) function, 26-27, 31-32, 47,
    83, 91-114, 122, 143, 191, 228,
    250, 278
    flags, 97-101
    return values, 104-106
    versatility, 374
printing
    %p format, 306
    %s format, 362
    %u format, 311
    characters, 63-64
    floating-point numbers, 67-78
    hexadecimal numbers, 55-56
    integer values, 54, 58-59
    long character strings, 106-110
    numbers, 349-354
    octal numbers, 55-56
    parameters, terminals, 273
    sorted data, 460-461
    strings, 360-361
printout.c file (listing 4.6), 93
priorities
    assignment operators, 182
    of operators, 172-173
prntval.c file listing 4.13., 106
program jumps, 662-663
program standards, 18-19
program state, 41
Programmer's WorkBench (PWB),
    15
programming
    automatic conversions, 154
    basic steps, 6
    expressions, 141-142

functions, 278-290
loops, 120-122, 211, 216-221
    comma operator, 219
    in word-counting program,
        225
    while loops, 121
operators, 122-133
parentheses, 212
publications, 642-643
statements, 142-145
switch statements, 235-237
symbolic constants, 213
with bitwise operators, 524-527
programming languages, 2, 637
programs
    buffered input problems, 263-269
    coding, 169-170
    controlling, 199-200
    data representation, 572-575
    debugger, 41
    debugging, 38-41
    designing, 583
    driver, 198
    echoing, 195-197
    exiting, 407-408
    file feeding with redirection,
        270-273
    geometric characters, 261-262
    interactive, user failure, 265
    line length, 271-273
    listings, see listings
    logic, pseudocode, 162
    modifying, 195-197
    multiple entries, 479-482
    navigating, 243-244
    repeating, 195-197
    setting structure vectors, 491
    similarities in symbols, 171-172
    sketching with characters,
        269-271
    statements, 142

structure, 33, 272-273
with multiple functions,
    compiling, 300-304
word-count, 224-227
promotions, 148
properties, integer, 584
proto1.c file (listing 9.5), 292
prototypes, 152
    ANSI C function prototype, 153
    functions, 291-293
pseudocode, 162
pt_ops.c file (listing 10.9), 333-334
publications
    C language, 641-642
    programming, 642-643
    reference, 643
put_out.c file (listing 11.7), 373
put_put.c file (listing 11.11), 376
put1.c file (listing 11.9), 375
put2.c file (listing 11.10), 376
putc( ) function, 409
putchar( ) function, 210-211,
  250-251
puts( ) function, 360, 373-374

Q

qualifiers, 656
queue.c file (listing 17.7), 606-608
queues, 598
    adding items to, 599, 604-606
    circular, 600-603
    data forms, 497-511
    deleting items, 599
    designing, 610-616
    full/empty, checking, 604
    simulating with, 610-616
    sizes, 601-603
    testing, 608-610
Quick C, compiling programs, 301
quotes.c file (listing 11.2), 362

R

\r (carriage return) escape sequence,
  61-62
r_drive1.c file (listing 13.4), 447
r_drive2.c file (listing 13.6), 449
ragged arrays, 366-368
rain.c file (listing 10.11), 338-339
rand( ) function, 446-452,
  611-612
rand0.c file (listing 13.3), 447
rand1( ) function, 451-452
random access files, 416-419, 616
    in text mode, 419-421
random numbers, 446-450
ranking types, 148
read_array( ) function, 349-351
readability, improving, 34
reading
    binary data, 426
    input, 110
    numbers, 349-354
    numeric data, 454-456
    strings, 360-361
reading loops, 162
    parameters, 194-197
reciprocal operators, 483-484
records, variably sized, 497-511
rectangular arrays, 366-368
recur.c file (listing 9.6), 294
recursion, 293-299
    characteristics, 295-296
    returns, 295
    reversal, 298-299
    statement execution, 295
    tail recursion, 296-298
    variables, 295
redirection
    AmigaDOS, 258-260
    characters, 249-250
    combined, 259-260
    DOS, 257-260

file feed to program, 270-273
I/O, 257, 260-261
output, 258-260
spacing symbols in filenames,
  258-260
UNIX, 257-260
redirection operators, 259-260
DOS, 258-260
executable program connection,
  260
UNIX, 258-260
reducto.c file (listing 12.2), 410-411
register variables, 444-445
REGS union, 532
relational expressions, 244, 647
values, 168-169, 174
relational operators, 139, 159-160,
  167-168, 646-647
floating-point numbers, 168
precedence, 172-177
representation, data, 572-575
return, 286-289
function termination, 288
recursions, 295
return statement, 32-44
return values, 104, 112
functions, 196-199
  printf( ), 104
  scanf( ), 161-162
  structures as, 487-490
with functions, 198-203
returning structures, 490
reversal, with recursion, 298-299
reverse.c file (listing 12.5), 416
revised while loop, 264-265
rewind( ) function, 412-413
rfactor.c file (listing 9.8), 297-298
rollem( ) function, 451-452
roots, 621
rounding errors, floating-point
  numbers, 69

rows 1.c file. (listing 6.15), 190-191
rows2.c file (listing 6.16), 192
rules.c file (listing 5.7), 132
running C programs, 7
running.c file (listing 5.16), 153-154
rvalue, 123-124

S

%s format, 362, 371
%s specifier, 81-83, 92, 109
s_and_r.c file (listing 13.5), 448
saving structure contents, 493-496
scalar variables, initializing, 320
scan_str.c file (listing 11.6), 372
scanf( ) function, 47, 83, 91-114,
  160-162, 206-207, 217, 250, 267,
  273, 305, 369-373
  * modifier, 112
  arguments, 73
  conversion modifiers, 109
  conversion specifiers, 109
  input termination, 371
  recommendations, 373
  return values, 112
scientific notation, 65
scope
  automatic variables, 437
  external variables, 439-440
  functions, 444
  storage classes, 434-436
scores_in.c file (listing 6.17), 194
searches
  binary, 618-619
  sequential, 618
SeekItem( ) function, 627
selecting
  entry/exit-condition loops,
    189-190
  for loops, 190
  while loops, 190

selection sort algorithm, 390
sequence points, 144-145, 223
sequential access, 616
sequential searches, 618
setvbuf( ) function, 427
shoe2.c file (listing 5.2), 121
shoes1.c file (listing 5.1), 120
short keyword, 49, 56-57, 70
show_array( ) function, 351-352
show_last( ) function, 421
showchar1.c file (listing 8.5),
   265-268
showfpt.c file (listing 3.6), 67
showinfo( ) function, 489-491
showmovies( ) function, 590
showr2.c file (listing 8.6), 267-270
side effects, 143
sign operators, 125-126, 649
sign-magnitude method, 515
signed integers, 70, 515, 653-654
simple statements, 147, 658
single-character I/O, 250
sizeof operator, 72, 80-85, 133
sizeof.c file (listing 5.8), 133
sizes
   array, 195-197
   queue, 601-603
   type, 71
sketcher statement, 271
sketcher.c file (listing 8.7), 269-270
skip.c file (listing 7.9), 229-230
skip2.c file (listing 4.17), 113
sort( ) function, 458-460
sort.c file (listing 13.12), 460
sort_int.c file (listing 13.9), 454
sort_str.c file (listing 11.22), 389
sorting
   numbers, 452-462
      getarray( ) function, 456-457
      getint( ) function, 457-458
      global decisions, 453-454

   printing sorted numbers,
      460-461
   reading numeric data, 454-456
   sort( ) function, 458-460
   testing sort, 461-462
selection sort algorithm, 390
strings, 388-390
   strcmp( ) function, 388
source code, 6
   compiling, 7
   debugging, 8
   files, 10
   testing, 8
sprintf( ) function, 386-387, 397
sqrt( ) function, 558
square root, returning, 558
squares.c file (listing 5.4), 127
srand( ) function, 612
srand1( ) function, 451
stacks, 153
   sizes 475-479
standard error output files, 406
   file pointers, 410
standard I/O package, 253-256,
   405-410
   command-line arguments,
      407-408
standard input (stdin), 257
standard input files, 406
   file pointers, 410
standard output files, 406
   file pointers, 410
standards, 18-19
   naming, 29
start-up code, 11
statements, 142-147, 658
   assignment, 30-31, 143
   branching, 207
   break, 662-663
   compound, 145-149, 658
   continue, 230-231, 270-273, 663

control, 175
declaration, 29, 35, 143
do while, 659-660
execution, 295
for, 181-182, 659
function, 143
goto, 240-244, 663
if, 206-208, 264-265, 660-661
if else, 208-221, 272-273
in loops, 143
jump, 243-244
NULL, 166-167
return, 32-44
simple, 147, 658
structured, 143
switch, 235-237, 661-662
while, 143-146, 173-174,
    658-659
static
    arrays, 322
    functions, 444, 594
    storage, 362, 436
    variables, 322, 442-443
        declaring, 442
        in structures, 474-477
static keyword, 445
static.c file (listing 13.2), 442
status, changing, 171-172
stdin (standard input), 254-257
stdio.h header file, 25-27, 410
stdlib.h header file, 397, 559
stdout (standard output), 254
stillbad.c file (listing 2.5), 39
storage classes, 321
    automatic variables, 321, 437-438
    choosing, 445-446
    comments, 322
    dynamic memory allocation, 566
    external static variables, 443
    external variables, 321-322,
        438-441
    properties, 655

register variables, 444-445
scope, 434-436
    linkage, 436
    storage duration, 436
static variables, 322, 442-443
storage files, differences, 253-256
storing
    data types, 498-511
    pointers, 575-579
str_cat.c file (listing 11.13), 378
strcat( ) function, 378-379, 387
strchr( ) function, 387
strcmp( ) function, 379-383,
    387-388
    collating sequence, 382
    identical characters, 382
    input termination, 382-383
strcpy( ) function, 383-387
    arguments, 384
    source, 384
    string pointers, 384
    target, 384
streams
    associating with files, 254
    data I/O, 253-256
    screen output, 254
string arrays, 362-368
    automatic arrays, 362
    external array, 362
    initializing, 362
string constants, 361-362, 397
    static storage, 362
string length, 83-89
string-related functions, 84
string.h header file, 84
strings, 397
    arrays of, 366
    converting to numbers, 396-397
    defining, 360-362
        pointer notation, 363
    functions, 387-388
        string-handling, 377-388

header files, 378
input, 368-373
macro arguments, 543-544
output, 373-375
printing, 360-361
reading, 360-361, 369-371
sorting, 388-390
storage space, 369
with pointers, 367-368
strings.c file (listing 11.1), 360-361
strlen( ) function, 81-89, 278,
    377-378, 388, 489-490
strncat( ) function, 387
strncmp( ) function, 387
strncpy( ) function, 387
strpbrk( ) function, 388
strrchr( ) function, 388
strstr( ) function, 388
structure initializers, 474
structure of simple program, 33
structure operators, 649-650
structure pointers
    declaring, 482-483
    initializing, 482-483
    two-way communications,
        487-490
structure templates, 491-496
structured statements, 143
structures
    accessing members, 474-475
        by pointers, 483-484
    allocating, 575-579
    arrays, 475-479
        declaration, 477
        member indentification,
            477-478
    arrays of, 491-496
    as first elements of arrays,
        493-496
    as function return values, 487-490
    book subscripts, 474-475

fields, 471
formats, 475
guy, 483
identifying to functions, 483-484
initializing, 473-477
inventory uses, 470-471
linking, 498-511
member operators, 474-475
members, 471
memory, 475-479
    allocating, 472-473
    stack sizes, 475-479
nested, 479-482
    declaring in templates, 481
new data forms, 497-511
passing as arguments, 484-487
pointer operator, 483-484
pointers, 481-482
pointers to, defining, 481-482
returning, 490
saving contents in file, 493-496
setting vectors in programs, 491
template/variable definition,
    combining, 473
templates, 469-470
    constructing, 471-472
variables
    defining, 472-473
    external, 474-477
    static, 474-477
versus pointers to structures,
    490-491
structuring programs, 272-273
subarrays, applying functions to,
    344-345
subexpressions, 141
subscripts
    array elements, 193
    arrays, 478
    in book structures, 474-475
subst.c file (listing 16.3), 544

subtraction (-) operator, 646
subtrees, 620
sum( ) function, 485, 493-496
sum_arr1.c file (listing 10.6), 329
sum_arr2.c file (listing 10.7), 331
summing.c file (listing 6.1), 160-161
swap1.c file (listing 9.14), 307
swap2.c file (listing 9.15), 307-308
swap3.c file (listing 9.16), 311
sweetie1.c file (listing 6.8), 174-175
sweetie2.c file. (listing 6.9), 175-182
switch keyword, 661
switch statement, 235-237, 661-662
    break statement, 243
    in loops, 236
    structure, 236-237
    versus if else statements, 239-240
symantic errors, 39-40
symbolic constants, 86, 213
    defining, 86
    naming, 88
    NULL, 577
symbols
    EOF (end of file), 255-257
    similarities in programs, 171-172
syntax
    errors, 38-39
    pointers, 165-168
system requirements, 256-257

T

\t (horizontal tab) escape sequence,
    32, 61-62
t_and_f.c file. (listing 6.5), 168
tail recursion, 296-298
talkback.c file (listing 4.1), 80
templates
    character arrays, 471-472
    combining definition with
        variables, 473
    external function placement, 472
    float variables, 471-472
    funds, 487
    internal function definition, 472
    structure, 469-470, 491-496
        book structure, 471-472
        constructing, 471-472
        declaring nested structures,
            481
    union, 499-511
temporary pointers, 606
terminals, printing parameters, 273
terminating
    for loops, 180-182
    keyboard input, 253-256
    loop structures, 161-162
    programs, 267
    while loops, 163-164
    with input values, 268-271
test conditions
    do while loop, 189
    end of file, 260-263
    for loop, 176
    nonzero values, 169-170
    status changing, 171-172
    while loop, 165-169
test.c file (listing 11.12), 377-378
testing
    functions, 196-199
    program source code, 8
    queues, 608-610
    while loop conditions, 161-162
text file view, 404-405
text files, 257-260
    end-marking, 255-257
    word counts, 260-263
Think C compiler, 17-18
Think C programming language,
    637
    command line, 395-401
    compiling programs, 301

tokens (#define directive), 540
ToLeft( ) function, 625-627
tolower( ) function, 392
ToRight( ) function, 625-627
toupper( ) function, 392
Traverse( ) function, 590, 596,
  627-628
tree.c file (listing 17.11), 628-631
tree.h (listing 17.10), 622-624
TreeItems( ) function, 624
trees
    AVL, 635
    binary search, 620-621
        drawbacks, 635-636
        implementing, 624-631
        removing nodes, 622
        traversing, 627
trouble.c file (listing 6.7), 170
truncation, 129
truth.c file (listing 6.6), 169
Turbo C, compiling programs, 301
turning off bits, 522
turning on bits, 521-522
two_func.c file (listing 2.3), 36
two's complement method, 515
type cast, 152
type conversions, 147-150
    assignment statements, 148
    automatic, 149
    cast operators, 149-150
    demotion, 148
    lint program, 147
    promotions, 148
    ranking, 148
    rules, 147
    selecting, 149-150
type errors, declaring functions, 292
typedef facility, 469-470
types
    declaring in functions, 280
    defining, 572, 583-584

    enumerated, 552-555
        assigned values, 553-554
        constants, 553
        default values, 553
        uses, 554-555
    operations, designing, 585-586
    queue, defining, 598
    sizes, 71

U

%u format, 311, 362
%u specifier, 92, 109
#undef directive, 548-549
unary operators, 125
unbuffered input, 251-252
underflow, floating-point numbers,
  68
unechoed input, 252
ungetc( ) function, 423
union
    operators, 649-650
    templates, 499-511
    variables, 499-511
unions, storing data types, 498-511
UNIX
    C programs, 11-13
    compiling programs, 12-13, 300
    end of file signal, 256
    input redirection, 257-260
    operators, 260
    output redirection, 257-260
    redirection operators, 258-260
unsigned integers, 70, 654
unsigned keyword, 49, 56, 70
updating
    assignment operators variables,
      185-186
    for loop expressions, 179-182
use.qc (listing 17.8), 609-610
user failure, interactive programs,
  265
user interface, accessing, 263-269

V

\v (vertical tab) escape sequence, 61-62

values
  array
    assigning, 325-326
    displaying, 351-352
  comparison, relational operators, 174
  enumerated type, 553-554
  EOF (end of file), 255-257
  expressions, 141-142
  floating-point (Borland C), 475-479
  identifying errors, 273
  of ASCII in for loops, 178-182
  printing
    integer, 54
    long, 58-59
  relational expressions, 168-169, 174

variables, 49, 314
  automatic, 321
    initializing, 438
    linkage, 437
    scope, 437
    storage duration, 437
  combining definition with templates, 473
  constancy, 462-463
  declaring, 29-30, 47, 71, 654
    char, 60
    int, 52-53
  defining
    in structures, 472-473
    versus declaring, 441-442
  external, 321-322, 438-441, 474-477
    initializing, 441
    names, 441
    scope, 439-440
    storage duration, 439

  external static, 443
  float, 471-472
  floating-point numbers, 66
  functions, 472
  in structure, 469-470
  initializing
    char, 60
    int, 53
  linkage, 436
  naming, 29-30
  qualifiers, 656
  register, 444-445
  scalar, initializing, 320
  scope, 436-437
  static, 322, 442-443, 474-477
  storage duration, 436
  union, 499-511
  volatility, 463-464

variably sized records, 497-511
variations, nested loops, 191-193
varwid.c file (listing 4.16), 113
vectors, setting for structures, 491
vi editor, 15
volatile keyword, 463-464
vowels.c file (listing 7.12), 238

W

wheat.c file (listing 5.5), 127-128
when.c file. (listing 6.2), 164
while keyword, 658-659
while loop, 121-122, 163, 174-175, 375
  blocks, 122
  braces, 122
  comparisons to do while loop, 187-189
  conversion to for, 190
  entry-condition, 165, 173-174
  iterations, 163

multiple program entries,
479-482
newline input discarding,
264-265
revising, 264-265
selecting, 190
structure, 159-160
terminating, 163-164
test conditions, 161-165
nonzero values, 169-170
test expressions, 168-169
with function return value,
195-199
while statement, 143-146, 658-659
entry-condition loop, 165,
173-174
while1.c file (listing 6.3), 165-168
while2.c file (listing 6.4), 166-168
width.c file (listing 4.7), 97
word counts in text files, 260-263
word-count program
creating, 224-227
loops in, 225
requirements, 225
wordcnt.c file (listing 7.7), 226
words, 50
writing
binary data, 426
code, 6
functions for arrays, 329-330

X

\x (hexadecimal) escape sequence,
61-62
%X specifier, 93, 109
%x specifier, 92, 109

Y-Z

zeno.c file. (listing 6.12), 186
zippo1.c file (listing 10.12), 341
zippo2.c file (listing 10.13), 342

Dear Reader:

Thank you for considering the purchase of our book. Readers have come to know products from The Waite Group for the care and quality we put into them. Let me tell you a little about our group and how we make our books.

It started in 1976 when I could not find a computer book that really taught me anything. The books that were available talked down to people, lacked illustrations and examples, were poorly laid out, and were written as if you already understood all the terminology. So I set out to write a good book about microcomputers. This was to be a special book, very graphic, with a friendly and casual style, and filled with examples. The result was an instant best-seller. Today the Waite Group has over 70 computer books on the market, and many more are published each year. And no matter what your level of computer interest and expertise, we think The Waite Group has a title you'll like. Our books cover the DOS and Unix operating systems, as well and the C, C++, BASIC, and 80x86 assembler languages. Our titles cover the most popular compilers including those from Microsoft and Borland.

THE
WAITE
GROUP

We have honed the reader levels of our books into a number of best-selling approaches: our *Primer Plus*® and *Programming Primers* guide beginners from the introductory concepts through to a working knowledge of writing professional programs. Our *Bibles* have evolved into comprehensive reference books that appeal to intermediate and advanced programmers and power users. They include standard formats that make looking up any command or function quick and easy, provide clear examples, compatibility information, understandable syntax statements, jump tables and concise tutorials. Power users and programmers should check out our *Tricks of the Masters* books. These titles provide hints, tips, examples, and in-depth discussions that go far beyond the basic principles and facts found elsewhere. You'll discover obscure nuggets of information, work-arounds, and compelling discussions by experts that will hone your programming skills.

We're sure that you'll get to know the signature of "The Waite Group" on a book title as a stamp of a first quality book. A catalog of our titles can be obtained by filling out our reader response card, found in this book.

Thanks again for considering the purchase of this title. If you care to tell me anything you like (or don't like) about the book, please use our reader response card.

Sincerely,

Mitchell Waite
President

Primer Plus is a registered trademark of The Waite Group, Inc.

200 Tamal Plaza,   **Corte Madera,**   **CA**   **94926**   **415-924-2575**   **Fax 415-924-2576**

Code Typing Eliminator

Companion Disk Saves Time

There is absolutely no reason why anyone today would type in the program listings for a computer book unless they wanted to learn how to type. Suppose your time is worth $40 per hour (a not unusual rate for today's programmer). If it takes you 10 minutes to type in and debug a half page of code, then typing all the listings in this book will take you at least 1000 minutes, or 16.6 hours. At $40 per hour, that's $664. Contrast this with the $14.95 it takes to buy a disk with the code already on it. The companion disk for this book comes with all the listings in each chapter, numbered and organized into subdirectories named after chapters.

Ordering Details

Price: $14.95. Use order blank below. Order product CD-1-2E3 (3.5-inch diskette) or CD-1-2E5 (5.25-inch diskette.) California residents add 7.25% sales tax. Price includes first class shipping within the Continental U.S. Add $10 Canada, or $15 Foreign, for shipping and handling. Allow 3 to 4 weeks. Prices subject to change. Purchase orders subject to credit approval, and verbal purchase orders will not be accepted. Call for bulk or institutional orders.

Make check or Money Order payable to The Waite Group, Inc.
Signature is required for credit card orders.

Companion Disk for New C Primer Plus, 2E
from The Waite Group, Inc.

200 Tamal Plaza, Corte Madera, CA, 94925, (415) 924-2575. FAX: (415) 924-2576.

Waite Group Reader Feedback Card
Help Us Make A Better Book

To better serve our readers, we would like your opinion on the contents and quality of this book. Please fill out this card and return it to *The Waite Group*, 100 Shoreline Hwy., Suite A-285, Mill Valley, CA, 94941.

Name _____

Company _____

Address _____

City _____

State _____ ZIP _____ Phone _____

1. How would you rate the content of this book?

☐ Excellent   ☐ Fair

☐ Very Good   ☐ Below Average

☐ Good   ☐ Poor

2. Please mark an L for things you liked and a D for things you disliked about this book.

___ Pace   ___ Examples   ___ Cover

___ Content   ___ Index   ___ Price

___ Writing Style   ___ Listings   ___ Quizzes

___ Accuracy   ___ Ease of Use   ___ Construction

___ Jump Tables   ___ Design   ___ Appendixes

___ Compat. Boxes   ___ Illustrations   ___ Ref. Card

3. Please explain the one thing you liked *most* about this book. _____

4. Please explain the one thing you liked *least* about this book. _____

5. How do you use this book? For work, recreation, look-up, self-training, classroom, etc?

6. What is your level of computer expertise?

7. How did you learn about this book? _____

8. Where did you purchase this particular book?

☐ Book Chain   ☐ Direct Mail

☐ Small Book Store   ☐ Book Club

☐ Computer Store   ☐ School Book Store

☐ Other: _____

9. Can you name another similar book you like better than this one, or one that is as good, and tell us why?

10. How many Waite Group books do you own? _____

11. What are your favorite Waite Group books?

12. What topics or specific titles would you like to see The Waite Group develop?

13. What operating system and version are you using?

14. What programming languages do you know?

15. Any other comments you have about this book or other Waite Group titles?

16. ☐ Check here to receive a free Waite Group catalog.

Title of this book _____ ISBN: _____

Fold Here

From:

_____

_____

_____

The Waite Group, Inc.
100 Shoreline Highway, Suite A–285
Mill Valley, CA 94941

Staple or tape here

Branching

if Forms

```
if (expression)
    statement
```

```
if (expression)
    statement
else
    statement
```

```
if (expression)
    statement
else if (expression)
    statement
else
    statement
```

Example:

```
if (amt > 400)
    rate = 0.0056;
else
    rate = 0.0062;
```

switch

```
switch (expression)
{
    case label1 : statement(s)
    case label2 : statement(s)
...
    default     : statement(s)
}
```

The *expression* must evaluate to an integer value, and the labels should be integer constants (including char) or integer constant expressions.

Example:

```
switch(choice)
{
    case 'a' : act++;
               break;
    case 'b' : bct++;
               break;
    case 'c' : cct++;
               break;
    default  : otherct++;
               break;

}
```

Jumps

1. break is used inside a loop or switch. It causes program control to skip the rest of the loop or switch and to resume with the next command following the loop or switch.

2. continue is used inside a loop. It causes program control to skip the rest of the loop and to initiate the next cycle of the loop.

3. goto causes program control to jump to a statement bearing the indicated label. A statement label is followed by a colon.

Example:

```
while ((ch = getchar()) != EOF)
{
    if (ch == '\t' || ch == '\n')
        continue;   /* start next cycle */
    else if (ch == '#')
        break;       /* exit the loop */
    ct++;
}
```

OPERATOR PRECEDENCE

Operators (from high to low precedence)	Associativity
++ (postfix) -- (postfix) ( ) [ ] . ->	L–R
++ (prefix) -- (prefix) - + ~ ! sizeof * (dereference) & (address) (*type*) (all unary)	R–L
* / %	L–R
+ - (both binary)	L–R
<< >>	L–R
< > <= >=	L–R
== !=	L–R
&	L–R
^	L–R
|	L–R
&&	L–R
||	L–R
? : (trinary operator)	L–R
= *= /= %= += -= <<= >>= &= |= ^=	R–L
, (comma operator)	L–R

BASIC FORMATS FOR *printf()*

```
printf(controlstring, expression1,
    expression2, ...);
```

The controlstring consists of characters to be printed literally and of conversion specifications, which begin with a %. There should be one conversion specification for each expression value to be printed. The value of each expression is printed in the location indicated by the conversion specification.

Basic conversion specifications are

%d	prints an integer in decimal format
%o	prints an integer in octal format
%x	prints an integer in hexadecimal format

%u	prints an unsigned integer
%c	prints a character
%p	prints a pointer
%f	prints a floating-point number in fixed-decimal form
%e	prints a floating-point number in exponential form
%g	use %e or %f, depending on size of number
%s	prints a string

Modifiers may be placed after the % to indicate field width, precision, justification, and whether an int is long, to name a few.

%10d	print right-justified in a field 10 characters wide
%-6d	print left-justified in a field 6 characters wide
%5.2f	print 2 digits to right of decimal; field width = 5
%ld	print a long integer

Example:

```
printf("%s's score is %d out of 90\n", name,
    score);
```

could print the following:

```
Jim Dandy's score is 43 out of 90.
```

BASIC FORMATS FOR *scanf()*

The scanf() function works much like printf(). Here are the main differences:

1. The arguments following the control string must be addresses. They can use the address operator, as in &n, or an argument can be the name of a char array, which serves as the address of the first array element.

2. There is no %g format.

3. Both %e and %f work the same on input; each reads either floating-point format.

4. For reading a double value, use %le or %lf.

5. A %h specifier exists for reading short values.

6. The * modifier means to skip the indicated file; for example, %*s means to skip a word.

Example:

```
int n;
char title[20];

scanf("%d %s", &n, title);
```

The Waite Group's

New
C Primer Plus
Second Edition
Quick Reference Card

by Mitchell Waite and Stephen Prata

Owned or Sponsored by